PASO A PASO

Teacher's Edition

1

Myriam Met
Coordinator of Foreign Languages
Montgomery County Public Schools
Rockville, MD

Richard S. Sayers
Longmont, CO

Carol Eubanks Wargin
Glen Crest Junior High School
Glen Ellyn, IL

Prentice Hall

Glenview, Illinois
Needham, Massachusetts
Upper Saddle River, New Jersey

Visit our Web site at http://www.pasoapaso.com

ADDITIONAL WRITERS AND CONTRIBUTORS

The following individuals contributed their expertise and creativity in developing the many notes and features in this Teacher's Edition.

Lynn Andersen
Chattahoochee High School
Alpharetta, GA

Peggy Boyles
Foreign Language Coordinator
Putnam City Schools
Oklahoma City, OK

Mary Louise Carey
Natick (MA) High School

JoAnn DiGiandomenico
Natick (MA) High School

Susan Dobinsky
Niles North High School
Skokie, IL

Gail Glover
San Antonio, TX

Marjorie Hall Haley, Ph. D.
George Mason University
Fairfax, VA

Thomasina Pagán Hannum
Albuquerque, NM

Lucía Nuñez
Stanford University
Stanford, CA

Bernadette M. Reynolds
Parker, CO

Luz Nuncio Schick
Naperville, IL

Judith B. Smith, Ed. D.
Baltimore City (MD)
   Public Schools

Michael S. Werner
University of Chicago (IL)

ISBN: 0-673-58925-0

3 4 5 6 7 8 9 10 DOW 03 02 01 00

Prentice Hall
Upper Saddle River, New Jersey 07458

TABLE OF CONTENTS

PHILOSOPHY OF THE PROGRAM

Welcome to *PASO A PASO!*

This program is based on the belief that the purpose of learning Spanish is to communicate with the people who speak it and to understand their cultures. *PASO A PASO* is designed to help your students achieve that goal by getting them to communicate right from the start.

PASO A PASO reflects the most current thinking in the foreign language field. It reflects state-of-the-art research on how students learn languages and what teachers and materials need to do to help them become proficient language users, whether they are using their new language for oral or written communication.

Let's take a look at some basic premises about language and language learning, the components of *PASO A PASO,* and how each of these components contributes to developing language proficiency.

What is communication?

Communication is an authentic exchange of information for a real purpose between two or more people. By this we mean that people tell each other (through speech or writing) something the other person doesn't already know.

Communicating meaning has several aspects. Students need to learn to listen to and read Spanish in order to interpret intended meanings, to express meaning by conveying their own messages for a purpose and to a real audience, and to negotiate meaning through the natural give-and-take involved in understanding and in making oneself understood (Savignon, 1991). Research tells us that classroom activities must provide students practice in interpreting, expressing, and negotiating meaning through extensive and frequent peer interactions, preferably in pairs or small groups.

Communication is driven not only by meaning, but also by purpose. In real life, people communicate to get things done. They may communicate to transact business, to get to know someone else, or to find out something they really need to know. In authentic communication, people give and get new ideas or information. The information that one partner has and the other doesn't is often called an *information gap* or an *opinion gap.* How unlike the classrooms of old, where we typically asked students questions to which we (and everyone else) already knew the answer, questions such as, "Tom, what's your name?" and "Sally, are you a boy or a girl?" These questions are not heard in real life because they lack a communicative purpose: There is no information or opinion gap.

PASO A PASO is organized around the principle that just as meaning and purpose drive all language use, so too should they drive all language learning. Students are engaged in understanding messages, in sending their own messages, and thus in communicating on every page of every chapter. Because *PASO A PASO* structures almost all activities for pair or group interaction, students find themselves active participants in every lesson, every day. They communicate real ideas and real meanings for real purposes. Every component of *PASO A PASO* is designed with the goal of communication in mind.

Interpreting meaning

In the last decade we have learned more than ever before about how language is acquired. We know that students learn best when they have ample opportunities to internalize meanings before they have to produce them. That is, we know that comprehension precedes production. Many teachers will be familiar with the term "comprehensible input," first used by Stephen Krashen, who suggests that learners acquire language by understanding what they hear. Students need many opportunities to match what they hear with visual cues (pictures, video, or teacher pantomime) or experiences (physical actions) so that they can associate meanings with forms. This is as true for comprehending language structure and syntax as it is for vocabulary development.

In keeping with research on the importance of matching language with meaning, *PASO A PASO* gives students many opportunities to comprehend new language before producing it. The video allows students to hear native speakers using language in a contextualized format that makes the meanings of new words and structures clear. Students learn by matching what they hear with what they see. Numerous activities for providing comprehensible input are suggested in this Teacher's Edition, activities that involve visuals (transparencies and pictures) and that physically engage students as they acquire new language. Whenever possible, in the pupil's text, vocabulary is visualized, so that both video and print materials provide examples of language in context.

What kind of practice promotes communication skills?

The first and most critical step in the language development process is getting meaning—learning to understand by matching what is heard with what is seen or experienced. But by itself, understanding is not enough. Students also need to use their new knowledge.

Research tells us that students need extensive practice in using their new language to create and convey their own messages. While there may be a legitimate role for simply drilling new structures or vocabulary, the most valuable practice comes from using them to send messages that have meaning for the learner and serve a legitimate communicative purpose. When teachers (or texts) structure activities so there is only one right answer, clearly students are sending messages that convey someone else's thoughts, not their own, and are serving someone else's communicative purpose. In these kinds of activities students are *practicing* language, but they are not really *using* language to communicate.

In contrast, when the answers are determined by the students themselves—and are therefore unpredictable, with no single correct response—students are involved in authentic communication. In these information- or opinion-gap activities, answers will vary. Research suggests that these types of activities are extremely important. After all, if the purpose of learning Spanish is to communicate, then students will need practice in doing just that! In contrast, if practice consists only (or mainly) of producing right answers determined by others, students will have difficulty spontaneously creating their own messages when needed. Thus language activities and tasks should not proceed from rote or de-contextualized to meaningful practice. All practice should be meaningful, with a predominance of activities that are truly communicative, activities in which students' answers will vary.

Research also tells us that pair and group language practice is far more effective than student-teacher practice alone. Cooperative learning and pair and group work both provide increased time for communicative language practice and promote the give-and-take necessary for negotiating meaning.

Working with a partner to make and share meaning lies at the heart of *PASO A PASO*. Everything students learn in each chapter is tied together in a meaningful way. The parts of language are taught and practiced (with a partner) within the context of the whole, with vocabulary and related grammar closely intertwined. Students use language in context to convey meaning and for a real purpose. All activities involve meaning, and most allow students to choose the meanings they want to convey. These are the kinds of information- and opinion-gap events that are characteristic of real-life communication. Even in structured activities designed to provide specific practice of forms and to elicit certain responses, teachers will find that students may still respond in ways that are personal and true for them. The activities are, however, focused, and you will often find "answers will vary, but look for correct use of . . ." in the answer keys.

To promote the development of communicative ability, *PASO A PASO* integrates vocabulary and grammar. They are then re-integrated continually, with gradually increasing complexity. In addition to the personalized and open-ended responses found in the vocabulary and grammar sections of the chapter, the *Todo junto* feature specifically focuses on weaving together newly learned material with material from previous chapters. It promotes the use of all the language students have learned to that point, in oral tasks and through reading and writing.

Teaching for understanding:
The whole is greater than the parts

In many academic disciplines today, instructional practices are based on constructivist theory, which suggests that learners are more likely to be successful when instruction focuses on making meaning, on students' pursuing their natural inclination to try to make sense of what they are experiencing, and on ensuring that the parts are carefully integrated. In foreign languages, we traditionally taught the parts (grammar rules, vocabulary, pronunciation) hoping that eventually students would have the opportunity and ability to integrate them into the "whole" of communicating their own ideas. Today, integration of the parts of language takes place right from the start. It has been suggested that the relationship between learning the parts vs. integration with the whole is like learning to play a musical instrument. The focus is always on making music, and from the outset, learners need to have many experiences producing it. But they can't learn to play an instrument without knowing something about how to produce sounds (e.g., use the violin bow or play scales) or without practice.

Just as students learn the specific skills they need to produce a piece of music in learning to play an instrument, in language-learning we proceed today by identifying the learner's communicative needs (that is, the "music" they want to be able to produce) and then identifying the vocabulary, structures, and cultural skills needed

to accomplish their purpose. Vocabulary and grammar are thus taught in the context of the situations in which students will be communicating or the topics they will be communicating about. Everything ties together naturally.

All effective learning is rooted in a meaningful context. We know from research that information is most likely to be retained when it is connected to other information in a meaningful way. Thus, language learning is more successful and retention more likely when we present new language organized into topics or by situations. This also means that some things we have taught in the past may not get taught at the same point or in the same way. For example, students may need to learn the stem-changing verbs *jugar, perder,* and *querer* to describe leisure or sports activities. However, since *dormir, morir,* and *pedir* do not naturally fit with the theme of sports or leisure, they may not be introduced until another theme or situation arises that will logically involve the use of one or more of them.

PASO A PASO is organized into thematic chapters. All material—vocabulary, grammar, culture—is rooted in a context and used meaningfully. All the elements of a chapter tie together. Students learn the vocabulary related to the theme, the grammar they need to communicate about the theme, and the information that helps anchor language in its cultural context. The themes have been chosen to reflect what students want or need to talk about. And the end-of-chapter vocabulary list is organized to reflect how the new words are used to create and convey meaning.

Critical thinking:
Understanding and making meaning

We know from research that language learners are active makers of meaning. They learn by creating their own understandings, not by memorizing ours. This means that students are more likely to remember vocabulary when they have acquired it by figuring out its meaning in a logical context (video situation, visual, teacher pantomime). Grammar is most likely to be understood and rules applied when students have been guided to discover underlying patterns or have formulated the rules for themselves. In contrast, retention and applicability are greatly reduced when students simply memorize lists or rules without real understanding.

In order for students to construct their own understandings and generate rules of language usage, they need to be guided through interaction with teacher and text. Strategic questioning (in the text or by the teacher) plays an important role in this process, a process that is not at all the same as groping blindly to make a random discovery. Rather, through well-chosen examples and appropriate, inductive questioning, students can be led to make significant discoveries on their own, leading to a deep understanding that is much more likely to stay with them and be reflected in their own language use.

Understanding grammar

Understanding and critical thinking are reflected throughout *PASO A PASO*. This text is unique in its approach to the development of grammar skills, emphasizing as it does the critical roles that comprehensible input and student construction of knowledge play in language learning. New structures are foreshadowed through lexical presentation in the vocabulary section, and by the use of the *yo / tú* verb forms in vocabulary practice prior to the grammar presentation. Vocabulary activities familiarize students with new grammar before it is formally presented, allowing them to construct their own understanding.

To further facilitate grammar learning, students observe patterns of use in the comprehensible input that introduces the grammar section. This is done through a visualized context and strategic inductive questions. Through interaction with the teacher and the text, observation and analysis lead students to understand grammar, not merely to memorize formulas to be applied in rote fashion.

Understanding culture

Guided discovery is also an effective means of helping students construct an understanding of culture. Not only do we want our students to know about the cultures of the people who speak Spanish, we also want them to understand the cultural framework that determines what people say or do. In other words, we want students to understand the *why* of culture that determines the *what*. Whenever and wherever students may encounter speakers of Spanish, they will likely confront cultural practices and behaviors that are new to them. Cultural understanding begins with developing sensitivity to the possibility that people vary in how they think, live, and behave. Students must learn to observe other cultures without judging and to use what they see to help them discover the meanings that underlie cultural practices or behaviors. Specific information provides knowledge that aids in understanding the system of attitudes, values, and beliefs that frames cultural practices or behaviors. Students also need to understand other cultures in relation to their own, so that they may gain a deeper understanding of why they think, live, and behave as they do.

Background knowledge can serve as an important tool for the construction of meaning. It may be contextual (What normally happens in a restaurant?), topical (What are some typical leisure activities?), linguistic (What words do I already know that look like this new word?), or cultural (I know that interpersonal relationships are very important in Hispanic cultures, so that may be why people put so much value on greeting one another). This can serve to help students interpret new cultural information or contrast that information with values and practices common to their own culture. Students should be encouraged to understand the close relationship between language and culture. The social / cultural meanings of words (What does "friendship" mean in Hispanic cultures?) should be taught along with their dictionary meanings.

PASO A PASO develops important cultural understandings through a unique guided-discovery approach. It provides students with a progression of activities that lead them from thoughtful observation to knowledge and understanding of Hispanic cultures and then to reflection on their own culture. A photo essay with strategic inductive questions leads them to reflect on what they are observing. An informative reading then provides cultural information or insights that expand upon the visual information and allows students to validate or reject the ideas they formulated at the beginning. They are then asked thought-provoking questions to lead to reflection upon their own culture and their own cultural perspectives.

Strategies for success

Effective learners not only construct their own understanding of new concepts, they also know how to help themselves be successful learners. One way they do this is by using specific problem-solving strategies. When confronted with unknown words in a reading passage, successful learners don't run for a dictionary or just give up. They know how to get around that obstacle.

PASO A PASO teaches students to use strategies to be effective listeners, readers, and writers. Each reading selection takes students through a multi-step process (Phillips, 1984). Before reading, they are encouraged to use their background knowledge to help them predict or anticipate information they are likely to encounter in the text. A first reading helps them focus on general ideas (gist) without getting mired in details or difficult expressions. Reading closely for specific information, with specific strategies for dealing with difficult aspects of a text, is a strategy frequently emphasized in the reading sections. Students are then encouraged to use what they have learned in the reading by applying it in a new way. Thus, from the start, students are empowered to deal with authentic print materials.

Effective writing is promoted through a process

approach in *PASO A PASO*. In the pre-writing stage, students think about the topic, generate needed language, and organize their ideas. They then write a first draft. Reviewing this draft with a peer yields insights into needed revisions or clarification and results in a revision that may be published or placed in a portfolio. This approach is consistent with the ways in which many students are learning to write in their English classes. It also provides them with a strategy or model for independent writing.

Authenticity in language learning

Language teaching today places great value on authenticity. The content that students are expected to learn and how they practice it (objectives and tasks) should be authentic to the learner's interests and to real-life uses. Tasks should require an authentic exchange of meaning (an information or opinion gap) and should have an authentic purpose. Students should be taught authentic, not "textbook," language. Most important, information and, to the extent possible, materials should be culturally authentic.

PASO A PASO opens authentic avenues to communication and culture. Students continually engage in authentic communicative tasks. Pair and group activities in which students fill information or opinion gaps constitute the great majority of exercises. These activities allow students to express their own views on topics and questions of interest to them. The language presented is culturally accurate. Videos show native speakers engaged in real-life situations and experiences. Videos, photos, realia, and readings provide authentic contacts with the cultures of Spanish speakers.

PASO A PASO and the student

PASO A PASO is a learner-friendly series. It is friendly to the interests of students and provides extensive opportunities for them to talk about themselves, to explore with peers, and to be engaged, thoughtful learners. Each chapter opens with clearly stated communicative objectives that help focus on what students are expected to learn. Knowing what's expected of them makes students more comfortable.

Because we know that it is impossible for students to learn all the vocabulary related to a given theme at one time, and because we know that it is unusual for students to "master" the grammar the first time they are exposed to it, *PASO A PASO* reviews each Book 1 theme in Book 2. However, the review is not simply repetition, re-entry, or recycling. Rather, our approach is recursive: Each review allows students to expand to new levels of achievement, so that their language becomes more refined, more elaborate, and more complex. Students will find comfort in knowing that there is more than one chance to learn the material and that they don't need to know everything perfectly all at once. *PASO A PASO* is a program in which students are continually getting better at communicating in Spanish and are regularly made aware of their progress at specific points in every chapter.

The student book and tests convey a powerful message. Both emphasize knowledge in action. Students are asked to use what they know to communicate real messages to a real audience for a real purpose. Practice activities make it clear to students that they are expected to learn to communicate in the language. End-of-chapter tests reinforce the message, assessing students' ability to use what they have learned for receptive and productive purposes and allowing them to demonstrate their understanding of related aspects of Hispanic cultures.

We know more today than ever about how foreign languages are learned. Using that knowledge to help students become proficient communicators, and to acquire an understanding and appreciation of other cultures, can be facilitated by appropriate instructional materials. *PASO A PASO* is based on solid research on second-language acquisition, on accepted theories about the

teaching of culture, and on sound pedagogical practices that are common to all disciplines. We are sure that you and your students will find this an exciting, engaging, and enormously successful approach to learning Spanish.

Bibliography

Adair-Hauck, Bonnie, Richard Donato and Philomena Cumo. 1994. "Using a Whole Language Approach to Teach Grammar," in Eileen Glisan and Judith Shrum, Eds. *Contextualized Language Instruction.* Boston: Heinle and Heinle Publishers, pp. 90–111.

Brooks, Jacqueline and Martin G. Brooks. 1993. *In Search of Understanding: The Case for Constructivist Classrooms.* Alexandria, VA: Association for Supervision and Curriculum Development.

Doughty, Catherine and Teresa Pica. 1986. "Information Gap Tasks: Do They Facilitate Second Language Acquisition?" *TESOL Quarterly.* 20:3, 305–325.

Ellis, Rod. 1993. "The Structural Syllabus and Second Language Acquisition." *TESOL Quarterly.* 27:1, 91–112.

Kagan, Spencer. 1992. *Cooperative Learning.* San Juan Capistrano, CA: Resource for Teachers Inc.

Krashen, Stephen. 1982. *Principles and Practice in Second Language Acquisition.* Oxford: Pergamon Press.

Nunan, D. 1991. "Communicative Tasks and the Language Curriculum." *TESOL Quarterly.* 25:2, 279–295.

Phillips, June K. "Practical Implication of Recent Research in Reading." *Foreign Language Annals.* 17:4 (September 1984), 285–299.

Resnick, Lauren B. 1989. *Knowing, Learning, and Instruction: Essays in Honor of Robert Glaser.* Hillsdale, New Jersey: Lawrence Erlbaum Associates, Publishers.

Savignon, S. J. 1991. "Communicative Language Teaching: State of the Art." *TESOL Quarterly.* 25:2, 261–277.

Swain, Merrill. 1985. "Communicative Competence: Some Roles of Comprehensible Input and Comprehensible Output in Its Development." In Susan Gass and Madden, C. (Eds.) *Input in Second Language Acquisition.* Rowley, MA: Newbury House.

PASO A PASO AND THE NATIONAL STANDARDS

National standards provide an important and useful framework to guide the teaching and learning of foreign languages. This framework should result in a new generation of language learners prepared to meet the demand for competence in other languages that our nation will face as we move toward an increasingly interdependent world. The work of teachers and students will be facilitated by instructional resources aligned with the National Standards. *PASO A PASO* provides these resources. The program at all levels, with its rich array of ancillary materials (including print and technological resources), is designed to help students develop the competencies delineated in the *Standards for Foreign Language Learning*.

Goal 1. Communication

Communicate in Languages Other than English

Standard 1.1:	Students engage in conversations, provide and obtain information, express feelings and emotions, and exchange opinions.
Standard 1.2:	Students understand and interpret written and spoken language on a variety of topics.
Standard 1.3:	Students present information, concepts, and ideas to an audience of listeners or readers on a variety of topics.

From the very first oral activity in *PASO A PASO,* students work with a partner. They use language to convey meaning and for a real purpose that allows them to choose the meanings *they* want to convey, which is the basic characteristic of real-life communication. Even in structured activities designed to provide practice of specific forms, students may still interact with partners to exchange real information.

PASO A PASO gives students many opportunities to comprehend new language before producing it. The video allows students to hear native speakers using new vocabulary and grammar in a context that makes the meanings clear. Numerous activi-

ties for providing comprehensible input are suggested in this Teacher's Edition, including hands-on activities that physically engage students as they acquire new language. In the student book, vocabulary is visualized, rather than translated or buried in cartoons or *fotonovelas,* so that print and video materials provide different but complementary examples of language in context.

An important characteristic of both the audio and video materials is that they do not repeat material from the text, but rather extend it. Simply hearing what they read does not develop students' ability to understand Spanish when it is spoken, because spoken language and written language are not alike. Even more important, students need to develop the ability to understand the spoken message without being able to predict every word they will hear.

Reading activities can also be found in every chapter and at every level of *PASO A PASO.* As students begin to gain control of new chapter material, they are presented with short reading passages. Later in the chapter, more extensive reading selections are presented, along with strategies that empower students to be successful independent readers. In Book 2, cultural essays are presented in Spanish. As students progress through the program, reading selections increase in challenge level, culminating in a 68-page *Fondo literario* in Book 3. The various Web-based activities at www.pasoapaso.com provide still more opportunities for reading authentic materials.

The presentational mode (Standard 1.3) differs from the interpersonal mode (Standard 1.1) in that the opportunity for direct interaction (conversational give-and-take) between speaker and listener (or reader and writer) is absent. Examples of the former include leaving messages and giving speeches. At the earliest stages of language development, students are more likely to engage in the presentational mode in writing than in speaking. Nonetheless, students have many opportunities for making oral presentations in the *Todo junto* sections at the end of each chapter. As they move through the program, the presentational speaking activities become more frequent and more challenging.

Various challenge levels of writing occur throughout each chapter of *PASO A PASO*. Initial writing tasks are limited in scope and audience, but at the end of every chapter at every level a more extended and comprehensive writing task requires student communication on the chapter topic. Because writing always has an intended audience and purpose, these are made clear in each writing task, with suggestions for ways in which students can publish their writing.

The interactive CD-ROMs *(Pasos vivos 1* and *Pasos vivos 2: La Catrina)* provide outstanding opportunities for both spoken and written presentations. The Word Processor, Slide Presentation Maker, and Video Presentation Maker are the three magic multimedia features aimed at achieving Standard 1.3.

Goal 2. Cultures
Gain Knowledge and Understanding of Other Cultures

Standard 2.1:	Students demonstrate an understanding of the relationship between the practices and perspectives of the culture studied.
Standard 2.2:	Students demonstrate an understanding of the relationship between the products and perspectives of the culture studied.

Cultural understanding is at the heart of Goal 2. Cultural information (knowing about the practices and products of other cultures) is important. However, it is equally important for students to understand that the perspectives of a culture (its attitudes, values, beliefs) both determine that culture's practices and products and may in turn be influenced by them. Resources for teaching toward Goal 2 of the Standards are found throughout the student books in cultural photo essays *(¡Piensa en la cultura!)*, cultural readings

(Perspectiva cultural), and in cultural notes *(Pasos culturales)*. There are also culture notes throughout this Teacher's Edition. Significant cultural information abounds in the video program.

Too often in teaching foreign languages, it is easier to focus on the informational aspects of culture and to ignore the perspectives that underlie them. *PASO A PASO* helps students know about the cultures of the people who speak Spanish, but it also highlights the cultural framework that determines what people say or do. In other words, we want students to understand the *why* of culture that determines the *what*.

These important cultural understandings are developed through guided discovery, an approach unique to *PASO A PASO*. The program provides students with a progression of activities that lead them from thoughtful observation, to knowledge and understanding of Hispanic cultures, as well as to reflection on their own culture. A photo essay (in the video and in the opening section of the textbook chapter) with strategic inductive questions leads students to reflect on what they are observing. An informative cultural reading provides information and insights that expand upon the visual information in the photo essay and allows students to validate or reject the ideas they formulated earlier. Most important, students are asked thought-provoking questions for reflection upon the cultural perspectives they have encountered.

Goal 3. Connections
Connect with Other Disciplines and Acquire Information

Standard 3.1:	Students reinforce and further their knowledge of other disciplines through the foreign language.
Standard 3.2:	Students acquire information and recognize the distinctive viewpoints that are only available through the foreign language and its cultures.

In *PASO A PASO A-B, 1,* and *2* a section of each chapter, entitled *Conexiones,* gives students an opportunity to use their language skills to acquire information in other disciplines (mathematics, science, social studies, etc.). Certain chapter themes (the environment, health, art) directly relate to the content of the school curriculum. The Internet-based activities found at www.pasoapaso.com provide activities that connect to other curriculum areas as well as access to information that is available only through the Spanish language. In the Teacher's Editions of Books 1–3, cross-curricular connections are noted at the beginning of each chapter, including suggestions for student activities.

Another important way in which *PASO A PASO* connects with other disciplines is through the development of learning strategies, learning processes, and higher order thinking skills. We teach students to use strategies to be effective readers, listeners, and writers. For example, the *¡Vamos a leer!* takes students through a multistep process similar to the strategic approach they may be using in their language arts courses. Similarly, effective writing is promoted through a process approach. In the pre-writing stage, students think about the topic, generate needed language, and organize their ideas. They then write a first draft. Reviewing this draft with a peer results in a revision, which may be published or placed in a portfolio. This approach is not only consistent with the ways in which many students are learning to write effectively in their English classes, but it also provides them with a strategy or model for independent writing.

Higher order thinking skills are emphasized throughout, with suggestions for developing critical thinking and for enrichment activities included in the Teacher's Edition. In addition, deep understanding, rather than rote memorization, is a key feature of grammar and culture instruction. *PASO A PASO* is unique in its approach to the development of grammar understanding. It emphasizes the critical roles that comprehensible

input and the construction of knowledge play in language learning. To provide comprehensible input, new structures are foreshadowed through lexical presentation in the vocabulary section, for example, by the use of first- and second-person singular verb forms in vocabulary practice prior to the grammar presentation. Both the video and vocabulary activities familiarize students with new grammar before it is formally presented, allowing students to construct their own understanding. Students then discuss with a partner the grammatical patterns under observation. This is done through actual or simulated realia highlighted by inductive questions in the text. This approach of observation and analysis leads students to *understand* the grammar, eventually leading to a more consistently correct use of the structures being studied.

Goal 4. Comparisons

Gain Insight into the Nature of Language and Culture

Standard 4.1:	Students demonstrate understanding of the nature of language through comparisons of the language studied and their own.
Standard 4.2:	Students demonstrate understanding of the concept of culture through comparisons of the cultures studied and their own.

Myriad opportunities exist in *PASO A PASO* for students to compare their own language and culture to Spanish and to Hispanic cultures. Take, for example, the very first chapter of Books A and 1. Students are introduced to the concept that most adjectives change if they are describing a boy or a girl. They note how this can help them as a reading strategy (was the self-descriptive poem "Yo" written by a male or a female?). They learn the very different cultural connotations of the supposedly equivalent words *amigo(a)* and "friend."

Such comparisons between the student's own langauge and culture and the target language and culture(s) are found in every chapter. Guided discovery is a prime feature of *PASO A PASO* as a means to help students gain insight into language and culture. For example, at the end of every culture section, students are asked to reflect upon what they have read from their own cultural perspective. This heightened consciousness of their own language and cultural beliefs and practices can only evoke a deeper understanding of those being studied.

Goal 5. Communities

Participate in Multilingual Communities at Home and Around the World

Standard 5.1:	Students use the language both within and beyond the school setting.
Standard 5.2:	Students show evidence of becoming life-long learners by using the language for personal enjoyment and enrichment.

Of the five goals in the National Standards, Goal 5 involves application of Goals 1–4, and is most closely aligned with experiences that take place outside the classroom. These experiences may be within the school itself, but are also likely to be in the community and even beyond the student's enrollment in a given course.

For students with direct access to Spanish speakers in their school or community, there are many suggestions in *PASO A PASO* that address Standard 5.1. Many of these are found in the Teacher's Edition (labeled "Spanish in Your Community"). Other opportunities to use Spanish in or beyond the school setting are included in suggestions for publishing student writing, in activities that involve collecting information from the local community, and in chapters related to the environment (Books A-B, 1, and 2) and community service (Book 3). In fact, two chapters in Book 3 directly address Standard 5.1: a chapter on community service and another on the importance of knowing another language. Indeed, the latter chapter also addresses Standard 5.2, for the

personal enrichment derived from knowing Spanish is highlighted. Each chapter provides at least two Internet links that take students into the Spanish-speaking world.

As for Standard 5.2, it is hard to do much more than promote this Standard, for it is neither text- nor schoolroom-based. However, users of the first edition of *PASO A PASO* share with us their students' enthusiasm for the study of Spanish, of going beyond the textbook, of wanting to interact with Spanish speakers both in school and in the community. And we also know that the award-winning *telenovela, La Catrina*, that accompanies *PASO A PASO 2* moves students toward achieving Standard 5.2, for we have seen the essays, reports, and taped sequels that it has prompted individuals and small groups of students to create.

Page-by-Page Correlations to the Standards

In this Teacher's Edition, you will find page-by-page correlations to the Standards. These are located in the bottom left- or right-hand corner of each page. All material in the Teacher's Edition pages and in the reduced Student Edition are correlated. So when the audio program is listed in the margin of the Teacher's Edition, Standard 1.2 will be noted; if an activity in *Un paso más* requires writing, Standard 1.3 will be noted; if a video activity asks students to compare cultures, Standard 4.2 is noted, and so on.

Each chapter supports the Standards, but not all Standards are supported on every page. Some pages contain no correlations, because the material on those pages is not Standard-specific. It is important to recognize that not every activity in a textbook or ancillary component supports a Standard, and we have been very strict in our interpretation. For example, a fill-in-the-blank exercise designed for skill-building writing practice is a valid activity, but it is *not* aimed at fulfilling a Standard.

COMPONENTS OF THE PROGRAM

PASO A PASO is a complete, three-level series with a full range of ancillary components that allow you to tailor the materials to the needs of your students and to your teaching style.

Student's Edition

Presentation material begins with maps of Spanish-speaking countries and *El primer paso,* a preliminary unit focusing on basic, high-frequency communication objectives. This is followed by fourteen thematic chapters and an appendix offering verb charts, a grammar index, and Spanish-English / English-Spanish vocabularies.

Ancillaries

Multisensory / Technology

 Overheads: A package of 90 full-color overhead visuals that reproduce the vocabulary-teaching illustrations without labels or captions. Also included are maps, a pronoun chart, a clock, the realia from the *Gramática en contexto,* and additional teaching transparencies. Suggestions for use are provided in a separate booklet.

 Audio Cassettes / CDs: A set of ten 60-minute audio tapes on cassette or CD containing listening activities for each chapter and separate tapes for assessment, pronunciation and vocabulary, and songs. The primary focus is on developing listening comprehension, with secondary emphasis on supporting the beginning stages of speaking, including practice with pronunciation and some focused speaking opportunities.

 Vocabulary Art Blackline Masters for Hands-On Learning/CD-ROM: All teaching vocabulary art reproduced on blackline masters and available on the Resource Pro® CD-ROM, ideal for making manipulatives or flashcards.

 Classroom Crossword: A wall-size crossword puzzle to be completed over the course of the school year.

 En vivo: A set of chapter-by-chapter videos taped on location in Miami, Guadalajara, and Madrid. Available on both tape and disc, the videos focus on culture, vocabulary, and real-life situational interactions. A Teacher's Guide is included with complete transcriptions, cultural information, teaching suggestions, and reduced reproductions of the Video Activities pages *(see next page)* with overprinted answers.

 Pasos vivos CD-ROM: Chapter-by-chapter real-world activities based on *En vivo* offer creative, interactive practice opportunities for listening, speaking, reading, and writing, while extending students' knowledge of Hispanic cultures.

 Internet-based activities at www.pasoapaso.com: Chapter-by-chapter support for the culture and content of each chapter through engaging internet-based activities. Students can explore sites from around the Spanish-speaking world via selected web sites and can interact with the information provided at each while expanding language skills and cultural understanding. Additional chapter-by-chapter activities provide games and drill-and-skill practice with vocabulary and grammar.

TPR Stories for *PASO A PASO*: Complete Support for 14 Thematic Units. This blackline master book provides TPR-Storytelling support for each chapter. Fun, creative *mini-cuentos* utilize the chapter's vocabulary as guide words. A longer *cuento principal* provides reinforcement while additional readings, writing, picture stories, and speaking activities integrate all aspects of TPR-S.

 At-Home Vocabulary Videos: This at-home study video contains the second vocabulary segment *(Vocabulario para conversar B)* from all chapters of the *En vivo* video program. Additional comprehension activities and at-home language tasks are provided on the video for each chapter.

Print

 Practice Workbook: (with separate Teacher's Answer Key): Worksheets for basic, one-step writing practice for all vocabulary and grammar sections of the student text. Exercises include the support of learning strategies. Each chapter also has an Organizer that allows students to record and keep track of new vocabulary and structures.

 Writing, Audio & Video Activities: Writing Activities provide chapter-by-chapter practice that is at the same or a slightly higher level than that in the student text. Audio Activities offer exercises necessary to focus attention on listening comprehension as students work with the audio tapes. Video Activities focus attention as students view the video. Follow-up activities verify and extend their understanding of what they have seen.

Teacher's Edition: Writing, Audio & Video Activities: Student material with overprinted answers and a complete tapescript of the audio tapes.

 Communicative Activities Blackline Masters (Pair and Small-Group Activities with Situation Cards): Oral activities for pair and group practice.

 Un paso más: Actividades para ampliar tu español: A worktext for Spanish-speaking students designed to supplement the textbook activities.

Assessment

 Assessment Program: Blackline master quizzes *(Pruebas)* for each vocabulary section and each grammar topic in the student text; fourteen chapter quizzes *(Pruebas cumulativas);* fifteen chapter proficiency tests *(Exámenes de habilidades);* and a *Banco de ideas,* a set of cumulative proficiency sections for use in creating mid-term and special end-of-year tests to highlight teachers' own objectives or areas of concern. Suggestions for administering and scoring proficiency tests are included.

 ¿Lo sabes bien? Video Quiz: This end-of-chapter video quiz provides ten multiple-choice questions that review key concepts. The questions appear on the monitor and are read aloud.

 Test Generator: A multiple-choice test generator. Teachers can add their own questions to the question bank.

Teacher's Resource File: This convenient, desk-top organizer contains the Teacher's Edition of the Writing, Audio & Video Activities, the Assessment Program, and the Communicative Activities Blackline Masters.

RESOURCE PRO®

Resource Pro®: Teachers have complete support for developing lesson plans through this multipurpose CD-ROM. The Teaching Resources Library allows teachers to view and print out all print ancillaries. Planning Express builds complete lesson plans for regular and block scheduling with objectives and correlations to local and national standards. The Vocabulary Clip Art Library contains clip art for all visualized vocabulary in all levels of the program. Teacher and students can copy and use images for manipulatives and flashcards.

CHAPTER ORGANIZATION

Organization of the Text

PASO A PASO 1 contains a preliminary chapter *(El primer paso)* and 14 thematically organized chapters in which students learn to communicate about their own lives and how to interact with Hispanic cultures. The 14 themes are:

CAPÍTULO 1   Friendship

CAPÍTULO 2   School

CAPÍTULO 3   Sports and leisure activities

CAPÍTULO 4   Food

CAPÍTULO 5   Family

CAPÍTULO 6   Clothing

CAPÍTULO 7   Leisure and vacation

CAPÍTULO 8   Home

CAPÍTULO 9   Health

CAPÍTULO 10 Community

CAPÍTULO 11 Movies and TV

CAPÍTULO 12 Restaurants

CAPÍTULO 13 The environment

CAPÍTULO 14 Parties and celebrations

Using *El primer paso*

El primer paso is designed as a 10-day teaching unit to give students a successful start in Spanish. In this chapter students will:

1 gain insight into the importance of Spanish in the global community, in the United States, and in their own community

2 recognize the importance of Spanish in the workplace

3 begin to communicate with their peers

4 develop successful learning strategies

5 understand the book's chapter organization

Chapter organization

The 14 chapters follow a consistent organization that increases student confidence while allowing for easy classroom management. Chapters are organized according to the latest research on how students learn a second language and follow a clear pedagogical model:

1 Introduce/Preview   **4** Apply

2 Present   **5** Summarize/Assess

3 Practice

Each chapter follows this model:

Chapter Sections	Pedagogical Support
Objectives	Introduce
¡Piensa en la cultura!	Preview

Vocabulario para conversar

• *Visualized vocabulary*	Present
• También necesitas …	Present
• Empecemos a conversar	Practice
• Empecemos a escribir (y a leer)	Apply
• ¡Comuniquemos!	Practice
• ¿Qué sabes ahora?	Practice / Assess

Perspectiva cultural	Preview / Present
•La cultura desde tu perspectiva	Apply

Gramática en contexto	Preview / Present / Practice
•Ahora lo sabes	Practice / Assess

Todo junto

•Actividades	Apply
•Conexiones	Apply
•¡Vamos a leer!	Apply
•¡Vamos a escribir!	Apply

Repaso: ¿Lo sabes bien?	Apply / Assess

Resumen del vocabulario	Summarize

USING A CHAPTER

Chapter Opener *(Introduce)*

The chapter theme is introduced through a photograph and related communicative and cultural objectives.

Teaching ideas for the Chapter Opener

Wrap-around notes give many suggestions. Here are a few basic ideas for these two pages:

1 Prior to discussing the objectives, have students look at the photos and skim the chapter. Ask them to suggest objectives based upon what they have seen. Write these on the chalkboard and see if they compare with those listed.

2 Show additional pictures, posters, or slides that preview the chapter theme.

3 You may wish to use the first video segment to provide a broad cultural overview of the chapter theme. (See the Video Guide for further suggestions.)

> **Objectives:**
> Relate to real-life, purposeful communication and relevant cultural information. These will be referred to throughout the chapter so that students can monitor their own progress. Chapter assessment is based on the objectives.

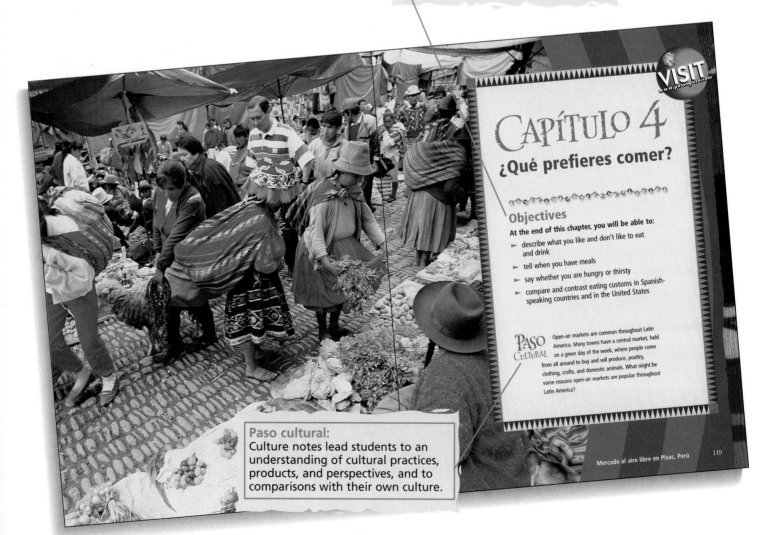

VISIT www.pasoapaso.com

CAPÍTULO 4
¿Qué prefieres comer?

Objectives

At the end of this chapter, you will be able to:

► describe what you like and don't like to eat and drink
► tell when you have meals
► say whether you are hungry or thirsty
► compare and contrast eating customs in Spanish-speaking countries and in the United States

PASO CULTURAL Open-air markets are common throughout Latin America. Many towns have a central market, held on a given day of the week, where people come from all around to buy and sell produce, poultry, clothing, crafts, and domestic animals. What might be some reasons open-air markets are popular throughout Latin America?

> **Paso cultural:**
> Culture notes lead students to an understanding of cultural practices, products, and perspectives, and to comparisons with their own culture.

Mercado al aire libre en Pisac, Perú   119

¡Piensa en la cultura! (Preview)

This section continues to preview the chapter theme. Students use their own experiences and background information to interact with the photographs.

Questions:
Students use critical thinking to answer inductive questions.

Teaching ideas for ¡Piensa en la cultura!

1 Ask students to study the photographs and to suggest as many words, phrases, or short sentences as they can about them.

2 Use the inductive questions to elicit the similarities and differences. Focus on the similarities.

3 If you haven't yet done so, use the first video segment to preview the cultural theme.

4 At the end of the chapter, return to these photos. See how extensively students can describe the pictures. Choose a photo and have students bring it to life by acting out the situation.

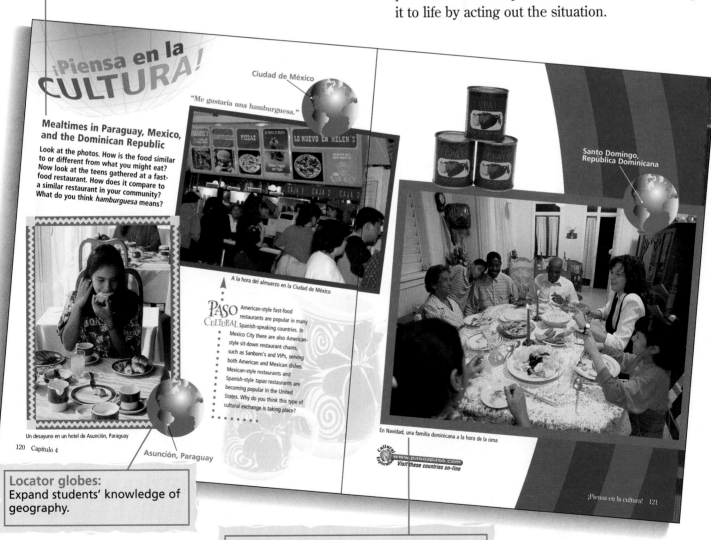

¡Piensa en la CULTURA!

Ciudad de México

"Me gustaría una hamburguesa."

Mealtimes in Paraguay, Mexico, and the Dominican Republic

Look at the photos. How is the food similar to or different from what you might eat? Now look at the teens gathered at a fast-food restaurant. How does it compare to a similar restaurant in your community? What do you think *hamburguesa* means?

A la hora del almuerzo en la Ciudad de México

PASO CULTURAL American-style fast-food restaurants are popular in many Spanish-speaking countries. In Mexico City there are also American-style sit-down restaurant chains, such as Sanborn's and VIPs, serving both American and Mexican dishes. Mexican-style restaurants and Spanish-style *tapas* restaurants are becoming popular in the United States. Why do you think this type of cultural exchange is taking place?

Un desayuno en un hotel de Asunción, Paraguay

120 Capítulo 4

Asunción, Paraguay

Santo Domingo, República Dominicana

En Navidad, una familia dominicana a la hora de la cena

www.pasoapaso.com
Visit these countries on-line

¡Piensa en la cultura! 121

Locator globes:
Expand students' knowledge of geography.

Captions:
Easy-to-guess cognates and recycled vocabulary help build students' confidence. New vocabulary and structures are previewed.

ocabulario para conversar *(Present, Practice & Apply)*

New vocabulary is presented in a visualized context in two short, manageable sections.

Teaching ideas

1 Use the Overheads, the Vocabulary Audio Tape, the Vocabulary Art Blackline Masters/CD-ROM, and / or the second video segment to introduce the new vocabulary.

2 Combine auditory, visual, and kinesthetic activities. Present the vocabulary using comprehensible input. Here are several suggestions:

> **Visualized vocabulary:**
> Research indicates that we learn best in logical sets or categories and through immediately associating words with objects.

A. Getting meaning from comprehensible input

The purpose of these activities is to allow students to match new language with its meaning.

- Using the Overhead, point to pictures as you simply and clearly name and talk about them in Spanish. Students should be able to understand new vocabulary from your body language and gestures. For example: *Es una manzana. La manzana es una fruta. Ésta es una manzana también. Tengo muchas manzanas.*

- You might also pantomime new vocabulary.

- As you progress through *PASO A PASO,* your descriptions will expand to include previously learned language.

> **También necesitas . . . :**
> Non-visualizable vocabulary and lexical preview of grammar. Do *not* treat these *as grammar.* The more students can master without explanation, the more easily and thoroughly they will learn it.

> **¿Y qué quiere decir . . . ?:**
> Cognates and word families are the focus of this section.

B. Demonstrating comprehension through physical response

The purpose of these activities is to allow students to demonstrate their comprehension non-verbally.

■ After presenting two or three pictures of new vocabulary, review by asking yes / no questions, e.g., *¿Es un plátano? ¿Es una naranja? ¿Te gusta comer naranjas?* Students may respond as a group with thumbs up / down *(sí / no).* Individuals may also be asked to respond in this way.

■ As students become more proficient, vocabulary from previous chapters can be used in these questions, e.g., *¿Necesitas beber leche en la cena?*

■ Continue alternating the steps in the first two paragraphs until all new vocabulary has been presented.

■ Distribute Vocabulary Art BLMs or make photocopies from the CD-ROM printout. As you name each new item, point to it on the transparency. Have students point to the corresponding picture. Tell students: *Señalen el plátano. Señalen la naranja.* This time, do not point to the picture on the transparency until students have pointed to it on their worksheet. Confirm student responses on the transparency.

■ Have students point to pictures on the Overhead as you describe the picture, e.g., *A Miguel le gusta comer zanahorias* (student points to picture of carrots).

■ Have students open their books and point to pictures you name or describe: *Señalen dos cosas que les gusta comer. Señalen dos cosas que no les gusta comer.*

■ Have students pantomime vocabulary.

■ Have students respond to commands: *Dale la hamburguesa a María. Muestra el sandwich a la clase.*

■ Provide each student with a worksheet from the Vocabulary Art BLMs/CD-ROM. Direct them to cut out each picture. Have students move the pictures as you direct: *Pongan los guisantes a la derecha de las papas. Pongan la lechuga entre las uvas y las cebollas. Pongan las comidas en dos columnas: Comidas que me gustan y comidas que no me gustan.* Or students may use them to make your sentence true by arranging pictures to match your oral description, e.g., *Hay uvas y manzanas en la mesa.*

Each chapter provides suggestions for Learning Spanish Through Action (TPR).

C. Limited verbal response

Once students have had an opportunity to internalize meaning and to demonstrate comprehension of new language physically, they may respond verbally.

■ Ask yes / no or true / false questions, e.g., *¿Comes cereal en el desayuno? La lechuga es una fruta.*

■ Ask questions that require comprehension of new vocabulary but do not require using it in the answer. Responses will use language from previous chapters, e.g., *¿Prefieres ver la tele o ir al cine los fines de semana?*

■ Ask questions in which the correct answer is embedded: *¿Es una manzana o es una naranja? ¿Prefieres beber leche o té helado?*

■ Have students repeat after you for pronunciation practice.

3 On subsequent days, add details by recycling previously learned vocabulary. Retell an earlier narration without visual support. Ask students to draw their own visual representation of what has been said.

4 Have students re-view the video segment. Turn the sound off and let students provide their own narration.

Empecemos a conversar (Practice)

Students practice the new vocabulary in paired activities that provide models for real-life language.

Teaching ideas for *Empecemos a conversar*

1 Place students in pairs. (There are many ways of doing this.) You may want to pair students of different abilities. Assign "study buddies" for each week or chapter. They are not only pair-practice partners, but they also keep track of each other's papers and assignments. (Be sure they exchange phone numbers.) You might award extra credit for partners who work well together and show improvement.

2 Always model the pair practice. Quickly review the vocabulary so that students can be more successful.

3 Set a time limit. Finish an activity when approximately three fourths of the class have finished. Walk around the class, listening for areas of difficulty such as pronunciation or grammar. Focus on these at a later time.

4 Ask pairs of students to do selected items for the whole class.

5 Have students work in pairs to answer the questions, then with another group to compare responses. Ask individuals to write this section as homework. Use the more open-ended questions as one-on-one questions with students or as topics for class discussion.

6 See the list of ancillaries for additional resources to help students work with the new vocabulary.

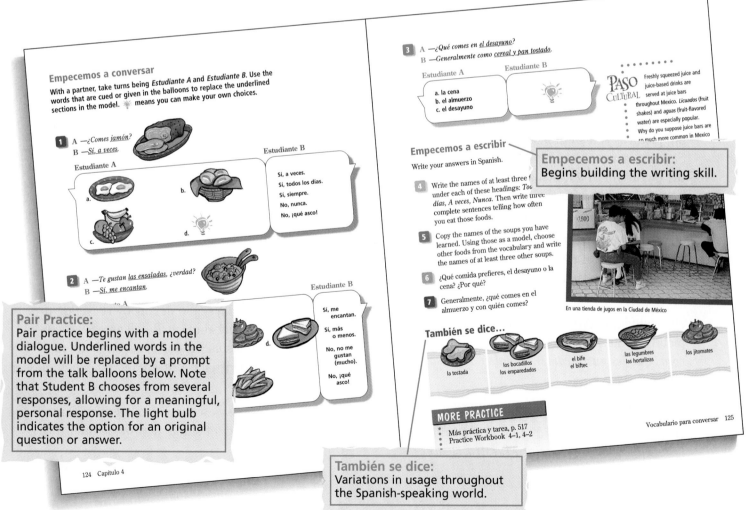

Pair Practice:
Pair practice begins with a model dialogue. Underlined words in the model will be replaced by a prompt from the talk balloons below. Note that Student B chooses from several responses, allowing for a meaningful, personal response. The light bulb indicates the option for an original question or answer.

Empecemos a escribir:
Begins building the writing skill.

También se dice:
Variations in usage throughout the Spanish-speaking world.

¡ Comuniquemos! *(Practice)*

This section offers additional practice with the new vocabulary. The varied activities guide students to personalized communication.

Teaching ideas

Follow the guidelines for paired practice. At this point, students are familiar with the new vocabulary and the activities should go quickly, but choose from among them. Do not attempt to do them all.

¡COMUNIQUEMOS!

¡NO OLVIDES!
If you need help spelling, ask
¿Cómo se escribe . . . ?

1
You and a friend are deciding what to order at a restaurant. Take turns asking each other about your food preferences.

A —¿Prefieres ___ o ___?
B —Prefiero ___.
A —Yo prefiero ___ también.
  o: Yo prefiero ___.
  o: A mí no me gusta(n) ni el (la, los, las) ___ ni el (la, los, las) ___.

2
Help a friend prepare a shopping list. Ask what he or she needs, and write down the responses.

A —¿Qué necesitas para la sopa?
B —Necesito zanahorias, tomates y cebolla.

a. los sandwiches
b. la ensalada de frutas
c. la ensalada de verduras
d. el desayuno
e. el almuerzo
f. la cena

3
Your family is having guests this weekend and you are expected to attend at least three of the meals. Find out what time each of the is and what will be served. With your partner, take turns playing the two roles. For example:

A —¿A qué hora es el almuerzo el sábado?
B —A las doce.
A —¿Qué vamos a comer?
B —Pollo y ensalada.

4
Have the following conversation with a partner. Keep your conversation going as long as you can.

• Find out if your partner is hungry.
• Your partner answers affirmatively.
• Ask what he/she wants/prefers/ would like to eat.
• Your partner answers.

¿Qué sabes ahora?
Can you:
▶ tell someone that you are hungry / thirsty?
  —Tengo ___ / ___.
▶ tell someone what you like or do not like to eat and drink?
  —Me encanta comer ___, pero (no) me gusta beber ___.
▶ say that you like certain foods because they are healthful or tasty?
  —Me gustan las uvas ___ son ___.

Vendedora de frutas en Concón, Chile

130 Capítulo 4

Vocabulario para conversar 131

¿Qué sabes ahora?:
Students begin to check their own progress toward achieving the chapter objectives.

Perspectiva cultural (Preview, Present & Apply)

This section offers a unique perspective into understanding the richness of Hispanic cultures. Using a combination of a photographic and narrative essay, it asks students to think about culture in such a way as to develop real cross-cultural understanding and sensitivity.

Teaching ideas for the *Perspectiva cultural*

1 Have students answer the inductive questions as a whole-class or small-group activity. Write their responses on the board. This will activate background information, prompt and recycle related vocabulary, and show that, even in their own class, they will find a variety of customs and traditions.

2 Use the photographs to encourage students to make observations about Hispanic cultures. Describe the photos in Spanish, adding more information.

3 Add personal information or anecdotes. If any students have traveled to a Spanish-speaking country, let them share their experiences. Ask Spanish speakers to share family traditions.

4 In small groups or as a whole class, have students answer the questions in *La cultura desde tu perspectiva*. This is your best opportunity for helping students understand their own culture and the beliefs and attitudes they have formed.

5 You may want to ask how Spanish-speaking students coming to the U.S. might react to being in a culture with traditions such as those described by students when they answered the inductive questions.

Cultural reading: Cultural information and insights that expand upon the information in the photos. Students validate or reject the ideas they formulated earlier.

Critical questioning: A series of inductive questions focusing on students' background knowledge and on the photos.

La cultura desde tu perspectiva: Students reflect upon and interact with new cultural information from the perspective of their own culture.

Perspectiva cultural
Las horas de las comidas

¿A qué hora es el desayuno, el almuerzo y la cena en los Estados Unidos? ¿Qué comemos en el desayuno, por ejemplo? En las fotos, ¿a qué hora comen los hispanos?

El desayuno, which generally takes place between 7:00 and 8:30, is usually a light meal that consists of coffee or *café con leche,* which is half coffee and half hot milk, and bread or rolls with butter and jam. Children and teenagers sometimes drink hot chocolate or chocolate milk instead of coffee.

El almuerzo (called *la comida* in Spain and Mexico) is the largest and most important meal of the day. It is eaten between noon and 3:00. Many businesses and schools close so that families can enjoy *el almuerzo* together at home. Although this lengthy midday break is still common, more and more

...pting a *jornada continua* or ... (uninterrupted schedule) ... hours in the United States. ... time for employees to go

...ening meal. It may start ...much later, especially in ...ave a late midday meal. In Spain, *la cena* may start as late as 10:00 or 11:00, since most Spaniards enjoy going out after work or school and it is customary to wait until all family members are present before sitting down to eat. *La cena* is usually a light meal, and it may include leftovers from *el almuerzo.*

In some countries, there is also a late afternoon meal called *la merienda.* It may be like a *desayuno,* or it may resemble an English tea, with sandwiches, pastries, or rolls and *café con leche,* tea, or hot chocolate.

A la hora de cenar en Escazú, Costa Rica

Una familia salvadoreña comiendo el almuerzo

La cultura desde tu perspectiva

1 In what ways are mealtimes in Spanish-speaking countries similar to or different from those in the United States?

2 Why would a late-afternoon snack probably be necessary for someone from the United States who was visiting a Spanish-speaking country? Are there any other times of day when a snack might be needed?

En Xochimilco, México, ...

2:00 PM 5:00 PM 9:30 PM

www.pasoapaso.com

Perspectiva cultural 133

Gramática en contexto (*Preview, Present & Practice*)

A realia-based reading provides comprehensible input for the new grammar. This gives students meaningful understanding of the structures by letting them intuit the rules. This inductive approach allows students to internalize and gain a deeper understanding of the grammar. Students were shown these structures in the vocabulary presentation and have practiced using them. They should not be uncomfortable with the structures themselves.

Realia-based reading:
The reading combines cognates and previously learned vocabulary with the chapter's key grammar concepts.

Teaching ideas for *Gramática en contexto*

1 Show the Overhead. Activate students' own experience by asking questions such as: How many students like cheese? What types of cheese? Ask what they might expect to find in an ad such as this. Have them skim the ad. Did they find what they expected?

2 Read the headline and ask what it means. Can students identify any of the flags? Read aloud the subhead. Can students tell you what it means? Have pairs of students read the ad and answer the questions. Let them verify their answers with another pair or as a whole-class activity.

3 As students generate an explanation, write it on the chalkboard along with examples from the reading.

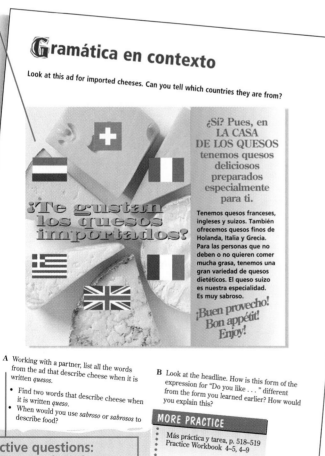

Inductive questions:
Students scan for information that leads them to produce their own explanation for the structures used.

¡No olvides!:
This recycling feature reminds students at appropriate moments of previously taught concepts and vocabulary.

Easy-to-understand grammar explanations:
Rules developed by the student are reinforced in easily understood explanations. Grammar terminology is kept to a minimum.

In a truly thematic approach, grammar is tied to the communicative objectives. What is not relevant is not presented. Here, for example, students work with three *-er* verbs appropriate to the theme: *deber, beber,* and *comer.* Additional *-er* verbs are, of course, taught in later chapters.

This thematic approach builds in regular review and recycling as students are reminded of the *-er* conjugation through the *¡No olvides!* feature. There are three to four grammar topics per chapter, each followed by a variety of activities.

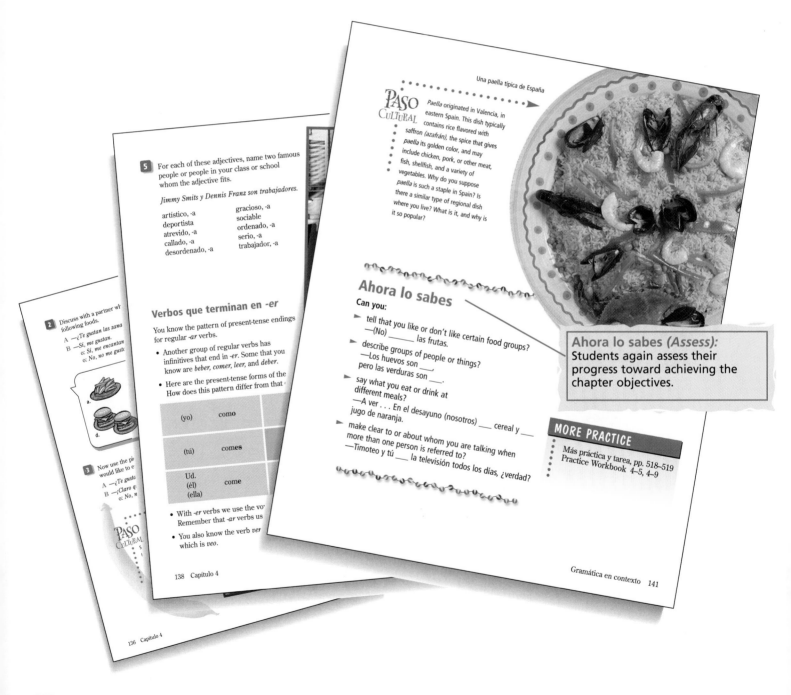

5 For each of these adjectives, name two famous people or people in your class or school whom the adjective fits.

Jimmy Smits y Dennis Franz son trabajadores.

artístico, -a
deportista
atrevido, -a
callado, -a
desordenado, -a

gracioso, -a
sociable
ordenado, -a
serio, -a
trabajador, -a

Verbos que terminan en *-er*

You know the pattern of present-tense endings for regular *-ar* verbs.

- Another group of regular verbs has infinitives that end in *-er.* Some that you know are *beber, comer, leer,* and *deber.*

- Here are the present-tense forms of the How does this pattern differ from that

(yo)	como
(tú)	comes
Ud. (él) (ella)	come

- With *-er* verbs we use the vo Remember that *-ar* verbs us

- You also know the verb *ver* which is *veo.*

138 Capítulo 4

136 Capítulo 4

Una paella típica de España

PASO CULTURAL
Paella originated in Valencia, in eastern Spain. This dish typically contains rice flavored with saffron *(azafrán),* the spice that gives paella its golden color, and may include chicken, pork, or other meat, fish, shellfish, and a variety of vegetables. Why do you suppose paella is such a staple in Spain? Is there a similar type of regional dish where you live? What is it, and why is it so popular?

Ahora lo sabes

Can you:

▶ tell that you like or don't like certain food groups?
—(No) _____ las frutas.

▶ describe groups of people or things?
—Los huevos son _____, pero las verduras son _____.

▶ say what you eat or drink at different meals?
—A ver . . . En el desayuno (nosotros) _____ cereal y _____ jugo de naranja.

▶ make clear to or about whom you are talking when more than one person is referred to?
—Timoteo y tú _____ la televisión todos los días, ¿verdad?

Ahora lo sabes (Assess): Students again assess their progress toward achieving the chapter objectives.

MORE PRACTICE

Más práctica y tarea, pp. 518–519
Practice Workbook 4–5, 4–9

Gramática en contexto 141

Todo junto (Apply)

Todo junto is composed of four integrative sections: *Actividades, Conexiones, ¡Vamos a leer!,* and *¡Vamos a escribir!*

Teaching ideas for *Actividades*

1 To complement this section, use the third video segment in *En vivo.*

2 You may want to use different activities for different ability groupings.

3 Use activities for performance-based assessment. Refer to the section in the Assessment Program book on the development and use of rubrics to evaluate student performance.

Teaching Ideas for *Conexiones*

1 Use these activities to extend the chapter language skills.

2 Include additional activities if students express interest in the connection. Work with other subject area teachers for ideas or let students develop their own ideas.

> **Actividades *(Apply):***
> Pick and choose from among these activities.

> **Conexiones:**
> Activities connect to other disciplines through the chapter theme and content.

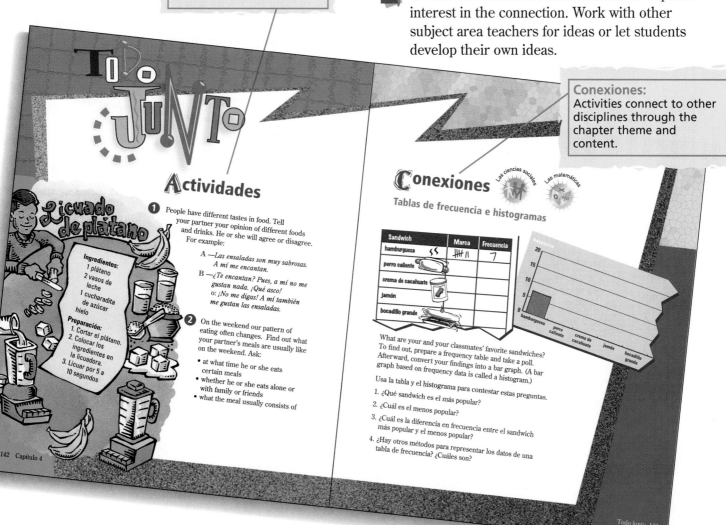

¡**V**amos a leer! *(Apply)*

Students learn how to become efficient readers through a four-step process. Real comprehension is achieved through strategies, questions, and activities in the *Infórmate* and *Aplicación*. Students encounter unknown vocabulary, but gain confidence by realizing they don't need to know every word to read successfully.

Teaching ideas

1 *Antes de leer:* Use the maps in the textbook or on the Overheads to point out where the Mayas and Aztecs lived. Use a world map to show the routes the Spaniards followed to reach Mexico. Ask students if they like chocolate and if anyone knows its origin.

2 *Mira la lectura:* Have students work in groups and report back to the class. Write the names of the products students mention on the chalkboard to reinforce the concept of cognates.

3 *Infórmate:* This can best be done as an individual task or as pair work.

4 *Aplicación:* Students will complete this activity successfully because of the careful structuring of the early steps in the reading process. You might have students compare their lists in pairs or small groups.

• Step 1
Antes de leer: Activates students' background knowledge to help them predict or anticipate.

• Step 2
Mira la lectura: Pre-reading section focusing on a specific reading strategy.

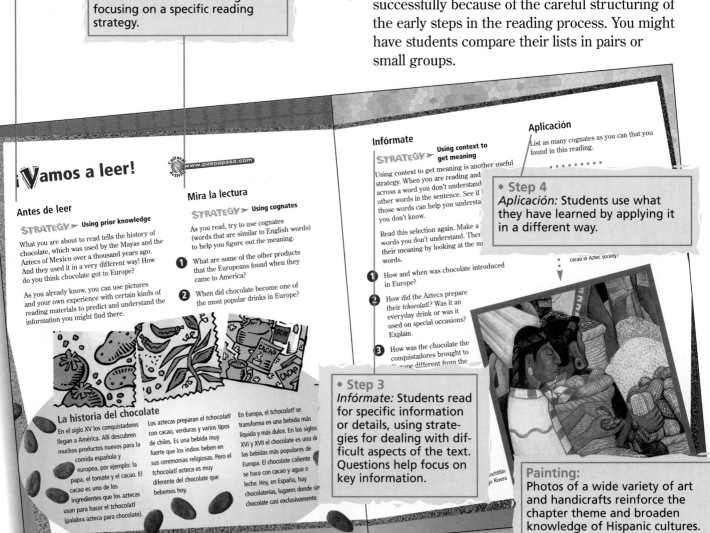

• Step 4
Aplicación: Students use what they have learned by applying it in a different way.

• Step 3
Infórmate: Students read for specific information or details, using strategies for dealing with difficult aspects of the text. Questions help focus on key information.

Painting:
Photos of a wide variety of art and handicrafts reinforce the chapter theme and broaden knowledge of Hispanic cultures.

144 Capítulo 4

¡Vamos a escribir! (Apply)

As with reading, students develop effective writing through a process approach consistent with the way they are learning to write in their English classes. It also provides a strategy or model for writing independently. Each writing task provides a creative, personalized opportunity to expand the chapter theme.

• **Step 1**
Pre-writing questions have students think about the topic, generate needed language, and organize their ideas. They then write the first draft.

• **Steps 2–4**
Through peer review students gain insights into needed revisions or clarifications for preparing the final draft.

Teaching ideas

1 This may be done in class or as homework. Students can work individually, in pairs, or in small groups to brainstorm the topic and needed vocabulary. They can jot down answers to the questions and share them with other students. They then use the questions and responses as a starting point for writing their first draft. You might have students skip lines on the first draft so that there is room for comments during the peer review.

2 Have students share their first draft with one or more partners. Peer reviewers should check for thoroughness and comprehensibility, as well as for errors in spelling, grammar, and punctuation. (You may want to make sure that each reviewer says at least one good thing about the writing sample.)

3 You might want to include final drafts in the students' writing portfolios.

¡Vamos a escribir!

Think about what, when, and where you eat on a typical day. Then write a short paragraph about your favorite meal of the day. Follow these steps.

1 Answer these questions, then use the answers to write your paragraph.

- ¿A qué hora comes tu comida favorita?
- ¿Dónde comes: en la casa, en la escuela o en un restaurante?
- ¿Con quién comes?
- ¿Qué comes y qué bebes?

Comprando frutas para la merienda en Cartagena, Colombia

Letrero de un restaurante en Santiago, Chile

OFERTA
HOT-DOG COMPLETO
$50

2 Show your paragraph to a partner. Does he or she have any ideas to suggest? Did you use the answers to all the questions in your paragraph? Think about any changes you may want to make, then write a second draft.

3 Check for correct spelling and punctuation. Did you use the *yo* form of the verbs? Did you use *me gusta(n)* or *me encanta(n)?* Does your partner have any further suggestions?

Comiendo alcapurrias *(fritters)*, una comida popular para la merienda en el Viejo San Juan, Puerto Rico

4 Write your final draft. Add the corrected paragraph to your writing portfolio.

Photographs:
Ask students to describe the pictures or write new captions. Have pairs create questions and ask them of another pair.

146 Capítulo 4

Cocinando arepas en el mercado en Saquisilí, Ecuador

¡Vamos a escribir! 147

Repaso: ¿Lo sabes bien? *(Apply, Assess & Summarize)*

In this section students practice tasks similar to those they will encounter on the *Examen de habilidades.* They focus on the chapter objectives and show what they can do with the language.

Teaching ideas

1 Point out how this pre-test and the vocabulary on the following page prepare for the *Examen de habilidades.*

2 Do this as a whole-class activity or have pairs complete the section at home and then compare their responses with those of a partner. Or, with a partner, they can work through each section in class and then compare their answers with those of another pair.

3 Students who do well should feel confident about performing well on the test. Those having difficulty will know where they need to focus attention as they study for the test.

Resumen del vocabulario *(Summarize)*

This section organizes the chapter vocabulary to reflect how it can be used to meet the communicative objectives. The objectives were stated in the chapter overview, and students have been given regular opportunities to assess their progress in the *¿Qué sabes ahora?, Ahora lo sabes,* and *Repaso: ¿Lo sabes bien?*

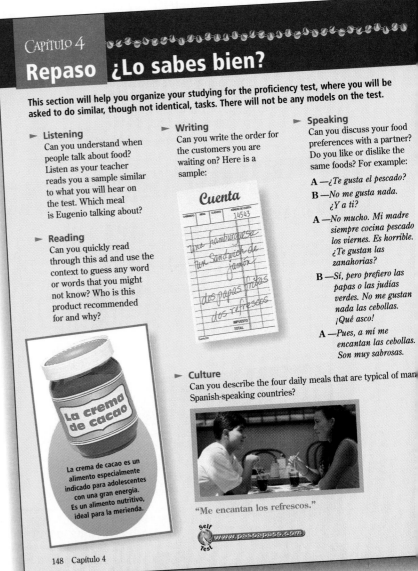

CAPÍTULO 4

Repaso ¿Lo sabes bien?

This section will help you organize your studying for the proficiency test, where you will be asked to do similar, though not identical, tasks. There will not be any models on the test.

► **Listening**
Can you understand when people talk about food? Listen as your teacher reads you a sample similar to what you will hear on the test. Which meal is Eugenio talking about?

► **Reading**
Can you quickly read through this ad and use the context to guess any word or words that you might not know? Who is this product recommended for and why?

La crema de cacao es un alimento especialmente indicado para adolescentes con una gran energía. Es un alimento nutritivo, ideal para la merienda.

► **Writing**
Can you write the order for the customers you are waiting on? Here is a sample:

Cuenta
14543
Una hamburguesa
Un sandwich de jamón
dos papas fritas
dos refrescos

► **Speaking**
Can you discuss your food preferences with a partner? Do you like or dislike the same foods? For example:

A —*¿Te gusta el pescado?*
B —*No me gusta nada. ¿Y a ti?*
A —*No mucho. Mi madre siempre cocina pescado los viernes. Es horrible. ¿Te gustan las zanahorias?*
B —*Sí, pero prefiero las papas o las judías verdes. No me gustan nada las cebollas. ¡Qué asco!*
A —*Pues, a mí me encantan las cebollas. Son muy sabrosas.*

► **Culture**
Can you describe the four daily meals that are typical of many Spanish-speaking countries?

"Me encantan los refrescos."

Self Test www.pasoapaso.com

148 Capítulo 4

Teaching ideas

1 Have pairs review the vocabulary. They might make up a sentence or dialogue in each category. For example, *Tengo hambre ahora* or:

— *¿Qué bebes cuando tienes sed?*
— *Bebo agua.*

2 If students have created flashcards, have them organize these according to the communicative categories.

3 Have students quiz each other using the list in the book or their flashcards. Ask them to indicate any words their partner had trouble with by writing them on a sheet of paper or placing a check on the flashcard. This will focus their test preparation on problem areas.

Assessment options

1 The *Prueba cumulativa* is a prochievement instrument that focuses on students' knowledge of the chapter vocabulary and grammar in a communicative context.

2 The *Examen de habilidades* is a proficiency-oriented instrument that focuses on what students can do with the language in a real-world context.

3 The Test Generator provides a test bank of multiple-choice questions to which you can add your own questions.

esumen del vocabulario

the vocabulary from this chapter to help you:

escribe what you like and don't like to eat
nd drink

tell when you have meals

say whether you are hungry or thirsty

ndicate hunger or thirst
er hambre / sed

describe meals
er: (yo) bebo
        (tú) bebes
ner: (yo) como
        (tú) comes
cena
comida
desayuno
el desayuno / el almuerzo /
la cena

talk about foods
arroz
bistec
cereal
ensalada
as frutas
    la manzana
    la naranja
    el plátano
    la uva
a hamburguesa
el huevo
el jamón
el pan
    el pan tostado
la papa
    las papas al horno
    las papas fritas

el pescado
el pollo
el queso
los sandwiches
    el sandwich de jamón
        y queso
la sopa de pollo / de tomate /
    de verduras
las verduras
    la cebolla
    los guisantes
    las judías verdes
    la lechuga
    el tomate
    la zanahoria

to talk about drinks
las bebidas
    el agua (f.)
    el café
    el jugo de naranja
    la leche
    la limonada
    el refresco
    el té
    el té helado

to describe foods
bueno, -a (para la salud)
horrible
malo, -a (para la salud)
sabroso, -a

to express likes or preferences
más o menos
me encanta(n)
me gusta(n)
preferir: (yo) prefiero
            (tú) prefieres

to express an opinion
Creo que sí / no.
¡Qué asco!

to ask for an explanation
¿Por qué?

to give an explanation
porque

to elicit agreement
¿verdad?

to refer to obligation
deber: (yo) debo
        (tú) debes

to indicate frequency
nunca
siempre

to refer to something you cannot name
algo

other useful words
son
unos, unas

Resumen   149

USING THE TEACHER'S EDITION

This Teacher's Edition provides all the support needed to work with the wide range of students in today's Spanish classes.

Each teacher chapter begins with a spread that provides organizational and cultural information for instructional planning.

> Additional information and insight into the chapter's cultural theme

> List of the chapter communication, culture, and grammar objectives

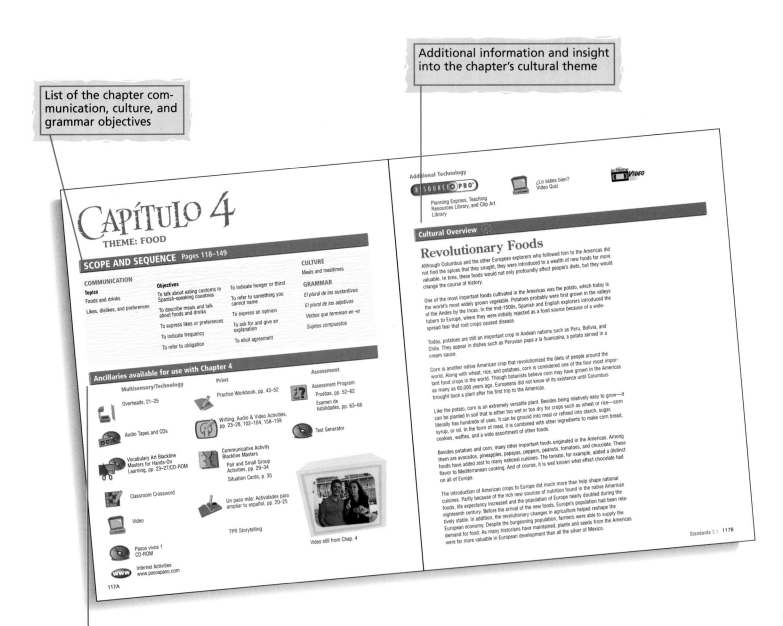

> List of ancillaries available, each represented by an icon that will be shown at suggested point of use

This Teacher's Edition is organized to provide for maximum ease of use. The student page is slightly reduced. Teacher notes appear regularly in the same place on the page.

Sidenotes are organized around the five-step pedagogical model used throughout *PASO A PASO:*

- **Introduce / Preview**
- **Present**
- **Practice**
- **Apply**
- **Summarize / Assess**

Notes provide answers, teaching suggestions, ancillary cross-references, recycling references, and other useful information.

Previously taught vocabulary sets that are re-entered in the chapter

Activities that expand the chapter theme into other curricular areas

Activities in which students can look beyond the classroom to find the influence of Hispanic cultures

Ideas for planning, strategies for reaching all students, and expansions on cultural themes

References to help with planning and instruction

Chapter theme

Communicative objectives

Icons for ancillary references

Ideas for recycling previously taught material

Additional perspectives from throughout the Spanish-speaking world

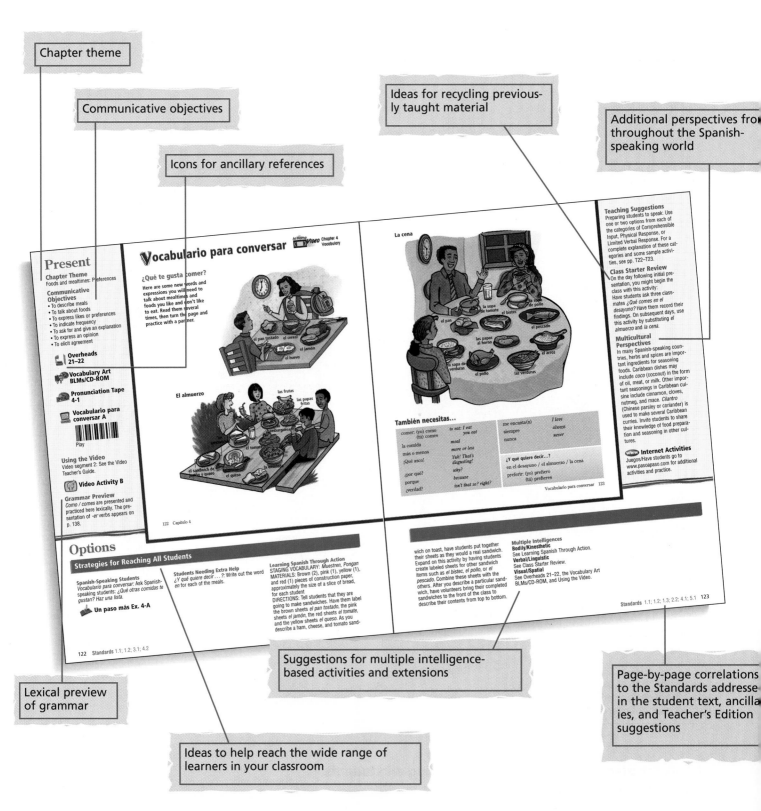

Lexical preview of grammar

Ideas to help reach the wide range of learners in your classroom

Suggestions for multiple intelligence-based activities and extensions

Page-by-page correlations to the Standards addressed in the student text, ancillaries, and Teacher's Edition suggestions

CLASSROOM MANAGEMENT AND LESSON PLANS

PASO A PASO 1 has been carefully developed to provide the instructional materials for one school year. The authors had as a goal the development of a realistically paced and easy-to-manage program that would relieve teacher and student frustration. There is flexibility and choice among the textbook activities and ancillaries. To help work with the wide variety of learners in your classroom, *PASO A PASO 1* offers unprecedented support on every page. We developed the Scope and Sequence to give students the tools needed to communicate about their interests. Thematic chapter organization allows for real integration of vocabulary, grammar, and culture, while avoiding unneeded grammatical content.

We present vocabulary in logical sets and, when possible, with visuals. Research shows that both of these approaches lead to more efficient and more permanent learning. Above all, lexical and contextual introduction of grammar allows students to learn structures in a truly natural way. *Fui* is not "the first-person singular preterite of the verb *ir*," but, quite simply, "I went"—a concept that presents no difficulty. (This is particularly true for students who neither know nor care that "I went" is a past-tense form of the verb "to go.")

We would urge you to allow this process to unfold. Avoid explanations in the vocabulary section. Allow students to use the words naturally. By the time they reach the explanations they will feel confident in their ability to use the language.

Management and Lesson Plans for the Traditional Class Schedule

Teachers working in a traditional class schedule (meeting daily for approximately 40–50 minutes) should comfortably reach Chapter 12 in one school year.

Pacing for *El primer paso*

Do **not** spend more than two weeks on *El primer paso*. While students will need to recognize the vocabulary through listening and reading, they will not need spelling mastery at this point. Use this chapter to let students learn the beginning communication tools, cultural insights, and learning strategies. All of the concepts presented will be recycled throughout the text.

Pacing for Chapters 1–14

We suggest that approximately 11–13 instructional days be spent on each chapter, including assessment. This time will vary based upon the amount of instructional time and the range of students in the class.

As you begin teaching with *PASO A PASO 1,* you will sense a rhythm, a flow within each chapter that helps students move smoothly and successfully. The thematic integration and spiraling within a chapter, the extensive use of context and comprehensible input for vocabulary and grammar, the inductive questioning that leads to real understanding, and the recycling of previously taught material are part of the carefully thought-out chapter design. You should be able to move quickly through the chapters in the suggested time period.

The following Lesson Plans show how Chapter 1 might be organized for instruction. Feel free to adapt these sample lessons to your teaching style, students, and schedule. As you become more familiar with the program, you will find many more ways to use all of the *PASO A PASO* components.

Capítulo 1 Y tú, ¿cómo eres?

	Instructional Process	Tasks/Activities	Components
Day # 1	Introduction	Chapter 1 Objectives	Text, p. 27
	Preview/Presentation	Cultural Overview *¡Piensa en la cultura!*	Text, pp. 25B, 26–27 *En vivo: ¡Piénsalo bien!*
	Practice	Discussion Video Activity	Text, pp. 28–29 WAVA: Video Activity, p. 152, A
	Presentation	Vocabulary Presentation/Input	Text, pp. 30–31 Overheads 6–7 Vocabulary Art BLMs
	Closing/Assignments	Review day's objectives and tasks to be done Preview Day #2	Practice Wkbk. 1-1 Vocabulary Art BLMs
Day # 2	Introduction/Review	Class Starter Review Vocabulary Review Pronunciation Review Review homework	Text, p. 31 Vocabulary Art BLMs Pronunciation Tape 1-1 Practice Wkbk. 1-1
	Presentation	*También necesitas ...*	Text, p. 31
	Practice	Paired Practices 1, 2	Text, p. 32
	Application	Video Activity	*En vivo: Vocabulario para conversar* WAVA: Video Activities, p. 152, B: 1, 2, 4
	Closing/Assignments	Review day's objectives and tasks to be done Preview Day #3	Practice Wkbk. 1-2, 1-3, Organizer p. 22
Day # 3	Introduction/Review	Vocabulary Review Review homework	Text, pp. 30–31 Vocabulary Art BLMs Practice Wkbk. 1-2, 1-3
	Practice	Paired Practices 3, 4	Text, p. 33
	Application	Audio Activities	WAVA: Audio Activities 1.1, 1.2
	Assessment	Quiz	*Prueba* 1-1
	Closing/Assignments	Review day's objectives and tasks to be done Preview Day #4	Text, p. 33, *Empecemos a escribir* (and/or) WAVA: Writing Activities 1-A, 1-B

	Instructional Process	Tasks/Activities	Components
Day # 4	Introduction/Review	Review homework	Text, p. 33 (and/or)
			WAVA: Writing Activites 1-A, 1-B
	Assessment	Quiz	*Prueba* 1-2
	Presentation	Vocabulary Presentation/Input	Text, pp. 34–35
			Overheads 8–9
			Vocabulary Art BLMs
	Practice	Video Activity	*En vivo: Vocabulario para conversar*
			WAVA: Video Activities, p. 152, B: 3
	Closing/Assignments	Review day's objectives and tasks to be done	Practice Wkbk. 1-4, 1-5
		Preview Day #5	Vocabulary Art BLMs
Day # 5	Introduction/Review	Class Starter Review	Text, p. 35
		Pronunciation Review	Pronunciation Tape 1-2
		Review homework	Practice Wkbk. 1-4, 1-5
			Vocabulary Art BLMs
	Practice	Paired Practices 1–4	Text, pp. 36–37
	Practice	Communicative Activity	Communicative Activity BLMs 1-1
	Assessment	Quiz	*Prueba* 1-3
	Closing/Assignments	Review day's objectives and tasks to be done	Text, p. 37, *Empecemos a escribir y a leer*
		Preview Day #6	Practice Wkbk. Organizer p. 22
Day # 6	Introduction/Review	Review homework	Text, p. 37
			Practice Wkbk. Organizer p. 22
	Practice	*¡Comuniquemos!*	Text, pp. 38–39
	Application	Choose from:	
		Audio Activities	WAVA: Audio Activities 1.3, 1.4
		Communicative Activity	Communicative Activity BLMs 1-2
		CD-ROM activities	*Pasos vivos 1* CD-ROM
	Closing/Assignments	Review day's objectives and tasks to be done	Text, p. 39, *¿Qué sabes ahora?*
		Preview Day #7	

	Instructional Process	Tasks/Activities	Components
Day # 7	Introduction/Review	Review homework	Text, p. 39
	Assessment	Quiz	*Prueba* 1-4
	Presentation/Practice	*Perspectiva cultural*	Text, pp. 40–41
	Presentation/Practice	Grammar: *Los adjetivos*	Text, pp. 42–43
	Closing/Assignments	Review day's objectives and tasks to be done Preview Day #8	Practice Wkbk. 1-6, 1-7
Day # 8	Introduction/Review	Review homework	Practice Wkbk. 1-6, 1-7
	Presentation/Practice	Grammar: *Ni . . . ni*	Text, p. 44
	Presentation/Practice	Grammar: *Sí/Tampoco*	Text, p. 45
	Application	Self-assessment	Text, p. 45, *Ahora lo sabes*
	Closing/Assignments	Review day's objectives and tasks to be done Preview Day #9	Practice Wkbk. 1-8, 1-9, Organizer p. 22
Day # 9	Introduction/Review	Review homework	Practice Wkbk. 1-8, 1-9, Organizer p. 22
	Practice	Communicative Activity	Communicative Activity BLMs 1-3
	Assessment	Quizzes	*Pruebas* 1-5, 1-6, 1-7
	Application	Choose from: Video Activity CD-ROM activities	*En vivo: Todo junto* WAVA: Video Activity, p. 153, C *Pasos vivos 1* CD-ROM
	Closing/Assignments	Review day's objectives and tasks to be done Preview Day #10	WAVA, pp. 7–8
Day # 10	Introduction/Review	Review homework	WAVA, pp. 7–8
	Presentation/Practice	*¡Vamos a leer!*	Text, pp. 48–49
	Application	Choose from: *Todo junto* activities *Actividades en grupo* CD-ROM activities	Text, pp. 46–47 Communicative Activity BLMs, p. 13 *Pasos vivos 1* CD-ROM
	Presentation	*¡Vamos a escribir!*	Text, p. 50
	Closing/Assignments	Review day's objectives and tasks to be done Preview Day #11	Text, p. 50, #1–3

	Instructional Process	Tasks/Activities	Components
Day # 11	Introduction/Review	Review and continue homework	Text, p. 50, 1–6
	Application	Self-assessment	Text, p. 52
	Closing/ Assignments	Review for chapter test	
Day # 12	Assessment	Chapter Test	Assessment Program: Choose from *Prueba cumulativa* or *Examen de habilidades* (or) Use components such as: WAVA, pp. 9–10; Situation Cards, Communicative Activities BLMs, p. 14; Test Generator
	Closing/Assignments	Preview Day #1 of *Capítulo 2*	Text, pp. 54–55

Management and Lesson Plans for the Block Schedule

PASO A PASO is ideal for the block schedule. The theme-based approach in each chapter allows for a more holistic presentation of content. Since the vocabulary, grammar, and culture are based upon the theme and recycle naturally throughout the chapter, there is flexibility in the way the material can be presented. The wide range of activities in the student book and the many ancillary components allow for individual, paired, and small group activities, as well as for the incorporation of different learning modalities. A variety of formal and informal assessment options are provided.

For teachers using the block schedule (85–90 minutes of instructional time), you should comfortably reach between Chapters 10–12 in one block.

Do not spend more than six days on *El primer paso*. While students will need to recognize the vocabulary through listening and reading, they will not need spelling mastery at this point. Use this chapter to let students learn the beginning communication tools, cultural insights, and learning strategies. All of the concepts presented will be recycled throughout the text.

We suggest approximately 6–8 instructional days for each chapter. Start planning by looking at the year as a whole. Determine how many class periods you will have for instruction and how these are grouped around grading periods, testing, and vacation. Determine what your goals will be and then develop a general plan for the entire year using the following sample lesson plans as a guide. To develop a daily lesson plan, you might want to divide each day into a five- or six-step instructional sequence: Introduction/Review; Preview/Presentation; Practice; Application; Assessment; and Closing/Assignments. The amount of time devoted to each and how it is sequenced each day will vary based upon daily goals. You will notice variations in these sample plans. Feel free to adapt them to your teaching style, students, and class schedule. As you become more familiar with the program, you will find many more ways to use all of the *PASO A PASO* components.

Capítulo 1   Y tú, ¿cómo eres?

	Instructional Process	Tasks/Activities	Components
Day # 1	Introduction	Outline day's objectives	Text, p. 30
	Presentation	Vocabulary presentation/Input	Text, pp. 30–31 Overheads 6–7 Vocabulary Art BLMs
	Practice	Paired Practices 1, 2	Text, p. 32
	Application	Video Activity	*En vivo: Vocabulario para conversar* WAVA: Video Activities, p. 152, B: 1, 2, 4
	Closing/Assignments	Review day's objectives and tasks to be done Preview Day #2	Practice Wkbk. 1-1 Vocabulary Art BLMs
Day # 2	Introduction/Review	Class Starter Review Vocabulary Review Pronunciation Review	Text, p. 31 Vocabulary Art BLMs Pronunciation Tape 1-1
	Presentation	*También necesitas …*	Text, p. 31
	Practice	Paired Practices 3, 4 *Empecemos a escribir*	Text, p. 33
	Application	Audio Activities *Todo junto #3*	WAVA: Audio Activities 1.1, 1.2 Text, p. 47
	Assessment	Recognition quiz	*Prueba* 1-1
	Closing/Assignments	Review day's objectives and tasks to be done Preview Day #3	Practice Wkbk. 1-2, 1-3, Organizer p. 22
Day # 3	Introduction/Review Assessment	Review homework Vocabulary quiz	Practice Wkbk. 1-2, 1-3, Organizer p. 22 *Prueba* 1-2 WAVA: Writing Activities 1-A, 1-B
	Presentation	Vocabulary Presentation/Input	Text, pp. 34–35 Overheads 8–9 Vocabulary Art BLMs
	Practice	Paired Practices 10, 11	Text, p. 36

	Instructional Process	Tasks/Activities	Components
Day # 3 *continued*	Application	Choose from: Video Activity *Gramática en contexto* CD-ROM activities	*En vivo: Vocabulario para conversar* WAVA: Video Activity, p. 152, B: 3 Text, p. 42 *Pasos vivos 1* CD-ROM
	Closing/Assignments	Review day's objectives and tasks to be done Preview Day #4	Practice Wkbk. 1-4, 1-5 Vocabulary Art BLMs
Day # 4	Introduction/Review	Class Starter Review Vocabulary Review Pronunciation Review	Text, p. 35 Vocabulary Art BLMs Pronunciation Tape 1-2
	Practice	Paired Practice 12, *Empecemos a escribir y a leer* Communicative Activity	Text, p. 37 Communicative Activity BLMs 1-1
	Assessment Application	Quiz Audio Activity CD-ROM activities	*Prueba* 1-3 WAVA: Audio Activity 1.3 *Pasos vivos 1* CD-ROM
	Closing/Assignments	Review day's objectives and tasks to be done Preview Day #5	Text, p. 39, #3 Practice Wkbk. Organizer p. 22
Day # 5	Introduction/Review	Partner work based on homework	Text, p. 39, #3 Practice Wkbk. Organizer p. 22
	Presentation/Practice	*Perspectiva cultural*	Text, pp. 40–41
	Presentation/Practice	Grammar: *Los adjetivos* *Ni … ni*	Text, pp. 43–45
	Application	Choose from: Audio Activities Self-assessment CD-ROM activities	WAVA: Audio Activities 1.4, 1.5 Text, p. 39 *¿Qué sabes ahora?* *Pasos vivos 1* CD-ROM
	Closing/Assignments	Review day's objectives and tasks to be done Preview Day #6	Practice Wkbk. 1-6, 1-7, 1-8
Day # 6	Introduction/Review	Review homework	Practice Wkbk. 1-6, 1-7, 1-8
	Assessment	Quizzes	*Pruebas* 1-4, 1-5

	Instructional Process	Tasks/Activities	Components
Day # 6 *continued*	Presentation/Practice	Grammar: *Sí/Tampoco*	Text, p. 45
	Application	Choose from: Communicative Activity Self-assessment Video Activity CD-ROM activities	Communicative Activity BLMs 1-2 Text, p. 45, *Ahora lo sabes* *En vivo: Todo junto* WAVA: Video Activity, p. 153, C *Pasos vivos 1* CD-ROM
	Closing/Assignments	Review day's objectives and tasks to be done Preview Day #7	Practice Wkbk. 1-9, Organizer p. 22 WAVA, pp. 7–8
Day # 7	Introduction/Review	Review homework	Practice Wkbk. 1-9, Organizer; WAVA
	Assessment	Quizzes	*Pruebas* 1-6, 1-7
	Presentation/Practice	*¡Vamos a leer!*	Text, pp. 48–49
	Application	Choose from: *Aplicación* *Todo junto* #1, 2 *¡Vamos a escribir!* Communicative Activity *Actividades en grupo* CD-ROM activities	Text, p. 49 Text, pp. 46–47 Text, p. 50 Communicative Activity BLMs 1-3 Communicative Activity BLMs, p. 13 *Pasos vivos 1* CD-ROM
	Application	Self-assessment	Text, p. 52
	Closing/Assignments	Review for chapter test	
Day # 8	Assessment	Chapter Test	Assessment Program: Choose from *Prueba cumulativa* or *Examen de habilidades* (or) Use components such as: WAVA, pp. 9–10 or Situation Cards, Communicative Activity BLMs, p. 14; *Pasos vivos 1* CD-ROM; Test Generator
	Preview/Presentation	Chapter 2 Objectives Cultural Overview *¡Piensa en la cultura!*	Text, pp. 54–55 Text, p. 53B *En vivo: ¡Piénsalo bien!*
	Practice	Discussion Video Activity	Text, pp. 56–57 WAVA: Video Activities, p. 154, A
	Closing	Preview Day #2	Text, pp. 58–59

Bridging to *PASO A PASO 2*

As students move into *PASO A PASO 2,* it is expected that they will have completed at least the content in Chapters 1–12 of Book 1. The vocabulary and grammar in Chapters 13–14 of Book 1 are retaught in *PASO A PASO 2.*

Review and reteaching

As students move into *PASO A PASO 2,* they will continually be exposed to previously learned material from Book 1.

PASO A PASO 2 begins with a lively, communicative magazine-like section entitled *Pasodoble* that reactivates the major vocabulary sets and structures of the early chapters of *PASO A PASO 1.*

The chart below shows the reteaching and expansion of specific grammar points in *PASO A PASO 2* that students first learned in *PASO A PASO 1.* (For information on grammar re-entry in *PASO A PASO 3,* see the equivalent Front Matter pages in Book 2.)

Grammar	PASO A PASO 1	PASO A PASO 2
ser	1, **5***	*Pasodoble,* **4, 7**
adjectives	**1,** 3, **4, 5, 6, 7, 8, 9**	*Pasodoble,* **1, 3**
negatives	**1,** 2, **14**	**8**
regular *-ar* verbs	**2**	*Pasodoble*
tener	2, 4, **5**	*Pasodoble,* **1**
ir	**3**	*Pasodoble*
estar	**3**	*Pasodoble,* **8**
stem-changing verbs: *o→ue*	3, **7, 9**	**2**
stem-changing verbs: *e→ie*	3, 4, **7, 8**	**2**
regular *-er* verbs	**4**	*Pasodoble*
possessive adjectives	**5, 8**	**7**
demonstrative adjectives	**6**	**1, 3**
direct object pronouns	**6,** 10, **11, 12,** 13	**1, 9**
preterite	6, 7, 9, **10, 11, 12,** 13	**3, 4, 6, 9, 10**
salir	**7**	**1**
personal *a*	**7**	*Pasodoble*
regular *-ir* verbs	**8**	*Pasodoble*
hacer	**8**	*Pasodoble*
poner	**8**	**8**
indirect object pronouns	**9, 11, 12**	**2,** 3, **5,** 9
dar	11, **14**	**6**
comparatives / superlatives	**11**	**1, 3**
stem-changing verbs: *e→i*	**12**	**2, 6**
traer	**12**	**1,** 9
saber	**13**	**4, 8**
decir	**13**	**7**
tú affirmative commands	**13**	**12**
conocer	**14**	**1,** 5
present progressive	**14**	**8,** 9

*Lightface numbers represent lexical introduction or quick review; boldface numbers represent presentation of the grammar point.

INTEGRATING TECHNOLOGY IN THE *PASO A PASO* CLASSROOM

PASO A PASO provides a complete, state-of-the-art technology package for each chapter at all levels, including Internet-based activities, award-winning video programs, lively audio activities, interactive CD-ROMs that combine practice and performance-based tasks, easy-to-use test generators, and vocabulary art on CD-ROM. *PASO A PASO* also provides extensive overheads that build upon the time-tested approach of presenting vocabulary visually.

Throughout this Teacher's Edition, there are clear cross-references to the various technology components. The following chart shows how to integrate these in a chapter.

Chapter section	Technology component
¡Piensa en la cultura!	*En vivo* video
Vocabulario para conversar	*En vivo* video
	Pasos vivos CD-ROM
	Audio program
	www.pasoapaso.com
	Vocabulary Art CD-ROM
	Overheads
Perspectiva cultural	www.pasoapaso.com
	Pasos vivos CD-ROM
Gramática en contexto	Overheads
	Pasos vivos CD-ROM
	Audio program
Todo junto: Actividades	*En vivo* video
	Pasos vivos CD-ROM
Todo junto: ¡Vamos a leer!	www.pasoapaso.com
Todo junto: ¡Vamos a escribir!	*Pasos vivos* CD-ROM
Resumen: Exámenes	Audio program
	Test generator
	Pasos vivos CD-ROM

Internet-based Activities:
www.pasoapaso.com
Standards: 1.2; 1.3; 2.1; 2.2; 3.1; 3.2; 4.1; 4.2; 5.1; 5.2

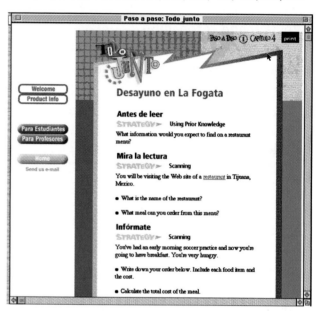

A quick trip via cyberspace to www.pasoapaso.com provides access to a wide range of activities, from authentic sources and cultural resources found on web sites to vocabulary and grammar games and extra drill-and-skill opportunities. All chapters in *PASO A PASO* have specific activities that integrate vocabulary, grammar, and culture. You will also find additional resources, articles, updates, teaching ideas, and ways to network with other *PASO A PASO* users.

En vivo Video Program
Standards: 1.2; 2.1; 2.2; 3.1; 3.2; 4.1; 4.2; 5.1; 5.2

En vivo (available on videocassettes or videodiscs) is integrated throughout each chapter in *PASO A PASO 1*. Student activity sheets are found in the Writing, Audio, and Video Activities workbook. An extensive Teacher's Guide offers many suggestions for use of the video.

Each episode is divided into three segments. The first, *¡Piénsalo bien!*, provides a visual montage of the chapter cultural theme. This almost entirely visual sequence provides an overview, allowing students to anticipate the situations they will encounter. It also provides a visual context for the language and cultural information they will be learning and reinforces and expands the cultural presentation of *¡Piensa en la cultura!*

The second segment, *Vocabulario para conversar,* presents the chapter's vocabulary as teenage hosts from Madrid, Guadalajara, and Miami show students their world. New language is presented through comprehensible input in culturally authentic situations. This segment is then repeated, the second time with key vocabulary words appearing on the screen.

The final segment, *Todo junto,* is designed to be shown after all new chapter vocabulary and grammar have been presented and practiced. This segment requires students to apply their newly acquired knowledge in slightly different contexts. The segment is repeated with additional visual cues as needed to aid comprehension.

Teachers will find *En vivo* to be a powerful tool in promoting the acquisition of new language, in developing listening comprehension skills, and in bringing the cultures of the Spanish-speaking world into the classroom in a lively, involving way.

Vocabulary Art CD-ROM

Standards: 1.1; 1.2

This clip art (part of the Resource Pro® CD-ROM) includes all visualized vocabulary from Books 1–3 of *PASO A PASO*. Teachers can modify the clip art to create a variety of hands-on learning tools, such as flashcards, posters, and games.

Audio Program

Standards: 1.2; 3.1

Each chapter contains a variety of audio activities, including vocabulary/pronunciation practice, contextualized listening activities, songs, and listening comprehension tests. The audio activities help students learn the vocabulary and grammar of each chapter. Student activity sheets appear in the Writing, Audio, and Video Activities workbook.

Pasos vivos 1 CD-ROM

Standards: 1.2; 1.3; 2.1; 2.2; 3.1; 3.2; 4.2; 5.1; 5.2

Students enter the world of broadcast station KPSO, where they encounter a wide range of interactive games and activities that allow them to practice and apply the chapter vocabulary and grammar, to view short video clips from *En vivo,* to record their own voices, and to produce a slide presentation, a video presentation, or a writing project using the built-in word processor. Students can develop oral and written portfolios and explore the many open-ended resources. Cultural notes, music, and beautiful, theme-based photographs expand the cultural support for each chapter.

Test Generator

Standards: 1.2; 1.3; 2.1; 2.2; 4.2

Teachers can access ready-made tests for each chapter that contain multiple choice, true/false, matching, fill-in-the-blank, short answer, and essay questions. You can integrate these as intra-chapter quizzes, prepare end-of-chapter tests, or combine questions from various chapters to create semester or year-end tests. The templates can also be used to create your own questions.

Overheads

Standards: 1.1; 1.2

Each chapter provides complete overheads for vocabulary and grammar presentation and practice.

STRATEGIES FOR REACHING ALL STUDENTS

PASO A PASO 1 provides teachers the support and strategies needed to reach all students in the Spanish classroom. We offer an unprecedented commitment to providing materials that help meet the realities of today's classroom. This article focuses on strategies from *PASO A PASO 1* that will help you and all of your students enjoy a successful year learning Spanish . . . step by step!

1 Material that builds upon students' experiences

Language students learn best by using what they know, by building new knowledge on old, and by experiencing and doing. As you use the text, you will see that *PASO A PASO 1* provides for an authentic, meaningful experience for the learner. The fourteen chapter themes were developed by asking, "What do students want to talk about?" The vocabulary taught is high-frequency language that students want to learn. The grammar supports communication and is practiced communicatively. The cultural content provides a means toward understanding and a global perspective that will be meaningful to all students. The activities ask students to interact, to become active participants in the learning process, and to express real ideas and real meanings for real purposes.

2 A multisensory approach to learning

Each student enters the Spanish classroom with different learning styles and abilities. Some work best with an aural / oral approach; others need a strong visual approach. Many need to touch and be physically involved in learning. An approach that addresses the needs and strengths of each student lays the groundwork for reaching all.

PASO A PASO 1 provides a strong multisensory approach to language learning. Students have varied opportunities for success by working with activities that recognize different learning styles and employ more than one modality. Each chapter provides suggestions for incorporating TPR, which we call Learning Spanish Through Action. The *Todo junto* offers activities that involve different learning skills and interests (creating a collage, preparing a skit, drawing a house).

The cornerstone of success in Scott Foresman's foreign language programs has always been our strong visual approach. We have expanded this in *PASO A PASO 1*. Each chapter opens with culturally authentic photographs (*¡Piensa en la cultura!*) that call upon students' background knowledge in discussing the chapter theme. Vocabulary presentation is facilitated by contextual visualization that is then recycled in the practice activities to reinforce learning. This approach is supported by the Overheads and the Vocabulary Art Blackline Masters/CD-ROM. We have enhanced the visual approach through a photo essay in the *Perspectiva cultural*. A new, realia-based approach offers students an opportunity to study grammar in a real-life context. And reading and writing practice are made more accessible through the strong use of visual cues.

The multisensory approach is further expanded through use of the chapter-by-chapter audio tapes, video, and the interactive multimedia CD-ROM. The video program brings the culture to students while providing support for the chapter's content. Language use is presented in an authentic context. The CD-ROM, *Pasos vivos*, provides opportunities for students to work at their own pace while engaging all learning styles.

3 Learning strategies

PASO A PASO 1 reinforces the strategies and skill-building techniques that students are using in their other classes. Some of these may be new to you but are easily implemented in the Spanish classroom. Strategies include building on background knowledge and experience, making lists or webs to organize their learning, inductive questioning, and consistent application of reading strategies and process writing.

4 Higher-order and inductive thinking

It sometimes seems that every day researchers are discovering new facts about the workings of the brain. We now know that information is stored in many areas of the brain and connected by a rich network of neurons. The goal of instruction should be to maximize the use of this network by helping students make connections and to learn information from a variety of perspectives and in a variety of ways. Activities aimed toward this goal are inherently interesting and motivating.

Students learn more successfully when they create their own understanding. Throughout *PASO A PASO 1* you will find activities that ask students to do just this. Inductive questions, for example, are the starting point of the following chapter features: *¡Piensa en la cultura!, Perspectiva cultural, Gramática en contexto,* and *¡Vamos a leer!* Activities that engage students in higher-level thinking skills are the initial focus in each of these sections, as well as in the *Actividades/Conexiones* and *¡Vamos a escribir!* We sequence these activities so that all students can be successful.

Another important learning strategy, informed guessing, is embedded in the vocabulary section entitled *¿Y qué quiere decir . . . ?* and is focused on in the inductive questions about photographs, as well as in the process reading and writing sections of each chapter.

5 Multiple learning opportunities

We know that students will improve at different rates and will be stronger in some areas than in others. In addition, developing proficiency takes time for everyone, no matter how gifted. Therefore, instruction must provide multiple opportunities for learning and improvement.

PASO A PASO 1 offers these opportunities. New vocabulary is presented, practiced, and recycled throughout a chapter and in subsequent chapters. Students are first exposed to grammar lexi-

cally, use it as they practice, and have some degree of understanding and control of it before it is presented and practiced as grammar. It is presented in easy-to-deal-with increments. Direct object pronouns, for example, are first explained in Chapter 6, with reminders and/or additional information being presented in Chapters 10–13; similarly with the preterite, which is first presented lexically in Chapter 6, and later explained in Chapters 10–13. In addition, recursive themes from one level to the next allow for regular review, expansion, and elaboration.

Throughout the text you will find reminder notes to students entitled *¡No olvides!* These focus on previously learned concepts that students will need in order to do a particular exercise or to understand better an extension of a given structure. These reminders are not crutches, but rather important tools for mastery.

6 Additional opportunities for students who need them

A regular on-page feature of this Teacher's Edition entitled "Strategies for Reaching All Students" provides you support for working with:

- Spanish-speaking students
- those having difficulty learning
- the gifted
- cooperative learning groups
- students needing extra practice
- multiple intelligences

For working with Spanish speakers, there are suggestions throughout the text, as well as a specially written supplemental worktext, *Un paso más: Actividades para ampliar tu español.* Notes under the heading "Students Needing Extra Help" suggest adaptations of the textbook activities or grammar explanations for those with real learning difficulties. Enrichment suggestions allow students who are capable of doing so to move beyond the textbook.

Varied assessment options

Students will do better in assessment situations if they have a clear understanding of the objectives and of how they will be assessed, and if they are assessed in such a way as to focus on their strengths.

PASO A PASO 1 offers a variety of options. Besides the *Pruebas* and *Exámenes de habilidades* in the Assessment Program, the *Actividades/ Conexiones* in the integrative *Todo junto* offer you different types of opportunities for assessment, asking students to draw upon auditory, visual, and kinesthetic strengths. The Communicative Activities Blackline Masters include Situation Cards that are ideal for use in assessing speaking proficiency. (For additional ideas, see the article on assessment, pp. T54–T58, and the Introduction to the Assessment Program itself.)

Through the clearly stated objectives at the beginning of each chapter and the mini-assessments within the chapter *(¿Qué sabes ahora?* and *Ahora lo sabes),* students are able to monitor their own progress. In addition, the end-of-chapter pretest *(Repaso: ⊅ ¿Lo sabes bien?)* gives them a clear picture of how they will be assessed on the *Examen de habilidades.*

PASO A PASO 1 is committed to helping every teacher reach every student in the Spanish class. By providing materials that are strategy-based and that have built-in teacher support, we believe that we are enabling both you and your students to experience real enjoyment and unparalleled success.

MULTIPLE INTELLIGENCES

Education, like most institutions, has weathered storms of quick fix-it methodologies or theories that look promising on paper but have little or no practical application or realistic hope of success in an actual classroom. The Multiple Intelligences Theory is in no way intended to be a quick fix-it approach for teaching second languages, yet it is easily applicable in any classroom with careful planning and reflection on the teacher's part. Additionally, the Multiple Intelligences Theory does not demand that you teach in a certain way or falsely promise an easy ten-step process which, if followed precisely, will transform the entire class into straight A students! However, what the theory does do is remind us of what we already know: Everyone learns in different ways, and if you present new material in a variety of formats, then more students will likely learn and be able to demonstrate proficiency with the new material.

The notion that a person's intellectual worth can be based on a narrowly focused standardized test was challenged in 1983 by Howard Gardner in his book, *Frames of Mind,* which proposed the theory of Multiple Intelligences. Gardner believes that a person has many different ways of both acquiring and demonstrating intelligence (Armstrong, 1994). For instance, some students can remember just about anything as long as it is learned to the tune of a jingle, while someone else may be able to grasp an idea, concept, or grammatical form provided it is presented visually in the form of a graph, chart, or picture. Gardner has identified and labeled eight main styles of acquiring and demonstrating knowledge; those eight intelligences are Verbal/Linguistic, Visual/Spatial, Bodily/Kinesthetic, Logical/Mathematical, Interpersonal/Social, Intrapersonal/Introspective, Musical/Rhythmic, and Naturalist. Allowing students the opportunity to learn and acquire knowledge in the manner in which they are most receptive maximizes their potential to become successful students (Armstrong, 1994; Beckman, 1998).

When Gardner introduced his theory of Multiple Intelligences in 1983, he marked a new trend in cognitive psychology, broadening perspectives on human brain functions and views on human potential in terms of learning, and facilitating attempts to explain human differences. Gardner presents the notion that there is no "general intelligence," but rather that the mind is organized around distinct functional capacities, which he defines as "intelligences." Though each of the intelligences is developed independently of the others over the course of a lifetime, they usually work together and do not often appear in isolation.

In this Teacher's Edition you will find frequent specific suggestions for accommodating and teaching to the Multiple Intelligences. This is not meant to be construed as a paradigm for labeling every student in your class. On the contrary, we must continue to recognize each student as unique, complex, and highly individualistic. Therefore, we must regard students holistically and as individuals, recognizing that they are intelligent in many ways and that their overall "intelligence" is based on the sum of all of their intelligences.

Given the nature of the subject, foreign language teachers traditionally work most often with the **Verbal/Linguistic Intelligence.** Individuals who demonstrate strength in this area think and express themselves through words and have a strong ability to understand and use language to communicate effectively (Chapman, 1993). They enjoy reading, writing, telling stories, playing word games, and often excel in memorizing.

Musical/Rhythmic Intelligence is reflected in an individual's ability to analyze or create musical compositions. This intelligence can be used in a foreign language classroom in a variety of ways, such as teaching about culture through music or having students create their own raps or jingles to enhance vocabulary/grammar learning. It is important to note that Gardner does not believe that music played in the background during an activity or test is necessarily engaging the Musical Intelligence. If it is merely background music, its function is "unlikely to be different from that of a dripping faucet or a humming fan" (Gardner, 1995). The following are opportunities for accommodating this intelligence: Students research Spanish dances and are prepared to discuss them and teach them to the class; students compose a song about traveling and favorite places to visit; students make up rhymes to practice vocabulary; students create and demonstrate an aerobic exercise routine.

Interpersonal/Social Intelligence operates primarily through person-to-person relationships and communication. A common misconception is that it applies only to extroverted individuals (Gardner, 1995). One of the most effective ways to utilize this intelligence is through pair, group, and cooperative learning activities.

Intrapersonal/Introspective Intelligence is the ability to understand oneself and to think introspectively. Such students often enjoy working alone, being allowed to pursue their own interests, being provided with individualized projects and self-paced instruction. The following activities will provide opportunities to accommodate this intelligence: Students write poems describing themselves; students write a report on their views about recycling; students write a personal agenda for improving the environment.

Bodily/Kinesthetic Intelligence is related to physical movement and the ability to manipulate objects. These students enjoy most physical activities, e.g., moving, touching, body language, jumping, and running. Learning Spanish Through Action provides a wide variety of activities that accommodate this intelligence. Other production activities include role-playing, drama, creative movements, and gross motor and whole body activities.

Visual/Spatial Intelligence relies on the sense of sight and being able to visualize an object through mental images or pictures. These students enjoy opportunities to work with art and construction materials and to create projects. The use of video, movies, slides, imagination games, mazes, and puzzles will accommodate this intelligence.

Logical/Mathematical Intelligence deals with inductive and deductive reasoning, numbers, and the recognition of abstract patterns. Individuals who enjoy analyzing similarities and differences and manipulating numbers and graphs are strong in this intelligence. These students will perform well by working with numbers, exploring patterns and relationships, and using manipulatives. The following activities will provide opportunities to accommodate this intelligence: Students use a Venn diagram to compare Spanish and U.S. homes; students create a survey to determine what one should do to prevent catching a cold and display the results in a graph or chart; students use a logic puzzle to figure out which primary colors combine to produce the secondary colors on their TV screen.

Naturalist Intelligence is the latest intelligence added by Gardner. It includes the capacity to recognize flora and fauna, to make distinctions in the natural world, and to use this ability productively in activities such as gardening, farming, and biological science. This intelligence involves the ability to see the natural world from a larger perspective—an understanding of how nature interacts with civilization, the symbiotic relationships inherent in nature, and the life cycles of nature. Students exhibiting this intelligence will learn best through working in nature, exploring living things, learning about plants and natural events.

It should be stressed that the eight intelligences were not designed to be used as a new set of labels for teachers to assign to students (Edwards, 1998). Instead, by identifying a student's preferred intelligence, you can encourage the learning process while also fostering the other intelligences through appropriate activities.

As a rule, the eight intelligences should not be thought of as independent and isolated approaches, but rather should be intertwined and used in conjunction with each other to create the best possible learning experience for all students (Armstrong, 1994).

Integrating the use of Multiple Intelligences into the classroom does not require a major overhaul of lesson plans or a reworking of the curriculum. Generally, all that is required is supplementing and enhancing already existing lesson plans with a few creative and imaginative activities (Campbell, 1997). Some first-hand accounts are reassuring because many teachers find that in a very short time thinking and planning within the framework of the eight intelligences becomes second nature and quite painless (Campbell, 1989). Another suggestion from veteran Multiple Intelligences teachers is to team teach or team plan with teachers who have strengths in the intelligences that complement your own (Campbell, 1997).

The idea of Multiple Intelligences is a wonderful concept because it recognizes and validates the fact that every person is an individual who acquires and demonstrates knowledge through different means. However inclined, students should all be given the same opportunity to function in the manner in which they are most receptive and proficient. Some of those students may even discover that they actually enjoy learning—and that is the goal of every teacher: to instill the love of learning for learning itself.

References

Armstrong, Thomas. *Multiple Intelligences in the Classroom.* State of Virginia: Association for Supervision and Curriculum Development (1994).

Beckman, Marian S. *Multiple Ways of Knowing: Howard Gardner's Theory of Multiple Intelligences Extend and Enhance Student Learning.* http://www.earlychildhood.com/articles/artmi.html (1998).

Campbell, Bruce. "Multiplying Intelligences in the Classroom." New Horizons for Learning: *On the Beam,* IX, No. 2, (Winter 1989).

Campbell, Linda. "Variations on a Theme: How Teachers Interpret MI Theory." *Educational Leadership,* Vol. 55, No. 1 (September 1997).

Campbell, L., B. Campbell, and D. Dickinson. *Teaching and Learning Through Multiple Intelligences.* Tucson, AZ: Zephyr Press (1996).

Chapman, C. *If the Shoe Fits . . . How to Develop Multiple Intelligences in the Classroom.* Palatine, IL: IRI/Skylight (1993).

Edwards, Jack. *Multiple Intelligences and Technology.* http://www.firn.edu/~face/about/dec95/multi_int.html (1995).

Gardner, Howard. *Frames of Mind: The Theory of Multiple Intelligences.* New York: Basic Books (1983).

————. *Multiple Intelligences: The Theory in Practice: A Reader.* New York: Basic Books (1993).

ASSESSMENT

Various methods of assessment are appropriate in a standards-driven classroom. Chapter tests, student conferences, teacher notes, checklists, portfolios, and performance demonstrations are all part of a well-rounded assessment program. All have advantages and disadvantages, and to use any one method exclusively would block your view of the total student picture. *PASO A PASO 1* offers a multi-faceted assessment program based on the premise that the main purpose of learning a language is to communicate in a meaningful and culturally appropriate way. As you begin to use the assessment program, you might want to start by asking yourself a few key questions: What do I expect my students to learn? What do I want them to be able to do? and How can I assess what I am looking for in student performance? Your answers to these questions can help define your philosophy in regard to assessment.

Self-Assessment of Chapter Objectives

Essential to any assessment program is the inclusion of self-assessment opportunities, which allow students to become independent evaluators of their own progress and to take more responsibility for their own learning. They engage students in the process of learning and promote greater involvement and reflection. The *chapter objectives* offer the basis for a self-assessment checklist of what each student should be able to do at the end of the chapter. The stated objectives can be rewritten by you and distributed as "I can . . ." statements to be used as a checklist as students move through the chapter. For example, a checklist for *El primer paso* might look like this:

Student Checklist	*El primer paso*	
Using the Spanish I have learned . . .	**Yes**	**No**
1. I can greet people and introduce myself.	☐	☐
2. I can ask how someone is feeling and can tell someone else how I am feeling.	☐	☐
3. I can ask where someone is from and can tell where I am from.	☐	☐
4. I can say good-by.	☐	☐
5. I can use the Spanish alphabet to spell words aloud.	☐	☐
6. I can use numbers to count and to tell my age, my phone number, and the date.	☐	☐
7. I can ask questions such as "How do you say . . .?" and "How do you write . . .?"	☐	☐
8. I can respond correctly to the teacher's requests in the classroom, such as *Saquen una hoja de papel* or *Date la vuelta*.	☐	☐
9. I can describe, in English, at least one influence of the Spanish language and Hispanic culture.	☐	☐
10. I can use my textbook to help me understand vocabulary, conversations, and cultural information.	☐	☐

Two Types of Assessment

Both traditional and authentic assessment are part of the *PASO A PASO 1* program. *Traditional assessments* test knowledge of limited materials presented in a given chapter, and therefore are achievement based. *Authentic assessments* evaluate what learners can *do* with the language being learned, and are therefore competency-based.

Both have a valid place in today's classroom. While the former assess for "coverage," the latter assess for "uncoverage." In other words, it is important to know that students can prove mastery of the material covered, but it is also important to "uncover" how they can use this language to express their own meanings.

PASO A PASO 1 offers you opportunities to assess the students' knowledge of specific vocabulary and grammar points through the use of several *pruebas* provided for each chapter. These prompt the student to progress from simple vocabulary recognition to limited production of a specific grammatical structure. The *prueba cumulativa* can be used as a final quiz to assess students' ability to apply learned material in a new context. The *Test Generator,* a bank of multiple-choice questions, offers yet another option for end of chapter assessment. It serves especially well as a make-up assessment for those who were unable to attend class on final quiz day.

A unique assessment tool in *PASO A PASO 1*, the *Examen de habilidades,* provides a vehicle for evaluating students' ability to apply what they have learned in a realistic, yet controlled context. For example, students may be asked to role-play a situation in which they are buying clothes. These more revealing, performance-based assessments provide engaging tasks from which to evaluate students' ability to use acquired language more creatively. Both the *Test Generator* and the *Banco de ideas* section offer additional test questions and assessment tasks, providing students opportunities to demonstrate real-life applications of the language they are learning.

Many of the activities in the *Todo junto* and *¡Vamos a escribir!* sections of the textbook provide the basis for *performance demonstrations,* such as individual writing projects, small group presentations, and paired conversations. Tasks in the very engaging CD-ROM package, *Pasos vivos 1,* include making videos and replying to faxes in the imaginary setting of radio station KPSO. Such performance assessments allow you to see the students' actual use of language in several types of tasks. Another source of mini-performance asssessments can be found in the *Communicative Activity Blackline Masters,* which offer small group tasks, paired activities, and situation cards.

Grading Performance Assessments

PASO A PASO 1 provides you with several templates for *scoring rubrics.* These include numerical values associated with performance levels, such as Below Average (1 point), Average (3 points), and Good (5 points). The criteria are precisely defined in terms of what students actually do to demonstrate performance at that level and they reflect what are considered to be appropriate communication skills and strategies. These criteria can be changed at any time to reflect a different emphasis. A rubric should be explained in advance to the students so that they have a clear understanding of what is expected of them and the level of performance needed to receive the highest score.

Grading a Paired Conversation

Throughout *PASO A PASO 1,* there are many activities that can serve as a basis for a performance assessment. For example, in the *Todo junto* section of Chapter 2, students interview each other concerning the classes they are taking. What would your expectations be for your students in this activity? How can you be consistent in the way you grade performances? The following rubric can serve as a template for this paired activity, as well as for many similar tasks in any chapter:

Paired Conversation Rubric

	1 point	3 points	5 points
Language Use	Heavy reliance on English words, word order, and pronunciation.	Frequently uses English words, word order, and pronunciation.	Can "talk around" an exact word in order to maintain conversation in Spanish.
Ability to Sustain Conversation	Can only answer partner's direct questions.	Can both ask and answer questions.	Can state opinions and give reasons for them.
Conversational Interaction	Interaction is nonexistent. No conversational reaction to what is said by partner.	Limited conversational reaction to what is said by partner. Responds, but quickly moves to next question.	Natural interaction between partners. Each responds by following up on what the other person says.

15 pts. = A; 11–13 pts. = B; 7–9 pts. = C; 3–5 pts. = D

This particular rubric makes clear to students that getting their message across to their partners and maintaining a conversational flow are your top priorities at this point.

Although performance levels will vary greatly, your expectations are firmly anchored in the rubric's descriptors and in the models you give as examples of the different levels. For example, *Me* (pronounced as the English 'me') *gusta my Spanish clase* is an example of *language use* at the 1-point level, whereas *Me gusta mi clase español* is at the 3-point level. *Me gusta mi clase de . . . de . . . Sra. Stafford* is at the 3-point level because even while forgetting the Spanish word for English, the student was able to substitute the teacher's name instead. A student able both to answer and ask questions would receive 3 points for *ability to sustain conversation*. To perform at the 5-point level, the student would offer a reason by saying something such as, *Me gusta mi clase de español. La Sra. Stafford es muy paciente.*

Conversational interaction focuses on whether the partners are listening and responding appropriately. For example, after hearing that one's partner really likes Spanish class, the student responds at the 1-point level by ignoring the information and saying *Mi clase de historia empieza a las diez.* At the 3-point level, the student might respond with *A mí también.* A performance in conversational interaction at the 5-point level would elicit a response such as *A mí también. La Sra. Stafford es muy paciente e interesante.*

Grading a Writing Sample

Throughout *PASO A PASO 1,* students are led through the writing process to enable them to organize both their thinking and writing. There are several writing tasks strategically placed in each chapter's *¡Vamos a escribir!* sections. These can serve as stand-alone writing assessments, or as writing assignments for homework. In either case, you want to be able to grade the sample objectively and fairly. For example, students are asked in Chapter 2 to compose a letter, based on process writing strategies, to a Spanish-speaking friend outside of the class. The following rubric could be used for this activity and many similar writing tasks in the program:

Writing Rubric

Criteria	1 point	3 points	5 points
Use of pre-writing strategies	Only turns in final product.	Turns in lists or planning notes along with final product.	Turns in planning notes, first draft, and final product.
Accuracy	Many spelling errors and repeated patterns of subject/verb agreement errors.	Several spelling errors and repeated patterns of subject/verb agreement errors.	Few spelling or subject/verb agreement errors.
Content	Gives no examples or details about the topic.	Gives a few examples or details about the topic.	Consistently adds examples and/or details about topic.

15 pts. = A; 11–13 pts. = B; 7–9 pts. = C; 3–5 pts. = D

Assessment of Cultural Awareness

Both the *Foreign Language Standards* and *PASO A PASO 1* emphasize the importance of students' using their language and cultural understanding outside of the classroom in order to connect to and reflect on their own and the target culture. At several points in each chapter, students are called upon to reflect about the products, practices, and perspectives of people in the Spanish-speaking world, and as they progress through the program, they gain increasing awareness of Hispanic influences around them.

In the *Examen de habilidades,* students are consistently asked to compare their own culture to that of the Spanish-speaking world and to reflect about the differences and similarities. For example, they might be asked to compare the customs and practices in Mexican schools with those in their own, or to think of ways in which the Spanish-speaking world has influenced the U.S. in the areas of food, music, or clothing. Since the students respond in English, they are able to express more sophisticated thoughts in regard to the cultural prompt. You might give half the allotted points to the student for stating the factual information, and the additional half for evidence of having reflected on the whys and hows of the cultural issue.

Personal Culture Logs

In order to encourage cultural awareness, you might want to ask students to keep a log of at least ten instances in which they have encountered the target language or target culture in their own communities. Their entries might include chance meetings with Spanish speakers, snippets of conversation in movies or TV programs, street or store signs, product information, references noted from other classes where Spanish culture or language was mentioned, or any other experience in which students realized that "something Spanish" was going on.

Each of the ten entries would be graded as 2-point, 4-point, or 6-point entries. The following rubric could be distributed to students and used for giving an objective grade to their log entries. The rubric guides students to go beyond the recognition level to a more reflective level of thinking about culture and language. The following is an example of a student entry in a culture log that would earn six points because of the evidence of reflection:

Personal Language and Culture Log

Date	Recognition—2 points	Comprehension—4 points	Reflection—6 points
	"Hey, that's Spanish!"	"Hey, that's Spanish and I know what it means!"	"Hey, that's Spanish and I think I know why they did that!"
1.			We went to the arts festival in the city's Paseo District. *Paseo* means "walk" in Spanish. I bet they named it that because it is one of the few places where there are sidewalks for people who like to walk!

Portfolios

A portfolio is a purposeful collection that exhibits a student's performance efforts, progress, and achievement over a period of time. Some teachers, especially those working on a block schedule, have found that portfolios have given their students an avenue to pursue some things outside of class that they don't have time to develop in the class period. For example, students could compare the reporting of a major international news story in newspapers from around the Spanish-speaking world to that in the United States by accessing foreign newspapers on the Internet outside of class. Portfolios can allow students to document aspects of their learning that do not show up well in traditional assessments, yet are part of the overall assessment program.

One of the most common uses of portfolios is to showcase the students' favorite examples of their work. This type of portfolio can include both assigned and student-selected projects. Since the student chooses some of the work to be showcased, the portfolio can link the student personally to his or her own assessment in a way that traditional assessment can never create. The final portfolio can then be shared with parents, friends, and other teachers.

Another type of portfolio might have the focus of documenting student progress over time. You could collect baseline samples of work, such as the first piece of writing for the year and the first oral interview, and then regularly update and add to the portfolio. It can be a unique opportunity for your students to monitor and evaluate their own progress.

INDEX OF CULTURAL REFERENCES

PASO A PASO

1

Unas molas de San Blas, Panamá

These *molas* are hanging out to dry. *Molas* are decorative handsewn blouse inserts made and used by members of the Cuna Indians from the San Blas Islands, Panama. They are embroidered by reverse appliqué (a technique in which patterns are cut out and stitched over other fabrics, thus revealing the colors of the underlying fabrics). Their designs are traditionally abstract, often based on the patterns of coral in the local waters.

1

Myriam Met
Coordinator of Foreign Languages
Montgomery County Public Schools
Rockville, MD

Richard S. Sayers
Longmont, CO

Carol Eubanks Wargin
Glen Crest Junior High School
Glen Ellyn, IL

Prentice Hall

Glenview, Illinois
Needham, Massachusetts
Upper Saddle River, New Jersey

Visit our Web site at http://www.pasoapaso.com

3 4 5 6 7 8 9 10 DOC 03 02 01 00

Prentice Hall
Upper Saddle River, New Jersey 07458

Contributing Writers

Eduardo Aparicio
Miami, FL

Margaret Juanita Azevedo
Stanford University
Palo Alto, CA

Thomasina Pagán Hannum
Albuquerque, NM

Mary de López
Río Rancho Public Schools
Río Rancho, NM

Jacqueline Hall Minet
Brooklyn, NY

Reader Consultants

The authors and editors would like to express our heartfelt thanks to the following team of reader consultants. Each of them read the manuscript, chapter by chapter, offering suggestions and providing encouragement. Their contribution has been invaluable.

Rosario Martínez-Cantú
Northside Health Careers High School
San Antonio, TX

Greg Duncan
InterPrep
Marietta, GA

Barbara A. Gordon
Apopka High School
Apopka, FL

Walter Kleinmann
Sewanhaka Central High School District
New Hyde Park, NY

Bernadette M. Reynolds
Parker, CO

Rudolf L. Schonfeld, Ph.D.
Parsippany-Troy Hills School District
Parsippany, NJ

Marcia Payne Wooten
Starmount High School
Boonville, NC

Tabla de materias

X

CAPÍTULO 9 ¿Cómo te sientes?

283

Theme

► Health

Objectives

► Describe how you are feeling
► Tell what parts of your body hurt
► Suggest things you or others can do to feel better
► Discuss attitudes toward health and health practices in the Spanish-speaking world

CAPÍTULO 10 ¿Qué hiciste ayer?

313

Theme

► Community

Objectives

► Name various places in your community
► Name activities or errands you do
► Identify different means of transportation available in your area
► Compare and contrast a Hispanic community with a community you are familiar with

CAPÍTULO 13 Para proteger la Tierra 415

Theme

▶ The Environment

Objectives

▶ Describe the natural environment

▶ List actions to protect the environment

▶ Discuss environmental dangers

▶ Name species in danger of extinction in the United States and the Spanish-speaking world and say what can be done to protect them

CAPÍTULO 14 ¡Vamos a una fiesta! 447

Theme

▶ Parties and Celebrations

Objectives

▶ Make plans for giving or attending a party

▶ Describe gift-giving

▶ Make and acknowledge introductions

▶ Compare parties that Spanish-speaking teenagers go to with those you usually attend

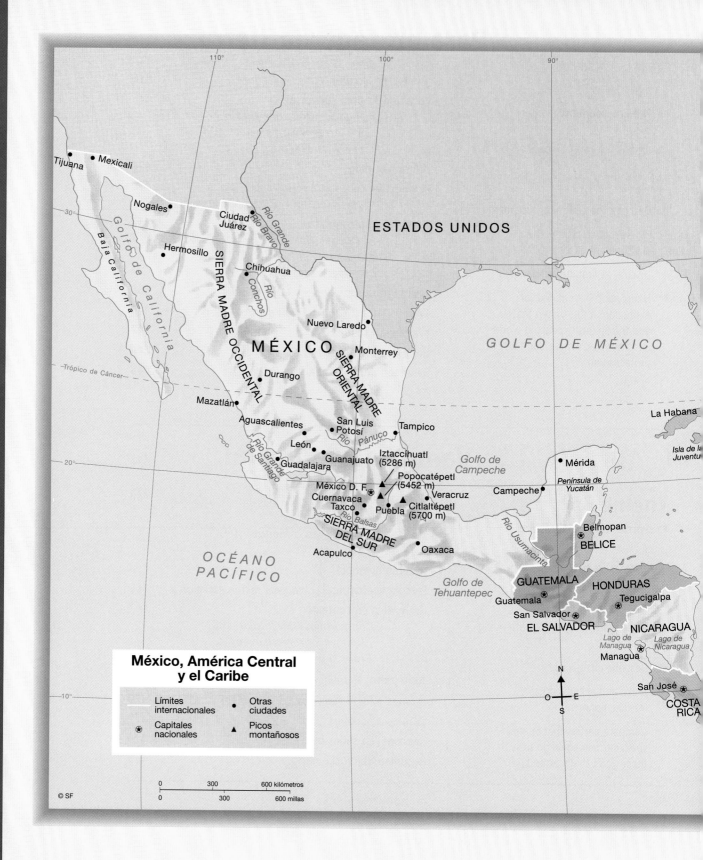

México, América Central y el Caribe

Límites internacionales

Capitales nacionales

Otras ciudades

Picos montañosos

| 0 | 300 | 600 kilómetros |
| 0 | 300 | 600 millas |

© SF

ESTADOS UNIDOS

GOLFO DE MÉXICO

OCÉANO PACÍFICO

MÉXICO

Tijuana
Mexicali
Nogales
Ciudad Juárez
Hermosillo
Chihuahua
Nuevo Laredo
Monterrey
Durango
Mazatlán
Aguascalientes
San Luis Potosí
Tampico
León
Guanajuato
Guadalajara
Iztaccíhuatl (5286 m)
Popocatépetl (5452 m)
México D. F.
Cuernavaca
Veracruz
Taxco
Puebla
Citlaltépetl (5700 m)
Acapulco
Oaxaca
Mérida
Campeche
Belmopan
BELICE
GUATEMALA
HONDURAS
Guatemala
Tegucigalpa
San Salvador
EL SALVADOR
NICARAGUA
Managua
San José
COSTA RICA
La Habana
Isla de la Juventud

Golfo de California
Baja California
SIERRA MADRE OCCIDENTAL
SIERRA MADRE ORIENTAL
SIERRA MADRE DEL SUR
Río Grande
Río Bravo
Río Conchos
Río Pánuco
Río Grande de Santiago
Río Balsas
Río Usumacinta
Golfo de Campeche
Península de Yucatán
Golfo de Tehuantepec
Lago de Managua
Lago de Nicaragua

Trópico de Cáncer

110°   100°   90°
30°
20°
10°

N
O   E
S

XIV

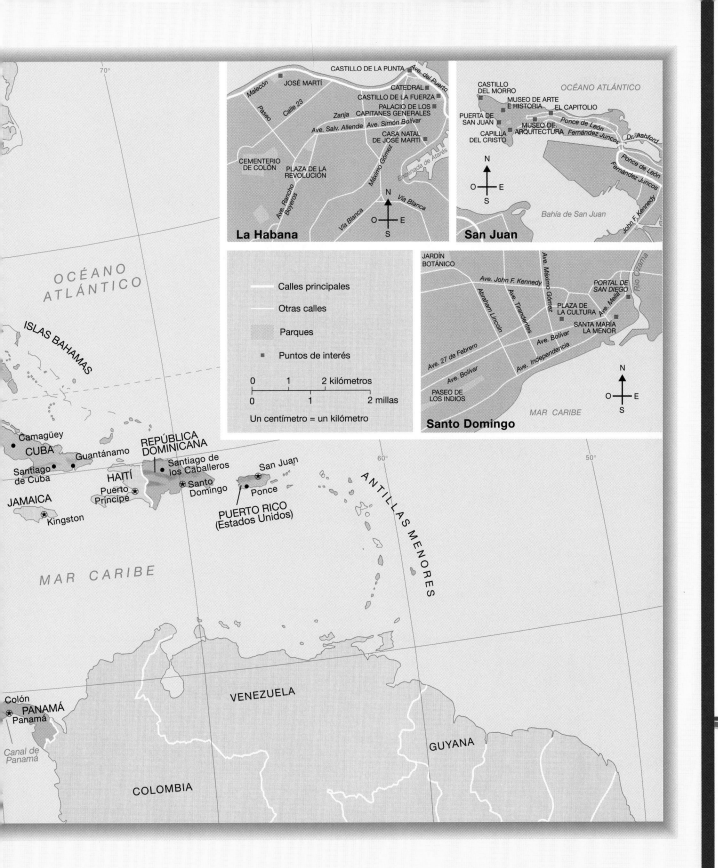

La Habana

CASTILLO DE LA PUNTA
Ave. del Puerto
Malecón
JOSÉ MARTÍ
CATEDRAL
CASTILLO DE LA FUERZA
Paseo
Calle 23
PALACIO DE LOS CAPITANES GENERALES
Zanja
Ave. Salv. Allende   Ave. Simón Bolívar
CASA NATAL DE JOSÉ MARTÍ
CEMENTERIO DE COLÓN
Máximo Gómez
Ensenada de Atarés
PLAZA DE LA REVOLUCIÓN
Ave. Rancho Boyeros
Vía Blanca
Vía Blanca
Vía Blanca

San Juan

CASTILLO DEL MORRO
OCÉANO ATLÁNTICO
MUSEO DE ARTE E HISTORIA
EL CAPITOLIO
PUERTA DE SAN JUAN
Ponce de León
Fernández Juncos
MUSEO DE ARQUITECTURA
Dr. Ashford
CAPILLA DEL CRISTO
Ponce de León
Fernández Juncos
Bahía de San Juan
John F. Kennedy

OCÉANO ATLÁNTICO

ISLAS BAHAMAS

Camagüey
CUBA
Guantánamo
Santiago de Cuba
HAITÍ
Puerto Príncipe
JAMAICA
Kingston

REPÚBLICA DOMINICANA
Santiago de los Caballeros
Santo Domingo
San Juan
Ponce
PUERTO RICO (Estados Unidos)

Calles principales
Otras calles
Parques
Puntos de interés

| 0 | 1 | 2 kilómetros |
| 0 | 1 | 2 millas |

Un centímetro = un kilómetro

Santo Domingo

JARDÍN BOTÁNICO
Ave. John F. Kennedy
Ave. Máximo Gómez
Abraham Lincoln
Ave. Tiradentes
Ave. Máximo Gómez
PORTAL DE SAN DIEGO
Ave. Mella
PLAZA DE LA CULTURA
SANTA MARÍA LA MENOR
Río Ozama
Ave. 27 de Febrero
Ave. Bolívar
Ave. Bolívar
Ave. Independencia
PASEO DE LOS INDIOS
MAR CARIBE

MAR CARIBE

ANTILLAS MENORES

Colón
PANAMÁ
Panamá
Canal de Panamá

VENEZUELA

GUYANA

COLOMBIA

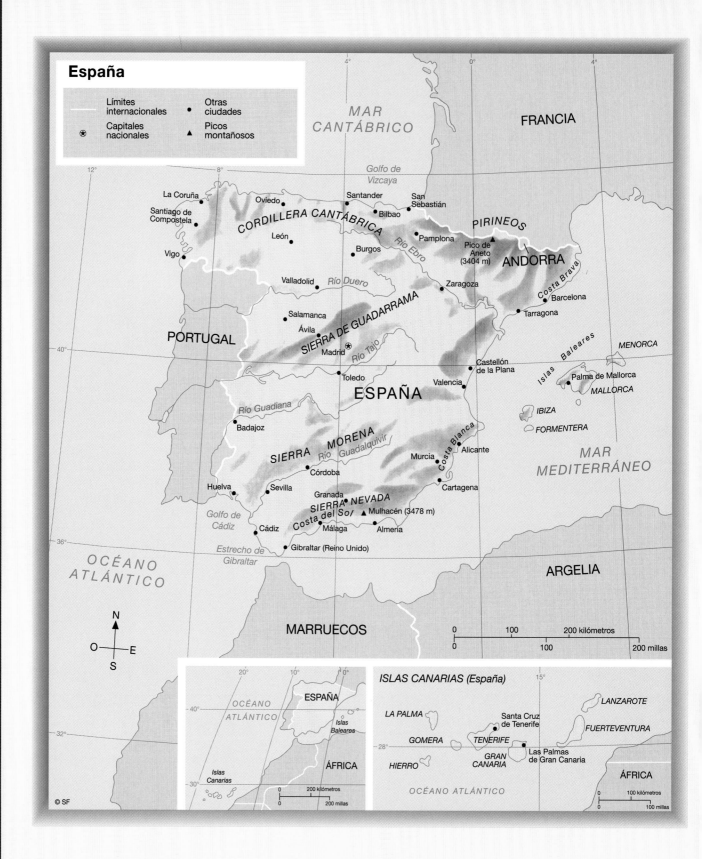

España

Límites internacionales
Capitales nacionales
Otras ciudades
Picos montañosos

FRANCIA

MAR CANTÁBRICO

Golfo de Vizcaya

La Coruña
Santiago de Compostela
Oviedo
Santander
San Sebastián
Vigo
Bilbao
CORDILLERA CANTÁBRICA
León
Burgos
PIRINEOS
Pamplona
Pico de Aneto (3404 m)
ANDORRA
Río Ebro
Valladolid
Río Duero
Zaragoza
Costa Brava
Barcelona
Salamanca
Tarragona
Ávila
SIERRA DE GUADARRAMA
PORTUGAL
Madrid
Río Tajo
Toledo
ESPAÑA
Castellón de la Plana
Valencia
Islas Baleares
MENORCA
Palma de Mallorca
MALLORCA
Río Guadiana
IBIZA
FORMENTERA
Badajoz
SIERRA MORENA
Río Guadalquivir
Costa Blanca
Alicante
Murcia
MAR MEDITERRÁNEO
Córdoba
Cartagena
Huelva
Sevilla
Granada
SIERRA NEVADA
Mulhacén (3478 m)
Costa del Sol
Golfo de Cádiz
Cádiz
Málaga
Almería
Estrecho de Gibraltar
Gibraltar (Reino Unido)
OCÉANO ATLÁNTICO
ARGELIA
MARRUECOS

N
O   E
S

0   100   200 kilómetros
0   100   200 millas

OCÉANO ATLÁNTICO
ESPAÑA
Islas Baleares
ÁFRICA
Islas Canarias

0   200 kilómetros
0   200 millas

© SF

ISLAS CANARIAS (España)
LA PALMA
LANZAROTE
GOMERA
TENERIFE
Santa Cruz de Tenerife
FUERTEVENTURA
HIERRO
GRAN CANARIA
Las Palmas de Gran Canaria
OCÉANO ATLÁNTICO
ÁFRICA

0   100 kilómetros
0   100 millas

XVI

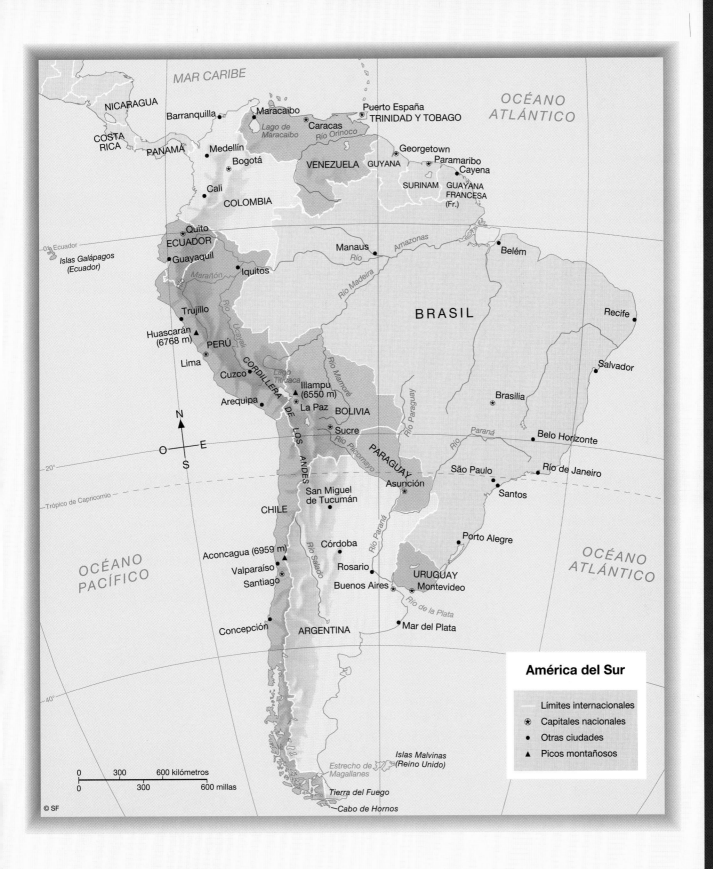

MAR CARIBE

NICARAGUA

Barranquilla

COSTA RICA

PANAMÁ

Maracaibo

Lago de Maracaibo

Caracas

Río Orinoco

Puerto España

TRINIDAD Y TOBAGO

OCÉANO ATLÁNTICO

Medellín

Bogotá

VENEZUELA

GUYANA

Georgetown

Paramaribo

Cayena

Cali

COLOMBIA

SURINAM

GUAYANA FRANCESA (Fr.)

0° Ecuador

Quito

ECUADOR

Islas Galápagos (Ecuador)

Guayaquil

Manaus

Río

Amazonas

Belém

Iquitos

Marañón

Trujillo

Río Madeira

BRASIL

Recife

Huascarán (6768 m)

PERÚ

Ucayali

Lima

CORDILLERA

Cuzco

Lago Titicaca

Illampu (6550 m)

Río Mamoré

Salvador

Arequipa

DE

La Paz

BOLIVIA

Brasília

N

O   E

S

LOS

Sucre

Río Pilcomayo

PARAGUAY

Río Paraguay

Río

Paraná

Belo Horizonte

20°

ANDES

Asunción

São Paulo

Río de Janeiro

Trópico de Capricornio

San Miguel de Tucumán

Santos

CHILE

Córdoba

Río Salado

Río Paraná

Porto Alegre

OCÉANO PACÍFICO

Aconcagua (6959 m)

Valparaíso

Santiago

Rosario

Buenos Aires

URUGUAY

Montevideo

OCÉANO ATLÁNTICO

Río de la Plata

Concepción

ARGENTINA

Mar del Plata

40°

América del Sur

— Límites internacionales

⊛ Capitales nacionales

• Otras ciudades

▲ Picos montañosos

0   300   600 kilómetros

0   300   600 millas

© SF

Islas Malvinas (Reino Unido)

Estrecho de Magallanes

Tierra del Fuego

Cabo de Hornos

EL PRIMER PASO

THEME: INTRODUCTION TO THE WORLD OF SPANISH

COMMUNICATION

Topics

Greetings and leave-takings

Names of countries

Professions

Classroom objects

Alphabet / Numbers 0–31

Classroom expressions

Objectives

To discuss the influence of Spanish language and culture

To greet people and say good-by

To tell how you feel

To ask someone's name and tell your name

To acknowledge introductions

To ask for and give information

To say when something takes place

To count or give dates

To say thank you

To talk about the classroom

CULTURE

Names and locations of Spanish-speaking countries

Spanish names

Ancillaries available for use with *El primer paso*

Multisensory/Technology

 Overheads, 1–5

 Audio Tapes and CDs

 Vocabulary Art Blackline Masters for Hands-On Learning, pp. 3–7/CD-ROM

Classroom Crossword

Video

 Pasos vivos 1 CD-ROM

 Internet Activities www.pasoapaso.com

Print

 Practice Workbook, pp. 1–11

 Writing, Audio & Video Activities, pp. 1–4, 91–92, 151

 Communicative Activity Blackline Masters

Pair and Small Group Activities, pp. 1–6

Situation Cards, p. 7

TPR Storytelling

Assessment

 Assessment Program

Examen de habilidades, pp. 1–8

Video still from *El primer paso*

1A

Planning Express, Teaching
Resources Library, and Clip Art
Library

¿Lo sabes bien?
Video Quiz

Cultural Overview

The Richly Diverse Hispanic Americans

According to the 1990 census, 22,354,000 people (about 9 percent of the total population in the U.S.) classified themselves as being of Spanish or Hispanic descent. Out of that number, 17,268,000 indicated that they were of either Mexican, Puerto Rican, or Cuban descent. The remaining 5,086,000 people checked "Other Spanish / Hispanic" on their census question-naires. This broad category included people who came from or who had ancestral ties to other Spanish-speaking countries in the Caribbean, Central and South America, or Spain.

The nation's Hispanic population is growing at a tremendous rate. Between 1980 and 1990 it grew by an astounding 53 percent. In contrast, the nation as a whole expanded only 9.8 per-cent. Between 1990 and 1996, the Hispanic population grew by another 27 percent. The Census Bureau estimates that by 2050, people in the Spanish or Hispanic group will number almost 100 million and constitute almost 25 percent of the population. Collectively, the group would outnumber African Americans by 2010.

The influence of the many diverse Hispanic cultures is everywhere. The Southwestern look, drawing on traditional Spanish architecture as well as contemporary influences, has emerged as an important design style. Ethnic groceries specializing in ingredients essential to many of the traditional dishes served in Hispanic cultures have sprung up across the country. The music of Celia Cruz, Gloria Estefan, Rubén Blades, and Los Lobos has introduced Spanish vocabulary into everyday English. Hispanic actors such as Edward James Olmos and Rosie Pérez have earned great acclaim in recent years for their outstanding work. Motion pictures such as *La Bamba, Stand and Deliver,* and *Like Water for Chocolate* were hits at the box office.

Perhaps most important, Hispanic Americans have increased their political power in recent years. During the last several presidential administrations, Hispanics have been appointed to many major political posts. In 1988 President Reagan appointed Lauro F. Cavazos, a Mexican American, as Secretary of Education. He was the first Hispanic American appointed to the Cabinet. In 1990, Dr. Antonia Coello Novello, with roots in Puerto Rico, became the first woman and the first Hispanic American to become Surgeon General. Many other Hispanic Americans also have achieved success in national, state, and local politics, and their num-bers in the House of Representatives continue to increase.

(p. XVIII, top photo)
Combining Spanish and Native American traditions, Mexico's *charros* are known for their handsome outfits and precision horsemanship. Some Mexican American horsemen join U.S. rodeos, but most perform in shows called *charreadas* in the U.S. and Mexico. Many U.S. cowboy terms come from *charrismo*. Ask students if they can name the English words derived from Spanish *la reata* (lariat) and *vaquero* (buckaroo).

(p. XVIII, bottom photo)
In the seventeenth and eighteenth centuries, Spanish priests established missions throughout the present-day southwestern U.S. San Xavier del Bac, established in 1700 near what is now Tucson, is considered a masterpiece of mission architecture and was restored by architects who supervised the restoration of Rome's Sistine Chapel. Have students discuss challenges restorers might have faced in their task.

LA PRESENCIA HISPANA EN LOS ESTADOS UNIDOS

Estados con una población hispana bastante grande (más de 500.000)

Estados con una población hispana notable (más de 100.000)

Estados con una pequeña población hispana (menos de 100.000)

Charro con la bandera mexicana en The Dalles, Oregon

La Misión de San Xavier del Bac en Tucson, Arizona

XVIII   El primer paso

Planning

Cross-Curricular Connections

Math Connection *(p. 4)*
Have students add the Spanish-speaking populations of the listed cities. Of the total population, what percentage is from a certain city? Have them add the populations of the countries listed and calculate the same percentage for a country of their choice. For example, the Spanish-speaking population of New York is about 3% of the listed cities, and the U.S. represents about 9% of the Spanish speakers in these countries.

Geography Connection *(p. 4)*
In pairs, have one student call out the different countries shown on the graph as the other locates them on the maps in the front of their books (pp. XIV–XVII). Then have them reverse roles where one student says a country and the other says the capital.

Language Arts Connection *(p. 10)*
Assign portions of the glossary in the back of the book to groups or pairs of students. Have them look for cognates and note the spelling differences between the Spanish and English. For example: *-ología* and *-ology; -dad* and *-ty; -mente* and *-ly.*

Músicos tocando instrumentos andinos en Minneapolis, Minnesota

Celebrando el Día del puertorriqueño en Nueva York

Mural en la Pequeña Habana, Miami, Florida

Cultural Notes
(pp. XVIII–1, realia)
Mexican salsa is so popular in the U.S. that it is now consumed more than catsup. The vegetarian taco in the photo is made with avocado, tomato, and onion, and is accompanied by *salsa casera* (homemade). Though not frequently served in U.S. Mexican restaurants, a lime wedge and chopped cilantro are very common as garnish in Mexico.

(p. 1, top left photo)
Traditional Andean music is played by small groups of musicians on folk instruments like these. The musician on the right is playing the *charango,* and the three others are playing *zampoñas.* The musician second from the left is also playing *chachis,* which are hooves from llamas or goats sewn on a cloth and shaken to keep time. Ask students to name similar folk instruments from American or other cultures.

Cultural Notes ☼

Spanish in Your Community
How has Hispanic culture influenced your community? Have small groups of students brainstorm ideas and then develop lists of the various ways. If students have difficulty, you might suggest broad categories, such as politics or sports, under which students can supply specific examples. Groups can then share their findings with the class. In addition, ask students to explore their community to find out if there are store signs in Spanish, streets with Hispanic names, and so on.

(p. 1, top right photo)
The U.S. acquired the Caribbean island of Puerto Rico in 1898 as a result of the Spanish-American War, and Puerto Ricans were granted U.S. citizenship in 1917. Today, more Puerto Ricans live in New York City than in San Juan, the largest city in Puerto Rico. The New York Puerto Rican Day Parade is held every year in early June. Ask students to name other U.S. cities that have a large Puerto Rican community.

(p. 1, bottom photo)
Settled by Cuban emigrés after the 1959 Cuban Revolution, Miami's Little Havana neighborhood is the largest Cuban American community in the U.S. The arts also thrive there, with the Cuban Museum of Arts and Culture exhibiting both pre-Revolutionary art and work by contemporary Cuban American artists. Many neighborhood buildings feature murals such as this one. Ask students what this mural presents about Cuba.

Introduce

 ¡Piénsalo bien!

Play

 Video Activity A

Using the Video
This chapter's video provides an overview of the video series and introduces the *En vivo* hosts: Alexander in Miami, Karina in Guadalajara, and Gracia and Jorge in Madrid. Alexander interviews Spanish-speaking patrons at Miami's Bayside Marketplace, asking them about their cultural backgrounds and interests.

Before students watch the video, ask them to predict what it will be about.

For future chapters, you may want to show the first segment of the video as an introduction to the chapter theme, the second segment as an introduction to chapter vocabulary, and the third segment as reinforcement.

Video segment 1: For more teaching suggestions, see the Video Teacher's Guide.

Options

Strategies for Reaching All Students

Students Needing Extra Help
Students who have had learning problems are often intimidated by a foreign language. This opening section gives you an opportunity to calm their fears with non-threatening activities. Emphasize how very little Spanish they may know now and how much they will soon know.

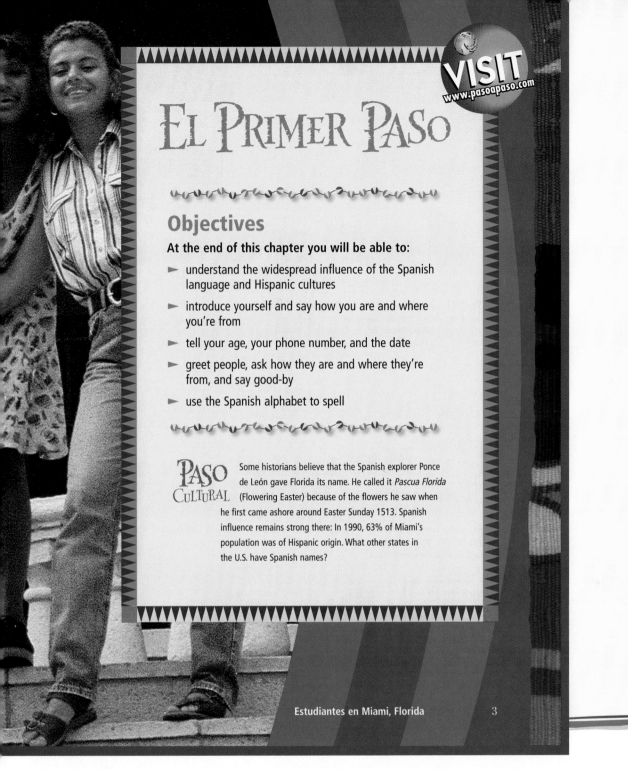

EL PRIMER PASO

Objectives

At the end of this chapter you will be able to:

► understand the widespread influence of the Spanish language and Hispanic cultures

► introduce yourself and say how you are and where you're from

► tell your age, your phone number, and the date

► greet people, ask how they are and where they're from, and say good-by

► use the Spanish alphabet to spell

PASO CULTURAL Some historians believe that the Spanish explorer Ponce de León gave Florida its name. He called it *Pascua Florida* (Flowering Easter) because of the flowers he saw when he first came ashore around Easter Sunday 1513. Spanish influence remains strong there: In 1990, 63% of Miami's population was of Hispanic origin. What other states in the U.S. have Spanish names?

Estudiantes en Miami, Florida

3

Cultural Notes

Paso cultural
Possible answers: Arizona, Colorado, Montana, Nevada, Texas.

Present & Apply

Cultural Objective
- To discuss the influence of Spanish language and culture

Vocabulario para conversar

Play

Step

Video Activity B

Using the Video
Video segment 2: See the Video Teacher's Guide.

Teaching Suggestions
The names of countries, Spanish names, Spanish alphabet, and classroom expressions presented in this chapter are for recognition only.

Remind students that the numbers shown in the first two graphs are in millions.

Current usage dictates the use of the country's name without a definite article *(Perú* rather than *el Perú,* for example). In this book, names of countries will appear without the definite article, with the exception of *El Salvador, la República Dominicana,* and *los Estados Unidos.*

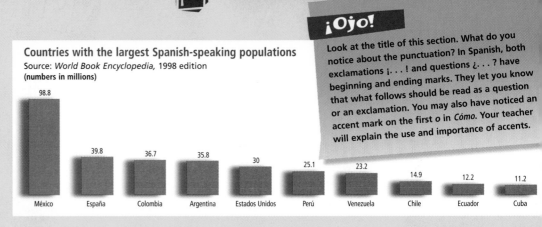

¡Ojo!
Look at the title of this section. What do you notice about the punctuation? In Spanish, both exclamations ¡ . . . ! and questions ¿ . . . ? have beginning and ending marks. They let you know that what follows should be read as a question or an exclamation. You may also have noticed an accent mark on the first o in *Cómo.* Your teacher will explain the use and importance of accents.

Countries with the largest Spanish-speaking populations
Source: *World Book Encyclopedia,* 1998 edition
(numbers in millions)

México 98.8 | España 39.8 | Colombia 36.7 | Argentina 35.8 | Estados Unidos 30 | Perú 25.1 | Venezuela 23.2 | Chile 14.9 | Ecuador 12.2 | Cuba 11.2

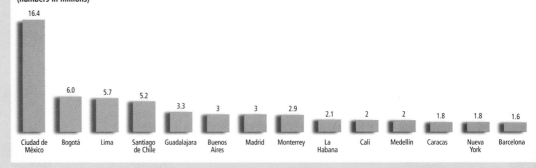

Cities with the largest Spanish-speaking populations*
*Population figures are for metropolitan areas.
Source: *The Statesman's Year-Book,* 1997-98 edition
(numbers in millions)

Ciudad de México 16.4 | Bogotá 6.0 | Lima 5.7 | Santiago de Chile 5.2 | Guadalajara 3.3 | Buenos Aires 3 | Madrid 3 | Monterrey 2.9 | La Habana 2.1 | Cali 2 | Medellín 2 | Caracas 1.8 | Nueva York 1.8 | Barcelona 1.6

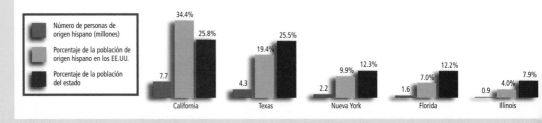

Seventy-five percent of the people of Spanish-speaking origin in the United States live in the following five states.
Source: *U.S. Bureau of the Census,* 1990

- Número de personas de origen hispano (millones)
- Porcentaje de la población de origen hispano en los EE.UU.
- Porcentaje de la población del estado

California 7.7 / 34.4% / 25.8% | Texas 4.3 / 19.4% / 25.5% | Nueva York 2.2 / 9.9% / 12.3% | Florida 1.6 / 7.0% / 12.2% | Illinois 0.9 / 4.0% / 7.9%

4   El primer paso

Options

Strategies for Reaching All Students

Students Needing Extra Help
Review basic graph-reading skills, if necessary. Have students locate the countries listed in the top graph on p. 4 on the maps in the front of their books (pp. XIV–XVII) or on a wall map.
Ex. C: Tell students that they are so used to these words that they don't realize that they are borrowed from another language.

Ex. D: Emphasize the word *cognate.* Tell students that a cognate is a tool for helping them understand the meaning of words. Say the Spanish words aloud so students can hear the difference in pronunciation from English.

Enrichment
As a written assignment, have students research a city or town near them that has a significant Spanish-speaking population. Ask them to include such census data as the estimated size, countries of origin, and average age of that population.

A Look at the graph of the countries with the largest Spanish-speaking populations. Where does the United States fall in rank order?

Now look at the graph of the cities. Where does a U.S. city fall in rank order?

B Discuss the information with a partner. Which fact was most surprising to you? Which facts did you know before you saw these graphs?

C There are many words we use every day that come from Spanish. You probably already know how to pronounce a few of these words and phrases. See how many more you can add:

ANIMALS: armadillo, pinto, . . .
BUILDINGS: adobe, patio, . . .
CLOTHING: poncho, sombrero, . . .
EXPRESSIONS: adiós, hasta la vista, . . .
FAMOUS PEOPLE: *(past and present, real or fictional)*: Andy García, Don Quijote, . . .
FOODS: tacos, tamales, . . .
GAMES/SPORTS: piñata, jai alai, . . .
GEOGRAPHY: chaparral, mesa, . . .
MUSIC/DANCE: mariachi, tango, . . .
PEOPLE: matador, señor, . . .
PLACE NAMES: Nevada, Santa Fe, . . .

D Spanish is a Romance language, meaning that it comes from Latin, the language of the Romans. Because of the great influence of Latin on the English language, there are also many words in Spanish that look and/or sound similar to English words. These are called cognates. Take advantage of this!

Can you guess the meaning of these Spanish words?

- *carnaval*
- *comunicación*
- *delicioso*
- *fabuloso*
- *farmacia*
- *libertad*
- *limón*
- *parque*
- *oficina*

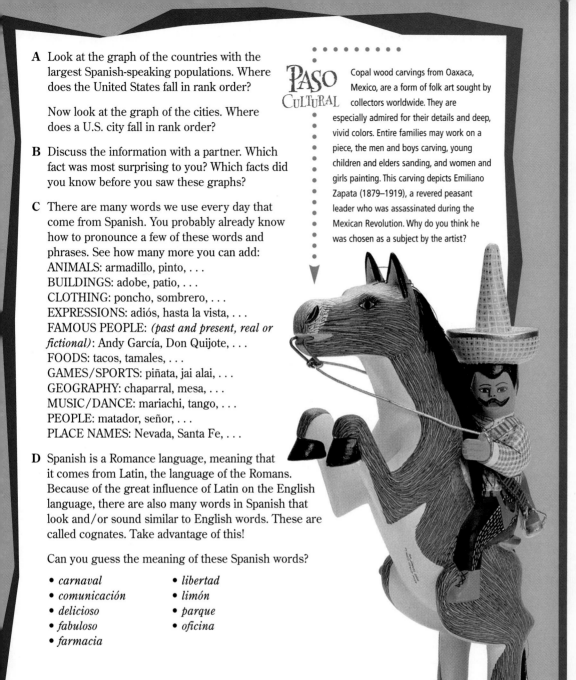

PASO CULTURAL

Copal wood carvings from Oaxaca, Mexico, are a form of folk art sought by collectors worldwide. They are especially admired for their details and deep, vivid colors. Entire families may work on a piece, the men and boys carving, young children and elders sanding, and women and girls painting. This carving depicts Emiliano Zapata (1879–1919), a revered peasant leader who was assassinated during the Mexican Revolution. Why do you think he was chosen as a subject by the artist?

Cultural Notes

Apply

Teaching Suggestions

To prepare for the discussion of professions, post pictures of people working at the jobs mentioned on this page. Label each picture in Spanish.

Answers

E Photo captions: *dentista* (dentist); *fotógrafa* (photographer); *veterinario* (veterinarian); *policía* (police officer)
List: actor, actress; architect; astronaut; banker; carpenter; chauffeur; scientist; engineer; mechanic; doctor; pilot; politician; president; professor; secretary; supervisor

Answers will vary.

Answers will vary, but might include: working at a clothing store or fast-food restaurant, delivering newspapers, babysitting, volunteering at a hospital. An employer would probably hire a teenager who spoke Spanish so he or she could communicate with more people. If any of these jobs are in a Spanish-speaking community, knowing Spanish would be especially helpful.

E Look at these photos and read the captions.

Can you guess what these professions are in English? Here is an additional list for you to practice with:

> el actor/la actriz
> el arquitecto/la arquitecta
> el/la astronauta
> el banquero/la banquera
> el carpintero/la carpintera
> el/la chofer
> el científico/la científica
> el ingeniero/la ingeniera
> el mecánico/la mecánica
> el médico/la médica
> el piloto/la pilota
> el político/la política
> el presidente/la presidenta
> el profesor/la profesora
> el secretario/la secretaria
> el supervisor/la supervisora

"Soy dentista y soy de Miami."

"Soy fotógrafa y soy de Costa Rica."

"Soy veterinario y soy de Ecuador."

"Soy policía y soy de la Ciudad de México."

- With a partner, discuss why knowing Spanish would be valuable in these careers. What career(s) are you considering? How will knowing Spanish help you with your goals?

- With your partner, make a list of the six most popular jobs or volunteer positions that students might have. If you were hiring a teenager, would you prefer one who spoke Spanish? Why? Are there summer jobs in which knowing Spanish would be especially helpful?

You have made a great decision to study Spanish. Let's take it *PASO A PASO*, step by step. You'll be communicating in Spanish very soon.

MORE PRACTICE

Más práctica y tarea, p. 505

6   El primer paso

¡Ojo!

Did you know that, according to research, high-school students with two years of a foreign language score up to 12% higher on the S.A.T. verbal exam—and their scores continue to rise by at least 5% for each additional year of foreign-language study?

Options

Strategies for Reaching All Students

Students Needing Extra Help
Help students pronounce the names of the occupations. With cognates, some students may be tempted to pronounce them as they would in English.

Enrichment
Bring in photocopies of the classified ads page from a Spanish-language newspaper. Have students look for cognates.

Multiple Intelligences
Visual/Spatial
Have students add the functional expressions to their notebooks. Have them illustrate the intonation pattern of the phrase *¿Y tú?* by writing the words on the board or on an overhead transparency and drawing a line that curves upward above the words.

Vocabulario para conversar

In the next four sections you will find some study notes to help you learn about the various parts of each chapter. Here are some words you will need to greet people and introduce yourself.

¡Hola!

¡Buenos días!

¿Cómo te llamas?

Me llamo Anita. ¿Y tú?

Roberto.

¿Cómo estás?

Bien, gracias.

¡Ojo!

You will need to learn the new words pictured in *Vocabulario para conversar* and the words in *También necesitas...* ("You also need ..."). To learn them, you might want to keep a vocabulary section in your notebook by categories, or make flashcards with the Spanish word on one side and a picture or the English word on the other. Practice these from time to time with a classmate or family member. Maybe they can learn some Spanish too!

También necesitas...

Mucho gusto.	*Pleased / Nice to meet you.*	Muy bien.	*Very well.*
		Así, así.	*So-so.*
Igualmente.	*Likewise.*		

El primer paso   7

Present

Chapter Theme
Greetings

Communicative Objectives
• To greet people and say good-by
• To tell how you feel
• To ask someone's name and tell your name
• To acknowledge introductions

Overhead 1

Vocabulary Art BLMs/CD-ROM

Pronunciation Tape P-1

Teaching Suggestions
Preparing students to speak: Use one or two options from each of the categories of Comprehensible Input, Physical Response, or Limited Verbal Response. For a complete explanation of these categories and some sample activities, see pp. T22–T23.

Explain the use of punctuation marks at the beginning of questions and exclamations. Elicit how these provide a clue about the type of sentence that follows.

Present & Practice

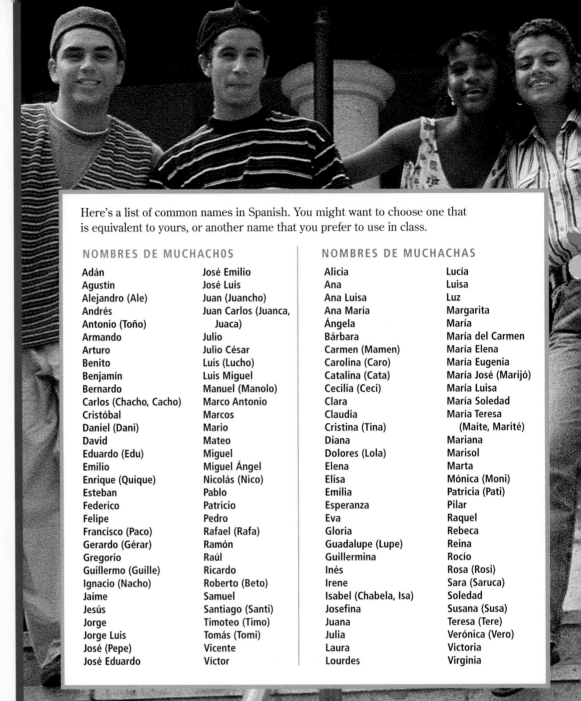

Here's a list of common names in Spanish. You might want to choose one that is equivalent to yours, or another name that you prefer to use in class.

NOMBRES DE MUCHACHOS

Adán	José Emilio
Agustín	José Luis
Alejandro (Ale)	Juan (Juancho)
Andrés	Juan Carlos (Juanca,
Antonio (Toño)	Juaca)
Armando	Julio
Arturo	Julio César
Benito	Luis (Lucho)
Benjamín	Luis Miguel
Bernardo	Manuel (Manolo)
Carlos (Chacho, Cacho)	Marco Antonio
Cristóbal	Marcos
Daniel (Dani)	Mario
David	Mateo
Eduardo (Edu)	Miguel
Emilio	Miguel Ángel
Enrique (Quique)	Nicolás (Nico)
Esteban	Pablo
Federico	Patricio
Felipe	Pedro
Francisco (Paco)	Rafael (Rafa)
Gerardo (Gérar)	Ramón
Gregorio	Raúl
Guillermo (Guille)	Ricardo
Ignacio (Nacho)	Roberto (Beto)
Jaime	Samuel
Jesús	Santiago (Santi)
Jorge	Timoteo (Timo)
Jorge Luis	Tomás (Tomi)
José (Pepe)	Vicente
José Eduardo	Víctor

NOMBRES DE MUCHACHAS

Alicia	Lucía
Ana	Luisa
Ana Luisa	Luz
Ana María	Margarita
Ángela	María
Bárbara	María del Carmen
Carmen (Mamen)	María Elena
Carolina (Caro)	María Eugenia
Catalina (Cata)	María José (Marijó)
Cecilia (Ceci)	María Luisa
Clara	María Soledad
Claudia	María Teresa
Cristina (Tina)	(Maite, Marité)
Diana	Mariana
Dolores (Lola)	Marisol
Elena	Marta
Elisa	Mónica (Moni)
Emilia	Patricia (Pati)
Esperanza	Pilar
Eva	Raquel
Gloria	Rebeca
Guadalupe (Lupe)	Reina
Guillermina	Rocío
Inés	Rosa (Rosi)
Irene	Sara (Saruca)
Isabel (Chabela, Isa)	Soledad
Josefina	Susana (Susa)
Juana	Teresa (Tere)
Julia	Verónica (Vero)
Laura	Victoria
Lourdes	Virginia

8   El primer paso

Options

Strategies for Reaching All Students

Spanish-Speaking Students
Have students add names to the list: *Haz una lista de otros nombres posibles. Empecemos a conversar:* Pair bilingual with non-bilingual students whenever possible for oral exercises. Bilingual students can model pronunciation.

Students Needing Extra Help
Every chapter in this book has an Organizer, found in the *Practice Workbook*. The purpose of the Organizer is to provide students with access to vocabulary and grammar points that, because of certain disabilities or learning styles, they may have difficulty recalling. It can be used as a type of clipboard sheet of important information they will be filling in so that they can perform the exercises and activities in the chapter.

Begin the vocabulary section of the Organizer.
Ex. 1: Choose a student to help you model the dialogue. This will make it clear from the beginning that the dialogues in the *Empecemos a conversar* throughout the text are active, involving two contributing students as partners. Point out the use of dashes before each line in the model dialogue. Explain that these markers indicate

Empecemos a conversar

In these exercises you will create conversations according to a model. With a partner, take turns at being *Estudiante A* and *Estudiante B.* Use the words that are cued or given in the balloons to replace the underlined sections in the model.

 means you can make your own choices for that item or exercise.

¡Ojo!

You might want to scan the exercise first in order to get the gist of doing it. If you need help, review the *Vocabulario para conversar* or *También necesitas...* sections.

1 Estudiante A —*¡Hola! Me llamo <u>María</u>. ¿Cómo te llamas?*

Estudiante B —*Me llamo <u>Rafael</u>.*

Estudiante A —*Mucho gusto, <u>Rafael</u>.*

Estudiante B —*Igualmente, <u>María</u>.*

Estudiante A   Estudiante B

Did you use your own name in the conversation? Now redo it with five other classmates. Play both roles. Your teacher may ask you to tell your classmates' names, so remember their answers.

2 A —*Buenos días. ¿Cómo estás, <u>Pilar</u>?*

B —*Muy bien, gracias. ¿Y tú?*

A —*Así, así.*

Estudiante A   Estudiante B

Did you keep using the same answers for how you feel? Repeat this conversation with four other classmates and vary your answers.

Saludos entre amigos en Chile

MORE PRACTICE

- Más práctica y tarea, p. 505
- Practice Workbook P–1

---

a dialogue exchange. Remind students to reverse roles with their partner as they work through the exercises. Encourage them to give logical responses when appropriate.

Multiple Intelligences
Verbal/Linguistic
See Exs. 1–2.

Cultural Notes

(p. 9, photo)
In most of Latin America men greet each other with a handshake or even an *abrazo.* In daily conversation they generally maintain eye contact and stand much closer to each other than in the U.S. Ask students to compare this with body language in other cultures that they know. Also ask whether they think body language is harder or easier to learn than spoken language, and why.

Present & Practice

Chapter Theme
Greetings, leavetakings, and introductions

Communicative Objectives
- To greet people and say good-by
- To tell how you feel
- To ask for and give information
- To say thank you

 Overhead 2

 Vocabulary Art BLMs/CD-ROM

 Pronunciation Tape P-2

Teaching Suggestions
Preparing students to speak: Use one or two options from each of the categories of Comprehensible Input, Physical Response, or Limited Verbal Response. For a complete explanation of these categories and some sample activities, see pp. T22–T23.

Vocabulario para conversar

Here are some more words and expressions you will need to greet people and tell where you are from.

> Buenas tardes, Señora García. ¿Cómo está Ud.?*

> Bien, gracias, ¿y tú?

> Buenas noches. Me llamo Anita. ¿Qué tal?

> Me llamo Miguel. Muy bien, gracias.

¡Ojo!
Look at the words in the section titled *¿Y qué quiere decir...?* You will see this section often. These are cognates, or are closely related to words you have already learned.

También necesitas...

		¿Y qué quiere decir...?		
¿De dónde eres (tú)?	*Where are you from?*	sí	Adiós.	señor (Sr.)
Yo soy de ___.	*I am from ___.*	no		señora (Sra.)
¿Y usted?	*And you?*	o		señorita (Srta.)
Hasta luego.	*See you later.*			

*Usted is often abbreviated Ud. in writing.

10   El primer paso

Options

Strategies for Reaching All Students

Spanish-Speaking Students
Ask: *¿A quién le hablas de "Ud."? ¿A quién le hablas de "tú"?*

Multiple Intelligences
Visual/Spatial
Once students are familiar with the names of the Spanish-speaking countries, write them on the board or transparency and have them identify which are North, Central, and South America.

Students Needing Extra Help
También necesitas . . . : Explain that the words in parentheses are optional.
Point out the two ways of saying "How are you?" and the concept of respect or formality in the Spanish language. (See Enrichment.) This is presented later in Chap. 2.

Enrichment
Explain that the important distinction between "you" formal *(usted)* and "you" familiar *(tú)* still exists in many languages. See Chap. 2, p. 72 for an explanation of the distinction.

Empecemos a conversar

For Exercise 1, refer to the map below.

1   A —*¡Hola! Me llamo <u>Benito</u>. ¿Y tú?*
    B —*Me llamo <u>Luisa</u>. ¿De dónde eres?*
    A —*Soy de <u>Costa Rica</u>. ¿Y tú?*
    B —*Soy de <u>Bolivia</u>.*

¡Ojo!

Do you remember *¿Y tú?* and *¿Cómo estás?* There is another way to say "How are you?" in Spanish. We use *usted* to show respect when speaking to an older person.

Estudiante A   **Estudiante B**

Did you use your own name and country? Now repeat this dialogue with three classmates. Pretend to be someone else, and use different names and countries.

2   Now repeat the conversation with five classmates, using a city name from page 4.

Saludos entre un amigo y una amiga
en Xalapa, México

El primer paso   11

¿Y qué quiere decir...?

Explain that this section will appear from time to time in the *También necesitas* . . . to facilitate language learning through the use of cognates and word families. Use comprehensible input to introduce this new vocabulary without giving students an English equivalent.

Answers: Empecemos a conversar

1–2 Answers will vary. You may wish to use Overheads 78–81 for the maps of Spanish-speaking countries with the Spanish names from the list on p. 8. Students can then choose their name and their country of origin at the same time.

Point out that Spanish is one of the official languages spoken in the West African country of Guinea Ecuatorial.

Learning Spanish Through Action
Learning Spanish Through Action (LSTA), based on James Asher's Total Physical Response (TPR), is a strategy modeled on the way children acquire their native language. Through positive reinforcement, confidence building, and realia, students begin to comprehend, communicate, and even think in Spanish without native-language interference. See the front section of this Teacher's Edition for more information.

STAGING VOCABULARY: *Apunten, Señalen*
MATERIALS: transparency of a map of the Spanish-speaking world (Overheads 78–81) or a wall map of the same areas
DIRECTIONS: Tell students to imagine that they are from the country you announce. In pairs, have them point to the country and ask: *¿De dónde eres?* They should respond orally.

Cultural Notes

(p. 11, photo)
Male and female friends greet each other in most of Latin America by brushing cheeks and "kissing air," or they may simply shake hands. The man and woman in this picture are students at the University of Art in Xalapa, Veracruz, near the Gulf coast of Mexico. Discuss with students how this way of greeting friends of the opposite sex compares with the way they greet their friends of either sex.

Apply

Answers: Empecemos a escribir

3 Answers will vary, but may include: *buenos días, buenas tardes, buenas noches, ¿cómo está usted?, ¿cómo estás?, ¡hola!, ¿qué tal?*

4 *adiós, hasta luego*

5–7 Answers will vary.

Answers: Empecemos a escribir y a leer

8 Answers will vary, but look for the *usted* form: *Buenas tardes, señora. ¿Cómo está usted?*

9 a. *no;* b. *sí;* c. *sí;* d. *no*

 Practice Wkbk. P-2

 Audio Activity P.1

 Writing Activity P-B

Empecemos a escribir

Write your answers in Spanish.

3 List four ways to greet someone.

4 What are two ways to say "good-by"?

5 ¿Cómo te llamas?

6 ¿Cómo estás?

7 ¿De dónde eres?

> **¡Ojo!**
>
> In this section you will write your answers and ideas in Spanish. Above all, communicate the message. After you finish, you can refer to *Vocabulario para conversar* and *También necesitas . . .* or the *Resumen* at the end of the chapter to check your spelling.

Empecemos a escribir y a leer

In this section you will write your answers and also do some reading.

Write your answers in Spanish.

8 How do you greet an older person and ask how he or she is feeling?

9 Read the following conversation, then reply *sí* or *no* to the statements.

PROFESORA:	Buenas tardes. Me llamo Señora Guzmán. ¿Y tú?
ESTUDIANTE:	Me llamo Ana María Hernández. Mucho gusto.
PROFESORA:	Igualmente. ¿De dónde eres? ¿De los Estados Unidos?
ESTUDIANTE:	No, soy de Costa Rica. ¿Es usted de Argentina o de Chile?
PROFESORA:	Soy de Uruguay. Adiós, Ana María. Hasta luego.
ESTUDIANTE:	Adiós, profesora.

a. The people in the dialogue know each other.
b. The teacher is a woman.
c. We know the last names of both people.
d. The student is from the United States.

> **¡Ojo!**
>
> You might want to read the passage twice, once to get the general meaning, and a second time to try to figure out words you don't know. Many times you can guess the meaning of a word just by how it is used. YOU DON'T HAVE TO UNDERSTAND EVERY WORD TO GET THE OVERALL MEANING.

 www.pasoapaso.com

MORE PRACTICE

Más práctica y tarea, p. 506
Practice Workbook P–2

Options

Strategies for Reaching All Students

Spanish-Speaking Students
Empecemos a escribir: Ask students if they know other ways to say hello or good-by. *¿Sabes otras maneras de saludar a alguien o de despedirte? ¿Cuáles son? Escríbelas.*

Students Needing Extra Help
Empecemos a escribir: These sections serve as an opportunity to help develop students' writing skill. You may wish to use them as homework assignments throughout the chapters, in addition to the Extended Written Practice/Homework sections.
Emphasize the importance of keeping track of their progress.

Have students create a chart with four columns with headings: Greetings, Ways to ask how someone is, Responses, and Ways to end a conversation.
Point out the gender differences in the vocabulary words. One way to help students remember gender is to color-code flashcards.

Vocabulario para conversar

la sala de clases

la pizarra

el profesor

pl. los estudiantes

la estudiante

la profesora

el estudiante

pl. los compañeros

el compañero

la compañera

el pupitre

la mesa

la hoja de papel

el libro

el bolígrafo

También necesitas...

¿Cómo se dice ___ en español?	*How do you say ___ in Spanish?*
¿Cómo se escribe___?	*How do you spell ___?*
Se escribe ___.	*It's spelled ___.*

El primer paso   13

Present

Teaching Suggestions

In April of 1994, the Association of Spanish Language Academies *(La Real Academia)* voted 17–1 to eliminate *ch* and *ll* as separate letters from the Spanish alphabet. The sole opposition came from Ecuador, while Panama, Nicaragua, and Uruguay abstained. The change was made primarily to simplify dictionaries and make the language more computer compatible. Spelling, pronunciation, and usage are not, of course, affected.

Some sources indicate that the *rr* is only a sound and not a distinct letter of the alphabet. We have opted to retain the *rr* as a letter and have listed it as so.

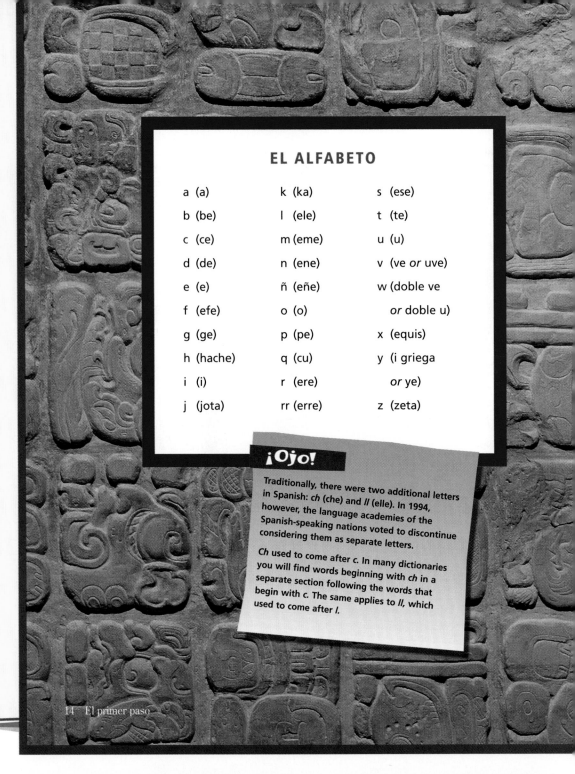

EL ALFABETO

a (a)	k (ka)	s (ese)
b (be)	l (ele)	t (te)
c (ce)	m (eme)	u (u)
d (de)	n (ene)	v (ve *or* uve)
e (e)	ñ (eñe)	w (doble ve
f (efe)	o (o)	*or* doble u)
g (ge)	p (pe)	x (equis)
h (hache)	q (cu)	y (i griega
i (i)	r (ere)	*or* ye)
j (jota)	rr (erre)	z (zeta)

¡Ojo!

Traditionally, there were two additional letters in Spanish: *ch* (che) and *ll* (elle). In 1994, however, the language academies of the Spanish-speaking nations voted to discontinue considering them as separate letters.

Ch used to come after *c.* In many dictionaries you will find words beginning with *ch* in a separate section following the words that begin with *c.* The same applies to *ll,* which used to come after *l.*

14 El primer paso

Options

Strategies for Reaching All Students

Students Needing Extra Help
Allow extra practice time with the alphabet. Encourage students to return to this page for review as needed.

Enrichment
Tell students that when they are spelling aloud, they should say *acento* after a vowel that has an accent mark on it: *país se escribe pe-a-i acento-ese.* You might also have them say *mayúscula* after a capital letter: *Manolo se escribe eme mayúscula-a-ene-o-ele-o.*

Learning Spanish Through Action
STAGING VOCABULARY: *Digan, Levanten*
MATERIALS: sheets of paper labeled with the letters of the Spanish alphabet
DIRECTIONS: Pass a letter or letters to each student. As you recite the letters, have students raise their sheets, pronouncing the letters as they do so.

Empecemos a conversar

1 A —¿Cómo se dice "table" en español?
B —Mesa.

Estudiante A   **Estudiante B**

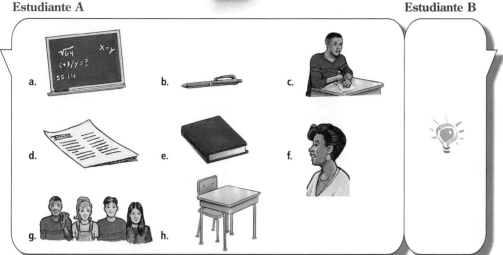

a. b. c.
d. e. f.
g. h.

2 A —¿Cómo se escribe <u>libro</u>?
B —Se escribe <u>ele-i-be-ere-o</u>.

Estudiante A   **Estudiante B**

a. b. c. d.

Empecemos a escribir

Write your answers in Spanish.

3 Your teacher will spell some names. Listen carefully and write them down. Later, compare your paper with a partner's.

MORE PRACTICE

Más práctica y tarea, p. 506
Practice Workbook 4–1, 4–2

El primer paso   15

Cultural Notes

Multiple Intelligences
Bodily/Kinesthetic
Name an item in the classroom and have students point to it or pick it up from among items you have displayed on a table.
Musical/Rhythmic
Have students sing the Spanish alphabet to "The Alphabet Song."
Verbal/Linguistic
See Ex. 3.

(p. 14, background photo)
Mayan calendar glyphs from a Palenque (Chiapas) site in Mexico. The ones shown in the photo date from the late classic period, around A.D. 600–900. The ancient Maya devised a calendar as exact as the one we use today. The Maya also had the most advanced writing system in pre-Columbian America. Glyphs inscribed on monuments were used to tell about a king's life and his accomplishments.

Chapter Theme
Calendar expressions and numbers 0–31

Communicative Objectives
- To ask for and give information
- To say when something takes place
- To count or give dates

 Overheads 4–5

 Vocabulary Art BLMs/CD-ROM

 Pronunciation Tape P-4

Teaching Suggestions
Preparing students to speak: Use one or two options from each of the categories of Comprehensible Input, Physical Response, or Limited Verbal Response. For a complete explanation of these categories and some sample activities, see pp. T22–T23.

Vocabulario para conversar

el día   el mes   la semana

ENERO

LUNES	MARTES	MIÉRCOLES	JUEVES	VIERNES	SÁBADO	DOMINGO
						1 UNO
2 DOS	**3** TRES	**4** CUATRO	**5** CINCO	**6** SEIS	**7** SIETE	**8** OCHO
9 NUEVE	**10** DIEZ	**11** ONCE	**12** DOCE	**13** TRECE	**14** CATORCE	**15** QUINCE
16 *DIECISÉIS	**17** DIECISIETE	**18** DIECIOCHO	**19** DIECINUEVE	**20** VEINTE	**21** VEINTIUNO	**22** VEINTIDÓS
23 VEINTITRÉS	**24** VEINTICUATRO	**25** VEINTICINCO	**26** VEINTISÉIS	**27** VEINTISIETE	**28** VEINTIOCHO	**29** VEINTINUEVE
30 TREINTA	**31** TREINTA Y UNO					

¿Cuándo es tu cumpleaños?

Mi cumpleaños es el 6 de junio.

¡Ojo!
Spanish calendars begin the week with Monday (*lunes*) and end with Sunday (*domingo*).

* You will also see the numbers 16–19 spelled *diez y seis, diez y siete, diez y ocho, diez y nueve.* The numbers 21–29 may also be written *veinte y uno, veinte y dos,* and so on.

16   El primer paso

Options

Strategies for Reaching All Students

Students Needing Extra Help
Demonstrate on the chalkboard how *diez y seis* becomes *dieciséis.*
También necesitas . . . : Have students put these phrases in an organizer / notebook so that they will have them throughout the year for easy reference.

Learning Spanish Through Action
STAGING VOCABULARY: *Escriban, Pasen a la pizarra*
MATERIALS: cards with numbers 0–31 written on them
DIRECTIONS: Direct four to eight students to go to the chalkboard to write numbers. Show the class the card as you say the number while students at the chalkboard write the numeral.

Multiple Intelligences
Bodily/Kinesthetic
Have students make Bingo cards using the numbers 0–31 and then play the game.
Interpersonal/Social
Read the Multicultural Perspectives section aloud to the class. Then have students correspond with a Spanish-speaking "key pal" via the Internet. Ask them to find out the date of their pal's birthday and the name of his or her patron saint.

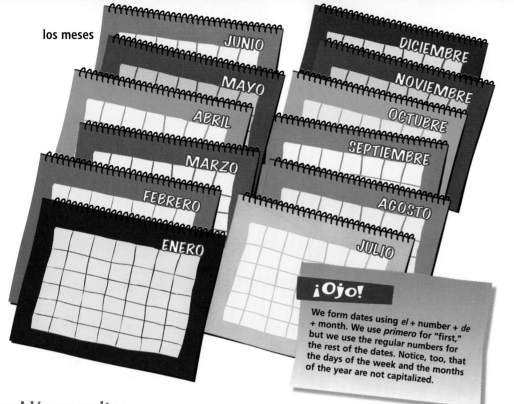

los meses

JUNIO
MAYO
ABRIL
MARZO
FEBRERO
ENERO

DICIEMBRE
NOVIEMBRE
OCTUBRE
SEPTIEMBRE
AGOSTO
JULIO

¡Ojo!

We form dates using *el* + number + *de* + month. We use *primero* for "first," but we use the regular numbers for the rest of the dates. Notice, too, that the days of the week and the months of the year are not capitalized.

También necesitas...

¿Cuántos(as) ___ hay?*	*How many ___ are there?*
¿Cuántos años tienes?	*How old are you?*
Tengo ___ años.	*I'm ___ years old.*
el año	*year*
¿Cuál es tu número de teléfono?	*What's your phone number?*
¿Cuándo es ___?	*When is ___?*
¿Cuál es la fecha de hoy?	*What's the date today?*
Hoy es ___.	*Today is ___.*
Mañana es ___.	*Tomorrow is ___.*

¿Qué día es hoy?	*What day is today?*
Mi / Tu cumpleaños	*My / Your birthday*
el 6 de febrero	*the 6th of February / February 6*
el primero de mayo	*the first of May / May 1*
por favor	*please*
Hay	*There is / are*
Mi	*My*

¿Y qué quiere decir...?
cero
en

* We use *cuántos* with masculine nouns and *cuántas* with feminine nouns.

El primer paso 17

Class Starter Review
On the day following vocabulary presentation, you might start the class with either of these activities:
1) Have students count to ten (and later to 20 and 30), forward and backward.
2) Have students share the date of their birthday with a partner. Partners should then be prepared to share the information with the class.

Multicultural Perspectives
Many Catholics in Latin America and Spain not only celebrate their birthday, but their *día santo* as well. Each day of the Catholic Church calendar is dedicated to one or more saints. Many people are named after their *día santo*. For example, a girl born on December 4 might be named Bárbara because this date is *el día de Santa Bárbara*. Ask students to find out if any of them share their names with a saint. Encourage them to find out how people in other cultures celebrate birthdays.

Logical/Mathematical
Have students practice counting in Spanish using number patterns, e.g., 2, 4, 6, 8; 1, 3, 5, 7; 3, 8, 13, 18.
Musical/Rhythmic and Bodily/Kinesthetic
Write the words to the song "Uno de enero" (see Writing, Audio & Video Activities, p. 135) on the board or on an overhead transparency. Play the song and ask students to hold up the correct number of fingers every time they hear a number sung. Invite them to sing along or dance the second time you play the song.

Empecemos a conversar

1 With a partner, continue these sequences as far as you can.

A —*cero, dos, cuatro, . . .*   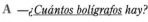 `0, 2, 4, . . .`
B —*seis, ocho, diez, . . .*

a. 5, 10, . . .
b. 1, 3, 5, . . .
c. 0, 3, 6, . . .

2

A —*¿Cuántos bolígrafos hay?*
B —*Hay tres bolígrafos.*

Estudiante A   Estudiante B

3 With a partner, continue these sequences to the end.

A —*enero*
B —*febrero*

A —*lunes*
B —*martes*

Now take turns naming a day or month at random.
Can your partner name the day or month that follows?

Celebrando el Cinco de Mayo en San Francisco

18   El primer paso

Options

Empecemos a escribir y a leer

Write your answers in Spanish.

4 Find out when these popular Hispanic holidays occur and write down the dates for each of them: *el Año Nuevo* (New Year's Day), *el Día de los Reyes* (Twelfth Night/Epiphany), *el Día de la Raza* (Columbus Day), *el Día de los Muertos* (Day of the Dead/All Souls' Day), *la Navidad* (Christmas).

5 Count the items listed below and write the answer in Spanish. Compare your answer with a partner's.

a. books on your desk
b. girls in the class
c. countries in Latin America
d. people wearing jeans
e. letters in your teacher's last name

6 Read the following sentences and rewrite them, making the necessary corrections:

a. Mi cumpleaños es el 15 de diciembre.
b. El cumpleaños de Martin Luther King, Jr. es en octubre.
c. El Día de San Patricio es el 14 de enero.
d. El Día de San Valentín es en junio.
e. Chanuka es en febrero.

7 ¿Cuál es la fecha de hoy? ¿Y de mañana?

8 ¿Cuándo es tu cumpleaños?

9 ¿Qué día es hoy? ¿Y mañana?

10 ¿Cuál es tu número de teléfono? ¿Y el número de teléfono de tu compañero(a) de clase?

MORE PRACTICE

Más práctica y tarea, p. 507
Practice Workbook P–4, P–6

PASO CULTURAL

This is an example of *papel picado*, the product of a Mexican technique of cutting layers of fine paper to create delicate designs or scenes. After cutting, the layers are separated and strung along a cord as decorations. The scene on the paper shown here is for a *Día de los Muertos* celebration.

www.pasoapaso.com

El primer paso   19

Cultural Notes

(p. 18, photo)
On May 5, 1862, invading French troops reached the city of Puebla, expecting little resistance on their way to Mexico City. At Puebla, however, they were overwhelmed by Mexican forces and forced to withdraw from battle. Although the French eventually established an empire in Mexico (1863–1867), this victory is commemorated as a national holiday.

Practice

Todo junto A

Play

Todo junto B

Play

Video Activity C

Using the Video
Video segment 3: See the Video Teacher's Guide.

Audio Activities
P.3, P.4

¡COMUNIQUEMOS!

¡Ojo!
In the ¡Comuniquemos! section, you are free to use the language you already know. Try to use different expressions for the same ideas. Are you aware that you are now REALLY COMMUNICATING IN SPANISH?

1

Find out when your classmates' birthdays are. Then tally the results to find out which month has the most birthdays.

A —¿Cuándo es tu cumpleaños?
B —Es el cinco de julio.

2

Role-play a conversation with a partner in which you:

- greet each other
- find out each other's names
- ask and answer how you are
- say good-by

3

With a partner, role-play a meeting between you and a new student in which you:

- greet each other and ask each other's names
- say that you are glad to meet each other
- ask each other your ages and where you are from
- ask for each other's phone numbers
- give the information and then say good-by

Los Cumpleaños

enero	febrero	marzo	abril	mayo	junio
₩₩|		||	||	

julio	agosto	septiembre	octubre	noviembre	diciembre
₩| |||	₩||		|||	

20   El primer paso

Options

Strategies for Reaching All Students

Spanish-Speaking Students
Ask students to mention any variations they know for the list of requests and instructions on pp. 21–23.

Cooperative Learning
Divide the class into groups of three. Provide students with an index card and tell them that they are going to assume the identity of a Hispanic American by completing some sentences. On the chalkboard, write *Me llamo* _____. Have students write out the sentence and tell them to fill in a name from the list on p. 8. After they write the sentence, have them pass their cards to the left. On the chalkboard, write *Tengo*

_____ *años*. Have them write out the sentence, fill in the blank with a number, and then pass their cards to the left. Finally, write *Soy de* _____. Have them write out the sentence and fill in the blank with the name of a Spanish-speaking country. Call on individual students to read their "autobiographies." Ask if the information given could correspond to the student reading the card.

Expresiones para la clase

Por favor

Here is a list of requests and instructions. You will need to know what to do when your teacher says them, but you will **not** need to know how to say or write them.

Levántate, por favor.

Siéntate, por favor.

Pasa a la pizarra.

Trabajen con un compañero.

Saquen una hoja de papel.

Entreguen las hojas.

Abran el libro en la página 19.

Cierren el libro.

El primer paso   21

Present

Teaching Suggestions

Present the classroom expressions and vocabulary from pp. 21–23 a few at a time, starting with four and adding one or two every day. (You may want to write these on strips of paper, have them laminated, and then display them around the classroom for reference.) Start with the most common commands. Review each time before presenting new ones. Act out each command so that students have a visual image.

Multiple Intelligences
Bodily/Kinesthetic
To practice using classroom expressions, play "Simon Says" *(Simón dice)*.
Interpersonal/Social
See Cooperative Learning.

Present

Teaching Suggestions

Have pairs of students play the roles of student and teacher. The student asks permission to do something and the teacher responds appropriately.

If students ask, here are some additional computer/Internet terms in Spanish. Remind them that these are for enrichment/recognition only:

browser *(el navegador, el examinador, el explorador)*
to click *(hacer clic)*
to delete *(eliminar, borrar)*
e-mail *(el correo electrónico)*
file *(el archivo)*
folder *(la carpeta)*
hard disk *(el disco duro)*
Internet *(la Red, la Internet)*
link *(el enlace)*
to quit *(abandonar, salir)*
to save *(guardar)*
to shut down *(apagar el sistema)*
to surf the net/to browse
    (navegar por la red)
Website *(el sitio Web)*

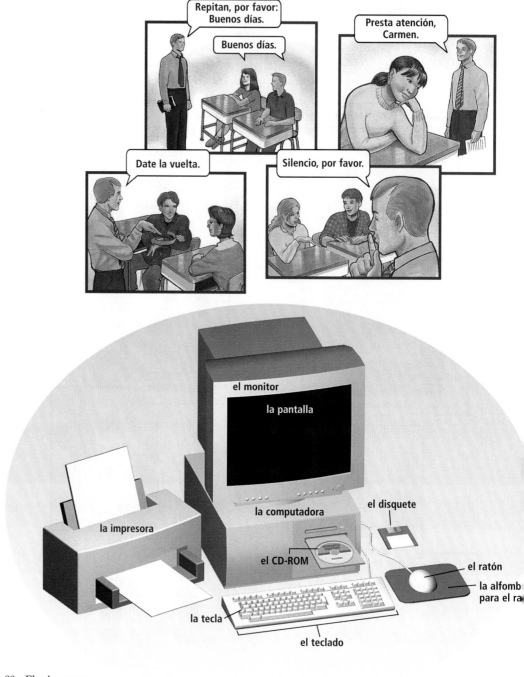

Repitan, por favor: Buenos días.

Buenos días.

Presta atención, Carmen.

Date la vuelta.

Silencio, por favor.

el monitor
la pantalla
la computadora
el disquete
la impresora
el CD-ROM
el ratón
la alfomb para el ra
la tecla
el teclado

22   El primer paso

Options

Strategies for Reaching All Students

Students Needing Extra Help
Make sure students understand each class expression by having individuals act out or mimic the expressions.

Enrichment
Have pairs of students make a set of index cards, with each card bearing one of the questions and responses on p. 23. Students can practice the material by pulling a card from the deck, reading it aloud, and having their partner give appropriate responses.

Multiple Intelligences
Bodily/Kinesthetic
See Enrichment.
Logical/Mathematical
Read the Multicultural Perspectives aloud and have students calculate the approximate percentage of schools in Spain which are *not* run by the government (33%).
Visual/Spatial
Mount the classroom expressions on placards and have students respond appropriately as you point to them.

Profesor(a), ¿puedo . . . ?

When you need to ask for permission to do something, you should ask in Spanish. Here are some questions that you may frequently ask in class, and some of the expected answers.

Profesor(a),
¿puedo ir al baño?

Profesor(a),
¿puedo ir a mi armario?

Profesor(a),
¿puedo ir a la oficina del director (de la directora)?

OFICINA

Profesor(a),
¿puedo sacarle punta a mi lápiz?

Profesor(a),
¿puedo abrir la ventana?

Profesor(a),
¿puedo cerrar la ventana?

Your teacher may respond to your requests in any of the following ways:

Sí/No.	*Yes/No.*
Sí, ve (al baño, a tu armario, etc.).	*Yes, go ahead (to ___).*
Sí, ábrela/ciérrala.	*Yes, open/close it.*
Claro.	*Of course.*
Ahora no.	*Not now.*
No, lo siento.	*No, I'm sorry.*

El primer paso   23

Multicultural Perspectives

In Spain, the federal government runs about two-thirds of all the primary and secondary schools. Approximately one out of every six students attends a school run by the Roman Catholic Church. (About 99 percent of Spain's population is Roman Catholic.) Spanish law requires that students attend school until they are 14. Ask students if they are familiar with the laws or regulations regarding school attendance in their area.

Practice Wkbk. P-7, P-8, P-9

Writing Activities P-G, P-H

Comm. Act. BLMs P-4, P-5

Internet Activities
Have students go to www.pasoapaso.com for additional activities and practice.

Assess & Summarize

Test Preparation

You may want to assign parts of this section as homework or as an in-class writing activity prior to administering the *Examen de habilidades.*

Answers

Listening:
—*Buenas tardes. ¿Cómo te llamas?*
—*Me llamo Luis. ¿Y tú?*
—*Me llamo Claudia. ¿De dónde eres, Luis?*
—*Soy de Bogotá, Colombia.*
—*Tengo catorce años. Y tú, ¿cuántos años tienes?*
—*Quince. Claudia, ¿cuál es la fecha de hoy?*
—*El veintiséis de enero. ¡Es mi cumpleaños!*

The students find out about their names, origin, age, and birthdays.

Reading: Yes, he has two friends or classmates who speak Spanish. / There are 29 students in his class. / He gives his name, origin, age, birthday, and teacher's origin.

Writing: Classroom objects: *bolígrafo, pizarra* / Months of the year: *agosto, enero* / Numbers: *cuatro, quince* / Greetings or Saying good-by: *Buenas noches, Hasta luego*

Repaso ¿Lo sabes bien?

This section will help you organize your studying for the proficiency test, where you will be asked to do similar, though not identical, tasks. There will not be any models on the test.

► **Listening**
Can you understand a brief conversation between two students who have just met? Listen as your teacher reads a sample similar to what you will hear on the test. What do the students find out about each other in this conversation?

► **Reading**
Can you read a note and find out some information about that person? Read the following description about Arturo. Does he have any friends who speak Spanish? How many students are there in his class? What other information does he give?

Me llamo Arturo. Soy de Boston, Massachusetts. Tengo dieciséis años. Mi cumpleaños es el 20 de noviembre. En mi sala de clases hay veintinueve estudiantes. El profesor es de la República Dominicana. En la sala de clases tengo dos compañeras de Venezuela.

► **Writing**
Can you put the words in the list under the appropriate categories: Classroom objects, Months of the year, Numbers, and Greeting or Saying good-by?

agosto	enero
bolígrafo	Hasta luego.
Buenas noches.	pizarra
cuatro	quince

► **Culture**
What influences have the Spanish language and Hispanic cultures had on the United States? Can you give some examples?

► **Speaking**
Can you and your partner play the roles of a teacher and a student greeting and introducing yourselves? Here is a sample dialogue:

A —*Buenos días. ¿Cómo está usted?*
B —*Muy bien, gracias. Y tú, ¿qué tal?*
A —*Así, así. Me llamo Miguel. ¿Y usted?*
B —*Me llamo Alfonso Beltrán.*
A —*Mucho gusto, Señor Beltrán.*

Self Test www.pasoapaso.com

24   El primer paso

Options

Strategies for Reaching All Students

Students Needing Extra Help
Have students write out this section so they can keep track of what they have mastered. Emphasize that this is just a sample of what the actual test will be like.
Listening: Read the conversation more than once, if necessary. Review the types of questions that are asked when you first meet someone. Brainstorm for which words students should be listening and let them know how much information is required for an acceptable answer.

Reading / Writing: Have students use the Organizer.
Culture: In the culture sections for each chapter, students will be encouraged to take notes that they can later review for the *¿Lo sabes bien?* section in preparation for the chapter test. Have them reread pp. 5–6 for possible answers.
Speaking: Allow students to use the Organizer to prepare for this section. Limit the number of lines for the dialogue.

Resumen del vocabulario

Use the vocabulary from this chapter to help you:

► greet people and ask how they are feeling

► talk about classroom items

► tell numbers and dates and use the Spanish alphabet to spell

to greet people and say good-by
Buenos días.
Buenas tardes.
Buenas noches.
¿Cómo está usted?
¿Cómo estás?
¡Hola!
¿Qué tal?
Adiós.
Hasta luego.

to tell how you feel
Así, así.
(Muy) bien.

to ask someone's name and tell your name
¿Cómo te llamas?
(Yo) me llamo ___.

to acknowledge introductions
Mucho gusto.
Igualmente.
señor / señora / señorita

to ask for and give information
¿Cómo se dice ___ en español?
Se dice ___.
¿Cómo se escribe ___?
¿Cuál es la fecha de hoy?
Hoy es ___.

Mañana es ___.
¿Cuál es tu número de teléfono?
Mi/Tu (cumpleaños)
¿Cuándo es ___?
el año
¿Cuántos años tienes?
Tengo ___ años.
¿Cuántos, -as ___ hay?
Hay
¿De dónde eres?
(Yo) soy de ___.
¿Qué día es hoy?
es
¿Y tú?
¿Y usted?
no
sí
o

to say when something takes place
el día/el mes/la semana
en
el + *number* + de + *month*
lunes   viernes
martes   sábado
miércoles   domingo
jueves

enero   julio
febrero   agosto
marzo   septiembre
abril   octubre
mayo   noviembre
junio   diciembre

to count or give dates
el primero de
cero, uno, dos, tres, cuatro,
   cinco, seis, siete, ocho,
   nueve, diez
once, doce, trece, catorce,
   quince, dieciséis, diecisiete,
   dieciocho, diecinueve, veinte
veintiuno, veintidós, veintitrés,
   veinticuatro, veinticinco,
   veintiséis, veintisiete,
   veintiocho, veintinueve,
   treinta
treinta y uno

to say please and thank you
por favor/gracias

to talk about the classroom
el bolígrafo
el compañero, la compañera
   pl. los compañeros
el/la estudiante
   pl. los estudiantes
la hoja de papel
el libro
la mesa
la pizarra
el profesor, la profesora
el pupitre
la sala de clases

Culture: Answers will vary. Students may mention place names, music, foods, language, and so on.

Speaking: Dialogues will vary.

Assessment

 Examen de habilidades

Additional Assessment Options

 Comm. Act. BLMs
Small Group Activities
Situation Cards

 ¿Lo sabes bien? Video Quiz

 **Internet Activities**
Self-Test

CAPÍTULO 1

THEME: FRIENDSHIP

SCOPE AND SEQUENCE   Pages 26–53

COMMUNICATION

Topics

Friendship

Likes and dislikes

Personality characteristics

Sports and leisure activities

Objectives

To talk about the concept of friendship in Spanish-speaking countries

To talk about activities

To say what you like and do not like

To ask someone what he or she likes

To ask if a statement is accurate

To say what you are like or what someone else is like

To ask someone what he or she is like

To describe yourself or others

CULTURE

Concept of friendship

GRAMMAR

Los adjetivos

Ni...ni

Sí / tampoco

Ancillaries available for use with Chapter 1

Multisensory/Technology

 Overheads, 6–10

 Audio Tapes and CDs

 Vocabulary Art Blackline Masters for Hands-On Learning, pp. 8–12/CD-ROM

 Classroom Crossword

 Video

 Pasos vivos 1 CD-ROM

 Internet Activities www.pasoapaso.com

Print

 Practice Workbook, pp. 13–22

 Writing, Audio & Video Activities, pp. 5–10, 93–95, 152–153

 Communicative Activity Blackline Masters

  Pair and Small Group Activities, pp. 8–13

  Situation Cards, p. 14

 Un paso más: Actividades para ampliar tu español, pp. 1–6

TPR Storytelling

Assessment

 Assessment Program

  Pruebas, pp. 9–18

  Examen de habilidades, pp. 19–22

 Test Generator

Video still from Chap. 1

Planning Express, Teaching
Resources Library, and Clip Art
Library

¿Lo sabes bien?
Video Quiz

Cultural Overview

The Foundations of Friendship

Friendship has many components which include individual personality traits and cultural values. For example, when people of different Latin American nationalities meet, they may form friendships partly based on shared interests and personality traits and partly on common cultural values they share as Latin Americans.

Adriana and Ricardo are two teenagers who have recently immigrated to Chicago from Mexico and Argentina, respectively. They have become friends because they share a similar sense of humor and a great love of soccer, which is a favorite sport in Latin America. The former is a largely idiosyncratic trait, while the latter has much to do with their Latin American backgrounds.

For many young Latin Americans, two very strong influences in their lives are family and a close-knit group of friends. Adriana and Ricardo are part of a larger group of friends from diverse Hispanic nations, including Guatemala, Colombia, and El Salvador. There are several sets of brothers and sisters in the group and, as is common in Latin America, these siblings act as peers. For example, Adriana and her younger sister Rosalba are very close and share their social lives as well as their family life.

These friends spend free time and study time at each other's houses and all know each other's family members. Close friends, rather like extended family, are often included in family events and celebrations. Parties that Adriana and Ricardo attend commonly include several generations, from babies to grandparents.

Intimate friendship among Latin Americans is sometimes marked by *apodos,* or nicknames, denoting the special relationship. In Mexico, *primo(a), hermano(a),* or *cuate* (for males, meaning "pal" or, literally, "twin") are used. (Adriana can often be heard hailing Ricardo in the halls with *"¡Oye, primo!")* Other terms, more frequently employed by Spanish-speaking adults, are *compadre* or *comadre* (godfather or godmother with respect to each other's child and, literally, "co-father, co-mother"), *maestro(a)* (master or teacher), *cuñado(a)* (in-law), or, in Venezuela, *poeta* (poet).

While friendship is a universal phenomenon, each friendship is unique. As the camaraderie between Adriana and Ricardo illustrates, the expression of friendship is a singular blending of personal affinities and shared culture.

Introduce

26   Capítulo 1

Planning

Cross-Curricular Connections

Career Connection (pp. 34–35)
Have students bring in pictures of people in various occupations. Ask them to name a personality characteristic that might contribute to success in that occupation.

Civics Connection (pp. 42–43)
Have pairs of students make illustrated posters for a person, real or imaginary, who is running for president of the U.S. Allow students creative latitude, but make sure posters include a list of the candidates' good characteristics.

Geography Connection (pp. 48–49)
Have students refer to a map of Mexico to locate and count the different states. Then have them refer to a map of the U.S. Invite students to make size comparisons between states in each nation.

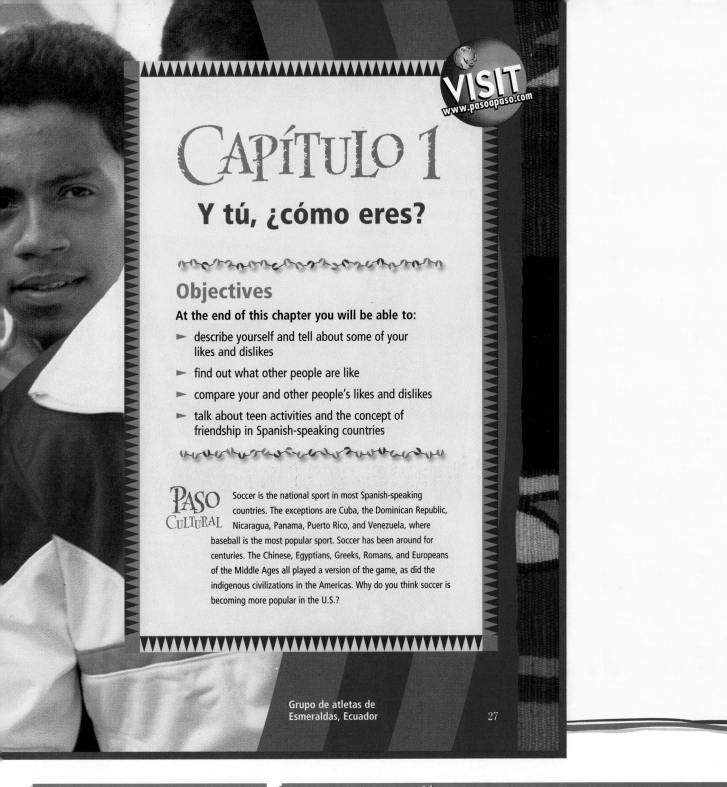

VISIT
www.pasoapaso.com

CAPÍTULO 1
Y tú, ¿cómo eres?

Objectives

At the end of this chapter you will be able to:

► describe yourself and tell about some of your likes and dislikes

► find out what other people are like

► compare your and other people's likes and dislikes

► talk about teen activities and the concept of friendship in Spanish-speaking countries

PASO CULTURAL Soccer is the national sport in most Spanish-speaking countries. The exceptions are Cuba, the Dominican Republic, Nicaragua, Panama, Puerto Rico, and Venezuela, where baseball is the most popular sport. Soccer has been around for centuries. The Chinese, Egyptians, Greeks, Romans, and Europeans of the Middle Ages all played a version of the game, as did the indigenous civilizations in the Americas. Why do you think soccer is becoming more popular in the U.S.?

Grupo de atletas de
Esmeraldas, Ecuador

27

Cultural Notes

Spanish in Your Community
How many students in your school came from or have parents who came from a Spanish-speaking country? Conduct a survey in class and at home in your neighborhood to get a rough idea of how many students there might be and the countries from which they came. Record the countries on the chalkboard. As you do so, have volunteers point to or flag each country on a world map.

(pp. 26–27, photo)
The faces of the members of this soccer team and of their friends reflect the racial makeup of inhabitants of Esmeraldas, Ecuador. The population of the seaport is composed mostly of descendants of African slaves. However, there is a mix in some faces of African, European, and indigenous traits. Esmeraldas, the first place in Ecuador where the Spanish *conquistadores* landed, now is a popular spot for tourists.

Paso cultural
Possible answers: Immigration from countries where soccer is popular. The 1994 World Cup was held in the U.S.

Cultural Objective
• To talk about teen activities and the concept of friendship in Spanish-speaking countries

 ¡Piénsalo bien!

Play

 Video Activity A

Teaching Suggestions
Point out the use of quotation marks in the photo captions on pp. 28–29. Tell students that these indicate a statement from a person in the photo. Contrast this with a caption that gives an explanation of the photo content, as on p. 27.

Using the Video
This chapter's video focuses on friendship, what people are like, and what they like to do. Students will see our host in Miami interviewing several people and also talking about himself.
To prepare students for the video, first ask them to predict what this chapter's tape will be about. Then have students watch the segment several times. After the first time, you may wish to have them brainstorm possible vocabulary and expressions they will need to talk

¡Piensa en la CULTURA!

Spending time with friends in Spain and Mexico

Look at the photographs. In the captions these teens tell us something about themselves.

PASO CULTURAL It's a common practice in Spanish-speaking countries to take a break at an outdoor café. In addition to coffee and pastries, patrons can order soft drinks and even light meals. Why do you think it's so enjoyable for people in Spanish-speaking countries to go to cafés?

"Soy de Madrid. Me gusta mucho estar con mis amigos."
What is this group of friends doing?

Madrid, España

28 Capítulo 1

Options

Strategies for Reaching All Students

Spanish-Speaking Students
Ask individual students the following: *¿Eres como uno de estos chicos? ¿Quién es como tus amigos? ¿Te gustan estas actividades? ¿Por qué? Describe a las personas en las fotos.*

 Un paso más Ex. 1-A

Students Needing Extra Help
¡Piensa en la cultura!: If students define *estudiar* correctly, ask them how they arrived at their answer. Show them how it resembles the English word study, and how this is a good technique for learning vocabulary.

Cultural Notes

Paso cultural
Possible answers: nice climate in general, facilitates socializing

Barcelona, España

"Soy de Barcelona. Me gusta hablar por teléfono con mis amigos."
What do you think the girl is saying in the caption?

"Me gusta estudiar con Mariana. Es muy amable."
What do you think *estudiar* might mean?

www.pasoapaso.com
Visit these countries on-line

Quintana Roo, México

29

about what they saw on the video. Ask students to identify things they saw that looked familiar but were somewhat different from what they might see in their own community.

Video segment 1: For more teaching suggestions, see the Video Teacher's Guide.

Class Starter Review

Explain that because this chapter teaches ways to describe yourself and others, it is important to know your classmates' names. Have students ask the names of four classmates sitting near them. (Remind students that they saw *¿Cómo te llamas?* and *Me llamo ___* in *El primer paso.*)

Answers: ¡Piensa en la cultura!

(p. 28, photo) See if students can guess through visual context clues.

(p. 29, top photo) Have students use cognates *(teléfono)* and familiar vocabulary *(amigos)* to guess the meaning.

(p. 29, bottom photo) See if students can guess the meaning by associating the word with a cognate in English. Encourage students to look at the photo and see if they can recognize *estudiar* as a cognate.

(p. 28, photo)
This group of friends has gathered at an outdoor café in Madrid's Plaza Mayor, one of the largest public squares in Europe. Designed by Juan de Herrera, architect to Felipe II, the Plaza Mayor has been the site of a wide variety of public events since its inauguration in 1620: the canonization of saints, royal weddings, coronations, bullfights, and masked balls.

(p. 29, top photo)
This Barcelona teenager is enjoying a privilege few of her peers are lucky enough to have—a telephone extension in her own bedroom. The Spanish telephone system is jointly run by government and private companies. In 1997, Spain, with a population of 40.5 million, had about 16 million telephones in use. In comparison, the U.S., with a population of 267 million, has roughly 157 million telephones in use.

(p. 29, bottom photo)
In most traditional Latin American societies, girls often form close friendships with each other, such as these two girls studying together. The friendships between girls may extend entire lifetimes, as women choose childhood friends to be the godmothers, or *madrinas,* of their children. Discuss with students whether these kinds of friendships are found in other societies.

Chapter Theme
Friendship: Things friends do together

Communicative Objectives
• To talk about activities
• To say what you like and do not like
• To ask someone what he or she likes
• To ask if a statement is accurate

 Overheads 6–7

 Vocabulary Art BLMs/CD-ROM

 Pronunciation Tape 1-1

 Vocabulario para conversar A

Play

Using the Video
Video segment 2: See the Video Teacher's Guide.

 Video Activity B

Grammar Preview
Emphatic *sí* and *tampoco* are presented lexically. A brief explanation and practice exercise appear on p. 45.

Vocabulario para conversar

 **At Home** **VIDEO** Chapter 1 Vocabulary

¿Qué te gusta hacer?

Here are some new words and expressions you will need to talk about your likes and dislikes. Read them several times, then turn the page and practice with a partner.

ir a la escuela

nadar

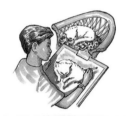

dibujar

ir al cine

practicar deportes

escuchar música

patinar

ayudar en casa

hablar por teléfono

30 Capítulo 1

Options

Strategies for Reaching All Students

Students Needing Extra Help
Point out the *¡No olvides!* feature on p. 31. These notes will appear as needed in future chapters.

Enrichment
También necesitas…: To reinforce *me gusta (más / mucho)* and *no me gusta (mucho / nada),* have students do a written assignment rating fast-food restaurants, entertainers, or TV programs, making sure to use each of the expressions at least once.

Learning Spanish Through Action
STAGING VOCABULARY: *Señalen, Toquen*
MATERIALS: transparency of activities in the *Vocabulario para conversar* or pictures of similar activities from magazines
DIRECTIONS: Using the overhead or pictures placed along the chalkboard edge, ask students to touch or point to various activities you call out at random.

Multiple Intelligences
Bodily/Kinesthetic
Play charades as a way of identifying the activities shown.
Bring in props that match the various activities and have students identify them while wearing/touching/holding the items.
Logical/Mathematical
Have students conduct a survey of activity preferences among their classmates and then make a graph, chart, or table to represent the findings.

estudiar

ver la televisión (la tele)

cocinar

leer

tocar la guitarra

También necesitas...

¿Qué te gusta (hacer)?	*What do you like (to do)?*
¿Te gusta ___?	*Do you like ___?*
estar con amigos	*to be with friends*
(A mí) me gusta ___.	*I like ___.*
más ___.	*___ better. (I prefer.)*
mucho ___.	*___ a lot.*
¿Y a ti?	*And you?*
(A mí) sí me gusta ___.	*I do like ___.*
A mí también.	*I do (like it) too.*
(A mí) no me gusta ___.	*I don't like ___.*
mucho ___.	*___ very much.*
nada ___.	*___ at all.*
___ tampoco.	*___ either.*
¿De veras?	*Really?*
Pues	*Well . . .*
y	*and*

¡NO OLVIDES!

Remember that in Spanish we use an upside-down punctuation mark at the beginning of questions and exclamations and a regular one at the end.

Vocabulario para conversar 31

Teaching Suggestions
Preparing students to speak: Use one or two options from each of the categories of Comprehensible Input, Physical Response, or Limited Verbal Response. For a complete explanation of these categories and some sample activities, see pp. T22–T23.

By introducing new vocabulary via overheads or video, students will begin to learn and acquire the language by matching what they see or read to what they hear. This is known as comprehensible input. Students can also deduce the meaning of new grammatical structures or endings by listening or reading in a context that makes their meaning apparent.

Use the Overheads or Vocabulary Art BLMs/CD-ROM for initial vocabulary presentation. Later, you may wish to use the Vocabulary Art to make your own copies for additional written or oral assessment.

Class Starter Review
On the day following initial presentation, you might begin the class with this activity:
Using visuals, state each of the vocabulary activities and have students indicate *Me gusta* or *No me gusta*.

www Internet Activities
Juegos/Have students go to www.pasoapaso.com for additional activities and practice.

Visual/Spatial
1) Use Overheads 6–7 or the Vocabulary Art BLMs/CD-ROM to make flashcards for oral practice.
2) See Using the Video.

Practice & Apply

Answers: Empecemos a conversar

1 ESTUDIANTE A

a. ¿Qué te gusta hacer? ¿Te gusta patinar?

b. ...¿Te gusta escuchar música?

c. ...¿Te gusta dibujar?

d. ...¿Te gusta cocinar?

e. ...¿Te gusta estudiar?

f. Questions will vary, but look for *¿te gusta* + inf.? in second question.

ESTUDIANTE B

a.–f. Answers will vary according to selected choice.

2 ESTUDIANTE A

a. ¿Qué te gusta más, dibujar o leer?

b. ... ir a la escuela o ayudar en casa?

c. ... ir al cine o ver la tele(visión)?

d. ... escuchar música o tocar la guitarra?

e. Questions will vary, but look for *¿qué te gusta más?* + inf.

ESTUDIANTE B

a.–e. Answers will vary, but should include one of the infinitives suggested by *Estudiante A*.

3 Answers will vary. Encourage at least three exchanges.

Empecemos a conversar

With a partner, take turns being *Estudiante A* and *Estudiante B*. Use the words that are cued or given in the balloons to replace the underlined sections in the model. 🔆 means you can make your own choices.

1 A —*¿Qué te gusta hacer? ¿Te gusta nadar?*
   B —*Sí, me gusta.*

Estudiante A   Estudiante B

Sí, me gusta.
o: No, no me gusta.
o: No, no me gusta nada.

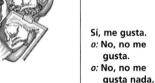

2 A —*¿Qué te gusta más, practicar deportes o hablar por teléfono?*
   B —*Pues, me gusta más hablar por teléfono.*

Estudiante A   Estudiante B

32   Capítulo 1

Options

Strategies for Reaching All Students

Spanish-Speaking Students
To model pronunciation, pair bilingual and non-bilingual students for Exs. 1–2. For more advanced practice, pair Spanish-speaking students with each other for Exs. 3–4.

📖 **Un paso más Exs. 1-B, 1-C**

Students Needing Extra Help
Have students fill in their Organizers (available in the *Practice Workbook*) before doing the exercises that require them to make choices. As students continue through the chapter, have them add to the Organizer whenever they are required to use newly presented vocabulary.
Ex. 1: Explain when to use each response. Do some examples aloud for those students who don't see the possible choices. Model at least one negative item.

Ex. 2: Review *pues*. Show what remains the same in the sentence when substitutions occur. Emphasize that *Estudiante B* creates his or her own answer when a situation is open ended.
Ex. 3: Model both possibilities for *Estudiante B*. Explain the use of the responses.
Ex. 4: Point out that *o:* indicates a choice. Have students use the Organizer for possible answers.
Exs. 5–6: To keep the possibilities orderly, have students create an organizer with three

3 A —No me gusta mucho <u>ver la televisión</u>.

    B —<u>A mí no me gusta tampoco.</u>

Estudiante A   Estudiante B

A mí no me gusta tampoco.

o: ¿De veras? A mí sí me gusta.

4 A —A mí me gusta <u>tocar la guitarra</u>. ¿Y a ti?

    B —Pues, a mí me gusta <u>practicar deportes</u>.

        o: Pues, a mí también.

Estudiante A   Estudiante B

Empecemos a escribir

Write your answers in Spanish.

5 Categorize the activities on pages 30–31 either as entertainment or as duties. Make two lists. Put a check next to any duties you enjoy.

6 Make a list of all those activities that you do on a normal school day.

7 ¿Qué te gusta hacer? ¿Qué no te gusta hacer?

8 ¿Qué te gusta más, leer o ver la tele?

También se dice...

People in different English-speaking countries often use different words to refer to the same thing. For example, what we call an "apartment" the English call a "flat." Similarly, in various Spanish-speaking countries, there are sometimes different words for the same thing.

mirar la televisión
(la tele)

> **MORE PRACTICE**
>
> Más práctica y tarea, p. 508
> Practice Workbook 1-1, 1-3

4 Answers will vary, but look for *a mí me gusta* + inf.

Answers: Empecemos a escribir

Note that Exs. 7–8 are directed to students in Spanish for further comprehension practice in the target language.

5–6 Answers will vary.

7 Answers will vary, but look for *me gusta* and *no me gusta* + inf.

8 Answers will vary.

También se dice

This feature offers examples of how Spanish vocabulary differs from region to region and discourages viewing vocabulary choice as a matter of right or wrong. These sections are for enrichment only. They point out to students that they might hear variant forms depending on the speaker's native country or region. Allow Spanish-speaking students who may use other words or expressions to add to this section.

 Practice Wkbk. 1-1, 1-2, 1-3

 Audio Activities 1.1, 1.2

 Writing Activities 1-A, 1-B

 Pruebas 1-1, 1-2

---

columns labeled "Entertainment," "Duties," and "School Activities."

Empecemos a escribir: For additional practice, have students categorize the activities from this vocabulary section as things they like to do, things they don't like to do much, and things they don't like to do at all.

Enrichment

Ex. 1: Encourage pairs of students to extend their dialogues by having *Estudiante B* ask *Estudiante A* what he or she likes: *¿Y a ti? ¿Qué te gusta hacer?*

Extended Written Practice/Homework

These exercises provide extended written practice with emphasis on correct spelling and punctuation. Many of them allow for oral or written follow-up with other students.

1. Choose seven activities from pp. 30–31. For each activity, write a sentence telling how much you like or dislike it. Add the question, *"¿Y a ti?"* to each sentence.
2. Write three questions asking a person which of two activities he or she prefers.

Multiple Intelligences

Interpersonal/Social

Have students make personalized Bingo cards using vocabulary words on pp. 30–31 and play as teams, in groups, or in pairs.

Present

Chapter Theme
Friendship: Describing friends

Communicative Objectives
- To say what you are like or what someone else is like
- To ask someone what he or she is like
- To describe yourself or others

 Overheads 8–9

 Vocabulary Art BLMs/CD-ROM

 Pronunciation Tape 1-2

 Vocabulario para conversar B

Play

Step

Using the Video
Video segment 2: See the Video Teacher's Guide.

 Video Activity B

 Pasos vivos 1 CD-ROM
Clip Art Album

Vocabulario para conversar

 Chapter 1 Vocabulary

¿Cómo eres?

Here's the rest of the vocabulary you will need to describe yourself and others.

generoso generosa

tacaño tacaña

impaciente

paciente

deportista

artístico artística

atrevido atrevida

prudente

34   Capítulo 1

Options

Strategies for Reaching All Students

Learning Spanish Through Action
STAGING VOCABULARY: *Señalen, Toquen*
MATERIALS: transparency of adjectives in the *Vocabulario para conversar* or magazine pictures of people in professions such as police officer, firefighter, judge, athlete, comedian, talk-show host, mime, stuntperson, artist, and chess player

DIRECTIONS: Have students touch or point to the appropriate overhead image or magazine picture as you call out various adjectives. If you do this activity with magazine pictures after presenting the grammar, have students listen carefully to masculine and feminine forms.

Multiple Intelligences
Bodily/Kinesthetic
Using Overheads 8–9, have students come up to the projector and identify a scene as you describe it.
Verbal/Linguistic
See Pronunciation Tape 1-2.
Visual/Spatial
See Overheads 8–9, the Vocabulary Art BLMs/CD-ROM, and Using the Video.

ordenado ordenada

desordenado desordenada

trabajador trabajadora

perezoso perezosa

gracioso graciosa

serio seria

I·C·T INSTITUTO COSTARRICENSE DE TURISMO
COSTA RICA

También necesitas...

¿Cómo eres?	*What are you like?*	callado, -a	*quiet*
(Yo) soy ___.	*I am (I'm) ___.*	pero	*but*
(Tú) eres ___.	*You are (You're) ___.*	a veces	*sometimes, at times*
muy	*very*		
amable	*nice, kind*	**¿Y qué quiere decir...?**	
		sociable	

Vocabulario para conversar 35

Grammar Preview
Allow students to use these adjectives *before* presenting rules of agreement. The visuals will help them intuit the rule, making the understanding of grammar a natural outgrowth of its use and facilitating learning.

Teaching Suggestions
Preparing students to speak: Use one or two options from each of the categories of Comprehensible Input, Physical Response, or Limited Verbal Response. For a complete explanation of these categories and some sample activities, see pp. T22–T23.

¿Y qué quiere decir...?: Remind students that the vocabulary in this section is either cognates or previously seen words or expressions.

Class Starter Review
On the day following initial presentation, you might begin the class with this activity:
Have students turn to a partner and describe themselves, using three adjectives. On the next day, have students do this same activity in written form.

www Internet Activities
Juegos
Have students go to www.pasoapaso.com for additional activities and practice.

Cultural Notes

(p. 35, realia)
Brochure from the Costa Rican Institute of Tourism. This brochure invites tourists to come to Costa Rica to go parasailing *(subir al paracaídas acuático)* and for other water sports. With its tropical rainforests and two oceans, Costa Rica is also one of the world's most popular destinations for ecotourism.

Practice & Apply

Re-enter / Recycle
Ex. 15: greetings from *El primer paso*

Grammar Preview
The explanation of adjective agreement appears on p. 43. If students ask why it is *-o* in some cases, *-a* in others, encourage them to develop their own explanation. They will almost certainly decide on the right answer and teach themselves the grammar rule.

Answers: Empecemos a conversar

9 Model this carefully, alternating between male and female students.

ESTUDIANTE A

a. ¿Cómo eres, gracioso(a) o serio(a)?

b. ... atrevido(a) o prudente?

c. ... generoso(a) o tacaño(a)?

d. ... impaciente o paciente?

e. ... trabajador(a) o perezoso(a)?

ESTUDIANTE B

a.–e. Answers will vary, but look for correct adjective agreement.

10 Questions and answers will vary, but look for correct adjective agreement.

Empecemos a conversar

9 A —¿*Cómo eres, ordenado(a) o desordenado(a)?*
   B —*Soy ordenado(a), pero a veces soy desordenado(a).*

Estudiante A   Estudiante B

a.   b.   c.   d.   e.

10 A —¿*Eres serio(a)?*
   B —*Sí, y soy callado(a) también.*
      o: *No, no soy serio(a).*

Estudiante A   Estudiante B

Options

Strategies for Reaching All Students

Spanish-Speaking Students
Have pairs of Spanish-speaking students write out at least three questions and answers for Ex. 10. With Ex. 11, have them write three short sentences describing themselves.

 Un paso más Ex. 1-D

Students Needing Extra Help
Have students add *tampoco* and *también* to their Organizers.
Ex. 13: Have students create an organizer with four columns for the exercise.
Exs. 14–15: Show students the number of tools (cognates, patterns, etc.) they have to help them, and the number of times they have already seen these words.

Enrichment
Ex. 9: Preview the grammar by asking students why there are two adjective endings. Ask what an adjective is and what it does.
Ex. 12: For each of the three words describing themselves, have students write a logical sentence telling what they like or dislike doing.

11

A —¿Te gusta _nadar_?

B —Sí, soy _deportista_.

   o: _No, no soy muy **deportista**._

Estudiante A

Estudiante B

a.
b.
c.
d.

Empecemos a escribir y a leer

Write your answers in Spanish.

12 Look at the vocabulary on pages 34–35 and write down three words that describe you.

13 Make a list of the words that you would use to describe:
- the ideal student
- the ideal teacher
- the ideal parent
- the ideal friend

14 ¿Cómo eres? ¿Eres amable? ¿Sociable? ¿Trabajador(a)?

15 ¡Hola! Me llamo Esteban. A mí me gusta nadar y patinar. También me gusta estar con mis amigos o hablar por teléfono. No me gusta ni cocinar ni ayudar en casa. ¿Cómo soy?

Eres . . .

MORE PRACTICE

- Más práctica y tarea, p. 509
- Practice Workbook 1–4

Vocabulario para conversar 37

11 Remind students that _Estudiante B_ must make a logical response to _Estudiante A._

ESTUDIANTE A

a. ¿Te gusta practicar deportes?

b. . . . dibujar?

c. . . . ayudar en casa?

d. . . . patinar?

ESTUDIANTE B

a. Sí, (No, no) soy muy deportista.

b. . . . artístico(a).

c. . . . trabajador(a).

d. . . . atrevido(a).

Answers: Empecemos a escribir y a leer

12–13 Answers will vary, but look for correct adjective agreement.

14 Answers will vary, but look for _soy_ + correct adjective agreement.

15 Likely answers: _Eres deportista y sociable. No eres trabajador._

 Practice Wkbk. 1-4

 Audio Activity 1.3

 Writing Activities 1-C, 1-D

¿? **Pruebas 1-3, 1-4**

Extended Written Practice/Homework

1. Choose six adjectives from pp. 34–35. For each, write a sentence saying whether you are or are not like this.

2. Write five questions in which you ask other students if they are described by one adjective or another (_gracioso o serio_).

Multiple Intelligences

Bodily/Kinesthetic

Display pictures of well-known personalities on the board. Have students come up and write adjectives from their vocabulary list to describe them.

Verbal/Linguistic and Bodily/Kinesthetic

Have each student pick an adjective from pp. 34–35 and begin to "act" that way. Ask for a volunteer to walk from desk to desk and try to guess each student's adjective: _¿Eres gracioso(a)?_

Standards 1.1; 1.2 **37**

Practice

Teaching Suggestions
The *¡Comuniquemos!* section allows for integrated practice of both vocabulary sections of the chapter.

Answers:
¡Comuniquemos!
1–2 Answers will vary, but look for the correct infinitive used:
escuchar música
cocinar
leer
hablar por teléfono
ver la tele(visión)
ayudar en casa

¡COMUNI

1

Find out how many of the pictured activities both you and your partner enjoy. Take turns asking the questions. Be sure to choose only those activities you really like.

A —*A mí me gusta escuchar música. ¿Y a ti?*
B —*A mí me gusta también.*
   o: *A mí no me gusta.*

2

Now take turns finding out if you and your partner dislike the same things. Use the pictures, and this time choose only those activities you <u>don't</u> like.

A —*No me gusta cocinar. ¿Y a ti?*
B —*A mí no me gusta tampoco.*
   o: *A mí sí me gusta.*

38   Capítulo 1

Options

Strategies for Reaching All Students

Spanish-Speaking Students
For the *¡Comuniquemos!* section, have Spanish-speaking students describe themselves in four or five sentences, concentrating on telling what activities they like and do well.

Students Needing Extra Help
Exs. 1–2: Have students provide at least five examples of likes and dislikes. Remind them that *o:* indicates a choice.

Enrichment
For extra practice, begin by asking someone what he or she is like. That person should answer and then ask someone else the same question. Continue until everyone has participated. To save time, you may want to let each row or section do its own question-and-answer exercise. For example:
A —*Luis, ¿cómo eres?*
B —*Soy (muy) paciente y (muy) sociable también. Enrique, ¿cómo eres?*
C —*Pues, soy . . . .*

¡QUEMOS!

What have you and your partner learned about each other? Write a two-sentence description of your partner. Include two words that describe him or her and two activities that he or she likes. Read your description aloud, pausing to allow your partner to say *Sí* or *No* to your statements.

You are going to be an exchange student in Costa Rica and your host family wants to know what you are like. Write a few sentences telling them what you are like and some things you like to do. Then, with a partner, compare what you wrote about yourselves.

¿Qué sabes ahora?

Can you:

► ask someone what he or she likes to do?
—¿Qué ___ hacer?

► tell someone what you like or do not like to do?
—___ ir a la escuela.

► ask someone what he or she is like?
—¿Cómo ___?

► tell someone what you are like?
—Soy ___.

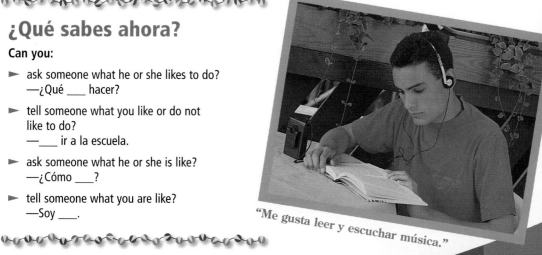

"Me gusta leer y escuchar música."

Vocabulario para conversar 39

---

3 Answers will vary, but look for adjective agreement and use of the infinitive.

4 Answers will vary, but look for *soy* + correct adjective agreement and use of *me gusta* + inf.

Answers: ¿Qué sabes ahora?
• te gusta
• (No) me gusta
• eres
• Answers will vary, but should contain correct adjective agreement.

 Audio Activity 1.4

 Writing Activities 1-E, 1-F, 1-G

 Comm. Act. BLMs 1-1, 1-2

 Pasos vivos 1 CD-ROM
Slide Projector, Laboratorio de grabar

Cooperative Learning
Prepare four cards numbered 1–4, each listing one of the activities in Ex. 1. After placing a card in each corner of the room, ask students, in groups, to write and then recite in Spanish the number and name of the activity that they least like among the four. After reciting, each student goes to the appropriate corner and gives one reason why his or her group disliked the particular activity they chose. A spokesperson for each group then summarizes the reasons given.

Multiple Intelligences
Bodily/Kinesthetic, Interpersonal/Social, and Verbal/Linguistic
See Cooperative Learning.
Intrapersonal/Introspective
See *¿Qué sabes ahora?*

Cultural Notes

(p. 39, photo)
Most Latin Americans place a premium on education, and families strive to give their children time and space for study. During the economic crises of the 1980s and 1990s, however, many teenagers were forced to leave their studies for full time jobs to help support their families. Discuss this role of teenagers as family providers with your students, emphasizing how they are indicative of Hispanic family loyalty and love.

Standards 1.1; 1.2; 1.3; 2.1; 3.1; 5.1 **39**

Cultural Objective
- To talk about the concept of friendship in Spanish-speaking countries

Teaching Suggestions
In order to prepare students for a meaningful discussion about the similarities and differences between the concept of friendship in the U.S. and in Spanish-speaking countries, you might wish to have them read the text the night before you present the lesson in class. Ask them to begin thinking about what friendship means to them.

Critical Thinking: Comparing and Contrasting
Although friendship is defined somewhat differently in the U.S. than it is in some Spanish-speaking countries, there are some aspects of friendship that would apply to both cultures. Ask students to suggest what some of these aspects might be and if some of them might be universally applicable.

Multicultural Perspectives
Have students list similarities, differences, and common interests of teens from a Spanish-speaking culture and of those from the U.S.

Perspectiva cultural

La amistad

Children in Latin America often give these cloth bracelets to each other as tokens of friendship.

Te gusta estar con tus amigos, ¿no? ¿Qué te gusta hacer con tus amigos? ¿Les gusta ir al cine? ¿Hablar por teléfono? ¿Practicar deportes? Sí, probablemente. Pero, ¿qué quiere decir esa palabra mágica, "amigo"?

Look at the people in the photos. How can you tell that they might be friends?

"Mike, this is my friend Luis." That is how my classmate introduced

"Soy de Chile. Me gusta tocar la guitarra."

me to another boy in our class. It was my first day of school here. I was in the seventh grade. My family had come from El Salvador in July, so I had not met any English speakers my age. And here was someone introducing me as his friend when we had just met that morning! What a strange place I was in!

Options

Strategies for Reaching All Students

Spanish-Speaking Students
After reading the text, ask Spanish-speaking students: *¿Te gusta salir con tus amigos? ¿Cuándo salen Uds. juntos? ¿Adónde van? ¿Salen los fines de semana? ¿Qué hacen?*

 Un paso más Ex. 1-E

Enrichment
Tell students that in Mexican Spanish, the word *cuate* is used to name a very special, trusted friend. Point out that the other meaning of this word is "twin." Ask students if they can think of any words in English that would be the equivalent of *cuate* (buddy, pal, etc.).

Multiple Intelligences
Verbal/Linguistic
Have students bring in a photo of a friend. In pairs or groups have them describe this person.

Estudiantes mexicanos
en la escuela

By the end of that year, I did have friends, friends in the Spanish sense. They are still my friends. I think that they will always be, because that is what we mean by *amigo,* a friend for life.

Where I came from, people didn't move around a lot. You would probably grow up in one neighborhood or town and might even live there your whole life. Yes, you might miss out on a few things, but you would form deep friendships and keep them. You would know people well, and would usually see your friends every day. You'd also get to know each other's families well.

And we share a lot. We share our true feelings and thoughts with our friends. We also share what we have. If a friend borrows money from me, I don't keep track or get an I.O.U. Or if I do a favor for a friend, I don't think any more about it. I know that my friend will always help me out. In the long run, it will probably turn out even.

Of course, we are warm and welcoming to people we don't know very well, people you might call friends but whom we would call *conocidos* (acquaintances). We may get along quite well, but they are not *amigos.* Perhaps some day they will be, but that takes time. An *amigo* is someone you can count on all your life.

La cultura desde tu perspectiva

1 What are some similarities and differences between who is considered a friend in a Spanish-speaking country and in the United States?

2 What could you expect to occur if you became friends with someone in a Spanish-speaking country?

Perspectiva cultural   41

Cultural Notes

(p. 40, photo)
Students in Santiago, Chile. The guitar remains a popular instrument among students in most Spanish-speaking countries. Chileans place a high value on the arts, culture, and education. As a result of an intensive literacy campaign initiated in 1980, the rate of adult literacy rose from 89 percent in 1970 to 93.4 percent in 1990.

(pp. 40–41, realia)
If students ask, inform them that the pictured items are friendship bracelets from El Salvador.

(p. 41, photo)
This photo of Mexican schoolgirls walking arm in arm is similar to what you might see in many parts of Latin America. Friends are more likely to show their affection physically than their counterparts in the U.S. School uniforms are also typical throughout the region.

Teaching Suggestions
This poem serves as a summary of the structures students have been using and a preview of *ni...ni.* As they work through the poem and the questions, students will formulate for themselves the rules given on the following pages. *Encourage this to occur as students work with and examine the building blocks of the language.*

Answers
Answers will vary, but may include: adjectives or words that describe the author.

A Answers may vary, but could include that the author is not extremely one way or another, that she is sometimes talkative and sometimes quiet, etc.

B The poet is female, since almost all of the adjectives end in *-a: callada, generosa, tacaña, atrevida, ordenada, desordenada.*

C See if students can guess the meaning from context.

D Answers will vary, but may include: Words ending in *-o* refer to males and words ending in *-a* refer to females. Yes; *amable, deportista, impaciente, paciente, prudente, trabajador, sociable.*

Gramática en contexto

Here is a descriptive poem entitled "Yo." What kind of information would you expect to find in such a poem?

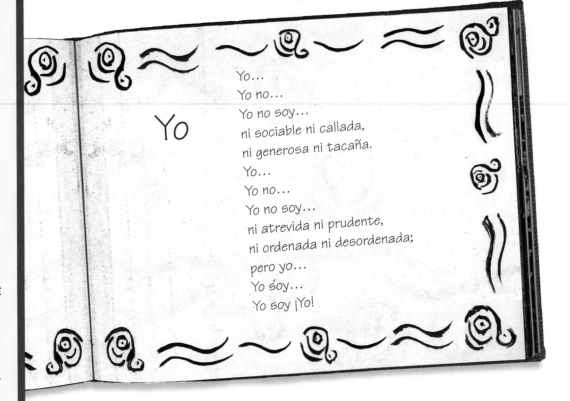

Yo...
Yo no...
Yo no soy...
ni sociable ni callada,
ni generosa ni tacaña.
Yo...
Yo no...
Yo no soy...
ni atrevida ni prudente,
ni ordenada ni desordenada;
pero yo...
Yo soy...
Yo soy ¡Yo!

A Think about the predictions you made before you read the poem. Did you find the information that you thought you would find in the poem? What did you find out about the person who wrote it?

B Is the poet male or female? How do you know? Find at least three words that give you that information.

C *Ni . . . ni* appears four times in the poem. What do you suppose it means?

D Think of a guideline that could help you decide whether to use the words *generoso* or *generosa* and *serio* or *seria* to describe a person. Are there any adjectives (descriptive words) on pages 34–35 that your rule does not cover? Which ones?

42 Capítulo 1

Options

Strategies for Reaching All Students

Students Needing Extra Help
For sections A–D, model aloud so that students hear everyone's responses. Write any responses on the board for visual learners.
Ex. 1: Make sure students understand that they should choose words from the list.
Ex. 2: Point out to students that they can answer with a negative statement.

Enrichment
Ask for a male volunteer to read the poem aloud, making the necessary changes in adjective forms.
Ex. 1: Have students play a memory game in which they turn over cards with adjectives on them and try to match a feminine adjective with its masculine form (exclude adjectives ending in *-e).* Play with at least ten sets of adjectives (20 cards). A variation of this game is to have students match an adjective with its opposite meaning.

(This will be more challenging if separate cards are made for masculine and feminine forms. For example, the correct match for *perezosa* has to be *trabajadora,* not *trabajador.)*

Los adjetivos

Words describing people and things are called adjectives.

- In Spanish, adjectives describing females usually end in *-a*.

- Adjectives describing males usually end in *-o*. However, there are some exceptions, such as *deportista,* which can describe both males and females.

- Adjectives that end in *-e* can describe either females or males, for example: *amable.*

Here are the adjectives you already know:

amable	impaciente
artística	ordenada
artístico	ordenado
atrevida	paciente
atrevido	perezosa
callada	perezoso
callado	prudente
deportista	seria
desordenada	serio
desordenado	sociable
generosa	tacaña
generoso	tacaño
graciosa	trabajador
gracioso	trabajadora

1 Look at the list of adjectives. Seventeen of the words can be used to describe a boy. Which ones are they? Which ones can be used to describe a girl? How many of the words can be used to describe a boy *or* a girl? Which ones are they?

2 Students are preparing a who's who that describes each member of the class. Ask your partner what he or she is like. Each of you should choose four or more words from the list to describe yourselves.

A —¿*Cómo eres?*

B —*Soy graciosa, artística, paciente y sociable.*
   o: *Soy gracioso, artístico, paciente y sociable.*

3 With a partner, take turns describing these fictional characters. Afterward, compare your descriptions with those of another pair of students.

Mary Poppins

A —¿*Cómo es Mary Poppins?*

B —*Es muy paciente.*

¡NO OLVIDES!

To describe a third person (he or she), use *es.*

a. Ricitos de Oro (Goldilocks) f. Robin Hood
b. Donald Duck   g. La Cenicienta (Cinderella)
c. Curious George   h. Scrooge
d. Garfield   i. Pocahontas
e. Superman   j. el león de El Mago de Oz

4 Choose a person, real or fictional, whom your partner is likely to know about. Describe that person. If necessary, pantomime any other hints that might be helpful. Can your partner figure out whom you are describing?

Gramática en contexto   43

Present & Practice

Class Starter Review

On the day following the presentation of adjectives, you might begin the class with this activity: Write these professions in English on the chalkboard: auto racer, politician, salesperson, sculptor, judge, comedian, baseball player, accountant. Ask students to choose adjectives that would describe the quality or qualities that a person wanting to enter one of these professions should have.

Answers

1 Six adjectives can describe either a boy or a girl: *amable, deportista, impaciente, paciente, prudente,* and *sociable.*

2–4 Answers will vary, but look for adjective agreement. Possible responses for Ex. 3:
a. Es muy sociable.
b. ... gracioso.
c. ... amable.
d. ... perezoso.
e. ... atrevido.
f. ... generoso.
g. ... trabajadora.
h. ... tacaño.
i. ... seria.
j. ... prudente.

 Practice Wkbk. 1-5, 1-6, 1-7

 Prueba 1-5

Extended Written Practice/Homework
1. Write four sentences saying what you are like, and then what you are like sometimes: *Soy prudente y a veces soy tacaño.*
2. Write three sentences saying what you are like, but what you are not like: *Soy desordenada pero no soy perezosa.*

Multiple Intelligences
Bodily/Kinesthetic
See notes under Enrichment, Ex. 1.
Visual/Spatial
Have students rewrite the poem on p. 42 substituting those adjectives which best describe them as individuals.

Present & Practice

Answers

5 a. Me gusta ir al cine y escuchar música, pero no me gusta ni nadar ni hablar por teléfono.

b. Me gusta leer y practicar deportes, pero no me gusta ni ver la tele(visión) ni ayudar en casa.

c. Me gusta nadar y tocar la guitarra, pero no me gusta ni estudiar ni ir a la escuela.

d. Me gusta cocinar y dibujar, pero no me gusta ni leer ni practicar deportes.

Ni . . . ni

- If you want to say that you do not like either of two choices, use *ni . . . ni* to mean "neither . . . nor" or "not . . . or."
  For example:
  No me gusta **ni** nadar **ni** dibujar.

- Use *ni . . . ni* to say that neither of two descriptions fits you.
  No soy **ni** deportista **ni** artístico.

5 Imagine that these are new students in your Spanish class. Tell what each person might say about his or her likes and dislikes.

María

Me gusta dibujar y tocar la guitarra, pero no me gusta ni cocinar ni patinar.

a. Pablo

b. Enrique

c. Elena

d. Isabel

44   Capítulo 1

Options

Strategies for Reaching All Students

6 Take turns asking and answering questions to find out what your partner is like. Discuss whether your partner is *sociable* or *callado(a)*, *paciente* or *impaciente*, *prudente* or *atrevido(a)*, and *trabajador(a)* or *perezoso(a)*.

A —¿Eres generoso(a) o tacaño(a)?
B —Soy (muy) generoso(a).
  o: Soy tacaño(a).
  o: No soy ni generoso(a) ni tacaño(a).

Sí / Tampoco

- Use *sí* + *me gusta* to contrast something you like with something you or someone else dislikes. For example:
  —A mí no me gusta hablar por teléfono. ¿Y a ti?
  —A mí **sí me gusta**.

- Use *no me gusta* + *tampoco* to agree with someone who dislikes something. For example:
  —A mí no me gusta practicar deportes. ¿Y a ti?
  —A mí **no me gusta tampoco**.

7 You and your partner are discussing activities that you like and don't like. Choose some activities that you don't like, and find out whether or not your partner agrees.

A —A mí no me gusta patinar. ¿Y a ti?
B —Pues, a mí sí me gusta.
  o: A mí no me gusta tampoco.

MORE PRACTICE

Más práctica y tarea, p. 510
Practice Workbook 1–5, 1–9

Ahora lo sabes

Can you:

- describe yourself or someone else?
  —Yo soy ___, pero tú eres ___.

- say that you do not like either of two choices?
  —No me gusta ___ ver la tele ___ ir al cine.

- say that neither of two descriptions fits you?
  —No soy ___ perezoso(a) ___ sociable.

- emphasize that you do like something?
  —¿No te gusta? ¡A mí ___!

- say that you do not like something either?
  —A mí ___.

Gramática en contexto   45

6 Answers will vary, but look for correct adjective agreement. Ask how *Estudiante A* might continue the dialogue by responding to *Estudiante B*. Encourage *Estudiante A* to respond using *también* and / or *tampoco*.

7 Look for correct placement of *sí* and *tampoco*.

Answers: Ahora lo sabes
- Answers will vary, but look for correct adjective agreement.
- ni, ni
- ni, ni
- sí (me gusta)
- no me gusta tampoco

 Practice Wkbk. 1-8, 1-9

 Audio Activity 1.5

 Pruebas 1-6, 1-7

 Comm. Act. BLM 1-3

 Pasos vivos 1 CD-ROM
Bulletin Board, Slide Presentation Maker, Spindle, Treadmill

Extended Written Practice/Homework
1. Write three dialogues following this pattern:
Person A—Ask whether Person B prefers to do one activity or another.
Person B—Say that you do not like either choice.
2. Choose three pairs of adjectives that do *not* describe you. Write three sentences in which you say that neither one description nor another fits you.

Multiple Intelligences
Bodily/Kinesthetic
Have students use the previously made activity flashcards (pp. 30–31). Each student is to randomly select four activities and talk about each one using *me gusta, no me gusta*, and *ni ... ni*.
Allow individuals to distribute flashcards to other classmates to continue the activity.
Intrapersonal/Introspective
See *Ahora lo sabes*.

Pronunciation Tape 1-3

Todo junto A

Play

Todo junto B

Play

Using the Video
Video segment 3: See the Video Teacher's Guide.

Video Activity C

Pasos vivos 1 CD-ROM
Video Monitor, Video Presentation Maker

Answers: Actividades
You might assign Ex. 1 as written homework in preparation for doing either it or Ex. 2 orally in class for pair or small-group practice.

1 Answers will vary, but look for *soy* + correct adjective agreement and use of *me gusta* + inf.

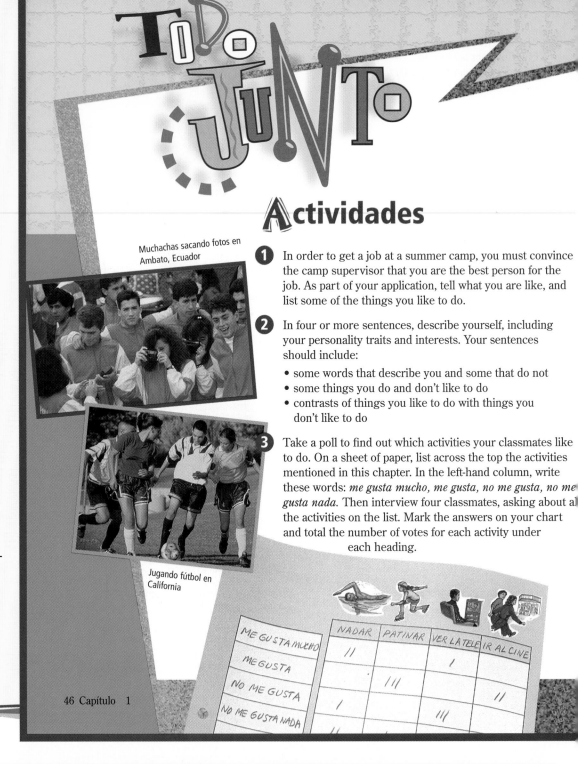

Todo junto

Actividades

Muchachas sacando fotos en Ambato, Ecuador

Jugando fútbol en California

46 Capítulo 1

1 In order to get a job at a summer camp, you must convince the camp supervisor that you are the best person for the job. As part of your application, tell what you are like, and list some of the things you like to do.

2 In four or more sentences, describe yourself, including your personality traits and interests. Your sentences should include:
- some words that describe you and some that do not
- some things you do and don't like to do
- contrasts of things you like to do with things you don't like to do

3 Take a poll to find out which activities your classmates like to do. On a sheet of paper, list across the top the activities mentioned in this chapter. In the left-hand column, write these words: *me gusta mucho, me gusta, no me gusta, no me gusta nada*. Then interview four classmates, asking about all the activities on the list. Mark the answers on your chart and total the number of votes for each activity under each heading.

	NADAR	PATINAR	VER LA TELE	IR AL CINE
ME GUSTA MUCHO	//			/
ME GUSTA		.	///	
NO ME GUSTA	/	///		//
NO ME GUSTA NADA			///	

Options

Strategies for Reaching All Students

Students Needing Extra Help
Exs. 1–3: Use the Organizer. For Ex. 3, have students base their chart on the model shown. Remind them that the verbs listed are examples, and that they should choose from all the verbs in the chapter.

Multiple Intelligences
Intrapersonal/Introspective
See *Actividades* 1–2.
Verbal/Linguistic and Visual/Spatial
See *Actividades* 3 and *Conexiones.*

Enrichment
Ex. 1: As a follow-up, you might have pairs of students act out a job interview in which the camp supervisor questions the applicant's qualities and the applicant must contradict him or her. For example:
—¿Eres impaciente?
—¡No! No soy impaciente. Soy paciente (y ordenado).
Make sure students begin the interview with appropriate greetings and introductions (soy, me llamo, ¿cómo está Ud.?, etc.).

Cooperative Learning
Divide the class into groups of four or five students. Instruct each student to write his or her name at the top of an index card and then to pass the card to the left. Using an appropriate adjective, each student should write a compliment about the student named on the card. Cards should then be circulated until every student has written a complimentary description for each person in the group. Collect the cards and read the descriptions to the class.

Conexiones

El arte

La personalidad y la pintura

What can we learn about people from a painting? Here are two famous paintings of young boys: *El príncipe Baltasar Carlos* by Diego Velázquez (1599–1660) and *Paulo sobre un asno* by Pablo Picasso (1881–1973).

- Look at each portrait. In what ways are the paintings similar? In what ways are they different?

- What is your impression of the boys? Write a list of adjectives to describe each of them.

Bring to class a picture of a portrait or self-portrait by an artist or a photo of a person cut from a magazine. Tell what you think the person is like. What are his or her likes and dislikes?

Write a four-line caption in which the person describes himself or herself: *Tengo . . . años, Soy . . ., Me gusta (mucho) . . . , No me gusta (nada) . . .* In small groups, look at the pictures and read the captions.

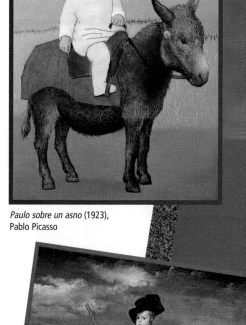

Paulo sobre un asno (1923), Pablo Picasso

El príncipe Baltasar Carlos (1634–35), Diego Velázquez

Todo junto   47

2 Answers should include *(no) soy* + adjective, *(no) me gusta* + inf., and correct adjective agreement.

3 Remind students to use *¿te gusta* + inf.? in their questions.

Teaching Suggestions
Conexiones: Encourage discussion by asking students if they agree or disagree with each other's descriptions. As an alternative to the activity, students might choose a person in a photo from the chapter to describe.

Answers: Conexiones
Answers will vary, but students may focus on the fact that the boy in the painting by Velázquez is dressed elegantly and is seated on a rearing pony, while the boy in Picasso's painting is dressed simply and is seated on a motionless donkey. Encourage students to guess at the boys' ages and to use chapter vocabulary such as *serio, atrevido, prudente,* and *paciente.* Captions will vary, but look for use of chapter vocabulary.

 Comm. Act. BLMs 1-4, 1-5

 Pasos vivos 1 CD-ROM
A Jugar, Boom Box, Laboratorio de grabar, Maps, Spindle

Cultural Notes

(p. 46, top photo)
With a population of 140,000, Ambato is the fourth-largest city in Ecuador. It is about a two-and-a-half hour drive south of Quito on the scenic Pan American highway. In 1949 a major earthquake almost completely destroyed Ambato, which has been known since colonial times as *la ciudad de frutas y flores.* Ambato is famous for its *Fiesta de frutas y flores* every February and as a center for the production of distinctive Persian-knot rugs.

(p. 47, top photo)
Painted in 1923, *Paulo sobre un asno* is a realistic portrait of Picasso's first child Paulo. Picasso went through many transformations as a painter, and is perhaps best known for "cubism" and other abstract styles. His personal life was also full of transformation and turmoil, but this portrait of his son seems to reflect a time of relative tranquility.

(p. 47, bottom photo)
Court painter and personal confidant of King Philip IV of Spain, Diego Velázquez (1599–1660) is considered one of the premier artists of seventeenth-century Europe. His equestrian portrait of Prince Baltasar Carlos, Philip IV's son and heir apparent, makes the child into a heroic, almost monumental figure. Ask students to discuss how the colors and shapes in the painting link the prince both to the earth and the clouds.

Apply

Process Reading

Make sure students understand the four headings in this section and the tasks they represent:

- *Antes de leer:* pre-reading activity for activating prior knowledge; emphasis on one or more strategies for overcoming the tendency to read slowly, word by word, and instead to focus on receiving the message being communicated in the text.
- *Mira la lectura:* scanning / skimming for general ideas or information, looking for cognates, proper nouns, headings, numbered or bulleted items, familiar words, etc.
- *Infórmate:* reading for more detailed information
- *Aplicación:* post-reading activity

Critical Thinking: Classifying

Ask students to name the student or students from *Buscando amigos* who would most likely get along well with an American student who enjoys music as well as sports (Santiago).

Answers

Antes de leer

1 Age of the target readership.

2 Answers will vary, but may include names, addresses, ages, likes and dislikes, or hobbies.

Mira la lectura

Answers will vary.

¡Vamos a leer!

Antes de leer

   www.pasoapaso.com

STRATEGY ➤ **Using prior knowledge**

We usually make new friends through personal acquaintances, but sometimes we meet people through correspondence. For example, you might want to look through a pen pal column in a Spanish-language magazine to start a correspondence with someone from another country.

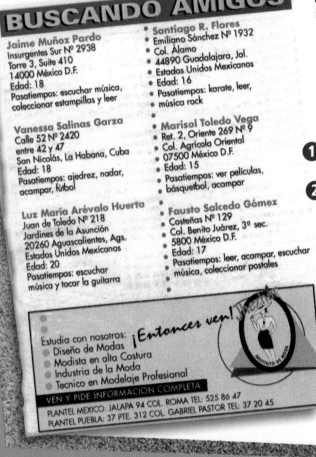

You can help yourself read in Spanish by using certain strategies. One strategy is using what you know to predict what a reading might contain. For example, you already know the kinds of information you might find in the various sections of a newspaper or magazine.

Buscando amigos is the name of the pen pal section in the Mexican magazine *15 a 20.*

1 What do you think the name *15 a 20* refers to?

2 List three things you might expect to find in a pen pal section.

Mira la lectura

STRATEGY ➤ **Scanning**

Look at this pen pal section. Does it include the three things you expected to find? What, if anything, is missing? What additional types of information did you find?

48 Capítulo 1

Options

Strategies for Reaching All Students

Spanish-Speaking Students

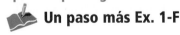 **Un paso más Ex. 1-F**

Students Needing Extra Help

Do all the activities in *¡Vamos a leer!* as a class or in small groups. The latter might work better at first. Use the Organizer as needed.

Enrichment

Aplicación: You may want to have students create a bulletin-board display with their written responses. Encourage them to use photos.

Infórmate

STRATEGY ➤ **Scanning**

Scanning is another strategy you can use. When you scan you only look for certain information. You do not have to read and understand every word.

1 Look at the first listing, for Jaime Muñoz Pardo. In what order does Jaime provide the following information?

address age hobbies name

2 Look at the first names of the people seeking pen pals. On a separate sheet of paper, list them in the three categories shown below. How many are girls? How many are boys? What clue(s) did you use to help you decide?

Boys   Girls   Not sure

3 Read about each person's pastimes.

a. List the pastimes that two or more of them share.

b. List five pastimes that are not shared.

c. Are there any pastimes whose meaning you cannot guess? If so, you and a partner should choose two that you can't figure out. Each of you should find out the meaning of one of the words and share it with the class.

Aplicación

Imagine that you are seeking a pen pal. Provide information about yourself that you think is important to share. You may want to use the following categories:
- Nombre
- Dirección
- Edad
- Pasatiempos

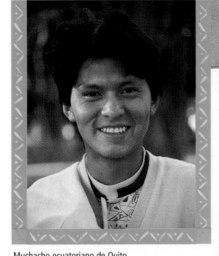
Muchacho ecuatoriano de Quito

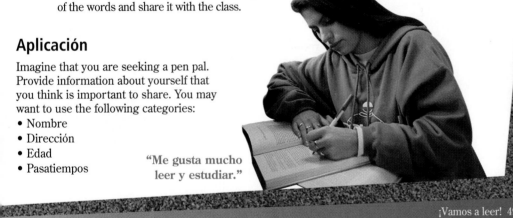
"Me gusta mucho leer y estudiar."

¡Vamos a leer! 49

Cultural Notes ☀

(p. 48, realia: left postage stamp)
The Tlaquepaque neighborhood southeast of downtown Guadalajara, Jalisco, was once a quiet, separate village where the city's wealthy families built spacious country retreats. Today these buildings are used as studios and shops by artists and artisans who produce some of the most prized works in all of Mexico. Tlaquepaque is particularly known for its exquisite blown glass, an outstanding example of which appears on this stamp.

(p. 48, realia: center postage stamp)
Jalisco is one of many Mexican states known for its production of textiles hand-loomed from wool. Because handicrafts are central to culture and commerce in Mexico, the federal as well as many state governments fund artisans by providing them with training and places to show their work. Handicraft showrooms, such as FONART, subsidize artisans and assure shoppers that they are buying authentic, quality crafts.

(p. 48, realia: right postage stamp)
The oldest university in the Americas, the Universidad Nacional Autónoma de México (UNAM) was founded in 1551 in Mexico City as the Royal and Pontifical University. It was run by the Roman Catholic church until 1867, when it was closed by the government. In 1910 the university re-opened as part of a new national school system. In 1929 it became autonomous, the occasion commemorated by this stamp.

Apply

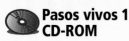
¡Vamos a escribir!

"A mí me gusta estar con mis amigos." ►

Write a poem about yourself similar to the one on page 42. Follow these steps:

1. Read the poem on page 42 again.

2. Look at the vocabulary on pages 34–35 and write down five adjectives that apply to you and five that don't. Use the headings *Soy* and *No soy*.

   Then, using the vocabulary on pages 30–31, write down at least three things that you like to do and three things that you don't like to do. Use the headings *Me gusta mucho* and *No me gusta nada*.

3. Write your poem based on the lists that you made. Focus on arranging your ideas in a way that you like.

4. Now show your poem to a partner. Ask which parts of the poem he or she likes and which ones might be changed. Decide whether or not you agree, then rewrite your poem, making any changes that you have decided on.

5. Check to make sure that everything is spelled correctly. Are capital letters used where they are needed? Are accents used correctly? Did you use question marks and exclamation points at the beginning and end of a sentence?

6. Now recopy your corrected poem. Add drawings or pictures if you like.

"¡Hola! Soy de Guatemala."

"Soy de Argentina. Soy seria y paciente."

"Soy colombiano y soy muy amable."

50   Capítulo 1

Options

Strategies for Reaching All Students

Spanish-Speaking Students
Extend the assignment by having Spanish-speaking students write a poem describing their best friend or an ideal friend.

 Un paso más Ex. 1-G

Students Needing Extra Help
Step 2: Review the definition of an adjective, reminding students that it is a word that describes someone or something. Refer to the Organizer.
Step 5: Use the Organizer.

Multiple Intelligences
Naturalist
Using vocabulary from this chapter, have students write a journal entry in which they describe activities they like to do outdoors (*al aire libre*).

¡Vamos a escribir! 51

Cultural Notes ☼

(p. 50, top photo)
This young weaver from Santiago Atitlán, Guatemala, is wearing a blouse that richly demonstrates the beauty of the hand-woven textiles for which her village is famous. Like other villages in the Maya highlands, Santiago Atitlán produces clothing that often tells a complex story of the local people and history through symbols, patterns, and colors.

(p. 51, photo)
Friendship in Spanish-speaking countries is characterized by much more physical contact than in the U.S. In Mexico, for example, teens and even adult women express their friendship by walking together in a way that many Americans might consider excessive or an invasion of personal space—hand in hand or with their arms around each other's shoulders.

Assess & Summarize

Test Preparation

You may want to assign parts of this section as written homework or as an in-class writing activity prior to administering the *Examen de habilidades*.

Answers

Listening: *Soy callado. No me gusta hablar por teléfono. No me gusta ir al cine tampoco.* The person would be more likely to read at home.

Reading: The paragraph describes a boy who likes to skate and go to the movies. He is sometimes impatient, but nice and generous.

Writing: Letters will vary.

Culture: Answers will vary, but students may say that, in a Spanish-speaking country, a friend is a person who grew up with you. Friendship involves sharing, trusting, knowing each other's families very well, and so on.

Speaking: Answers will vary.

Repaso ¿Lo sabes bien?

This section will help you organize your studying for the proficiency test, where you will be asked to do similar, though not identical, tasks. There will not be any models on the test.

► **Listening**

Can you understand when someone talks about personality traits and interests? Listen as your teacher reads you a sample similar to what you will hear on the test. Would the person making the statements be more likely to participate in a school play or read at home?

► **Reading**

Can you understand a written description of a person's traits and interests? Scan the paragraph below. What is the person like? Is it a description of a boy or a girl?

Me gusta mucho patinar.
También me gusta ir al cine.
A veces soy impaciente,
pero soy amable y generoso.

► **Writing**

Can you write a letter describing your personality and interests? Here is an example of an appropriate letter.

¡Hola, Alfredo!

Soy trabajador y me gusta ayudar en casa. También me gusta ir a la escuela y tocar la guitarra. No soy prudente. No soy callado tampoco. Y tú, ¿cómo eres?

Saludos,
Antonio

► **Culture**

Can you explain what the word *amigo* might mean to a person from a Spanish-speaking country?

En Otavalo, Ecuador

► **Speaking**

Can you describe yourself and tell what you like to do? Here is one example of a good response:

—*Pues, yo soy seria y callada, pero no soy ni deportista ni artística. Me gusta mucho leer y estar con amigos. No me gusta nada hablar por teléfono.*

Self
Test
www.pasoapaso.com

52   Capítulo 1

Options

Strategies for Reaching All Students

Students Needing Extra Help
Have students write out this section so they can check off what they have mastered.

Use the vocabulary from this chapter to help you:

► describe yourself and tell about some of your likes and dislikes

► find out what other people are like

► compare your and other people's likes and dislikes

to talk about activities
ayudar en casa
cocinar
dibujar
escuchar música
estar con amigos
estudiar
hablar por teléfono
  el teléfono
ir a la escuela
ir al cine
  el cine
leer
nadar
patinar
practicar deportes
tocar la guitarra
ver la televisión (la tele)

to say what you like
(A mí) me gusta ___.
        más ___.
        mucho ___.
(A mí) sí me gusta ___.
A mí también.

to say what you do not like
(A mí) no me
  gusta ___.
     mucho ___.
     nada ___.
     ___ tampoco.

to say what you or someone else is like
(Yo) soy ___.
(Tú) eres ___.

to ask someone what he or she likes
¿Qué te gusta (hacer)?
¿Te gusta ___?
¿Y a ti?

to ask someone what he or she is like
¿Cómo eres?
¿Eres (tú) ___?

to describe yourself or others
amable
artístico, -a
atrevido, -a
callado, -a
deportista
desordenado, -a
generoso, -a
gracioso, -a
impaciente
ordenado, -a
paciente
perezoso, -a
prudente
serio, -a
sociable
tacaño, -a
trabajador, -a

to ask if a statement is accurate
¿De veras?

other useful words and expressions
a veces
muy
ni . . . ni
pero
pues
también
tampoco
y

Assessment

 Prueba cumulativa

 Examen de habilidades

 Test Generator

Additional Assessment Options

 Comm. Act. BLMs

Small Group Activities
Situation Cards

 Pasos vivos 1 CD-ROM

Slide Presentation Maker, Video Presentation Maker, Word Processor, Spindle

 ¿Lo sabes bien? Video Quiz

www Internet Activities
Self-Test

Cultural Notes

(p. 52, photo)
The Saturday market in Otavalo is the most famous of the Ecuadorian Indian markets and one of the largest in South America. It dates to pre-Incan times, when the Cara Indians (ancestors of the modern *otavaleños)* prospered as traders with neighboring tribes. Today the market is best known for the textiles sold by the *otavaleños* who, like their ancestors, demonstrate remarkable weaving skills.

Standards 1.1; 1.2; 1.3; 2.1; 2.2; 3.1 **53**

Capítulo 2

THEME: SCHOOL

SCOPE AND SEQUENCE Pages 54–85

COMMUNICATION

Topics

School supplies

School subjects

Class schedules

Time-telling

Numbers 32–59

Objectives

To compare school systems in the U.S. and in Spanish-speaking countries

To talk about school subjects and supplies

To talk about what people need

To say what something is for

To express possession

To express quantity

To ask for information

To express regret / hesitation

To talk about location

To ask and tell when something takes place / To ask and tell the time

CULTURE

Mexican vs. U.S. school systems

Levels of speech: *tú / Ud. / Uds.*

GRAMMAR

Los pronombres personales

Verbos que terminan en -ar

Los sustantivos

Ancillaries available for use with Chapter 2

Multisensory/Technology

 Overheads, 11–15

Audio Tapes and CDs

Vocabulary Art Blackline Masters for Hands-On Learning, pp. 13–17/CD-ROM

 Classroom Crossword

Video

Pasos vivos 1 CD-ROM

 Internet Activities www.pasoapaso.com

Print

Practice Workbook, pp. 23–32

Writing, Audio & Video Activities, pp. 11–16, 96–98, 154–155

 Communicative Activity Blackline Masters

Pair and Small Group Activities, pp. 15–20

Situation Cards, p. 21

Un paso más: Actividades para ampliar tu español, pp. 7–12

TPR Storytelling

Assessment

Assessment Program

Pruebas, pp. 23–33

Examen de habilidades, pp. 34–36

Test Generator

Video still from Chap. 2

Additional Technology

Planning Express, Teaching
Resources Library, and Clip Art
Library

¿Lo sabes bien?
Video Quiz

Cultural Overview

Educational Traditions

Although educational goals in Spain, Latin America, and the U.S. are fundamentally the same—most educators, for example, want to foster good citizens—their educational traditions are quite distinct.

Many of the educational traditions of Latin America have their origin in Spanish traditions. The Spanish school system is divided into four different levels of education: 1) preschool, 2) *Educación General Básica* (EGB), which is primary education, 3) *Bachillerato Unificado y Polivalente* (BUP), which is a program of study aimed at university requirements, or *Formación Profesional* (FP), which is high-school-level training in technical fields, and 4) university study. In order to enter a university, the *Curso de Orientación Universitaria* (COU) must be completed.

Children in Spain may enter free preschool programs. Primary schooling begins at age 6 and continues to age 16. *Educación General Básica* provides a background in languages, mathematics, social and natural sciences, and artistic expression. Children attend around 25 hours of instruction a week. Though school books are free in some special cases, Spanish families usually pay for books as well as school supplies, transportation, lunch service, and voluntary extracurricular activities. This is generally true throughout Latin America as well.

If students complete the EGB before age 16, they receive the certificate of *Graduado Escolar* and may choose to continue their education in either a secondary (BUP) program or a technical-training school (FP). Those who do not complete their studies by age 16 receive a certificate of *Escolaridad* and are eligible only for technical training schools.

BUP is geared toward academics and FP is hands-on training in the areas of science and technology, health-care technology, or business. Evaluation in either option is through exams in each subject area. A final comprehensive exam is given twice a year. Students who wish to continue their studies must pass this exam.

Perhaps the most significant contrast between the U.S. and Spanish educational systems is the "tracking" of students for college. In the U.S., high school graduates have theoretically received a general academic preparation enabling them to attend any of a variety of post-secondary educational institutions. In Spain, however, secondary education more specifically gears students to either university studies or further technical and business education.

Introduce

Re-entry of Concepts

The following list represents words, expressions, and grammar topics re-entered from *El primer paso* to Chap. 1:

El primer paso
School supplies
Numbers 0–31
Greetings
School vocabulary

Chapter 1
Activities
Gustar expressions
Adjectives describing personality

Planning

Cross-Curricular Connections

Math Connection *(p. 58)*
Explain the difference between ordinal and cardinal numbers. Have students be responsible for looking up words for 9th through 20th and then writing them on a poster or on the chalkboard. They may want to make a list for their notebooks.

Graphic Arts Connection *(pp. 58, 62–63)*
Have students plan a study schedule for the afternoon or evening based on the subjects that they study in school. Have them design and illustrate the time (beginning and ending) devoted to the study of each subject. Students could draw pictures to illustrate descriptions of activities.

Geography Connection *(pp. 80–81)*
Obtain two maps of Mexico from a travel agency or tourist office. Post one on the wall. From the second, cut out picture features, names of cities and sites, etc. Give pairs of students these cutouts and have them locate and pin them on the map. Continue by giving each pair a blank map and have them make a pictorial of an area. Have each pair pick one aspect or location and do a brief follow-up paragraph in English.

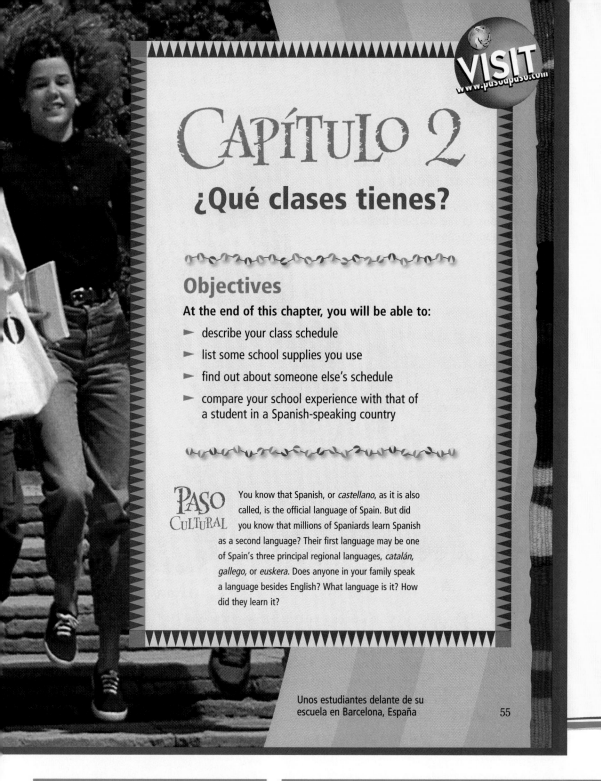

CAPÍTULO 2

¿Qué clases tienes?

Objectives

At the end of this chapter, you will be able to:

► describe your class schedule

► list some school supplies you use

► find out about someone else's schedule

► compare your school experience with that of a student in a Spanish-speaking country

PASO CULTURAL You know that Spanish, or *castellano*, as it is also called, is the official language of Spain. But did you know that millions of Spaniards learn Spanish as a second language? Their first language may be one of Spain's three principal regional languages, *catalán*, *gallego*, or *euskera*. Does anyone in your family speak a language besides English? What language is it? How did they learn it?

Unos estudiantes delante de su escuela en Barcelona, España

55

Cultural Notes ☼

Spanish in Your Community
Besides in your school, where else in the community is it possible to learn Spanish or other foreign languages? Have students suggest other learning sources or explore their community. Possible answers might include: community colleges, universities, private language schools such as Berlitz, tapes, and libraries. Ask: What languages are taught in our community? What foreign language do you think is the most popular in our community?

Paso cultural
Answers will vary.

Preview

Cultural Objective

• To compare your school experience with that of a student in a Spanish-speaking country

 ¡Piénsalo bien!

Play

 **Video Activity A**

Using the Video

This chapter's video focuses on school—classes, supplies, and schedules. Students will see our hosts in Madrid visiting a high school and interviewing students in class.

Since the videos for this chapter and for Chapters 3, 4, 6, 8, and 9 were filmed in Spain, students will hear the forms of *vosotros* being used. You may want to prepare your students by reviewing those verb forms.

To prepare students for the video, first ask them to predict what this chapter's tape will be about. Then have students watch the segment several times. After the first time, you may wish to have them brainstorm possible vocabulary and expressions they will need to talk about what they saw on the video. Ask students to identify: a) things they saw that looked familiar but

¡Piensa en la CULTURA!

School activities in Costa Rica, Spain, and Mexico

Look at the pictures and read the captions. In the captions these teens talk about school.

"Los miércoles tengo ciencias en la primera hora. La clase empieza a las siete y media."

When do you have your *clase de ciencias?*

"Me gusta mucho la clase de inglés, pero no es nada fácil."

Which of your classes is most like this *clase de inglés?*

Málaga, España

Escazú, Costa Rica

 PASO CULTURAL

In Costa Rica, the government spends 20 percent of its annual budget on education. This is a remarkably high percentage, and the country's 93 percent literacy rate ranks among the highest in the world. What differences, if any, do you think there might be between a biology class in Costa Rica and one in your school?

56   Capítulo 2

Chetumal, México

En la Escuela Secundaria Adolfo López

"Los estudiantes de mi clase tienen un 10 . . ."

What do you think getting a grade of 10 in a Spanish-speaking school means?

www.pasoapaso.com
Visit these countries on-line

Answers: ¡Piensa en la cultura!

(p. 56, left photo) Answers will vary.

(p. 56, right photo) Students would probably say their Spanish class is most like this one.

(p. 57, photo) Most students would say this is equivalent to receiving an A or A+ in a U.S. school.

(p. 56, left photo)
Costa Ricans of African descent, like the teacher in this photo, make up only three percent of that country's population and are mainly descendants of Jamaican and West Indian immigrants who came in the late nineteenth century. Guide students in a discussion of racial diversity in Hispanic countries, emphasizing the history of the different groups and how their cultures have blended.

(p. 56, right photo)
For almost 40 years under General Francisco Franco's rule, foreign language instruction in Spain was either of very poor quality or nonexistent. The government also forbid the teaching of indigenous languages of Spain, such as *catalán* and *vasco*. After Franco's death in 1975 and with Spain's entry into the European Community in 1992, Spaniards have hastened to study languages, particularly English, to keep pace commercially with the rest of the world.

(p. 57, photo)
Mexico's schools use a 1–10 grading system. A 6 is sufficient to pass a course, but to move from *primaria* to *secundaria*, a student needs an average of 7. Other Latin American countries use different systems. In Peru, for example, students are given number grades between 1 and 20.

Standards 1.2; 2.1; 3.1; 4.1; 4.2 **57**

Present

Chapter Theme
School subjects and supplies

Communicative Objectives
- To ask and tell when something takes place
- To talk about school subjects
- To talk about school supplies
- To talk about what people need
- To say what something is for
- To express possession
- To express quantity
- To ask for information
- To express regret
- To express hesitation
- To talk about location

 Overheads 11–12

 Vocabulary Art BLMs/CD-ROM

 Pronunciation Tape 2-1

 Vocabulario para conversar A

Play

Using the Video
Video segment 2: See the Video Teacher's Guide.

 Video Activity B

Vocabulario para conversar

¿Qué clases tienes?

 At Home VIDEO Chapter 2 Vocabulary

Here are some new words and expressions you will need to talk about your class schedule and school supplies. Read them several times, then turn the page and practice with a partner.

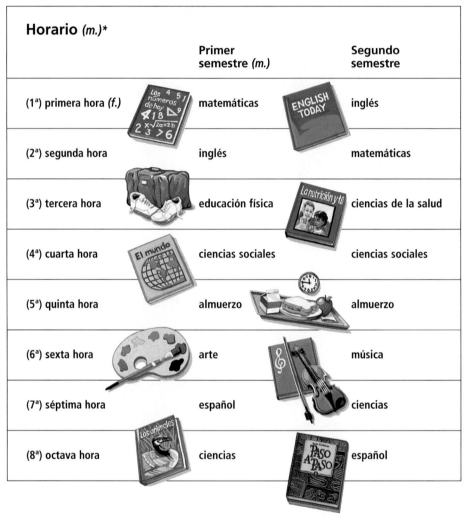

Horario *(m.)**	Primer semestre *(m.)*	Segundo semestre
(1ª) primera hora *(f.)*	matemáticas	inglés
(2ª) segunda hora	inglés	matemáticas
(3ª) tercera hora	educación física	ciencias de la salud
(4ª) cuarta hora	ciencias sociales	ciencias sociales
(5ª) quinta hora	almuerzo	almuerzo
(6ª) sexta hora	arte	música
(7ª) séptima hora	español	ciencias
(8ª) octava hora	ciencias	español

* The letters in parentheses indicate the gender of the noun: masculine *(m.)* or feminine *(f.)*.

58   Capítulo 2

Strategies for Reaching All Students

Spanish-Speaking Students
Spanish-speaking students can make their own vocabulary lists with additional classes and supplies. If necessary, help students with spelling. (You may wish to label classroom supplies and objects around the room with note cards for the benefit of all students.)

Students Needing Extra Help
Have students start filling in their Organizers.

Enrichment
Enhance the vocabulary presentation by bringing in class schedules, course descriptions, etc., from schools in Spanish-speaking countries.
If students should ask: *novena hora* (ninth period / hour), *décima hora* (tenth period / hour).

Vocabulario para conversar: As a written assignment, have students use adjectives they've learned to describe their behavior in different classes, perhaps pointing out how behavior may vary according to the class they're in. Example: *Soy perezoso(a) en la clase de matemáticas, pero muy trabajador(a) en la clase de ciencias.*

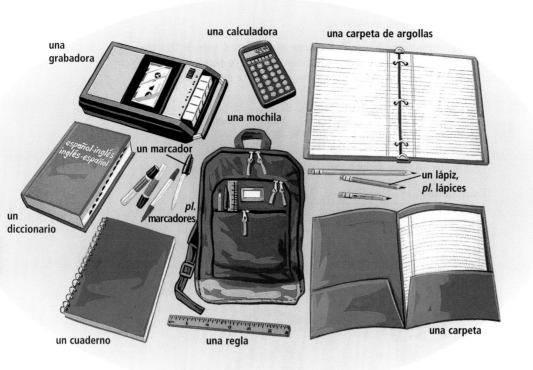

una grabadora

una calculadora

una carpeta de argollas

una mochila

un marcador

español-inglés inglés-español

un diccionario

pl. marcadores

un lápiz, pl. lápices

un cuaderno

una regla

una carpeta

¡NO OLVIDES!

tú = *you*
tu = *your*

También necesitas...

la clase de ___	___ *class*	para	*for*
difícil	*difficult, hard*	tu	*your*
fácil	*easy*	¿Qué?	*What?*
la tarea	*homework*	Lo siento.	*I'm sorry.*
aprender: (yo) aprendo (tú) aprendes	*to learn: I learn* *you learn*	A ver . . .	*Let's see . . .*
		Aquí / Allí está.	*Here / There it is.*
necesitar: (yo) necesito (tú) necesitas	*to need: I need* *you need*		
tener: (yo) tengo (tú) tienes	*to have: I have* *you have*	¿Y qué quiere decir . . . ? mucho, -a	

Vocabulario para conversar 59

Grammar Preview
Necesito and *necesitas* are presented lexically. The explanation of -ar verbs appears in the grammar section, along with nouns and articles, on pp. 71–76.

Teaching Suggestions
Preparing students to speak: Use one or two options from each of the categories of Comprehensible Input, Physical Response, or Limited Verbal Response. For a complete explanation of these categories and some sample activities, see pp. T22–T23.

The indefinite articles *un* and *una* are used with school supplies for more natural language use in this vocabulary section. (The formal explanation of singular indefinite articles is on p. 76.)

Formation of plural nouns will be taught in Chap. 4. For now, students will use them, but they will not be expected to form them.

Class Starter Review
On the day following initial presentation, you might begin the class with this activity:
Name a class subject and have students signal *sí* or *no* as you mention school supplies that might be necessary for that class.

www Internet Activities
Juegos
Have students go to www.pasoapaso.com for additional activities and practice.

Multiple Intelligences
Bodily/Kinesthetic
1) Using books and other props to represent the vocabulary, have students go to the board and place the items in the order in which they occur in their own daily schedule.
2) Have students identify three items in their book bags.
Logical/Mathematical
Have students create a new class schedule for themselves using the ordinal numbers.

Visual/Spatial
Use Overheads 11–12, the Vocabulary Art BLMs/CD-ROM, and Using the Video.

Learning Spanish Through Action
STAGING VOCABULARY: *Levanten, Muestren, Señalen, Toquen*
1) MATERIALS: transparency of school supplies in the *Vocabulario para conversar* or the actual items
DIRECTIONS: Using the transparency or actual school supplies, have pairs of students touch or point to the items that you mention. If the actual items are available, you may wish to have students raise the item, then ask them *¿Qué tienes?*
2) MATERIALS: transparency of school subjects in the *Vocabulario para conversar*
DIRECTIONS: Using the transparency, mention a class subject and have pairs of students touch or point at the appropriate illustration. Continue until each class subject is mentioned.

Standards 1.1; 1.2; 4.1; 5.1 59

Practice & Apply

Re-enter / Recycle
Ex. 8: *gustar* expressions from Chap. 1

Critical Thinking: Classifying Information
As a written activity, have students use the *Vocabulario para conversar* to list the supplies they aren't using this semester or year. Then ask them to list the ones they would use in almost *every* class.

Answers: Empecemos a conversar

1 ESTUDIANTE A
a. ¿Tienes mucha tarea en tu clase de matemáticas?
b. ...ciencias de la salud?
c. ...ciencias sociales?
d. ...español?
e. ...inglés?

ESTUDIANTE B
a.–e. Answers will vary.

2 ESTUDIANTE A
Questions will vary, but should include school supplies. Encourage *Estudiante A* to ask at least three or four questions.

ESTUDIANTE B
Answers will vary depending on whether *Estudiante B* has the object mentioned. Ask students to show the object if they have it.

Empecemos a conversar

With a partner, take turns being *Estudiante A* and *Estudiante B*. Use the words that are cued or given in the balloons to replace the underlined sections in the model. 💡 means you can make your own choices.

1 A —¿Tienes mucha tarea en tu clase de <u>ciencias</u>?
B —Sí, tengo mucha tarea.
o: No, no tengo mucha tarea.

Estudiante A   Estudiante B

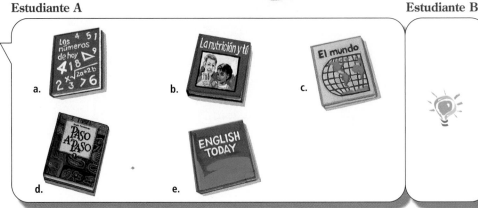

a.   b.   c.

d.   e.

2 A —¿Tienes <u>una calculadora</u>?
B —A ver . . . Sí, aquí está.
o: Sí, allí está.
o: A ver . . . No, lo siento.

Estudiante A   Estudiante B

Una clase de matemáticas en San Miguel de Allende, México

Strategies for Reaching All Students

Spanish-Speaking Students
Pair bilingual with non-bilingual students for Exs. 1 and 3. You may wish to have them write out Ex. 2, using at least three questions.

 Un paso más Exs. 2-B, 2-C

Students Needing Extra Help
Ex. 2: Explain the responses before moving ahead. Model with other school supplies.
Ex. 3: Explain that when we speak, we often repeat all or part of the question to be sure we understand what was asked. Model one or two examples in English.
Ex. 5: If students don't have supplies with them, have them list what they should have, including all classes in which they use those supplies.

Ex. 8: Remind students of *ni . . . ni.*
Empecemos a escribir: For additional practice, have students make a two-column chart. In the left column they should write the heading *Clase* and list their classes. In the right column, have them write the heading *Necesito* and list the school supplies they need next to each class.

3

A —¿Qué clase tienes en la _primera_ hora?

B —¿En la _primera_ hora? Pues, tengo _matemáticas_.

Estudiante A   Estudiante B

a. 2ª

b. 3ª

c. 4ª

d. 5ª

e. 6ª

f. 7ª

g. 8ª

4 Find out which class your partner likes the most and which one he or she does not like at all. Say whether or not you too like or dislike those classes. For example:

A —¿Qué clase te gusta más?

B —Me gusta más la clase de ciencias.

A —A mí también. ¿Y qué clase no te gusta nada?

B —Pues, la clase de inglés.

A —¿De veras? A mí sí me gusta.

Empecemos a escribir

Write your answers in Spanish.

5 List the school supplies you have with you right now. Next to each item, write the name of at least one class in which you use it.

6 In two columns, under the headings _Fácil_ and _Difícil_, list the subjects you are taking this year.

7 ¿Qué necesitas para tu primera clase?

8 ¿Qué te gusta más, hacer la tarea de español o hablar con tus compañeros(as) en la clase de español?

9 ¿Qué tienes en tu mochila?

También se dice...

el lapicero
la pluma
el boli

la carpeta de anillas
el archivador

MORE PRACTICE

- Más práctica y tarea, p. 511
- Practice Workbook 2–1, 2–2

Vocabulario para conversar   61

---

3 ESTUDIANTE A

a. ¿Qué clase tienes en la segunda hora?

b. ...tercera hora?

c. ...cuarta hora?

d. ...quinta hora?

e. ...sexta hora?

f. ...séptima hora?

g. ...octava hora?

ESTUDIANTE B

Make sure students say: _Tengo el almuerzo._

a. ¿En la segunda hora? Pues, tengo ... (Possible answers: educación física, ciencias sociales, el almuerzo, arte, español, ciencias, inglés)

b. ...tercera hora? ...

c. ...cuarta hora? ...

d. ...quinta hora? ...

e. ...sexta hora? ...

f. ...séptima hora? ...

g. ...octava hora? ...

4 Dialogues will vary.

Answers: Empecemos a escribir

5–9 Answers will vary, but look for appropriate school supplies in Exs. 5 and 7.

Practice Wkbk. 2-1, 2-2

Audio Activity 2.1

Writing Activities 2-A, 2-B, 2-C

Pruebas 2-1, 2-2

Comm. Act. BLM 2-1

Extended Written Practice/Homework

1. Write a sentence for each class that you have, listing one or more objects that you need for each class.
2. Choose three classes on p. 58 and tell how much you like or dislike each one.
3. Choose three classes on p. 58 and tell whether each is hard or easy.
4. Choose three classes on p. 58 and tell if there is or isn't a lot of homework in each.

Multiple Intelligences

Intrapersonal/Social
See Exs. 5–9.

Verbal/Linguistic
See Ex. 3.

Cultural Notes

(p. 60, photo)

Although most of the basic high school subjects studied in Hispanic countries are the same as in the U.S., teachers tend to use traditional methods such as memorization more, and students generally work in groups. Discuss with students some advantages and disadvantages of these methods for the presentation and mastery of different subjects.

Present

Chapter Theme
School: Time-telling

Communicative Objectives
- To talk about school subjects
- To ask and tell when something takes place
- To ask and tell the time
- To tell who performs an action

 Overheads 13–14

 Vocabulary Art BLMs/CD-ROM

 Pronunciation Tape 2-2

 Vocabulario para conversar B

Play

Step

Using the Video
Video segment 2: See the Video Teacher's Guide.

 Video Activity B

 Pasos vivos 1 CD-ROM
Clip Art Album

Vocabulario para conversar

¿Qué hora es?

 **Ar Home** **VIDEO** Chapter 2 Vocabulary

Here's the rest of the vocabulary you will need to talk about your class schedule.

Es la una.

Son las dos.

Son las tres.

Son las cuatro.

Son las cinco.

Son las seis.

Son las siete.

Son las ocho.

Son las nueve.

Son las diez.

Son las once.

Son las doce.

 2:05
Son las dos y cinco.

 2:15
Son las dos y cuarto. (Son las dos y quince.)

2:20
Son las dos y veinte.

 2:30
Son las dos y media. (Son las dos y treinta.)

 2:45
Son las dos y cuarenta y cinco.

  2:58
Son las dos y cincuenta y ocho.

62   Capítulo 2

Strategies for Reaching All Students

Learning Spanish Through Action
STAGING VOCABULARY: *Escriban, Muestren, Vayan*
1) MATERIALS: toy or student-made analog clocks (enough for the whole class or groups)
DIRECTIONS: Using a model clock, set a time and then say it out loud. Have a pair of students set the hands of their clocks to the proper positions. Ask students to show their clocks for verification and then show the correct time on your clock before proceeding to the next time.
2) MATERIALS: index cards with various times written on them
DIRECTIONS: Have volunteers go to the chalkboard to complete digital clocks. Say the time while showing the rest of the class the index card. Once the clocks are filled in, students can check their own work against the index cards.

Multiple Intelligences
Bodily/Kinesthetic
Have students stand and use their arms as hands on a clock while you say, *son las tres, son las dos y cuarto,* etc.
Musical/Rhythmic
In pairs, have students begin clapping a slow, steady beat. Student 1 says *primera hora* in any rhythm which fits the beat. Student 2 answers with the name of his or her first class without losing the beat. Student 1 says *segunda hora* on the next

62   Standards 1.1; 1.2; 3.1; 4.2

El reloj del Parque Hundido, Ciudad de México

32 treinta y dos
33 treinta y tres
34 treinta y cuatro
35 treinta y cinco
36 treinta y seis
37 treinta y siete
38 treinta y ocho
39 treinta y nueve
40 cuarenta
41 cuarenta y uno...
49 cuarenta y nueve
50 cincuenta
51 cincuenta y uno...
59 cincuenta y nueve

¡NO OLVIDES!

You worked with the numbers 0 to 31 in *El primer paso.*

También necesitas...

enseñar: enseña	*to teach: (he / she) teaches*	terminar: termina	*to end: it ends*
a	*at*	es	*he / she / it is*
¿A qué hora _____?	*At what time _____?*	¿Qué hora es?	*What time is it?*
empezar: empieza	*to begin: it begins*	¿Quién?	*Who? Whom?*

Vocabulario para conversar 63

Grammar Preview
Enseña and *termina* are presented lexically here for communication skills. These will appear in the grammar explanation of *-ar* verbs on pp. 73–74.

Teaching Suggestions
Preparing students to speak: Use one or two options from each of the categories of Comprehensible Input, Physical Response, or Limited Verbal Response. For a complete explanation of these categories and some sample activities, see pp. T22–T23.

Discuss the system of telling time on the 24-hour clock (8:00 P.M. = 20:00). Note that there are other time-telling formats. For example, 1:40 could be read as *(Faltan) veinte para las dos* or *Son las dos menos veinte*. (Use Overhead 77 to present the concept of telling time.)

Tell students that when we use a number that ends in *-uno* before a masculine noun, we drop the *o*: *Tengo* **treinta y un cuadernos**. (Note that *veintiún* has an accent mark.) When a number ending in *-uno* precedes a feminine noun, this ending becomes *-una*: *Tengo* **veintiuna carpetas**.

Using Photos
Ask: *¿Qué hora es en la foto?*

www Internet Activities
Juegos/Have students go to www.pasoapaso.com for additional activities and practice.

Cultural Notes ☀

beat and so on. If one student misses the beat or doesn't say the name of a class, the pair switches roles and starts again. Have each pair report the highest number of class names chanted with no errors. Ask for volunteer pairs to "perform" for the class.
Visual/Spatial
Use Overhead 13 and randomly place numbers next to each clock. Call out a time and have students identify it correctly by the number. Reverse the procedure for further practice.

(p. 63, photo)
Mexico City's parks, gardens, and monuments provide residents with many opportunities to take a break from the fast pace of life in the largest city in the world. This colorful spot is on the southern extension of the 18.5-mile-long Avenida Insurgentes, one of the city's two main traffic arteries.

Practice & Apply

Re-enter / Recycle

Exs. 10–15: numbers 0–31 from *El primer paso*

Ex. 16: *gustar* expressions and activities from Chap. 1

Answers: Empecemos a conversar

10 ESTUDIANTE A

a. ¿Qué hora es? ¿Son las once?

b. ...¿Son las doce y media (treinta)?

c. ...¿Son las diez?

d. ...¿Es la una y cuarto (quince)?

ESTUDIANTE B

a. No, son las once y veinticinco.

b. No, son las doce y cuarenta.

c. No, son las nueve y cincuenta y cinco.

d. No, es la una y treinta y cinco.

11 ESTUDIANTE A

a. ¿A qué hora empieza tu clase de ciencias?

b. ...ciencias de la salud?

c. ...matemáticas?

d. ...arte?

ESTUDIANTE B

a. Empieza a las nueve y termina a las nueve y cincuenta.

b. ...las dos ...las dos y cincuenta.

c. ...las diez ...las diez y cincuenta.

d. ...la una ...la una y cincuenta.

Empecemos a conversar

10 A —*¿Qué hora es? ¿Son las dos?*

   B —*No, es la una y cuarenta y cinco.*

Estudiante A

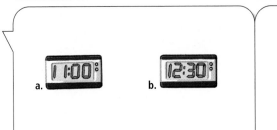

a. b. c. d.

Estudiante B

a. b. c. d.

11 A —*¿A qué hora empieza tu clase de educación física?*

   B —*Empieza a las diez y termina a las diez y cincuenta.* 10:00-10:50

Estudiante A

a. b. c. d.

Estudiante B

9:00- 9:50   2:00- 2:50

10:00-10:50   1:00- 1:50

a. b. c. d.

64   Capítulo 2

Strategies for Reaching All Students

Spanish-Speaking Students

Have Spanish-speaking students write out Ex. 10. Pairs of bilingual and non-bilingual students can write out Exs. 11–12. Encourage them to expand their answers, where possible.

 Un paso más Ex. 2-D

Students Needing Extra Help

Have students fill in their Organizers.

Exs. 10–12: Point out that these questions all ask about time, but in different ways.

Ex. 11: If students have difficulty, explain why *tu clase de educación física* is after the verb form in the model (inversion in questions). This explanation comes later in the chapter's grammar presentation of *-ar* verbs.

Ex. 12: Have students use their Organizers.

Ex. 13: Structure this activity for students and give them a model. Times should include minutes, and most students' schedules should have at least five classes.

Enrichment

Exs. 10–11: Encourage students to invent mini-dialogues naming other classes and times.

12

A —¿Cuándo tienes la clase de _ciencias_?

B —A ver . . . A _las ocho y diez_.

A —¿Quién es tu profesor(a)?

B —_La profesora González_.

Estudiante A

Estudiante B

Empecemos a escribir y a leer

Write your answers in Spanish.

13 Redesign your school schedule. You decide when classes begin and end and how long each period lasts.

14 ¿A qué hora es el almuerzo? ¿Cuándo termina?

15 ¿Quién es tu profesor(a) favorito(a)? ¿Qué enseña? ¿A qué hora empieza la clase? ¿Cuándo termina?

16 Federico dice: "Yo soy artístico. Me gusta mucho dibujar," pero Ernesto responde:
"A mí no me gusta nada dibujar, pero me gusta mucho practicar deportes, especialmente nadar y patinar." Ana dice:
"A mí me gusta más leer libros de historia," pero Susana responde: "A mí no me gusta mucho leer, pero sí me gustan los números y los cálculos."

¿Quién dice . . .

a. "Mi clase favorita es matemáticas"?

b. "Mi clase favorita es educación física"?

c. "Mi clase favorita es arte"?

MORE PRACTICE

- Más práctica y tarea, p. 511
- Practice Workbook 2–3, 2–4

www.pasoapaso.com

La Estación del Norte en Valencia, España

Vocabulario para conversar 65

¡NO OLVIDES!

Remember that when using _señor(a)_, _profesor(a)_ or any other title to talk about a person, we need to add the definite article to the title: _El señor López enseña inglés._ However, when addressing a person, we do not use the article: _¿Cómo está, señor López?_

12 ESTUDIANTE A
Questions will vary.
ESTUDIANTE B
Answers will vary, but look for appropriate times given.

Answers: Empecemos a escribir y a leer

13 Look for appropriate use of time-telling, names for school subjects, and class periods.

14–15 Answers will vary.

16 a. Susana, b. Ernesto, c. Federico

Multicultural Perspectives

With variances from one Spanish-speaking country to another, many schools have instruction from 9:00 A.M. to 1:30 P.M. before breaking for lunch. Students often go home for their midday meal where they are joined by other family members. The meal may last from 2:00 P.M. until 4:30 P.M. They then return for their afternoon classes, which may last until 7:00 P.M. or later. Ask students familiar with other cultures to share any information they know about school schedules.

 Practice Wkbk. 2-3, 2-4

 Audio Activity 2.2

 Writing Activity 2-D

 Pruebas 2-3, 2-4

Extended Written Practice/Homework
1. Write five clock times using numerals, including hours and minutes. For each time, write a sentence saying what time it is.
2. Using vocabulary from pp. 58, 59, 62, and 63, write four interview questions that you can ask a classmate about classes.
3. Write three sentences telling who teaches different classes.
4. Write two sentences telling when first hour begins and last hour ends.

Multiple Intelligences
Visual/Spatial
See Exs. 13–16.

Practice

Re-enter / Recycle

Ex. 1: *gustar* expressions from Chap. 1

Answers:
¡Comuniquemos!

1 ESTUDIANTE A
¿Qué clase te gusta más . . . (música, ciencias sociales, matemáticas, inglés, ciencias de la salud, arte, español, educación física, ciencias)?

ESTUDIANTE B
Answers will vary.

2 ESTUDIANTE A
¿Qué necesitas para tu clase de . . . ?

ESTUDIANTE B
A ver . . . Necesito . . . *(Answers will vary, but may include:* una regla, una calculadora, un lápiz, un marcador, un cuaderno, una carpeta, una carpeta de argollas.*)*

3 Questions will vary. Look for logical combinations.

¡COMUNI

1

Find out which classes your partner prefers.

A —*¿Qué clase te gusta más, ciencias o ciencias sociales?*

B —*Me gusta más la clase de ciencias.*

¡NO OLVIDES!
To say that you don't like either of two things, use *ni . . . ni.* See page 44.

66   Capítulo 2

Strategies for Reaching All Students

Spanish-Speaking Students
Ex. 1: Have Spanish-speaking students write out the questions they ask their partners about their preferences.

Students Needing Extra Help
Ex. 2: Use the Organizer.
¿Qué sabes ahora?: Have students write out this section to keep in their notebooks. Students will check off concepts as they are mastered.

Enrichment
Ex. 1: Have pairs of students vary and extend their dialogues by having *Estudiante A* express surprise, disagreement, or agreement with *Estudiante B*'s reply. Example: *¿De veras? Pues, a mí me gusta más la clase de . . .* or: *¿De veras? A mí también.*

2

You are planning to go shopping for school supplies with a friend. Find out from each other what supplies you need for each class you are taking.

A —*¿Qué necesitas para tu clase de ciencias sociales?*
B —*A ver . . . Necesito un cuaderno y un bolígrafo.*

 Audio Activity 2.3

 Writing Activity 2-E

 Comm. Act. BLM 2-2

 Pasos vivos 1 CD-ROM
Slide Projector, Laboratorio de grabar

3

Make up questions using a word or phrase from each column to find out three things about your partner.

¿Cómo	es	la clase de ___?
¿Cuál	necesitas	para la clase de ___?
¿Cuándo	se escribe	tu cumpleaños?
¿Qué	tienes	tu nombre?
¿Quién		tu número de teléfono?
		tu profesor(a) de ___?

¿Qué sabes ahora?

Can you:

► ask someone what he or she needs for a certain class?
—¿Qué ___ para la clase de inglés?

► tell someone what you need for a class?
—___ un bolígrafo o ___ lápiz y ___ cuaderno.

► ask someone what classes he or she has?
—¿Qué clases ___ el primer semestre?

► tell someone what classes you have?
—___ ciencias, español y matemáticas.

Vocabulario para conversar   67

Cooperative Learning
Have groups of three or four students prepare a TV advertisement for a store offering school items for sale. The ad should have a poster display of items with prices clearly marked. Items should be discounted at different times during the day for special sales.

Once the display is ready, ask students to give pertinent details. For example: *A las ocho (tengo) carpetas. ¡25 pesos!* Students should be encouraged to include as many school vocabulary items as possible. At the end of the activity the class can select the store most likely to succeed.

Multiple Intelligences
Interpersonal/Social
See Cooperative Learning.
Verbal/Linguistic
See Enrichment.

Present & Apply

Cultural Objective
- To talk about similarities and differences between a Mexican and a U.S. high school

Teaching Suggestions
You might wish to prepare a list of additional discussion questions to ask students after they have read the material. Suggestions: Do you think American students spend more or less time on homework than Mexican students? How much time do you spend on homework each day? Do Mexican schools seem more or less structured than American schools? Do you think Mexican students or American students are more respectful of their teachers? Why?

If students ask: *Ciencias naturales,* Science; *Tecnología,* Computer or another technology-related class; *Receso,* Break; *Educación artística,* Art; *Orientación vocacional,* Career Counseling; *Libre,* Free period.

Point out to students that there is no lunch break in the schedule, because most students would go home for lunch at 1:00 or 2:00. (Have them notice that they use the 24-hour clock system.) The class schedule varies from day to day, and there is no passing period, since the teachers move from room to room, not the students.

Perspectiva cultural

Las escuelas mexicanas

Los estudiantes en los países hispanos tienen muchas clases. Y tú, ¿qué clases tienes? ¿Qué clases te gustan más? ¿Qué clases no te gustan?

Look at the photo of public school students and the school schedule below. What do you notice that you didn't expect?

Although an *escuela secundaria* in Mexico City has a lot in common with a high school in the United States, there are some striking differences. And even though there are differences among Mexican schools, you might find that any or all of these things happen.

- In most schools, when a teacher enters the classroom, the students stand.
- The teacher probably calls the students by their last name.
- The students, on the other hand, are more likely to address their teacher simply as *maestro* or *maestra,* without a last name.
- The average amount of time students spend on homework ranges from 15 to 30 minutes per class.

HORA	HORAS	LUNES	MARTES	MIÉRCOLES	JUEVES	VIERNES
1a	7:30 a 8:15	Ciencias naturales	Educación física	Inglés	Ciencias sociales	Ciencias naturales
2a	8:15 a 9:00	Ciencias naturales	Tecnología	Español	Ciencias sociales	Ciencias naturales
3a	9:00 a 9:45	Inglés	Tecnología	Ciencias sociales	Matemáticas	Español
4a	9:45 a 10:30	Ciencias sociales	Ciencias sociales	Ciencias sociales	Ciencias naturales	Matemáticas
	10:30 a 10:50	R E C E S O				
5a	10:50 a 11:35	Español	Ciencias sociales	Matemáticas	Ciencias naturales	Tecnología
6a	11:35 a 12:20	Matemáticas	Inglés	Ciencias naturales	Educación artística	Tecnología
7a	12:20 a 13:05	Tecnología	Educación artística	Tecnología	Educación física	Orientación vocacional
8a	13:05 a 13:50	Tecnología	Español	Tecnología	LIBRE	LIBRE

68   Capítulo 2

Strategies for Reaching All Students

Spanish-Speaking Students
Ask Spanish-speaking students: *¿Te gustaría tener las clases que tiene este estudiante? ¿Qué clases te gustarían más? ¿Deben los estudiantes usar uniformes en la escuela? ¿Por qué?* Have students design a school uniform and describe it to the class.

 Un paso más Exs. 2-E, 2-F

Students Needing Extra Help
Have students use their Organizers for reading the schedule.

Enrichment
Elicit opinions from students regarding which kind of instruction they prefer: teacher lecture or class discussion. Ask them for reasons for their preference. Have students divide a sheet of paper in half and, by making two lists, compare or contrast Mexican and U.S. schools based on the information in the text.

a clase de ciencias
n el Colegio Tulum,
Ciudad de México

- Teachers usually collect the homework the next day rather than reviewing it in class.

- The grading scale in Mexico ranges from a low of 1 to a high of 10, with 6 being the lowest passing grade. A grade of 6 or 7 is roughly equivalent to a C, 8 to a B, and 9 and 10 to an A.

- Grades are based much more on test results and homework than on class participation.

- Class time is generally spent with the teacher lecturing rather than with class discussion.

- Many public schools require uniforms at least four days a week.

La cultura desde tu perspectiva

 1 If you attended school in Mexico City, what might you find that might be familiar to you? What would you have to adjust to?

 2 Based on what you now know about schools in Mexico City, list five suggestions that might help an exchange student from Mexico City adjust to your school's system.

www.pasoapaso.com
Cultural Activity

Estudiantes en la Ciudad de México

Perspectiva cultural 69

Answers

Possible answers to inductive question: Students may say that the class schedule varies from day to day with the student taking more classes than they do. There is no passing period. Some courses last for two class periods. Students should notice that they are wearing uniforms in the photo. Discuss your school's dress code policy (if any).

Answers: La cultura desde tu perspectiva

1 Answers will vary, but students may mention the following as similarities or differences: student-teacher relationships, amount of homework, grading system, and teaching methods.

2 Answers may include suggestions for the exchange student to be prepared to see possible relaxed rules or regulations for the classroom; changes in student-teacher relationships; different treatment of homework, grades, and testing; and differences in the school day with respect to number of courses, class length, and schedules.

Pasos vivos 1 CD-ROM
Notas culturales, Maps

Internet Activities
Perspectiva cultural
Have students go to www.pasoapaso.com for additional activities and practice.

Cultural Notes

Multiple Intelligences
Interpersonal/Social
In groups, have students compare their schedules to the one on p. 68.
Visual/Spatial
See Enrichment.

(p. 68, photo)
High school graduates in Mexico are expected to have a solid foundation in biology, chemistry, and physics. Yet jobs in science generally have low salaries and, although Mexican scientists enjoy a solid international reputation, government funding for their projects must be renegotiated each year. Ask students to discuss reasons (economic, social, political) for the way the Mexican government funds science.

(p. 69, photo)
Schoolgirls in Mexico City. While girls in Mexico nearly equal boys in enrollment in the lower primary grades, their numbers diminish progressively at the higher grades in primary and secondary levels. At the secondary-school level, the ratio is approximately four boys to every three girls.

Preview

Critical Thinking: Identifying Evidence in the Text

Ask students what part or parts of the letter suggest that the teacher expects students to study at home (end of first paragraph).

Answers

Answers will vary, but may include an explanation of what the students can expect to learn in the course, course content, etc.

In the first paragraph of the letter, explain the abbreviation for *noveno (9°)*.

A *preparan, trabajan, necesitan* / Answers will vary, but see if students mention that the verb endings correspond to the subject (person) in the sentences. The *-s* ending tells you that the subject of the verb is *tú*.

B "we use"

Gramática en contexto

This is a letter that a science teacher sent home before school started. What information would you expect to find in a letter like this?

28 de agosto

Estimados padres y estudiantes:

En mi clase de ciencias tengo los estudiantes de 9° grado. Es una clase importante y muy interesante. Los estudiantes preparan experimentos en el laboratorio y trabajan mucho en la clase; pero también necesitan estudiar mucho en la casa.

Para la clase de ciencias, los estudiantes necesitan lápices, papel y una carpeta. También usamos frecuentemente una calculadora y una regla en la clase.

Si Uds. necesitan más información, favor de llamar al 222-89-67 durante la tercera hora, que empieza a las 10 y termina a las 10:50.

Atentamente,

Margarita Hernández Sevilla

A Find all the words in the letter that end in *-an*. Why do you think they end in those two letters? (Hint: *Necesito* and *tengo* both end in *-o*. Think about what the *o* might tell you. *Necesitas* and *tienes* also have similar endings. What might their *-s* ending tell you?)

B Now look at the word *usamos* in the second paragraph. Can you guess at the meaning of this word?

70 Capítulo 2

Strategies for Reaching All Students

Students Needing Extra Help
Have students write out the letter so that they can highlight, underline, and so on. Or, use the transparency so that you can highlight for them. Point out that *estudiantes* is plural and that the corresponding verb ends in *-an*. Compare this to *necesito / necesitas* and *tengo / tienes* where the *-o* signals "I" and the *-as / -es* signal "you."

Show the subject pronoun chart by putting it on the chalkboard or overhead. Explain grammatical terms (pronouns, infinitives, etc.) to avoid discouraging students who have had difficulty with these in English.

Los pronombres personales

We often use people's names to tell who is doing an action.
We also use what we call subject pronouns.

Singular	Plural	
yo	nosotros	nosotras
tú	vosotros*	vosotras*
usted (Ud.)	ustedes (Uds.)	
él	ellos	
ella	ellas	

* There are two additional pronouns that are used mostly in Spain: *vosotros* and *vosotras*. They are used when speaking to two or more people whom you would call *tú* individually: *tú + tú = vosotros* or *vosotras*. We will include these pronouns when we present new verb forms, and we will use them occasionally in situations that take place in Spain. So you should learn to recognize them.

Compañeros de clase en Santiago de Chile

PASO CULTURAL

Chile's capital, Santiago, is home to three of South America's most prestigious universities: la Universidad de Chile, la Universidad de Santiago, and la Universidad Católica. Can you name some of the cities in the United States that have several outstanding universities? Do you think that the courses offered at Chilean universities are similar to or different from courses taught in the U.S.? Why?

Gramática en contexto   71

Present

Teaching Suggestions
Explain the use of art with icons in the chart. These pictures indicate about whom we are speaking. (Use Overhead 76 to introduce subject pronouns. Refer to it when teaching verbs throughout the book.)

Stress the importance of the accent mark on *tú* and *él* by writing *el / él, tu / tú* on the chalkboard along with these sentences: *Él necesita el diccionario. Tú necesitas tu calculadora.*

Cultural Notes

(p. 71, photo)
University students in Santiago, Chile. Chileans have one of the lowest rates of population growth in South America, roughly 1.5 percent a year, and their mortality rate has been steadily dropping to 6 per 1,000. These figures notwithstanding, Chile is a country of young people, with over half of the population under 20. Because of this, traditional ways of life have changed greatly in recent years, with more young people being educated, earning incomes, and becoming part of a growing consumer middle class.

Paso cultural
Possible answers: Cambridge (MA), New Haven (CT), New York, Princeton (NJ), Chicago, Berkeley (CA), Los Angeles./ Students may mention that courses in Chilean universities would focus more on that country's history, heritage, and themes.

Present & Practice

Teaching Suggestions

Point out that a question in Spanish may omit the subject if it is clearly known. Example: *¿Cocina Juan en la clase de ciencias?* → *¿Cocina en la clase de ciencias?*

1 Answers
a. ella
b. Ud.
c. él
d. ellos
e. Uds.
f. tú
g. ellas
h. nosotras

• *Yo* means "I."

• *Tú, usted,* and *ustedes* mean "you."

 a. Use *tú* with family members, close friends, people around your age or younger, and anyone you call by a first name.

 b. Use *usted* with adults and anyone you would address with a title of respect, such as *señor, señora,* etc. *Usted* is usually written as *Ud.*

 c. Use *ustedes* when speaking to two or more people, even if you would call them *tú* individually. We usually write it as *Uds.*

• There are two forms for "we" in Spanish: *nosotras* for females, and *nosotros* for males or for a mixed group of males and females.

• There are also two forms for "they." *Ellos* refers to a group of males or to a mixed group of males and females. *Ellas* refers to a group of females only.

• In Spanish, subject pronouns may be omitted because most verb forms indicate who the subject is: ***Tengo** ciencias en la primera hora.*

• Subject pronouns are usually used for emphasis or contrast, or if the subject is not clear: ***Él** es trabajador, pero **ella** es perezosa.*

1 With a partner, take turns telling which subject pronouns Ana would use to speak to or about these people.

a.   b.   c.   d.

e.   f.   g.   h.

Strategies for Reaching All Students

Students Needing Extra Help
Ex. 1: Have students turn to their Organizers to review subject pronouns.
Ex. 2: Use further examples from your school and community to show students the distinction between the three forms of "you."

Enrichment
Ex. 2: Ask students to name three people they would address as *tú* in Spanish, and three people they would address as *Ud.*

Multiple Intelligences
Bodily/Kinesthetic
See Class Starter Review.
Visual/Spatial and Bodily/Kinesthetic
Prepare three sections on the bulletin board or three large blank pieces of paper, one labeled *tú,* one labeled *usted,* and one *ustedes.* Ask students to bring in old magazines from home and cut out pictures showing individuals and groups of people whom they would address as *tú, usted,* or *ustedes.* Have students glue, tape, or pin each picture

2 Now tell which form of "you" you would use if you were speaking to these people.

a. your father
b. the principal
c. the girl next door
d. your teacher
e. your mother and sister
f. your cousin
g. an older person sitting next to you on the bus
h. three classmates

Verbos que terminan en -ar

A verb usually names the action in a sentence. We call the verb form that ends in -r the infinitive. It is the form you would find in a Spanish dictionary. It means "to ___." On the right are some of the infinitives you already know. We call these -ar verbs.

ayudar	nadar
cocinar	necesitar
dibujar	patinar
enseñar	practicar
escuchar	terminar
estudiar	tocar
hablar	

• In Spanish, the last letter or letters of the verb tell you who does the action.

• To change an infinitive to a form that tells who is doing the action, remove the -ar and add the appropriate ending.

estudiar			
SINGULAR		PLURAL	
(yo)	estudio	(nosotros) (nosotras)	estudiamos
(tú)	estudias	(vosotros) (vosotras)	estudiáis
Ud. (él) (ella)	estudia	Uds. (ellos) (ellas)	estudian

* Verb forms ending in -áis, such as *estudiáis*, are used mainly in Spain. We will use them occasionally and you should learn to recognize them.

Gramática en contexto   73

2 Answers
a. tú (Ud.)
b. Ud.
c. tú
d. Ud.
e. Uds.
f. tú
g. Ud.
h. Uds.

 Practice Wkbk. 2-5, 2-6

 Prueba 2-5

Class Starter Review
On the day following initial presentation of -ar verbs, you might begin the class with this activity: Prepare a sheet of paper with the personal pronoun icons or use the overhead of pronouns (no words), photocopy a class set, and cut into flashcards. (You may wish to mount these on index cards.) Call out an -ar verb. Have pairs of students take turns showing each other their personal pronoun flashcards and saying the correct verb form. Change verbs at regular intervals.

on one of the three collages according to the pronoun being used.

• The verb forms in the chart are in the present tense. They are the equivalent of both "I study, you study, he or she studies" and "I'm studying, you're studying, he's or she's studying," and so on.

• When you want to say that you do *not* do something, use *no* before the verb form.

    Yo **no cocino** en la clase de educación física.

• When we ask a question in Spanish, we usually put the subject after the verb or sometimes at the end of the sentence.

    ¿Cocina **Juan** en la clase de ciencias?

    ¿Estudia mucho **Paulina?**

3 Imagine that someone from Colombia has just arrived at your school. Which of these statements could you use to tell this student what you personally do and what you need at school?

En Caracas, Venezuela

a. Necesitamos bolígrafos y marcadores.
b. Hablo inglés.
c. Practico deportes.
d. Necesitan un cuaderno para la clase de español.
e. Tocamos la guitarra en la clase de música.
f. Habla inglés.
g. Necesito una mochila.
h. Estudian mucho para la clase de ciencias.
i. Cocinamos en la clase de ciencias sociales.
j. Dibuja en la clase de arte.
k. Estudia inglés.
l. Necesita un diccionario para la clase de inglés.
m. Habla inglés y español.
n. Nadamos en la clase de educación física.
o. Escuchan música en la clase de inglés.

"Nadamos en la clase de educación física."

Strategies for Reaching All Students

Spanish-Speaking Students
Ex. 6: Have Spanish-speaking students write out their answers and expand them where possible.

Students Needing Extra Help
Exs. 3–5: Have students fill in the verb chart in the Organizer so that they can refer to it when necessary.

Enrichment
Ex. 3: As a written exercise, have students group the sentences according to their verb endings. Then have them insert subjects into each of these sentences, using personal pronouns or proper nouns as required. They may also change each sentence by turning it either into a negative statement or into a question.
Ex. 6: Have students expand each answer by stating what school supplies they need as they study for each class.

4 Which sentences in Exercise 3 could you use to tell about a friend? Which could you use to tell about your friend and yourself? Which ones could you use to tell about two friends?

5 What school supplies do you and your classmates need for different classes? When necessary, ask the people what they need for a certain class and then report back to your partner.

a. what you need
b. what you and a person sitting next to you need
c. what the person sitting behind or in front of you needs
d. what any two people you choose need

SELECTIP® NOVEDAD

Descubra un Bolígrafo que es un ROTULADOR; un Rotulador que es un Roller; un Roller que es un Marcador; un Marcador que es un Bolígrafo...

El 4x4 de CROSS

Bolígrafo con super-carga Jumbo. Rotulador de fibra. Roller. Marcador de documentos. Cuatro cargas compatibles para un sólo instrumento de escritura. SELECTIP®: El 4x4 de CROSS, con garantía de por vida.

Disponible en Townsend, Century y Solo Classic

CROSS
SINCE 1846
ABSOLUTA PERFECCIÓN MECÁNICA

6 Tell what subjects you and your classmates are studying this year.

Ramona estudia ciencias de la salud.

a. (nombre)

b. (nombre) y (nombre)

c. yo

d. (nombre) y (nombre)

e. (nombres) y yo

f. (nombre)

Gramática en contexto 75

4 Your friend: f., j., k., l., m.
Your friend and yourself:
a., e., i., n.
Two friends: d., h., o.

5 a. Necesito . . . *(Answers will vary for school supplies.)*
b. Necesitamos . . .
c. Necesita . . .
d. Necesitan . . .

6 a. . . . estudia . . .
b. . . . estudian . . .
c. . . . estudio . . .
d. . . . estudian . . .
e. . . . estudiamos . . .
f. . . . estudia . . .

 Practice Wkbk. 2-7, 2-8

 Writing Activity 2-F

 Prueba 2-6

 Comm. Act. BLM 2-3

Extended Written Practice/Homework
1. Refer to the list of -ar verbs on p. 73. Write four sentences telling which of your friends do these actions. Use the correct verb form and other necessary words.
2. Write three sentences saying what you and your friends or you and your family do or do not do.
3. Think of teachers in your school who teach the same subject. Choose three of those subjects and write three sentences telling which ones two or more teachers teach.

Multiple Intelligences
Verbal/Linguistic
Have students use their completed sentences from Ex. 6 to form questions or make negative sentences:
Ramona estudia ciencias de la salud./¿Estudia ciencias de la salud Ramona?
or: *Ramona estudia ciencias de la salud./Ramona no estudia ciencias de la salud.*

Cultural Notes ☀

(p. 75, realia)
Linguists use the term "loanwords" for words that have crossed from one language to another. Mexican Spanish is full of loanwords from *náhuatl*, the Aztec language, among others. Recent decades have seen a dramatic influx of loanwords into Spanish from English. Ask students what English loanwords they can spot in this ad. Also ask them to name any Spanish loanwords that are used in contemporary English.

Present & Practice

Re-enter / Recycle
Ex. 9: school supplies from
El primer paso

Teaching Suggestions
Ex. 7: Refer students to the list in the margin on p. 73 for suggestions on which verbs to use. You may want to tell students why they must use *-ar* verbs.

Answers
7 Answers will vary, but look for subject-verb agreement.

8 *Calculadora, carpeta, carpeta de argollas, grabadora, mochila,* and *regla* are feminine.
Diccionario, marcador, cuaderno, and *lápiz* are masculine.

9 a. la *or* una
b. La
c. el *or* un
d. la
e. el *or* un
f. un
g. la *or* una
h. la

---

7 Write four sentences telling what you and your classmates do in your free time. Choose which four letters from a–h you want to use before you begin. Afterward, let two classmates read your sentences.

Esteban, Ana María y yo practicamos deportes.

a. (nombre)

b. (nombres) y yo

c. (nombre) y (nombre)

d. yo

e. (nombre) y (nombre)

f. (nombre)

g. (nombres) y yo

h. (nombre) y yo

Los sustantivos

Nouns refer to people, animals, places, and things. In Spanish, nouns have gender. They are either masculine or feminine.

• Most nouns that end in *-o* are masculine. Most nouns that end in *-a* are feminine. For example:
    el libro   la calculadora
There are a few exceptions. You know one: *el día.*

• Other Spanish nouns end in *-e* or a consonant. Some of these are masculine, and some are feminine. For example:
    el cine   el marcador
    la clase   la televisión

• A few nouns can be both masculine and feminine. For example: *el / la estudiante.*

• *El* and *la* are called definite articles and are the equivalent of "the" in English. We use *el* with masculine nouns, *la* with feminine nouns.

• *Un* and *una* are indefinite articles, like "a" and "an" in English. We use *un* with masculine nouns, *una* with feminine nouns.

It is a good idea to learn a noun with its definite article, *el* or *la,* because that will usually tell you the gender.

Strategies for Reaching All Students

Students Needing Extra Help
Los sustantivos: Point out that the concept of masculine and feminine in Spanish deals with the spelling of the word, not with the actual definition in English of "masculine" and "feminine."
Ahora lo sabes: Have students write out this section so that they can chart their progress.

Extended Written Practice/Homework
1. Make two columns with the headings "Masculine Nouns" and "Feminine Nouns." Under these headings, list at least 12 things that can be found in your school. Refer to pp. 13 and 59.
2. Refer to your lists in #1. Write six sentences saying what you and your classmates need for different classes.

Multiple Intelligences
Bodily/Kinesthetic
1) Make flashcards from the Vocabulary Art BLMs/CD-ROM for the vocabulary on p. 59. Display them on the board at the front of the room. Ask students to write the appropriate definite article with each picture.
2) Place several items (see pp. 13 and 59) in a book bag and ask students to reach

8 Turn back to page 59. Decide which of the words in the picture are masculine and which are feminine. Make a list of these words in random order, leaving out the words *un* and *una*. Give the list to your partner and have him or her write the correct definite article *(el* or *la)*. Check your partner's answers.

9 Write these sentences on a sheet of paper, adding the definite or indefinite article *(el/la* or *un/una)* according to which makes the best sense. Do any of them make sense both ways? Discuss your answers with your partner.

a. Necesito ___ calculadora.
b. ___ clase de ciencias es difícil.
c. Tengo ___ marcador en mi mochila.
d. Toco ___ guitarra.
e. Necesito ___ diccionario.
f. ¿Hay ___ bolígrafo en la mesa?
g. ¿Tienes ___ regla?
h. ¿A qué hora empieza ___ clase de inglés?

MORE PRACTICE

Más práctica y tarea, pp. 512–513
Practice Workbook 2–5, 2–9

Ahora lo sabes

Can you:

► state who is doing an action without using people's names?
—¿Practican deportes Marta y Teresa?
—Sí, ___ nadan y patinan.

► use the correct verb form to tell what you and others do regularly?
—¿Estudian Uds. para la clase de matemáticas?
—No, pero (nosotros) ___ para la clase de ciencias.

► say that you do *not* do something?
—(Yo) ___ cocino en la clase de matemáticas.

► use the appropriate subject pronouns when addressing someone?
—Miguel, ¿tocas ___ la guitarra?
—Señora, ¿habla ___ inglés?
—Jorge y Juan, ¿practican ___ deportes?

Gramática en contexto   77

inside without looking and select an item. They must correctly name each item with the appropriate definite article. This can be done in groups, pairs, or as cooperative learning.
Visual/Spatial
Use an overhead transparency or laminated flashcards printed with the name of an item and the appropriate definite article, *el* or *la.*

Apply

 Pronunciation Tape 2-3

 **Todo junto A**

Play

Todo junto B

Play

Using the Video
Video segment 3: See the Video Teacher's Guide.

 Video Activity C

 **Pasos vivos 1 CD-ROM**
Video Monitor, Video Presentation Maker

Re-enter / Recycle
Ex. 1: numbers 0–31 from *El primer paso*, *gustar* expressions from Ch. 1
Ex. 2: numbers 0–31 from *El primer paso*

Answers: Actividades
1 Dialogues will vary, but encourage students to use the full range of chapter vocabulary.

2 Schedules will vary. Look for appropriate use of time-telling, names for school subjects, and class periods.

Todo Junto

Actividades

1 Ask a partner:
- which classes he or she is taking
- who the teacher is
- what time each class begins
- when each class ends
- whether or not he or she likes the class

Afterward you can create a class schedule for each other, showing teachers' names and times.

2 Make a schedule in Spanish for a family member to follow at Open House at your school. Use your regular schedule, but make each period only 20 minutes long. Include the name of each class, who teaches it, which period, and when it begins and ends. When you have finished, compare your schedule with that of a partner.

78   Capítulo 2

Strategies for Reaching All Students

Spanish-Speaking Students
Ex. 1: Have Spanish-speaking students expand their reasons why they like or don't like certain classes. You may wish to have them write out this exercise.

Students Needing Extra Help
Ex. 2: Give guidelines for when the Open House begins and ends. Work out the time schedule on the chalkboard to help speed time computations.

Enrichment
As a written assignment, students can list all the class subjects they now know in a chart with two columns: one with the heading *Me gusta la clase de . . .* and the other with *No me gusta la clase de . . . .*

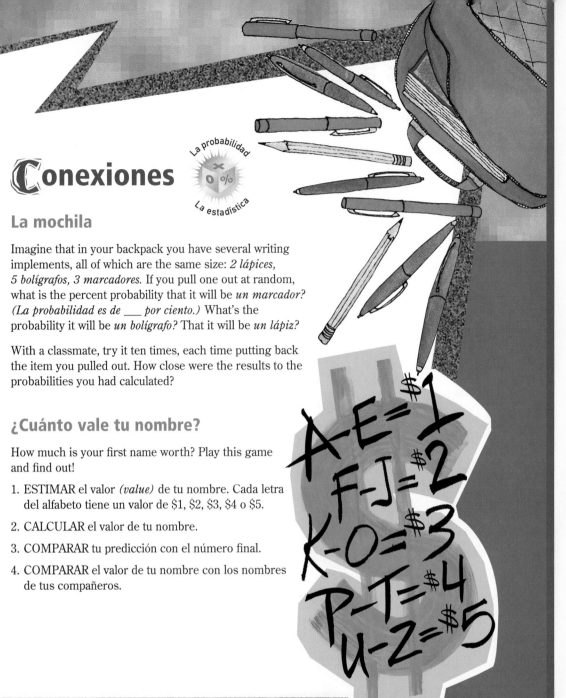

Conexiones

La probabilidad × 0 % *La estadística*

La mochila

Imagine that in your backpack you have several writing implements, all of which are the same size: *2 lápices, 5 bolígrafos, 3 marcadores.* If you pull one out at random, what is the percent probability that it will be *un marcador?* *(La probabilidad es de ___ por ciento.)* What's the probability it will be *un bolígrafo?* That it will be *un lápiz?*

With a classmate, try it ten times, each time putting back the item you pulled out. How close were the results to the probabilities you had calculated?

¿Cuánto vale tu nombre?

How much is your first name worth? Play this game and find out!

1. ESTIMAR el valor *(value)* de tu nombre. Cada letra del alfabeto tiene un valor de $1, $2, $3, $4 o $5.

2. CALCULAR el valor de tu nombre.

3. COMPARAR tu predicción con el número final.

4. COMPARAR el valor de tu nombre con los nombres de tus compañeros.

A-E = $1
F-J = $2
K-O = $3
P-T = $4
U-Z = $5

Todo junto   79

Teaching Suggestions
¿Cuánto vale tu nombre?:
Encourage students to pronounce aloud the letters and numbers in Spanish as they work.

Answers: Conexiones
Un marcador, 30%; un bolígrafo, 50%; un lápiz, 20%. Percentages are reached by dividing the number of a given writing implement by the total number of implements (10) and multiplying by 100. For example, the two pencils would be divided by the total number of implements. That number (.2) is then multiplied by 100, which results in the final answer of 20%.

Answers will vary. For example, the name Jane (2+1+3+1) Doe (1+3+1) is worth $12.

 Comm. Act. BLMs 2-4, 2-5

 Pasos vivos 1 CD-ROM
A Jugar, Boom Box, Laboratorio de grabar, Maps, Spindle

Cooperative Learning
In groups of three or four, have students use Ex. 3 on p. 74 to list those activities that specifically apply to them during a normal school day. Ask one member from each group to tabulate everybody's responses, and then graph the results so that the information can be shared with the class or compiled to form a whole-class survey.

Multiple Intelligences
Interpersonal/Social
See Cooperative Learning.
Logical/Mathematical
See *Conexiones.*
Verbal/Linguistic
See Pronunciation Tape 2-3.
Visual/Spatial
See Using the Video.

Apply

Process Reading
For a description of process reading, see p. 48.

Multicultural Perspectives
In most Spanish-speaking countries, students may take up to seven courses per school year. These may include: trigonometry, anatomy, history, geography, Spanish, English, French, physical education, and courses in fine arts. Ask students to compare their courses with those taken by their Spanish-speaking counterparts.

Answers
Antes de leer
Answers may include the student's name, class schedule, year in school, subjects, teachers' names, grades, comments, etc.

Mira la lectura
Answers will vary depending on what the student expected to find in the previous section.

¡Vamos a leer!

Antes de leer

STRATEGY ➤ **Using prior knowledge**

Depending on the kind of document we are reading, we can often predict the kind of information it will include. For example, in a menu we expect to find the names and prices of different dishes. In a bus schedule, we look for the time of arrival and departure of buses throughout the week, as well as ticket prices.

Make a list of four things you might expect to find on a report card.

Mira la lectura

STRATEGY ➤ **Scanning**

Remember that scanning is a strategy to help you look for certain information.

Here is a report card for a student in Mexico. Of the four things you listed, how many can you find on this report card?

PART 1

SEP SECRETARÍA DE EDUCACIÓN PÚBLICA
SUBSECRETARÍA DE EDUCACIÓN

BOLETA DE EVALUACIÓN

EXPEDIDA POR LA

Dirección General de Educación

en _____ CHIHUAHUA

Escuela _____ "AMADO NERVO" T. VESPERTINO.

CLAVE CENTRO DEL TRABAJO
0 8 D P R 1 7 5 5 X

VALLE NACIONAL Y JAZMINAL S/N
domicilio   calle   número   código postal

A nombre del alumno (a)

RAMOS SUAREZ JOSE RAUL

MATRÍCULA	EDAD AÑOS MESES	GRADO	GRUPO
394		9º	B

Strategies for Reaching All Students

Students Needing Extra Help
Antes de leer: Have students brainstorm and list *all* possibilities, not just four.
Aplicación: Model a blank report card that your school uses. Use the Organizer to review the vocabulary for class subjects. You may wish to do this as a whole-class activity.

Multiple Intelligences
Visual/Spatial
See *Aplicación.*

Infórmate

STRATEGY ➤ Scanning

As you read, match what you expected to find with the information given.

1 Study Part 1 of the *Boleta de evaluación*.

a. What is the name of the school?

b. Where is it located?

c. What is the name of the student?

d. What grade is he in? How old do you think he is?

PART 2
RESULTADOS DEL APRENDIZAJE

ÁREAS	UNIDAD PROGRAMÁTICA								RESULTADO ANUAL
	I	II	III	IV	V	VI	VII	VIII	
INGLÉS	9	8	9	8	10	10	10	10	9
MATEMÁTICAS	9	8	9	7	8	10	10	9	9
CIENCIAS NATURALES	9	9	9	9	9	10	10	10	9
CIENCIAS SOCIALES	9	9	9	8	9	10	10	10	9
EDUCACIÓN ARTÍSTICA	8	9	9	9	9	9	9	9	9
EDUCACIÓN FÍSICA	8	8	8	10	10	10	10		9
EDUC. TECNOLÓGICA	8	9	9	8	8	10	10	10	9

PART 3
ASISTENCIA

	SEPTIEMBRE	OCTUBRE	NOVIEMBRE	DICIEMBRE	ENERO	FEBRERO	MARZO	ABRIL	MAYO	JUNIO	TOTAL
DÍAS HÁBILES	20	22	20	10	22	19	15	17	21	20	186
INASISTENCIAS	–	–	–	1	–	–	1	1	–		3

PART 4

RESULTADO FINAL	ESCALA DE EVALUACIÓN	
✓ PROMOVIDO	10 EXCELENTE 9 MUY BIEN 8 BIEN 7 REGULAR	} ACREDITADO
◯ NO PROMOVIDO	6 SUFICIENTE 5 NO SUFICIENTE	} NO ACREDITADO

2 Examine Part 2, *Resultados del aprendizaje*.

a. How many subjects did the student take?

b. How many grading periods were there during the school year?

c. Did the student's grades generally improve or decline during the year? In which subject(s) did he improve the most? In which was he most consistent? In which subject did he receive his lowest mark?

d. Using the scale explained in the *Escala de evaluación*, which words would you use to describe the student's overall academic work?

3 Read Part 3, *Asistencia*.

a. How many school days were there? How many days was the student absent?

b. In which month were there the fewest days of instruction?

4 Look at Part 4, *Resultado final*. Were you surprised by the student's final results for the year? Why or why not?

Aplicación

Design a report card in Spanish for your classes this year.

Infórmate

Part 1:

a. Amado Nervo (*T. vespertino* means *turno vespertino*. This indicates that the student attends afternoon classes.)

b. Chihuahua, Mexico (Point out this state on a map.) Mention that the letters *S / N* in the student's home address stand for *sin número*. This means that he probably lives in a small village area where the street number is not required.

c. José Raúl Ramos Suárez

d. Ninth grade, around 13–14 years old

Part 2:

a. seven

b. eight

c. His grades generally improved. He improved the most in math and in computer class (computer science). He was most consistent in art. His lowest mark was in math.

d. *muy bien*

Part 3:

a. 189, 3

b. December

Part 4:

Answers will vary.

Aplicación

Guide this activity and show students a model.

🌐 Internet Activities

Have students go to www.pasoapaso.com for additional activities and practice.

Cultural Notes ☀

(pp. 80–81, realia)
As this report card from Mexico indicates, the grading system in most Mexican schools has traditionally been based on a scale of 1 to 10, with 10 being the highest grade and 6 or 7 the minimum passing grade. Letter grades similar to those in the U.S. are also used by some private secondary schools and institutions of higher education. The *Resultado final* of promotion or non-promotion is determined by the teacher's general evaluation of the student and not by any exam scores.

(p. 80, realia)
The novels *Eva Luna* by Isabel Allende and *Como agua para chocolate* by Laura Esquivel are examples of "magical realism," a literary style that originated in Latin America. Allende is the niece of former Chilean president Salvador Allende. She fled Chile when her uncle's government was overthrown by General Augusto Pinochet in 1973. Esquivel, a Mexican, also wrote the screenplay for the successful movie based on her novel.

Apply

Process Writing
For information regarding developing a writing portfolio, see p. 50.

 Writing Activity 2-G

 Pasos vivos 1 CD-ROM
Word Processor

¡Vamos a escribir!

Una estudiante prepara su tarea para las clases. ▶

Write a letter to a Spanish-speaking friend about your school day. Follow these steps.

1 Write out your class schedule. Put a check mark beside those classes in which you have a lot of homework. Underline the classes that you like a lot.

2 Write your letter using the class schedule and the information you've added to it. On the right is an outline that will help you get started.

3 Now show your letter to a partner. Ask which parts might be changed. Decide whether or not you agree, then rewrite your letter, making any changes that you have decided on.

4 Check your letter for spelling and punctuation, including accents. Did you begin with the date and the greeting *Hola?* Did you end with a closing expression and your name?

5 Make any corrections and recopy. You might send your letter to:
- a new pen pal
- a student of Spanish in another school
- a student in another Spanish class at your school
- a student in your Spanish class

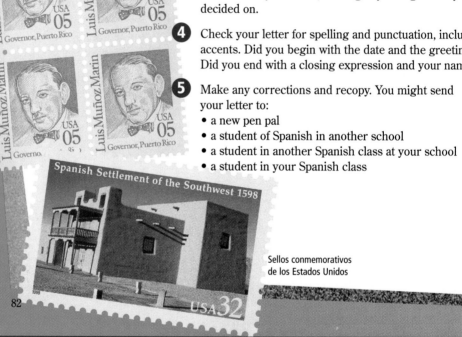

Sellos conmemorativos de los Estados Unidos

Strategies for Reaching All Students

Spanish-Speaking Students
Have Spanish-speaking students answer the letter of one of the non-bilingual students. They can then compare classes and tell about a favorite class.

 Un paso más Exs. 2-G, 2-H

Students Needing Extra Help
Have students use their Organizers to check for spelling.

Enrichment
One organization through which you can arrange pen pals is: International Youth Service / PB 125 / SF-20101 / Turku, Finland.

"¡Hola! A mí me gustan muchas clases, pero me gusta más la clase de ciencias sociales."

Un muchacho de Colombia

¡Vamos a escribir! 83

Cultural Notes ☀

Multiple Intelligences
Interpersonal/Social
Using Step 3 on p. 82, have students compare their suggested changes. Ask volunteers to share theirs with the rest of the class.

(p. 82, realia)
These stamps issued by the U.S. Postal Service honor Hispanics and their culture. The stamp at the top, for example, commemorates Cinco de Mayo, an important civic holiday in Mexico. On May 5, 1862, Mexican troops at Puebla stopped a French invasion force that was advancing toward Mexico City. Ask students to name some other commemorative stamps with a U.S. or world historical event for their theme.

(p. 83, bottom photo)
This teenager is wearing a traditional outfit from the Colombian highlands: a straw hat known as a *jipijapa* and a *ruana* (a woolen cloak that measures about four square feet with an opening in the center for the head). Although traditional clothing is still common in rural Colombia, increasing numbers of people are adopting Western dress, which is now worn by nearly everyone in the cities.

Assess & Summarize

Test Preparation
You may want to assign parts of this section as written homework or as an in-class writing activity prior to administering the *Examen de habilidades.*

Answers
Listening: *Hoy tengo la clase de ciencias sociales en la séptima hora y la clase de arte a las 3:55.* He is talking about his afternoon schedule.

Culture: Answers will vary, but may include: School uniforms, class schedules, length of school day, grades, homework, testing, student-teacher relationships, etc.

Reading: Mauricio has the following classes: English for first period, math for second, science for third, physical education for fourth, and lunch is fifth.

Writing: Lists will vary, but students should use the chapter vocabulary. Look for logical items. Remind them of *un / una* with masculine and feminine nouns.

Speaking: Answers will vary, but look for expressions with *me / te gusta.* Encourage use of vocabulary from this chapter.

Repaso ¿Lo sabes bien?

This section will help you organize your studying for the proficiency test, where you will be asked to do similar, though not identical, tasks. There will not be any models on the test.

► **Listening**
Can you understand when people talk about their class schedules? Listen as your teacher reads you a sample similar to what you will hear on the test. Would you say the student making the statement is talking about his morning or afternoon schedule?

► **Culture**
Can you list some possible differences between your school and one in Mexico City?

► **Reading**
How well can you understand a person's written schedule? Scan the paragraph below. Can you chart out Mauricio's schedule based on this description?

Mauricio tiene muchas clases. En la primera hora tiene clase de inglés, su clase favorita. En la segunda hora tiene clase de matemáticas. La clase de ciencias es a las 10:00. La clase de educación física empieza a las 11:00 y termina a las 11:50. El almuerzo es a las 12:00.

► **Writing**
Can you write a list of supplies you need for school? Your parents want to discuss the school supplies you need to buy. To prepare for the discussion, list under the headings provided below the supplies and the classes you need the supplies for. For example:

¿Qué? ¿Para qué clases?

regla matemáticas, arte

► **Speaking**
Ask a partner which classes he or she likes better, and which ones he or she doesn't like at all. Do you and your partner like and dislike the same classes? Here is a sample dialogue:

A —*¿Qué clase te gusta más?*

B —*Me gusta mucho la clase de música. También me gustan mucho la clase de ciencias y las matemáticas.*

A —*¿Qué clase no te gusta nada?*

B —*La clase de educación física. Yo soy muy perezosa. ¿Y tú?*

Self Test www.pasoapaso.com

Strategies for Reaching All Students

Students Needing Extra Help
You may wish to have students write out this section so that they can check off what they have mastered.

Multiple Intelligences
Intrapersonal/Introspective
See *¿Lo sabes bien?*

Resumen del vocabulario

Use the vocabulary from this chapter to help you:

► describe your class schedule

► list some school supplies you use

► find out about someone else's schedule

to talk about school subjects
el almuerzo
el arte (f.)
las ciencias
las ciencias de la salud
las ciencias sociales
la clase de ___
la educación física
el español
el inglés
las matemáticas
la música
difícil
fácil
aprender: (yo) aprendo
       (tú) aprendes
enseñar: enseña
la tarea

to talk about school supplies
la calculadora
la carpeta (de argollas)
el cuaderno
el diccionario
la grabadora
el horario
el lápiz, pl. los lápices
el marcador, pl. los marcadores
la mochila
la regla

to talk about what people need
necesitar: (yo) necesito
      (tú) necesitas

to express possession
tener: (yo) tengo
     (tú) tienes
tu

to express quantity
mucho, -a
un, -a

to ask for information
¿Qué?

to ask and tell when something takes place
a
¿A qué hora ___?
empezar: empieza
terminar: termina
es
la hora
   la primera hora
   la segunda hora
   la tercera hora
   la cuarta hora
   la quinta hora
   la sexta hora
   la séptima hora
   la octava hora
el semestre
   el primer semestre
   el segundo semestre

to ask and tell the time
¿Qué hora es?
Es la una (y ___).
Son las ___ (y ___).
cuarto
media
treinta y dos
treinta y tres
treinta y cuatro . . .
cuarenta
cincuenta

to express regret
Lo siento.

to hesitate
A ver . . .

to talk about location
aquí
   Aquí está.
allí
   Allí está.

to say what something is for
para

to tell who performs an action
yo
tú
usted (Ud.)
él, ella
nosotros, -as
vosotros, -as
ustedes (Uds.)
ellos, -as
¿Quién?

 Prueba cumulativa

 Examen de habilidades

 Test Generator

Additional Assessment Options

 Comm. Act. BLMs

Small Group Activities
Situation Cards

 Pasos vivos 1 CD-ROM

Slide Presentation Maker, Video Presentation Maker, Word Processor, Spindle

 ¿Lo sabes bien? Video Quiz

www Internet Activities
Self-Test

CAPÍTULO 3

THEME: SPORTS AND LEISURE ACTIVITIES

SCOPE AND SEQUENCE Pages 86–117

COMMUNICATION

Topics

Public buildings and places

Seasons

Sports and leisure activities

Objectives

To compare leisure-time activities in Spanish-speaking countries with those in the U.S.

To tell how someone feels or where someone is

To tell where someone is going

To talk about activities

To say when and with whom you do an activity

To express surprise, enthusiasm, or disappointment

To express possession

To extend, accept, or decline invitations

CULTURE

Leisure-time activities

Parks and *plazas*

GRAMMAR

El verbo ir

Ir + a + *infinitivo*

La preposición con

El verbo estar

Ancillaries available for use with Chapter 3

Multisensory/Technology

 Overheads, 16–20

 Audio Tapes and CDs

 Vocabulary Art Blackline Masters for Hands-On Learning, pp. 18–22/CD-ROM

 Classroom Crossword

Video

 Pasos vivos 1 CD-ROM

 Internet Activities www.pasoapaso.com

Print

 Practice Workbook, pp. 33–42

 Writing, Audio & Video Activities, pp. 17–22, 99–101, 156–157

 Communicative Activity Blackline Masters

  Pair and Small Group Activities, pp. 22–27

  Situation Cards, p. 28

 Un paso más: Actividades para ampliar tu español, pp. 13–19

TPR Storytelling

Assessment

 Assessment Program

  Pruebas, pp. 37–47

  Examen de habilidades, pp. 48–51

Test Generator

Video still from Chap. 3

85A

Planning Express, Teaching
Resources Library, and Clip Art
Library

¿Lo sabes bien?
Video Quiz

Cultural Overview

Teen Activities

Unlike in the U.S., where teen couples often go alone to a concert, movie, or a meal, young people in Latin America tend to socialize in groups until a couple's relationship is more serious. Generally, relationships are carefully scrutinized by parents, and family life has a strong influence on young people. Brothers and sisters often share the same group of friends and accompany each other on outings.

Night life in large Latin American cities such as Buenos Aires, Montevideo, Santiago de Chile, and Mexico City often begins late. During holidays, vacation, or on weekends, many teens often do not meet with friends until 10 P.M. or later. This late-night schedule is an inheritance from Mediterranean cultures where warm climates encouraged people to stay in during the heat of the day.

Besides going to movies, video arcades, and restaurants, teens in Latin America often meet at city parks. These parks, such as Chapultepec Park in Mexico City, attract pedestrians who stroll along the paths on their way to other destinations. Some rest for a while on park benches, chatting with friends or reading. Young couples may use the parks as meeting places where they can spend some time away from the scrutiny of family or friends.

Parks are lively places populated with many vendors who sell food, drinks, *paletas* (popsicles or ice cream bars), gum, small toys, and other treats. Some parks even include museums, small amusement parks, or zoos. Especially on weekends, parks have a very festive atmosphere and are a favorite destination for people of all ages.

Smaller towns are built around a *plaza,* which is a central square or public space where people meet to spend leisure time. *Cafés* and businesses surround the *plaza,* with concerts and other civic events held there. With trees and formal flower plantings, *plazas* are similar to our town squares and are comfortable spots for young people to gather and have fun.

Introduce

Re-entry of Concepts
The following list represents words, expressions, and grammar topics re-entered from *El primer paso* to Chap. 2:

El primer paso
Calendar expressions

Chapter 1
Activities
Gustar expressions
Adjectives describing personality

Chapter 2
School subjects
Time expressions
Possession
Personal pronouns

Planning

Cross-Curricular Connections

Geography Connection *(pp. 90–91)*
Have students create a map of North and South America and write in the current seasons above and below the equator. In pairs, they can select five states or countries from above and below the equator, and report on the current temperatures.

Business Education Connection *(pp. 90–91)*
Have students record on a daily basis the time and location of their activities for an entire week. Using this record as a personal profile, have them develop a time-management plan for the following week, including school and recreational activities.

Geography Connection *(pp. 94–95)*
In pairs, have students create a drawing of their ideal weekend vacation spot. Have them draw or cut out pictures to indicate featured activities and label each one. On the back, have them locate the vacation spot in a country or state, give the price for the trip, and provide some information on the weather in each season. Post these around the room and give points for the most creative or artistic pictures.

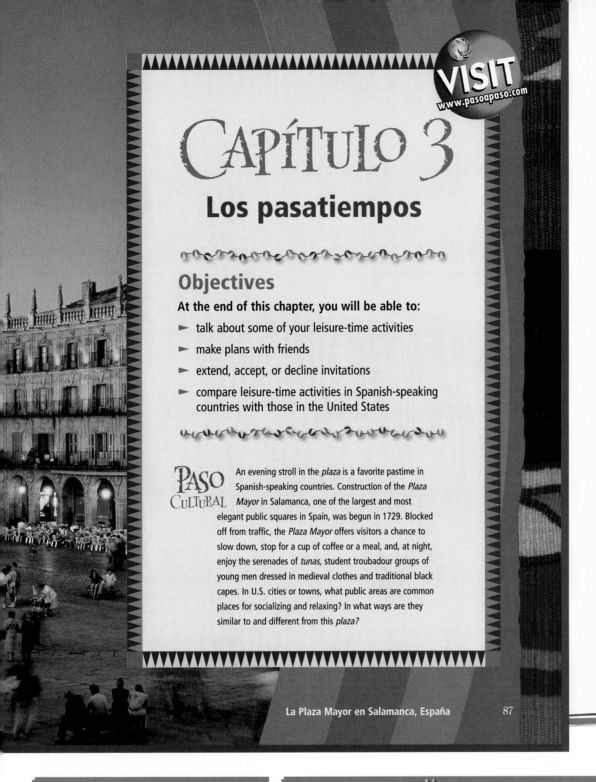

CAPÍTULO 3
Los pasatiempos

Objectives

At the end of this chapter, you will be able to:

► talk about some of your leisure-time activities

► make plans with friends

► extend, accept, or decline invitations

► compare leisure-time activities in Spanish-speaking countries with those in the United States

PASO CULTURAL

An evening stroll in the *plaza* is a favorite pastime in Spanish-speaking countries. Construction of the *Plaza Mayor* in Salamanca, one of the largest and most elegant public squares in Spain, was begun in 1729. Blocked off from traffic, the *Plaza Mayor* offers visitors a chance to slow down, stop for a cup of coffee or a meal, and, at night, enjoy the serenades of *tunas,* student troubadour groups of young men dressed in medieval clothes and traditional black capes. In U.S. cities or towns, what public areas are common places for socializing and relaxing? In what ways are they similar to and different from this *plaza?*

Cultural Notes

Spanish in Your Community
Which sport in your community (or in the U.S.) has been most greatly influenced by Hispanic culture? Ask students to explore their community or the Internet for a list of these sports. Have them report back to class with their results. Have students choose from the sports listed in the second vocabulary section (p. 94) or suggest any other sport. Have them explain their responses with specific reasons.

Paso cultural
Answers will vary. Students may mention shopping malls, cafés, restaurants, and so on./Answers will vary.

(pp. 86–87, photo)
Salamanca is one of the artistic and cultural treasures of Europe, and its Plaza Mayor is one of many impressive landmarks there. Considered a masterpiece of Baroque architecture, the *plaza* features arches adorned with medallions of illustrious Spaniards. Ask students if they know of buildings with elaborate architecture in their community and if they can describe them.

Preview

Cultural Objective

- To compare leisure-time activities in Spanish-speaking countries with those in the U.S.

 ¡Piénsalo bien!

Play

 Video Activity A

Teaching Suggestions

Bring several sports or leisure magazines or newspapers from Spanish-speaking countries to class. Share photos of the activities with your students, encouraging a discussion about how these activities compare with theirs.

Using the Video

This chapter's video focuses on sports and leisure activities. Students will see our hosts in Madrid visiting a famous park and interviewing athletes.

To prepare students for the video, first ask them to predict what this chapter's tape will be about. Then have students watch the segment several times. After the first time, you may wish to have them brainstorm possible vocabulary and expressions they will need to talk about what they saw on the video. Ask students to identify: a) things

¡Piensa en la CULTURA!

Leisure activities in Argentina, Spain, and California

Look at the photos and read the captions. How do the leisure activities of these teens compare to what you and your friends do? Which of these activities would you be most likely to do with your friends?

"Me encanta celebrar los días festivos y bailar sevillanas."

What do you think these teens might be celebrating? Do you have similar festivals in your community?

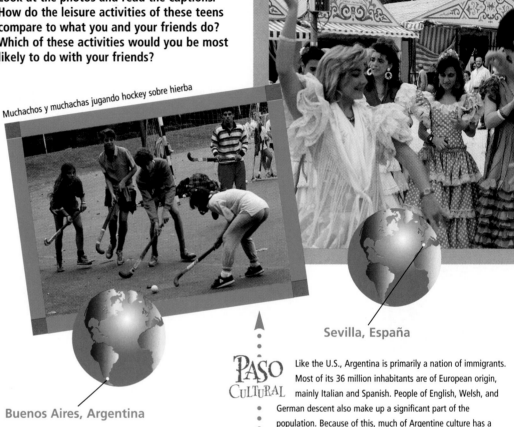

Muchachos y muchachas jugando hockey sobre hierba

Sevilla, España

Buenos Aires, Argentina

PASO CULTURAL

Like the U.S., Argentina is primarily a nation of immigrants. Most of its 36 million inhabitants are of European origin, mainly Italian and Spanish. People of English, Welsh, and German descent also make up a significant part of the population. Because of this, much of Argentine culture has a distinct European flavor to it. What are some reasons people immigrate to another country?

88   Capítulo 3

Options

Strategies for Reaching All Students

Spanish-Speaking Students
¡Piensa en la cultura!: Ask students to describe what they see in the photos. In addition, you may want to ask: *¿Qué te gusta hacer con tus amigos? ¿Cuándo sales con tus amigos? ¿Cuándo vas a fiestas?*

Students Needing Extra Help
¡Piensa en la cultura!: Discuss other activities that students engage in during weekends.

"Me gusta mucho ir al parque de diversiones y montar en la montaña rusa. ¡Pero a mi amiga Lupe no le gusta nada!"

What do you think a *parque de diversiones* might be? And can you guess what a *montaña rusa* is?

www.pasoapaso.com
Visit these countries on-line

En California

Vendedor de buñuelos en Otavalo, Ecuador

they saw that were familiar to them, and b) things they saw that they probably would not see in a park where they live.
Video segment 1: For more teaching suggestions, see the Video Teacher's Guide.

Multicultural Perspectives
In many urban Hispanic neighborhoods, *bodegas* (grocery stores) are an informal meeting place for people and for sharing news. Ask students, especially Spanish-speakers, if they know about any other types of informal meeting places in different cultures.

Answers: ¡Piensa en la cultura!
Answers to inductive questions will vary.

(p. 88, right photo) Students may say that they are celebrating some kind of festival. Answers will vary.

(p. 89, photo) Students should be able to guess from context that a *parque de diversiones* means "amusement park." If students have difficulty with *montaña rusa* (roller coaster), tell them the literal translation ("Russian mountain"), and then see if they can guess the meaning.

Cultural Notes ☼

Paso cultural
Possible answers: To find better work or educational opportunities, to escape war or political repression, to find out what another country is like.

(p. 88, right photo)
The *sevillana,* a very popular kind of dance that originated in Sevilla, is now well known in many other areas of Spain. Distinct from the *flamenco,* the *sevillana* is traditionally performed on three occasions: at *ferias* (town fairs), at spring parties known as *Cruces de mayo,* and on the annual pilgrimage to Nuestra Señora del Rocío.

(p. 89, bottom photo)
This boy from Otavalo, Ecuador is helping his family by selling *buñuelos*— deep-fried doughballs sprinkled with sugar. The dough used to make *buñuelos* is similar to that used to make *churros* (see Chap. 12, p. 385), but *buñuelos* are small and sphere-shaped while *churros* are long and thin.

Present

Chapter Theme
Leisure-time activities: Places to go

Communicative Objectives
- To tell where someone is going
- To say when and with whom you do an activity
- To talk about activities
- To express surprise, enthusiasm, or disappointment
- To express possession

 Overheads 16–17

 Vocabulary Art BLMs/CD-ROM

 Pronunciation Tape 3-1

 Vocabulario para conversar A

Play

Using the Video
Video segment 2: See the Video Teacher's Guide.

 Video Activity B

Vocabulario para conversar

¿Cuándo vas al parque?

Here are some new words and expressions you will need to talk about your leisure-time activities. Read them several times, then turn the page and practice with a partner.

At Home **VIDEO** Chapter 3 Vocabulary

90   Capítulo 3

Options

Strategies for Reaching All Students

Learning Spanish Through Action
STAGING VOCABULARY: *Señalen, Toquen*
MATERIALS: seasons from the Vocabulary Art BLMs/CD-ROM or transparency
DIRECTIONS: Have students touch or point to one of the seasons. Then have them name an activity they like to do in that particular season.

Multiple Intelligences
Naturalist
Have students create a collage showing their favorite outdoor leisure-time activities and places. Have them label each one in Spanish.
Verbal/Linguistic
See Pronunciation Tape 3-1.
Using Overheads 16–17, have students practice the names of the seasons while reviewing *me gusta, no me gusta,* etc.

Visual/Spatial
See Overheads 16–17, the Vocabulary Art BLMs/CD-ROM, and Using the Video.

las estaciones
(*sing.,* la estación)

la primavera

el verano

el otoño

el invierno

¡NO OLVIDES!

What do you think the difference is between *tu* and *tus?* When do you think you might use each one? And what is the difference between *tu* and *tú?*

También necesitas...

a	here: *to*
a la, al (a + el)	*to the*
el pasatiempo	*hobby, pastime*
el lunes el martes ...	*on Monday* *on Tuesday* ...
los lunes los martes ...	*on Mondays* *on Tuesdays* ...
los fines de semana	*on the weekends*
después (de)	*after*
después de las clases	*after school*
(por) la mañana la tarde la noche	*(in) the morning* *the afternoon* *the evening*

generalmente	*usually, generally*
todos los días	*every day*
¡No me digas!	*Really?* *You don't say!*
mi, mis	*my*
tus	*your*

¿Y qué quiere decir ... ?
¿Dónde?
ir: (yo) voy
    (tú) vas
con
el amigo, la amiga
la familia
solo, -a

Vocabulario para conversar   91

Grammar Preview
Voy / vas are previewed here. The complete paradigm of *ir* appears in the grammar section on p. 105.

Teaching Suggestions
Preparing students to speak: Use one or two options from each of the categories of Comprehensible Input, Physical Response, or Limited Verbal Response. For a complete explanation of these categories and some sample activities, see pp. T22–T23.

¡No olvides!: Explain the difference between the singular and plural form of *tu(s).* The formal explanation of possessive adjectives appears in Chap. 5.

Class Starter Review
On the day following initial presentation, you might begin the class with this activity:
Have students use *¿Cuándo tienes la clase de. . . ?* and *por la mañana / tarde* so that they can take turns asking for and giving information about their school schedules. Use visuals to elicit responses.

www Internet Activities
Juegos
Have students go to www.pasoapaso.com for additional activities and practice.

Practice & Apply

Reteach / Review: Vocabulary

Exs. 1–2: Expand this dialogue by having *Estudiante B* ask: *¿Y tú?* *Estudiante A* either gives the same answer using *también* or, in Ex. 2, *tampoco,* or gives a different answer.

Ex. 3: Elicit another expression that can be used in place of *¡No me digas! (¿De veras?)*

Re-enter / Recycle

Exs. 3 and 5: *me/te gusta* + activities from Chap. 1
Ex. 7: *me / te gusta* from Chap. 1

Answers: Empecemos a conversar

1 ESTUDIANTE A
a. ¿Cuándo vas a la piscina?
b. . . . a la escuela?
c. . . . a la playa?
d. . . . a la clase de matemáticas?
ESTUDIANTE B
a.–d. Answers will vary.

2 ESTUDIANTE A
a. ¿Cuándo vas al campo?
b. . . . al gimnasio?
c. . . . al centro comercial?
d. . . . al parque de diversiones?
ESTUDIANTE B
a.–d. Answers will vary.

Empecemos a conversar

With a partner, take turns being *Estudiante A* and *Estudiante B.* Use the words that are cued or given in the balloons to replace the underlined sections in the model.
 means you can make your own choices.

1 A —¿Cuándo vas *a la clase de inglés?*
B —Voy *por la tarde.*

Estudiante A

Estudiante B

después de las clases

los lunes, los martes . . .

en el verano

los fines de semana

por la mañana / tarde

2 A —¿Cuándo vas *al parque?*
B —Voy *los viernes.*
o: *Pues, generalmente no voy.*

Estudiante A

Estudiante B

los lunes, los martes . . .

los fines de semana

todos los días

por la mañana / tarde / noche

después de las clases

92   Capítulo 3

Options

Strategies for Reaching All Students

Spanish-Speaking Students
In Ex. 5, Spanish-speaking students should mention a few activities for each season.
In Ex. 8, also ask: *¿Por qué?*

 Un paso más Ex. 3-A

Students Needing Extra Help
Empecemos a conversar: Have students begin filling in their Organizers.
Exs. 1, 2, and 4: Point out that *voy* and *vas* are used to state where someone is going. Explain why *vas* changes to *voy* in the response. Remind students that they need *a(l)* before the location. In Exs. 1–2, explain that *Estudiante B*'s responses are choices and are not to be used in the order given. Show the full verb chart to students who may need to see the pattern right away.

Ex. 6: Model on the chalkboard. Divide possibilities into interrogatives for people and places. Show students that they have practiced these questions in Exs. 1, 2, and 4.
Empecemos a escribir: For additional practice, have students make four columns, labeling each one with a season. Using the vocabulary for places (p. 90), have them think about when they usually go there, and write the places in the appropriate columns.

3 A —¿Qué te gusta hacer en *el verano*?

B —Me gusta *nadar e* ir a la playa con mis amigos*.

A —¡No me digas! A mí también.

Estudiante A

a.

b.

c.

d.

Estudiante B

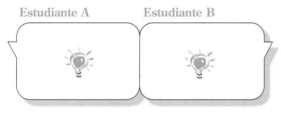

4 A —¿Con quién vas *al parque de diversiones*?

B —Generalmente voy *con mis amigos*.

o: Generalmente voy *solo(a)*.

Estudiante A   **Estudiante B**

Empecemos a escribir

Write your answers in Spanish.

5 For each season write one activity that you enjoy doing.

6 Write questions to ask your partner about when and with whom he or she goes to three different places. Record your partner's answers.

7 ¿Te gusta más el verano o el invierno? ¿Qué estación no te gusta?

8 Generalmente, ¿adónde vas después de las clases? ¿Cuál es tu pasatiempo favorito?

* The Spanish word *y* becomes *e* before a word beginning with *i* or *hi*.

También se dice...

la alberca
la pileta

el parque de atracciones

> **MORE PRACTICE**
>
> Más práctica y tarea, p. 514
> Practice Workbook 3–1, 3–2

Vocabulario para conversar   93

3 ESTUDIANTE A

a. ¿Qué te gusta hacer en la primavera?

b. ...el verano?

c. ...el otoño?

d. ...el invierno?

ESTUDIANTE B

a.–d. Answers will vary. Look for *me gusta* + inf.

4 Questions and answers will vary.

Answers: Empecemos a escribir

5 Answers will vary, but look for use of *me gusta* + inf.

6 Answers will vary. Look for *¿cuándo?* and *¿con quién?* along with use of *voy / vas*.

7 Answers will vary.

8 Answers will vary, but encourage students to use chapter vocabulary.

 Practice Wkbk. 3-1, 3-2

 Audio Activity 3.1

 Writing Activities 3-A, 3-B

 Pruebas 3-1, 3-2

 Comm. Act. BLM 3-1

Enrichment

Ex. 3: Students can prepare for this exercise by asking each other: *¿Qué te gusta más, la primavera, el verano, el otoño o el invierno?*

Ex. 5: Students can also write about what they need to do in each season.

Ex. 8: Expand this exercise by having students tell with whom they go to that place.

Extended Written Practice/Homework

1. Choose five places from the list on p. 90. List them in order of where you go most frequently to least frequently. Write complete sentences saying how often you go to each place *(todos los días, los fines de semana, a veces)*.

2. Write two sentences telling where you go and what you like to do after school and on the weekends.

3. Refer to the list of *-ar* verbs on p. 73. Write three sentences saying what you and your friends do in different seasons.

Multiple Intelligences

Interpersonal/Social
See Ex. 6.

Intrapersonal/Introspective
See Exs. 5, 7, and 8.

Visual/Spatial
See Students Needing Extra Help.

Present

Chapter Theme
Leisure-time activities: Sports

Communicative Objectives
- To tell where someone is
- To talk about activities
- To extend, accept, or decline invitations
- To tell how someone feels
- To tell where someone is going
- To say when and with whom you do an activity
- To express surprise, enthusiasm, or disappointment

 Overheads 18–19

 Vocabulary Art BLMs/CD-ROM

 Pronunciation Tape 3-2

 Vocabulario para conversar B

Play

Step

Using the Video
Video segment 2: See the Video Teacher's Guide.

 Video Activity B

Vocabulario para conversar

¿Te gustaría ir conmigo?

 **VIDEO** Chapter 3 Vocabulary

Here's the rest of the vocabulary you will need to talk about your leisure-time activities and to extend, accept, or decline invitations.

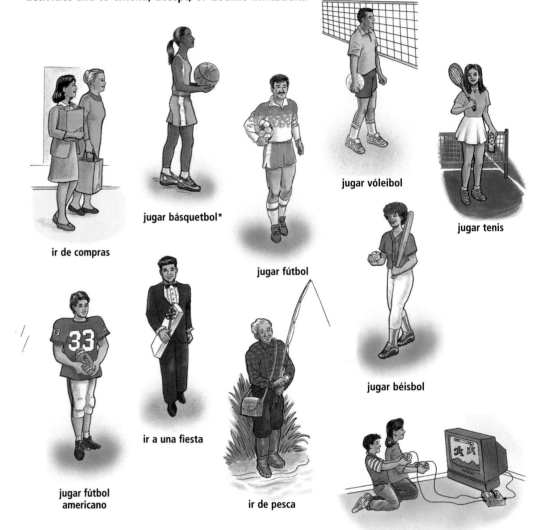

jugar vóleibol

jugar básquetbol*

ir de compras

jugar fútbol

jugar tenis

ir a una fiesta

jugar béisbol

jugar fútbol americano

ir de pesca

jugar videojuegos

* The names for these sports are all masculine, for example: el *básquetbol*.

94   Capítulo 3

Options

Strategies for Reaching All Students

Spanish-Speaking Students
Ask Spanish-speaking students to talk about their favorite leisure-time activities.

 Un paso más Exs. 3-B, 3-C

Enrichment
También necesitas. . . : Reinforce the difference between *mañana* and *por la mañana* by having students tell where they are going tomorrow morning. For example: *Mañana por la mañana voy al (a la). . . .*

Learning Spanish Through Action
STAGING VOCABULARY: *Señalen, Toquen*
MATERIALS: transparency of activities in the *Vocabulario para conversar* or pictures of similar activities from magazines
DIRECTIONS: Arrange the pictures on a bulletin board or use the transparency. Ask students to touch or point to one of the activities. You may wish to ask: *¿Te gustaría (name of activity)?* Encourage students to use any appropriate response in *También necesitas. . .* for their answers.

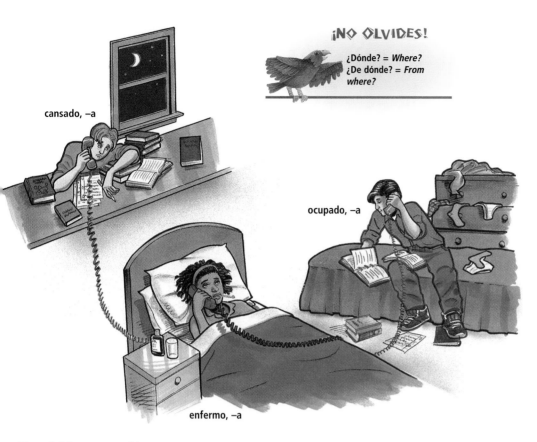

cansado, –a

¡NO OLVIDES!

¿Dónde? = Where?
¿De dónde? = From where?

ocupado, –a

enfermo, –a

También necesitas...

estar: (yo) estoy	*to be: I am*	
(tú) estás	*you are*	
¿Adónde?	*(To) where?*	
conmigo, contigo	*with me, with you*	
¿(A ti) te gustaría ___?	*Would you like ___?*	
(A mí) me gustaría ___.	*I would like ___.*	
poder: (yo) puedo	*can: I can*	
(tú) puedes	*you can*	
querer: (yo) quiero	*to want: I want*	
(tú) quieres	*you want*	

¡Claro que sí!	*Of course!*
¡Claro que no!	*Of course not!*
De nada.	*You're welcome.*
¡Genial!	*Great! Wonderful!*
¡Qué lástima!	*That's too bad! That's a shame!*

¿Y qué quiere decir...?
hoy no
mañana*

* *Mañana* alone means "tomorrow"; *la mañana* means "morning."

Vocabulario para conversar 95

Pasos vivos 1 CD-ROM
Clip Art Album

Grammar Preview
Estoy / estás are previewed here. The complete paradigm of *estar* appears in the grammar section on p. 108.

Teaching Suggestions
Preparing students to speak: Use one or two options from each of the categories of Comprehensible Input, Physical Response, or Limited Verbal Response. For a complete explanation of these categories and some sample activities, see pp. T22–T23.

Note: An explanation of stem-changing verbs and the conjugation of *jugar* appear on p. 233.

In current usage, native Spanish speakers tend to omit *a* + definite article after the verb *jugar*.

Class Starter Review
On the day following initial presentation, you might begin the class with this activity:
Call out each of the leisure-time activities. Have students signal (for example, thumbs up or thumbs down) if they like or don't like to do them. Have a volunteer keep a tally on the board of the activities that the class enjoys the most.

Internet Activities
Juegos/Have students go to www.pasoapaso.com for additional activities and practice.

Multiple Intelligences
Bodily/Kinesthetic
See Learning Spanish Through Action.
Intrapersonal/Introspective
See Class Starter Review.
Verbal/Linguistic
See Pronunciation Tape 3-2.
Visual/Spatial
See Overheads 18–19, the Vocabulary Art BLMs/CD-ROM, and Using the Video.

Standards 1.2; 4.1; 5.1   95

Practice

Re-enter / Recycle

Ex. 9: calendar expressions from *El primer paso*

Answers: Empecemos a conversar

9 ESTUDIANTE A

a. ¿Adónde vas el martes? / ¡No me digas! Yo también.

b. ...el miércoles? / ...

c. ...el jueves? / ...

d. ...el viernes? / ...

e. ...el sábado? / ...

f. ...el domingo? / ...

g. ...mañana? / ...

ESTUDIANTE B

a.–g. *Answers will vary.*
Suggested places include: Voy al centro comercial. / ...al campo. / ...al gimnasio. / ...a la playa. / ...al parque de diversiones.

10 ESTUDIANTE A

a. ¿Te gustaría jugar básquetbol conmigo?

b. ...ir de pesca...

c. ...jugar videojuegos...

d. ...ir de compras...

e. ...ir al cine...

f. ...jugar tenis...

ESTUDIANTE B

a.–f. Answers will vary. Encourage students to select a different response each time.

Empecemos a conversar

  A —*¿Adónde vas <u>el lunes</u>?*   el lunes

B —*Voy <u>al parque</u>.*

A —*¡No me digas! Yo también.*

Estudiante A   Estudiante B

a. el martes

b. el miércoles

c. el jueves

d. el viernes

e. el sábado

f. el domingo

g. mañana

10 **A** —*¿Te gustaría <u>ir a una fiesta</u> conmigo?*

B —*¿Contigo? <u>Sí, me gustaría (mucho)</u>.*

Estudiante A   Estudiante B

a.   b.   c.

d.   e.   f.

Pues, ¡claro que sí!

Lo siento, pero no puedo.

No puedo. Tengo mucha tarea.

¡Sí, genial! ¡Gracias!

¡Qué lástima! No puedo.

Sí, me gustaría (mucho).

Options

Strategies for Reaching All Students

Students Needing Extra Help

Empecemos a conversar: Have students continue filling in their Organizers.

Ex. 9: Remind *Estudiante B* to use *al* or *a la* before the pictured word.

Ex. 10: You may wish to explain responses for *Estudiante B*.

Extended Written Practice/Homework

1. Choose four activities from p. 94 and write sentences telling what you want to do and with whom.

2. Choose four activities and write questions that you could use to invite someone to do the activity with you. Indicate when you want to do the activity.

Multiple Intelligences

Musical/Rhythmic

Have the class review the days of the week with this simple chant:

Lunes, martes, miércoles, ¡tres!
(Clap, clap, clap, clap)
Jueves, viernes, sábado, ¡seis!
(Clap, clap, clap, clap)
Y domingo, siete. (Clap)

Verbal/Linguistic

See Exs. 9–11.

11

A —¿Puedes *ir al cine* conmigo?

B —Hoy no; lo siento. Estoy *ocupado(a)*.
o: ¡Claro que no! Estoy *enfermo(a)*.

Estudiante A

a.   b.   c.

d.   e.   f.

Estudiante B

a. ¿Puedes estudiar conmigo?
b. … ir de pesca …
c. … ir de compras …
d. … jugar fútbol …
e. … jugar vóleibol …
f. Questions will vary.
ESTUDIANTE B
a.–f. Answers will vary, but may include: … *Estoy ocupado(a)*, … *cansado(a)*, … *enfermo(a)*.

Practice & Apply

Ex. 12: Students can do a variation of this exercise with *Estudiante A* asking *¿Te gustaría...?* and *Estudiante B* answering *Me gustaría, pero necesito....*

Re-enter / Recycle

Ex. 12: activities from Chap. 1
Ex. 13: calendar expressions from *El primer paso*, time-telling from Chap. 2

Answers: Empecemos a conversar

12 Review activities vocabulary from Chap. 1.

ESTUDIANTE A

a. ¿Quieres ver la tele(visión)?
b. ...escuchar música?
c. ...jugar básquetbol?
d. ...jugar béisbol?
e. ...jugar fútbol americano?
f. ...jugar fútbol?
g. ...jugar vóleibol?

ESTUDIANTE B

a.–g. Answers will vary, but may include: ... *Necesito ayudar en casa,* ...*estudiar,* ...*leer,* ...*cocinar.*

12
A —¿Quieres *jugar videojuegos?*
B —Quiero, pero no puedo. Necesito *ir de compras.*
A —¡Qué lástima!

Estudiante A

a. b. c. d.
e. f. g.

Estudiante B

Options

Strategies for Reaching All Students

Spanish-Speaking Students
Ex. 12: Pair bilingual and non-bilingual students. Have them write two or three more responses for *Estudiante B*.

 Un paso más Exs. 3-D, 3-E

Students Needing Extra Help
Exs. 13–17: Have students refer to their Organizers.

Enrichment
Ex. 16: Students can also write answers to *¿Qué no te gusta hacer los fines de semana?*

Empecemos a escribir y a leer

Write your answers in Spanish.

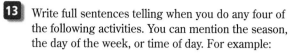

13 Write full sentences telling when you do any four of the following activities. You can mention the season, the day of the week, or time of day. For example:

En el otoño, voy a la playa los fines de semana.
or: *En la primavera, voy al campo los domingos.*

14 Write three excuses that you have learned how to say in this chapter.

15 ¿Qué te gustaría hacer hoy después de las clases?

16 ¿Qué quieres hacer el sábado por la noche?

17 ¿Es lógico o no?

"No soy nada atrevido. Al contrario, soy muy prudente. Generalmente voy al parque de diversiones cuando estoy cansado."

"¡Qué lástima! Estoy enferma hoy y no puedo ir de compras contigo."

"Soy paciente y me gusta estar sola. En el verano, cuando no estoy ocupada los fines de semana, me gusta mucho ir de pesca."

MORE PRACTICE

Más práctica y tarea, p. 515
Practice Workbook 3–3, 3–4

También se dice...

jugar baloncesto

jugar balonvolea

Vocabulario para conversar   99

Answers: Empecemos a escribir y a leer

13 Suggested activities include: *ayudar en casa, ir a la escuela, ir de compras, ir de pesca, ir a la playa, ir al cine, practicar deportes, nadar, ir al gimnasio.*

14 Answers may include: *no puedo, estoy . . .; hoy no; me gustaría, pero . . . .*

15–16 Answers will vary.

17 No es lógico; Sí, es lógico; Sí, es lógico.

 Practice Wkbk. 3-3, 3-4

 Audio Activity 3.2

 Writing Activities 3-C, 3-D

 Pruebas 3-3, 3-4

 Comm. Act. BLM 3-2

Extended Written Practice/Homework
1. Using the adjectives on p. 95, write three sentences telling what you cannot do and giving your reasons.
2. Make two columns with the headings (+) and (–). Write four or more expressions from p. 95 that you could use to accept or decline an invitation.

Multiple Intelligences
Bodily/Kinesthetic
Have students mime the activities for the vocabulary on pp. 94–95 while the rest of the class tries to guess what they are.
Interpersonal/Social
In pairs, have students talk about their "ideal" weekend.
Intrapersonal/Introspective
See Exs. 13 and 15–16.

Practice

Re-enter / Recycle
Exs. 1–3: time-telling from
Chap. 2

**Answers:
¡Comuniquemos!**

1–3 Dialogues will vary, but
encourage students to use the full
range of chapter vocabulary.

**Answers: ¿Qué sabes
ahora?**
• Me gustaría
• Quiero, no puedo
• Quieres
• gracias (no puedo, no quiero)

¡COMUNI

Your partner wants to get together with you,
but you are always busy.

A —*¿Estás ocupado(a) el sábado a las nueve?*

B —*Sí. Voy . . .*

A —*¡Qué lástima!*

Create a week's calendar on a sheet of paper.
Then for every afternoon, write in an activity
that you would like to do or might have to do.
With a partner, take turns asking each other
to join you in that activity. Your partner will
refuse politely and explain why he or she
cannot join you.

A —*¿Quieres ir al cine conmigo el jueves por
la tarde?*

B —*Me gustaría, pero voy de pesca
con Raúl.*

Options

Strategies for Reaching All Students

Spanish-Speaking Students
Ex. 3: Have students write out the
questions.

 Un paso más Exs. 3-F, 3-G

Students Needing Extra Help
Review time-telling from Chap. 2.
Ex. 3: Model the exercise. Refer to time-
telling in Chap. 2.
¿Qué sabes ahora?: Have students write out
this section so that they can check off what
they have mastered.

Enrichment
Ex. 1: Have students expand this dialogue
with *Estudiante A* asking about another time
(*¿Y el viernes a las tres?*) and *Estudiante B*
either making another excuse or saying that
he or she is free and then asking what
Estudiante A would like to do.
Ex. 2: As a written assignment, students can
continue this dialogue with *Estudiante A*
asking about another day to do the activity
and the two of them settling on a time.

You're going to a party Friday night. Find out from a partner what time the party begins and with whom he or she is going. If your partner is going alone, ask if he or she would like to go with you.

¿Qué sabes ahora?

Can you:

► say what you would like to do after class?
 —___ ir al cine después de las clases.

► say that you want to do an activity but cannot?
 —___ ir a la playa, pero ___.

► invite someone to do something with you?
 —¿___ ir de compras conmigo?

► accept or decline an invitation?
 —¿Te gustaría ir al cine el sábado?
 —Sí (No), ___.

Multicultural Perspectives

Ball games similar to soccer were popular in the Americas long before the Spaniards arrived. The Mayas played a team game on large stone courts in which the players tried to hit a large rubber ball—with their elbows, hips, or knees—through vertical wood or stone rings placed about 20 feet above the ground. Such games had a religious significance for their participants. Some scholars believe the ball represented the sun and that the two teams fought a symbolic struggle between the forces of light and darkness, or life and death. Evidence suggests that the losing team was some-times offered up as a sacrifice to the Mayan gods. Ask students to share with the class any informa-tion that they might have about games played by other cultures.

 Audio Activity 3.3

 Pasos vivos 1 CD-ROM
Slide Projector, Laboratorio de grabar

Cooperative Learning
Supply each student with a blank index card. Divide the class into groups of three. First ask students to write down a season of the year, and then to pass their cards to the right. Next, have them write an activity they like to do, based on the season written on the card they have. Finally, have them pass

the cards once more to the right. Tell them to write down an expression of frequency (for example: *todos los días, los sábados, por la mañana,* etc.). Ask a member from each group to summarize. Have the class compile all the information in a chart to find out which seasons, activities, or expressions of frequency were listed the most.

Multiple Intelligences
Interpersonal/Social
See Cooperative Learning.
Intrapersonal/Introspective
See *¿Qué sabes ahora?*
Verbal/Linguistic
See Enrichment.

Cultural Objective
- To talk about parks and leisure-time activities

Teaching Suggestions
Before they read the text, ask students to look at the photos and then discuss any similarities or differences between these parks and those in their neighborhood.

Critical Thinking: Identifying Evidence
After students have read the text, ask them: Which paragraphs provide information that parks in Spanish-speaking countries have a wide variety of family-oriented activities? (Paragraph two mentions an amusement park and a zoo. Paragraph four talks about a playground with vendors selling ice cream or balloons.)

Multicultural Perspectives
The area we now know as Chapultepec Park was developed by the Aztecs in the fourteenth century. In 1325, the Aztecs built the magnificent city of Tenochtitlán on the present-day site of Mexico City. The city, the capital of the Aztec Empire, had a population of around 100,000 in 1519, when the Spanish arrived.

Perspectiva cultural

Plazas y parques

Muchas personas, generalmente, van al parque los fines de semana. Van con la familia, con los amigos o van solas a practicar deportes, leer, visitar museos o a hacer un picnic y conversar.

El parque de Chapultepec en la Ciudad de México

Look at the photos. Why might a family often choose to spend time together in these places?

Mexico City's Chapultepec Park is one of the largest in the world. It has a castle, a zoo, a botanical garden, and a world-famous anthropological museum. It also contains an amusement park, which offers a variety of

rides—*la montaña rusa* (roller coaster), *la rueda de feria* (Ferris wheel), *los carros locos* (bumper cars), and so on.

In the Retiro Park in Madrid you could visit the Crystal Palace, where numerous expositions are held, or row a boat in the *estanque* (lake).

El parque del Retiro en Madrid, España

102   Capítulo 3

Options

Strategies for Reaching All Students

Spanish-Speaking Students
Ask: *¿Dónde está tu parque favorito? ¿Cómo es? ¿Con quién vas allí? ¿Cómo son los parques cerca de tu casa o tu escuela? ¿Qué te gustaría tener en un parque ideal? ¿Cómo sería tu parque ideal?* (Responses can be oral or written.)

 Un paso más Exs. 3-H, 3-I, 3-J

Enrichment
Additional questions for discussion: How have parks changed since you were a child? What do you think parks will be like in the future? What kinds of things do you like to do in parks? What would your ideal park be like?

Multiple Intelligences
Intrapersonal/Introspective
See Enrichment.
Have students bring in pictures of well-known American parks and ask them to compare them to those shown in the photos.

La plaza de Armas en Iquitos, Perú

However, most parks are not very big. In small cities and towns, the main outdoor gathering place would be a *plaza,* a small green area that usually includes a small playground. Like the park, the *plaza* is where people meet to exchange news and local gossip, and where vendors sell *paletas* (popsicles or ice cream bars) or *globos* (balloons). In many cities, the *plaza,* or town square, is truly the heart of town. Many families will often spend an entire Sunday afternoon in a *plaza* or a park.

▲▲▲▲▲▲▲▲▲▲▲▲▲▲▲▲▲▲▲▲▲▲▲▲▲▲▲

La cultura desde tu perspectiva

1 In what ways are parks in Spanish-speaking countries similar to or different from parks that you know? Have you ever visited a park that has facilities similar to the ones in Chapultepec or El Retiro?

2 If you lived near El Retiro or Chapultepec, how often do you think you would go there? Why?

▼▼▼▼▼▼▼▼▼▼▼▼▼▼▼▼▼▼▼▼▼▼▼▼▼▼▼

Cultural Activity · www.pasoapaso.com

Perspectiva cultural   103

Although Chapultepec Park may be enjoyed by everyone today, its use originally was restricted to Aztec emperors. Ask students to share any information that they might have about the Aztecs.

Answers
Possible answers to inductive questions: Students may say that families might often choose to spend time together in parks, such as the ones in the photos, because they offer attractive, well-equipped facilities that appeal to people.

Answers: La cultura desde tu perspectiva
1 Answers will vary. Similarities may include: gardens, paths, lakes, fountains, monuments, etc. Differences may include: castles, zoos, restaurants, and amusement parks. / Answers will vary.

2 Answers will vary.

 Pasos vivos 1 CD-ROM
Notas culturales, Maps

 Internet Activities
Perspectiva cultural
Have students go to www.pasoapaso.com for additional activities and practice.

Cultural Notes
(p. 103; bottom photo) ice cream vendor in San José, Costa Rica.

Cultural Notes ☀

(p. 102, bottom photo)
El parque del Retiro in Madrid is a large, elegantly planned park. Dating to 1630, it was originally intended to be a *buen retiro* (nice retreat) for Felipe IV. Today it serves that function for the millions who go there to stroll, picnic, rent rowboats on its central lake (which is graced by a statue of Spain's twentieth-century monarch, Alfonso XII), and enjoy puppet theater, art exhibits, and concerts.

(pp. 102–103, top photo)
El parque de Chapultepec is the largest and most important park in Mexico City. The area is also a very old recreation spot, having been used by Aztec kings as a summer residence. Chapultepec is especially crowded on Sundays, when families come to stroll, picnic, and otherwise enjoy the many attractions the park has to offer. Among them are a world-famous zoo, an amusement park, fountains, lakes, museums, and art galleries.

(p. 103; top right photo)
The chief town of Peru's jungle region, Iquitos, is located right on the Amazon and is linked to the rest of Peru only by river and air. During the rubber boom of the late nineteenth century, Iquitos became known as the "Pearl of the Amazon" for the luxurious residences of its rubber barons. Discuss with students the ideas people have about frontier or boom towns and how these kinds of towns in the U.S. compare with Iquitos.

Gramática en contexto

Look at the brochure describing a family vacation camp. What kind of information would you expect to find in a brochure such as this?

A Find the sentence that tells where the camp is located. What verb is used? How many times does it appear in the brochure?

B What activities are planned for guests? What verb is used with each pair of activities? (HINT: You already know two forms of the verb *ir: voy* and *vas*.) What do you think the *ustedes* and *nosotros* forms of the verb *ir* might be?

C In the brochure, *van a* is always followed by a verb. What do you think *van a nadar* and *van a escuchar música* mean? Based on what you've seen here, could you create a rule for this?

104   Capítulo 3

Options

Strategies for Reaching All Students

Students Needing Extra Help
Have students fill in the *ir* chart in the grammar portion of the Organizer.
Ex. 2: Remind students that the verb form changes in some responses. Show how the *a* in *adónde* is shown again in the answers as *al* or *a la.*

Extended Written Practice/Homework
1. Write three sentences telling where you and your friends or you and your family go. Tell when you go to those places.
2. Using *mis profesores,* write three sentences telling how often you think your teachers go to different places.

Multiple Intelligences
Bodily/Kinesthetic
On a piece of cubed plastic foam, write in bold letters the subject pronouns. Toss out the cube to students and when they catch it, ask them to give the appropriate form of the verb *ir* that matches the subject pronoun. Ask for volunteers to form complete sentences.

El verbo *ir*

You know that verbs whose infinitives end in *-ar* follow a pattern. The endings show who is doing the action: *(yo) cocino, (tú) cocinas,* and so on.

- Verbs that follow certain patterns are called regular verbs. Those that do not follow those patterns are called irregular. The verb *ir,* "to go," is irregular. It is often followed by the word *a:* *¿Vas a la escuela? Voy al cine.* Here are its present-tense forms.

(yo)	**voy**	(nosotros) (nosotras)	**vamos**
(tú)	**vas**	(vosotros) (vosotras)	**vais**
Ud. (él) (ella)	**va**	Uds. (ellos) (ellas)	**van**

1 Based on the chart, with which of the following people would you use the verb form *van?* What forms of *ir* would you use with the other people?

a. Julia y Nicolás
b. Carlos
c. José Luis
d. Bárbara y tú
e. María Elena
f. mis amigos
g. Lourdes y Andrés
h. Marcos y yo

2 Find out from three people where they are going this weekend. For example:

A —*¿Adónde vas el sábado por la tarde?*

B —*Voy a la (al) . . .*

Then tell your partner where each of them is going.

Esteban va al gimnasio. Rosa y Miguel van al centro comercial.

Gramática en contexto   105

Present & Practice

Re-enter / Recycle
Exs. 3–5: activities from Chap. 1

Answers
3 Answers a, d, and h happen regularly. Answers b, c, e, f, and g are going to happen in the future.

4 a.–h. Look for correct use of *¿Vas a* + inf.? and *Sí (No), voy a* + inf.

5 Statements will vary, but look for correct use of *(No) va a* + inf.

 Practice Wkbk. 3-6

 Writing Activity 3-F

 Prueba 3-6

Cultural Notes
(p. 106, realia)
Originally a tailor's shop in Madrid, El Corte Inglés was bought in 1928 by Ramón Areces Rodríguez, who expanded and transformed it into a luxury department store with branches throughout Spain. El Corte Inglés now also has travel, insurance, and publishing businesses. This ad invites readers to experience the adventure of their lives. The cover shows fanciful Chinese figures, an idealized pre-Columbian Mexican landscape, and vacationers on a roller coaster swooping down between herds of bison. Ask

Ir + a + infinitivo

We also use a form of the verb *ir + a* + infinitive to tell what someone is going to do.

> Yo **voy a nadar.** Y tú, **¿vas a jugar** fútbol?

3 Which of these things happen regularly and which ones are going to happen in the future?

  a. Voy a la piscina los sábados.
  b. Voy a nadar.
  c. Vamos a ayudar en casa mañana.
  d. Ella va a la escuela todos los días.
  e. Van a jugar fútbol por la tarde.
  f. Vas a tener mucha tarea.
  g. Va a estar cansada.
  h. Generalmente voy al gimnasio.

4 With a partner, take turns asking and answering whether or not you're going to do these things tomorrow.

ir al cine

  A —*¿Vas a ir al cine mañana por la tarde?*
  B —*Sí, voy a ir.*
     o: *No, voy a ir al centro comercial.*

a. estudiar	e. jugar básquetbol
b. ayudar en casa	f. jugar fútbol americano
c. ir al centro comercial	g. jugar vóleibol
d. ir a una fiesta	h. jugar béisbol

5 Based on the answers your partner gave in Exercise 4, tell another student two things your partner will and will not do tomorrow.

Juan va a jugar béisbol mañana pero no va a ir al centro comercial.

If there is something that both of you—or neither of you—will do, report that too.

(No) vamos a . . .

Niños paseando en bote en el estanque de la Plaza de España, Sevilla

¡NO OLVIDES!
Infinitives always end in *-r* in Spanish

Options

Strategies for Reaching All Students

Spanish-Speaking Students
Ex. 4: Have students write five statements about themselves.
Ex. 5: Have them write five statements about their partners.

Students Needing Extra Help
Ex. 4: Model, emphasizing the *ir + a* + inf. construction. Point out that in the example and in c and d the infinitive is *ir,* as this may cause confusion. Have students write out responses in preparation for Ex. 5.
Ex. 5: Point out that *voy* in the responses for Ex. 4 becomes *va* when referring to another person.
La preposición con: Have students fill in this grammar portion of their Organizers.

Ex. 6: Remind students that *conmigo* is answered with *contigo.*
Ex. 7: Show students how a female name is replaced with *ella* and a male name with *él.* Students may need a model to see that *Uds.* becomes *nosotros (-as)* in the answer, and that *tú* will become *contigo* and will be answered with *conmigo.*

La preposición *con*

Con may be used with the names of people or in the following ways:

conmigo	con nosotros / nosotras
contigo	con vosotros / vosotras
con Ud. / él / ella	con Uds. / ellos / ellas

6 With a partner, take turns asking each other about doing these activities together.

estudiar

A —*¿Quieres estudiar conmigo después de las clases?*

B —*¿Contigo? ¡Claro que sí!*
   o: *¿Estudiar contigo? Me gustaría, pero no puedo.*

a. ver la tele
b. practicar deportes
c. ir al gimnasio
d. ir de compras
e. jugar videojuegos
f. jugar tenis
g. jugar fútbol
h.

7 Take turns asking a partner with whom he or she would like to do these activities.

A —*¿Con quién te gustaría ir al cine el sábado?*

B —*Con Alicia.*

A —*¿Con ella?*

B —*Sí, con ella.*

Alicia

a. Susana y Julia

b. Marcelo y Graciela

c. Uds.

d. Marcos

e. Ana María

f. tú

Gramática en contexto   107

students why they think this ad would appeal to potential tourists in Spain, and how they would change it for a U.S. audience.

6 ESTUDIANTE A
a. ¿Quieres ver la tele conmigo después de las clases?

b. . . . practicar deportes . . .
c. . . . ir al gimnasio . . .
d. . . . ir de compras . . .
e. . . . jugar videojuegos . . .
f. . . . jugar tenis . . .
g. . . . jugar fútbol . . .
h. Questions will vary.

ESTUDIANTE B
a.–h. Answers will vary.

7 ESTUDIANTE A
a. ¿Con quién te gustaría ir de compras el sábado? / ¿Con ellas?
b. . . . ir al parque de diversiones . . . / ¿Con ellos?
c. . . . ir a una fiesta . . . / ¿Con nosotros(as)?
d. . . . ir al gimnasio . . . / ¿Con él?
e. . . . patinar . . . / ¿Con ella?
f. . . . nadar . . . / ¿Conmigo?

ESTUDIANTE B
a. Con Susana y Julia. / Sí, con ellas.
b. Con Marcelo y Graciela. / Sí, con ellos.
c. Con Uds. / Sí, con Uds.
d. Con Marcos. / Sí, con él.
e. Con Ana María. / Sí, con ella.
f. Contigo. / Sí, contigo.

Practice Wkbk. 3-7

Writing Activity 3-G

Prueba 3-7

Cultural Notes

Enrichment
Ex. 4: As a written assignment, students can tell what they are going to do on each day of the weekend, specifying whether they'll be doing it alone or with family or friends.

Extended Written Practice/Homework
1. Using activities from pp. 30–31 and p. 94, write four sentences telling what your friends are going to do.
2. Write four questions that you can ask your classmates to find out when they are going to do different activities.

3. Write an invitation. Include a question inviting the person to go to a place with you and a statement telling what you are going to do there.

Multiple Intelligences
Verbal/Linguistic
See Exs. 4–7.
Visual/Spatial
See Practice Wkbk. 3-7 and Writing Activity 3-G.

(p. 106, photo)
Sevilla is a historic city full of beautiful palaces and cathedrals. It was the home of Don Juan Tenorio and the setting for the operas *Carmen* and *El barbero de Sevilla*. La plaza de España is located in the Parque María Luisa, and contains two towers that were designed by Aníbal González, Sevilla's most prominent architect of the twentieth century.

Class Starter Review
On the day following the initial presentation of *estar,* you might begin the class with this activity: Use the Vocabulary Art BLMs/ CD-ROM showing the places in the *Vocabulario para conversar* and Overhead 76 (subject pronouns). Have pairs of students alternate saying where different people are.

Answers
8 ESTUDIANTE A

a. ¿Dónde está Rosa?

b. ...está José Antonio?

c. ...están Uds.?

d. ...están Carolina y Lucía?

e. ...está Silvia?

f. ...estás (tú)?

ESTUDIANTE B

a. Está en el parque.

b. Está en el parque de diversiones.

c. Estamos en el centro comercial.

d. Están en el gimnasio.

e. Está en la piscina.

f. *Answers will vary, but should begin with* Estoy.

El verbo *estar*

Estar ("to be") is an irregular verb. We use it to tell how someone feels or where someone is. Here are its present-tense forms.

(yo)	**estoy**	(nosotros) (nosotras)	**estamos**
(tú)	**estás**	(vosotros) (vosotras)	**estáis**
Ud. (él) (ella)	**está**	Uds. (ellos) (ellas)	**están**

• In writing, be sure to use the accent mark on all forms except *estoy* and *estamos*.

8 With a partner, take turns asking and answering where these people are.

A —¿Dónde está Alejandro?

B —Está en el campo.

Alejandro

a. Rosa	**b. José Antonio**	**c. Uds.**

d. Carolina y Lucía	**e. Silvia**	**f. tú**

Options

Strategies for Reaching All Students

Students Needing Extra Help
Have students fill in the *estar* chart in the grammar portion of the Organizer.
Ex. 8: Have students use the Organizer.
Ahora lo sabes: Have students write out this section so that they can check off what they have mastered.

Extended Written Practice/Homework
1. Choose four members of your class and tell how they are feeling using *bien, enfermo(a), ocupado(a),* or *cansado(a).*
2. Write two or more sentences telling what things are in your desk and backpack.

Multiple Intelligences
Bodily/Kinesthetic
Use the cube made of plastic foam with the subject pronouns. (See Multiple Intelligences, p. 104). Toss the cube out to students and ask for the correct present-tense verb form of *estar.* Ask for volunteers to make complete sentences, questions, or negative statements.
Interpersonal/Social
See Ex. 10.
Verbal/Linguistic
See Exs. 8 and 10.

9 Can you find the answers in column B to the questions in column A?

A	**B**
a. ¿Cómo está Paco?	Estamos enfermos.
b. ¿Cómo está Ud.?	Estoy cansado(a).
c. ¿Cómo estás?	Está enfermo.
d. ¿Cómo están Uds.?	

10 Find out from several classmates how they are feeling today. Take turns asking and answering using *bien, enfermo(a),* or *cansado(a)*. Keep a log for reporting this information. For example:

You ask Bárbara: *¿Cómo estás hoy?*

She answers: *Estoy cansada.*

You write in your log: *Bárbara está cansada.*

Ahora lo sabes

Can you:

► say where someone is going?
—Mariana y yo ___ a la piscina.

► say what someone is going to do?
—Alejandro y Marta ___ jugar básquetbol mañana.

► say who does an activity with you?
—Mis amigos estudian ___ después de las clases.

► say how someone feels?
—Felipe ___ muy cansado hoy.

► say where someone is?
—José y Ana ___ aquí.

MORE PRACTICE

- Más práctica y tarea, p. 515–516
- Practice Workbook 3–5, 3–9

Jugando béisbol en la República Dominicana

PASO CULTURAL

American sailors introduced baseball to Cuba well over 100 years ago. From there its popularity spread to other Spanish-speaking countries of the Caribbean. Today, only the U.S. has produced more baseball superstars than the small nation of the Dominican Republic. Although baseball in Spanish has its own terms, such as *golpe* (strike), *lanzador* (pitcher), and *sencillo* (single), some terms are taken from English. What do you think *jonrón* might mean?

Gramática en contexto 109

9 a. Está enfermo.
b. Estoy cansado(a).
c. Estoy cansado(a).
d. Estamos enfermos.

10 Questions and answers will vary, but look for correct *estar* forms + adjective agreement.

Answers: Ahora lo sabes
- vamos
- van a
- conmigo
- está
- están

 Practice Wkbk. 3-8, 3-9

 Audio Activity 3.4

 Writing Activity 3-H

 Prueba 3-8

 Comm. Act. BLM 3-3

 Pasos vivos 1 CD-ROM

Bulletin Board, Slide Presentation Maker, Spindle, Treadmill

Apply

 Pronunciation Tape 3-3

 Todo junto A

Play

Todo junto B

Play

Using the Video
Video segment 3: See the Video Teacher's Guide.

 Video Activity C

 Pasos vivos 1 CD-ROM
Video Monitor, Video Presentation Maker

Re-enter / Recycle
Exs. 1–2: days of the week from *El primer paso*

Answers: Actividades
1 Questions and answers will vary, but look for correct use of *ir* forms. Places may include: *el centro comercial, el campo, la playa, el cine, el parque de diversiones, la piscina, el gimnasio, el parque.*

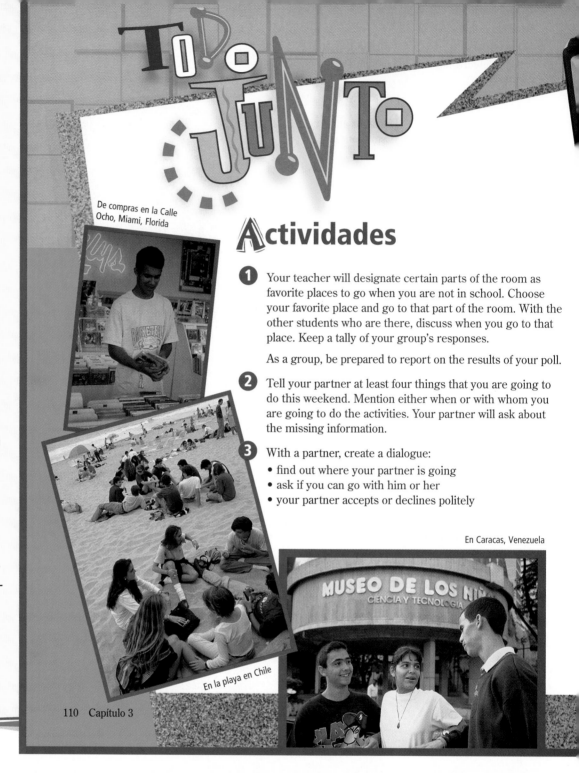

De compras en la Calle Ocho, Miami, Florida

Todo junto

Actividades

1. Your teacher will designate certain parts of the room as favorite places to go when you are not in school. Choose your favorite place and go to that part of the room. With the other students who are there, discuss when you go to that place. Keep a tally of your group's responses.

   As a group, be prepared to report on the results of your poll.

2. Tell your partner at least four things that you are going to do this weekend. Mention either when or with whom you are going to do the activities. Your partner will ask about the missing information.

3. With a partner, create a dialogue:
   • find out where your partner is going
   • ask if you can go with him or her
   • your partner accepts or declines politely

En Caracas, Venezuela

MUSEO DE LOS NIÑOS
CIENCIA Y TECNOLOGIA

En la playa en Chile

110   Capítulo 3

Options

Strategies for Reaching All Students

Spanish-Speaking Students
Pair bilingual and non-bilingual students for the activities in this section.

Students Needing Extra Help
Ex. 1: Brainstorm possibilities for places. (See Exs. 1–2, p. 92.)
Ex. 2: Remind students of interrogatives for asking questions in this activity: *¿cuándo?/¿con quién(es)?*
Ex. 3: Model and have students use the Organizer.

Enrichment
Ex. 3: As a written assignment, students can modify the dialogue to include asking with whom their partner is going.

Multiple Intelligences
Interpersonal/Social
See Cooperative Learning.
Logical/Mathematical
See *Conexiones*.
Visual/Spatial
See Using the Video.

Cooperative Learning
Divide the class into groups of four. Have each group brainstorm and prepare a list of activities that they and their friends are going to do this weekend. After a time limit of five minutes, have one member from each group share the results with the class.

Conexiones

 La estadística

Las ciencias sociales

Los pasatiempos

The table below, based on one from the Spanish magazine *Cambio 16,* shows the results of a poll concerning how people spend their free time. How does this compare with your favorite leisure-time activities?

Working in groups of four, ask each person how often he or she does the activities listed in the table. For example: *¿Con qué frecuencia practicas deportes?* Designate one person as *secretario(a)* to keep a tally.

• Collect your group's data. As a whole-class activity, total each group's tally to make a class total for each activity.

• Convert each total to a percentage.

• Create a double bar graph that compares the Spanish statistics to your class's statistics.

FRECUENCIA CON QUE PRACTICAN DEPORTES

 = Clase de España
 = Esta clase

	CON FRECUENCIA	A VECES	NUNCA
Practicar deportes	12	11	65
Ir a competiciones deportivas	6	14	62
Ver la televisión	51	36	4
Ir al cine/teatro	6	20	49
Ir a conciertos/óperas	2	8	76
Ir al campo, al parque, etc.	6	24	48
Ir de compras	7	42	21
Leer	22	23	30
Ayudar en casa	4	10	74

Todo junto 111

2 Dialogues will vary, but encourage students to use the full range of previously learned vocabulary.

3 Dialogues will vary, but look for correct use of *ir* forms, *puedo / puedes,* and *conmigo / contigo.* To decline an invitation, remind students that they can use expressions such as: *Tengo mucha tarea. / No me gusta ___. / Necesito ___.*

Answers: Conexiones
Graphs will vary.

Teaching Suggestions
Remind students that, in order to calculate the percentages, they divide the number of students that do an activity *con frecuencia, a veces,* or *nunca* by the total number of students in the class and multiply the result by 100.

Writing Activity 3-I

Comm. Act. BLMs 3-4, 3-5

Pasos vivos 1 CD-ROM
A Jugar, Boom Box, Laboratorio de grabar, Maps, Spindle

Cultural Notes

(p. 110, top photo)
Cuba has long been a cultural crossroads, and its music draws on a variety of international influences. Combining African rhythms and harmonies with European instrumentation, *salsa* and *son* have set the standard for Latin dance music. Ask students to compare Cuban music with different kinds of American music that have also been influenced by African rhythms and harmonies.

(p. 110, center photo)
Chile's coastline is 2,800 miles long, but on average the country is no more than 120 miles wide. This means that no Chilean is more than a day's drive from the coast. During the summer months, residents of the central valley flock to the beach, and even the Chilean congress and president relocate to the coast. Ask students to discuss what they know about the geography of various Latin American countries.

(p. 110, bottom photo)
Caracas's Parque Central is a popular gathering place for local teenagers. Among its attractions are the Museo de los Niños, which is a sophisticated modern science museum, the Museo Audiovisual, the Museo del Teclado *(keyboard),* and the Museo de Arte Contemporáneo. Ask students which of these museums appeals most to them and to name museums in the U.S. that have similar focuses or specialties.

Apply

Process Reading

For a description of process reading, see p. 48.

Teaching Suggestions

For sections 3–4 in *Infórmate*, emphasize the concepts rather than the content. For example, in Mexico, Spain, and South America, the 24-hour clock tends to be used in advertisements for events.

Explain that people from the U.S. making purchases in other countries will need to know the exchange rate and use a little math to calculate prices.

Using a map or globe, refer to the calendar of events and ask students: Do you know in what country this city is located? (Mexico) Do you know what major U.S. city Ciudad Juárez borders on? (El Paso, Texas)

Answers
Antes de leer

Answers will vary, but may include activities along with their respective information for location, date, time, and price of admission.

Mira la lectura

1 Friday, Saturday, and Sunday

2 Saturday offers the greatest selection of activities with theater, sports (soccer), and music (concerts).

3 Answers will vary.

¡Vamos a leer!

Antes de leer

STRATEGY > Using prior knowledge

Earlier you used your own experience with certain kinds of reading materials to predict the types of information you might find in a pen pal column or report card. If you are looking at a calendar of events, what types of information would you expect to find?

Remember that what you already know about a newspaper section like this in English can help you predict, look for, and even understand information in Spanish.

Mira la lectura

STRATEGY > Skimming

Look at the calendar of events, noting the title, format, illustrations, and boldface headings.

1 Which days of the week are featured?

2 Which day offers the greatest selection of activities? What kinds of events are there?

3 Do you find the display ad effective? Does it contain all the information a reader would need? Did you find what you expected to find?

112 Capítulo 3

Options

Strategies for Reaching All Students

Students Needing Extra Help

Some of your students may not be familiar with the newspaper format. Have one available for reference.
Infórmate: This would make a good small-group or whole-class activity. For section 4, explain the concept of money having different values in foreign countries. Bring in samples of foreign currency along with the exchange rate from the business pages of a newspaper.

Enrichment

Bring in calendars of events from local newspapers and discuss the cultural differences between the events listed there and in those in the text.
Ask students to pick an event to go to, tell a partner about it, and invite him or her to come along. The partner can accept or

decline, in the latter case giving a reason why he or she cannot go.
As an extension activity, have students make a newspaper listing for an activity taking place in their school or community this weekend. Follow the same format that is used in this section and provide the same kind of information.

Infórmate

STRATEGY ➤ **Scanning**

Using the ad, make plans for Saturday night.

1 Look at the calendar of events and identify four places to go on Saturday, then choose the one you would like to go to.

2 Find the following information for the place you choose:

- Lugar (cine; concierto; partido de fútbol; teatro)
- Nombre de la película / del grupo musical / del equipo de fútbol / de la obra de teatro
- Dirección
- Hora
- Admisión

3 What seems unusual about some of the times given? How else could you express 20:00?

The following movie times are based on the 24-hour clock. How would they read according to the 12-hour clock?

11:15   13:45   16:20   18:50   21:30

4 N$ means *nuevos pesos*. When the Mexican government revalued the peso in the spring of 1993, N$ 3 equaled US $1. Given this information, figure out the price of admission to the place you selected in United States dollars.

Aplicación

Take a poll to see which of the activities mentioned in the calendar of events would be the most popular among your classmates.

¡Vamos a leer! 113

Cultural Notes

(p. 112, realia)
The Mexico City Ballet Folklórico Nacional Aztlán performs twice weekly in the elegant Teatro de la Ciudad, a stately, neoclassical building inaugurated in 1912. Tickets are less expensive and easier to obtain for performances of the newer, yet very distinguished troupe than for those of the world-famous Ballet Folklórico, whose spectacular repertoire of traditional dances is performed in the theater of the Palacio de Bellas Artes.

(p. 112, realia)
With a population of approximately 1 million, Ciudad Juárez is the largest city in the state of Chihuahua. Twin city to El Paso, Texas, Ciudad Juárez is the *maquiladora* (U.S.-owned factory) center of Mexico, with an estimated 65 percent of its working population employed in industry.
As in many cities in Mexico, Ciudad Juárez is strongly influenced by American culture just as El Paso, for example, is by Mexican culture.

(p. 113, realia)
As of 1998, ten Mexican *nuevos pesos* equaled one U.S. dollar. Emiliano Zapata, hero from the early twentieth-century Mexican revolution, is pictured on the ten-peso bill. The current *zapatista* rebel group from Chiapas is named after him. The fifty-peso bill pictures José María Morelos, leader in the nineteenth-century revolt against Spain.

Apply

Teaching Suggestions
If students ask why *estar* is used in the invitation *(¡La fiesta va a estar fantástica!)* instead of *ser,* tell them we often use *estar* for emphatic use in describing things in Spanish. (All the present-tense forms of *ser* will be taught in Chap. 5.)

**Pasos vivos 1
CD-ROM**
Word Processor

¡Vamos a escribir!

You and a friend are giving a party. Plan your party and write the invitation you will send to your friends. Follow these steps.

1 Think about what you are going to do at the party. A checklist will help you plan. With a partner, write a list in Spanish of the activities and when each might begin. For example:

Actividad   Hora

Vamos a . . .   a las . . .

2 Next, write the invitation. Include the day and time, your names, the address, and what you are going to do. Here is a model blank invitation:

_____ y _____ te invitan a una

FIESTA

Cuándo: el _____ de _____ a la(s) _____

Dónde: _____

Actividades: En la fiesta vamos a
_____
_____
_____

¡LA FIESTA VA A ESTAR FANTÁSTICA!

Fiesta de cumpleaños en
Quintana Roo, México ►

114   Capítulo 3

Options

Strategies for Reaching All Students

Spanish-Speaking Students
Have students respond in writing to the invitation. If they cannot go to the party, they should express regrets and tell why.

 Un paso más Ex. 3-K

Students Needing Extra Help
If you elect not to use the model, brainstorm and develop an invitation. Give each student a copy or make one on the chalkboard or overhead. Have students use the Organizer for Chaps. 2 and 3.
Step 4: Have students use their Organizers.

Enrichment
Encourage students to be creative with their invitations, using different kinds of lettering, pictures, and layout to present the information. Students might also want to include sentences indicating acceptance or refusal with a blank space after them for invitees to check off.

3 Exchange invitations with another group and share any suggestions for improvement. Is there enough information, or should something be added?

4 Think about their suggestions and any other changes you may want to make. Rewrite your invitation. Check it for spelling and punctuation, including accents. Let the other group check it too. Ask them if you have included all the necessary information.

5 Now recopy your corrected invitation. You may want to file it in a writing portfolio.

¡Vamos a escribir! 115

Multiple Intelligences
Bodily/Kinesthetic
See Enrichment.
Logical/Mathematical and Musical/Rhythmic
Have students create a "singing telegram" inviting a special friend to a party. Then have the class create a scale with categories (most original, best singing, etc.) for evaluating the telegrams. After several volunteers perform their telegrams, have the class choose the top one in each category.

Cultural Notes

(p. 115, photo)
In much of Mexico, U.S.-style birthday parties are popular, but in traditional Mexican families girls especially look forward to their fifteenth birthday, or *quinceañera*. This celebration combines a church service and a formal party in which family members reaffirm their faith in and love for one another. Ask students to discuss what they know of similar celebrations in other cultures for young people coming of age.

Assess & Summarize

Test Preparation

You may want to assign parts of this section as written homework or as an in-class writing activity prior to administering the *Examen de habilidades*.

Answers

Listening:
—Margarita, ¿te gustaría ir al cine el domingo por la tarde?
—Claro que sí, Luis; pero no puedo. Tengo mucha tarea.
No, Margarita is not going to the movies with Luis.

Reading: Ruth would like to go shopping Friday. Saturday morning she wants to go swimming at the beach and in the evening go skating with friends. On Sunday she needs to sleep, but would like to go to the movies in the afternoon. / She is spending the weekend in Miami.

Writing: Paragraphs will vary, but look for the use of *me / te gustaría*, *quiero / quieres*, and *puedo / puedes* + inf.

This section will help you organize your studying for the proficiency test, where you will be asked to do similar, though not identical, tasks. There will not be any models on the test.

▶ **Listening**
Can you understand when people talk about their free-time activities? Listen as your teacher reads you a sample similar to what you will hear on the test. Is Margarita going to the movies with Luis or not?

▶ **Reading**
Can you look at this letter and get an idea of how Ruth is planning to spend her weekend? In what city is Ruth spending the weekend?

> Querida Isabel:
> Voy a estar contigo tres días allí en Miami. El viernes me gustaría ir de compras todo el día. ¿Puedes ir conmigo? El sábado por la mañana quiero ir a la playa a nadar y por la noche quiero ir a patinar con mis amigos. El domingo necesito dormir. Soy muy perezosa, pero me gustaría ir al cine por la tarde. Y tú, ¿qué prefieres?
>
> Saludos,
> Ruth

▶ **Writing**
Can you write a note to a classmate in which you decline an invitation and say why? You should also suggest other days when you are free and what you would like to do. Here is a sample:

> Rebeca:
> Me gustaría mucho ir de compras contigo el viernes, pero estoy ocupada. El sábado, claro que sí, no tengo ni clase ni tarea. Me gustaría ir a nadar por la mañana, y por la noche me gustaría ir al cine. También me gustaría ir contigo al campo el domingo. ¿Quieres ir?
>
> Cecilia

▶ **Culture**
Can you compare a *plaza* to a park such as El Retiro or Chapultepec?

▶ **Speaking**
Can you invite your partner to do an activity with you? You and your partner should agree on what to do, where, and when. For example:

A —¿Te gustaría jugar básquetbol?
B —Sí, pero prefiero ir a patinar.
A —¡Genial! ¿Adónde vamos? ¿Al parque?
B —Sí. ¿A qué hora? ¿Puedes ir a las 9:00?
A —No, necesito ir de compras con mi familia. ¿Y a las 11:00?
B —Sí, a las 11:00.

La Plaza de Armas en Santiago, Chile

self Test · www.pasoapaso.com

Options

Strategies for Reaching All Students

Spanish-Speaking Students
 Un paso más Ex. 3-L

Students Needing Extra Help
Have students write out this section so that they can check off what they have mastered.

Resumen del vocabulario

Use the vocabulary from this chapter to help you:

► talk about some of your leisure-time activities

► make plans with friends

► extend, accept, or decline invitations

to tell how someone feels or where someone is
¿Dónde?
estar: (yo) estoy
        (tú) estás

to tell where someone is going
¿Adónde?
ir: (yo) voy
    (tú) vas
a
a la, al (a + el)
el campo
el centro comercial
el gimnasio
el parque
el parque de diversiones
la piscina
la playa

to talk about activities
ir a una fiesta
ir de compras
ir de pesca
jugar básquetbol
jugar béisbol
jugar fútbol
jugar fútbol americano
jugar tenis

jugar videojuegos
jugar vóleibol
el pasatiempo

to say when you do an activity
la estación, *pl.* estaciones
    la primavera
    el verano
    el otoño
    el invierno
el lunes, el martes . . .
los lunes, los martes . . .
el fin (los fines) de semana
después de (las clases)
(por) la mañana
        la tarde
        la noche
generalmente
hoy no
mañana
todos los días

to say with whom you do an activity
con
conmigo, contigo
el amigo, la amiga
la familia
solo, -a

to extend, accept, or decline invitations
¿(A ti) te gustaría ___?
(A mí) me gustaría ___.
poder: (yo) puedo
        (tú) puedes
querer: (yo) quiero
        (tú) quieres
¡Claro que sí!
¡Claro que no!
De nada.
cansado, -a
enfermo, -a
ocupado, -a

to express surprise, enthusiasm, or disappointment
¡No me digas!
¡Genial!
¡Qué lástima!

to express possession
mi, mis
tus

Resumen   117

Culture: Answers will vary, but may include: A *plaza* is usually a small green area with a playground that may serve as the town square. A park such as Chapultepec contains an amusement park, a castle, a zoo, a botanical garden, and a museum.

Speaking: Dialogues will vary, but look for *me / te gustaría, puedo / puedes,* and *quiero / quieres* + inf.

Assessment

 Prueba cumulativa

 Examen de habilidades

 Test Generator

Additional Assessment Options

 Comm. Act. BLMs

Small Group Activities
Situation Cards

 Pasos vivos 1 CD-ROM

Slide Presentation Maker, Video Presentation Maker, Word Processor, Spindle

 ¿Lo sabes bien? Video Quiz

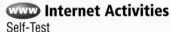 **Internet Activities**
Self-Test

Cultural Notes

(p. 116, photo)
The skyline of Santiago, Chile combines ornate colonial architecture with contemporary steel-and-glass highrises. The old Plaza de Armas, shown in this photo, is at the heart of the city. Ask students to describe cities throughout the U.S. in which the original or historic district has been preserved or showcased as the rest of the city has developed around it.

Capítulo 4

THEME: FOOD

SCOPE AND SEQUENCE   Pages 118–149

COMMUNICATION

Topics

Foods and drinks

Likes, dislikes, and preferences

Objectives

To talk about eating customs in Spanish-speaking countries

To describe meals and talk about foods and drinks

To express likes or preferences

To indicate frequency

To refer to obligation

To indicate hunger or thirst

To refer to something you cannot name

To express an opinion

To ask for and give an explanation

To elicit agreement

CULTURE

Meals and mealtimes

GRAMMAR

El plural de los sustantivos

El plural de los adjetivos

Verbos que terminan en -er

Sujetos compuestos

Ancillaries available for use with Chapter 4

Multisensory/Technology

 Overheads, 21–25

 Audio Tapes and CDs

 Vocabulary Art Blackline Masters for Hands-On Learning, pp. 23–27/CD-ROM

Classroom Crossword

Video

 Pasos vivos 1 CD-ROM

 Internet Activities www.pasoapaso.com

Print

 Practice Workbook, pp. 43–52

 Writing, Audio & Video Activities, pp. 23–28, 102–104, 158–159

 Communicative Activity Blackline Masters

  Pair and Small Group Activities, pp. 29–34

  Situation Cards, p. 35

 Un paso más: Actividades para ampliar tu español, pp. 20–25

TPR Storytelling

Assessment

 Assessment Program

  Pruebas, pp. 52–62

  Examen de habilidades, pp. 63–66

 Test Generator

Video still from Chap. 4

Planning Express, Teaching
Resources Library, and Clip Art
Library

¿Lo sabes bien?
Video Quiz

Cultural Overview

Revolutionary Foods

Although Columbus and the other European explorers who followed him to the Americas did not find the spices that they sought, they were introduced to a wealth of new foods far more valuable. In time, these foods would not only profoundly affect people's diets, but they would change the course of history.

One of the most important foods cultivated in the Americas was the potato, which today is the world's most widely grown vegetable. Potatoes probably were first grown in the valleys of the Andes by the Incas. In the mid-1500s, Spanish and English explorers introduced the tubers to Europe, where they were initially rejected as a food source because of a widespread fear that root crops caused disease.

Today, potatoes are still an important crop in Andean nations such as Peru, Bolivia, and Chile. They appear in dishes such as Peruvian *papa a la huancaína,* a potato served in a cream sauce.

Corn is another native American crop that revolutionized the diets of people around the world. Along with wheat, rice, and potatoes, corn is considered one of the four most important food crops in the world. Though botanists believe corn may have grown in the Americas as many as 60,000 years ago, Europeans did not know of its existence until Columbus brought back a plant after his first trip to the Americas.

Like the potato, corn is an extremely versatile plant. Besides being relatively easy to grow—it can be planted in soil that is either too wet or too dry for crops such as wheat or rice—corn literally has hundreds of uses. It can be ground into meal or refined into starch, sugar, syrup, or oil. In the form of meal, it is combined with other ingredients to make corn bread, cookies, waffles, and a wide assortment of other foods.

Besides potatoes and corn, many other important foods originated in the Americas. Among them are avocados, pineapples, papayas, peppers, peanuts, tomatoes, and chocolate. These foods have added zest to many national cuisines. The tomato, for example, added a distinct flavor to Mediterranean cooking. And of course, it is well known what effect chocolate had on all of Europe.

The introduction of American crops to Europe did much more than help shape national cuisines. Partly because of the rich new sources of nutrition found in the native American foods, life expectancy increased and the population of Europe nearly doubled during the eighteenth century. Before the arrival of the new foods, Europe's population had been relatively stable. In addition, the revolutionary changes in agriculture helped reshape the European economy. Despite the burgeoning population, farmers were able to supply the demand for food. As many historians have maintained, plants and seeds from the Americas were far more valuable in European development than all the silver of Mexico.

Introduce

Re-entry of Concepts

The following topics represent words, expressions, and grammar points re-entered from Chaps. 1 to 3:

Chapter 1
Activities
Gustar expressions
Adjectives to describe personality

Chapter 2
School subjects
School supplies
Possession and need
Time expressions

Chapter 3
Destinations
Pastimes
Adverbs describing when things take place
Invitations (accepting / declining)
Expressions of emotion (*¡Claro que sí!*)

Planning

Cross-Curricular Connections

Geography Connection *(pp. 122–123)*
West of Buenos Aires, the capital of Argentina, is the fertile farming region of the Pampas, which is responsible for most of the nation's food production. Have students research the Pampas and create maps indicating the food products of the region.

Art Connection *(pp. 126–127)*
Have students draw the food vocabulary on index cards so that they can be used as flashcards. Assign each student one of the fruits or vegetables listed in the *Vocabulario para conversar*. Then have them draw their food in a collage format. These can then be posted around the room.

Health Connection *(pp. 146–147)*
Have students make a pyramid of the food groups (grains, fruits, vegetables, meat, dairy) using cutouts or drawings. Have them write how many portions are recommended and highlight their favorite food from each group.

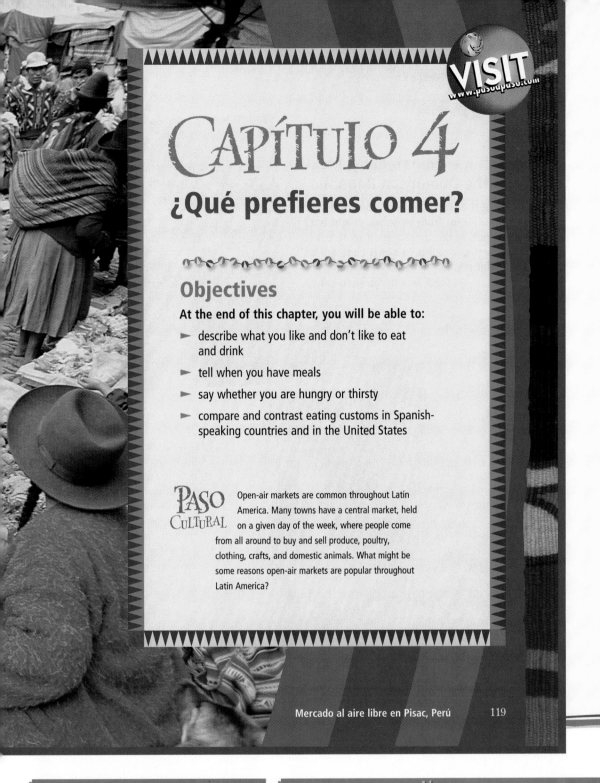

CAPÍTULO 4

¿Qué prefieres comer?

Objectives

At the end of this chapter, you will be able to:

► describe what you like and don't like to eat and drink

► tell when you have meals

► say whether you are hungry or thirsty

► compare and contrast eating customs in Spanish-speaking countries and in the United States

PASO CULTURAL Open-air markets are common throughout Latin America. Many towns have a central market, held on a given day of the week, where people come from all around to buy and sell produce, poultry, clothing, crafts, and domestic animals. What might be some reasons open-air markets are popular throughout Latin America?

VISIT
www.pasoapaso.com

Mercado al aire libre en Pisac, Perú   119

Cultural Notes

Spanish in Your Community
What foods from Spanish-speaking countries are available in your community? Have students visit a local Hispanic grocery store and make a list of at least ten foods sold there. As students share their lists with the class, compile a master list on the chalkboard.

(pp. 118–119, photo)
Shown here is the Sunday market in Pisac, a small town in the Peruvian Andes north of Cuzco. This kind of weekly market has been a fixture in villages throughout Latin America for centuries. Families in outlying areas rise before dawn to bring their goods to market. Ask students: Are there weekly markets where you live? How are they similar to or different from this one?

Paso cultural
Possible answers: The climate is generally warmer, there are no supermarkets or even grocery stores in many areas, markets are places where people can socialize.

Preview

Cultural Objective
- To compare and contrast eating customs in Spanish-speaking countries and in the U.S.

¡Piénsalo bien!

Play

 **Video Activity A**

Using the Video

This chapter's video focuses on food. Students will go with our hosts to the San Miguel Market in Madrid to discover the different types of food for sale there.

To prepare students for the video, first ask them to predict what this chapter's tape will be about. Then have students watch the segment several times. After the first time, you may wish to have them brainstorm possible vocabulary and expressions they will need to talk about what they saw on the video. Ask students to identify: a) things they saw that were familiar to them, and b) things they saw that they probably would not see in a market or grocery store where they live.

Video segment 1: For more teaching suggestions, see the Video Teacher's Guide.

¡Piensa en la CULTURA!

Ciudad de México

"Me gustaría una hamburguesa."

Mealtimes in Paraguay, Mexico, and the Dominican Republic

Look at the photos. How is the food similar to or different from what you might eat? Now look at the teens gathered at a fast-food restaurant. How does it compare to a similar restaurant in your community? What do you think *hamburguesa* means?

Un desayuno en un hotel de Asunción, Paraguay

Asunción, Paraguay

A la hora del almuerzo en la Ciudad de México

PASO CULTURAL American-style fast-food restaurants are popular in many Spanish-speaking countries. In Mexico City there are also American-style sit-down restaurant chains, such as Sanborn's and VIPs, serving both American and Mexican dishes. Mexican-style restaurants and Spanish-style *tapas* restaurants are becoming popular in the United States. Why do you think this type of cultural exchange is taking place?

120   Capítulo 4

Options

Strategies for Reaching All Students

Spanish-Speaking Students
Ask Spanish-speaking students: *¿Qué comidas ves aquí? ¿Comes tú las mismas comidas? ¿A qué hora desayunas? ¿Cuándo almuerzas? ¿Con quién almuerzas?*

Students Needing Extra Help
Discuss the mealtimes of your students. Compare and contrast this information in a chart form, after presenting the *Perspectiva cultural* (pp. 132–133).

Multiple Intelligences
Bodily/Kinesthetic
See Teaching Suggestions.
Interpersonal/Social
See Students Needing Extra Help.
Visual/Spatial
See Using the Video.

Santo Domingo,
República Dominicana

En Navidad, una familia dominicana a la hora de la cena

Cultural
Exploration
www.pasoapaso.com
Visit these countries on-line

If possible, bring to class samples of several foods that are eaten regularly in Spanish-speaking countries. Choose nonperishables that can be easily divided and shared with the class. As an alternative, you might ask student volunteers to bring in food samples at various times during their study of the chapter. Be aware of any food allergies or religious/personal preferences that your students may have.

Answers:
¡Piensa en la cultura!
Answers will vary. / Students should recognize *hamburguesa* as a cognate.

Multicultural Perspectives
Many foods grown in the Americas today were brought from Europe, Asia, and Africa; others are native to the hemisphere. Corn, tomatoes, papayas, pineapples, and pumpkins were cultivated in the Americas; cocoa was used as a seasoning for foods and as a beverage by the Aztecs. Green beans, onions, lettuce, apples, and grapes were brought to the Americas from Europe, and rice, tofu/soybean, and curry spices from Asia. Bananas, okra, coffee, and sugar cane came from Africa. Invite students to share their knowledge about the histories of various foods.

Cultural Notes ☼

Paso cultural
Possible answers: Increased awareness of ethnic dishes, growth of immigration of some Hispanic groups, and so on.

(p. 121, realia)
Ask students if they are familiar with the different kinds of *salsa* available now in the U.S.

(p. 120, left photo)
This young woman is having breakfast at a restaurant on the top floor of the Guaraní Hotel in Asunción, the capital of Paraguay. A port on the Río Paraguay, Asunción is Paraguay's oldest city, founded in 1537 by Spanish explorers. It is also the largest city (800,000) and the commercial and industrial center of the country.

(p. 121, photo)
Christmas dinner in the Dominican Republic. In some Spanish-speaking countries, gifts are not exchanged on Christmas Day, but rather on January 6, the Feast of the Epiphany (Three Kings' Day). A dinner is generally enjoyed after midnight mass. It often includes *sancocho,* a stew made with vegetables, plaintains, and several kinds of meat.

Present

Chapter Theme
Foods and mealtimes: Preferences

Communicative Objectives
- To describe meals
- To talk about foods
- To express likes or preferences
- To indicate frequency
- To ask for and give an explanation
- To express an opinion
- To elicit agreement

 Overheads 21–22

 Vocabulary Art BLMs/CD-ROM

 Pronunciation Tape 4-1

 Vocabulario para conversar A

Play

Using the Video
Video segment 2: See the Video Teacher's Guide.

 **Video Activity B**

Grammar Preview
Como / comes are presented and practiced here lexically. The presentation of *-er* verbs appears on p. 138.

Vocabulario para conversar

¿Qué te gusta comer?

Here are some new words and expressions you will need to talk about mealtimes and foods you like and don't like to eat. Read them several times, then turn the page and practice with a partner.

el pan tostado   el cereal

el jamón

el huevo

El almuerzo

las frutas

las papas fritas

los sandwiches

la hamburguesa

el tomate

el sandwich de jamón y queso

el queso

la ensalada

122   Capítulo 4

Options

Strategies for Reaching All Students

Spanish-Speaking Students
Vocabulario para conversar: Ask Spanish-speaking students: *¿Qué otras comidas te gustan? Haz una lista.*

📖 **Un paso más Ex. 4-A**

Students Needing Extra Help
¿Y qué quiere decir . . . ?: Write out the word *en* for each of the meals.

Learning Spanish Through Action
STAGING VOCABULARY: *Muestren, Pongan*
MATERIALS: Brown (2), pink (1), yellow (1), and red (1) pieces of construction paper, approximately the size of a slice of bread, for each student
DIRECTIONS: Tell students that they are going to make sandwiches. Have them label the brown sheets *el pan tostado,* the pink sheets *el jamón,* the red sheets *el tomate,* and the yellow sheets *el queso.* As you describe a ham, cheese, and tomato sand-

La cena

la sopa de tomate
la sopa de pollo
el pan
el bistec
el pescado
las papas al horno
el arroz
la sopa de verduras
el pollo
las verduras

También necesitas...

comer: (yo) como (tú) comes	*to eat: I eat you eat*
la comida	*meal*
más o menos	*more or less*
¡Qué asco!	*Yuk! That's disgusting!*
¿por qué?	*why?*
porque	*because*
¿verdad?	*isn't that so? right?*

me encanta(n)	*I love*
siempre	*always*
nunca	*never*

¿Y qué quiere decir...?

en el desayuno / el almuerzo / la cena

preferir: (yo) prefiero (tú) prefieres

Vocabulario para conversar 123

Practice & Apply

Answers: Empecemos a conversar

1 ESTUDIANTE A

a. ¿Comes huevos?

b ... pan?

c. ... frutas?

d. Questions will vary.

ESTUDIANTE B

a.–d. Answers will vary depending on *Estudiante B*'s preferences.

2 ESTUDIANTE A

a. Te gustan las papas al horno, ¿verdad?

b. ... las verduras ...

c. ... los tomates ...

d. ... los sandwiches ...

e. ... las hamburguesas ...

f. ... los sandwiches de jamón y queso ...

g. ... las papas fritas ...

ESTUDIANTE B

a.–g. Answers will vary depending on *Estudiante B*'s preferences.

Empecemos a conversar

With a partner, take turns being *Estudiante A* and *Estudiante B*. Use the words that are cued or given in the balloons to replace the underlined sections in the model. means you can make your own choices.

1 A —¿Comes <u>jamón</u>?

B —<u>Sí, a veces.</u>

Estudiante A

a. b. c. d.

Estudiante B

Sí, a veces.

Sí, todos los días.

Sí, siempre.

No, nunca.

No, ¡qué asco!

2 A —<u>Te gustan las ensaladas</u>, ¿verdad?

B —<u>Sí, me encantan.</u>

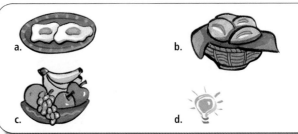

Estudiante A

a. b. c. d.

e. f. g.

Estudiante B

Sí, me encantan.

Sí, más o menos.

No, no me gustan (mucho).

No, ¡qué asco!

Options

Strategies for Reaching All Students

Spanish-Speaking Students

Try to pair bilingual students with non-bilingual students for Exs. 1–3. This will help both. The former will learn to speak clearly and carefully, and the latter will have good models.

 Un paso más Exs. 4-B, 4-C

Students Needing Extra Help

Have students begin to fill in their Organizers.

Exs. 1–2: Review the meanings of the responses. Point out that Column B contains choices and that it is not a linear match for answers.

Ex. 3: Have students write the names of the three meals in columns so as to organize them. Model a sentence.

Ex. 7: Remind students that they answered this type of question in Ex. 3.

Enrichment

Ex. 2: Do a similar exercise with you taking the place of *Estudiante A* and forming your questions using *te gusta* and singular nouns. Preview the grammar by asking students why you used *te gusta* instead of *te gustan* in your questions. Have them note the difference between *me / te gusta* + inf. and *me / te gusta(n)* + noun by contrasting these sentences: *Me gustan las ensaladas. Me gusta comer ensaladas.* Explain that *las* is not used here after the infinitive.

3 A —*¿Qué comes en el desayuno?*

B —*Generalmente como cereal y pan tostado.*

Estudiante A

a. la cena
b. el almuerzo
c. el desayuno

Estudiante B

PASO CULTURAL

Freshly squeezed juice and juice-based drinks are served at juice bars throughout Mexico. *Licuados* (fruit shakes) and *aguas* (fruit-flavored water) are especially popular. Why do you suppose juice bars are so much more common in Mexico than they are in the United States?

Empecemos a escribir

Write your answers in Spanish.

4 Write the names of at least three foods under each of these headings: *Todos los días, A veces, Nunca.* Then write three complete sentences telling how often you eat those foods.

5 Copy the names of the soups you have learned. Using those as a model, choose other foods from the vocabulary and write the names of at least three other soups.

6 ¿Qué comida prefieres, el desayuno o la cena? ¿Por qué?

7 Generalmente, ¿qué comes en el almuerzo y con quién comes?

En una tienda de jugos en la Ciudad de México

También se dice...

la tostada

los bocadillos
los emparedados

el bife
el biftec

las legumbres
las hortalizas

los jitomates

MORE PRACTICE

- Más práctica y tarea, p. 517
- Practice Workbook 4–1, 4–2

Vocabulario para conversar   125

---

3 ESTUDIANTE A
a. ¿Qué comes en la cena?
b. . . . el almuerzo?
c. . . . el desayuno?
ESTUDIANTE B
a.–c. Answers will vary depending on *Estudiante B's* preferences.

Answers: Empecemos a escribir

4 Answers will vary, but encourage students to use chapter vocabulary.

5 La sopa de verduras, la sopa de tomate, la sopa de pollo. / La sopa de queso, la sopa de pescado, la sopa de papa.

6–7 Answers will vary.

Practice Wkbk. 4-1, 4-2

Audio Activity 4.1

Writing Activities 4-A, 4-B

Pruebas 4-1, 4-2

Multicultural Perspectives

Aguas frescas, or flavored waters, are popular beverages in Mexican eating places. These include *agua de sandía, agua de limón, agua de tamarindo,* and *horchata* (made with rice flour). *Aguas frescas* are sold in restaurants, at market lunch counters, and by street vendors. Invite students to share their knowledge of popular beverages from other cultures.

Cultural Notes ☀

For an additional written assignment, ask small groups to rate the meals at three or four local restaurants with which they are familiar. Students can list the restaurants in one column and then put a check mark under columns with the headings: *Me encanta, Me gusta,* and *¡Qué asco!* or *No me gusta.* Another assignment could be about the time dinner begins and ends at home, with students answering these questions: *¿A qué hora, más o menos, empieza la cena en tu casa? ¿A qué hora termina?*

Extended Written Practice/Homework
1. Choose six foods. Write sentences saying at which meal you usually eat them.
2. Write four questions asking a person which of two foods he or she prefers.
3. Write two sentences: a. Mention three foods that you always eat. b. Mention two foods that you never eat.
4. Write three sentences telling what you are going to eat at each meal tomorrow.

Paso cultural
Possible answers: Awareness of nutrition and healthful foods. Greater variety of fruits available.

Present

Chapter Theme
Foods: Fruits, vegetables, and beverages

Communicative Objectives
- To talk about foods and drinks
- To describe meals and foods
- To refer to obligation
- To indicate hunger or thirst
- To talk about something you cannot name
- To express an opinion

Overheads 23–24

Vocabulary Art BLMs/CD-ROM

Pronunciation Tape 4-2

Vocabulario para conversar B

Play

Step

Using the Video
Video segment 2: See the Video Teacher's Guide.

Video Activity B

Vocabulario para conversar

¿Tienes hambre?

  Chapter 4 Vocabulary

tener hambre

Here's the rest of the vocabulary you will need to tell what you like and don't like to eat and drink and to say whether you are hungry or thirsty.

la lechuga

los guisantes

las judías verdes

las zanahorias

la naranja

las cebollas

la manzana

las papas

la uva

el plátano

126   Capítulo 4

Options

Strategies for Reaching All Students

Spanish-Speaking Students
Ask: *¿Qué otras frutas y verduras puedes nombrar?*

 Un paso más Exs. 4-D, 4-E

Students Needing Extra Help
Have students continue to fill in their Organizers.

Enrichment
The names of many fruits and vegetables in Mexico are derived from *náhuatl*, a very ancient language spoken by the Aztecs in central Mexico and still spoken today in various dialects in Mexico and Central America. Words derived from *náhuatl* are distinguishable by their *-te* (formerly *-tl*) ending: *aguacate, chocolate, cacahuate, tomate, elote* (corn), *ejote* (string bean).

tener sed

la leche el café el té

el agua (f.)* la limonada los refrescos el jugo de naranja el té helado

También necesitas...

beber: (yo) bebo	*to drink: I drink*
(tú) bebes	*you drink*
bueno, -a	*good*
(para la salud)	*(for your health)*
malo, -a (para la salud)	*bad (for your health)*
sabroso, -a	*delicious, tasty*
Creo que sí.	*I think so.*
Creo que no.	*I don't think so.*
algo	*something*

deber:	*ought to, should*
(yo) debo	*I ought to, should*
(tú) debes	*you ought to, should*
son	*(they) are*
unos, unas	*some*

¿Y qué quiere decir...?
horrible

*Note that *agua* is a feminine noun. However, we use the article *el* with feminine nouns beginning with stressed *a* or *ha*.

Vocabulario para conversar 127

 Pasos vivos 1 CD-ROM
Clip Art Album

Grammar Preview
Bebo / bebes and *debo / debes* are presented here lexically. The explanation of *-er* verbs appears on p. 138.

Teaching Suggestions
Preparing students to speak: Use one or two options from each of the categories of Comprehensible Input, Physical Response, or Limited Verbal Response. For a complete explanation of these categories and some sample activities, see pp. T22–T23.

Class Starter Review
On the day following initial presentation, you might begin the class with this activity:
As you call out the visualized items in this vocabulary section, ask students to categorize them as *frutas, verduras,* or *bebidas.*

www Internet Activities
Juegos
Have students go to www.pasoapaso.com for additional activities and practice.

Learning Spanish Through Action
STAGING VOCABULARY: *Den, Levántense, Muestren, Pongan*
MATERIALS: Three 8 1/2 X 11 sheets of paper labeled *frutas, verduras,* and *bebidas;* index cards with pictures of all the fruits, vegetables, and beverages in the *Vocabulario para conversar.* If possible, use plastic toys or magazine cutouts.
DIRECTIONS: Have three volunteers go to the front of the class. Give each volunteer one of the sheets, instructing him or her to hold it up for the class. Distribute the index cards to individuals in the class. As you recite each food or beverage, have the student who has the corresponding card for that item get up and give it to the appropriate volunteer. Continue until all of the foods and beverages are properly categorized.

Multiple Intelligences
Bodily/Kinesthetic
See Learning Spanish Through Action.
Verbal/Linguistic
See Class Starter Review.
Visual/Spatial
See Overheads 23–24, the Vocabulary Art BLMs/CD-ROM, and Using the Video.

Answers: Empecemos a conversar

8 In this exercise, the indefinite article is not included with the items *cereal, agua,* and *leche.* Whereas in English we might say <u>some</u> cereal or <u>some</u> milk, the most common usage in Spanish with certain nouns would be to simply omit the article.

ESTUDIANTE A
Make sure students alternate roles for this exercise.

ESTUDIANTE B
¿Te gustaría una manzana?
. . . una naranja?
. . . una zanahoria?
. . . un sandwich?
. . . unas uvas?
. . . cereal?
. . . un plátano?
. . . agua?
. . . un té helado?
. . . un jugo de naranja?
. . . una limonada?
. . . leche?
. . . un refresco?

9 Preview adjective agreement here by asking students to predict why *buenas* and *sabrosas* end in *as.*

Empecemos a conversar

8 A —*Necesito comer algo.*
B —*¿Te gustaría una manzana?*

Estudiante A

a. Debo comer algo.
b. Tengo sed.
c. Necesito beber algo.
d. Tengo hambre.
e. Debo beber algo.

Estudiante B

9 A —*Las verduras son buenas para la salud, ¿verdad?*
B —*Sí, y son sabrosas también.*

Estudiante A

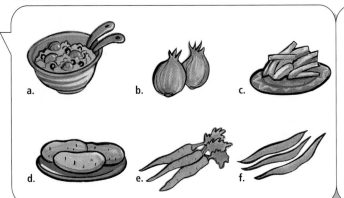

a.
b.
c.
d.
e.
f.

Estudiante B

Sí, y son sabrosas también.
Sí, pero no me gustan mucho.
Sí, pero no son sabrosas.
Sí, pero son horribles.
Creo que sí.
No, creo que no.
No, son malas para la salud.
Más o menos.

Options

Strategies for Reaching All Students

Spanish-Speaking Students
Exs. 8–9: Pair Spanish-speaking students. For Ex. 9, ask students to explain their answers.
Ex. 11: Ask Spanish-speaking students to find out about their classmates' beverage preferences for breakfast. Then have them write short paragraphs about their findings.

For example: *Pregúntales a tus compañeros qué beben en el desayuno. Luego escribe un párrafo sobre las bebidas más populares.* Guide students in their writing and provide further questions to be answered in paragraph form.

 Un paso más Exs. 4-F, 4-G

Students Needing Extra Help
Ex. 8: Emphasize that *hambre, comer,* and the foods go together and that *sed, beber,* and the beverages go together.
Ex. 10: Put a few choices on the chalkboard.
Exs. 11–13: Have students use their Organizers.

Empecemos a escribir y a leer

Write your answers in Spanish.

10 Imagine that you are waiting tables and need to write yourself a reminder. Write down what comes with the hamburgers, and at least four ingredients that are in the vegetable soup today.

11 ¿Qué bebida prefieres en el desayuno, en el almuerzo y en la cena? ¿Por qué?

12 ¿Qué verduras te gustan?

13 Unos animales hablan de lo que prefieren comer.

el cerdo
el pato
el mono
el conejo
la gallina

¿Quién dice . . . ?

a. —A ver . . . Me encantan el pan y el agua. Sí, sí. Me gusta mucho beber agua, y como mucho pan en el parque.

b. —En el desayuno siempre como plátanos. En el almuerzo a veces como más plátanos. ¿Y en la cena? Pues . . . generalmente como plátanos también. Son muy buenos para la salud, ¿verdad?

c. —¿Comer huevos? ¡Ay, no! ¿Huevos? ¡Nunca!

d. —Como mucho todos los días. ¡Pero no puedo comer jamón! ¡Nunca voy a comer jamón!

e. —Yo como muchas zanahorias. ¡A mí me encantan las zanahorias! Me gustaría comer zanahorias en todas las comidas.

MORE PRACTICE

- Más práctica y tarea, p. 517–518
- Practice Workbook 4–3, 4–4

También se dice...

las bananas
los guineos

las chinas

la chaucha (sing.)
las habichuelas verdes
los ejotes

las patatas

las arvejas
los chícharos

el zumo de naranja

 www.pasoapaso.com

Vocabulario para conversar   129

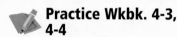

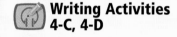
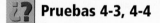
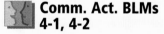

Enrichment

Ex. 8: Have *Estudiante B* expand his or her answer by saying if the foods named are healthful.

Empecemos a escribir y a leer: For additional practice, have students plan a dinner menu for some friends.

Extended Written Practice/Homework

1. Write three questions asking if someone drinks certain beverages every day.
2. Write six sentences telling someone what he or she should or should not drink.
3. Write two sentences: a. Say that you are hungry and tell what you want to eat. b. Say that you are thirsty and tell what you want to drink.
4. Write five questions asking someone if he or she wants certain foods or beverages.

Multiple Intelligences

Naturalist
Ask students to research information on organic gardening. Have them list the names of any fruits or vegetables in Spanish that can be organically grown.

Verbal/Linguistic
See Audio Activity 4.2.

Visual/Spatial
See Practice Wkbk. 4-3 and 4-4, Writing Activities 4-C and 4-D, and Comm. Act. BLMs 4-1 and 4-2.

Standards 1.1, 1.2; 3.1   **129**

Practice

Re-enter / Recycle

Ex. 2: *necesito / necesitas* from Chap. 2
Ex. 3: time-telling from Chap. 2.

Answers:
¡Comuniquemos!

1 Dialogues will vary. Remind students to include definite articles in their responses if they elect the last option for *Estudiante A*.

2 ESTUDIANTE A

a. ¿Qué necesitas para los sandwiches?
b. . . . la ensalada de frutas?
c. . . . la ensalada de verduras?
d. . . . el desayuno?
e. . . . el almuerzo?
f. . . . la cena?

ESTUDIANTE B

a.–f. Answers will vary depending on what *Estudiante B* needs. Encourage students to use the full range of chapter vocabulary. Suggest that *Estudiante B* respond with at least three foods for each item.

¡COMUNI

¡NO OLVIDES!

If you need help spelling, ask
¿Cómo se escribe . . . ?

1

You and a friend are deciding what to order at a restaurant. Take turns asking each other about your food preferences.

A —¿Prefieres ___ o ___?
B —Prefiero ___.
A —Yo prefiero ___ también.
 o: Yo prefiero ___.
 o: A mí no me gusta(n) ni el (la, los, las) ___ ni el (la, los, las) ___.

2

Help a friend prepare a shopping list. Ask what he or she needs, and write down the responses.

A —¿Qué necesitas para la sopa?
B —Necesito zanahorias, tomates y cebolla.

a. los sandwiches
b. la ensalada de frutas
c. la ensalada de verduras
d. el desayuno
e. el almuerzo
f. la cena

130 Capítulo 4

Options

Strategies for Reaching All Students

Spanish-Speaking Students

Exs. 1–4: Pair bilingual and non-bilingual students.

Students Needing Extra Help

Ex. 2: Have students use their Organizers.
Ex. 3: Review time and days of the week. Have students use their Organizers.
¿Qué sabes ahora?: Have students write out this section so they can check off what they have mastered. In item 1, repeat *tengo* for the second blank. In item 3, create a negative sentence also.

Enrichment

Ex. 3: As a written assignment, have students invent a dialogue in which they are responsible for fixing lunch on Saturday for the family and guests. Have them ask for help from a sibling who declines, perhaps giving an elaborate excuse why he or she can't help. Encourage students to be creative in their presentation, using as much known vocabulary as possible.

Your family is having guests this weekend and you are expected to attend at least three of the meals. Find out what time each of those meals is and what will be served. With your partner, take turns playing the two roles. For example:

A —¿A qué hora es el almuerzo el sábado?

B —A las doce.

A —¿Qué vamos a comer?

B —Pollo y ensalada.

Have the following conversation with a partner. Keep your conversation going as long as you can.

- Find out if your partner is hungry.
- Your partner answers affirmatively.
- Ask what he/she wants/prefers/ would like to eat.
- Your partner answers.

¿Qué sabes ahora?

Can you:

► tell someone that you are hungry / thirsty?
—Tengo ___ / ___.

► tell someone what you like or do not like to eat and drink?
—Me encanta comer ___ , pero (no) me gusta beber ___.

► say that you like certain foods because they are healthful or tasty?
—Me gustan las uvas ___ son ___.

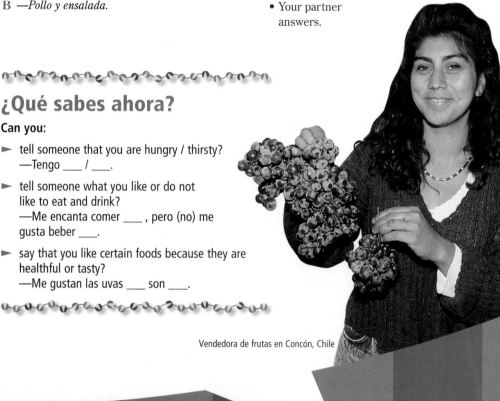

Vendedora de frutas en Concón, Chile

Audio Activity 4.3

3 ESTUDIANTE A
¿A qué hora es el desayuno (el almuerzo, la cena) el sábado (el domingo)?

ESTUDIANTE B
Dialogues will vary, but encourage students to use the full range of chapter vocabulary.

4 Conversations will vary. Encourage students to use the full range of chapter vocabulary.

Answers: ¿Qué sabes ahora?
- hambre / sed
- Answers will vary.
- Answers will vary, but may include: . . . porque / buenas para la salud (sabrosas)

Pasos vivos 1 CD-ROM
Slide Projector, Laboratorio de grabar

Cooperative Learning
In groups of four or five, have students plan a complete lunch menu for each day of the school week. Each lunch should include an item from the dairy, meat, vegetable, bread, and fruit groups, a beverage, and some extras. Have a volunteer from each group write the menus on butcher paper, making sure to label each meal with the day on which it will be served. Post the menus on a bulletin board and discuss them. To extend the activity, have student "critics" rate the menus on a scale of 1–5.

Multiple Intelligences
Interpersonal/Social
See Cooperative Learning.

Present & Apply

Cultural Objective
• To compare and contrast eating customs in Spanish-speaking countries and in the U.S.

Critical Thinking: Making Hypotheses
After students read the text, have them speculate as to how the adoption of a *jornada continua* or *horario continuado* in some businesses in large Mexican cities will affect family traditions.

Multicultural Perspectives
In Colombia it is proper etiquette for someone who is eating to offer to share his or her food. Eating food while walking down the street is considered improper. Discuss these customs with students. Ask: How is eating and meal etiquette different in the U.S. and Colombia? How is it the same? Invite students to share information they have about food etiquette in other cultures.

Answers
Answers will vary: *a las 8:00, a las 12:00 y a las 6:00 / cereal, huevos, pan tostado, etc. / a las 2:00, a las 5:00 y a las 9:30*

Perspectiva cultural

Las horas de las comidas

¿A qué hora es el desayuno, el almuerzo y la cena en los Estados Unidos? ¿Qué comemos en el desayuno, por ejemplo? En las fotos, ¿a qué hora comen los hispanos?

Look at the mealtimes shown in the photos. Based on those times, do you think there might be another meal not pictured? Explain your answer.

In Spanish-speaking countries, as in the United States, there are three main meals—*el desayuno, el almuerzo,* and *la cena.*

El desayuno, which generally takes place between 7:00 and 8:30, is usually a light meal that consists of coffee or *café con leche,* which is half coffee and half hot milk, and bread or rolls with butter and jam. Children and teenagers sometimes drink hot chocolate or chocolate milk instead of coffee.

El almuerzo (called *la comida* in Spain and Mexico) is the largest and most important meal of the day. It is eaten between noon and 3:00. Many businesses and schools close so that families can enjoy *el almuerzo* together at home. Although this lengthy midday break is still common, more and more

En Xochimilco, México, a la hora de la merienda

5:00 PM

Options

Strategies for Reaching All Students

Spanish-Speaking Students
Ask students: *¿Cuáles son tus comidas favoritas? ¿A qué hora cenas? ¿Cena toda la familia junta? ¿Comes algo entre el almuerzo y la cena? ¿Qué comes? ¿Vas con tus amigos a comer después de las clases?*

 Un paso más Ex. 4-H

Enrichment
Have students consult various up-to-date guidebooks in the library to do a brief written or oral report on fast-food restaurants in Spanish-speaking countries. For another assignment, ask students to watch any local television programs broadcast in Spanish and to take note of the content and format of commercials from supermarket chains, small grocery stores, fast-food chains, and restaurants. Ask them to watch with these questions in mind: What's different about these commercials? What's the same? Are there any slogans? What are they? Do you think the same slogans would be effective in English?

Multiple Intelligences
Visual/Spatial
See Enrichment.

businesses are adopting a *jornada continua* or *horario continuado* (uninterrupted schedule) similar to working hours in the United States. This does not leave time for employees to go home for lunch.

La cena is the evening meal. It may start around 7:00 or much later, especially in countries that have a late midday meal. In Spain, *la cena* may start as late as 10:00 or 11:00, since most Spaniards enjoy going out after work or school and it is customary to wait until all family members are present before sitting down to eat. *La cena* is usually a light meal, and it may include leftovers from *el almuerzo*.

In some countries, there is also a late afternoon meal called *la merienda*. It may be like a *desayuno,* or it may resemble an English tea, with sandwiches, pastries, or rolls and *café con leche,* tea, or hot chocolate.

Una familia salvadoreña comiendo el almuerzo

A la hora de cenar en Escazú, Costa Rica

9:30 PM

La cultura desde tu perspectiva

1 In what ways are mealtimes in Spanish-speaking countries similar to or different from those in the United States?

2 Why would a late-afternoon snack probably be necessary for someone from the United States who was visiting a Spanish-speaking country? Are there any other times of day when a snack might be needed?

www.pasoapaso.com

Perspectiva cultural   133

Cultural Notes

(p. 132, photo)
The floating gardens of Xochimilco, Mexico, have flourished since the thirteenth century, when the Chinampaneca Indians established themselves in this area about 13 miles west of what is today the center of Mexico City. A popular attraction for tourists and residents alike, the gardens can be viewed from gondolas like this one, called *trajineras.*

(pp. 132–133, photo)
The time shown for this photo is the usual time for the evening meal in Hispanic countries, although on occasion *la cena* may be served earlier or later. When guests are present or when the family wants to linger, the meal may be followed by the *sobremesa,* which is a time to savor coffee and other treats while prolonging the table conversation. Ask students: Are there *sobremesas* in U.S. culture? Explain.

(p. 133, top photo)
In Hispanic countries, *el almuerzo* is traditionally much more than a meal; it is a daily ritual that binds family, friends, and business associates together. It usually lasts about two hours, giving everyone a chance to join in the leisurely conversation. Ask students: What do you think about this ritual of sharing the midday meal? Could this work in the U.S.? Explain.

Preview

 Overhead 25

Answers

Countries (starting with top flag and moving clockwise): Switzerland, Italy, France, Great Britain, Greece, Netherlands. Discuss more common types of cheese that students may see or buy: American, cheddar, parmesan, Swiss, etc.

A *importados, deliciosos, preparados, franceses, ingleses, suizos, finos, dietéticos / suizo, sabroso /* Answers will vary, but look for explanations such as: You use *sabroso* when describing one item and *sabrosos* when describing more than one item.

B It ends in *-n*. Students may refer to the word as being plural.

Gramática en contexto

Look at this ad for imported cheeses. Can you tell which countries they are from?

A Working with a partner, list all the words from the ad that describe cheese when it is written *quesos*.

- Find two words that describe cheese when it is written *queso*.
- When would you use *sabroso* or *sabrosos* to describe food?

B Look at the headline. How is this form of the expression for "Do you like . . . " different from the form you learned earlier? How would you explain this?

134   Capítulo 4

Options

Strategies for Reaching All Students

Students Needing Extra Help
A: Review what students have already learned about the singular endings of adjectives. Have them use their Organizers from Chap. 3 to review other adjectives.
B: Write a *¿Te gustan . . . ?* question, underlining the plural word.
El plural de los sustantivos: Have students fill in the first chart in the grammar portion of their Organizers.

Extended Written Practice/Homework
1. Choose eight foods. For each food, write a sentence saying how much you like or dislike it.
2. Choose a number of foods that you do not like. Write three sentences saying that you like neither one food nor another.

Multiple Intelligences
Bodily/Kinesthetic
1) Cut out pictures of food from magazines. Write the articles *el, la, los, las, un, una, unos,* and *unas* on index cards. Have students practice using the correct definite or indefinite article by placing the card next to the appropriate picture.
2) Ask students to bring in Spanish-language food labels and make a collage to be displayed in the room.

El plural de los sustantivos

- In Spanish, to make nouns plural, we generally add -s to words ending in a vowel (*libro* → *libros*) and -es to words ending in a consonant (*papel* → *papeles*).

- The plural definite articles are *los* and *las*. *Los* is used with masculine plural nouns, *las* with feminine plural nouns.
  los cereal**es**   **las** pap**as**

- *Los* is also used with a plural noun that includes both males and females.
  el profesor Sánchez y la profesora Romero
  = **los** profesor**es**

- Singular nouns that end in the letter *z* change the *z* to *c* in the plural.
  el lápi**z** → los lápi**ces**

- To keep the stress on the correct syllable, we sometimes have to add or remove an accent mark in the plural.
  el ex**amen** → los ex**ámenes**
  el jam**ón** → los jam**ones**

- The plural indefinite articles are *unos* and *unas*. They mean "some" or "a few."
  No tengo mucha hambre, pero voy a comer **unas** papas fritas.

- We use *me gustan* and *me encantan* to talk about a plural noun.
  No me gust**an** las manzanas pero me encant**an** las uvas.

¡NO OLVIDES!
The singular definite articles are *el* and *la*. The singular indefinite articles are *un* and *una*.

Aquí las vitaminas están…

Espinacas en Hojas

…garantizadas.

Espinacas en Hojas

Después de cosechar las espinacas, sus vitaminas empiezan a desaparecer. Por eso, Frudesa aplica un estricto control de tiempo. Las Espinacas Frudesa se congelan inmediatamente después de recogerlas, para mantener sus propiedades nutritivas. Así te lo garantiza el Sello de Vitaminas.

Frudesa, Vitaminas y Sabor. Garantizados. frudesa

1 Write sentences using an appropriate expression from the left-hand column with each of the words in the two right-hand columns. Afterward, read any four of your sentences to a partner to find out if he or she agrees.

(no) me gusta	a. las manzanas	f. las verduras
(no) me gustan	b. la leche	g. los tomates
me encanta	c. las cebollas	h. el jugo de naranja
me encantan	d. la sopa de pollo	i. los huevos
	e. la sopa de verduras	j. el pescado

Gramática en contexto   135

Present & Practice

Re-enter / Recycle
Exs. 2–4: *gustar* expressions from Chap. 1
Ex. 3: invitations from Chap. 3

Reteach / Review: Definite & Indefinite Articles
Ex. 3: Contrast the use of indefinite and definite articles in this exercise to do a variation of Ex. 2: *¿Te gustaría comer unas papas al horno? / Sí, me encantan las papas al horno. / No, gracias. No me gustan las papas al horno.*

Answers
2 Explain that the definite article is used with foods when they occur with *gusta(n)*.

ESTUDIANTE A
a. ¿Te gustan las papas fritas?
b. ...las verduras?
c. ...los guisantes?
d. ...las hamburguesas?
e. ...los plátanos?
f. ...los huevos?

ESTUDIANTE B
a.–f. Answers will vary depending on what *Estudiante B* likes or dislikes.

---

2 Discuss with a partner whether or not you like the following foods.

A —*¿Te gustan las zanahorias?*
B —*Sí, me gustan.*
   o: *Sí, me encantan.*
   o: *No, no me gustan nada.*

a.   b.   c.
d.   e.   f.

3 Now use the pictures in Exercise 2 to ask if your partner would like to eat those foods.

A —*¿Te gustaría comer unas zanahorias?*
B —*¡Claro que sí! A mí me encantan.*
   o: *No, no tengo hambre. Gracias.*

PASO CULTURAL Stuffed pastries such as these *empanadas* are a popular snack food in Spanish-speaking countries. How do these compare with what you might have as an after-school snack?

Comida para la merienda en la Ciudad de México

Options

Strategies for Reaching All Students

Spanish-Speaking Students
Ex. 3: Have Spanish-speaking students write questions such as those used by *Estudiante A* for each of the foods listed. Ask them to add four or five other foods.
Ex. 4: Pair bilingual and non-bilingual students for this exercise.

Enrichment
Ex. 2: Have *Estudiante B* expand his or her answer by telling why he or she likes or dislikes the food named.

Students Needing Extra Help
Ex. 2: Explain the difference in degree between *me gustan* and *me encantan* and how both phrases include the idea of "them." (I like them. / I love them.)
Ex. 3: Review *te gusta* and *te gustaría.*
Ex. 4: Review possible responses *también* and *tampoco.*
El plural de los adjetivos: Have students continue to fill in the first chart (adjective endings) in the grammar portion of their Organizers.

Extended Written Practice/Homework
1. Write two sentences telling what foods or drinks are tasty or horrible.
2. Write two sentences telling what foods or drinks are good or bad for your health.
3. Write a sentence saying that two or more classes are difficult. Then write a sentence saying that two or more classes are easy.

4 These foods might be served in your school cafeteria this week. Take turns with a partner telling whether you like them or not.

A —*Me gustan las papas al horno.*

B —*A mí también.*
    o: *A mí no.*

A —*No me gustan las papas al horno.*

B —*A mí tampoco.*
    o: *A mí sí.*

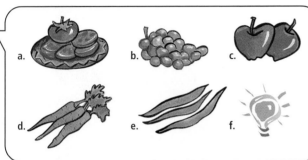

El plural de los adjetivos

You know that in Spanish most adjectives have different masculine and feminine singular forms: *La leche es sabrosa; el cereal es bueno para la salud.* If the noun is plural, the adjective too must be plural:

La**s** papa**s** frita**s** son sabrosa**s** pero no son buena**s** para la salud.

Lo**s** guisante**s** son bueno**s** para la salud.

- To make adjectives plural, add -*s* to the final vowel. If the adjective ends in a consonant, add -*es*.

    horrible   horrible**s**
    trabajador   trabajador**es**

- When an adjective describes both masculine and feminine nouns, use the masculine plural ending.

    Los plátanos y las manzanas son sabros**os**.

Llevando pan a los mercados en Málaga, España

Gramática en contexto   137

3 **ESTUDIANTE A**

a. ¿Te gustaría comer unas papas fritas?

b. . . . unas verduras?

c. . . . unos guisantes?

d. . . . unas hamburguesas?

e. . . . unos plátanos?

f. . . . unos huevos?

ESTUDIANTE B

a.–f. Responses will vary.

4 **ESTUDIANTE A**

a. (No) me gustan los tomates.

b. . . . las uvas.

c. . . . las manzanas.

d. . . . las zanahorias.

e. . . . las judías verdes.

f. Statements will vary.

ESTUDIANTE B

a.–f. Statements will vary depending on *Estudiante B*'s preferences.

 Practice Wkbk. 4-5

 Prueba 4-5

Cultural Notes

Multiple Intelligences
Bodily/Kinesthetic and Visual/Spatial
Play Tic-Tac-Toe labeling the grid as follows: *una, gustan, la, un, gusta, el, los, unos,* and *unas.* Show the first player from the *X* team a flashcard of a food item (such as *jugo*), and he or she can put the *X* on a square with an article or verb form used with that word (*el, un* or *gusta*). The *O* team takes the next turn, and so on.
Verbal/Linguistic
See Exs. 2–4.

Paso cultural
(p. 136, photo)
Answers will vary.
In most parts of Latin America one can find street vendors offering *empanadas,* or stuffed pastries. Every region has its own version of the pastry, which comes in different sizes, shapes, and fillings. This vendor in a Mexico City park is selling the enormous sweet *empanadas* of Michoacán, a mountainous state in western Mexico. Ask students: What foods similar to *empanadas* are sold in your area?

(p. 137, photo)
In much of Spain and Latin America, where cars are often expensive and public transportation can be unreliable, motorcycles are put to various uses. Shopkeepers and tradespeople often will use their *moto* to pick up supplies and deliver goods, distributing the load onto attached racks, trailers, and sidecars. Ask students: How does this delivery method compare to those in the U.S.?

Present & Practice

Re-enter / Recycle

Ex. 5: adjectives to describe personality from Chap. 1

Answers

5 Answers will vary. Make sure that students use correct adjective agreement.

 Practice Wkbk. 4-6

 Writing Activity 4-E

 Prueba 4-6

6 a. *Lavan, apagas, descansas,* and *pagamos* are *-ar* verb forms.
b. *Recoges, creemos, ponen, traen, vende,* and *lees* are *-er* forms.
c. *Regreso* and *corto* could be either.

The infinitive forms of the verbs in lists (a) and (b) are *lavar, apagar, descansar, pagar, recoger, creer, poner, traer, vender,* and *leer.*

7 ESTUDIANTE A
a. ¿Qué bebe Anita en el desayuno?
b. . . . beben Pilar y Pablo en el almuerzo?
c. . . . beben Graciela y Juan en la cena?
d. . . . bebe Carlitos en el desayuno?
e. . . . beben Uds. en la cena?
f. . . . bebes tú en el almuerzo?

---

5 For each of these adjectives, name two famous people or people in your class or school whom the adjective fits.

Jimmy Smits y Dennis Franz son trabajadores.

artístico, -a	gracioso, -a
deportista	sociable
atrevido, -a	ordenado, -a
callado, -a	serio, -a
desordenado, -a	trabajador, -a

Maltratar a los traviesos resulta verdaderamente innecesario. Por el simple motivo de que la mayoría de estos muchachos y muchachas se hacen daño a sí mismos al no recibir suficiente calcio. Por lo tanto, tome 3 vasos de leche diarios. Su cuerpo se lo agradecerá. Sobre todo si no tenemos que repetírselo.

LECHE
¿Dónde está *su bigote?*

Para más información
1-888-LECHESI

Verbos que terminan en *-er*

You know the pattern of present-tense endings for regular *-ar* verbs.

- Another group of regular verbs has infinitives that end in *-er.* Some that you know are *beber, comer, leer,* and *deber.*

- Here are the present-tense forms of the verb *comer.* How does this pattern differ from that of *-ar* verbs?

(yo)	como	(nosotros) (nosotras)	comemos
(tú)	comes	(vosotros) (vosotras)	coméis
Ud. (él) (ella)	come	Uds. (ellos) (ellas)	comen

- With *-er* verbs we use the vowel *-e* in all forms except *yo.* Remember that *-ar* verbs use the vowel *-a* except in the *yo* form.

- You also know the verb *ver.* It is regular except in the *yo* form, which is *veo.*

¡NO OLVIDES!

The pattern of present-tense *-ar* verbs is:

hablo	hablamos
hablas	habláis
habla	hablan

Options

Strategies for Reaching All Students

Spanish-Speaking Students
Ex. 8: Have Spanish-speaking students write out the exercise, paying close attention to spelling and the use of accents.

Students Needing Extra Help
Verbos que terminan en -er: Have students fill in the verb chart in the grammar portion of their Organizers.
Ex. 8: Model some examples on the chalkboard. There are really three verbs involved in this exercise. Show how the verb in the first sentence becomes an infinitive in the second sentence.

Extended Written Practice/Homework
1. Write five sentences listing foods that you and your family or you and your friends often eat.
2. Write three questions that can be asked to a group of students *(ustedes)* to find out what fruits and vegetables they eat and what beverages they drink.
3. Write three sentences of advice saying what students should do to be successful at school: *Los estudiantes deben escuchar en clase.*

6 Here are some present-tense verb forms. You do not yet know most of these verbs. With a partner, make lists of (a) those that are *-ar* verb forms, (b) those that are *-er* forms, and (c) those that could be either. Working together, can you write the infinitive form of each of the verbs in lists (a) and (b)?

lavan	creemos	descansas	corto
apagas	regreso	traen	pagamos
recoges	ponen	vende	lees

7 With a partner, take turns asking and answering what the following people drink at different meals.

A —*¿Qué beben tus amigos en el almuerzo?*

B —*Beben refrescos.*

tus amigos / almuerzo

 a. Anita / desayuno

 b. Pilar y Pablo / almuerzo

 c. Graciela y Juan / cena

 d. Carlitos / desayuno

 e. Uds. / cena

f. tú / almuerzo

8 These people do not eat certain foods. With your partner, discuss why they should eat them.

A —*Juan Carlos no come judías verdes.*

B —*¡Pero debe comer judías verdes! Son buenas para la salud.*

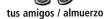
Juan Carlos

 a. Víctor y Tomás

 b. Inés

 c. Raúl

 d. Carmen y yo

 e. Gloria y Victoria

f. yo

Gramática en contexto   139

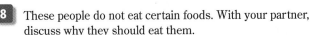

Cultural Notes

Present & Practice

Re-enter / Recycle
Ex. 9: activities from Chap. 1; pastimes, destinations, expressions of emotion, and adverbs describing when things take place from Chap. 3

9 Answers
a. dibujamos
b. practican
c. hablan
d. ayudamos
e. comen
f. debemos
g. vamos
h. leemos
i. hablan
j. ven

Sujetos compuestos

- When you talk about yourself and someone else, you really mean "we." Therefore, you should use the *nosotros* form of the verb.

  Alejandro y yo (nosotros) estudi**amos** por la noche.
  Tú y yo (nosotros) com**emos** a las doce.

- When speaking to more than one person—even if you call one of them *tú*—use the *ustedes* form of the verb.
  Tú y Tomás (ustedes) practi**can** deportes.

- When you talk about more than one person or thing, use the *ellos / ellas* form of the verb.
  Marta y él (ellos) beb**en** jugo de uva.
  Marta y ella (ellas) escuch**an** música.

9 Imagine that these students are talking about activities they usually do or activities they are planning to do. Choose the correct verb form to complete each of the following sentences.

a. Mis amigos y yo *(dibujamos / dibujan)* en el parque.
b. ¡No me digas! Pablo y ella *(practican / practicamos)* deportes también.
c. Esteban y tú *(hablan / hablamos)* por teléfono todos los días, ¿verdad?
d. Juan va a cocinar hoy. Él y yo siempre *(ayudan / ayudamos)* en casa.
e. Él y ella *(comemos / comen)* en casa los fines de semana.
f. Tú y yo *(deben / debemos)* ir de compras mañana por la mañana.
g. ¡Qué lástima! Patricia y yo no *(vamos / van)* a ir de pesca en el verano.
h. Elena nunca lee, pero mis amigos y yo *(leen / leemos)* todos los días.
i. José y mis amigas siempre *(hablamos / hablan)* después de las clases.
j. No veo la tele por la tarde, pero Juanita y tú *(ves / ven)* la tele todos los días por la tarde.

■ Alimentación
Plátano, rico para comer

■ Anualmente se producen 84 millones de toneladas de plátanos en el mundo.

■ La producción en Canarias es de 406.000 toneladas al año, de las cuales 372.000 se consumen fuera de las islas.

■ El plátano es uno de los frutos con más calorías: 66 kcal por cada 100 gramos (el peso aproximado de 1 unidad).

■ Es una fruta que contiene vitamina C, B1, B2 y A. Además es muy rica en potasio, hierro, calcio, fósforo y sodio, pero no tiene nada de colesterol.

■ Existen más de 500 variedades de bananas.

■ Las dimensiones de los plátanos pueden variar desde los 5 centímetros hasta el medio metro.

■ En Canarias viven del plátano unas 35.000 personas. El negocio supera los 30.000 millones de pesetas.

■ Nueva Guinea es el país donde má se consumen, unos 250 kg por persona

This item from the Spanish magazine *Muy interesante* contains so many cognates that you will probably be successful in reading it. With a partner, make a list of the cognates. If a section seems difficult, can you work together to understand the gist of it? In English, write down any three facts that you learned from reading this.

Options

Strategies for Reaching All Students

Students Needing Extra Help
Ahora lo sabes: Have students write out this section so they can check off what they have mastered.

Enrichment
Ex. 9: As a written assignment, students may write sentences using the verb forms not used in this exercise, creating correct subjects for them, and any reasonable variations on the vocabulary in the original sentences.

Extended Written Practice/Homework
1. Write two sentences telling where you and your friends eat at different times.
2. Write two sentences telling where you and your family go at different times.
3. Write two sentences telling what activities you and one of your friends do after school or on the weekends.

Una paella típica de España

PASO CULTURAL

Paella originated in Valencia, in eastern Spain. This dish typically contains rice flavored with saffron *(azafrán)*, the spice that gives *paella* its golden color, and may include chicken, pork, or other meat, fish, shellfish, and a variety of vegetables. Why do you suppose *paella* is such a staple in Spain? Is there a similar type of regional dish where you live? What is it, and why is it so popular?

Ahora lo sabes

Can you:

► tell that you like or don't like certain food groups?
—(No) _____ las frutas.

► describe groups of people or things?
—Los huevos son ___,
pero las verduras son ___.

► say what you eat or drink at different meals?
—A ver . . . En el desayuno (nosotros) ___ cereal y ___ jugo de naranja.

► make clear to or about whom you are talking when more than one person is referred to?
—Timoteo y tú ___ la televisión todos los días, ¿verdad?

MORE PRACTICE

Más práctica y tarea, p. 518–519
Practice Workbook 4–5, 4–9

Gramática en contexto   141

Cultural Notes ☀

Multiple Intelligences
Bodily/Kinesthetic
Bring in various kinds of fruits and place them in a large bowl on a table. Place a blindfold on a student and let the class select a piece of fruit. See if the student can guess what it is by smelling and touching it.
Verbal/Linguistic
Have students, in pairs, describe their favorite ingredients in a fruit salad *(ensalada de fruta)*.

Paso cultural
(p. 140) Responses will vary.

(p. 141) Paella's popularity may be owed to Spain's long coastline and abundant seafood./Jambalaya from the Cajun region of Louisiana is one example of a similar dish from the U.S. Students may mention other similar dishes./Answers will vary.

(p. 140, realia)
Plantains and bananas are a staple throughout Latin America. Plantains are closely related to bananas, but are much starchier and are fried or boiled rather than eaten raw. Plantains are not as popular as bananas in the U.S., but increasing amounts are being imported each year for the Latino market. Ask students: What are some Latin American countries that export bananas to the U.S.? (Brazil, Ecuador, Mexico, Honduras, Colombia, Costa Rica)

Standards 1.1; 1.2; 2.1; 2.2; 3.1; 4.1; 4.2   **141**

Apply

 Pronunciation Tape 4–3

 Todo junto A

Play

Todo junto B

Play

Using the Video
Video segment 3: See the Video Teacher's Guide.

 Video Activity C

 Pasos vivos 1 CD-ROM
Video Monitor, Video Presentation Maker

Critical Thinking: Synthesizing
Actividades: Have small groups create an invitation to a dinner party that they will be hosting. Invitations should include a brief menu. Have other groups accept or decline the invitation. (Review Chap. 3 vocabulary related to accepting or declining invitations.)

Answers: Actividades
1–2 Dialogues will vary, but encourage students to use the full range of chapter vocabulary.

Todo junto

Actividades

1 People have different tastes in food. Tell your partner your opinion of different foods and drinks. He or she will agree or disagree. For example:

A —*Las ensaladas son muy sabrosas. A mí me encantan.*

B —*¿Te encantan? Pues, a mí no me gustan nada. ¡Qué asco!*
o: *¡No me digas! A mí también me gustan las ensaladas.*

2 On the weekend our pattern of eating often changes. Find out what your partner's meals are usually like on the weekend. Ask:

• at what time he or she eats certain meals
• whether he or she eats alone or with family or friends
• what the meal usually consists of

142   Capítulo 4

Options

Strategies for Reaching All Students

Spanish-Speaking Students
Ex. 2: Have pairs of students write out the exercise. Then have them present the exercise orally.

Students Needing Extra Help
Exs. 1–2: Create some worksheets in which parts of a complete dialogue are missing, as in a cloze activity. For example, in the first dialogue a few words can be missing that the students will fill in. Then have a dialogue where *Estudiante B*'s responses are missing. Finally, have the students create a complete dialogue. Build up to this carefully so as not to overwhelm.

Ex. 1: Have students use their Organizers. Talk through students' likes and dislikes of foods. Write some on the chalkboard.
Ex. 2: Review time-telling from Chap. 2. Have students use their Organizers.

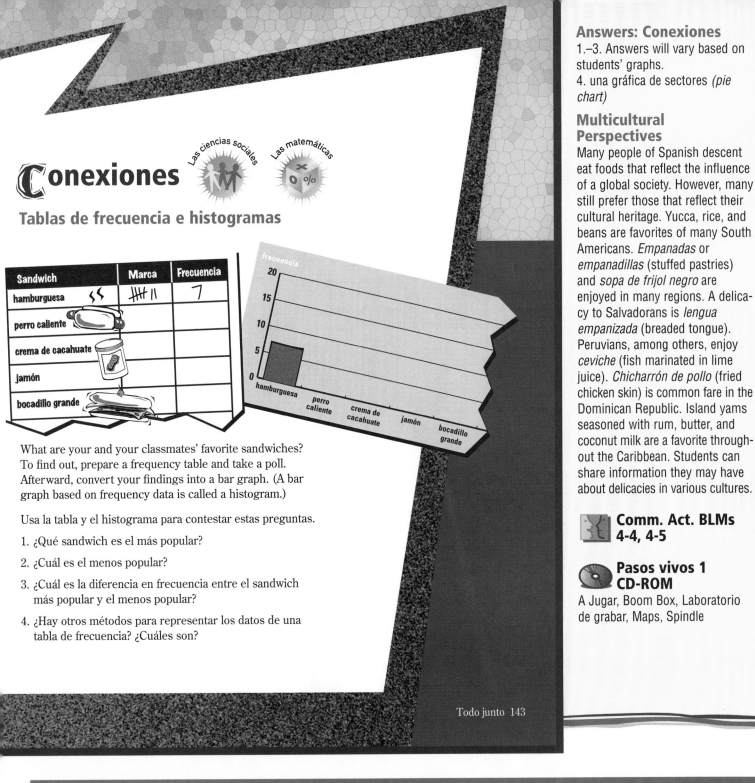

Conexiones

Las ciencias sociales Las matemáticas

Tablas de frecuencia e histogramas

Sandwich	Marca	Frecuencia
hamburguesa	⌇⌇ ₩II	7
perro caliente		
crema de cacahuate		
jamón		
bocadillo grande		

frecuencia

20
15
10
5
0

hamburguesa · perro caliente · crema de cacahuate · jamón · bocadillo grande

What are your and your classmates' favorite sandwiches? To find out, prepare a frequency table and take a poll. Afterward, convert your findings into a bar graph. (A bar graph based on frequency data is called a histogram.)

Usa la tabla y el histograma para contestar estas preguntas.

1. ¿Qué sandwich es el más popular?

2. ¿Cuál es el menos popular?

3. ¿Cuál es la diferencia en frecuencia entre el sandwich más popular y el menos popular?

4. ¿Hay otros métodos para representar los datos de una tabla de frecuencia? ¿Cuáles son?

Multicultural Perspectives

Many people of Spanish descent eat foods that reflect the influence of a global society. However, many still prefer those that reflect their cultural heritage. Yucca, rice, and beans are favorites of many South Americans. *Empanadas* or *empanadillas* (stuffed pastries) and *sopa de frijol negro* are enjoyed in many regions. A delicacy to Salvadorans is *lengua empanizada* (breaded tongue). Peruvians, among others, enjoy *ceviche* (fish marinated in lime juice). *Chicharrón de pollo* (fried chicken skin) is common fare in the Dominican Republic. Island yams seasoned with rum, butter, and coconut milk are a favorite throughout the Caribbean. Students can share information they may have about delicacies in various cultures.

Comm. Act. BLMs 4-4, 4-5

Pasos vivos 1 CD-ROM
A Jugar, Boom Box, Laboratorio de grabar, Maps, Spindle

Cooperative Learning
In groups of three or four, have students compile a list of foods and beverages they like to eat and drink. Then have them decide as a group which food or beverage items are good for them (healthful), or which ones they *should* eat or drink. Ask a member from each group to summarize. Later, have all groups compile a whole-class list. Which items were mentioned most often?

Multiple Intelligences
Bodily/Kinesthetic
1) Have students set up a restaurant scene in which two students order and one student writes down the information.
2) Have students create vocabulary Bingo cards using food words. Play this as a game or final review.
Interpersonal/Social
1) Have students make menus with a choice of American-style foods on one side and

Latin American or Caribbean-style foods on the other. Display these around the room.
2) See Cooperative Learning.
Logical/Mathematical
1) Have students survey the class for their favorite fast-food restaurant. Show results in a chart, bar, or graph.
2) See *Conexiones*.
Visual/Spatial
See Students Needing Extra Help.

Apply

Process Reading
For a description of process reading, see p. 48.

Answers
Antes de leer
Answers will vary.

Mira la lectura

1 potatoes, tomatoes, and cocoa

2 in the sixteenth and seventeenth centuries

¡Vamos a leer!

Antes de leer

STRATEGY ➤ **Using prior knowledge**

What you are about to read tells the history of chocolate, which was used by the Mayas and the Aztecs of Mexico over a thousand years ago. And they used it in a very different way! How do you think chocolate got to Europe?

As you already know, you can use pictures and your own experience with certain kinds of reading materials to predict and understand the information you might find there.

Mira la lectura

STRATEGY ➤ **Using cognates**

As you read, try to use cognates (words that are similar to English words) to help you figure out the meaning.

1 What are some of the other products that the Europeans found when they came to America?

2 When did chocolate become one of the most popular drinks in Europe?

La historia del chocolate

En el siglo XV los conquistadores llegan a América. Allí descubren muchos productos nuevos para la comida española y europea, por ejemplo: la papa, el tomate y el cacao. El cacao es uno de los ingredientes que los aztecas usan para hacer el *tchocolatl* (palabra azteca para chocolate).

Los aztecas preparan el *tchocolatl* con cacao, verduras y varios tipos de chiles. Es una bebida muy fuerte que los indios beben en sus ceremonias religiosas. Pero el *tchocolatl* azteca es muy diferente del chocolate que bebemos hoy.

En Europa, el *tchocolatl* se transforma en una bebida más líquida y más dulce. En los siglos XVI y XVII el chocolate es una de las bebidas más populares de Europa. El chocolate caliente se hace con cacao y agua o leche. Hoy, en España, hay chocolaterías, lugares donde sirven chocolate casi exclusivamente.

144 Capítulo 4

Options

Strategies for Reaching All Students

Spanish-Speaking Students

📖 **Un paso más Ex. 4-I**

Students Needing Extra Help
Place the reading in context by reminding students that the chapter theme is food.
Antes de leer: Remind students to use context clues in the text along with the visuals to help them understand the reading.

Mira la lectura: You may wish to provide students with a brief overview of the history of the Mayas and Aztecs.
Infórmate: Go over the questions with students before you begin the reading. Emphasize that they don't need to know every word in order to understand the text.

Infórmate

 STRATEGY **Using context to get meaning**

Using context to get meaning is another useful strategy. When you are reading and you run across a word you don't understand, look at the other words in the sentence. See if knowing those words can help you understand the one you don't know.

Read this selection again. Make a list of five words you don't understand. Then try to guess their meaning by looking at the surrounding words.

1 How and when was chocolate introduced in Europe?

2 How did the Aztecs prepare their *tchocolatl?* Was it an everyday drink or was it used on special occasions? Explain.

3 How was the chocolate the conquistadores brought to Europe different from the Aztecan *tchocolatl?*

Detalle de *La gran ciudad de Tenochtitlán* (1945), Diego Rivera

Aplicación

List as many cognates as you can that you found in this reading.

PASO CULTURAL This detail of a mural by Mexican artist Diego Rivera (1886-1957) in *el Palacio Nacional* in Mexico City shows the bustling market at Tenochtitlán, capital of the Aztec Empire. In the picture, we see cacao beans being traded. Aztecs believed that cacao seeds were brought by a prophet from paradise. How do you think this belief affected the value placed on cacao in Aztec society?

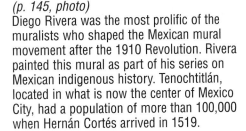

Infórmate
Lists will vary.

1 Chocolate was introduced in Europe in the sixteenth century as a sweeter and thinner liquid than its Aztec counterpart.

2 The Aztecs prepared *tchocolatl* with cocoa, vegetables, and different types of *chiles.* It was used in religious ceremonies.

3 Answers may vary, but may include that the chocolate differed in taste, appearance, and usage.

Aplicación
Lists will vary, but may include: *productos, cacao, ingredientes, aztecas, chocolate, preparan, tipos, chiles, indios, ceremonias religiosas, diferente, Europa, se transforma, líquida, populares, sirven, exclusivamente.*

www Internet Activities
Have students go to www.pasoapaso.com for additional activities and practice.

Cultural Notes ☀

Enrichment
Bring in a recipe for *mole* and show how it ties in with the Aztec recipe described in the text.

(p. 145, photo)
Diego Rivera was the most prolific of the muralists who shaped the Mexican mural movement after the 1910 Revolution. Rivera painted this mural as part of his series on Mexican indigenous history. Tenochtitlán, located in what is now the center of Mexico City, had a population of more than 100,000 when Hernán Cortés arrived in 1519.

Paso cultural
Answers will vary. Students may mention that the cacao seeds had a religious connection, that they were highly valued, and so on.

Apply

Process Writing
For information regarding developing a writing portfolio, see p. 50.

Multicultural Perspectives

With the influences and infusion of Hispanic cultures within the Americas, many restaurants cater to the varied tastes of their customers. Today, Hispanic cuisine can be classified as traditional or *nouveau,* vegetarian or *con carne,* Tex-Mex or Santa Fe, Salvadoran or Nicaraguan, and so on. Other establishments may feature only traditional Spanish dishes. Invite students to identify and describe other types of Hispanic cuisine.

 Pasos vivos 1 CD-ROM
Word Processor

¡Vamos a escribir!

Letrero de un restaurante en Santiago, Chile

Think about what, when, and where you eat on a typical day. Then write a short paragraph about your favorite meal of the day. Follow these steps.

1 Answer these questions, then use the answers to write your paragraph.

- ¿A qué hora comes tu comida favorita?
- ¿Dónde comes: en la casa, en la escuela o en un restaurante?
- ¿Con quién comes?
- ¿Qué comes y qué bebes?

Comprando frutas para la merienda en Cartagena, Colombia

Options

Strategies for Reaching All Students

Spanish-Speaking Students

 Un paso más Exs. 4-J, 4-K

Students Needing Extra Help
Step 1: Have students use their Organizers from earlier chapters to review time-telling, places, and *con.*
Step 3: Have students use their Organizers to check spelling.

Enrichment
If possible, bring in a poster of the food groups and have students make a poster showing similar items, but with the labels in Spanish. Students may wish to make original drawings or clip photographs from food magazines to make their posters more attractive.

Multiple Intelligences
Bodily/Kinesthetic
See Enrichment.
Intrapersonal/Introspective
See step 1.

2 Show your paragraph to a partner. Does he or she have any ideas to suggest? Did you use the answers to all the questions in your paragraph? Think about any changes you may want to make, then write a second draft.

3 Check for correct spelling and punctuation. Did you use the *yo* form of the verbs? Did you use *me gusta(n)* or *me encanta(n)*? Does your partner have any further suggestions?

4 Write your final draft. Add the corrected paragraph to your writing portfolio.

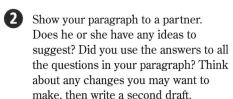
Comiendo alcapurrias *(fritters)*, una comida popular para la merienda en el Viejo San Juan, Puerto Rico

Cocinando arepas en el mercado en Saquisilí, Ecuador

¡Vamos a escribir! 147

Cultural Notes

(p. 146, bottom photo)
Fruit vendors are common on the streets of many Latin American countries. One reason for this is the abundance of a wide variety of fruits in tropical places such as Cartagena. U.S. consumers would easily recognize some of these, such as bananas and pineapples, and more recent imports such as mangos and papayas. Many other tropical fruits, however, have yet to become familiar or popular in the U.S.

(p. 147, left photo)
Green bananas are widely used in Puerto Rican cuisine. These girls from Viejo San Juan are enjoying *alcapurrias*—pastries made of green banana dough with pork inside.

(p. 147, right photo)
This vendor in Saquisilí, Ecuador, is preparing the Andean staple *arepas,* which are fried cornmeal cakes mixed with cheese. The Thursday market at Saquisilí is one of the most important indigenous markets in Latin America, occupying eight of the town's *plazas* and most of its streets. Ask students: What interests you about this photo? Why?

Standards 1.3; 2.2; 3.1 **147**

Assess & Summarize

Test Preparation

You may want to assign parts of this section as written homework or as an in-class writing activity prior to administering the *Examen de habilidades*.

Answers

Listening: *A esta hora siempre quiero comer cereal, huevos con jamón, pan tostado y café con leche. Prefiero comer frutas por la tarde.* Eugenio is talking about breakfast.

Reading: This product is recommended for physically active adolescents; it's a nutritious snack.

Writing: Writing samples will vary, but students should use the chapter vocabulary. Look for logical sentences.

Culture: Answers will vary, but may include: *El desayuno* is a light meal that consists of coffee and bread or rolls with butter and jam. *El almuerzo* or *la comida* is the largest and most important meal of the day. It is eaten between noon and 3:00. *La merienda* is a late afternoon meal that may resemble an English tea. *La cena* is the evening meal, which may be served around 7:00 or later.

Repaso ¿Lo sabes bien?

This section will help you organize your studying for the proficiency test, where you will be asked to do similar, though not identical, tasks. There will not be any models on the test.

► **Listening**

Can you understand when people talk about food? Listen as your teacher reads you a sample similar to what you will hear on the test. Which meal is Eugenio talking about?

► **Reading**

Can you quickly read through this ad and use the context to guess any word or words that you might not know? Who is this product recommended for and why?

La crema de cacao es un alimento especialmente indicado para adolescentes con una gran energía. Es un alimento nutritivo, ideal para la merienda.

► **Writing**

Can you write the order for the customers you are waiting on? Here is a sample:

Cuenta

una hamburguesa
un sandwich de jamón
dos papas fritas
dos refrescos

► **Culture**

Can you describe the four daily meals that are typical of many Spanish-speaking countries?

"Me encantan los refrescos."

www.pasoapaso.com

► **Speaking**

Can you discuss your food preferences with a partner? Do you like or dislike the same foods? For example:

A —*¿Te gusta el pescado?*

B —*No me gusta nada. ¿Y a ti?*

A —*No mucho. Mi madre siempre cocina pescado los viernes. Es horrible. ¿Te gustan las zanahorias?*

B —*Sí, pero prefiero las papas o las judías verdes. No me gustan nada las cebollas. ¡Qué asco!*

A —*Pues, a mí me encantan las cebollas. Son muy sabrosas.*

148   Capítulo 4

Options

Strategies for Reaching All Students

Students Needing Extra Help

Have students write out this section so they can check off what they have mastered.

Resumen del vocabulario

Use the vocabulary from this chapter to help you:

► describe what you like and don't like to eat and drink

► tell when you have meals

► say whether you are hungry or thirsty

to indicate hunger or thirst
tener hambre / sed

to describe meals
beber: (yo) bebo
    (tú) bebes
comer: (yo) como
     (tú) comes
la cena
la comida
el desayuno
en el desayuno / el almuerzo /
  la cena

to talk about foods
el arroz
el bistec
el cereal
la ensalada
las frutas
  la manzana
  la naranja
  el plátano
  la uva
la hamburguesa
el huevo
el jamón
el pan
  el pan tostado
la papa
  las papas al horno
  las papas fritas

el pescado
el pollo
el queso
los sandwiches
  el sandwich de jamón
   y queso
la sopa de pollo / de tomate /
  de verduras
las verduras
  la cebolla
  los guisantes
  las judías verdes
  la lechuga
  el tomate
  la zanahoria

to talk about drinks
las bebidas
  el agua *(f.)*
  el café
  el jugo de naranja
  la leche
  la limonada
  el refresco
  el té
  el té helado

to describe foods
bueno, -a (para la salud)
horrible
malo, -a (para la salud)
sabroso, -a

to express likes or preferences
más o menos
me encanta(n)
me gusta(n)
preferir: (yo) prefiero
     (tú) prefieres

to express an opinion
Creo que sí / no.
¡Qué asco!

to ask for an explanation
¿Por qué?

to give an explanation
porque

to elicit agreement
¿verdad?

to refer to obligation
deber: (yo) debo
    (tú) debes

to indicate frequency
nunca
siempre

to refer to something you cannot name
algo

other useful words
son
unos, unas

Resumen 149

Assessment

 Prueba cumulativa

 Examen de habilidades

 Test Generator

Additional Assessment Options

 Comm. Act. BLMs

Small Group Activities
Situation Cards

 Pasos vivos 1 CD-ROM

Slide Presentation Maker, Video Presentation Maker, Word Processor, Spindle

 ¿Lo sabes bien? Video Quiz

www Internet Activities
Self-Test

CAPÍTULO 5

THEME: FAMILY

SCOPE AND SEQUENCE Pages 150–179

COMMUNICATION

Topics

Family members

Personal physical characteristics

Age

Numbers 60–100

Objectives

To explain how names are formed in Spanish-speaking countries

To talk about family members

To tell someone's name

To ask and tell how old someone is

To indicate possession

To talk about what someone likes

To indicate number

To talk about people

To describe people, animals, and things

To name animals

CULTURE

The family

Spanish last names

GRAMMAR

El verbo tener

El verbo ser

Los adjetivos posesivos

Ancillaries available for use with Chapter 5

Multisensory/Technology

 Overheads, 26–30

 Audio Tapes and CDs

 Vocabulary Art Blackline Masters for Hands-On Learning, pp. 28–32/CD-ROM

Classroom Crossword

Video

Pasos vivos 1 CD-ROM

  Internet Activities www.pasoapaso.com

Print

 Practice Workbook, pp. 53–63

 Writing, Audio & Video Activities, pp. 29–34, 105–107, 160–161

 Communicative Activity Blackline Masters

Pair and Small Group Activities, pp. 36–41

Situation Cards, p. 42

 Un paso más: Actividades para ampliar tu español, pp. 26–31

TPR Storytelling

Assessment

 Assessment Program
Pruebas, pp. 67–76
Examen de habilidades, pp. 77–80

 Test Generator

Video still from Chap. 5

149A

Planning Express, Teaching
Resources Library, and Clip Art
Library

¿Lo sabes bien?
Video Quiz

Cultural Overview ☼

Family Ties

Strong family ties and allegiances are central to the social structures of many Spanish-speaking countries. The structure of family surnames, which contain both the mother's and the father's family names, reflects the great importance of the family unit. For example, if Sr. David Ramírez Tejeda is married to Sra. Ángela Díaz Contreras, their children will use the surname Ramírez Díaz.

Although strict gender-defined roles are gradually disappearing, vestiges of a patriarchal family structure can still be found in the different treatment of young men and women within some families. In working-class families, it is often assumed that the girls will help take care of their younger brothers and sisters and do other domestic work. Boys are largely exempt from these expectations. Boys often receive more education than girls do and have greater independence at an earlier age.

Until recent years, divorce was illegal in several Latin American countries. Although divorce is now possible, it remains socially unacceptable in many places and is often granted with stipulations. In Mexico, for example, a divorce judgment may stipulate that one or both parties may not remarry for a year or more. The Mexican Civil Code specifies such a restriction because marriage is viewed as the foundation of the family and is not to be entered into lightly or abandoned easily.

In many Spanish-speaking countries, it is considered a duty to spend time with one's family. People would almost never consider missing an important family event such as a baptism, wedding, or birthday. Parties for such events span several generations with all family members attending. Everyone from babies to grandparents can be seen at all kinds of parties.

Good friends are also included in many family events. In many cases, friends are considered part of the family. Friendship ties, like family bonds, are strong. Relatives and friends will help each other out and are regularly a part of the daily lives of each other's families.

Introduce

Re-entry of Concepts

The following list represents words, expressions, and grammar topics re-entered from *El primer paso* to Chap. 4:

El primer paso
Calendar expressions
Numbers 0–31
Greetings

Chapter 1
Activities
Gustar expressions
Adjectives describing personality

Chapter 2
School supplies
School subjects
Numbers 32–59
Possession and need

Chapter 3
Pastimes
Destinations
Adverbs describing when things
    take place

Chapter 4
Likes or preferences
Opinions
Adjective agreement

Planning

Cross-Curricular Connections

Drawing / Art Connection (pp. 158–159)
Have students draw an alien creature or monster as homework. The next day, pair students. As one student describes his or her creature in Spanish, the other student draws it. Then have the pairs switch roles. Pairs then compare drawings. Award a prize for the two drawings that are the most similar. Post some of the pairs of pictures on the walls and use for vocabulary warm-up questions.

Journalism Connection (pp. 170–171)
Have pairs of students each assume the identity of a famous person. Tell them that they will be interviewing each other for an article in the school newspaper. Give them several minutes to write a few appropriate questions before beginning their interviews. As homework, students can write out their interview and include a picture and headline.

Spanish in Your Community
Have students obtain a copy of a Spanish-language newspaper published in your community (if available). Ask them to look through the society section of this paper and find an announcement of a wedding, baptism, or funeral. Have them determine the family relationships mentioned in the article. As an alternative, have students look through the local phone book to see how many people in their community have common Spanish surnames such as González,

CAPÍTULO 5
¿Cómo es tu familia?

Objectives

At the end of this chapter you will be able to:

► describe family members and friends

► tell what someone's age is

► say what other people like and do not like to do

► explain how names are formed in Spanish-speaking countries

PASO CULTURAL

To a Spanish speaker, *familia* refers to extended family and long-standing friends as well as to parents and siblings. Despite social changes, family is still of highest importance in Hispanic cultures, and family members are always well represented at Sunday dinners and special occasions. Using what you know, explain why an *amigo* might also be considered *familia* to a Spanish speaker.

Cuatro generaciones de una familia puertorriqueña en San Juan

151

Cultural Notes ☀

García, and Pérez. Have students discover more surnames as they look through the phone book. (You may also wish to bring in any phone directories printed in Spanish.)

Paso cultural
Possible answers: An *amigo* is someone whose friendship you'll have for life, and whose family you also know well; *amigos* help each other and care for each other unconditionally.

(pp. 150–151, photo)
Respect and affection for elders are strong values in Hispanic culture. In daily life, elders often help their grown children with child care, keeping house, or even running a family business. As they advance in age, elders generally move in with their children to be cared for by the entire family. Ask students: How does this aspect of family life compare with those you might know of in other cultures?

Preview

¡Piénsalo bien!

Play

 Video Activity A

Using the Video

This chapter's video focuses on family. Students will join our host in her own Guadalajara home and meet her family. Then they will accompany her to meet a family in nearby Tlaquepaque.

To prepare students for the video, first ask them to predict what this chapter's video will be about. Then have students watch the segment several times. After the first time, you may wish to have them brainstorm possible vocabulary and expressions they will need to talk about what they saw on the video. Ask students to identify:

a) ways in which the Mexican families were similar to their own family, and b) ways in which the families were different from their own family.

Video segment 1: For more teaching suggestions, see the Video Teacher's Guide.

¡Piensa en la CULTURA!

Santiago, Chile

Families in Mexico and Chile

Look at the photos and compare the families to your own. How many people are in your family? Which family members do you think make up a family? Do you consider your grandparents, uncles, aunts, and cousins as your "family" or are they just "relatives"? Do you all get together sometimes?

San Miguel de Allende, México

"Me llamo Maricarmen y estoy con mi familia para celebrar el cumpleaños de mi abuelo. Tiene 67 años."

Who do you think the *abuelo* is? How did you know?

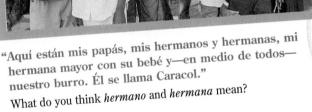

"Aquí están mis papás, mis hermanos y hermanas, mi hermana mayor con su bebé y—en medio de todos—nuestro burro. Él se llama Caracol."

What do you think *hermano* and *hermana* mean?

Options

Strategies for Reaching All Students

Spanish-Speaking Students
Ask Spanish-speaking students: *¿Qué es una familia? ¿Cómo es tu familia? ¿Es grande o pequeña? ¿Quiénes son los miembros de tu familia?*

 Un paso más Ex. 5-A

Students Needing Extra Help
Be sensitive to the fact that many of your students' families may not be typical. Discuss what an American family today may look like: single parent, stepsisters and half brothers, and so on. Not all students will want to discuss this issue. Some may have neighbors or others with whom they feel close. Be open to these ideas. Imaginary families or the family they would like to have when they become adults are alternative topics.

Multiple Intelligences
Bodily/Kinesthetic
See Teaching Suggestions.
Visual/Spatial
See Using the Video.

"Tenemos una familia grande. Nos gusta pasar los domingos y los días de fiesta juntos."

Ciudad de México

www.pasoapaso.com
Visit these countries on-line

¡Piensa en la cultura! 153

Cultural Exploration

PASO CULTURAL

In Latin America, as in the United States, pets are often treated like family members. Depending on landscape and climate, iguanas, boa constrictors, armadillos, and monkeys may be kept as pets, as well as dogs, cats, and birds. Would you or could you have an iguana or armadillo as a pet? Why or why not? What are some of the differences that you know of in the way various cultures view certain animals?

Teaching Suggestions

To enhance the discussion of families, bring to class photographs of families from a variety of different cultures. Ask students to clip photos from magazines and newspapers. Help them develop a bulletin-board display of the pictures, complete with Spanish captions.

Keep in mind that for many students the family is a sensitive topic for discussion. Whenever possible, offer an alternative to focusing on the student's own family by using a fictional family or that of a famous person.

Answers: ¡Piensa en la cultura!

(p. 152) Answers will vary.

(p. 152, top photo) See if students can guess the meaning of *abuelo* (grandfather) by using context clues. Can they associate *67 años* with the eldest man in the photo?

(p. 152, bottom photo) Assist students as needed with the meaning of *hermano* (brother) and *hermana* (sister).

Cultural Notes

Paso cultural
Answers will vary.

(p. 152, bottom photo)
In Hispanic countries, the *patio* is the center of family life, where members gather for special events and family photos. It's also where many women do much of the daily work of cooking and cleaning. The *patio* is often planted with seeds and cuttings handed down over generations. Ask students: What space in your home is the center of family life? Why? How is that space used by your family?

Present

Communicative Objectives
- To talk about family members
- To tell someone's name
- To ask and tell how old someone is
- To indicate possession
- To talk about what someone likes
- To indicate number

 Overheads 26–27

 Vocabulary Art BLMs/CD-ROM

 Pronunciation Tape 5-1

 **Vocabulario para conversar A**

Play

Using the Video
Video segment 2: See the Video Teacher's Guide.

 Video Activity B

Grammar Preview
Su and *de* are presented here lexically. The explanation of possessive adjectives appears in the grammar section on p. 170.

Vocabulario para conversar

¿Cómo se llama tu hermano?

Here are some new words and expressions you will need to talk about your family, to tell what someone's age is, and to say what other people like and do not like to do. Read them several times, then turn the page and practice with a partner.

mis abuelos

mi abuelo
Pedro, 80 años

mi abuela
Carmen, 75 años

mis padres — mis tíos

mi madre
María, 46 años

mi padre
Luis, 52 años

mi tía
Verónica, 50 años

mi tío
Tomás, 48 años

mis hermanos*

mis primos

mi hermano
José, 19 años

mi hermana
Gabriela, 23 años

yo
Mariana, 15 años

mi primo
Carlos, 16 años

mi prima
Ana, 18 años

Hermanos can mean either "brothers" or "brothers and sisters."

154   Capítulo 5

Options

Strategies for Reaching All Students

Students Needing Extra Help
Have students start to fill in the Organizer. Students often have difficulty reading a family tree, especially the reference to *yo*. Show them how the relationships change when *yo* becomes another person. For example, if Ana becomes *yo,* then Verónica becomes *la madre* and María becomes *la tía,* and so on. Point out the similarities between *abuelo / abuela, tío / tía,* etc.

También necesitas . . . : Point out that *único(a)* is used with nouns and age is expressed with *tener*—to "have" so many years.

Enrichment
También necesitas. . . : Elicit from students the English word for which *único(a)* might be a cognate. Explain that *único(a)* has two meanings in Spanish: "only," as in *hijo(a) único(a)* and "unique," as in *¡Eres único(a)!*

Learning Spanish Through Action
STAGING VOCABULARY: *Nombren, Señalen*
MATERIALS: transparency of family tree in the *Vocabulario para conversar*
DIRECTIONS: Using the transparency, have students take the part of Mariana by pointing at each relative as you mention the relationship.

60 sesenta
61 sesenta y uno . . .

70 setenta
71 setenta y uno . . .

80 ochenta
81 ochenta y uno . . .

90 noventa
91 noventa y uno . . .

100 cien

¡NO OLVIDES!

Solo, -a = alone:
Generalmente voy al
parque solo(a).

Sólo = only: María sólo
va al parque.

También necesitas...

el hijo / la hija	*son / daughter*	Tiene ___ años.	*He / she is ___ years old.*
el hijo único / la hija única	*only child (m.) / only child (f.)*	su	*his, her*
¿Cómo se llama?	*What is his / her name?*	de	*of*
¿Cómo se llaman?	*What are their names?*	(A + *person*) le gusta(n) / le encanta(n) ___.	*(He / she) likes / loves ___.*
Se llama(n) ___.	*His / her (their) name(s) is (are) ___.*	¿Cuántos, -as?	*How many?*
¿Cuántos años tiene ___?	*How old is ___?*	sólo	*only*

¿Y qué quiere decir...?
los hijos

Vocabulario para conversar   155

Teaching Suggestions
Preparing students to speak: Use one or two options from each of the categories of Comprehensible Input, Physical Response, or Limited Verbal Response. For a complete explanation of these categories and some sample activities, see pp. T22–T23.

Point out that after *ser,* the article *el / la* is not used with *hijo(a) único(a).*

Class Starter Review
On the day following initial presentation, you might begin the class with one of these activities:
1) Use the transparency of a family tree with one person labeled *yo.* Point to other members of the family and ask individual students who these relatives are in relation to *yo.* On the following day, label a different person *yo.* On the third day, arrange pictures of famous people in a family tree on the chalkboard and do the same activity.
2) Have pairs of students find out the name of at least one member of each other's family.

www Internet Activities
Juegos

Extended Written Practice/Homework
1. Choose four members of Mariana's family. Write sentences telling the names of the people and their relationship to Mariana.
2. Choose three other members of Mariana's family and write sentences telling their ages.

Multiple Intelligences
Bodily/Kinesthetic
See Learning Spanish Through Action.
Musical/Rhythmic
Write the numbers 1–100 on small squares of paper and have each student draw several numbers from a hat until none are left. Begin a rhythmical beat with the class using claps and/or snaps. The student who has the number 1 begins on any beat by saying *Uno* while clapping/snapping. The student who has the number 2 says *Dos,* and so on.

See how far the class can continue without missing a beat.
Verbal/Linguistic
See Pronunciation tape 5-1.
Visual/Spatial
See Overheads 26–27, the Vocabulary Art BLMs/CD-ROM, Using the Video, and Class Starter Review.

Standards 1.1; 1.2; 4.1; 5.1   155

Practice & Apply

Re-enter / Recycle

Ex. 2: numbers 0–31 from *El primer paso*, numbers 32–59 from Chap. 1

Exs. 4–5: activities from Chap. 1

Ex. 6: numbers 0–31 from *El primer paso*, numbers 32–59 from Chap. 2

Reteach / Review: Definite & Indefinite Articles

Do a quick practice exercise to review definite articles by naming a noun and calling on individuals to give the correct definite or indefinite article.

Answers: Empecemos a conversar

1 ESTUDIANTE A
a. ¿Cómo se llama el tío de Mariana?
b. ... el hermano ...
c. ... la hermana ...
d. ... el primo ...
e. ... la prima ...
f. ... el abuelo ...
g. Questions will vary.

ESTUDIANTE B
a. Se llama Tomás.
b. ... José.
c. ... Gabriela.
d. ... Carlos.
e. ... Ana.
f. ... Pedro.
g. Answers will vary.

Empecemos a conversar

With a partner, take turns being *Estudiante A* and *Estudiante B*. Use the words that are cued or given in the balloons to replace the underlined sections in the model. 💡 means you can make your own choices.

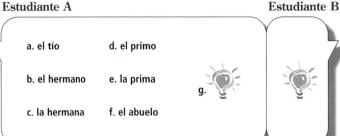

Celebrando un bautismo en San Juan, Puerto Rico

For Exercises 1 and 2, refer to the family tree on page 154.

1 A —¿Cómo se llama *la tía* de Mariana?
B —*Se llama Verónica.* | la tía |

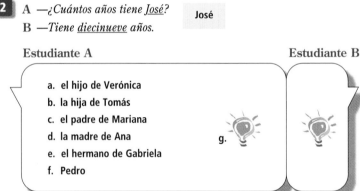

Estudiante A

a. el tío   d. el primo
b. el hermano   e. la prima
c. la hermana   f. el abuelo
g. 💡

Estudiante B

g. 💡

2 A —¿Cuántos años tiene *José*? | José |
B —*Tiene diecinueve años.*

Estudiante A

a. el hijo de Verónica
b. la hija de Tomás
c. el padre de Mariana
d. la madre de Ana
e. el hermano de Gabriela
f. Pedro
g. 💡

Estudiante B

g. 💡

Options

Strategies for Reaching All Students

Spanish-Speaking Students

Try to pair bilingual and non-bilingual students for Exs. 1–4.
Empecemos a escribir: Spanish-speaking students can expand on answers, especially for Ex. 6. Have them tell why they like particular relatives. (*¿Por qué son tus parientes favoritos?*)

 Un paso más Ex. 5-B

Students Needing Extra Help

Ex. 1: Some students may need a review for family relationship words in English. Go over these words before doing the exercise.

Enrichment

Ex. 2: After completing this exercise, have pairs of students ask and tell each other their names and ages.
Ex. 5: To extend this exercise, students can write about three things that they and another family member *don't* like to do.

Extended Written Practice/Homework

1. Write sentences about a friend of yours. Include the friend's name, age, a description (refer to pp. 34–35), and what he or she likes to do.
2. Write about one of your teachers who has children. Include the names and ages of the teacher's children: *El hijo de la señora García se llama Juan. Tiene 13 años.*

In Exercises 3 and 4, ask each other about your own family members or create ideal families to talk about.

3 A —¿Tienes _hermanos_?

B —Sí, tengo _un hermano y una hermana_.
  o: _No, no tengo hermanos._
  o: _No, no tengo. Soy hijo(a) único(a)._

A —¿Cómo se llama(n)?

B —_Mi hermano se llama Daniel y mi hermana se llama Laura_.

Estudiante A   Estudiante B

4 A —¿Qué le gusta hacer a tu _primo_?

B —_Le gusta dibujar_
  o: _Le encanta dibujar._

Estudiante A   Estudiante B

Empecemos a escribir

Write your answers in Spanish.

5 Mention at least three interests you share with other family members. For example: _A mi hermana le gusta practicar deportes. A mí también._

6 Give the name and age of your favorite relatives: _Mi tía favorita se llama Gloria. Tiene cuarenta años (más o menos)._

7 ¿Eres hijo(a) único(a)? Si no, ¿cuántos hermanos tienes?

8 ¿Cuántos primos tienes?

Madre aymará del Sol (1996), por el artista boliviano Roberto Mamani Mamani

Madre e hija en Saquisilí, Ecuador

MORE PRACTICE

Más práctica y tarea, p. 520
Practice Workbook 5–1, 5–2

Vocabulario para conversar   157

2 ESTUDIANTE A
a. ¿Cuántos años tiene el hijo de Verónica?
b. ... la hija de Tomás?
c. ... el padre de Mariana?
d. ... la madre de Ana?
e. ... el hermano de Gabriela?
f. ... Pedro?
g. Questions will vary.

ESTUDIANTE B
a. Tiene dieciséis años.
b. ... dieciocho años.
c. ... cincuenta y dos años.
d. ... cincuenta años.
e. ... diecinueve años.
f. ... ochenta años.
g. Answers will vary.

3–4 Questions and answers will vary.

Answers: Empecemos a escribir

Students may use imaginary people or invent answers.

5–8 Answers will vary, but encourage students to use chapter vocabulary.

 Practice Wkbk. 5-1, 5-2

 Audio Activity 5.1

 Writing Activities 5-A, 5-B

 Pruebas 5-1, 5-2

 Comm. Act. BLM 5-1

Cultural Notes

(p. 156, photo)
For Hispanic Roman Catholics, baptism marks not only the beginning of a child's religious life, but also of the cherished relationship between families that is known as _compadrazgo,_ or co-parenting. A child's godparents, who are called _compadre_ or _comadre_ by the parents, and _padrino_ or _madrina_ by the child, are expected to help in raising the child. Ask students: Why would this relationship be considered a valuable part of a culture?

(p. 157, top photo)
A member of the Aymara people of Bolivia, artist Roberto Mamani Mamani was discouraged from formally studying art because of his ethnic background. Nevertheless, he persevered and in 1991 received his country's most prestigious art award. He has said that his artistic training was in _los talleres_ (workshops) _de mi cultura._ Ask students: Can you name an artist whose works reflect his or her ethnic roots?

(p. 157, bottom photo)
The Thursday market in Saquisilí, Ecuador, is one of the most colorful and crowded Indian markets in the country. It is distinct from other popular Indian markets in Ecuador in that it is aimed primarily at the people of the region, and not at tourists interested in baskets, weavings, or other souvenirs. Ask students: What differences other than the goods sold might there be between this market and other Indian markets in Ecuador?

Present

Chapter Theme
Describing friends and family

Communicative Objectives
- To talk about family members
- To talk about people
- To describe people, animals, and things
- To name animals
- To indicate possession and number

 Overheads 28–29

 Vocabulary Art BLMs/CD-ROM

 Pronunciation Tape 5-2

 Vocabulario para conversar B

Play

Step

Using the Video
Video segment 2: See the Video Teacher's Guide.

 Video Activity B

Vocabulario para conversar

¿Cómo es tu abuelo?

 At Home VIDEO Chapter 5 Vocabulary

Here's the rest of the vocabulary you will need to describe family members and friends.

el hombre
Juan

la mujer
Gloria

el pelo castaño

el pelo rubio

el muchacho
Marcos

la muchacha
Adela

baja

alto

pelirrojos

bonito

feo

el perro

los gemelos
Paco y Pepe

158   Capítulo 5

Options

Strategies for Reaching All Students

Students Needing Extra Help
One way of approaching this vocabulary is to categorize it in the Organizer under "Words That Describe People" according to eyes, hair, etc., or by opposites.
También necesitas. . .: Have students continue filling in their Organizers.

Learning Spanish Through Action
STAGING VOCABULARY: *Dibujen, Señalen*
1) MATERIALS: transparency of people in the *Vocabulario para conversar* or pictures from magazines
DIRECTIONS: Using the transparency or magazine pictures, have students point to the person as you describe eye and hair color and other physical characteristics.

2) MATERIALS: colored chalk
DIRECTIONS: Have volunteers go to the chalkboard to draw people as you describe them. You may wish to use pictures of famous people as models for your descriptions.

viejo
Ramón
el pelo canoso

las gemelas Clara y Claudia
el pelo negro

joven
Daniel

grande

pequeño

el gato

los ojos verdes

los ojos azules

los ojos grises

los ojos negros

los ojos marrones

También necesitas...

mayor, *pl.* mayores	*older*	todos, -as *(pl.)*	*everyone*
menor, *pl.* menores	*younger*	nadie	*nobody*
guapo, -a	*handsome, good-looking*	que	*that, who*
cariñoso, -a	*affectionate, loving*	¿Quiénes?*	*who?*
simpático, -a	*nice, friendly*	**¿Y qué quiere decir . . . ?**	
tiene	*he / she has*	antipático, -a	inteligente
		atractivo, -a	la persona

* We usually use *¿Quiénes?* instead of *¿Quién?* if we know or expect that the answer will be more than one person.

Vocabulario para conversar   159

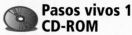

Pasos vivos 1 CD-ROM
Clip Art Album

Grammar Preview
Tiene is presented here lexically. The complete paradigm of *tener* appears on p. 167.

Teaching Suggestions
Preparing students to speak: Use one or two options from each of the categories of Comprehensible Input, Physical Response, or Limited Verbal Response. For a complete explanation of these categories and some sample activities, see pp. T22–T23.

Explain that although *hombre* and *mujer* are the terms for man and woman, Spanish speakers usually say *un señor* and *una señora* when speaking about someone whom they don't know.

Tell students that we say *Tiene el pelo rubio, castaño, negro*, etc., but we say *Es pelirrojo(a)*.

Explain that *ojos negros* literally means "black eyes," but the phrase refers to eyes darker than brown.

Class Starter Review
On the day following initial presentation, you might begin the class with this activity:
Have students state descriptions of two people in their families, including hair and eye color.

Internet Activities
Juegos

Extended Written Practice/Homework
1. Write sentences telling what color hair four different people you know have.
2. Describe your family's dog or cat (or your neighbor's dog or cat). Tell its name, age, and two things about it.
3. Write seven sentences describing the people on pp. 158–159.

Multiple Intelligences
Bodily/Kinesthetic
See Learning Spanish Through Action.
Bodily/Kinesthetic, Logical/Mathematical, and Interpersonal/Social
Have students copy a list of all class members' names and walk around the room finding out what color each person's hair or eyes are. Have students compare their results in pairs and make a graph showing the frequency of each hair or eye color.

Naturalist
Have students write a journal entry in which they describe their favorite outdoor activity spent with family members.
Verbal/Linguistic
See Class Starter Review.
Visual/Spatial
See Overheads 28–29, the Vocabulary Art BLMs/CD-ROM, and Using the Video.

Practice & Apply

Reteach / Review: Adjectives

Do a quick drill in which you name an adjective and call on individual students to give you its plural form.

Answers: Empecemos a conversar

9 ESTUDIANTE B

a. Se llama Esperanza.
b. Se llaman Raquel y Rebeca.
c. La mujer joven se llama Ana María. El hombre joven se llama Julio.
d. Marisol, Raquel y Rebeca tienen ojos azules.
e. Esperanza tiene pelo canoso. Antonio tiene pelo castaño.
f. Ana María, Raquel y Rebeca son pelirrojas.
g. Antonio, Benito y Bernardo tienen ojos marrones. Julio tiene ojos grises.
h. Answers will vary.
i. Nico es pequeño. Tigre es grande.
j. Answers will vary.

Empecemos a conversar

Antonio

Ana María

Julio

Nico

Tigre

Esperanza

Benito y Bernardo   Marisol

Dragón y Muñeca

Raquel y Rebeca

¡NO OLVIDES!

To make an adjective plural, add -s if the adjective ends in a vowel, and -es if it ends in a consonant.

Estudiante A

a. ¿Cómo se llama la mujer vieja?
b. ¿Cómo se llaman las gemelas?
c. ¿Cómo se llama la mujer joven? ¿Y el hombre joven?
d. ¿Quiénes tienen ojos azules?
e. ¿Quiénes tienen pelo canoso? ¿Y pelo castaño?
f. ¿Quiénes son pelirrojas?
g. ¿Quiénes tienen ojos marrones? ¿Y ojos grises?
h. ¿Cómo es Dragón? Y Muñeca, ¿cómo es?
i. ¿Es grande o pequeño Nico? Y Tigre, ¿cómo es?
j. ¿Cómo es Marisol? Y Benito, ¿cómo es?

Estudiante B

Options

Strategies for Reaching All Students

Spanish-Speaking Students
Ex. 14: Have Spanish-speaking students describe someone in their family. (*¿Cómo son tus padres?*)

Un paso más Exs. 5-C, 5-D, 5-E

Students Needing Extra Help
Ex. 9: Before students do this exercise, allow extra time for them to look over the pictures.
Ex. 10: Students may need your input to develop possibilities for *Estudiante A*.
Ex. 11: Before doing this exercise, ask students similar questions about their families. Explain responses.

Ex. 12: Before students do this exercise, have them describe each other. They should use their Organizers from previous chapters.

Enrichment
Ex. 12: For a continuation of this exercise, students can write questions they would ask someone whom they've never met.

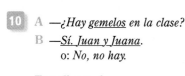

10 A —¿Hay *gemelos* en la clase? **gemelos**

B —*Sí. Juan y Juana.*
o: *No, no hay.*

Estudiante A   Estudiante B

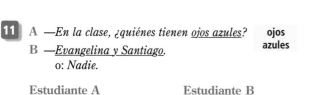

a. personas altas
b. personas rubias   c.

11 A —*En la clase, ¿quiénes tienen ojos azules?* **ojos azules**

B —*Evangelina y Santiago.*
o: *Nadie.*

Estudiante A   Estudiante B

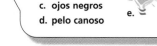

a. pelo rubio
b. ojos marrones
c. ojos negros
d. pelo canoso   e.

Empecemos a escribir y a leer

Write your answers in Spanish.

12 You are going to the airport to meet someone you haven't seen before. How would you describe yourself to that person?

13 Now describe your best friend.

14 On a separate piece of paper, write *sí* or *no* in response to the statements about the following paragraph. Rewrite incorrect statements to make them correct.

¡Hola! Me llamo Cristina. Soy la hermana mayor.
Tengo pelo castaño y ojos marrones. Tengo hermanas gemelas.
Son altas y tienen ojos verdes.

a. Cristina es hija única.
b. Cristina tiene ojos verdes.
c. Ella tiene dos hermanas menores.

También se dice...

los ojos de color café

güero, -a

colorín, colorina

la mamá
el papá

www.pasoapaso.com

MORE PRACTICE

Más práctica y tarea, p. 520–521
Practice Workbook 5–3, 5–4

Vocabulario para conversar   161

---

10 ESTUDIANTE A
a. ¿Hay personas altas en la clase?
b. ¿Hay personas rubias en la clase?
c. Questions will vary.
ESTUDIANTE B
a.–c. Answers will vary.

11 ESTUDIANTE A
a. En la clase, ¿quiénes tienen pelo rubio?
b. . . . ojos marrones?
c. . . . ojos negros?
d. . . . pelo canoso?
ESTUDIANTE B
a.–d. Answers will vary.

Answers: Empecemos a escribir y a leer

12–13 Answers will vary, but encourage stuents to use the full range of chapter vocabulary. Look for correct adjective agreement.

14 a. no/Cristina tiene hermanas gemelas.
b. no/Cristina tiene ojos marrones.
c. sí

 Practice Wkbk. 5-3, 5-4

 Audio Activity 5.2

 Writing Activities 5-C, 5-D

 Pruebas 5-3, 5-4

 **Comm. Act. BLM 5-2**

Extended Written Practice/Homework
1. Write two sentences telling the names of twins you know or have heard of and a description of them.
2. Write a description of a TV, music, or sports star. Include: personality, physical characteristics, age, and what he or she likes to do.

3. Write sentences telling the names and ages of your older or younger brothers and sisters. If you are an only child, write that down and then write sentences telling the names and ages of two other people you know.

Practice

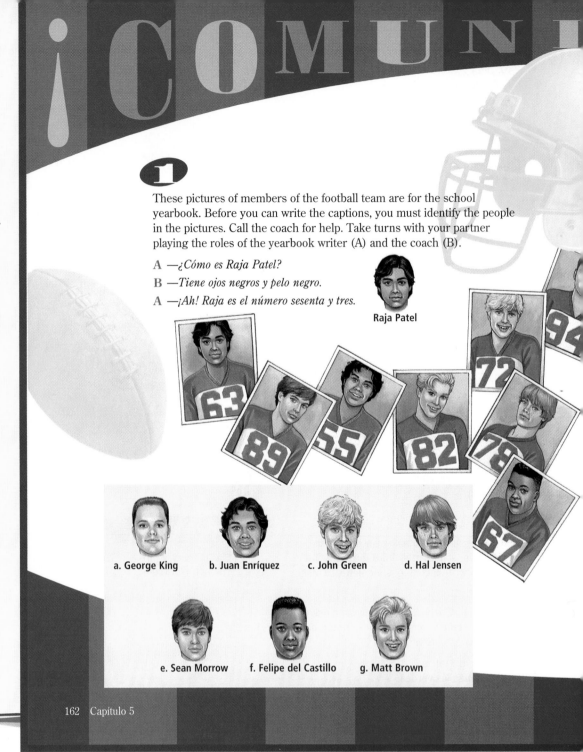

¡**COMUNI**

These pictures of members of the football team are for the school yearbook. Before you can write the captions, you must identify the people in the pictures. Call the coach for help. Take turns with your partner playing the roles of the yearbook writer (A) and the coach (B).

A —*¿Cómo es Raja Patel?*
B —*Tiene ojos negros y pelo negro.*
A —*¡Ah! Raja es el número sesenta y tres.*

Raja Patel

a. George King   b. Juan Enríquez   c. John Green   d. Hal Jensen

e. Sean Morrow   f. Felipe del Castillo   g. Matt Brown

Options

Strategies for Reaching All Students

Spanish-Speaking Students
Ex. 1: Have pairs of Spanish-speaking students work together on this exercise and then present it to the whole class.
Ex. 2: Pair bilingual and non-bilingual students.

 Un paso más Exs. 5-F, 5-G

Students Needing Extra Help
Ex. 1: Model a second example. Put paper numbers on some students in class. Have the rest of the class describe them according to the example.
Ex. 2: Have pictures of dogs and cats available to describe with true statements. Then make up some false statements. Keep them separate at first.

Have students use their Organizers for *perezoso, prudente,* etc. (Chap. 1); *ir de pesca, la piscina,* etc. (Chap. 3); *hambre, sed, bistec, pescado,* etc. (Chap. 4). Model the responses.
¿Qué sabes ahora?: Have students write out this section so that they can keep track of their progress. You may wish to expand on these concepts.

¡QUEMOS!

2

Describe either the cat or the dog to your partner.
To make sure your partner is listening, make two or
three untrue statements. Your partner will correct you.
Then your partner will describe the other animal to you.
For example:

Se llama . . .   (No) es . . .   (No) le gusta . . .   Tiene . . .

Chispa

Michi

3

Get together in groups of six
or seven. On a sheet of
paper, each person should
write a brief description of
one member of the group.
(Use complete sentences.)
Afterward, take turns
reading your descriptions,
one sentence at a time. Can
people guess whom you are
describing?

¿Qué sabes ahora?

Can you:

► describe what members of your family look like?
— Mi hermano tiene pelo ___ y ojos ___ .

► describe the personalities of family members?
— Mi abuela es ___ y ___.

► tell how old people in your family are?
— Mi primo ___ años.

► tell what members of your family like to do?
— A mi tía ___ gusta ___.

CHISPA

Vocabulario para conversar   163

Critical Thinking: Understanding Points of View

Tell students that married women in the U.S. were at one time almost exclusively formally addressed with the first name of their husbands (for example: Mrs. John Smith). Although some women may still prefer this form of address, this practice is deemed inappropriate to most women in the U.S. today. Discuss with students why most women would be offended if addressed by their husband's name.

Perspectiva cultural

Nombres y apellidos

Una boda en Chincheros, Perú

Look at the names on the wedding invitation and the passport. In what ways do the names resemble or not resemble those you are used to? Can you identify the last names?

In Spanish-speaking countries a person's full name consists of a first name *(nombre),* a middle name, and two surnames—the father's family name *(apellido paterno)* followed by the mother's family name *(apellido materno).* Take, for example, the bride's mother's name on the wedding invitation:

María Luisa González Prado de Enciso González is her *apellido paterno.* Prado is

her *apellido materno.* Enciso is her husband's last name. Now look at her husband's name. What are his *apellido paterno* and *apellido materno?*

Although a person's full name is used on all official documents, such as birth certificates, school records, passports, and identification cards, in daily life they usually use only one first name and one last name, most often the father's.

El Sr. Roberto Manuel Enciso Cuevas
y
la Sra. María Luisa González Prado de Enciso

El Sr. Antonio Miguel Ayala Arévalo
y
la Sra. Ana Clara Pérez Soler de Ayala

invitan cordialmente

a la celebración del matrimonio de sus hijos

Gloria Luisa y Hugo Eduardo

Options

Strategies for Reaching All Students

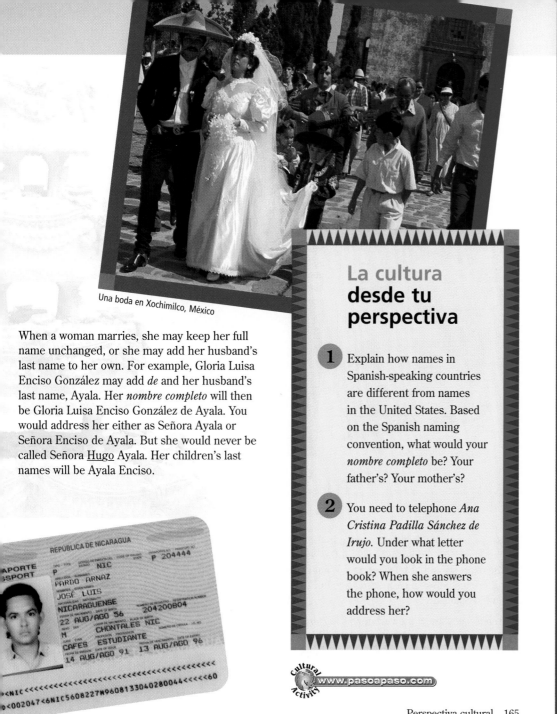

Una boda en Xochimilco, México

When a woman marries, she may keep her full name unchanged, or she may add her husband's last name to her own. For example, Gloria Luisa Enciso González may add *de* and her husband's last name, Ayala. Her *nombre completo* will then be Gloria Luisa Enciso González de Ayala. You would address her either as Señora Ayala or Señora Enciso de Ayala. But she would never be called Señora <u>Hugo</u> Ayala. Her children's last names will be Ayala Enciso.

La cultura desde tu perspectiva

1 Explain how names in Spanish-speaking countries are different from names in the United States. Based on the Spanish naming convention, what would your *nombre completo* be? Your father's? Your mother's?

2 You need to telephone *Ana Cristina Padilla Sánchez de Irujo.* Under what letter would you look in the phone book? When she answers the phone, how would you address her?

www.pasoapaso.com

Perspectiva cultural   165

Cultural Notes

(p. 164, photo)
The Quechua-speaking peoples of highland Peru are part of a broad group of cultures that once included the Incas. Many people in this region speak Spanish as a second language, if at all. Religious events such as weddings combine indigenous and European traditions. Ask students: Why would weddings be occasions for a combination of these traditions?

(p. 165, photo)
Mexican weddings, like this one in Xochimilco, are often lavishly planned affairs, including as many family members and friends as possible. A very special role in Mexican weddings is played by the bride and groom's godparents, who drape a gar-

land of beaded pearl leaves around the shoulders of the wedding couple, encircling them as they exchange vows. After the wedding mass the newlyweds bring a gift of roses and pray to the Virgen de Guadalupe, Mexico's patron saint.

A 24 / In English, age is expressed as "being" so many years old. In Spanish, it is expressed as "having" so many years with *tener*.

B *somos*

C *Me encanta la comida de Mamá. / de telenovelas, de mi mamá, de Sara / De* is used as a possessive here.

Teaching Suggestions

In a negative sentence, we generally don't use the indefinite article after the verb *tener* unless there is an adjective. *(No tengo lápiz. / No tengo un lápiz azul.)*

Class Starter Review

For the day after *tener* is presented: Give various classroom objects or school supplies to students. Then ask who has a specific item *(¿Quién tiene un(a) . . . ? Miguel, ¿tienes un(a) . . . ?* etc.). Remember to give a certain item to two students so that the plural forms are reviewed.

Re-enter / Recycle

Ex. 1: numbers 0–31 from *El primer paso*, classroom supplies from Chap. 2

Gramática en contexto

Look at this page from a Mexican magazine article about TV star Sara Sánchez. Now read the captions.

en casa con Sara Sánchez

Sara Sánchez, joven estrella de telenovelas, tiene 24 años. "Es maravilloso estar aquí en la casa de mi mamá. Somos madre e hija, sí, pero también somos muy buenas amigas." ►

▲ "A veces es un poco perezosa," dice la madre de Sara, "pero nunca cuando cocinamos." "Me encanta la comida de Mamá," dice Sara. "Sus enchiladas son sabrosas."

A Sara's age is one fact that is given in the captions. How old is she? Look at the verb in the expression that tells her age. What is the difference between expressing age in English and in Spanish?

B You already know the verb forms *soy, eres, es,* and *son.* They are all forms of the verb *ser.* Using what you know about verb endings, read the captions and find the form of *ser* that we use with *nosotros.*

C Find the expression that tells about Sara's mother's cooking *(comida).* Find two other places where an expression with *de* is used. What explanation can you give for this use of *de?*

MORE PRACTICE

Más práctica y tarea, p. 521–522
Practice Workbook 5–5, 5–10

166   Capítulo 5

Options

Strategies for Reaching All Students

Students Needing Extra Help

B: Put the verbs in chart form, using the pronouns. Then students can see that you have used all the forms except for "we." Remind them that they already know this setup from *-ar* verbs.
C: Discuss the English use of apostrophes to show ownership and how this concept is not used in Spanish. Give students a formula: object + *de* + person. Emphasize the

word order: In Spanish the object is first, followed by the person. Give some examples. *El verbo* tener: Ask students to identify what *tener* has in common with other *-er* verbs. What is different? Students may then complete the *tener* chart on their Organizers. Re-enter *¿Cuántos años tienes?* and *tengo / tienes, hambre / sed.*
Ex. 1: Model one or two more examples. Re-enter compound subjects and the verb forms they require.

Extended Written Practice/Homework

1. Write a sentence telling if you and your family have a cat or a dog.
2. Think of people who look like their relatives. Write four sentences describing what they have in common: *Anita y su mamá tienen pelo rubio.*
3. Using *nadie, muchas personas,* and *todos,* write five sentences telling what classroom objects (pp. 13 and 59) your classmates have.

El verbo *tener*

The verb *tener*, "to have," follows the pattern of other *-er* verbs. However, some forms of this verb are irregular. Here are all of its present-tense forms.

(yo)	**tengo**	(nosotros) (nosotras)	**tenemos**
(tú)	**tienes**	(vosotros) (vosotras)	**tenéis**
Ud. (él) (ella)	**tiene**	Uds. (ellos) (ellas)	**tienen**

You have already seen some of these verb forms. In what ways is *tener* irregular?

- As you know, *tener* is sometimes used where in English we use a form of the verb "to be": *tener sed / hambre / años.*

1 A class is getting ready to start a project. Several students have gathered the supplies they need. Find out who has them and how many they have.

A —*¿Quién tiene las carpetas de argollas?*
B —*Miguel.*
A —*¿Cuántas carpetas de argollas tiene?*
B —*Cuatro.*

carpetas de argollas

a. marcadores
b. reglas
c. diccionarios
d. cuadernos
e. lápices
f. carpetas
g. bolígrafos

Marcos, Yo (16)
Miguel (4)
Carlos, Jorge (14)
Yo (3)
Victoria (6)
Pilar, Sofía (8)
Anita (10)
Andrés (5)

Gramática en contexto   167

Present & Practice

1 Answers
a. A —¿Quién tiene los marcadores?
B —Anita.
A —¿Cuántos marcadores tiene?
B —Tiene diez.

b. A —. . . las reglas?
B —Andrés.
A —¿Cuántas reglas tiene?
B —Tiene cinco.

c. A —. . . los diccionarios?
B —Yo.
A —¿Cuántos diccionarios tienes?
B —Tengo tres.

d. A —. . . los cuadernos?
B —Pilar y Sofía.
A —¿Cuántos cuadernos tienen?
B —Tienen ocho.

e. A —. . . los lápices?
B —Marcos y yo.
A —¿Cuántos lápices tienen?
B—Tenemos dieciséis.

f. A —. . . las carpetas?
B —Victoria.
A —¿Cuántas carpetas tiene?
B —Tiene seis.

g. A —. . . los bolígrafos?
B —Carlos y Jorge.
A —¿Cuántos bolígrafos tienen?
B —Tienen catorce.

Multiple Intelligences
Bodily/Kinesthetic
In pairs, have students ask and answer questions about the contents of their book bags or backpacks using *tener* forms. Make sure each student shows his or her partner the contents.

Verbal/Linguistic
Read aloud several True/False statements about items that students have on their desks or in their book bags/backpacks. Ask students to verify your statements.

Visual/Spatial
See Students Needing Extra Help (B), *Gramática en contexto,* and Overhead 30.

Present & Practice

Re-enter / Recycle

Exs. 2–3: singular and plural adjective agreement from Chaps. 1 and 4

Ex. 4: singular and plural adjective agreement from Chaps. 1 and 4, adjectives describing personality from Chap. 1

Answers

2–3 Answers will vary, but encourage students to use chapter vocabulary.

A follow-up activity might include one student standing and reading a statement such as, *Daniel y yo tenemos 15 años.* All other students about whom the statement is true also stand. Then all students sit down. Another student stands and reads: *Sara y yo no tenemos hermanos.* All students about whom the statement is true also stand. Continue with other statements.

 Practice Wkbk. 5-5

 Writing Activity 5-F

 Prueba 5-5

2 Find out the ages and the number of family members of different students in your class. On a sheet of paper, copy the table below. As you ask students the questions, write their names and the information you receive. While talking to them, observe their hair and eye color and write that information in the appropriate columns.

A —¿*Cuántos años tienes?*

B —*Tengo 15 años.*

A —¿*Cuántos primos tienes?*

B —*Tengo nueve primos.*
   o: *No tengo primos.*

Estudiante	Años	Familia	Ojos	Pelo
Daniel	15	9 primos	azules	rubio

3 Using the information from Exercise 2, compare yourself with your classmates. Write as many statements as you can about similarities in age, number of family members, and appearance. Then report to the class.

Daniel y yo tenemos . . .

168   Capítulo 5

Options

Strategies for Reaching All Students

Spanish-Speaking Students
Exs. 2 and 4: Have Spanish-speaking students write out these exercises.

Students Needing Extra Help
Ex. 2: You may wish to have students draw another vertical line between *Familia* and *Ojos* to remind them that the information to the right of the line pertains to the classmate, not to his or her family members.

Ex. 3: Model different combinations.
El verbo ser: Have students fill in the chart in the grammar portion of their Organizers.
Ex. 4: Model two more examples.

Enrichment
Ex. 2: As a written assignment, students can make up questions to interview a classmate regarding whether he or she has cats or dogs at home. Encourage students to be as thorough and creative in their questions as

possible. For example, if the interviewee has no dogs or cats at home, students might turn their line of questioning to whether the interviewee likes cats or dogs, or whether they would like to have them but can't because another family member dislikes them. If there are cats or dogs at home, students can ask how many of each there are, their names and ages, what the pets are like, and what they like to do.

El verbo *ser*

The verb *ser,* "to be," is also an irregular verb. We use *ser* with adjectives to tell what someone or something is like.

• You already know some forms of *ser*. Here are all of its present-tense forms.

(yo)	**soy**	(nosotros) (nosotras)	**somos**
(tú)	**eres**	(vosotros) (vosotras)	**sois**
Ud. (él) (ella)	**es**	Uds. (ellos) (ellas)	**son**

¡NO OLVIDES!

Remember that adjectives agree in gender and number with the nouns they describe.

4 In each of these groups, two persons are alike in some way and the third is different. Describe their similarities and differences.

Ángela y Mónica son graciosas, pero Gregorio es serio.

Ángela y Mónica / Gregorio

a. José / Miguel y tú

b. Carolina / Luisa y yo

c. Juanito y David / tú

d. Barrabás / Turquesa y Condesa

e. Claudia y Marisol / yo

f. Jorge / Samuel y yo

g. Coqui/Napoleón y Sultán

Gramática en contexto   169

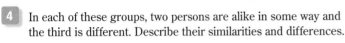

Class Starter Review
For the day after *ser* is presented: Using adjectives that students have learned, ask *¿Quién (no) es ...? ¿Eres...? ¿Son Uds....?* etc. Be aware of students' sensitivity to answering this type of question. You may wish to use the names of famous personalities instead of those of your students.

Reteach / Review: *Ser* with Adjective & Noun Agreement
To review agreement between adjectives and nouns as well as the verb forms of *ser,* call on individuals to answer questions about classmates or themselves.

Answers
4 Before beginning the activity, you may choose to practice making the adjectives agree in number and gender.
a. Miguel y tú son altos, pero José es bajo.
b. Luisa y yo somos deportistas, pero Carolina es artística.
c. Juanito y David son desordenados, pero tú eres ordenada.
d. Turquesa y Condesa son bonitas, pero Barrabás es feo.
e. Claudia y Marisol son tacañas, pero yo soy generoso.
f. Samuel y yo somos trabajadores, pero Jorge es perezoso.
g. Napoleón y Sultán son grandes, pero Coqui es pequeño.

Extended Written Practice/Homework
1. Choose four adjectives from the list on p. 170 that describe you and other people. Write sentences describing yourself and the other people: *Mi hermano y yo somos serios.*
2. Write three sentences saying how you and a person you know are different: *Yo soy alta pero mi prima es muy baja.*

Multiple Intelligences
Bodily/Kinesthetic
1) See Answers (p. 168), paragraph 2.
2) Have students create a poster in which they include a picture of themselves and/or their family and write five sentences using *ser.*
Interpersonal/Social
See Ex. 2 and Enrichment.
Intrapersonal/Introspective
See Ex. 3.
Verbal/Linguistic
See Reteach/Review.

Cultural Notes ☀

(p. 168, realia)
This ad talks about colored contact lenses. Ask students: What do you think the title at the top of the ad means? What do you think are the most popular colors? Why? (Answers will vary.)

Present & Practice

Re-enter / Recycle
Ex. 5: singular and plural adjective agreement from Chaps. 1 and 4, adjectives describing personality from Chap. 1.
Ex. 7: school supplies from Chap. 2

Answers
5 Questions and answers will vary, but look for correct adjective agreement.

 Practice Wkbk. 5-6, 5-7

 Writing Activity 5-G

 Prueba 5-6

---

5 Think of pairs of people in your class who are alike in at least one way. Your partner should tell you how these two classmates are alike. You may want to use the list on the right to help you.

> A —¿Cómo son Pablo y Pedro?
>
> B —Son altos.

Now ask your partner in what way you and various classmates are alike or different.

> A —¿Cómo somos Ignacio y yo?
>
> B —Uds. son trabajadores.
>   o: Ignacio es trabajador, pero tú eres perezoso.

alto, -a	impaciente
amable	inteligente
artístico, -a	joven
atrevido, -a	ordenado, -a
bajo, -a	paciente
bonito, -a	perezoso, -a
callado, -a	prudente
cariñoso, -a	serio, -a
deportista	simpático, -a
desordenado, -a	sociable
generoso, -a	tacaño, -a
gracioso, -a	trabajador, -a
guapo, -a	viejo, -a

Los adjetivos posesivos

To tell what belongs to someone or to show relationships, we use *de* + noun. For example:

> Tengo el cuaderno **de** Felipe.
> La hermana **de** María es amable.

- Another way to tell what belongs to someone and to show relationships is to use possessive adjectives. You already know some of them.

mi hermano	**mis** hermanos
tu abuela	**tus** abuelas
su hijo	**sus** hijos

- The possessive adjective must be singular if the noun is singular and plural if the noun is plural.

> Mi prima es alta.   Todas mi**s** prima**s** son alta**s**.
>
> —¿Son rubios los hermanos de Rafael?
> —No, su**s** herman**os** son pelirroj**os**.

¡NO OLVIDES!

Remember that *tú* with an accent means "you." *Tu* without an accent means "your."

170   Capítulo 5

Options

Strategies for Reaching All Students

Spanish-Speaking Students
Ex. 5: Pair bilingual and non-bilingual students.

Students Needing Extra Help
Ex. 5: Model, being careful to include students who might not otherwise be chosen for the comparison.
Los adjetivos posesivos: Have students fill in the grammar portion of their Organizers. Remind students of the information from Section C on p. 166. Discuss the idea of one owner, one thing; and one owner, two things. The *-s* in *mis, tus,* and *sus* automatically signals plural form. Give a few models.
Ex. 6: Have students do two true and one

false statement. First do all true statements. Then write false statements on the chalkboard. They may have to write these out to show how possessive adjectives work. In the example, show how *la* becomes *su,* and *de Mariana* disappears.
Ex. 7: Do two separate examples on the chalkboard, one for single items and one for plural.
Ahora lo sabes: Have students write out this section so they can check off what they have mastered. Add examples if necessary.

6 Using the family tree on page 154, make three true and false statements about Mariana's family to your partner. Your partner will look at the family tree and answer *sí* if a statement is correct. If a statement is incorrect, your partner will answer *no* and correct it.

A —*La hermana de Mariana tiene 23 años.*

B —*Sí, su hermana tiene 23 años.*

A —*Los abuelos de Mariana se llaman Pedro y Carolina.*

B —*No, sus abuelos se llaman Pedro y Carmen.*

7 Work in groups of three. Each of two students will choose three classroom items that they can "lose" for a moment. These students will turn their backs while their partner puts these objects out of sight. Then, when they turn around, one of them should ask where their things are.

A —*¿Dónde está mi carpeta?*

B —*¿Tu carpeta? Aquí está.*

A —*¿Dónde están sus libros?*
    o: *¿Dónde están los libros de Antonio?*

B —*¿Sus libros? Aquí están.*

Ahora lo sabes

Can you:

▶ tell what someone has?
  —Tomás y Mariana ____ doce libros.

▶ tell what a person's age is?
  —El abuelo de Celeste ____ 74 años.

▶ tell what someone or something is like?
  —Mi hermano ____ guapo.

▶ tell what belongs to someone?
  —¿Dónde está el cuaderno ____ Luis?
  —____ cuaderno está aquí.

MORE PRACTICE

Más práctica y tarea, pp. 521–522
Practice Workbook 5–5, 5–10

PASO CULTURAL

Colombian Fernando Botero (1932–) is one of today's best-known artists. All of his works of the past several years, including many large bronze sculptures, show figures with this same roundness. Botero once said that art is "bound to deform nature." Do you agree? Why?

En el parque (1996), Fernando Botero

Gramática en contexto   171

Answers
6 Statements will vary, but look for correct verb agreement.

7 Questions and answers will vary. Point out the plural form *aquí están.* (The singular form was introduced in Chap. 2.)

Answers: Ahora lo sabes
• tienen
• tiene
• es
• de, Su

 Practice Wkbk. 5-8, 5-9, 5-10

 Audio Activity 5.4

 Writing Activity 5-H

 Prueba 5-7

 Comm. Act. BLM 5-3

 Pasos vivos 1 CD-ROM
Bulletin Board, Slide Presentation Maker, Spindle, Treadmill

Extended Written Practice/Homework
1. Write three pairs of sentences telling about your friends and their family members: *Mi amiga Paula tiene dos hermanos. Sus hermanos son muy deportistas.*
2. Write four questions using *tu(s)* that you can ask a classmate to find out about his or her family members.

Multiple Intelligences
Bodily/Kinesthetic
See Ex. 7.
Verbal/Linguistic
See Audio Activity 5.4.
Visual/Spatial
See Ex. 6; Practice Wkbk. 5-6, 5-7, 5-8, 5-9, and 5-10; Writing Activities 5-G and 5-H; and Comm. Act. BLM 5-3.

Cultural Notes

Paso cultural
Answers will vary. Possible response: One cannot copy/paint anything exactly, so it will always be altered (i.e., deformed).
(p. 171, photo)
Botero is known for the full-figured subjects of his paintings and sculptures. Botero's influences include Spanish colonial art, the Mexican muralists, and the Spanish masters Goya and Velázquez. Discuss reasons why some artists' works become popular and those of others don't.

Apply

Using the Video
Video segment 3: See the Video Teacher's Guide.

 Video Activity C

 Pasos vivos 1 CD-ROM
Video Monitor, Video Presentation Maker

Teaching Suggestions
Other words your students may want to know: *divorciado, -a* (divorced); *casado, -a* (married); *soltero, -a* (unmarried, single).

Answers: Actividades
1–2 Descriptions will vary, but encourage students to use the full range of chapter vocabulary. Look for correct verb and adjective agreement.

Unos padres mexicanos

Unos abuelos en Madrid

172   Capítulo 5

Todo junto

Actividades

1 Write a brief description of your ideal family, including the number of grandparents, parents, aunts and uncles, cousins, and brothers and sisters that you have. Do not include their names.

Exchange papers with your partner. Find out about the members of your partner's ideal family by asking about their names, ages, and appearance or personalities. Take notes on the information you receive.

Using what you learned, write a two- or three-sentence description of one of the people in your partner's ideal family.

2 Cut a picture of a person from a magazine and write a description of the person on a separate sheet of paper. Bring the picture and description to class.

Without showing your partner the picture, read your description aloud. Your partner will draw what you are describing. Together, compare the drawing to the picture.

In groups of five or six, combine all of your pictures, drawings, and written descriptions. Exchange them with those of another group. Can the groups match all three pieces of each one?

Options

Strategies for Reaching All Students

Spanish-Speaking Students
 Un paso más Exs. 5-I, 5-J

Students Needing Extra Help
Ex. 1: Make a chart that includes relationship, name, age, and description of relatives for students to fill in before attempting the conversation. Before working in pairs, have a student carry on the conversation with you.
Conexiones: Review how to read a family tree. Remind students that a straight, horizontal line *directly* connecting two names indicates marriage. Vertical lines connected directly to names represent offspring.

Cooperative Learning
Divide the class into groups of three or four students. Have each individual write the name of one sports or entertainment personality on a notecard. Students should not see each other's cards. Now, have each group play "Guess the Personality." Designate one student in each group to serve as the moderator. Taking turns, each student gets to ask the moderator one question about the celebrity on the moderator's card. For example: *¿Es un hombre? ¿Tiene*

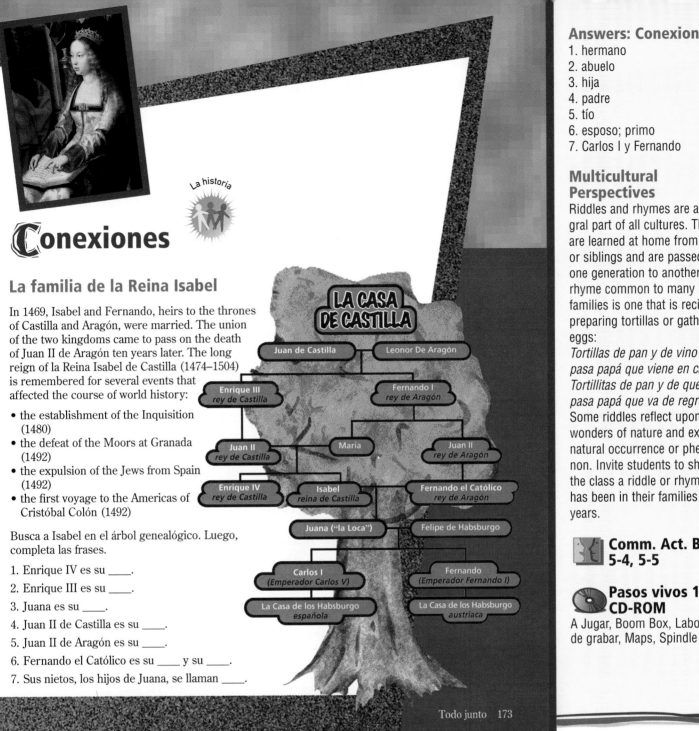

Conexiones

La historia

La familia de la Reina Isabel

In 1469, Isabel and Fernando, heirs to the thrones of Castilla and Aragón, were married. The union of the two kingdoms came to pass on the death of Juan II de Aragón ten years later. The long reign of la Reina Isabel de Castilla (1474–1504) is remembered for several events that affected the course of world history:

- the establishment of the Inquisition (1480)
- the defeat of the Moors at Granada (1492)
- the expulsion of the Jews from Spain (1492)
- the first voyage to the Americas of Cristóbal Colón (1492)

Busca a Isabel en el árbol genealógico. Luego, completa las frases.

1. Enrique IV es su _____.
2. Enrique III es su _____.
3. Juana es su _____.
4. Juan II de Castilla es su _____.
5. Juan II de Aragón es su _____.
6. Fernando el Católico es su _____ y su _____.
7. Sus nietos, los hijos de Juana, se llaman _____.

LA CASA DE CASTILLA

Juan de Castilla — Leonor De Aragón

Enrique III rey de Castilla

Fernando I rey de Aragón

Juan II rey de Castilla

María

Juan II rey de Aragón

Enrique IV rey de Castilla

Isabel reina de Castilla

Fernando el Católico rey de Aragón

Juana ("la Loca")

Felipe de Habsburgo

Carlos I (Emperador Carlos V)

Fernando (Emperador Fernando I)

La Casa de los Habsburgo española

La Casa de los Habsburgo austriaca

Todo junto   173

Multicultural Perspectives

Riddles and rhymes are an integral part of all cultures. They often are learned at home from parents or siblings and are passed from one generation to another. A rhyme common to many Hispanic families is one that is recited while preparing tortillas or gathering eggs:

*Tortillas de pan y de vino
pasa papá que viene en camino
Tortillitas de pan y de queso
pasa papá que va de regreso*

Some riddles reflect upon the wonders of nature and explain a natural occurrence or phenomenon. Invite students to share with the class a riddle or rhyme that has been in their families for many years.

Comm. Act. BLMs 5-4, 5-5

Pasos vivos 1 CD-ROM

A Jugar, Boom Box, Laboratorio de grabar, Maps, Spindle

---

pelo rubio? After each question, the moderator answers either *sí* or *no*. Students record the information on a piece of paper. Students alternate asking questions. Play continues until someone guesses the celebrity. Assign a new moderator and personality for the next round.

Multiple Intelligences
Interpersonal/Social
See Exs. 1–2, Students Needing Extra Help, and Cooperative Learning.
Visual/Spatial
See Using the Video and *Conexiones*.

Apply

Process Reading
For a description of process reading, see p. 48.

Teaching Suggestions
Elicit previously learned Spanish words: *(perros, gatos);* same as English *(hamsters);* sounds like English *(periquitos).*

Answers
Antes de leer
Compatibility of the personalities of the pet and the personalities and ages of family members; compatibility of the size of pet and the size of the house; indoor and outdoor needs of the pet; feeding, grooming, and medical care; affordability, etc. / Answers will vary.

Mira la lectura
1 Answers will vary. You may have to help students with the meaning of *mascota* (pet).

2 Four animals are listed: cats, dogs, hamsters, and parakeets.

¡Vamos a leer!

www.pasoapaso.com

Antes de leer

STRATEGY ➤ **Using prior knowledge**

What are some important considerations when choosing a family pet? What kinds of information would you hope to find in an article offering advice about pet choices?

Mira la lectura

STRATEGY ➤ **Using titles and context clues for meaning**

1 Does the title give a good idea about the subject of the article?

2 Look at the listings in the column entitled *mascota.* How many animals are considered here?

MI PRIMERA MASCOTA

MASCOTAS FAVORITAS

A los niños les gusta casi cualquier animal. Sin embargo, algunos animales no son recomendables para ellos. Es conveniente que los padres escojan una mascota de acuerdo a la edad de sus hijos. Los niños de entre cinco y diez años pueden tener un perro, por ejemplo, un pastor alemán, un dálmata o un collie. También pueden escoger otras clases de mascotas: gatos, conejos, periquitos, peces, tortugas, hámsters (ratoncillos domésticos), etc. Cuando escojan una mascota deben tener en consideración los siguientes aspectos: la longevidad, los cuidados y la alimentación.

Mascota	Gatos	Perros	Hámsters	Periquitos
Longevidad	15 años	15 años	2 años	5 años
Cuidados	Agua y comida todos los días. Vitaminas. Bañarlo con agua tibia una vez al mes.	Agua y comida todos los días. Vitaminas. Collar para pulgas. Bañarlo una vez a la semana.	Agua y comida especial todos los días. Limpiar la jaula cada cinco días.	Agua y comida todos los días. Lechuga, plátano y semillas. Limpiar la jaula una vez por semana.

Options

Strategies for Reaching All Students

Spanish-Speaking Students
Ask Spanish-speaking students to write about one or all of the following:
(1) ¿Tienes mascota? ¿Qué tienes? ¿Cómo es? (2) Describe la mascota ideal para ti. (3) Escribe un anuncio para vender un producto para una mascota. Puede ser una comida especial, un collar o un jabón, etc.

Students Needing Extra Help
Mira la lectura: Brainstorm as a class.
Infórmate #2: Remind students about the meaning of cognates. Give examples. Explain the term "longevity" in English.
Aplicación: Ask why these are good recommendations. Ask for specifics.
Have students explain why they would give certain jobs to certain family members.

Enrichment
As a written assignment, students can pretend that they are applying for a job at a pet-sitting service and name all of the characteristics that they have that would make them suitable for the job.

Infórmate

STRATEGY ▸ **Scanning**

Column and row headings identify the main categories. We can scan the entries relating to them for the specific information we need.

Scanning, or reading for specific information, is useful because charts and tables offer an efficient way to condense information in order to make quick comparisons.

❶ Scan the long paragraph and find the age range of children for whom these pets are recommended. Using what you know about cognates, can you identify the names of some of the dog breeds? From what you know, do you agree that these are good pets for children in this age range?

❷ Turning to the table, scan the information in the row entitled *Longevidad.* Do you know an English equivalent for *longevidad?* Does this information correspond to your own experience with pets? What do you think the row entitled *Cuidados* is about?

Dos hermanas con armadillos en Taxco, México

Aplicación

The recommendations given below are described in the table as necessary for the care of *los perros.* Can you figure out what these recommendations are? To which of these family members would you assign each of the first two tasks: *hijo mayor (10 años), hija menor (5 años), los padres?*

- bañarlo una vez a la semana
- comida y agua todos los días
- collar para pulgas
- vitaminas

¡Vamos a leer! 175

Infórmate

1 between 5 and 10 years old / German Shepherd, Dalmatian, Collie / Answers will vary.

2 longevity / Answers will vary. / care and feeding

Aplicación
Recommendations include: give it a bath once a week, food and water every day, flea collar, vitamins. / Answers will vary.

www **Internet Activities**

Cultural Notes ☼

Multiple Intelligences
Visual/Spatial
See Exs. 1–2 of *Mira la lectura.*

p. 175, photo)
These young girls holding armadillos live in Taxco, a town 104 miles southwest of Mexico City. Built on a hill where silver has been mined since pre-Columbian times, Taxco was founded in 1522 by Hernán Cortés. Today it is famous for its exquisitely crafted silver products and its eighteenth-century colonial architecture.

Apply

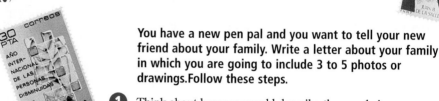

¡Vamos a escribir!

You have a new pen pal and you want to tell your new friend about your family. Write a letter about your family in which you are going to include 3 to 5 photos or drawings. Follow these steps.

1 Think about how you would describe the people in your photos or drawings: Who are they? What do they look like? What type of personality do they have? List your answers under each of these categories. Number your pictures so that you can refer to them easily.

2 Write a first draft of your letter describing three or four people in your family as completely as you can.

Una familia en México

Un abuelo con su nieta en Madrid

Options

Strategies for Reaching All Students

Spanish-Speaking Students
Have Spanish-speaking students answer one of the letters and compare his or her real, imaginary, or ideal family with the one in the letter. *Contesta la carta de un(a) compañero(a) de clase. Compara a tu familia con la de tu compañero(a).*

Students Needing Extra Help
Step 1: Some students might be very uncomfortable doing this activity with real family photos. Instead, let them create a family from magazine pictures or let them draw a family. Have students use their Organizers. Make a chart with the headings listed in the directions.

Step 2: Students have enough vocabulary so that they could expand on this example. Use a picture from a magazine and have the students do the exercise as a class.
Step 4: Have students use the Organizer.

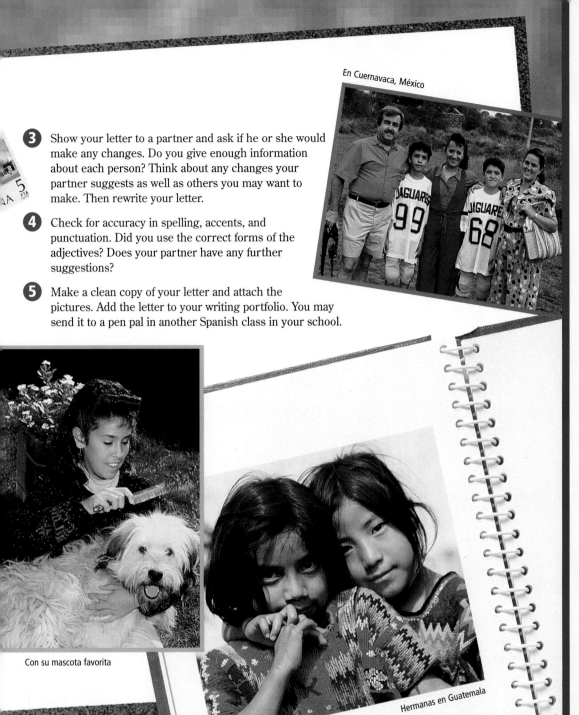

En Cuernavaca, México

3 Show your letter to a partner and ask if he or she would make any changes. Do you give enough information about each person? Think about any changes your partner suggests as well as others you may want to make. Then rewrite your letter.

4 Check for accuracy in spelling, accents, and punctuation. Did you use the correct forms of the adjectives? Does your partner have any further suggestions?

5 Make a clean copy of your letter and attach the pictures. Add the letter to your writing portfolio. You may send it to a pen pal in another Spanish class in your school.

Con su mascota favorita

Hermanas en Guatemala

Cultural Notes
(p. 176, realia)
Stamps such as these from Spain can provide clues about the history and culture of a country. The 30-*peseta* stamp commemorates the International Year of the Disabled, which occurred in 1981, and the thirteen-*peseta* stamp is a tribute to air-mail service in Spain. The five-*peseta* stamp at the top of the page honors Juan Bautista de la Salle, a saint from the seventeenth century who championed education for poor children. The five-*peseta* stamp underneath it marks the 100th anniversary of the Hospital del Niño Jesús (1879–1979), a children's hospital in Madrid.

Cultural Notes ☼

Multiple Intelligences
Bodily/Kinesthetic
See Teaching Suggestions.
Visual/Spatial
See step 2.

(p. 177, top photo)
As this photo of Mexican boys in football uniforms indicates, there is a strong American influence in Cuernavaca, the capital of the state of Morelos. Its cool climate and lush vegetation have made it an appealing home to Mexicans and foreigners since colonial times. Today Cuernavaca has a community of about 20,000 U.S. residents, and attracts many more *norteamericanos* with its numerous language schools.

(p. 177, bottom photo)
Descendants of the ancient Mayan civilization make up approximately half of Guatemala's 10 million people. The other half consists of *ladinos*—people of mixed Spanish and Indian ancestry.

Assess & Summarize

Test Preparation

You may want to assign parts of this section as written homework or as an in-class writing activity prior to administering the *Examen de habilidades*.

Answers

Listening: *Me llamo Enrique. En mi familia somos cuatro: mi padre, mi madre, mi hermano Alberto y yo. Mi padre es muy alto. Tiene ojos marrones y pelo castaño. Mi madre y Alberto tienen ojos verdes y pelo castaño. Mis ojos son verdes también, pero soy pelirrojo.* Enrique's hair is red. No, nobody else in his family has his hair color.

Culture: Ana Ríos

Reading: The chart lists four people with their name, age, and hair and eye color. / The dominant color of eyes is green. / Answers will vary: gray or dark-colored eyes.

Writing: Ads will vary, but students should use the chapter vocabulary. Look for logical sentences. Briefly explain the use of the personal *a* in the bottom phrase. The presentation of this grammar point will appear in Chap. 7.

Repaso ¿Lo sabes bien?

This section will help you organize your studying for the proficiency test, where you will be asked to do similar, though not identical, tasks. There will not be any models on the test.

► **Listening**

Can you understand when someone describes family members and friends? Listen as your teacher reads you a sample similar to what you will hear on the test. What color is Enrique's hair? Does any other member of his family have the same color hair?

► **Culture**

What version of her name would Ana Carmen most likely use to introduce herself to a new friend?

► **Reading**

Can you quickly glance through this chart and get an idea of its content? Now look at the information under the column entitled *Color de ojos*. What is the dominant color of eyes? Is there any common color of eyes missing?

Nombre	Edad	Color de pelo	Color de ojos
Rosalba	19	castaño	marrones
José Miguel	18	pelirrojo	verdes
Carlos	21	castaño	verdes
Maribel	19	rubio	azules

178   Capítulo 5

► **Writing**

Can you write an ad for actors for a school play? Here is a sample:

Necesito una mujer 50-60 años alta pelo canoso para representar a la madre

► **Speaking**

Can you talk with a partner about your families? For example:

A —*Tengo tres hermanos mayores. ¿Y tú?*

B —*Yo tengo una hermana mayor y una hermana menor. Mariana tiene dieciocho años y Roxana cinco.*

A —*Mis hermanos se llaman Roberto, Ramiro y Rafael. Todos son muy deportistas.*

B —*Mis hermanas son pelirrojas y tienen ojos verdes. Son muy simpáticas.*

Self Test   www.pasoapaso.com

Options

Strategies for Reaching All Students

Students Needing Extra Help
Have students write out this section so they can check off what they have mastered.

Resumen del vocabulario

Use the vocabulary from this chapter to help you:

► describe family members and friends

► tell what someone's age is

► say what other people like and do not like to do

to talk about family members
los abuelos: el abuelo
        la abuela
los hermanos: el hermano
         la hermana
los hijos: el hijo
      la hija
los padres: el padre
        la madre
los primos: el primo
        la prima
los tíos: el tío
     la tía
el hijo único, la hija única
los gemelos, las gemelas

to tell someone's name
¿Cómo se llama(n) ___?
Se llama(n) ___.

to ask and tell how old someone is
¿Cuántos años tiene ___?
Tiene ___ años.
sesenta (sesenta y uno . . .)
setenta (setenta y uno . . .)
ochenta (ochenta y uno . . .)
noventa (noventa y uno . . .)
cien

to talk about people
el hombre
el muchacho, la muchacha
la mujer
la persona
¿Quiénes?

to describe people, animals, and things
alto, -a
antipático, -a
atractivo, -a
bajo, -a
bonito, -a
cariñoso, -a
feo, -a
grande
guapo, -a
inteligente
joven
mayor, *pl.* mayores
menor, *pl.* menores
pequeño, -a
simpático, -a
viejo, -a
ser + *adjective*
el pelo: canoso
       castaño
       negro
       rubio

pelirrojo, -a
los ojos: azules
       grises
       marrones
       negros
       verdes

to name animals
el gato
el perro

to indicate possession
de
su, sus
tener

to talk about what someone likes
(A + *person*) le gusta(n) / le
  encanta(n)

to indicate number
¿Cuántos, -as?
nadie
sólo
todos, -as

other useful word
que

Resumen   179

CAPÍTULO 6
THEME: CLOTHING

SCOPE AND SEQUENCE Pages 180–215

COMMUNICATION

Topics
Clothing
Colors
Prices
Numbers 101–199

Objectives
To compare where people shop for clothes in Spanish-speaking countries and in the U.S.

To talk about articles of clothing, colors, and prices

To describe clothes

To indicate a specific item or items

To assist customers in a store

To address people

To start a conversation

To talk about shopping and places to shop for clothing

To talk about when something happened

To indicate location

CULTURE
Shopping for clothes
Types of clothing stores

GRAMMAR
La posición de los adjetivos

Los adjetivos demostrativos

El complemento directo: Los pronombres

Ancillaries available for use with Chapter 6

Multisensory/Technology

 Overheads, 31–35

 Audio Tapes and CDs

 Vocabulary Art Blackline Masters for Hands-On Learning, pp. 33–37/CD-ROM

 Classroom Crossword

 Video

 Pasos vivos 1 CD-ROM

 Internet Activities www.pasoapaso.com

Print

 Practice Workbook, pp. 64–72

 Writing, Audio & Video Activities, pp. 35–40, 108–110, 162–163

 Communicative Activity Blackline Masters
  Pair and Small Group Activities, pp. 43–48
  Situation Cards, p. 49

 Un paso más: Actividades para ampliar tu español, pp. 32–37

TPR Storytelling

Assessment

 Assessment Program
  Pruebas, pp. 81–90
  Examen de habilidades, pp. 91–94

 Test Generator

Video still from Chap. 6

179A

Additional Technology

Planning Express, Teaching
Resources Library, and Clip Art
Library

¿Lo sabes bien?
Video Quiz

Cultural Overview

Shopping

Throughout Latin America and Spain, people traditionally have shopped for clothing in small neighborhood specialty stores or at public marketplaces. These shopping habits are changing in many cities, however, as large department stores are becoming more commonplace.

Popular department stores include Colombia's San Andresito and Spain's El Corte Inglés and Galerías Primero. Shopping malls such as Mexico City's Perisur are also becoming more commonplace. Perisur, like malls in the U.S., features a variety of chain store branches *(sucursales)*. Among them are Liverpool, a fashionable clothing store, and Sanborn's, a department store and favorite lunch spot. Perisur has become a central place for friends to meet and spend time together as well as to shop. *Puntos de fábrica* (factory outlet stores) are becoming increasingly popular places to buy clothing.

Local indoor and outdoor markets still exist in many communities throughout Latin America. At El Mercado Oriental, a market that covers dozens of square blocks in Managua, Nicaragua, one can buy almost anything. In many smaller cities and towns in Mexico, *el día de plaza,* a once- or twice-weekly event, draws people from many surrounding communities. Vendors may travel from town to town depending on where the market will take place that day. Local residents rely on the market to supply them with clothes and other items. Customers can pay for their merchandise with cash or by credit without using a credit card. The merchant writes down the name of the client and how much she or he owes. For example, in Mexico, *botas de piel Alcalá* (fine leather boots) are very expensive. A customer can put a down payment on the boots and take them home. Every week the customer pays off a portion of the debt until the boots have been paid for.

Another common way of shopping is to wait for the *mercado a ruedas* (market on wheels) and *vendedores ambulantes* (door-to-door salespeople) to make a stop on the block. Shoppers appreciate the convenience as well as the congenial, personal service from familiar vendors.

Introduce

180 Capítulo 6

Planning

Cross-Curricular Connections

Geography Connection *(pp. 184–185)*
Have students find out the name of the currency for a Spanish-speaking country by using a reference book or calling a currency exchange or bank. Have them copy or draw an example of one of the bills and attach it by tape or string to a large map. If you don't have any foreign currency, ask consulates or travel agencies to help you.

Economics Connection *(pp. 184–185)*
Have students find out today's value of a currency from a Spanish-speaking country and convert the prices on p. 184. Have students then compare amounts among the different currencies.

Business Connection *(p. 200)*
Have pairs of students create an ad for a shop in a Spanish-speaking country showing three or four featured items and the prices in that country's currency and in U.S. dollars. They should name the store and write any other pertinent advertising information. Display the ads around the room.

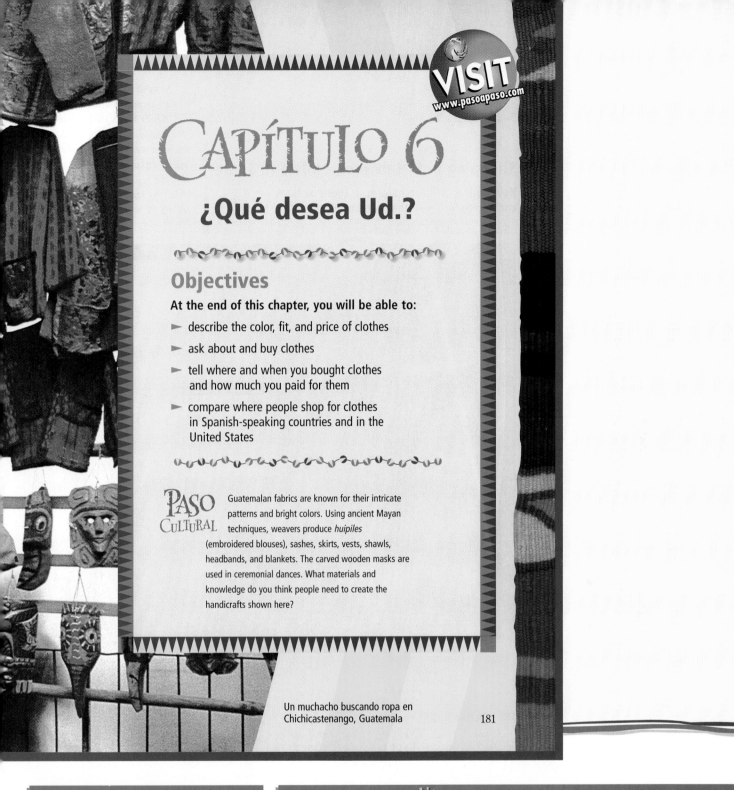

CAPÍTULO 6

¿Qué desea Ud.?

Objectives

At the end of this chapter, you will be able to:

► describe the color, fit, and price of clothes

► ask about and buy clothes

► tell where and when you bought clothes and how much you paid for them

► compare where people shop for clothes in Spanish-speaking countries and in the United States

PASO CULTURAL Guatemalan fabrics are known for their intricate patterns and bright colors. Using ancient Mayan techniques, weavers produce *huipiles* (embroidered blouses), sashes, skirts, vests, shawls, headbands, and blankets. The carved wooden masks are used in ceremonial dances. What materials and knowledge do you think people need to create the handicrafts shown here?

Un muchacho buscando ropa en Chichicastenango, Guatemala

181

Preview

Cultural Objective

• To compare where people shop for clothes in Spanish-speaking countries and in the U.S.

 ¡Piénsalo bien!

Play

 **Video Activity A**

Using the Video

This chapter's video focuses on shopping for clothing. Students will search for clothing bargains with our hosts in Madrid, visiting a major women's clothing store and a popular street market.

To prepare students for the video, first ask them to predict what this chapter's tape will be about. Then have students watch the segment several times. After the first time, you may wish to have them brainstorm possible vocabulary and expressions they will need to talk about what they saw on the video. Ask students to identify: a) things they saw that were familiar to them, and b) things they saw that they might not see in a clothing store in their home town or city. Video segment 1: For more teaching suggestions, see the Video Teacher's Guide.

 **¡Piensa en la CULTURA!**

Shopping in El Salvador, Chile and Spain

How do the malls and stores in these pictures compare with those that you know?

 PASO CULTURAL
Shopping malls in Spanish-speaking countries are not much different in appearance from those in the U.S. The differences are in the merchandise, which is often a specialty of the country or region. This mall includes shops specializing in textiles and shoes, two important industries in El Salvador. What merchandise do you think foreign tourists are likely to look for when visiting U.S. malls?

San Salvador, El Salvador

"¿Qué necesitas comprar?"

182   Capítulo 6

Options

Strategies for Reaching All Students

Spanish-Speaking Students
Ask Spanish-speaking students: ¿Tienen las mismas tiendas en los centros comerciales por donde vives tú? ¿Cuánto cuestan los artículos que ves en las fotos? ¿Vas a los centros comerciales con tus amigos? ¿Qué hacen allí?

 Un paso más Ex. 6-A

Multiple Intelligences
Interpersonal/Social
See Critical Thinking: Evaluating Information.
Visual/Spatial
See Using the Video.

Cultural Notes

Paso cultural
Possible answers: Small appliances, certain types of clothing, and other practical items that are hard to find in their own countries.

Critical Thinking: Evaluating Information

Ask small groups of students to prepare lists of factors they consider when making a clothing purchase. Lists might include price, quality, style, and so on. After students have prepared their lists, have them rank the factors according to importance. Discuss the lists.

Answers: ¡Piensa en la cultura!

Answers will vary, but students may say that some stores are the same as those in the U.S.

(p. 183, bottom photo) Assist students as needed with the meaning of *tienda de descuentos* (discount store). See if visual clues in the photo can help them.

"¡Qué bonito!"

Santiago, Chile

Barcelona, España

"Creo que la sección de jeans está allí."
What do you suppose *una tienda de descuentos* is?

www.pasoapaso.com
Cultural Exploration
Visit these countries on-line

¡Piensa en la cultura! 183

(p. 182, realia)
For over two thousand years, the brightly-colored textiles woven in Guatemala have communicated layers of meaning, including group identity, to Mayan peoples. Today, artesans buy their thread from factories rather than hand-dyeing it, and woven products such as this purse are sold internationally.

(p. 182, photo; p. 183, top photo)
For many Latin Americans, going to the mall has replaced the traditional evening stroll in the town *plaza*. People meet at the mall for a snack or meal, to browse or shop, or just to take a break. Ask students: How are socializing at the mall and at the *plaza* different? What aspects of Hispanic culture might be suffering or getting lost because people now go to malls instead of *plazas* to socialize?

(p. 183, bottom photo)
In Spain, large discount chain stores known as *hipermercados* are quite popular. These stores offer low prices and one-stop shopping for such basic items as food, clothing, and household goods. Although similar stores are popular in Latin America, in recent years they've been replaced by Sam's, Wal-Mart, and other U.S. warehouse chains. Discuss with students how stores like these affect a culture.

Present

Chapter Theme
Clothing and colors

Communicative Objectives
- To talk about articles of clothing, colors, and prices
- To describe clothes
- To talk about shopping
- To indicate a specific item or items
- To assist customers in a store
- To address people
- To start a conversation

 Overheads 31–32

 Vocabulary Art BLMs/CD-ROM

 Pronunciation Tape 6-1

 Vocabulario para conversar A

Play

Using the Video
Video segment 2: See the Video Teacher's Guide.

 Video Activity B

Vocabulario para conversar

¿Cuánto cuesta la camisa?

Here are some new words and expressions you will need to talk about clothes and colors. Read them several times, then turn the page and practice with a partner.

La ropa

la camiseta $7

la blusa $16

la camisa $18

la falda $30

la chaqueta $40

la chaqueta ¡Sólo 101 dólares!*

los pantalones cortos $12

la sudadera $14

el vestido $45

el suéter $27

los pantalones $21

los jeans $23

los tenis $30

los zapatos $65

las pantimedias $3

el calcetín pl. los calcetines $3

* Note that the number 100, *cien*, becomes *ciento* when followed by another number: *cien dólares*, but *ciento un dólares*. If followed by a feminine noun, we use *ciento una: ciento una camisas*.

184   Capítulo 6

Options

Strategies for Reaching All Students

Enrichment
To reinforce the new vocabulary, bring in pictures of clothing from magazines and mail-order catalogues. Have individual students or small groups present pictures to the class, naming the item of clothing, its price, and color. As a follow-up conversation, elicit opinions about the items from individual students, asking questions such as: *¿Te gusta(n)...? ¿Qué te gusta más? ¿Qué no te gusta nada? ¿Cuesta(n) mucho o poco...?*

Learning Spanish Through Action
STAGING VOCABULARY: *Levántense, Siéntense, Señalen, Toquen*
1) MATERIALS: transparency of clothing from the *Vocabulario para conversar*
DIRECTIONS: Using the transparency, point to an article of clothing. Ask students who are wearing that item to stand. While students remain standing, state a color.

Students wearing that color may then sit down. Continue naming colors until all students are seated, and then repeat with another article of clothing.
2) MATERIALS: none
DIRECTIONS: Ask students to touch or point to articles in the room as you mention a color.

Los colores

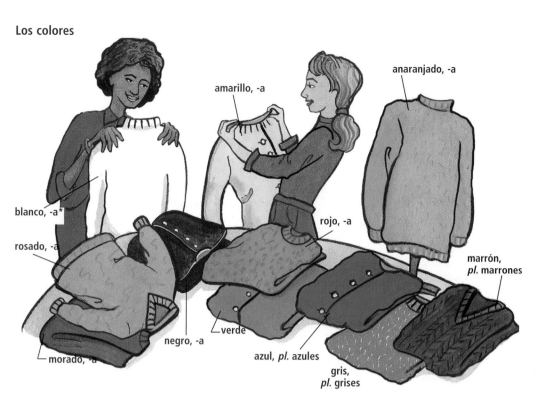

amarillo, -a

anaranjado, -a

blanco, -a*

rosado, -a

rojo, -a

marrón,
pl. marrones

negro, -a

verde

morado, -a

azul, *pl.* azules

gris,
pl. grises

También necesitas...

¿Cómo te queda(n)?	*How does it (do they) fit you?*	los, las	*them*
Me queda(n) bien.	*It fits (They fit) me well.*	¿Cuánto?	*How much?*
¿De qué color?	*What color?*	Cuesta(n) . . .	*It costs (They cost) . . .*
buscar	*to look for*	¿Qué desea (Ud.)?	*May I help you?*
comprar	*to buy*	el / la joven, *pl.* los jóvenes	*young person, pl. young people*
llevar	*to wear*	perdón	*excuse me*
para mí / ti	*for me / you, to me/ you*		
este, esta; ese, esa	*this; that*		
lo, la	*it*		

¿Y qué quiere decir . . . ?

el dólar

* When talking about individual colors, we use the masculine definite article: *Me gustan el rojo y el amarillo.*

Vocabulario para conversar   185

Grammar Preview
Demonstrative adjectives and direct object pronouns are previewed here. The explanation appears in the grammar sections on pp. 202 and 204–205.

Teaching Suggestions
Preparing students to speak: Use one or two options from each of the categories of Comprehensible Input, Physical Response, or Limited Verbal Response. For a complete explanation of these categories and some sample activities, see pp. T22–T23.

Point out that *marrón, gris, azul,* and *verde* do not change form in the feminine.

Remind students that they have seen *joven* as an adjective in Chap. 5. Explain that it can mean both "young man" and "young woman," and *jóvenes* can mean "young people," but as a form of address, *joven* is used mainly with males.

Class Starter Review
On the day following initial presentation, you might begin the class with this activity:
Call out different items of clothing. Have individuals point to these items if they are wearing them. Make this activity more specific by describing the colors.

www Internet Activities
Juegos

Multiple Intelligences
Bodily/Kinesthetic
See Learning Spanish Through Action and Class Starter Review.
Musical/Rhythmic
Write the words to the song "De colores" (see Writing, Audio & Video Activities, p. 137) on the board or on an overhead transparency. Divide the class into three groups: A, B, and C. Have group A sing the first three sentences of the song, group B the next two sentences, and group C the next three. Play the song and point to each group when it is their turn to sing along. (The order of singing will be A, B, C, B.)
Visual/Spatial
See Overheads 31–32, the Vocabulary Art BLMs/CD-ROM, and Using the Video.

Practice

Re-enter / Recycle

Exs. 1–2: numbers 0–31 from *El primer paso,* numbers 32–59 from Chap. 2, numbers 60–100 from Chap. 5

Answers: Empecemos a conversar

1 ESTUDIANTE A

a. Perdón, ¿cuánto cuesta la falda?

b. . . . la sudadera?

c. . . . la blusa?

d. . . . la camisa?

e. . . . el suéter?

f. . . . el vestido?

ESTUDIANTE B

a. Cuesta cuarenta y dos dólares.

b. . . . cuarenta . . .

c. . . . cincuenta y seis . . .

d. . . . veintiséis . . .

e. . . . treinta y tres . . .

f. . . . ochenta y cuatro . . .

2 ESTUDIANTE A

a. Perdón, ¿cuánto cuestan los zapatos?

b. . . . los pantalones?

c. . . . los calcetines?

d. . . . los pantalones cortos?

e. . . . las pantimedias?

f. . . . los tenis?

ESTUDIANTE B

a. Sólo cuestan cuarenta y ocho dólares.

b. . . . treinta y dos . . .

c. . . . cuatro . . .

d. . . . diecinueve . . .

e. . . . seis . . .

f. . . . cincuenta y siete . . .

Empecemos a conversar

With a partner, take turns being *Estudiante A* and *Estudiante B.* Use the words that are cued or given in the balloons to replace the underlined sections in the model. means you can make your own choices.

1 A —Perdón, ¿cuánto cuesta <u>la chaqueta</u>?

B —Cuesta <u>ciento veinticinco</u> dólares.

Estudiante A   Estudiante B

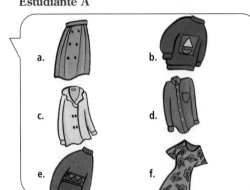

2 A —Perdón, ¿cuánto cuestan <u>los jeans</u>?

B —Sólo cuestan <u>treinta y seis</u> dólares.

Estudiante A   Estudiante B

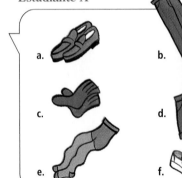

Options

Strategies for Reaching All Students

Spanish-Speaking Students
Pair bilingual with non-bilingual students for Exs. 1–4.

 Un paso más Ex. 6-B

Students Needing Extra Help
Have students begin filling in their Organizers. Explain the difference between the definite articles and direct object pronoun use of *la, los,* and *las.*
Exs. 1–2: Show students that they have to search for the answer. The *Estudiante B* response is not directly across from the *Estudiante A* clue. Explain the use of *cuesta(n)* with singular and plural nouns.
Ex. 3: Do a few of these aloud.

Ex. 4: Point out that the first response will be used if the requested color is there, and the second response if it isn't. Remind students that they have to search for the answer as in Exs. 1–2.

3

A —¿Qué desea, señor (señora/joven/señorita)? ¿Una camisa?

B —Sí, busco *una camisa amarilla* para mí y *una camisa rosada* para (nombre).

Estudiante A

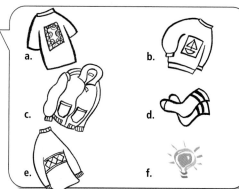

Estudiante B

4

A —Me encanta esa *camiseta* azul. ¿La tiene en amarillo?

B —¿Esta *camiseta*? Sí, aquí la tiene.
　　o: No, no la tenemos en amarillo.

Estudiante A

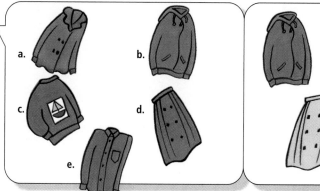

Estudiante B

Vocabulario para conversar　187

3 ESTUDIANTE A

a. ¿Qué desea, señor (señora/joven/señorita)? ¿Una camiseta?

b. . . . ¿Una sudadera?

c. . . . ¿Una chaqueta?

d. . . . ¿Unos calcetines?

e. . . . ¿Un suéter?

f. Questions will vary.

ESTUDIANTE B

a. Sí, busco una camiseta roja para mí y una camiseta amarilla para (nombre).

b. . . . una sudadera morada . . . una sudadera gris . . .

c. . . . una chaqueta verde . . .una chaqueta marrón . . .

d. . . . unos calcetines negros . . . unos calcetines azules . . .

e. . . . un suéter marrón . . . un suéter anaranjado . . .

f. Answers will vary.

4 In the model, note that the name of the color, *amarillo,* is a noun, and that there is no agreement: *¿La tiene en amarillo?*

ESTUDIANTE A

a. Me encanta esa blusa azul. ¿La tiene en amarillo?

b. . . . chaqueta . . .

c. . . . sudadera . . .

d. . . . falda . . .

e. . . . camisa . . .

ESTUDIANTE B

a. ¿Esta blusa? No, no la tenemos en amarillo.

b. ¿Esta chaqueta? No . . .

c. ¿Esta sudadera? Sí, aquí la tiene.

d. ¿Esta falda? Sí . . .

e. ¿Esta camisa? No . . .

Enrichment

Ex. 1: To practice *cien* and *ciento,* have students redo the entire exercise with prices ranging from $100 to $199.

Ex. 4: To preview the grammar, ask students the meaning of *esa.* You may want to make this preview more concrete by picking up pairs of objects and placing them so that you can touch one and point to the other to illustrate the difference between *esta / esa, este / ese.* Try not to place anything very far away so as to avoid *aquel(la).*

Extended Written Practice/Homework

1. Write three sentences telling which items of your own clothing fit you especially well.

2. Referring to the places on p. 90, write four sentences telling what you like to wear when you go to different places.

3. Write four sentences naming items of clothes that you need or want to buy.

Multiple Intelligences
Verbal/Linguistic
See Exs. 1–4.

Re-enter / Recycle
Ex. 6: seasons from Chap. 3
Ex. 9: *gustar* expressions from
Chap. 1

Answers: Empecemos a conversar

5 ESTUDIANTE A
a. ¿Cómo te quedan los pantalones?
b. . . . los jeans?
c. . . . los tenis?
d. . . . los pantalones cortos?
e. . . . los calcetines?

ESTUDIANTE B
a. No me quedan bien. Son muy grandes.
b. No me quedan bien. Son muy pequeños.
c. Me quedan bien. Los compro.
d. Me quedan bien. Los compro.
e. No me quedan bien. Son muy pequeños.

Answers: Empecemos a escribir

6–10 Answers will vary, but encourage students to use the chapter vocabulary. Look for correct adjective agreement.

5
A —*¿Cómo te quedan los zapatos?*
B —*Me quedan bien. Los compro.*
   o: *No me quedan bien. Son muy grandes (pequeños).*

Estudiante A

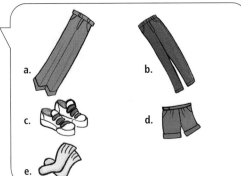

Estudiante B

Empecemos a escribir

Write your answers in Spanish.

6 The seasons affect how we dress. List a couple of clothing items you wear in each season of the year.

7 Choose five of those items and say which colors you prefer for each one.

8 ¿Qué ropa vas a llevar mañana? ¿De qué color es?

9 ¿Qué colores te gustan más? ¿Qué colores no te gustan nada?

10 ¿Qué ropa compras para ti?

Unos jóvenes chilenos en la playa

También se dice...

| el jersey
la chompa | el vaquero | la pollera | la remera
la franela
la playera | la chamarra
la campera |

188   Capítulo 6

Options

Strategies for Reaching All Students

Spanish-Speaking Students
Ex. 8: Ask Spanish-speaking students: *¿Qué llevas los fines de semana?*

Students Needing Extra Help
Ex. 6: Review the seasons.
Ex. 7: Review colors and adjective endings for colors not ending in *-o*.
Empecemos a escribir: For additional practice, tell students that they have $100 to spend on clothes at the shopping mall. Ask them to write a sentence telling what items they would like to buy and their cost: *Me gustaría comprar . . . .*

Multiple Intelligences
Intrapersonal/Introspective
See Exs. 6–10.
Naturalist
Have students create a pictograph in which they show the four seasons of the year on both the North and South American continents. Have them include people wearing clothing appropriate for each season.

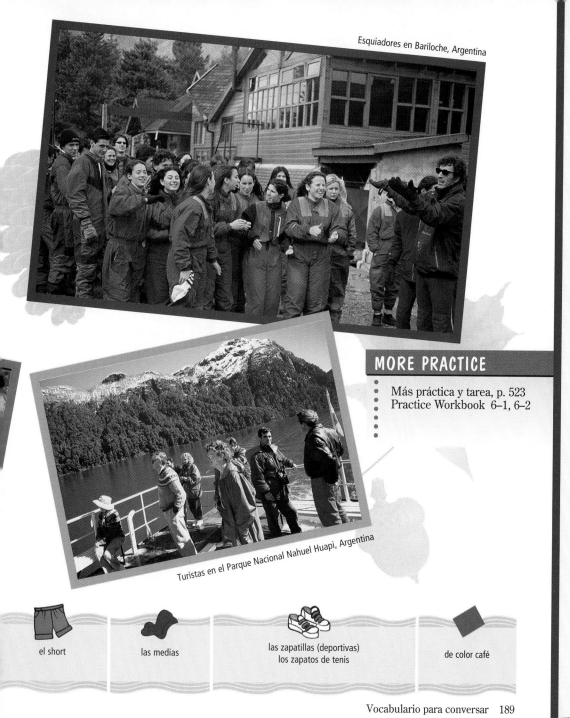

Esquiadores en Bariloche, Argentina

Turistas en el Parque Nacional Nahuel Huapi, Argentina

MORE PRACTICE

Más práctica y tarea, p. 523
Practice Workbook 6–1, 6–2

 Multicultural Perspectives
Latin American currencies tell much about the histories and cultures of the countries. The official currency of Venezuela, the *bolívar*, is named after Simón Bolívar, the great liberator who led the fight for independence in South America between 1810 and 1824. The *quetzal*—the official unit of money in Guatemala—is named after a rare, exotic bird found only in Central American rain forests. Ask students if they are familiar with other foreign currencies.

Practice Wkbk. 6-1, 6-2

Audio Activity 6.1

Writing Activities 6-A, 6-B

Pruebas 6-1, 6-2

Comm. Act. BLM 6-1

el short

las medias

las zapatillas (deportivas)
los zapatos de tenis

de color café

Vocabulario para conversar   189

Cultural Notes

(p. 188, photo)
The beach resort of Concón, Chile, lies north of Valparaíso, the country's principal port. The climate in this region is pleasant, with fresh breezes easing the summer heat and sunshine making the winters more tolerable. Swimming, fishing, camping, tennis, and horseback riding are some of the activities visitors enjoy there. An interesting wildlife attraction is a pelican colony near the beach.

(p. 189 , top photo)
Located at the northern edge of the Patagonian Andes, Argentina's Lake District is famous for its spectacular scenery and world-class skiing. During July (mid-winter in the southern hemisphere), thousands of high school students vacation at the Lake District town of Bariloche. Discuss Argentina's extremely varied geography with students, pointing out the different regions (desert, mountain, pampas).

(p. 189, bottom photo)
The Parque Nacional Nahuel Huapi includes 7,580 square kilometers of the Lake District's mountains, forests, and glaciers. Founded in 1903 as part of a worldwide drive to preserve wild places, the park has a forest research station that tests the latest techniques in wildlife management. Ask: What was happening in the early twentieth century that might explain this drive to preserve wild places? (Possible answer: awareness of increasing urbanization)

Present

Chapter Theme
Clothing stores

Communicative Objectives
- To talk about shopping and places to shop for clothing
- To talk about articles of clothing
- To describe clothes
- To indicate a specific item or items
- To talk about when something happened
- To indicate location

 Overheads 33–34

 Vocabulary Art BLMs/CD-ROM

 Pronunciation Tape 6-2

 Vocabulario para conversar B

Play

Step

Using the Video
Video segment 2: See the Video Teacher's Guide.

 Video Activity B

Vocabulario para conversar

At Home VIDEO Chapter 6 Vocabulary

¿Cuánto pagaste por el suéter?

Here's the rest of the vocabulary you will need to talk about where and when you bought clothes.

el almacén, *pl.* los almacenes

la tienda de ropa

la ropa

Options

Strategies for Reaching All Students

Students Needing Extra Help
También necesitas . . . : Show students how *qué* + adjective works. Teach *compré / compraste* as vocabulary only, not as a grammar point. Do the same with *hace* + time expression.

Learning Spanish Through Action
STAGING VOCABULARY: *Señalen, Vayan*
MATERIALS: cards with pictures of stores or transparency of stores
DIRECTIONS: Project the transparency or place the cards on the walls of your classroom. Ask students to point or go to the store as you call out each one. In addition, ask each student: *¿Qué vas a comprar?* or *¿Qué compraste?*

Multiple Intelligences
Bodily/Kinesthetic
See Learning Spanish Through Action.
Interpersonal/Social
See Class Starter Review.
Verbal/Linguistic
See Pronunciation Tape 6-2.
Visual/Spatial
See Overheads 33–34, the Vocabulary Art BLMs/CD-ROM, and Using the Video.

¡MUCHAS GANGAS!

la zapatería

la tienda de descuentos

¿Por qué pagar mucho?

También necesitas...

la ganga	*bargain*	pagar:	*to pay:*
barato, -a	*inexpensive*	(yo) pagué	*I paid*
		(tú) pagaste	*you paid*
caro, -a	*expensive*	por	*for*
nuevo, -a	*new*	estos, estas; esos, esas	*these; those*
¡Qué + *adjective!*	*How ___!*	otro, -a	*another, other*
comprar:	*to buy:*	hace + *time expression*	*___ ago*
(yo) compré	*I bought*	por aquí	*around here*
(tú) compraste	*you bought*		

Vocabulario para conversar   191

 Pasos vivos 1 CD-ROM
Clip Art Album

Grammar Preview
Demonstrative adjectives are previewed here. The explanation appears in the grammar section on p. 202. *[Aquel(los), aquella(s)* are presented in Book 2.]

Teaching Suggestions
Preparing students to speak: Use one or two options from each of the categories of Comprehensible Input, Physical Response, or Limited Verbal Response. For a complete explanation of these categories and some sample activities, see pp. T22–T23.

Class Starter Review
On the day following initial presentation, you might begin the class with this activity:
Have pairs of students ask their partners where they purchased certain clothing items and how much they paid for them. (If students are reluctant to discuss this topic, bring in department store catalogues to elicit the information.)

www Internet Activities
Juegos

Practice

Re-enter / Recycle
Ex. 13: numbers 0–31 from *El primer paso,* numbers 32–59 from Chap. 2, numbers 60–100 from Chap. 5

Reteach / Review: Spelling
Ex. 12: Stress the importance of the accent mark on *mí* by writing *mí / mi* on the chalkboard with these sentences: *Para mí esa camisa es muy cara. Yo compré mi camisa en un almacén.*

Answers: Empecemos a conversar

11 ESTUDIANTE A
a. ¿Dónde compraste esos pantalones cortos nuevos?
b. . . . zapatos . . .
c. . . . jeans . . .
d. . . . calcetines . . .
e. . . . tenis . . .

ESTUDIANTE B
a.-e. Answers will vary, but look for logical responses *(la tienda de ropa, el almacén, la zapatería, la tienda de descuentos, el centro comercial).*

12 ESTUDIANTE A
a. Estos zapatos son caros, ¿verdad?
b. . . . pantalones cortos . . .
c. . . . jeans . . .
d. . . . suéteres . . .
e. . . . vestidos . . .

Empecemos a conversar

11 A —*¿Dónde compraste esos <u>pantalones</u> nuevos?*
   B —*Los compré en <u>el almacén</u>.*

Estudiante A   Estudiante B

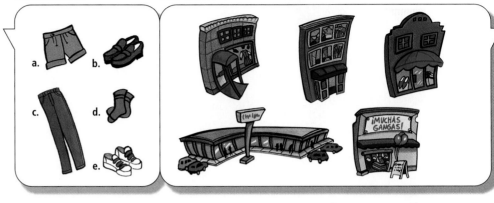

12 A —*Estos <u>calcetines</u> son caros, ¿verdad?*
   B —*Sí, para mí son muy caros. ¿Hay <u>otra tienda de ropa</u> por aquí?*

Estudiante A   Estudiante B

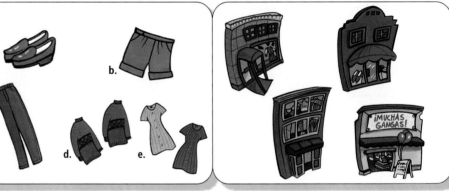

Options

Strategies for Reaching All Students

Spanish-Speaking Students
Pair bilingual with non-bilingual students for Exs. 11–14.

 Un paso más Ex. 6-C

Students Needing Extra Help
Ex. 11: Point out that *Estudiante B*'s response is not directly across from *Estudiante A*'s clue.
Ex. 12: Review the formation of plural nouns. Explain that because of the expense, *Estudiante B* is looking for another store to see if the prices are better.
Ex. 13: Again, point out that the response is not directly across from the clue. Keep in mind that the responses *¡Qué caro!* or *¡Qué barato!* are subjective.

Enrichment
Ex. 13: Pairs of students can extend this dialogue by having *Estudiante A* contrast what he or she paid for the item in question. Example: *¡Qué caro (barato)! Pues, por mi suéter, yo pagué . . . . Estudiante B* can then ask where *Estudiante A* bought the item.

13

A —¿Cuánto pagaste por <u>la falda</u>?

B —Pagué <u>veintiséis</u> dólares.

A —¡Qué cara (barata)!

Estudiante A	Estudiante B

14

A —Esa <u>blusa</u> es muy bonita. ¿Es nueva?

B —Más o menos. La compré <u>hace una semana</u>.

Estudiante A	Estudiante B

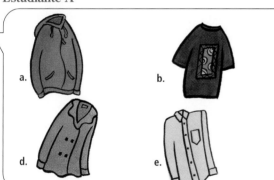

Vocabulario para conversar 193

ESTUDIANTE B

a.-e. Questions will vary, but look for logical choices (la tienda de ropa, la zapatería, el almacén, la tienda de descuentos).

13 ESTUDIANTE A

a. ¿Cuánto pagaste por el vestido?/¡Qué caro (barato)!

b. . . . la camiseta?/ . . . cara (barata)!

c. . . . la sudadera?/ . . . cara (barata)!

d. . . . la blusa?/ . . . cara (barata)!

e. . . . la camisa?/ . . . cara (barata)!

f. Questions will vary.

ESTUDIANTE B

a. Pagué treinta y cinco dólares.

b. . . . siete . . .

c. . . . sesenta y cinco . . .

d. . . . veintisiete . . .

e. . . . doce . . .

f. Answers will vary.

14 ESTUDIANTE A

a. Esa chaqueta es muy bonita. ¿Es nueva?

b. Esa camiseta . . .

c. Esa falda . . .

d. Esa blusa . . .

e. Esa camisa . . .

f. Esa sudadera . . .

ESTUDIANTE B

a.-f. Más o menos. La compré hace . . . (Answers will vary.)

Extended Written Practice/Homework

1. Write four sentences telling how much you paid for different items.

2. Write three sentences naming different types of stores that are or are not common in your area: *No hay muchas zapaterías por aquí.*

Multiple Intelligences
Verbal/Linguistic
See Exs. 11–14.

Apply

Re-enter / Recycle

Ex. 18: calendar expressions from *El primer paso*
Ex. 19: *gustar* expressions from Chap. 1, adjectives describing physical characteristics from Chap. 5

Answers: Empecemos a escribir y a leer

15–18 Answers will vary, but encourage students to use the full range of chapter vocabulary.

19 Answers
a. Marta
b. Silvia
c. una tienda de descuentos
d. Answers will vary.

Empecemos a escribir y a leer

Write your answers in Spanish.

15 Choose three of your favorite clothing items, and tell in what kinds of stores you bought them.

16 Describe your three favorite items of clothing.

17 Cuando vas de compras, ¿buscas gangas o no?

18 ¿Compraste algo hace dos semanas? ¿Qué? ¿Y hace un mes?

Dos jóvenes en un centro comercial en México

"¿A qué tienda quieres ir ahora?"

MORE PRACTICE

- Más práctica y tarea, pp. 523–524
- Practice Workbook 6–3, 6–4

www.pasoapaso.com

194   Capítulo 6

Options

Strategies for Reaching All Students

Students Needing Extra Help
Ex. 15: Model one example.

Enrichment
Have pairs of students invent a dialogue in which they go shopping. Encourage students to use extensive vocabulary to describe their favorite type of shopping companion. If students don't shop with anyone or don't like to go shopping, have them say so and give reasons for their shopping habits or preferences.

Extended Written Practice/Homework
1. Write three pairs of sentences telling how long ago you bought certain items of clothing.
2. Write three pairs of sentences telling how often you go to certain stores. Describe the clothing in each store.

19 Lee este diálogo.

SILVIA   Hola, Marta. ¡Qué bonito tu vestido!

MARTA   ¿Te gusta?

SILVIA   Sí, me gusta mucho. ¿Es nuevo?

MARTA   Pues, lo compré hace una semana.

SILVIA   ¿Dónde lo compraste?

MARTA   En la tienda de descuentos Nosotras.

SILVIA   ¿Y cuánto pagaste?

MARTA   ¡Diez dólares!

SILVIA   ¡No me digas! ¡Qué ganga! Yo también
necesito comprar un vestido nuevo.
¿Quieres ir de compras mañana?

MARTA   ¡Claro que sí!

a. ¿Quién tiene un vestido nuevo?
b. ¿Quién necesita un vestido nuevo?
c. ¿Qué es "Nosotras"?
d. En tu opinión, ¿la ropa en los almacenes es barata o cara?
¿Es necesario comprar ropa cara? ¿Por qué?

Vocabulario para conversar   195

Multicultural Perspectives

The indigenous people of Mexico and Central America may be seen wearing unique clothing. A *huipil* is an embroidered blouse. An *enredo* is a long, wrapped skirt. A *rebozo* is a shawl that can serve as a fashion accessory, as a head covering, or to cradle a baby. Men wear *sarapes* (ponchos), *huaraches de seis agujeros* (sandals with two rows of three eyelets, laced with leather cords) and *sombreros de palma* (straw hats). The patterns embroidered on the fabric of the clothing often contain information about community, marital status, or family affiliation. If you have students from other countries, ask them to share information about their traditional clothing.

 Practice Wkbk. 6-3, 6-4

 Audio Activity 6.2

 Writing Activity 6-C

 Pruebas 6-3, 6-4

Multiple Intelligences
Bodily/Kinesthetic
1) Use flashcards of seasons of the year or Overhead 17. Have students point to a season and call on a classmate to tell what item of clothing he or she bought and for what season: *Compré un suéter para el otoño.*
2) Write the lines of the dialogue in Ex. 19 on strips of paper and tape them in random order on the board. Then write the numbers 1–10 to the side. Have students go to the board one at a time and move the strips until they are all in order.
Intrapersonal/Introspective
See Exs. 15–19.
Verbal/Linguistic
1) With a permanent marker, draw stick figures on a transparency. Have students call out clothing descriptions while one student draws them on the stick figure.
2) See Audio Activity 6.2.

Cultural Notes

(p. 194, photo)
The majority of Mexico's consumer-product exports go to the U.S., and the majority of its imports come from the U.S. as well. Consequently, a mall such as this one in Mexico City could be initially mistaken for a U.S. one. Ask students: How do you imagine a trip to a Mexican mall would be different from a trip to one in the U.S.?

Practice

Re-enter / Recycle
Ex. 1: activities from Chap. 1, places and buildings from Chap. 3
Ex. 2: numbers 0–31 from *El primer paso,* school supplies from Chap. 2
Ex. 3: *me gustaría* from Chap. 3

**Answers:
¡Comuniquemos!**

1 ESTUDIANTE A
¿Qué ropa llevas cuando vas al gimnasio?
. . . al parque de diversiones?
. . . al centro comercial?
. . . a la escuela?
. . . al campo?
. . . al parque?
. . . al cine?

ESTUDIANTE B
Answers will vary.

2 ESTUDIANTE A
Questions will vary depending on the items chosen.

ESTUDIANTE B
Answers will vary depending on the prices of the items.

3 Dialogues will vary.

¡COMUNI

¡NO OLVIDES!

a + el = al

1

Find out what your partner usually wears when he or she goes to at least three different places.

A —*¿Qué ropa llevas cuando vas al parque?*

B —*Generalmente llevo . . .*
o: *Nunca voy al parque.*

Options

Strategies for Reaching All Students

Spanish-Speaking Students
Ex. 1: Have Spanish-speaking students write out part of the exercise: *Escribe seis oraciones que describen lo que llevas a diferentes lugares.*

 Un paso más Ex. 6-D

Students Needing Extra Help
Ex. 1: Have students use their Organizers for this chapter and from Chap. 3 to review the places.
Ex. 2: Have students use their Organizers from Chap. 2 for school supplies.
¿Qué sabes ahora?: Have students write out this section so they can track their progress.

Cooperative Learning
Divide the class into groups of three or four students. Using vocabulary from the *Vocabulario para conversar,* have each student prepare a list of the clothing they are wearing and their colors. Have one student in each group collect the lists and record the colors of one type (shoes, socks, etc.) of clothing. Have another student record colors for another type of clothing. Repeat until each type of clothing is recorded. Collect the responses and tally them. Before putting the

Find out how much your partner paid for at least five of his or her school supplies. For example:

A —¿Cuánto pagaste por . . . ?

B —Pagué cinco dólares, más o menos.

You want to buy some clothes for a trip or special event you will be attending. You have a budget of $100. Decide on three items you would like and what colors they will be. Your partner will estimate how much each item costs and keep a tally. Can you get what you will need and stick to your budget? For example:

A —Me gustaría comprar unos pantalones azules.

B —Cuestan 25 dólares.

A —También necesito . . .

¿Qué sabes ahora?

Can you:

► describe what you are wearing?
—Hoy llevo ___.

► tell where you bought something?
—___ mis jeans en ___.

► tell how much you paid for something?
—___ veinte dólares ___ la camisa.

► ask how much something costs?
—¿Cuánto ___ esa camisa?

Vocabulario para conversar   197

 Audio Activity 6.3

 Pasos vivos 1 CD-ROM

Slide Projector, Laboratorio de grabar

---

results on the chalkboard, ask students: What do you think is the most popular shoe color? The most popular color of jeans? and so on. (Combine some of the clothing categories for this exercise. For example, shoes / sneakers, pants / jeans.)

Multiple Intelligences
Interpersonal/Social
See Exs. 1–3 and Cooperative Learning.
Intrapersonal/Introspective
See *¿Qué sabes ahora?*
Logical/Mathematical
Have students list items in Ex. 2 from least to most expensive.
Verbal/Linguistic
See Audio Activity 6.3.

Cultural Notes

(pp. 196–197, realia)
Currency from Mexico, Honduras, and El Salvador. *Nuevos pesos mexicanos* coins are shown on the left. The currency of El Salvador is called the *colón,* named for Christopher Columbus. The Honduran *lempira,* however, is named for an indigenous leader who rallied native groups in rebellion against the Spaniards, and is seen as a symbol of national identity.

Cultural Objective
• To compare where people shop for clothes in Spanish-speaking countries and in the U.S.

Critical Thinking: Synthesis
Have students imagine they are owners of a small clothing store. Ask: How can you increase business in your store? Using learned vocabulary, have small groups of students create ads to attract customers of large stores to their small ones. Ask them to also create an inventory list of the merchandise their stores should carry.

Answers
Possible answers: clothing store, shopping malls.

Cultural Notes
(pp. 198–199, photos)
Shopping malls are now commonplace in most Spanish-speaking countries. Not only do they have clothing stores, bookstores, and fast-food restaurants, many of them have supermarkets as well. At the Alcampo mall in Zaragoza, Spain, shoppers can eat in their favorite restaurant, look at the latest fashion designs, and buy their groceries, all without leaving the complex.

Perspectiva cultural

Las tiendas en los países hispanos

¿Te gusta ir de compras en los almacenes o los centros comerciales? ¿Qué compras?

Look at the photos on these pages. What kinds of stores do you think are shown here?

In big cities in Spanish-speaking countries, you can usually find a variety of malls or shopping centers. The idea of the shopping mall originated in the United States, and other countries have

Centro comercial en Zaragoza, España

adopted the concept by creating malls of great beauty. However, there are also tailors and dressmaking stores where people can have their clothes custom-made at affordable prices.

Teenagers in Spanish-speaking countries like to window-shop at malls and clothing stores, just as they do here. And just as in other countries, there is a wide variety of materials, styles, and fashions to choose from. Teens in Spanish-speaking countries tend to be fashion-conscious and stylish in the way they dress, and many like to wear custom-made formal clothes on special occasions.

Fox Delicias Mall en Ponce, Puerto Rico

198   Capítulo 6

Options

Strategies for Reaching All Students

Spanish-Speaking Students
Ask Spanish-speaking students: *¿Hay tiendas pequeñas en tu comunidad que vendan productos de otros países? ¿Qué productos de otros países puedes comprar allí?*

 Un paso más Ex. 6-E

Students Needing Extra Help
The idea of specialized stores where you buy just one type of product may be unfamiliar to many students. Explain this concept to them.

Enrichment
If there is a sizable Hispanic population in your area, you may want to have pairs of students visit Hispanic neighborhood stores. Give each pair of students a topic on which to prepare a brief report, such as the products carried, the people who work and shop there, or how long the stores have been in existence.

Distrito comercial Sabana
Grande en Caracas, Venezuela

Tienda de ropa en la Ciudad de México

La cultura desde tu perspectiva

 1 What do you think are some of the advantages and disadvantages of shopping in a mall rather than in separate stores within several blocks?

 2 Do you think you would be able to find clothing brands that you are familiar with in the stores pictured? Why or why not?

www.pasoapaso.com

Perspectiva cultural   199

Teaching Suggestions

Ask students: What comparison can be made between a department store and a discount store in an ad like this? Find the place in the ad where the comparison is made (*¿Por qué pagar los precios altos . . .*).

Have students find these phrases from the ad: *precios altos, ropa espectacular.* Identify which of these words are nouns and which are adjectives. As a preview to the grammar, ask about the position of the adjectives in relation to the nouns.

Answers

Answers may include: name of the store, address, business hours, description of merchandise, prices, etc.

A *Esta* is used before *ropa* because it refers to a feminine, singular noun. *Este* refers to *mes* and is masculine. *Estas* would be used before *gangas* because it is feminine.

B *Las* refers to *camisas, blusas y faldas.* / *Ropa* determines the use of *la.* / If you were talking about a shirt, the phrase would be *la compro,* because *camisa* is feminine.

Gramática en contexto

Here is an ad for a store. What kinds of information would you expect to find in an ad for a discount clothing store?

A You know that *estos* and *estas* mean "these." Look at the ad. Which word is used before *ropa?* And before *mes?* Which form of the word would be used before *gangas?* Can you explain the difference?

B You know that *lo* and *la* can mean "it," and *los* and *las* can mean "them." In the question that begins *"¿Por qué pagar los precios altos . . . cuando nosotros las tenemos . . . ,"* what does *las* refer to? In the sentence that begins *"La Tienda de Descuentos Bolívar tiene . . . y ahora Ud. la puede comprar . . . ,"* why do you think *la* is used, and not *lo?* If you were talking about a shirt *(camisa),* would you say *lo compro* or *la compro?*

200   Capítulo 6

Options

Strategies for Reaching All Students

Spanish-Speaking Students
Ex. 1: Have Spanish-speaking students write out part of the exercise. *Escribe oraciones para estos artículos (estas prendas). Incluye tus colores preferidos.*

Students Needing Extra Help
Remind students that *la, las,* and *los* are also the definite articles meaning "the." Explain that the context makes clear which use is meant.
Be sure students understand the difference between *esta* (demonstrative adjective) and *está* (third person singular form of *estar*), and *estas* (demonstrative adjective) and *estás* (second person singular form of *estar*).

A: Remind students of adjective endings. Going from "these" to "this" will be a leap for some students. Walk them through this comparison.
B: Direct students back to the paragraph or write the sentences on the chalkboard so they can find out what *las* represents.
La posición de los adjetivos: Have students start to fill in the grammar portion of their Organizers.

La posición de los adjetivos

In Spanish, adjectives usually come after the noun they describe.

Me gusta más la camisa **blanca.**

Tenemos un perro **grande y feo.**

Adjectives agree in number (singular / plural) and gender (masculine / feminine) with the nouns they describe.

1 You and your partner are going shopping for clothing. Look at the items pictured and tell your partner which you would like to buy. Your partner will respond with his or her choice.

A —*Me gustaría comprar una camiseta blanca.*

B —*A mí también.*

o: *A mí no. Prefiero una camiseta roja.*

a.

b.

c.

d.

e.

f.

g.

h.

Gramática en contexto   201

Present & Practice

Reteach / Review: Indefinite Articles
Ex. 1: Do a quick review of the indefinite articles and the gender of nouns by mentioning a noun and calling on a student to give the correct indefinite article.

Re-enter / Recycle
Ex. 1: *me gustaría* from Chap. 3, adjective agreement from Chaps. 1 and 4

Answers
1 ESTUDIANTE A
a. Me gustaría comprar unos pantalones grises.
b. …una chaqueta marrón.
c. …una camisa azul.
d. …unos calcetines morados.
e. …unos zapatos negros.
f. …unos pantalones cortos verdes.
g. …un suéter rojo.
h. …una sudadera amarilla.
ESTUDIANTE B
a.–h. Statements will vary depending on *Estudiante B*'s preferences. Look for correct adjective agreement and placement.

Ex. 1: If *Estudiante B* chooses the second response, he or she will have to determine the color. Have students use the Organizer. *¡No olvides!:* Emphasize the terms singular / plural, masculine / feminine, rather than number and gender.

Extended Written Practice/Homework
1. Write four sentences naming items of your own clothing that you love. Include the color of the clothes.
2. Write three sentences saying where you can buy certain kinds of clothes: *Puedes comprar vestidos baratos en la tienda de descuentos Bolívar.*
3. Write two sentences describing a dog or cat that you or someone you know has: *Mi abuela tiene un gato muy grande y antipático.*

Multiple Intelligences
Bodily/Kinesthetic
Assign a clothing item to each student. Have them draw and color a picture of it on one side of an index card and write the Spanish word on the other. Distribute the cards to partners and have them ask for and give information about where they bought the item and how much they paid for it.
Musical/Rhythmic
Have students create a short radio or TV ad for a clothing item. Tell them that the ad should contain a jingle to be sung or chanted.

Present & Practice

Re-enter / Recycle

Ex. 2: adjective agreement from Chaps. 1 and 4, family and friends from Chap. 5
Ex. 4: numbers 0–31 from *El primer paso,* numbers 32–59 from Chap. 2, numbers 60–100 and *tener* from Chap. 5

Answers

2 Have students make a three-column "T" chart to help organize their answers. Use these headings: item/color/for whom

ESTUDIANTE A
a.–h. ¿Qué desea, señor (señora / joven / señorita)? / ¿Para Ud.?

ESTUDIANTE B
a. Busco un vestido *(student's choice of color).*/Answers will vary.
b. . . . unos pantalones cortos . . .
c. . . . un suéter . . .
d. . . . una sudadera . . .
e. . . . una camisa . . . y unos pantalones . . .
f. . . . una chaqueta . . .
g. . . . unas camisetas . . .
h. Statements will vary.

Colors will vary, but look for adjective agreement.

 Practice Wkbk. 6-5

 Prueba 6-5

---

2 Take turns with your partner playing the roles of a salesperson and a customer. The salesperson should find out what item the customer is looking for and for whom. The items can be for yourself or for a person of your choice. You decide the colors you want.

A —*¿Qué desea, señor (señora/joven/señorita)?*
B —*Busco unos calcetines rojos.*
A —*¿Para Ud.?*
B —*Sí, para mí.*
   o: *No, para . . .*

a.   b.   c.   d.

e.   f.   g.   h.

Los adjetivos demostrativos

We use demonstrative adjectives to point out people and things. You've already seen these forms: *este, esta, estos, estas* (this, these), and *ese, esa, esos,* and *esas* (that, those).

Demonstrative adjectives come before the noun. They have the same gender and number as the nouns that follow them.

SINGULAR	PLURAL
este vestido *(**this** dress)*	**estos** vestidos *(**these** dresses)*
esta blusa *(**this** blouse)*	**estas** blusas *(**these** blouses)*
ese suéter *(**that** sweater)*	**esos** suéteres *(**those** sweaters)*
esa sudadera *(**that** sweatshirt)*	**esas** sudaderas *(**those** sweatshirts)*

202   Capítulo 6

Options

Strategies for Reaching All Students

Spanish-Speaking Students
Pair bilingual with non-bilingual students for Exs. 2–4.

Students Needing Extra Help
Ex. 2: Point out the choices in the first line for *Estudiante A.* For the first *Estudiante B* response, review the indefinite articles. Model an example using a singular article of clothing.
Los adjetivos demostrativos: Have students fill in the chart in the grammar portion of their Organizers. The concept of "this,"

"that," "these," and "those" may be confusing for students. (Color-coding these words in sentences written on a transparency can help.) Associating the four letters in *este* with the four letters in "near" and the three letters in *ese* with the three in "far" also helps many students. Point out that the masculine, singular form of "this" and "that" end in *e,* not *o,* as students might expect.

3 With a partner, decide which words in this list you would use with the demonstrative adjective *este* or *ese*. Which would you use with *estos* or *esos? Esta* or *esa? Estas* or *esas?* Afterward write sentences using five of the words with an appropriate demonstrative adjective.

a. tienda
b. zapatos
c. sudaderas
d. calcetín
e. zapatería
f. ganga
g. pantimedias
h. vestido
i. suéteres
j. almacén
k. pantalones cortos
l. blusas
m. ropa
n. tienda de descuentos
o. colores

4 You are at a party and you want to get to know the guests. Find out from your partner their names and ages.

A —¿Cómo se llama esa muchacha alta y rubia?
B —Marta.
A —¿Cuántos años tiene?
B —Quince.

Marta

Lucía, 28

Pilar y
Conchita, 17

Carlitos, 9

Eva, 75

Marta, 15

Javier, 35

Miguel y Mateo, 14

Gramática en contexto   203

5 While shopping with a friend, you pick up and look at several items. Ask if your partner likes them.

A —¿Te gusta este suéter azul?

B —Sí, me gusta mucho.

   o: *No, no me gusta nada.*

a.

b.

c.

d.

e.

f.

6 Get together in groups of four or five. Each person should put at least two of his or her school supplies in a pile. Take turns holding up items and trying to find out to whom each one belongs. For example:

A —¿De quién es este marcador amarillo? ¿Es de (nombre)?

B —Sí. Ese marcador es de (nombre).

   o: *No, ese marcador no es de (nombre).*

El complemento directo: Los pronombres

A direct object tells who or what receives the action of the verb.

Quiero **esa falda.**

Compré **unos zapatos.**

To avoid repeating a direct object noun, we often replace it with a direct object pronoun ("it" or "them").

—¿Cuándo compraste **la falda?**

—**La** compré hace cinco días.

—Isabel, ¿tienes **mi suéter?**

—No, no **lo** tengo.

Disfruta la vida al natural.

Algodón. Naturalmente suave.

Options

Strategies for Reaching All Students

Students Needing Extra Help

El complemento directo: Los pronombres: This may be another difficult concept for students. Break the explanation into these steps:

1. Discuss what they already know about direct objects from English. Most students have been taught that direct objects answer the question "who" or "what" of the verb, or receive the action of the verb.

2. Remind students that pronouns replace nouns. Emphasize that once we have stated the noun, we usually replace it with "it" or "them."

3. Using Spanish nouns familiar to students, have them decide which object pronoun will replace each noun.

4. Using examples from the book and then creating others, have two students stand in front of the classroom, one holding a card that reads *Quiero* and the other *ese suéter.* The back of the *Quiero* card should read *quiero* and the back of the *ese suéter* card should read *Lo.* Read *Quiero ese suéter* and

its translation—"I want that sweater"—followed by "I want it." At this point the students should flip their cards. The second student moves to the other side of the first student, creating *Lo quiero.* This gives the class a memorable visual.

5. Repeat this process with variations, using sentences with *no* and a verb followed by an infinitive.

6. Delay the explanation of attaching the object pronoun to the infinitive. This will appear in Chap. 11.

SINGULAR			PLURAL	
lo	*it* (masculine)		**los**	*them* (masculine)
la	*it* (feminine)		**las**	*them* (feminine)

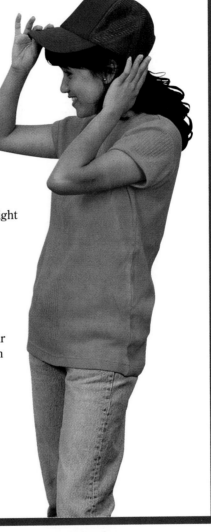

- The direct object pronoun usually comes right before the verb. If the verb is negative, the pronoun is placed between *no* and the verb.

  —¿Compras **esos pantalones?**
  —No, no **los** compro.

- When we have a verb followed by an infinitive, the direct object pronoun is usually placed right before the main verb (not the infinitive).

  —¿Quieres comprar **esa falda?**
  —Sí, **la** quiero comprar.

- Direct object pronouns have the same gender and number as the nouns they are replacing. When the pronoun replaces both a masculine and a feminine direct object noun, we use *los.*

  —¿Cuándo compraste **la falda y el vestido?**
  —**Los** compré el sábado.

7 Read each sentence on the left and tell which noun on the right has been replaced by a direct object pronoun.

No, no **la** necesito.   camisetas
Jorge **los** tiene.   chaqueta
Es caro pero **lo** quiero comprar.   tenis
Susana y Felipe **las** van a comprar.   vestido

8 Write four sentences similar to those in Exercise 7. Ask your partner to rewrite your sentences using an appropriate noun in place of the pronoun you used.

7. Remind students that they already know how to replace and combine a masculine and feminine subject with the masculine plural form.
Ex. 5: Remind students to use *gusta* with singular and *gustan* with plural nouns. This exercise may be made more realistic by bringing in actual items of clothing. This will help them visualize the difference between *este* and *ese.*

Extended Written Practice/Homework
1. Write three pairs of sentences. First, tell how long ago you bought an item of clothing. Then tell where you bought it: *Compré una sudadera hace tres meses. La compré en el almacén Super.*
2. Write three pairs of sentences. First, name a type of food or beverage you like. Then tell how often you eat or drink it: *Me gustan las manzanas. Las como todos los días.*

Multiple Intelligences
Bodily/Kinesthetic
See Class Starter Review and Students Needing Extra Help, part 4.

Practice

Re-enter / Recycle

Ex. 10: calendar expressions and numbers 0–31 from *El primer paso*, adjective agreement from Chaps. 1 and 4

Ex. 11: school supplies, school subjects, and *necesito / necesitas* from Chap. 2

Answers

9 ESTUDIANTE A

a. ¿De qué color prefieres los zapatos?

b. . . . los suéteres?

c. . . . las blusas?

d. . . . las camisetas?

e. . . . las chaquetas?

f. . . . las sudaderas?

g. . . . los calcetines?

h. Questions will vary.

ESTUDIANTE B

a. Los prefiero blancos (negros).

b. Los prefiero morados (azules).

c. Las prefiero rosadas (amarillas).

d. Las prefiero rojas (negras).

e. Las prefiero verdes (marrones).

f. Las prefiero grises (anaranjadas).

g. Los prefiero rojos (azules).

h. Answers will vary.

10 Order of students' exchanges may vary.

A—Tu chaqueta es nueva, ¿no?

B—Sí, la compré hace dieciocho días.

A—Tus calcetines son nuevos . . .

B— . . . los compré . . . quince días.

---

9 With a partner, take turns asking and answering.

A —*¿De qué color prefieres las camisas?*

B —*Las prefiero grises (blancas).*

Estudiante A Estudiante B

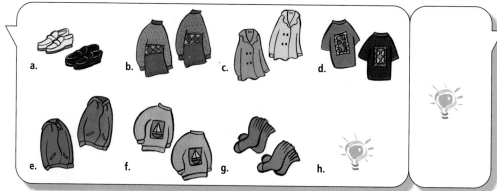

a.   b.   c.   d.

e.   f.   g.   h.

10 Today is January 28 and this month you have bought a lot of new clothes. Use the calendar to answer your partner's questions.

A —*Tu camisa es nueva, ¿no?*

B —*Sí. La compré hace tres semanas.*

206   Capítulo 6

Options

Strategies for Reaching All Students

Spanish-Speaking Students
Pair Spanish-speaking students for Exs. 9–11.

Students Needing Extra Help
Ex. 10: Review adjective agreement and *hace* + time expression. Show students how to arrive at the number of days (subtracting the date from January 28). Be aware that some math errors may occur. Point out that, like the direct object pronoun, *nueva* will change depending on the clothing item.
Ex. 11: Have students review their Chap. 2 Organizers for school supplies.
Remind students that they will be using direct object pronouns in the answers.

Multiple Intelligences
Verbal/Linguistic
See Audio Activity 6.4.
Visual/Spatial
See Comm. Act. BLMs 6-2 and 6-3 and Practice Wkbk. 6-7 and 6-8.

11 You're trying to help your partner clean out a messy locker. Ask whether or not he or she needs the objects pictured.

A —¿Necesitas la calculadora?

B —¡Claro que sí! La necesito para mi clase de matemáticas.
o: No, no la necesito.

Ahora lo sabes

Can you:

► identify and describe articles of clothing?
—Necesito un(a) ___.

► point out people and things?
—¿Qué bolígrafo prefieres?
—Prefiero ___ bolígrafo.

► avoid reusing a noun by replacing it with *lo, la, los,* or *las?*
—¿Tienes la calculadora y la regla?
—Sí, ___ tengo.

MORE PRACTICE

- Más práctica y tarea, pp. 524–525
- Practice Workbook 6–5, 6–8

A—Tu sudadera es nueva . . .
B—. . . la compré . . . dos semanas (catorce días).
A—Tus vestidos son nuevos . . .
B—. . . los compré . . . doce días.
A—Tus jeans son nuevos . . .
B—. . . los compré . . . ocho días.
A—Tu suéter y tu camiseta son nuevos . . .
B—. . . los compré . . . seis días.

11 ESTUDIANTE A
¿Necesitas los lápices (los cuadernos, la regla, etc.)? Assist students as needed.

ESTUDIANTE B
Answers will vary, but look for correct use of direct object pronouns./¡Claro que sí! Los necesito para . . . (No, no los necesito.)

Answers: Ahora lo sabes
- Answers will vary, but look for correct placement of adjectives.
- este (ese)
- las

 Practice Wkbk. 6-7, 6-8

 Audio Activity 6.4

 Writing Activities 6-E, 6-F

 Prueba 6-7

 Comm. Act. BLMs 6-2, 6-3

 Pasos vivos 1 CD-ROM
Fax Task, Slide Presentation Maker, Spindle, Treadmill

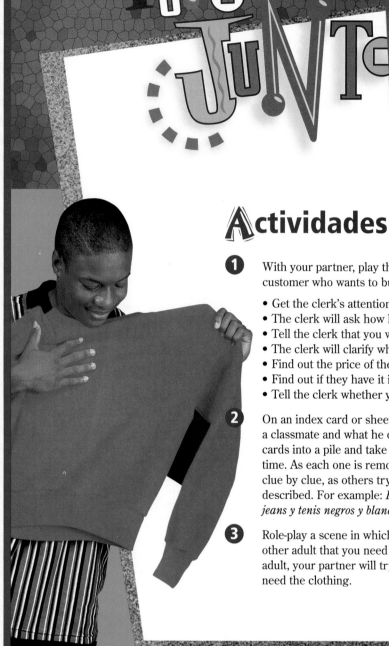

De compras en Madrid, España

Todo junto

Actividades

1 With your partner, play the roles of a store clerk and a customer who wants to buy an item of clothing:

- Get the clerk's attention
- The clerk will ask how he or she can help you
- Tell the clerk that you want to see an item
- The clerk will clarify which item you are talking about
- Find out the price of the item
- Find out if they have it in another color
- Tell the clerk whether you will buy it or not

2 On an index card or sheet of paper, write a description of a classmate and what he or she is wearing. Put all of the cards into a pile and take turns removing them one at a time. As each one is removed, someone reads it aloud, clue by clue, as others try to guess who is being described. For example: *Es un muchacho rubio. Lleva jeans y tenis negros y blancos. También lleva . . .*

3 Role-play a scene in which you try to convince a parent or other adult that you need to buy some new clothes. As the adult, your partner will try to convince you that you don't need the clothing.

208   Capítulo 6

Options

Strategies for Reaching All Students

Enrichment

Ex. 3: As a homework assignment, have students write a dialogue in which the parent wants the son or daughter to buy certain kinds or colors of clothes.

Conexiones: Have students tell where one of their own clothing items is made and have them calculate how many hours it would take the worker to work in order to buy that item in U.S. dollars.

Cooperative Learning

Have students work in groups of three or four to role play fashion designers. Their assignment is to come up with the best-looking outfit design for today's teenager. Using pictures and text, have one student in each group be responsible for presenting and explaining the new design to the class. Allow the class to vote for the best one.

Multiple Intelligences

Interpersonal/Social
See Cooperative Learning, *Actividades* Exs. 1–3, and Critical Thinking: Evaluating Information.

Logical/Mathematical
See *Conexiones.*

Verbal/Linguistic
See Pronunciation Tape 6-3.

Visual/Spatial
See Using the Video.

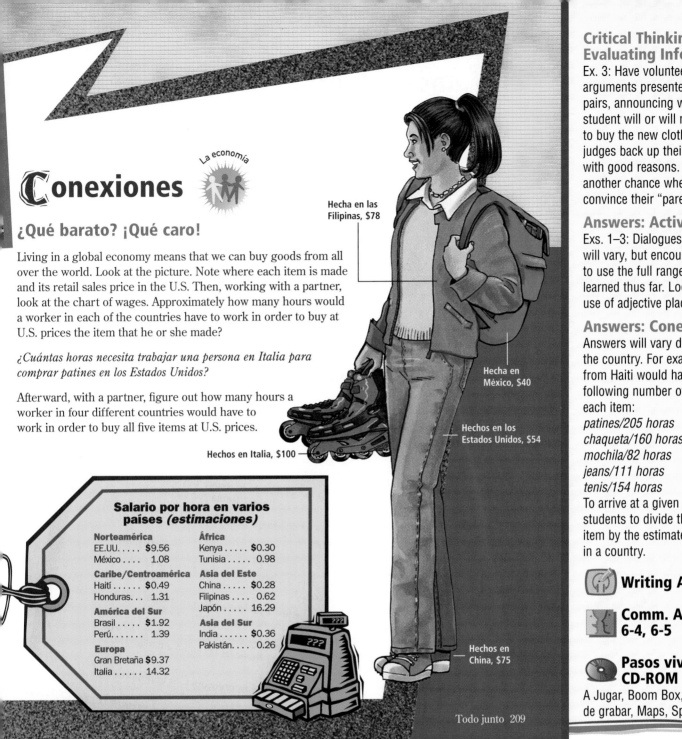

Conexiones

La economía

¿Qué barato? ¡Qué caro!

Living in a global economy means that we can buy goods from all over the world. Look at the picture. Note where each item is made and its retail sales price in the U.S. Then, working with a partner, look at the chart of wages. Approximately how many hours would a worker in each of the countries have to work in order to buy at U.S. prices the item that he or she made?

¿Cuántas horas necesita trabajar una persona en Italia para comprar patines en los Estados Unidos?

Afterward, with a partner, figure out how many hours a worker in four different countries would have to work in order to buy all five items at U.S. prices.

Hecha en las Filipinas, $78

Hecha en México, $40

Hechos en los Estados Unidos, $54

Hechos en Italia, $100

Hechos en China, $75

Salario por hora en varios países *(estimaciones)*

Norteamérica		África	
EE.UU.	$9.56	Kenya	$0.30
México	1.08	Tunisia	0.98
Caribe/Centroamérica		**Asia del Este**	
Haití	$0.49	China	$0.28
Honduras	1.31	Filipinas	0.62
		Japón	16.29
América del Sur			
Brasil	$1.92	**Asia del Sur**	
Perú	1.39	India	$0.36
		Pakistán	0.26
Europa			
Gran Bretaña	$9.37		
Italia	14.32		

Todo junto 209

Cultural Notes

(p. 208, top photo)
Madrid offers shoppers many choices in shopping settings. In addition to large department stores and malls, there's the Sunday outdoor flea market, El Rastro. Tucked into Madrid's old center are traditional shops selling handicrafts such as ceramics and classical guitars. Boutiques such as this one are also inviting. Ask students: In which of these settings would you like to shop if you were visiting Madrid?

Apply

Process Reading

For a description of process reading, see p. 48.

Answers
Antes de leer

Responses will vary. Students may mention that part of the story deals with clothing and someone's birthday.

Mira la lectura

a. He received two shirts as birthday gifts from his grandmother. He's invited to dinner at her place, and he doesn't know which shirt to wear.

b. He decides to wear the gray shirt.

c. She asks Juanito if he doesn't like the yellow one.

¡Vamos a leer!

Antes de leer

STRATEGY ➤ **Using titles and pictures to predict**

Look at the title and pictures to predict what the story is about.

Mira la lectura

STRATEGIES ➤ **Skimming
Identifying the main idea**

Skimming is another useful strategy. By quickly glancing through a reading selection, you can often get a general idea of the subject and content.

This story tells of a decision a boy has to make. Skim through it quickly to get the main ideas.

a. What is Juanito's problem?
b. What does he decide to do?
c. What is the grandmother's reaction?

El problema de las dos camisas

Juanito es un muchacho amable y sociable. Para su cumpleaños, Juanito recibe muchos regalos y muchísima ropa de su familia. Le encanta la ropa, pero una semana después de su cumpleaños, recibe una invitación para ir a cenar a la casa de su abuela.

Ahora tiene un problema: Su abuela le regaló dos camisas, una gris y otra amarilla. ¿Cuál va a llevar? Habla con su mamá.

Juanito: Mamá, ¿qué voy a llevar? Tengo las dos camisas nuevas de la abuela.

La mamá: Bueno, hijo, ¿por qué no llevas la camisa que te gusta más?

Juanito: Es que no quiero ofender a la abuela. Ella es un poco difícil a veces.

La mamá: Pues, hijo, puedes llevar una de las camisas para esta cena, y otro día puedes llevar la otra camisa.

Juanito decide llevar la camisa gris. Cuando él entra en la casa, la abuela le dice: "Y, ¿qué pasa? No llevas la camisa amarilla. ¿No te gusta?"

La mamá le dice a Juanito: "No te preocupes. Es imposible contentarles a todos."

210   Capítulo 6

Options

Strategies for Reaching All Students

Students Needing Extra Help

Mira la lectura: Make sure students understand the nature of skimming. You may wish to have students work in pairs, where one student answers the questions and the other records the responses. Set a limited amount of time for this activity.

Infórmate: Remind students of the saying "You can't please all of the people all the time."

Aplicación: Brainstorm some situations as a class. For example: (Chap. 3) Two friends can't decide whether to go to the amusement park or the mall. (Chap. 4) Two friends talk about what they want to eat for dinner.

Multiple Intelligences
Verbal/Linguistic
Have students role-play the parts of the narrator, Juanito, and *la mamá.*

Infórmate

STRATEGY > **Using context to get meaning**

Remember that when you are reading and you come across a word you don't understand, you should look at the other words in the sentence to see if they will help you understand.

As you read the story again, make a list of five words or phrases you don't understand.

a. What type of boy is Juanito? What words or phrases tell you that?

b. What do you think of the mother's advice? Would you have given the same advice? Why or why not?

c. What would you have done in Juanito's place?

d. What do you think the last line means?

Aplicación

Think of a similar situation where it seemed impossible to please someone. Create a short dialogue with a partner and end it with a solution that pleases both of you.

¡Vamos a leer! 211

Apply

Process Writing

Starting in this chapter, the revise and edit steps will appear in an abbreviated form.
For information regarding developing a writing portfolio, see p. 50.

Answers: ¡Vamos a escribir!

1–5 Look for correct use of adjectives and verbs. Encourage students to use all the vocabulary learned thus far.

Multicultural Perspectives

The fashion industry has been influenced by styles and designs typical of Spain and Latin America. (Two of the leading fashion designers in the world are from Latin America—Óscar de la Renta and Carolina Herrera.) *Gauchos* are the cowboys of the Pampas in Argentina. The word *gauchos* is also used to describe a type of women's baggy trousers that are often gathered at the ankles. Ask students to name other types of clothing from various cultures with which they are familiar.

 Pasos vivos 1 CD-ROM
Word Processor

¡Vamos a escribir!

"No cuesta mucho."

Many teens love to shop. They read fashion magazines and browse in stores to learn about the newest fashions, styles, and colors. Create an ad for an article of clothing to appear in a teen magazine or catalog.

1 First, think about what might appeal to you and your friends. What article of clothing are you going to sell? What colors does it come in? Where can you buy it? How much does it cost? Write out the answers to these questions in Spanish.

2 Invent a brand name for your clothing. Use it and the answers to the questions in Part 1 to help you design your ad. Be sure to give all the information and arrange it in a way that will catch the eye.

3 Show your ad to a partner. Does he or she want to suggest changes or additions? Think about any changes you might want to make, and rewrite your ad.

4 Check the ad for spelling, accents, and punctuation. Did you use the correct forms of the adjectives? If necessary, make a clean copy and add drawings or magazine pictures to illustrate your ad.

5 You can file your ad in your writing portfolio, or the entire class can collect the ads into a catalog ("ROPA DE PRIMAVERA / VERANO/ OTOÑO / INVIERNO 200__").

212   Capítulo 6

Options

Strategies for Reaching All Students

Spanish-Speaking Students

 Un paso más Exs. 6-F, 6-G, 6-H

Students Needing Extra Help
Step 1: Use the Organizer.
Step 2: If you elect to have students do this activity in groups, try to get an art-gifted student or visual learner in each one.
Step 4: Use Organizers from other chapters.

Enrichment
Groups of students might enjoy collaborating on a poster showing what clothes students will be wearing in the future. Encourage them to make up titles for their posters. Students should also label the clothes they display, indicating what they are and their color.

LOS NUEVOS **PAREDES**
¡ya están en las zapaterías!

Con éstos, de base de POLIURETANO
no sentirás el frío ni el calor, son ISOTÉRMICOS.
Su base es totalmente ANATÓMICA.
Caminar con ellos, es un auténtico placer.

Su diseño, te permite sin cambiarte
de zapatos, saltar directamente
de la pista de tenis, a tomar
una

...y, si te gusta cosido,

Ésta, es la nueva versión (mejorada)
del legendario modelo COMPETICIÓN

Su piel, es napa y está cosida a una estudiada
suela de caucho de gran agarre.
Se le ha incorporado una entresuela
de EVA para que amortigüe y absorba
los impactos que se producen en
el talón durante un partido
de tenis.

PAREDES
la estrella

DISEÑO: *Rafael*

Nuevas marcas

Green Coast

STUDIO CLASICS

NUDOS

BASS

ARCO IRIS

fórmul@ JOVEN

El Corte Inglés
PLANTA JOVEN

Cultural Notes

Multiple Intelligences
Interpersonal/Social and Visual/Spatial
See Enrichment.

(p. 212, photo)
In recent years large department store chains in the U.S. have realized that Latinos represent an increasingly significant market. These stores are increasing their bilingual staff and run slick, sophisticated ads in the Spanish media. Sears also publishes *Nuestra Gente,* a magazine primarily for women. Ask students: Why has the buying power of U.S. Hispanics increased so much recently?

(p. 213, realia)
Like most ads, those directed at a youth market do more than promote *nuevas marcas*—they also promote ideas. Ask students: What ideas about language and culture do the English-language *marcas* in the left ad imply? Do you agree with these ideas? Why or why not?

Assess & Summarize

Test Preparation

You may want to assign parts of this section as written homework or as an in-class writing activity prior to administering the *Examen de habilidades*.

Answers

Listening: *Este fin de semana voy a ir de compras. Necesito comprar un suéter, una sudadera, una chaqueta y dos camisetas, pero sólo tengo 120 dólares.* The person is planning to buy five items and spend approximately $120.

Reading: Inés prefers to go to shopping malls, because there are many types of stores and restaurants there.

Writing: Letters will vary, but students should use most of the chapter vocabulary. Look for logical sentences.

Culture: Answers will vary. Some students may say that they prefer a shopping center because of the convenience and variety of stores. Others may say that they would go to a tailor or dressmaker because of more personalized service.

Speaking: Answers will vary, but students should use the chapter vocabulary. Encourage use of vocabulary from previous chapters.

This section will help you organize your studying for the proficiency test, where you will be asked to do similar, though not identical, tasks. There will not be any models on the test.

► Listening

Can you understand when people talk about clothes? Listen as your teacher reads a sample similar to what you will hear on the test. How many items is the person planning to buy? Approximately how much money is he or she going to spend?

► Reading

Can you understand a description about shopping and clothes? Read through this paragraph to get the main idea. What kind of store does Inés prefer to go to, and why?

"A mí me gusta ir de compras en todas partes, pero lo que más me gusta es ir a los centros comerciales. Es agradable también ir a los almacenes, y a veces puedes comprar ropa buena y barata en las tiendas de descuentos. Pero hay muchas tiendas de todo tipo en los centros comerciales. También hay restaurantes allí, y si estás cansada puedes ir a beber un refresco y descansar."

► Writing

Can you write a letter to your parents similar to the one an exchange student might write home asking for money to buy school clothes? Here is an example:

Queridos papá y mamá:
Necesito comprar ropa nueva. Me gustaría comprar tres o cuatro camisetas. Hay camisetas muy bonitas y baratas. Sólo cuestan 10 dólares. No tengo pantalones cortos ni tenis. Necesito también unos pantalones y dos camisas. Los necesito para ir a fiestas. La ropa aquí es muy barata. Voy a necesitar sólo... 150 dólares.

Su hijo,
Luis

► Culture

If you were visiting a Spanish-speaking country, would you prefer to buy clothes at a shopping center or go to a tailor or dressmaker? Why?

Centro comercial en Buenos Aires, Argentina

► Speaking

Can you and a partner play the roles of a salesperson and a customer in a store? For example:

A —*¿Qué desea, señora (joven / señor / señorita)?*

B —*Busco un suéter blanco.*

A —*Sí, señora. Tenemos unos suéteres muy bonitos.*

B —*¿Cuánto cuestan?*

A —*Sólo 165 dólares.*

B —*¿Sólo 165 dólares? Perdón, señor... ¿hay otra tienda de ropa por aquí?*

Self Test www.pasoapaso.com

Options

Strategies for Reaching All Students

Students Needing Extra Help

Writing: Use the Organizer. Point out key phrases in the example or have students write out the paragraph so they can highlight their own copies.
Culture: Have students review the *Perspectiva cultural*.

Resumen del vocabulario

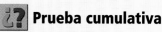
¿? Prueba cumulativa

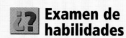
¿? Examen de habilidades

Test Generator

Additional Assessment Options

Comm. Act. BLMs

Small Group Activities
Situation Cards

Pasos vivos 1 CD-ROM

Slide Presentation Maker, Video Presentation Maker, Word Processor, Spindle

¿Lo sabes bien? Video Quiz

www Internet Activities
Self-Test

Use the vocabulary from this chapter to help you:

► describe the color, fit, and price of clothes

► ask about and buy clothes

► tell where and when you bought clothes and how much you paid for them

to talk about articles of clothing
la blusa
el calcetín, *pl.* los calcetines
la camisa
la camiseta
la chaqueta
la falda
los jeans
los pantalones (cortos)
las pantimedias
la ropa
la sudadera
el suéter
los tenis
el vestido
los zapatos

to describe clothes
la ganga
barato, -a
caro, -a
nuevo, -a
¿Cómo te queda(n)?
Me queda(n) bien.
¡Qué + *adjective!*

to talk about colors
el color
¿De qué color?
amarillo, -a
anaranjado, -a
azul, *pl.* azules
blanco, -a
gris, *pl.* grises
marrón, *pl.* marrones
morado, -a
negro, -a
rojo, -a
rosado, -a
verde

to talk about places to shop for clothing
el almacén, *pl.* los almacenes
la tienda de descuentos
la tienda de ropa
la zapatería

to talk about shopping
buscar
comprar: (yo) compré
　　　　 (tú) compraste
llevar
pagar: (yo) pagué
　　　 (tú) pagaste
para mí / ti
por

to indicate a specific item or items
ese, -a, esos, -as
este, -a, estos, -as
lo, la, los, las
otro, -a

to talk about prices
ciento un(o), una . . .
¿Cuánto?
Cuesta(n) . . .
el dólar, *pl.* los dólares

to assist customers in a store
¿Qué desea (Ud.)?

to address people
el / la joven, *pl.* los jóvenes

to start a conversation
perdón

to talk about when something happened
hace + *time expression*

to indicate location
por aquí

Resumen 215

Cultural Notes ☀

(p. 214, photo)
The Unicentro shopping center in Buenos Aires gives shoppers yet another locale for finding the same goods available in the shops along the city's downtown Calle Florida. Shoppers in Buenos Aires can also enjoy numerous Sunday markets, where souvenirs, antiques, clothes, books, and stamps are sold at bargain prices.

CAPÍTULO 7

THEME: LEISURE AND VACATION TIME

COMMUNICATION

Topics
Nature
Travel
Weather
Clothing

Objectives
To talk about how teens in Chile spend their vacations

To talk about vacation and planning a vacation

To talk about places to visit and things to do on vacation

To say that you want or would like something

To say where you went

To say when events occur

To name items to take on vacation

To ask about or describe weather

To express amazement or satisfaction

CULTURE
Leisure and vacation time

GRAMMAR

El verbo poder

Para + infinitivo

Los verbos querer *y* pensar

La a personal

Ancillaries available for use with Chapter 7

Multisensory/Technology

 Overheads, 36–40

 Audio Tapes and CDs

 Vocabulary Art Blackline Masters for Hands-On Learning, pp. 38–42/CD-ROM

 Classroom Crossword

 Video

 Pasos vivos 1 CD-ROM

Internet Activities www.pasoapaso.com

Print

 Practice Workbook, pp. 73–83

 Writing, Audio & Video Activities, pp. 41–46, 111–113, 164–165

 Communicative Activity Blackline Masters
Pair and Small Group Activities, pp. 50–55
Situation Cards, p. 56

 Un paso más: Actividades para ampliar tu español, pp. 38–43

 TPR Storytelling

 Assessment

Assessment Program
Pruebas, pp. 95–106
Examen de habilidades, pp. 107–110

 Test Generator

Video still from Chap. 7

Additional Technology

Planning Express, Teaching
Resources Library, and Clip Art
Library

¿Lo sabes bien?
Video Quiz

Cultural Overview

Vacations and Holidays

Many countries of the Spanish-speaking world are favorite international vacation spots. Many northern Europeans escape their winters by vacationing on the beaches of Spain, especially along the Costa del Sol. Many Canadians spend several weeks out of every year in one of several small fishing villages near Acapulco, Mexico. Countless others flock to sites such as Lake Titicaca, Bolivia.

People who live in the Spanish-speaking world may often vacation within the boundaries of their own country. In Argentina, for example, professionals and businesspeople commonly own small *pisos* (apartments) in coastal towns such as Mar del Plata, south of Buenos Aires. They use the *pisos* during vacations and sometimes on weekends. Middle-class families in Spain also share this custom of having a small country house for vacations.

In both Europe and in some Spanish-speaking countries, such as El Salvador, many people take vacations during August. Many private businesses as well as government offices shut down for two weeks. At this time of the year, el Lago Atitlán, in Guatemala, is a popular destination for Salvadorans. It becomes nearly impossible to find an empty hotel room in the small towns surrounding the lake.

Not everyone in Latin America and Spain may have a great amount of vacation time. Workers often receive days off only during holidays and festivals. In Mexico, for example, the Christmas-time *posadas* are a nine-day celebration ending on Christmas Eve. A different family hosts the *posada* for each of the nine nights, as people form a candlelight procession through the streets to reenact the travels of Mary and Joseph seeking shelter.

In addition to the *posada*, a number of other one- or two-day celebrations provide vacation time for the general public. For example, many towns celebrate the day of their local patron saint. Processions are held that day, the town square becomes the site of a general celebration, and fireworks illuminate the evening skies.

Introduce

Planning

Cross-Curricular Connections

Geography Connection *(pp. 218–219)*
Have small groups or pairs of students choose one of the countries mentioned in the chapter introduction. Have them use library resources to find out the special features, cultural sites, important products, and famous tourist or natural sites to create a pictorial map. When finished, ask them to share their work with the class. Display their work around the classroom.

Science / Geography Connection *(pp. 224–225)*
Have students prepare a weather chart for a city or region in a Spanish-speaking country of their choice for one month of each season. Charts should include average temperatures, average precipitation, and other facts. Encourage students to add pictures or drawings that illustrate various activities appropriate to each season.

Business Education / Advertising Connection *(pp. 232–233)*
Have small groups prepare tourist brochures for a Spanish-speaking country of their choice. Encourage the use of pictures or original drawings. On the back of their brochures, have students create a list of names of fictitious hotels with prices for various packages. Students should use the country's currency, give approximate equivalents in dollars, and include a phone number and address.

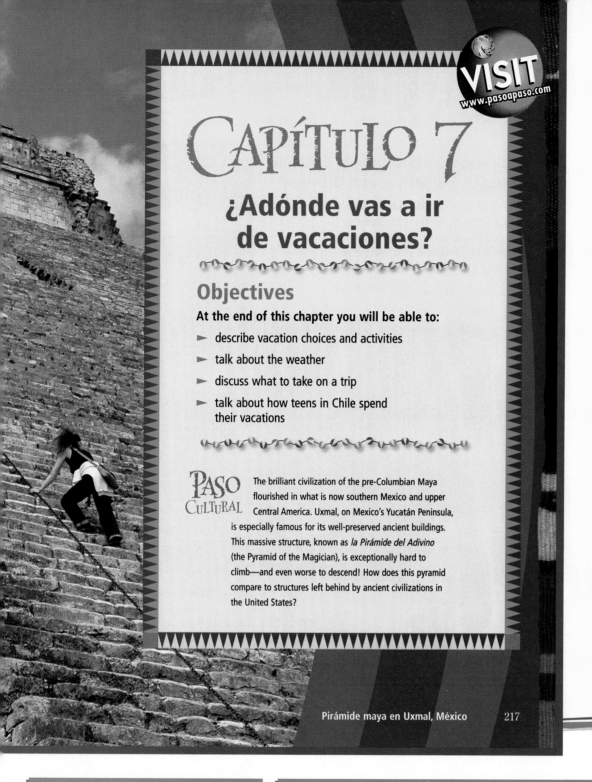

CAPÍTULO 7

¿Adónde vas a ir de vacaciones?

Objectives

At the end of this chapter you will be able to:

► describe vacation choices and activities

► talk about the weather

► discuss what to take on a trip

► talk about how teens in Chile spend their vacations

PASO CULTURAL

The brilliant civilization of the pre-Columbian Maya flourished in what is now southern Mexico and upper Central America. Uxmal, on Mexico's Yucatán Peninsula, is especially famous for its well-preserved ancient buildings. This massive structure, known as *la Pirámide del Adivino* (the Pyramid of the Magician), is exceptionally hard to climb—and even worse to descend! How does this pyramid compare to structures left behind by ancient civilizations in the United States?

Pirámide maya en Uxmal, México   217

Cultural Notes

Spanish in Your Community
Have small groups look through the travel sections of newspapers for advertisements or articles dealing with vacations in Spanish-speaking countries. They can also visit local travel agencies in their community. (Can they also find ads directed toward Spanish speakers?) Using learned vocabulary, students could then summarize the articles or ads for the class.

(pp. 216–217, photo)
The Mayan ruins at Uxmal differ from those of neighboring Chichén Itzá in that they are in the Puuc architectural style, which features complex geometric patterns of mosaics running along the upper façades of the buildings. The Pyramid of the Magician, shown here, stands 40 meters high. First occupied around 600 A.D., Uxmal was abandoned approximately 300 years later, possibly due to severe droughts.

Paso cultural
Answers will vary. Students may mention Native American burial mounds or the cliff dwellings of the Anasazi in the southwest. However, point out that we don't have existing ruins in the U.S. exactly like the ones in the photo.

Preview

Cultural Objective
• To talk about vacation and places to visit

¡Piénsalo bien!

Play

 Video Activity A

Using the Video

This chapter's video focuses on travel and vacations. Host Karina Romera takes viewers to her favorite places in and around Guadalajara, including a cathedral, a rodeo, a mariachi performance, and a waterfall. At various locations she interviews residents of Guadalajara about their vacation plans and preferences.

To prepare students for the video, ask them to predict what this chapter's tape will be about. Then have students watch the segment several times. After the first time, you may wish to have them brainstorm possible vocabulary and expressions they will need to talk about what they saw on the video. Ask students to identify: a) how a vacation in Guadalajara is similar to vacations they have taken, and b) anything they saw which they had not seen before.

¡Piensa en la CULTURA!

Vacation destinations in Ecuador, Mexico, Colombia, and Uruguay

Look at these photographs of four vacation destinations in Mexico, Colombia, Ecuador, and Uruguay. Which place would you most like to visit? Why?

. . . o explorar las Islas Galápagos en Ecuador. . .

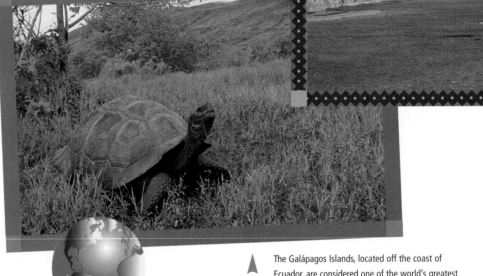

Islas Galápagos, Ecuador

"Quisiera ver la cancha de juego de Chichén Itzá en Yucatán . . .

In what ways is this playing field like or different from a football field or a basketball court that you know?

PASO CULTURAL

The Galápagos Islands, located off the coast of Ecuador, are considered one of the world's greatest natural history treasures. They are home to a richly diverse plant and animal life and were the first of Ecuador's national parks. Do you know the name of a famous nineteenth-century British scientist who visited the islands? What theory did he propose based on his observations of nature there?

218   Capítulo 7

Options

Strategies for Reaching All Students

Spanish-Speaking Students
Ask Spanish-speaking students: ¿Has estado en algún lugar como éstos? ¿Cómo se llama? ¿Cuál de estos lugares te gustaría visitar? ¿Por qué? ¿Qué te gusta hacer en las vacaciones?

 Un paso más Ex. 7-A

Students Needing Extra Help
Students may know very little about the Mayas and Mayan ruins. Provide information from reference books and show them the geographical area of this civilization on the map in the front of their books (p. XIV).

Multiple Intelligences
Visual/Spatial
See Using the Video.

Cultural Notes

(p. 218, left photo)
Ecuador's 400 Galápagos Islands, of which only five are inhabited, were declared a national park by the government in 1959. The islands are of volcanic origin and range in size from barren scraps of rock to larger islands filled with exotic animal and plant life whose adaptation Charles Darwin studied in 1835. This photo of the largest island, Isabela, shows one of the several thousand Galápagos tortoises that live on the slopes of Alcedo volcano.

Chichén Itzá, México

Bogotá, Colombia

. . . o visitar el Museo del
Oro en Bogotá, Colombia . . .

Punta del Este,
Uruguay

. . . o descansar en las playas
de Punta del Este, Uruguay."

Cultural Exploration
www.pasoapaso.com
Visit these countries on-line

¡Piensa en la cultura! 219

Video segment 1: For more teaching suggestions, see the Video Teacher's Guide.

Teaching Suggestions

Bring to class a variety of pictures of the four vacation destinations. Travel brochures and encyclopedias are good sources. If you've traveled to any of these places, bring in any slides, photographs, or realia.

Answers: ¡Piensa en la cultura!

Answers will vary.

(p. 218, top photo) Answers will vary, but may include the size and shape of the field.

(pp. 218–219, top photo)
The Mayan ruins at Chichén Itzá are the most extensive and renowned in Mexico's Yucatán peninsula. The ball court shown, the largest of the city's eight courts, was the site of games in which athletes tried to maneuver a ball through one of the stone hoops on the walls without using their hands. Carvings on the court's walls indicate that the losers were most likely decapitated in sacrificial rituals.

(p. 219, top photo)
This is one of the many treasure displays in the Museo del Oro in Bogotá. The museum is world famous for its unique collection of over 30,000 gold pieces. The collection includes earrings, rings, bracelets, masks, scepters, and various delicately wrought figures from a dozen pre-Columbian cultures, in addition to jewel-encrusted gold crosses from the colonial period.

(p. 219, bottom photo)
Uruguay's most glamorous beach resort is Punta del Este, a narrow peninsula with two beach areas: Playa Mansa, on the bay side for swimmers, and Playa Brava, on the Atlantic side for surfers. Punta del Este is a favorite spot among Argentines and other foreign tourists.

Paso cultural
Answers: Charles Darwin; the theory of evolution

Present

Chapter Theme
Vacation time

Communicative Objectives
- To talk about vacation
- To talk about places to visit and things to do on vacation
- To say that you want or would like something
- To say where you went
- To say when events occur
- To indicate use or purpose

 Overheads 36–37

 Vocabulary Art BLMs/CD-ROM

 Pronunciation Tape 7-1

 Vocabulario para conversar A

Play

Using the Video
Video segment 2: See the Video Teacher's Guide.

 Video Activity B

Grammar Preview
Para + inf. is presented here lexically. The complete presentation is in the grammar section on p. 235.

Vocabulario para conversar

¿Qué puedes hacer en México?

Ar Home **VIDEO** Chapter 7 Vocabulary

Here are some new words and expressions you will need to talk about vacation choices and activities. Read them several times, then turn the page and practice with a partner.

la selva tropical

explorar la selva

pasear en bote

el bote

el lago

los recuerdos

el museo

las montañas

sacar fotos

la foto

esquiar

220   Capítulo 7

Options

Strategies for Reaching All Students

Spanish-Speaking Students
 Un paso más Ex. 7-B

Students Needing Extra Help
Have students start filling in their Organizers.
También necesitas . . . : Point out that *quisiera* is a more formal or polite expression than *quiero.*

Learning Spanish Through Action
STAGING VOCABULARY: *Pongan, Señalen*
MATERIALS: large map of Spanish-speaking countries placed in front of the classroom; enlarged photocopies of the pictures in the *Vocabulario para conversar* from the transparency or Vocabulary Art BLMs/CD-ROM; thumbtacks or tape
DIRECTIONS: Direct students to point to the countries as you mention them. Then ask them to place a picture on the correct location on the map as you call out a country.

las cataratas

la pirámide
subir la pirámide

las ruinas

tomar el sol

la catedral

bucear

el mar

También necesitas...

la ciudad	*city*
el país	*country*
los lugares de interés	*places of interest*
descansar	*to rest*
quisiera	*I'd like*
ir: (yo) fui (tú) fuiste	*to go: I went you went*
pasado, -a	*last (year, month, week)*

no . . . ninguna parte	*nowhere, not anywhere*
para + *inf.*	here: *in order to*

¿Y qué quiere decir . . . ?

cuando*	ir de vacaciones
las vacaciones *(pl.)*	visitar

* When question words are used as conjunctions to join two parts of a sentence, we do not use
the accent mark: *¿Cuándo?* → *cuando, ¿Dónde?* → *donde,* etc.

Vocabulario para conversar   221

Teaching Suggestions
Preparing students to speak: Use one or two options from each of the categories of Comprehensible Input, Physical Response, or Limited Verbal Response. For a complete explanation of these categories and some sample activities, see pp. T22–23.

Class Starter Review
On the day following initial presentation, you might begin the class with this activity:
Ask students where they would like to go on vacation this summer. Keep track of responses on the chalkboard, then see which place was mentioned most often.

Multicultural Perspectives
Ecotourism is a growing industry for people wishing to travel to exotic, faraway places, but who also want to learn about a particular region or to encourage respect for the environment. The Amazon and other tropical rain forests in Latin America are increasingly attracting ecotourists. In Costa Rica, the government has declared many of the rain forests national parks. People travel to Monteverde to view exotic plant species, to see a rare *quetzal,* or just to experience the lushness of the forest. Ask students if they have heard of other examples of ecotourism.

www **Internet Activities**
Juegos

Extended Written Practice/Homework
1. Choose four places from pp. 220–221. Write four sentences telling when you went there last or saying that you didn't go there.
2. Write three sentences telling what you like to do when you go on vacation.
3. Choose a vacation spot and write a sentence naming two or more places of interest there: *En . . . los lugares de interés son . . .*

Multiple Intelligences
Bodily/Kinesthetic
See Learning Spanish Through Action.
Verbal/Linguistic
See Pronunciation Tape 7-1.
Visual/Spatial
See Overheads 36–37, the Vocabulary Art BLMs/CD-ROM, and Using the Video.

Practice & Apply

Reteach / Review: Vocabulary

Ex. 2: Pairs of students can extend this dialogue by having *Estudiante A* ask *Estudiante B* with whom he or she went. Encourage students to use vocabulary for family members.

Re-enter / Recycle

Ex. 1: activities from Chap. 1
Ex. 2: calendar expressions from *El primer paso,* seasons from Chap. 3
Ex. 3: activities from Chap. 1, seasons from Chap. 3
Ex. 5: calendar expressions from *El primer paso,* places and buildings from Chap. 3
Ex. 7: countries from *El primer paso*

Answers: Empecemos a conversar

1 ESTUDIANTE A

a. Cuando voy de vacaciones a la selva tropical, ¿qué puedo hacer?
b. ...al mar, ...
c. ...a la playa, ...
d. Questions will vary.

ESTUDIANTE B

a.–d. Puedes ... *(Answers will vary.)*

Empecemos a conversar

With a partner, take turns being *Estudiante A* and *Estudiante B.* Use the words that are cued or given in the balloons to replace the underlined sections in the model. means you can make your own choices.

1 A —*Cuando voy de vacaciones a <u>las montañas</u>, <u>¿qué puedo hacer</u>?*
    B —*Puedes <u>esquiar</u>. (También puedes . . .)*

Estudiante A   **Estudiante B**

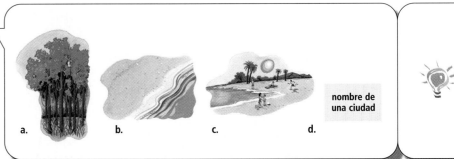

a.   b.   c.   d.   nombre de una ciudad

2 A —*¿Adónde fuiste <u>el verano pasado</u>?*   el verano pasado
    B —*Fui a <u>Los Ángeles</u>.*
      o: *No fui a ninguna parte.*

Estudiante A   **Estudiante B**

a. el año pasado   d. el invierno pasado

b. el mes pasado   e. el fin de semana pasado

c. la semana pasada   f.

Options

Strategies for Reaching All Students

Spanish-Speaking Students

 Un paso más Ex. 7-C

Students Needing Extra Help

Ex. 2: To ensure varied responses, give students a minute to think about their answers.
Ex. 3: Remind students that *primavera* is a feminine noun and will require *esta.*
Ex. 5: Have students refer back to Ex. 2.
Ex. 6: Have students brainstorm by using their Organizers from previous chapters.

Enrichment

Ex. 8: Ask students to expand this assignment by naming at least three *lugares de interés* in their city or region. For additional practice, tell students to imagine that they've just won a trip to any location of their choice. Ask them to write a sentence telling where they would like to go and what they would like to do there.

3 A —¿*Adónde vas a ir este verano?*
B —*Quisiera ir a la playa para tomar el sol.*

Estudiante A

Estudiante B

a.

b.

c.

d.

Empecemos a escribir

Write your answers in Spanish.

4 Write down three things that you would like to do on vacation.

5 ¿Adónde fuiste la semana pasada? ¿El mes pasado? ¿El año pasado? ¿Con quiénes fuiste a esos lugares?

6 ¿Adónde te gustaría ir de vacaciones?

7 ¿Qué países donde se habla español te gustaría visitar? ¿Por qué?

8 ¿Qué puede hacer un(a) turista en tu ciudad? ¿Qué lugares de interés puede visitar?

■ Turismo

A dónde va la gente con la maleta a cuestas

(Cifras en millones de visitantes)

Francia se encuentra a la cabeza de los destinos predilectos de los turistas del mundo, según datos de la Organización Mundial del Turismo. Nuestro país –con 41,3 millones de visitantes anuales– ocupa el tercer lugar del ranking.

Francia 62,4
Estados Unidos 46,3
España 41,3
Italia 32,8
Inglaterra 25,3
China 22,8
México 21,4
Hungría 20,7
Polonia 19,4
Canadá 17,2

INFOGRAFÍA: JOSÉ A. PIERA/FUENTE: ORGANIZACIÓN MUNDIAL DEL TURISMO

También se dice...

los suvenires

tomar fotos

MORE PRACTICE

- Más práctica y tarea, p. 526
- Practice Workbook 7–1, 7–2
-
-

Vocabulario para conversar   223

Present

Chapter Theme
Weather and vacation time

Communicative Objectives
- To talk about planning a vacation
- To name items to take on vacation
- To ask about or describe weather
- To express amazement or satisfaction

 Overheads 38–39

 Vocabulary Art BLMs/CD-ROM

 Pronunciation Tape 7-2

 Vocabulario para conversar B

Play

Step

Using the Video
Video segment 2: See the Video Teacher's Guide.

 Video Activity B

 Pasos vivos 1 CD-ROM

Clip Art Album

Vocabulario para conversar

¿Qué tiempo hace?

 Chapter 7 Vocabulary

Here's the rest of the vocabulary you will need to talk about the weather and to discuss what to take on a trip.

la lluvia

el viento

Hace viento.

Llueve.

Hace fresco.

el abrigo

el gorro

la bufanda

la nieve

los guantes

las botas

Nieva.

Hace frío.

224   Capítulo 7

Options

Strategies for Reaching All Students

Students Needing Extra Help
Have students continue to fill in their Organizers.
También necesitas . . . : Have students practice *pensar* + inf. in isolation. Ask how they would say "I plan to study."
Have them also practice *menos mal que* in isolation. Ask them to look at their previous Organizers to help them develop statements such as *Menos mal que tengo mi cuaderno.*

Enrichment
As a review of the months and to reinforce weather expressions, write this poem on the chalkboard or a transparency. (You will need to explain *neblina* and *tronar.*)
Los meses del año
En enero hace frío,
En febrero también.
En marzo hace viento,
En abril está bien.
En mayo hay flores,
En junio el amor.

En julio vacaciones,
En agosto el calor.
En septiembre hay neblina,
En octubre el tronar.
Noviembre trae lluvia,
Y diciembre el nevar.

los anteojos de sol

el traje de baño

el bronceador

Hace calor.

Hace mal tiempo.

Hace sol.

el sol

Hace buen tiempo.

el impermeable

la maleta   el paraguas

También necesitas...

llevar	here: *to take, to carry along*	¡Vaya!	*My goodness! Gee! Wow!*
salir*	*to leave*	Menos mal que ___.	*It's a good thing that ___.*
regresar	*to come back, to return*		
pensar + *inf.*: (yo) pienso (tú) piensas	*to plan: I plan you plan*	**¿Y qué quiere decir . . . ?**	
¿Qué tiempo hace?	*What's the weather like?*	la cámara fantástico, -a	el pasaporte

*Salir has an irregular *yo* form: *salgo.*

Vocabulario para conversar   225

Grammar Preview
Pienso / piensas are presented lexically. The complete paradigm of *pensar* appears in the grammar section on p. 236.

Teaching Suggestions
Preparing students to speak: Use one or two options from each of the categories of Comprehensible Input, Physical Response, or Limited Verbal Response. For a complete explanation of these categories and some sample activities, see pp. T22–T23.

Class Starter Review
On the day following initial presentation, you might begin the class with this activity:
Tell students to imagine they're getting ready to go out for the day. As you describe the weather, ask what clothes they are going to wear. Do this as a writing activity on a subsequent day, having students tell about their favorite season and weather.

www Internet Activities
Juegos

Learning Spanish Through Action
STAGING VOCABULARY: *Pongan, Saquen*
MATERIALS: manila folder to simulate a suitcase or a real one, enlarged photocopies of the pictures from the *Vocabulario para conversar* (available through the Overheads or the Vocabulary Art BLMs/CD-ROM)
DIRECTIONS: Ask students to put an item in the suitcase. Later, after stating a weather expression, have students take out an appropriate weather-related item. *(Hace sol. ¿Qué vas a sacar?* or *Hace sol. Saquen el*

(la) . . . .) You may wish to include clothing items from Chap. 6.

Multiple Intelligences
Bodily/Kinesthetic
See Learning Spanish Through Action.
Musical/Rhythmic
Have students recite the poem *Los meses del año* (see Enrichment). Students may choose to recite individually, in unison, or alternating lines with other group members.

Verbal/Linguistic
See Pronunciation Tape 7-2.
Visual/Spatial
See Overheads 38–39, the Vocabulary Art BLMs/CD-ROM, and Using the Video.

Standards 1.1; 1.2; 4.1; 5.1   **225**

Practice & Apply

Re-enter / Recycle

Ex. 9: calendar expressions from *El primer paso*

Ex. 10: possessive adjectives from Chap. 5, clothing from Chap. 6

Ex. 12: seasons from Chap. 3

Ex. 13: activities from Chap. 1

Ex. 15: clothing from Chap. 6

Answers: Empecemos a conversar

9 ESTUDIANTE A

a. ¿Qué tiempo hace en Miami en julio?

b. ... en Denver en enero?

c. ... en San Francisco en noviembre?

d. ... en Chicago en octubre?

e. ... en Washington, D.C., en abril?

f. Questions will vary.

ESTUDIANTE B

a. *(First part of responses will vary.)* ... Hace calor.

b. ... Hace frío.

c. ... Hace mal tiempo.

d. ... Hace viento.

e. ... Hace fresco.

f. Answers will vary.

10 ESTUDIANTE A

a. ¡Vaya! Hace sol (buen tiempo) hoy.

b. ... Llueve ...

c. ... Nieva ...

d. Statements will vary.

Empecemos a conversar

San Antonio / noviembre

9 A —¿*Qué tiempo hace en* <u>San Antonio</u> *en* <u>noviembre</u>?

B —<u>*Un tiempo fantástico*</u>. *Hace sol.*

Estudiante A

a. Miami / julio

b. Denver / enero

c. San Francisco / noviembre

d. Chicago / octubre

e. Washington, D.C. / abril

f.

Estudiante B

Miami · San Francisco · Washington, D.C.

Denver · Chicago

10 A —¡*Vaya!* <u>*Hace frío*</u> *hoy.*

B —*Menos mal que tienes* <u>*tu abrigo*</u>.

Estudiante A

a. · b. · c. · d.

Estudiante B

Options

Strategies for Reaching All Students

Spanish-Speaking Students

 Un paso más Ex. 7-D

Students Needing Extra Help

Exs. 9–10: Remind students that the responses depicted in the art for *Estudiante B* are not in sequential order with the phrases for *Estudiante A*.

Ex. 11: Have students brainstorm and use their Organizers.

Ex. 13: Have students use their Organizers from Chaps. 1 and 3.

Enrichment

Ex. 13: Students can also name activities they *don't* like to do in each type of weather.

11

A —¿Qué piensas llevar _a la playa_?

B —Pienso llevar _el bronceador y una cámara_.

Estudiante A

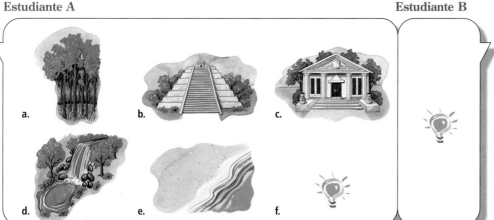

a.

b.

c.

d.

e.

f.

Estudiante B

Empecemos a escribir y a leer

Write your answers in Spanish.

12 Describe what the weather is like in your community in all four seasons. _En el invierno . . ._

13 Choose three types of weather and tell one activity you like to do in each one. _Cuando hace mal tiempo, . . ._

14 ¿Vas a ir de vacaciones este año? ¿Cuándo piensas salir? ¿Y regresar?

15 Cuando una persona va a esquiar, ¿qué ropa lleva en su maleta?

16 ¿Es lógico o no?

¡Vaya! Hace frío hoy. Me gustaría ir a la playa para tomar el sol.

¿Piensas ir a Argentina? Debes llevar tu pasaporte y una cámara para sacar fotos de los lugares de interés.

El año pasado no fui a ninguna parte. Este año voy a ir a la selva tropical para pasear en bote.

MORE PRACTICE

- Más práctica y tarea, p. 527
- Practice Workbook 7-3, 7-4

www.pasoapaso.com

También se dice...

la loción bronceadora
la crema para el sol

las gafas de sol
los lentes de sol

la máquina fotográfica

el bañador   la malla
la trusa   la ropa de baño

Vocabulario para conversar   227

Practice

Re-enter / Recycle
Ex. 1: *gustar* expressions and activities from Chap. 1

Reteach / Review: Vocabulary
Ex. 3: Students can continue this dialogue by taking turns asking and answering what clothes or other items they need to buy for their vacations.

Answers: ¡Comuniquemos!

1 ESTUDIANTE A

¿Qué te gusta hacer cuando hace fresco?

. . . hace sol (buen tiempo)?

. . . hace frío?

. . . llueve?

. . . nieva?

. . . hace calor?

. . . hace viento?

ESTUDIANTE B

Answers will vary.

2 a.–f. Responses will vary. Look for logical statements. For example: (a.) *Menos mal que no llueve mucho.*

1

With a partner, take turns asking and telling what activities you like to do in different kinds of weather. The list of verbs will help you answer. For example:

A —*¿Qué te gusta hacer cuando . . . ?*

B —*Pues, me gusta . . .*

beber	estar	nadar	salir
bucear	explorar	pasear	tocar
comer	hablar	patinar	tomar
descansar	ir	practicar	ver
esquiar	leer	sacar	visitar

228   Capítulo 7

Options

Strategies for Reaching All Students

Spanish-Speaking Students
Have Spanish-speaking students write a paragraph: *Escribe un párrafo acerca de tus vacaciones ideales. ¿Adónde te gustaría ir? ¿En qué estación del año te gustaría ir? ¿Qué puedes hacer allí? ¿Con quién te gustaría ir?*

Students Needing Extra Help
Ex. 1: Review the suggested verbs, especially *estar, ir,* and *ver,* since students will need to add an object or prepositional phrase. Model a few possibilities.
Ex. 3: Review interrogatives, then have students review Exs. 1–3 and 5–8 on pp. 222–223 to help them create a model. *¿Qué sabes ahora?:* Have students write out this section so that they can record their progress.

Enrichment
Ex. 3: As a written assignment, students can describe what they like to do or what they would like to do during summer and winter vacations.

Cooperative Learning
Have groups of three or four students write their names and birthdays (day and month only) on a sheet of paper. Next, have them pass their papers to the right. Students then write a sentence to describe what the weath-

2

With a partner, can you come up with good, logical exclamations using *Menos mal que . . .* in response to each of these statements? Afterward, compare your exclamations with those of another pair of students.

a. ¡Vaya! No tengo ni paraguas ni impermeable.
b. Yo pienso ir a la playa esta tarde.
c. ¡Estos recuerdos cuestan mucho!
d. Estoy enfermo(a).
e. ¡Nieva!
f. No esquío.

3

You and your partner are planning your vacations. Take turns asking and answering where and with whom you would like to go, and what activities you would like to do there. Don't forget to say when you are leaving and when you are planning to come back.

¿Qué sabes ahora?

Can you:

► tell what you can see or do on a vacation?
—En México puedo ___.

► tell what you plan to do on a vacation?
—En las vacaciones ___ visitar museos.

► tell what you will take on your vacation?
—Pienso llevar ___ a España.

► describe the weather at your vacation destination?
—___ en Orlando en el invierno.

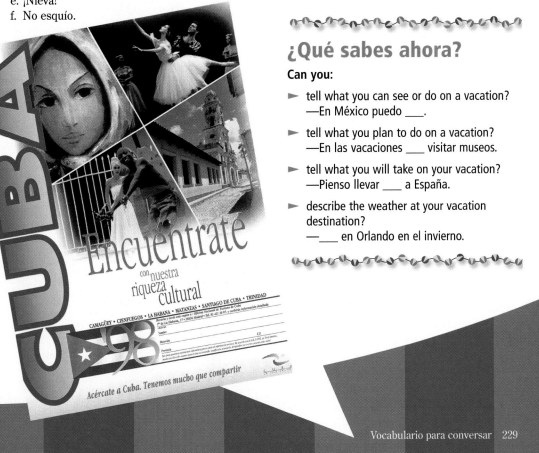

Vocabulario para conversar 229

3 Questions and answers will vary, but encourage students to use the full range of chapter vocabulary. Look for interrogatives such as *¿adónde?* and *¿con quién?*

Answers: ¿Qué sabes ahora?

• Answers will vary.
• pienso
• Answers will vary.
• Answers will vary, but may include: *Llueve* or *Hace . . . .*

 Audio Activity 7.3

 Writing Activity 7-D

 Pasos vivos 1 CD-ROM

Slide Projector, Laboratorio de grabar

---

er is like during that month. Students pass their papers to the right again. This time, they are to list one or two items that might be useful to have or wear during that month. Papers are now passed to owners. Call on individuals to read their papers, discussing other items that may not have been included.

Multiple Intelligences
Interpersonal/Social
See Cooperative Learning.
Intrapersonal/Introspective
See *¿Qué sabes ahora?*
Verbal/Linguistic
See Audio Activity 7.3.

Cultural Notes

(p. 229, realia)
With its world-class beaches, Spanish colonial architecture, and vibrant culture, Cuba is fast becoming a major tourist destination. Since the loss of Soviet subsidies in the 1980s, Cuba's socialist government has viewed tourism as an important source of income and has joined with European or Canadian firms to build new hotels. Ask students: What makes this ad inviting?

Multicultural Perspectives

The tourist bureaus in Spain and many Latin American countries advertise in the U.S. and Europe to attract visitors to their countries. Spain, for example, entices Scandinavians and other people living in cold winter climates through advertisements that feature its many beaches. The Dominican Republic and Puerto Rico use similar strategies to appeal to potential tourists in the northern sections of the U.S. Mexico also attracts many people with its advertisements of ancient ruins and beautiful beaches. Invite students to identify print or television ads directed at potential tourists. What methods do they use to attract people?

Perspectiva cultural

Las vacaciones de los jóvenes chilenos

Chile

En el verano, muchas personas van de vacaciones. A muchos jóvenes les gusta ir a la playa. A otros les gusta ir a las montañas. Y a ti, ¿qué te gusta hacer?

The two photos were taken in Chile. In which months might the activities be taking place?

January and February are summer months in Chile. Because of Chile's long coastline along the Pacific Ocean, going to the beach is very popular.

A Chilean teen reports, *"Me gusta ir a Viña del Mar con mi familia. Por la mañana, tomamos el sol y nadamos en el océano o en la piscina. Por la tarde, descansamos y por la noche, jugamos tenis, vamos al cine o vemos la tele. Hay muchas personas de mi edad allí."*

In July, Chilean students have a short winter vacation. Some may go to a ski resort in the Andes, but it is much more common for them to visit relatives and friends.

In Chile, most high-school students do not get a summer job. However, some may bag groceries at a supermarket or work at one of the growing number of fast-food restaurants.

Esquiando en Le Grand Mur, Valle Nevado, Chile

230   Capítulo 7

Options

Strategies for Reaching All Students

Spanish-Speaking Students
Ask Spanish-speaking students:
¿Qué haces durante las vacaciones? ¿Trabajas? ¿Practicas deportes? ¿Sales de viaje? ¿Qué tipos de trabajo puede tener un(a) joven en este país durante las vacaciones? ¿Te gustaría ir a la playa en enero? ¿Por qué? ¿Te gustaría pasar las vacaciones en otro país? ¿En cuál?

 Un paso más Ex. 7-E

Students Needing Extra Help
Discuss the equator and how climates change as you move away from it in either direction. On a map or globe, explain the difference in seasons for the month of December, for example, in Chile and in the northern section of the U.S.

Multiple Intelligences
Naturalist
Have students write a brief paragraph about their favorite vacation place. Ask them to include what outdoor activities they enjoy doing there.

En una playa de Chile

La cultura desde tu perspectiva

1 How is your vacation similar to or different from that of Chilean teens?

2 How does the geography affect vacation options for Chilean students? How does the geography of your area affect your vacation options?

Cultural Activity  www.pasoapaso.com

Perspectiva cultural   231

Cultural Notes ☼

(pp. 230–231, map and photos)
In Chile, the beach is never more than 125 miles from the mountains, all along the country's 2,800-mile coast. The official summer season extends from September 15 until March 15, when beaches are crowded even though the ocean is cold. The snow-ski season extends from late June to September or October, when vacationers have been known to ski in the mountains and sun on the beach in a single day.

Answers

Answers will vary for inductive questions, but may include: travel brochures, ads, promotional programs, etc.

A *puede* (you can) / *pueden* (they can), *quiere* (you want) / *queremos* (we want), *piensa* (you plan) / *pensamos* (we plan) / *Pensamos* doesn't contain *ie* in the stem of the verb.

B The infinitive follows *para.*

C The direct objects are *la familia* and *un suéter o su abrigo.* / The direct object is a thing in the second question; it is people in the first question. / The word before the direct object referring to people is *a.*

Gramática en contexto

Look at this ad for a travel agency. How does a travel agency attract new clients?

¿Qué piensa hacer Ud. este invierno?

¿Adónde puede ir Ud. para hacer todo esto y mucho más?

¡A la República Dominicana, el paraíso de las vacaciones!

¿Piensa llevar a la familia? Pues, debe ir a Puerto Plata, donde hay muchas actividades que sus hijos pueden hacer. ¿Piensa llevar un suéter o su abrigo? Pues, no los necesita. En Puerto Plata nunca hace frío. Hace buen tiempo todo el año.

Aquí en la Agencia de Viajes Cristal estamos para ayudar a nuestros clientes. Queremos y pensamos hacer de sus vacaciones algo fabuloso. Visite nuestra oficina en la Quinta Avenida 578, o llame al número:

1-555-523-3493

La República Dominicana, donde el verano nunca termina...

¿Quiere tomar el sol?

¿Quiere pasear en bote?

¿Quiere jugar tenis?

A Can you find in the ad at least one other form of each of these verbs: *puedo / puedes, quiero / quieres,* and *pienso / piensas?* What do these verb forms mean? How is the *nosotros* form of *pensar* different from its other forms?

B Look at the question in red that begins with *¿Adónde . . . ?* and the first sentence of paragraph 3. What form of the verb follows *para?*

C In paragraph 2, look at the two questions that begin, *¿Piensa llevar . . . ?* What are the direct objects? In which question is the direct object a thing? In which question is the direct object people? What word comes before the direct object that refers to people?

232   Capítulo 7

Options

Strategies for Reaching All Students

Students Needing Extra Help
Have students write out this section so that they can highlight the words.
Have them start to fill in the grammar portion of their Organizers.
B: Remind students that infinitives end in *-ar, -er,* and *-ir.*
C: Review direct object pronouns and how they replace a noun.

Write the complete sentences on the chalkboard, underlining the direct objects so that students can focus on them.
El verbo poder: Stem-changing verbs can be referred to as "boot" verbs. (If you outline the four forms that change, it resembles a boot and creates a memorable visual for the students. Or you can color-code the stems on a transparency.) Review *-er* endings.

Extended Written Practice/Homework
1. Refer to pp. 220–221. Write four sentences telling what tourists *(los turistas)* can do in different places.
2. Refer to p. 184. Write three sentences saying what different people can buy with a certain amount of money: *Con 27 dólares, Sara puede comprar una falda.*
3. Write three sentences telling what you and your friends can or cannot do: *No podemos ir al parque de diversiones los lunes.*

El verbo *poder*

Puedo and *puedes* come from the infinitive *poder,* "can, to be able to."

(yo)	**puedo**	(nosotros) (nosotras)	**podemos**
(tú)	**puedes**	(vosotros) (vosotras)	**podéis**
Ud. (él) (ella)	**puede**	Uds. (ellos) (ellas)	**pueden**

- When we drop the *-er* of the infinitive, the part that remains is called the stem. Notice that in four forms of *poder,* the *o* of the stem changes to *ue.* We call *poder* an *o → ue* stem-changing verb.*

- The endings follow the pattern of regular *-er* verbs.

- When the forms of *poder* are followed by another verb, the second verb is always in the infinitive. For example:

  No **puedo ir** al cine contigo el viernes.

Artesanía maya

PASO CULTURAL

Women were the ceramics artisans in ancient Mayan society. Working without a potter's wheel, they crafted beautifully shaped and decorated objects. The ruling class dictated the designs and motifs used by the artisans. As a result, these works of art repeatedly feature scenes from Mayan mythology and from the lives of the rulers. What are some other wonders that were created by ancient civilizations without the benefit of modern tools or inventions?

* The verb *jugar,* which you learned in Chapter 3, is also a stem-changing verb. The *u* of the stem changes to *ue* except in the *nosotros* and *vosotros* forms. Here are all of its forms: *juego, juegas, juega; jugamos, jugáis, juegan.*

Gramática en contexto   233

Teaching Suggestions

By introducing the *Gramática en contexto* section from the previous page, students will learn about stem-changing verbs in context. As they work through the exercises, they will formulate for themselves the rules given on the following pages. Remind them that they already know examples of stem-changing verbs from previous chapters: *puedo / puedes* and *quiero / quieres* (Chap. 3); *prefiero / prefieres* (Chap. 4).

For practice of *jugar,* use the Vocabulary Art BLMs/CD-ROM from Chapter 3. Have students tell what sports and games they and their friends and family play.

Cultural Notes

Multiple Intelligences
Visual/Spatial
See Exs. A–C.

Paso cultural
Possible answers: the pyramids of Egypt and the Americas, the Great Wall of China, Roman aqueducts, and other structures

Present & Practice

Re-enter / Recycle

Exs. 1 and 4: activities from Chaps. 1 and 3

Answers

1 ESTUDIANTE A
a. Puedes ir a pasear en bote conmigo este fin de semana?
b. . . . a esquiar . . .
c. . . . al museo . . .
d. . . . a tomar el sol . . .
e. . . . al gimnasio . . .
f. . . . de compras . . .
g. Questions will vary.

ESTUDIANTE B
a.–g. Answers will vary.

2 a.–g. Statements will vary, but look for subject/verb agreement and use of vocabulary from this and previous chapters.

 Practice Wkbk. 7-5

 Writing Activity 7-E

 Prueba 7-5

---

1 Respond to these invitations giving a reason why you can or cannot accept.

A —¿Puedes ir a nadar conmigo este fin de semana?
B —Sí, puedo. Tengo un traje de baño nuevo.
　　o: Lo siento, pero no puedo. No tengo traje de baño.

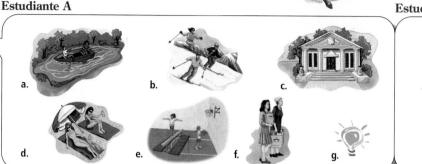

Estudiante A

a.
b.
c.
d.
e.
f.
g.

Estudiante B

2 The weather is terrible today. With a partner, take turns telling what these people can and cannot do as a result. Use as many different logical activities as you can think of.

Carlos puede visitar un museo.
o: *Carlos no puede ir a la playa porque llueve.*

a. (nombre de dos compañeros)
b. (nombre de una compañera)
c. yo
d. tú
e. mis amigos y yo
f. mis profesores
g. 💡

La Plaza de Cataluña
en Barcelona, España

234　Capítulo 7

Options

Strategies for Reaching All Students

Students Needing Extra Help
Ex. 1: Remind students that they saw *puedo / puedes* in Chap. 3. Students may find it helpful to think of possible responses that correspond to each item before beginning the exercise. Have students use their Organizers.

Ex. 3: If students need more practice with this structure, adapt the exercise in the following way: *Para estudiar, necesitamos un cuaderno.*
Ex. 4: Point out that *la casa de Felipe* becomes *allí.* Review compound subjects and how the verb form changes when answering a question. For example, questions with *tú* are answered with *yo,* and so on.

Enrichment
Ex. 2: As one student tells what the people can't do, have the other student name an activity he or she *can* do. For example: *Hace fresco y Marta no puede tomar el sol. Pero puede ir al cine.*
Ex. 3: To expand this exercise as homework, tell students to name five more items and explain why they need them.

Para + infinitivo

You know that *para* means "for" or "in order to." Whenever *para* is followed by a verb, the verb is in the infinitive form. For example:

Vamos a México **para bucear** y **tomar** el sol.

3 With a partner, take turns telling what you need these things for.

Necesitamos un cuaderno para estudiar. cuaderno

Estudiante A

a. piscina
b. hoja de papel
c. libro
d. papas
e. cámara
f.

Estudiante B

cocinar
sacar fotos
nadar
leer
dibujar

4 With a partner, take turns telling why these young people are going to a friend's house.

A —*Antonia va a la casa de Felipe, ¿verdad?*
B —*Sí, va allí para escuchar música.*

Antonia / Felipe

Estudiante A

a. Marisol / Yolanda
b. Eduardo y Raúl / David
c. Tú / Manuel
d. Lourdes / Andrea
e. Armando y tú / Sergio

Estudiante B

Gramática en contexto   235

---

3 Answers
a. Necesitamos una piscina para nadar.
b. ... una hoja de papel para dibujar.
c. ... un libro para leer.
d. ... papas para cocinar.
e. ... una cámara para sacar fotos.
f. Statements will vary.

4 ESTUDIANTE A
a. Marisol va a la casa de Yolanda, ¿verdad?
b. Eduardo y Raúl van a la casa de David, ...
c. Tú vas a la casa de Manuel, ...
d. Lourdes va a la casa de Andrea, ...
e. Armando y tú van a la casa de Sergio, ...
ESTUDIANTE B
(Endings may vary for statements.)
a. Sí, va allí para jugar básquetbol.
b. Sí, van allí para tomar el sol.
c. Sí, voy allí para tocar la guitarra.
d. Sí, va allí para ver la tele(visión).
e. Sí, vamos allí para nadar.

Practice Wkbk. 7-6

Writing Activity 7-F

Prueba 7-6

Extended Written Practice/Homework
1. Write four sentences telling why you would like to go to a place: *Me gustaría ir a la zapatería para comprar zapatos nuevos.*
2. Write three sentences of advice saying what you should/should not eat or drink in order to be in good health: *Para tener buena salud . . .*

Multiple Intelligences
Verbal/Linguistic
See Exs. 1, 3, and 4.
Visual/Spatial
See Practice Wkbk. 7-5 and 7-6 and Writing Activity 7-F.

Cultural Notes

(p. 234, photo)
Capital of the province of Cataluña and site of the 1992 Summer Olympics, Barcelona is Spain's most cosmopolitan city and its second largest. Since Roman times, the people of Cataluña have enjoyed close ties with the rest of Europe and, with their own language and culture, have maintained a strong identity separate from Spain. Discuss with students how a nation's culture can include regional cultures and still thrive.

Present & Practice

Class Starter Review

On the day following initial presentation of *querer* and *pensar,* you might begin the class by having students complete this sentence:
Voy al (a la) ___ (place) *para* ___ (activity).
On subsequent days, have them complete this sentence:
Voy al (a la) ___ (place), *porque quiero (pienso)* ___.
Ask follow-up questions, such as:
¿Quién quiere (piensa) ___?

Re-enter / Recycle

Ex. 5: activities from Chap. 3

Answers

5 ESTUDIANTE A

a. ¿Qué piensas hacer mañana?
b. ¿Qué piensan hacer tu amigo(a) y tú mañana?
c. ¿Qué piensas hacer para ayudar en casa este fin de semana?
d. ¿Qué piensan hacer tus amigos y tú este fin de semana?

ESTUDIANTE B

Answers will vary, but look for correct forms of *pensar.*
a. Pienso . . .
b. Pensamos . . .
c. Pienso . . .
d. Pensamos . . .

Los verbos *querer* y *pensar*

You know that we use *quiero* and *quieres* to tell what we want to do, and we use *pienso* and *piensas* to tell what we plan to do. These verb forms come from the infinitives *querer* and *pensar.* Here are their present-tense forms:

(yo)	pienso quiero	(nosotros) (nosotras)	pensamos queremos
(tú)	piensas quieres	(vosotros) (vosotras)	pensáis queréis
Ud. (él) (ella)	piensa quiere	Uds. (ellos) (ellas)	piensan quieren

• Notice that there is a stem change from *e* to *ie* in all except the *nosotros* and *vosotros* forms. *Querer* and *pensar* are called *e → ie* stem-changing verbs.

• The endings follow the pattern of regular *-ar* and *-er* verbs.

• When the forms of *querer* and *pensar* are followed by another verb, the second verb is always in the infinitive. For example:
—¿Quieres **estudiar** conmigo?
—No, pienso **ver** la tele.

5 With a partner, take turns asking and answering.

a. what each of you plans to do tomorrow

b. what you and a friend plan to do tomorrow

c. what your partner plans to do to help out around the house this weekend

d. what your partner and his or her friends plan to do this weekend

236   Capítulo 7

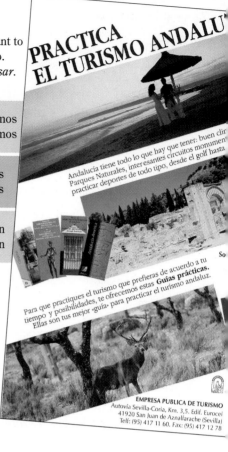

PRACTICA EL TURISMO ANDALU[...]

Andalucía tiene todo lo que hay que tener: buen clim[...] Parques Naturales, interesantes circuitos monumen[...] practicar deportes de todo tipo, desde el golf hasta [...]

Para que practiques el turismo que prefieras de acuerdo a tu tiempo y posibilidades, te ofrecemos estas **Guías prácticas.** Ellas son tus mejor -guía- para practicar el turismo andaluz.

EMPRESA PUBLICA DE TURISMO
Autovía Sevilla-Coria, Km. 3,5. Edif. Eurocei
41920 San Juan de Aznalfarache (Sevilla)
Telf: (95) 417 11 60. Fax: (95) 417 12 78

Turistas sacando fotos en la Alhambra
en Granada, España

Options

Strategies for Reaching All Students

Students Needing Extra Help
Ex. 5: Review compound subjects and the "boot" or color-coding for the verbs.
La a personal: Give students an example of an inanimate object that is used as a direct object. For example: *Quiero visitar el museo.*

Enrichment
To reinforce *querer* and *pensar,* give students an assignment in which they write two sentences for each verb—one in which the verbs are used alone, and the other in which they are used with another verb. For example: *Quiero ese libro. Lo quiero comprar hoy. Pienso que esa blusa es muy cara. No la pienso comprar.*

Extended Written Practice/Homework
1. Write three sentences telling what your friends plan to do or where they plan to go.
2. Write three sentences saying that a friend wants to do something but can't. Tell why he or she cannot do it: *Tere quiere esquiar pero no puede porque no hay nieve.*
3. Write two pairs of sentences telling where you and your family want to go on vacation and when you plan to go.

6 Choose four of the topics below and interview your partner about his or her preferences. Then report to the class what you and your partner would like.

¿Qué quieren tú y tu compañero(a)?

a. más tarea o menos tarea

b. leer más libros en la clase de inglés o leer menos libros

c. llevar ropa informal o llevar uniformes en la escuela

d. hablar más en la clase de español o hablar menos

e. más tiempo *(time)* para practicar deportes o menos tiempo

f. más días de vacaciones o menos días de vacaciones

g.

Nosotros(as) queremos menos tarea.
o: *Mi compañero(a) quiere menos tarea pero yo quiero más.*

6 a.–g. Answers will vary.

 Practice Wkbk. 7-7, 7-8

 Writing Activity 7-G

 Pruebas 7-7, 7-8

 Comm. Act. BLM 7-2

La *a* personal

You know that the direct object is the person or thing that receives the action of a verb. In Spanish, when the direct object is a specific person or group of people, we use *a* before it. That's why it's called the personal *a*.

Quiero visitar **a** mis abuelos.
Quiero visitar **al** señor López.

• To ask who receives the action of a verb, we use *¿A quién?*

—**¿A quién** quieres visitar?
—Quiero visitar **a** mis primos.

• We can also use the personal *a* when the direct object is an animal, especially a pet.

Busco **a mi perro**.

• We usually do not use the personal *a* after the verb *tener.*

Tengo muchos tíos.

237

Cultural Notes

Multiple Intelligences
Visual/Spatial
See Practice Wkbk. 7-7 and 7-8, Writing Activity 7-G, and Comm. Act. BLM 7-2.

(p. 236, realia)
This brochure invites tourists to "practice Andalusian tourism." People are drawn to Andalucía to visit renowned attractions such as the beaches of the Costa del sol and the Moorish architecture of the Alhambra. The region is also known for its warm, sunny climate and for flamenco music. Andalucía is Spain's southernmost region on the peninsula and is the entry point to the British-owned Rock of Gibraltar.

(p. 236, photo)
Seat of the sultanate of Granada, the last Moslem kingdom in Spain to fall to Christian forces in 1492, the Alhambra is named for the rich red clay of its ninth-century outer walls (Alhambra means "the red one" in Arabic). Within these walls stands the magnificent, thirteenth-century Alcázar, a palace adorned with ornate stonework and fountains. Ask students: Using what you know, describe the Arabs' influence on Spain.

Practice

Re-enter / Recycle

Exs. 7–8: family and friends from Chap. 5

Answers

7 ESTUDIANTE A

a. ¿A quién quieren visitar Anita y Claudia?

b. ...quieren visitar Armando y Andrea?

c. ...quieren visitar Paco y Marta?

d. ...quiere visitar Paco?

e. ...quiere visitar Graciela?

f. ...quiere visitar Ernesto?

ESTUDIANTE B

a. Quieren visitar a sus abuelos.

b. Quieren visitar a su hijo.

c. Quieren visitar a sus primas.

d. Quiere visitar a sus padres.

e. Quiere visitar a sus padres.

f. Quiere visitar a su hermana.

7 Imagine that the members of the Ramírez family live in different parts of the country. They all want to visit each other. Ask your partner which family member each person wants to visit. Your partner's answers will be based on the family tree.

A —¿A quién quiere visitar Claudia?

B —Quiere visitar a sus primos.

Claudia /
Marta y Paco

a. Anita y Claudia / Armando y Andrea

b. Armando y Andrea / Ernesto

c. Paco y Marta / Anita y Claudia

d. Paco / Gustavo y Graciela

e. Graciela / Armando y Andrea

f. Ernesto / Graciela

238   Capítulo 7

Options

Strategies for Reaching All Students

Students Needing Extra Help

Ex. 7: Review how to read a family tree. Do this as a whole-class activity, going step by step.

Ahora lo sabes: Have students write out this section so that they can track their progress.

Extended Written Practice/Homework

1. Write two sentences naming people you would like to visit and when.

2. Write two sentences naming places you would like to visit during different seasons.

Multiple Intelligences

Verbal/Linguistic

See Exs. 7–8 and Audio Activities 7.4 and 7.5.

Visual/Spatial

See Practice Wkbk. 7-9 and 7-10 and Writing Activity 7-H.

8 Tell your partner which of the following people and places you are planning or are *not* planning to visit this year. Remember to use the personal *a* when you talk about people.

primos
(nombre de un(a) amigo(a) que no vive en tu ciudad)
Puerto Rico
tíos
un parque de diversiones
un lago
países en Hispanoamérica
unas pirámides
Leonardo DiCaprio
el mar
los Everglades
abuelos
el (la) gobernador(a) del estado
Mark McGwire
una selva tropical

Ahora lo sabes

Can you:

► tell what someone can do, plans to do, and wants to do?
—Yo ___ nadar.
—Julio ___ visitar la selva tropical.
—Ellas ___ subir la pirámide.

► tell the reason for doing something?
—Luz va a la playa para ___.

► use the personal *a* correctly?
—¿___ quién ves?
—Veo ___ Antonio.

MORE PRACTICE

Más práctica y tarea, pp. 527–529
Practice Workbook 7–5, 7–10

SI QUIERES OLVIDARTE
DE TODO Y RELAJARTE,
ENCONTRARÁS UNO DE LOS CENTROS DE AGUAS TERMALES MÁS IMPORTANTES DEL MUNDO.

SI TE VUELVE LOCO IR DE COMPRAS, EN ANDORRA ENCONTRARÁS MÁS DE 4.000 COMERCIOS. SI TE GUSTA COMER BIEN, ENCONTRARÁS MÁS DE 400 RESTAURANTES. SI TE GUSTA HACER DEPORTE, ENCONTRARÁS LAS MEJORES INSTALACIONES DEL PIRINEO. SI QUIERES OLVIDARTE DE TODO Y RELAJARTE, ENCONTRARÁS CALDEA, CON MÁS DE VEINTE JACUZZIS, SAUNAS Y ZONAS DE RELAJACIÓN. SI TE APASIONA EL ROMÁNICO, ENCONTRARÁS UNO DE LOS MEJORES DEL MUNDO. SI QUIERES DISFRUTAR DE TODO ESTO Y DE MUCHO MÁS, ENCONTRARÁS MÁS DE 150 HOTELES DE TODAS LAS CATEGORÍAS DONDE PODER ALOJARTE. Y SI, ADEMÁS, ERES DE LOS QUE AMAN LA NATURALEZA, ENCONTRARÁS SESENTA Y CUATRO PICOS DE MÁS DE 2.500 METROS DE ALTURA.

·DISFRUTA. TU PAÍS ES ANDORRA.

▷ Andorra
EL PAÍS DE LOS PIRINEOS

PASO CULTURAL
Located in *los Pirineos* (the Pyrenees Mountains) between France and Spain, Andorra is one of the world's smallest countries. Its population of approximately 75,000 is made up mainly of Spanish and French speakers. The official language, however, is *catalán,* a Romance language that is also spoken in northeastern Spain in the region known as Cataluña. Like Spain, the U.S. has regions in which languages other than English have been spoken for generations. What are some of these regions and their languages?

Gramática en contexto 239

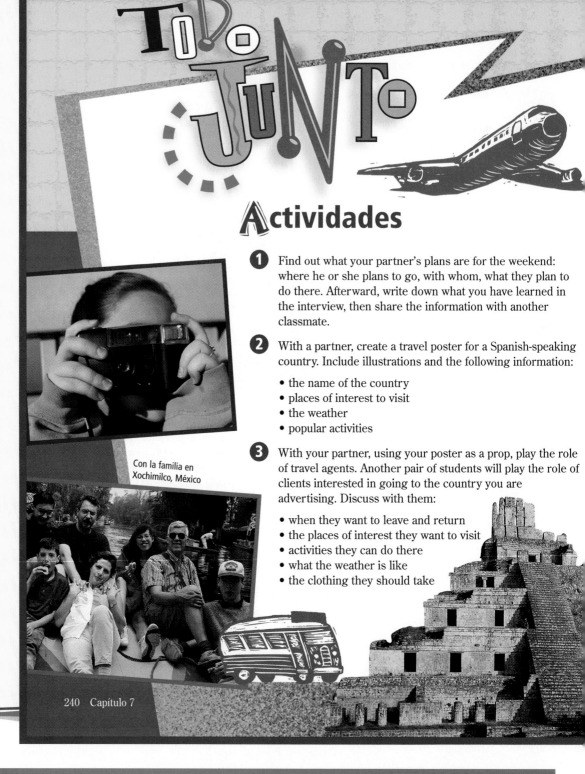

Todo junto

Actividades

1 Find out what your partner's plans are for the weekend: where he or she plans to go, with whom, what they plan to do there. Afterward, write down what you have learned in the interview, then share the information with another classmate.

2 With a partner, create a travel poster for a Spanish-speaking country. Include illustrations and the following information:

- the name of the country
- places of interest to visit
- the weather
- popular activities

3 With your partner, using your poster as a prop, play the role of travel agents. Another pair of students will play the role of clients interested in going to the country you are advertising. Discuss with them:

- when they want to leave and return
- the places of interest they want to visit
- activities they can do there
- what the weather is like
- the clothing they should take

Con la familia en Xochimilco, México

240   Capítulo 7

Options

Strategies for Reaching All Students

Conexiones

La geografía

Juego de geografía

How well do you know the countries of the world? On a sheet of paper, write the names of the countries from the list that are being referred to in each of these descriptions. Afterward, write similar descriptions in Spanish of three other countries. Can your partner tell what three countries they are?

1. Soy famoso por el chocolate, por las montañas y por organizaciones internacionales, como la Cruz Roja, que tienen oficinas aquí.
2. Puedes visitar unas ruinas antiguas de los incas en mis montañas altas.
3. Estoy al lado del Mar Rojo. Los sitios más santos del islam están aquí.
4. Tengo una civilización muy antigua y la población más grande del mundo.
5. Si quieres subir la montaña más alta del mundo, tienes que visitarme.
6. Mi capital es Rabat. El nombre de mi ciudad más grande quiere decir "white house" en español. Soy el país africano más cerca de España.
7. Puedes sacar fotos de pirámides mayas aquí.
8. Soy la isla más grande del Caribe.
9. Tengo la selva tropical más grande de las Américas. Las cataratas magníficas de Iguazú están en mi frontera con Argentina y Paraguay.
10. Soy una isla en el Océano Atlántico, una posesión de Dinamarca, pero ¡1550 veces más grande que ella!

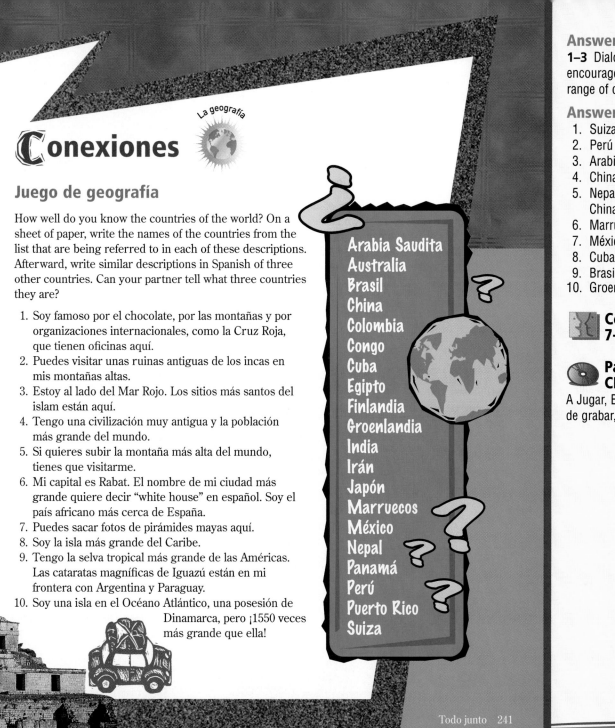

Arabia Saudita
Australia
Brasil
China
Colombia
Congo
Cuba
Egipto
Finlandia
Groenlandia
India
Irán
Japón
Marruecos
México
Nepal
Panamá
Perú
Puerto Rico
Suiza

Todo junto   241

Cultural Notes

(p. 240, bottom left photo)
Along with el Parque de Chapultepec, the floating gardens at Xochimilco have traditionally been a favorite spot for Mexico City's families to gather on Sundays. Riders on the colorful *trajineras* may bring their own food and drinks, or buy them from vendors. Mariachi bands, photographers, and souvenir vendors also navigate the canals, offering their wares and services to the Sunday crowds.

(pp. 240–241, photo)
The ancient Mayan site of Edzná, an important ceremonial center from 600 B.C. to A.D. 200, lies outside the city of Campeche in Mexico's Yucatán Peninsula. Its most impressive building is the Temple of the Five Stories, shown here, which stands 118 feet high and 236 feet wide. The four lower levels were living quarters for priests and the top was a shrine.

Apply

Process Reading
For a description of process reading, see p. 48.

Teaching Suggestions
Tell students that you will answer questions about word meanings only after they have applied coping strategies. Make sure there are dictionaries available.

Answers
Antes de leer
Answers will vary, but may include information about things to see and places to go. Activities that you might expect to find may include visiting cultural or archaeological sites, festivals, etc.

Mira la lectura
Mexico / archaeological sites and beaches / The aspect mentioned is hospitality. / You would receive more information.

¡Vamos a leer!

www.pasoapaso.com

Antes de leer

STRATEGY ► Using prior knowledge

Advertisements can give us lots of ideas about things to do in unknown locales. What kinds of information might you expect to find in this travel advertisement? Name three or four different kinds of activities that you would expect to find.

Mira la lectura

STRATEGY ► Scanning

Look at the title, photograph, and coupon.

- What country is advertised?
- What two tourist attractions does the photograph suggest it offers?
- What aspect of Mexico is mentioned in the coupon heading?
- What would you receive if you sent the coupon?

DEJA DE SOÑAR Y HAZ LA MALETA.

México.

México, un tesoro de 3,000 años de antiguas civilizaciones. Olmecas, Aztecas, Mixtecas y Mayas. Sus monumentos se encuentran por todas partes: Pirámides y templos, murales y frisos e, incluso, ciudades totalmente amuralladas. Todo en México es increíble.

Ven a México, tendrás mucho que recordar. Sus nobles ciudades coloniales, 10,000kms. de soleadas playas. Sus alegres mariachis. Su arte y escultura. Sus fiestas y folklore.

Tiendas de piel, plata, laca, tejidos. Y sus gentes que te reciben cordialmente, dándote siempre la bienvenida para que te sientas como en casa.

En México, vas a encontrar lo más moderno, elegante, lujoso y confortable. Con todo su pasado milenario a tu alrededor, México todavía sigue siendo México. Todavía sigue siendo mágico.

Visita México este año. Vas a tener las vacaciones que tú siempre has deseado. Ahora está a tu alcance. 14 días desde 123,050. pts.

Infórmate en tu agencia de viajes o envía este cupón a: Oficina de Turismo de México en España. Velázquez, 126. 28006 Madrid. Tel:261.18.27.

VENGA. VIVA LA HOSPITALIDAD DE MÉXICO.

Sírvase enviarme más información.   HO.2
Nombre _____
Dirección _____

Código postal
SECRETARÍA DE TURISMO DE MÉXICO.

242   Capítulo 7

Options

Strategies for Reaching All Students

Spanish-Speaking Students
Have Spanish-speaking students make a similar brochure. *Haz un anuncio o un folleto para un lugar de vacaciones en tu estado que atrae a los turistas. ¿Cómo se llama? ¿Dónde está? ¿En qué estación es más popular con los turistas? ¿Cuáles son algunas de las atracciones principales? ¿Cómo pueden recibir más información?*

 Un paso más Ex. 7-F

Students Needing Extra Help
Infórmate: Have students write out this exercise so they can number the items.

Multiple Intelligences
Interpersonal/Social
See Enrichment.

Enrichment
As an in-class assignment, have students work in pairs to list the cognates in this reading selection. Then have the entire class compare lists, discussing how they recognized the cognates and what the sentences in which they appear might mean.

As a homework assignment, ask students to create an ad for their hometown, region, or the U.S. in general. Ask them to think of the aspects of this country they would promote to appeal to foreign visitors.

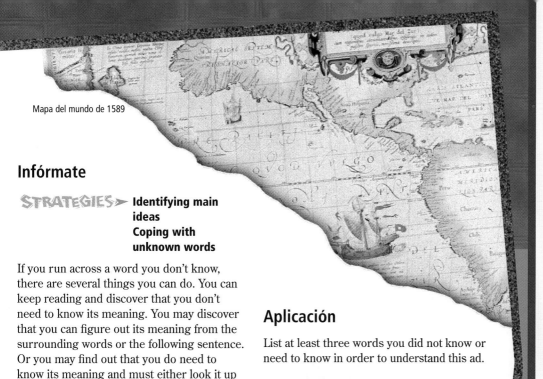

Mapa del mundo de 1589

Infórmate

STRATEGIES ► **Identifying main ideas**
Coping with unknown words

If you run across a word you don't know, there are several things you can do. You can keep reading and discover that you don't need to know its meaning. You may discover that you can figure out its meaning from the surrounding words or the following sentence. Or you may find out that you do need to know its meaning and must either look it up or ask someone. Use this strategy when you run across a word you don't understand.

1 Look at each paragraph to find the main idea, then tell in which paragraph (1–6) each of the following ideas is featured.

Affordable vacation package

Monuments of ancient civilizations

Modern and traditional features

Places and things to see

How to get more information

Opportunities for shopping

2 Which of the first four paragraphs describes the attractions that you find most appealing? Why do they appeal to you?

3 Scan the last paragraph to discover the country where this advertisement appeared.

Aplicación

List at least three words you did not know or need to know in order to understand this ad.

Montando en bicicleta en el Zócalo de la Ciudad de México

¡Vamos a leer! 243

Infórmate

1 1 = Monuments of ancient civilizations, 2 = Places and things to see, 3 = Opportunities for shopping, 4 = Modern and traditional features, 5 = Affordable vacation package, 6 = How to get more information

2 Answers will vary. Encourage student discussion and ask for reasons whenever possible.

3 Spain

Aplicación
Lists will vary.

www **Internet Activities**

Cultural Notes ☀

(p. 242, realia)
Toy ceramic bus from Mexico. It is common in many parts of Latin America for real buses to be loaded down like this toy one, with luggage, bags of produce, and other personal possessions piled on top. In Mexico, drivers often personalize the interior of the bus with elaborate decorations that frequently have a religious theme. Many drivers go one step further and give their bus a name.

(p. 242, realia)
As this ad from Spain indicates, the Mexican tourist office promotes the country as actually "three Mexicos," the archaeological, colonial, and resort. Every year, about seven million tourists visit Mexico (over 85 percent of them from the U.S.). The government, through various projects such as the one that transformed the fishing village of Cancún into a thriving tourist center, hopes to increase this number in the future.

(p. 243, photo)
Mexico City's main square, which stands on the site of what was once the central square of the magnificent Aztec city of Tenochtitlán, is officially named la Plaza de la Constitución. More commonly called el Zócalo (literally the "base" or "pedestal," but in Mexico the word refers to the central *plaza),* the area is today the site of events such as this bicycle race, religious ceremonies, and dance performances.

Apply

Pasos vivos 1 CD-ROM
Word Processor

¡Vamos a escribir!

Imagine that the government of Puerto Rico is offering a free vacation in San Juan to the student who writes the best short essay in Spanish on vacationing in Puerto Rico. Write an entry for this contest. Follow these steps.

1 First, think about what you want to say. Use the postcards to help you brainstorm some ideas. You may want to list your ideas under the headings Weather, Sights, Recreation, and Clothing.

San Juan

El Capitolio, San Juan

Puerto Rico

El Parque Nacional de Luquillo (El Yunque), Puerto Rico

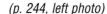

PASO CULTURAL

The Caribbean island of Puerto Rico became a U.S. territory in 1898 and a self-governing U.S. commonwealth in 1952. Its tropical climate and varied natural beauty make it a popular tourist destination. Puerto Rico's rain forest, El Yunque, is the only tropical National Forest in the U.S. Puerto Rico also offers well-preserved Spanish colonial architecture in *el viejo San Juan,* the second-oldest city in the Americas (after Santo Domingo), founded in 1521. Look at the postcard of El Morro. Keeping in mind the meaning of *puerto rico* (rich port), why do you think the Spaniards built this structure?

244 Capítulo 7

Options

Strategies for Reaching All Students

Students Needing Extra Help
Step 1: Have students use their Organizers.
Step 2: Help students with the first two or three sentences. Since students have just worked with ads (using incomplete sentences and single words), they might have to be encouraged to write in complete sentences.

Multiple Intelligences
Visual/Spatial
See Enrichment.

Enrichment
As a twist on this activity, have students write postcards from one of the places listed in the *Vocabulario para conversar* on pp. 220–221, explaining the weather and their activities, but without revealing the place. Students read their postcards aloud and classmates guess what places are being described.

Cultural Notes

(p. 244, left photo)
Puerto Rico's capitol, located in the section of San Juan known as Puerta de Tierra, was constructed in the 1920s under the direction of architect Rafael Carmoega. Inside the capitol dome are four murals representing scenes from Puerto Rican history. The original constitution, ratified in 1952 when the island became a U.S. commonwealth, is contained in an urn that stands at the center of the rotunda.

2 Write a first draft of your essay. Focus on communicating your ideas clearly.

3 Show your first draft to a partner. Ask what he or she likes about it and what should be changed. Think about any changes that you want to make, then revise it.

4 Check your work for spelling, accents, and question and exclamation marks.

5 Make a clean copy. You can file your work in your writing portfolio, or you can share it with your classmates, who can vote on the one that most makes them want to visit Puerto Rico.

La Plaza de Colón, San Juan

San Juan

La Casa de España, San Juan

El Castillo de El Morro, San Juan

¡Vamos a escribir! 245

Cultural Notes
(p. 245, top photo)
One of four *plazas* in Viejo San Juan, La Plaza de Colón was originally called St. James Square but was renamed in 1921 to commemorate the 400th anniversary of Columbus's exploration of Puerto Rico. Another *plaza,* La Plaza del Quinto Centenario, was opened in October, 1992 for the 500th anniversary of the journeys to the Americas and includes a 40-foot totemlike sculpture of black granite and ceramics representing the earthen roots of American history. Ask students: Comparing the style of the 1921 sculpture in the photo to the 1992 sculpture described, how do you think the public opinion of Columbus has changed in Puerto Rico?

(pp. 244–245, photo)
The Luquillo Division of the Caribbean National Forest, more commonly known as El Yunque (the Anvil) lies high in the mountains of northeastern Puerto Rico. It covers 28,000 acres of mountain area and is the habitat for 240 species of plants and trees.

Paso cultural
Possible answer: To protect themselves— and stored riches en route to Spain—from outside attack.

(p. 245, center photo)
The Casa de España in San Juan is one example of Spanish colonial architecture in the crowded old section of the city. Viejo San Juan is a historic landmark district with many of its buildings restored to their appearance in the sixteenth and seventeenth centuries. This section covers an area of several square blocks and lies on the tip of a long peninsula.

(p. 245, bottom photo)
The massive Castillo de San Felipe del Morro, known as El Morro, was built by the Spaniards over more than two centuries, beginning in 1539. El Morro is one of three fortresses built to protect San Juan, and it is said to be the strongest Spanish fortress in the Americas. Its walls are 20 feet thick in certain places and contain a network of stairways and ramps that were designed to facilitate quick movement of troops and artillery should the fort come under attack.

Assess & Summarize

Test Preparation

You may want to assign parts of this section as written homework or as an in-class writing activity prior to administering the *Examen de habilidades*.

Reteach / Review: Vocabulary

Speaking: Ask pairs of students to take turns naming various real or imaginary family members, describing their personalities, and then suggesting vacation destinations and activities they might enjoy. For example: *Mi hermana es deportista. Puede ir a Puerto Rico para bucear.*

Answers

Listening: *Llueve y quisiera visitar el museo. Menos mal que ayer fui a la catedral y a pasear en bote en el parque. Mañana, si hace buen tiempo, puedo ir a las cataratas.* Tomás may need the following: *las botas, el impermeable, el paraguas.* The weather was nice yesterday. Tomás will go to the waterfalls only if it's nice out.

Reading: The main idea is to attract people to Isla Mujeres in Mexico, because its beaches, the sea, and the weather all seem appealing.

Repaso ¿Lo sabes bien?

This section will help you organize your studying for the proficiency test, where you will be asked to do similar, though not identical, tasks. There will not be any models on the test.

► Listening

Can you understand when people talk about their vacation activities? Listen as your teacher reads a sample similar to what you will hear on the test. Can you name, in Spanish, at least two items that Tomás may need today? What do you think the weather was like yesterday? Is Tomás definitely going to the waterfalls tomorrow?

► Reading

Can you scan this travel ad and identify its author's main idea?

EN ISLA MUJERES EN MÉXICO

El mar es azul y las playas son blancas. En diciembre hace calor, hace sol y nunca llueve. Si no le gusta un invierno frío, venga a Isla Mujeres. Sólo necesita llevar su traje de baño, sus anteojos de sol y su pasaporte.

► Writing

Can you write a postcard telling about your vacation at a ski resort? Here is an example:

Hola, Marisol:

Hace mucho frío aquí, pero también hace sol. Mañana quiero ir a la tienda para comprar unos anteojos de sol. Esta tarde voy a visitar a mis nuevos amigos. El sábado pienso ir a esquiar con ellos.

Tu amiga,
Susana

► Culture

Based on what you know about vacation time in Chile, how would that affect the time of year you would visit that country?

► Speaking

Can you discuss vacation choices and activities with a partner? For example:

A —¿Adónde te gustaría ir este verano?

B —A mí me gustaría visitar las ruinas en Guatemala. ¿Y a ti?

A —Yo prefiero ir a una ciudad grande. Me gusta mucho visitar museos y comprar recuerdos. ¿Con quién piensas ir a Guatemala?

B —Con mi familia. Mi padre es de Guatemala. Y tú, ¿con quién piensas ir?

A —Con mi madre. A ella le gustan las ciudades grandes también.

Self Test — www.pasoapaso.com

Options

Strategies for Reaching All Students

Students Needing Extra Help

Listening: Have students write their answers.
Do an example in English, pointing out that they don't have to hear the words raincoat or umbrella, but because they hear the word rain, they know those items will be needed.

Writing: Have students use their Organizers to help them with their postcards.
Culture: Review the *Perspectiva cultural*.
Speaking: Do in smaller segments: A–B–A and then B–A. Give more examples.

Resumen del vocabulario

Use the vocabulary from this chapter to help you:

► describe vacation choices and activities

► talk about the weather

► discuss what to take on a trip

to talk about vacation
las vacaciones (pl.)
ir de vacaciones

to talk about places to visit on vacation
las cataratas
la catedral
la ciudad
el lago
los lugares de interés
el mar
las montañas
el museo
el país
la pirámide
las ruinas
la selva tropical

to talk about things to do on vacation
bucear
los recuerdos
descansar
esquiar
explorar (la selva)
llevar
pasear (en bote)
el bote
sacar fotos
la foto (f.)
subir (la pirámide)
tomar el sol
visitar

to talk about planning a vacation
pensar (e → ie) + inf.
regresar
salir

to name items to take on vacation
el abrigo
los anteojos de sol
las botas
el bronceador
la bufanda
la cámara
el gorro
los guantes
el impermeable
la maleta
el paraguas (sing.)
el pasaporte
el traje de baño

to ask about or describe weather
¿Qué tiempo hace?
fantástico, -a
Hace buen tiempo.
Hace calor.
Hace fresco.
Hace frío.
Hace mal tiempo.
Hace sol.
Hace viento.

la lluvia
la nieve
el sol
el viento
Llueve.
Nieva.

to say that you want or would like something
querer (e → ie)
quisiera

to say where you went
ir: (yo) fui
       (tú) fuiste
no . . . ninguna parte

to say when events occur
cuando
pasado, -a

to indicate use or purpose
para + inf.

to express amazement
¡Vaya!

to express satisfaction
menos mal que

to express ability or permission
poder (o → ue)

Resumen   247

Writing: Postcards will vary, but students should use the chapter vocabulary. Look for logical sentences.

Culture: Answers will vary. Students may include references to the opposite seasons for countries south of the equator.

Speaking: Dialogues will vary. Encourage use of vocabulary from previous chapters.

Assessment

 Prueba cumulativa

 Examen de habilidades

 Test Generator

Additional Assessment Options

 Comm. Act. BLMs
Small Group Activities
Situation Cards

 Pasos vivos 1 CD-ROM
Slide Presentation Maker, Video Presentation Maker, Word Processor, Spindle

 ¿Lo sabes bien? Video Quiz

 Internet Activities
Self-Test

CAPÍTULO 8
THEME: HOME

SCOPE AND SEQUENCE Pages 248–281

COMMUNICATION

Topics

Rooms in the house

Furniture

Household appliances

Household chores

Objectives

To talk about homes in Spanish-speaking countries

To talk about where someone lives

To talk about houses or apartments

To indicate possession

To name household chores

To indicate obligation

To name and describe household items

To indicate that someone is right or wrong

To indicate whether you agree with someone or something

CULTURE

Architecture and the home

GRAMMAR

Los verbos poner *y* hacer

Los verbos que terminan en -ir

El verbo preferir

Los adjetivos posesivos: su *y* nuestro

Ancillaries available for use with Chapter 8

Multisensory/Technology

Overheads, 41–45

Audio Tapes and CDs

Vocabulary Art Blackline Masters for Hands-On Learning, pp. 43–47/CD-ROM

Classroom Crossword

Video

Pasos vivos 1 CD-ROM

Internet Activities www.pasoapaso.com

Print

Practice Workbook, pp. 84–93

Writing, Audio & Video Activities, pp. 47–52, 114–116, 166–167

Communicative Activity Blackline Masters

  Pair and Small Group Activities, pp. 57–62

  Situation Cards, p. 63

Un paso más: Actividades para ampliar tu español, pp. 44–49

TPR Storytelling

Assessment

Assessment Program

  Pruebas, pp. 111–121

  Examen de habilidades, pp. 122–125

Test Generator

Video still from Chap. 8

247A

¿Lo sabes bien?
Video Quiz

Planning Express, Teaching
Resources Library, and Clip Art
Library

Architectural Influences

If you were to travel from the southwestern U.S. to the southern tip of South America, you would sense a certain familiarity in almost every place you visited. Although regional differences would quickly become apparent, you would still be conscious of a certain look shared by many southwestern U.S. and South American communities. This look in large part can be traced to the architecture of Moorish Spain. The Moors ruled most of the Iberian Peninsula from the early eighth century until the early thirteenth century.

Many elements common to Latin American architecture were first introduced in Moorish Spain. Patios, for example, became common in places such as Sevilla and Córdoba beginning in the early eleventh century. Because of widespread political and social upheaval during this time, houses were built with heavy doors and thick, fortresslike walls. Patios, positioned in the center of the house and accessible from all first-floor rooms, often had tiled floors. In the center, surrounded by lemon trees and flowers, was often a large clay pot filled with cool water. Patios were possibly the first naturally "air-conditioned" rooms of the house. Throughout Latin America today, as well as in Spain, they are still a popular feature in many commercial buildings as well as homes.

Another predominant element of Latin American architecture is the *balcón,* or *mirador.* In Moorish Spain, typical homes had balconies off of the second-floor sleeping areas. These balconies, which often included intricately fashioned iron railings and grates, overlooked the patio. During the colonial period, balconies became commonplace in Latin America as well. However, most of them did not face the patio as they did in Spain. Instead, they faced the street to facilitate the observation of street life.

Homes and other buildings in Moorish Spain stood apart from those in northern Europe in other ways. In traditional Spanish construction, thick walls helped shield inner rooms from the sun's heat. Although wood was used for ceiling beams, doors, and windows, it was not used as commonly as in northern Europe. Instead, adobe, stone, and brick were the popular building materials.

Today, builders in Latin America and the southwestern U.S. employ many of these same materials and techniques. In addition, they utilize many of the same building techniques and materials used for centuries by American Indians.

Introduce

Planning

Cross-Curricular Connections

Design Connection *(pp. 252–253)*
Have students create drawings of their ideal room, labeling all the items with descriptions including color, size, etc. Then divide the class into pairs. Have students describe their drawings without showing them to their partners. As one student describes a room, the other draws it. Students then switch roles. Display the drawings that are most alike.

Architecture Connection *(pp. 256–257)*
Using magazine cutouts or by drawing, have students create the house of a famous person. The house should have a cutaway view so that the interior is visible. (Provide an example.) Students should include items and a decor that characterize the person. Have them write a paragraph describing the house by means of a brief interview with the celebrity. When finished, students can display their houses, and the class can try to guess the owner.

Spanish in Your Community
See if students have ever noticed any houses or other structures in their community built in the Spanish architectural style. If they haven't, see if they can observe some on their daily commute to and from school. Ask: What are the characteristics of this style? Where are the buildings located?

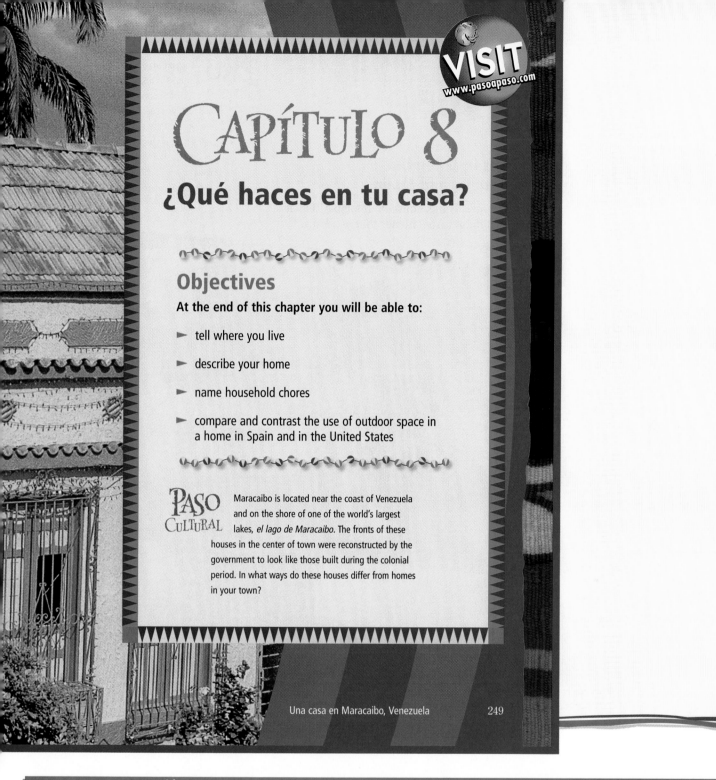

CAPÍTULO 8
¿Qué haces en tu casa?

VISIT www.pasoapaso.com

Objectives
At the end of this chapter you will be able to:

► tell where you live

► describe your home

► name household chores

► compare and contrast the use of outdoor space in a home in Spain and in the United States

PASO CULTURAL
Maracaibo is located near the coast of Venezuela and on the shore of one of the world's largest lakes, *el lago de Maracaibo*. The fronts of these houses in the center of town were reconstructed by the government to look like those built during the colonial period. In what ways do these houses differ from homes in your town?

Una casa en Maracaibo, Venezuela   249

Cultural Objective

• To talk about homes and rooms of the house

¡Piénsalo bien!

Play

 Video Activity A

Using the Video

This chapter's video focuses on the home. Students will visit the Madrid homes of each of our hosts and tour the El Escorial palace and monastery outside Madrid.

To prepare students for the video, first ask them to predict what this chapter's tape will be about. Then have students watch the segment several times. After the first time, you may wish to have them brainstorm possible vocabulary and expressions they will need to talk about what they saw on the video. Ask students to identify: a) things they saw that were familiar to them, and b) things they saw that they probably would not see where they live.

Video segment 1: For more teaching suggestions, see the Video Teacher's Guide.

¡Piensa en la CULTURA!

Homes in Colombia, Venezuela, and Spain

In what ways is this house in Colombia similar to and different from homes that you know?

En Cartagena, Colombia

Cartagena, Color

Caracas, Venezuela

"Nuestro dormitorio no es muy grande, pero hay espacio para todo."

250   Capítulo 8

PASO CULTURAL
The port city of Cartagena, Colombia, was founded in 1533 as a Spanish base for the conquest of the rest of South America. A series of massive forts and walls was built to protect the city from attack by sea or land. This colonial house is in the old walled city, which has been declared a World Cultural Heritage Site by UNESCO. How is the architectural style of this house different from that of colonial houses in New England or in the southeastern United States?

Options

Strategies for Reaching All Students

Spanish-Speaking Students
Ask Spanish-speaking students: *Describe la casa que ves en la foto. ¿Es como las casas en tu comunidad? Y el dormitorio, ¿es como el tuyo? ¿Cómo es diferente? ¿En qué se parece? ¿Se parece la cocina a la de tu casa o apartamento?*

 Un paso más Ex. 8-A

Enrichment
If possible, bring to class a collection of photographs of homes in Spanish-speaking countries. Strive for a sampling that includes homes representative of those from all socioeconomic groups. Students will be particularly interested in viewing the insides of homes, especially the bedrooms of teenagers.

Students Needing Extra Help
Relate *dormir* to *dormitorio* and *cocinar* to *cocina*. In talking about families, be sensitive to issues involving single-parent households, disadvantaged families, etc.

Multiple Intelligences
Visual/Spatial
See Using the Video.

En Madrid, España

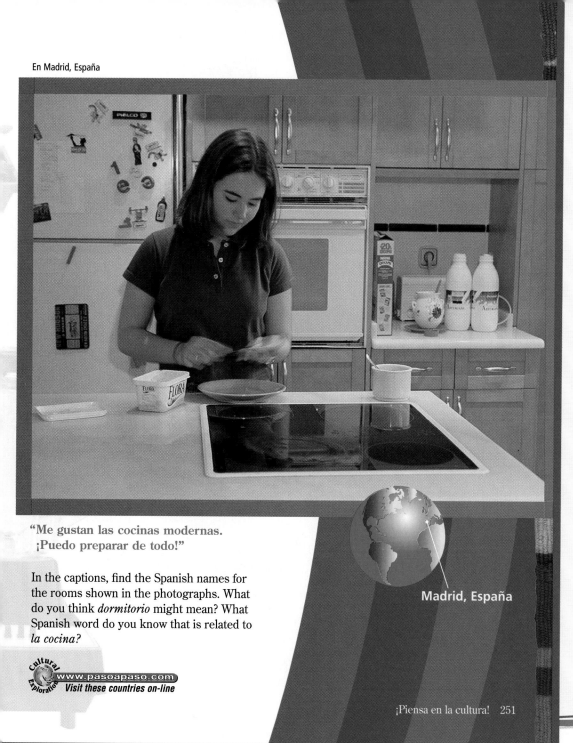

"Me gustan las cocinas modernas.
¡Puedo preparar de todo!"

In the captions, find the Spanish names for the rooms shown in the photographs. What do you think *dormitorio* might mean? What Spanish word do you know that is related to *la cocina?*

Cultural Exploration
www.pasoapaso.com
Visit these countries on-line

Madrid, España

¡Piensa en la cultura! 251

Multicultural Perspectives

In many countries in Latin America, adobe is the preferred building material for homes. Made of mud and / or clay, it is not only extremely strong, but also energy efficient, keeping houses cool in hot months and warm in cold ones. Ask students what types of materials are used to build houses in their neighborhoods.

Answers: ¡Piensa en la cultura!

(p. 250) Answers will vary.

(p. 251, photo) dormitorio, cocina /
See if students can guess from visual clues that *dormitorio* means "bedroom." You may wish to point out that this word is a false cognate and doesn't mean "dormitory" *(una residencia estudiantil)*. / cocinar

Using Photos

(pp. 250–251) Ask: ¿Qué hace el muchacho? ¿Y la muchacha?

Cultural Notes

Paso cultural
Possible answers: Most colonial houses in New England and the southeastern U.S. have cold-weather features such as glass windows, chimneys, slanted roofs, and wood or brick construction. The house in the photo has open windows covered with grating, no chimney, a flat roof, balconies with flowers growing, and walls made of cement or stucco.

(p. 250, bottom photo)
Because of space limitations, many Latin American teens share a room with one or more siblings. Ask students: How do you think Latin American teens who share bedrooms adapt to not having their own space?

(p. 251, photo)
This modern kitchen might be found in any part of the world. Yet the housing situation in Spain and Latin America varies greatly. Acceptable, affordable housing can be hard to find. This is especially true for large cities like Madrid, which have seen rapid increases in new residents seeking jobs. Ask students: Is there a housing shortage in your town or city? If there is, what's being done to solve it?

Present

Chapter Theme
Home: Rooms of a house and household chores

Communicative Objectives
- To talk about where someone lives
- To talk about houses or apartments
- To indicate possession
- To name household chores
- To indicate obligation

 Overheads 41–42

 Vocabulary Art BLMs/CD-ROM

 Pronunciation Tape 8-1

 Vocabulario para conversar A

Play

Using the Video
Video segment 2: See the Video Teacher's Guide.

 Video Activity B

Vocabulario para conversar

 Chapter 8 Vocabulary

¿Cómo es tu casa?

Aquí tienes palabras y expresiones necesarias para hablar sobre dónde vives, cómo es tu casa y algunas cosas que tienes que hacer en casa. Léelas varias veces y practícalas con un(a) compañero(a) en las páginas siguientes.

una casa de dos pisos

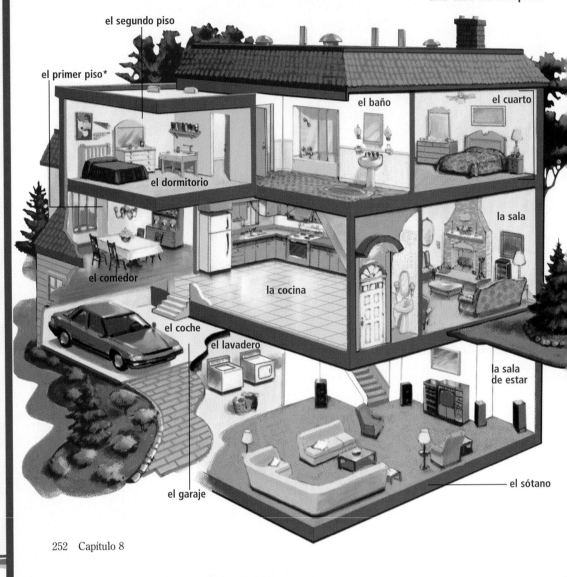

el segundo piso
el primer piso*
el baño
el cuarto
el dormitorio
el comedor
la cocina
el coche
el lavadero
la sala
la sala de estar
el garaje
el sótano

252   Capítulo 8

Options

Strategies for Reaching All Students

Students Needing Extra Help
Have students begin to fill in their Organizers.
To facilitate learning, present the rooms and chores separately.
También necesitas . . . : To help reinforce meaning, give some examples of *tener que* using activities vocabulary from Chap. 1. Note that from this point on, exercise directions are in Spanish. Words that would be difficult to understand are translated for the

first few times. Help students see this as part of the reading process. Encourage them to use strategies that they are developing in *¡Vamos a leer!*
Remind students of the expression *ayudar en casa* from Chap. 1.

Learning Spanish Through Action
STAGING VOCABULARY: *Señalen* and the commands for household chores listed in the *Vocabulario para conversar*

1) MATERIALS: none
DIRECTIONS: Tell students that they are going to help you clean your house on Saturday. Direct them to act out the chores that you mention.
2) MATERIALS: transparency of the *Vocabulario para conversar* or an enlarged photocopy of the page
DIRECTIONS: Direct students to point to rooms as you tell where people in your family are. Be sure to include pets.

el apartamento

hacer la cama

sacudir los muebles

lavar los platos

quitar la mesa

pasar la aspiradora

limpiar el baño

arreglar el cuarto

poner la mesa

310

lavar la ropa

cortar el césped

sacar la basura

También necesitas...

cerca (de)	*near*	hacer:	*to do, to make:*
lejos (de)	*far (from)*	(yo) hago	*I do / make*
vivir: (yo) vivo	*to live: I live*	(tú) haces	*you do / make*
(tú) vives	*you live*	el quehacer	*(household) chore*
el piso	*floor*	(de la casa)	
bastante	*rather, quite*	tener que + *inf.*	*to have to ___*
nuestro, -a	*our*	más	here: *else*

* In a multistory building, we usually call the ground floor *la planta baja,* the second floor *el primer piso,* the third floor *el segundo piso,* the fourth floor *el tercer piso,* and so on. Note that for "first" and "third," we use *primer* and *tercer* in front of a masculine singular noun.

Vocabulario para conversar   253

Practice & Apply

Re-enter / Recycle

Ex. 2: places from Chap. 3
Ex. 4: numbers 0–31 from *El primer paso*
Ex. 5: activities from Chaps. 1 and 3
Ex. 6: *gustar* expressions from Chap. 1

Reteach / Review: Vocabulary

Ex. 3: Students can extend this dialogue by having *Estudiante A* say that he or she can't do the chore because he or she has something else to do, somewhere to go, or doesn't feel well.

Answers: Empecemos a conversar

1 ESTUDIANTE A
a. ¿Dónde está el coche?
b. . . . el dormitorio?
c. . . . la sala?
d. . . . el comedor?
e. . . . el baño?
f. . . . la sala de estar?
g. . . . el lavadero?

ESTUDIANTE B
a. Está en el garaje.
b. . . . el segundo piso.
c. . . . el primer piso.
d. . . . el primer piso.
e. . . . el segundo piso.
f. . . . el sótano.
g. . . . el sótano.

Empecemos a conversar

Túrnate con un(a) compañero(a) para ser *Estudiante A* y *Estudiante B*. Reemplacen las palabras subrayadas con las palabras representadas o escritas en los recuadros. quiere decir que puedes escoger tu propia respuesta. Para el Ejercicio 1, ve *(see)* el dibujo de la casa en la página 252.

1 A —¿Dónde está *la cocina*?
  B —Está en *el primer piso*.

Estudiante A   **Estudiante B**

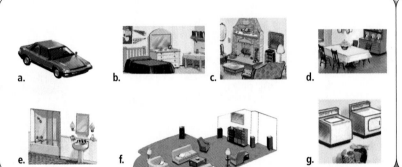

a.   b.   c.   d.

e.   f.   g.

el garaje

el primer piso

el segundo piso

el sótano

2 A —¿Vives cerca de *un almacén*?
  B —*Sí, bastante cerca.*
    o: *No, vivo lejos.*

Estudiante A   **Estudiante B**

a.   b.

c.   d.

254   Capítulo 8

Options

Strategies for Reaching All Students

3

A —¿*Tienes que* <u>*lavar los platos*</u>?

B —<u>*Sí, todos los días.*</u>
  o: *Sí, a veces.*
  o: *No, nunca.*

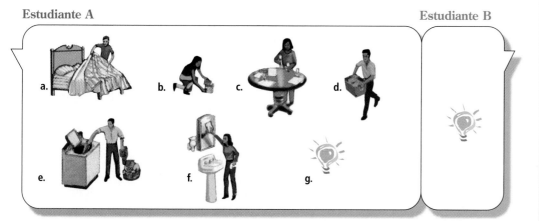

Estudiante A | Estudiante B

a. b. c. d.
e. f. g.

Empecemos a escribir

Escribe tus respuestas en español.

4 ¿Cuántos pisos y cuántos cuartos hay en tu casa o apartamento?

Nuestra casa / Nuestro apartamento tiene…

5 ¿En qué cuarto de la casa prefieres estudiar? ¿Por qué? ¿En qué cuarto prefieres escuchar música? ¿Ver la tele? ¿Hablar por teléfono?

6 ¿Te gusta más cortar el césped, pasar la aspiradora o sacudir los muebles? ¿Por qué?

7 ¿Qué quehaceres tienes para este fin de semana? ¿Qué más vas a hacer?

www.pasoapaso.com

MORE PRACTICE

Más práctica y tarea, p. 529–530
Practice Workbook 8–1, 8–2

También se dice…

el living

la recámara   la habitación (de dormir)
la alcoba   la pieza   el cuarto

el carro
el auto
la máquina

el zacate   la hierba
el pasto   la grama

Vocabulario para conversar   255

Present

Chapter Theme
Home: Household items

Communicative Objectives
• To name and describe household items
• To indicate that someone is right or wrong
• To indicate whether you agree with someone or something

 Overheads 43–44

 Vocabulary Art BLMs/CD-ROM

 Pronunciation Tape 8-2

 Vocabulario para conversar B

Play

Step

Using the Video
Video segment 2: See the Video Teacher's Guide.

 Video Activity B

Vocabulario para conversar

¿Cómo es tu dormitorio?

 At Home VIDEO Chapter 8 Vocabulary

Aquí tienes el resto del vocabulario necesario para hablar sobre las cosas que hay en una casa.

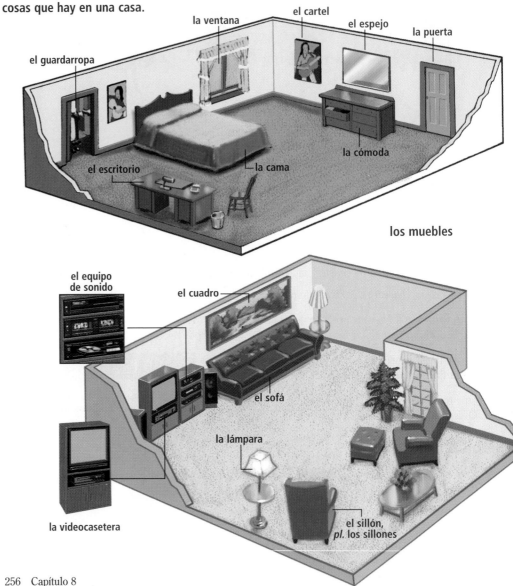

el guardarropa
la ventana
el cartel
el espejo
la puerta
el escritorio
la cama
la cómoda
los muebles

el equipo de sonido
el cuadro
el sofá
la lámpara
la videocasetera
el sillón, pl. los sillones

256　Capítulo 8

Options

Strategies for Reaching All Students

Learning Spanish Through Action
STAGING VOCABULARY: *Pongan*
MATERIALS: floor plan with room labels drawn on the chalkboard; pictures of furniture cut out from magazines or newspapers, tape
DIRECTIONS: Tell students that they are helping you move into a new house. Give them the furniture pictures. As you tell what item goes in which room, students go to the chalkboard and place the furniture in the appropriate room.

Extended Written Practice/Homework
1. Write three sentences telling what new household items you would like to have for different rooms of your house.
2. Write three sentences describing different pieces of furniture in your house that are or are not comfortable. Include in which room they are found.
3. Refer to the descriptions of furniture on p. 257. Write four sentences describing pieces of furniture in your house.

Multiple Intelligences
Bodily/Kinesthetic
See Learning Spanish Through Action.
Interpersonal/Social
See Class Starter Review.
Verbal/Linguistic
See Pronunciation Tape 8-2.
Visual/Spatial
See Overheads 43–44, the Vocabulary Art BLMs/CD-ROM, and Using the Video.

256　Standards 1.1; 1.2

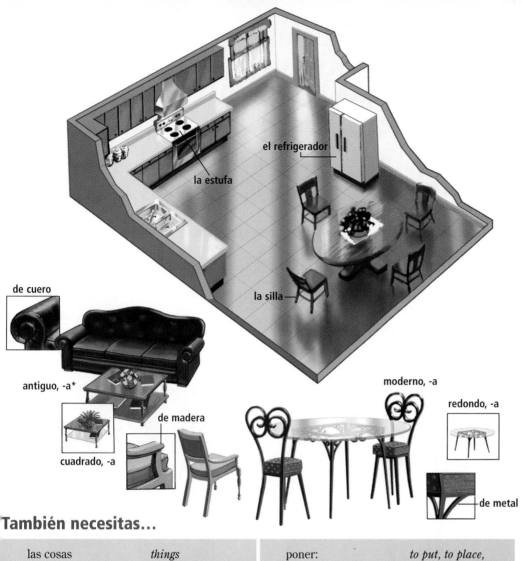

de cuero

antiguo, -a*

cuadrado, -a

de madera

la estufa

el refrigerador

la silla

moderno, -a

redondo, -a

de metal

También necesitas...

las cosas	*things*	poner:	*to put, to place, to set*
cómodo, -a	*comfortable*	(yo) pongo	*I put*
incómodo, -a	*uncomfortable*	(tú) pones	*you put*
limpio, -a	*clean*	(no) tener razón	*to be right (wrong)*
sucio, -a	*dirty*	(no) estar de acuerdo	*to (dis)agree*

* In general, we use the adjective *antiguo, -a* for things, whereas we can use *viejo, -a* for either people or things. *Antiguo, -a* can imply value, as in *muebles antiguos.*

Vocabulario para conversar   257

 Pasos vivos 1 CD-ROM
Clip Art Album

Grammar Preview
The verb forms *pongo / pones* are presented lexically. The complete paradigm appears on p. 267.

Teaching Suggestions
Preparing students to speak: Use one or two options from each of the categories of Comprehensible Input, Physical Response, or Limited Verbal Response. For a complete explanation of these categories and some sample activities, see pp. T22–T23.

Class Starter Review
On the day following initial presentation, you might begin the class with one of these activities:
1) Ask students to write a list of three things in their *(name a room of the house).*
2) Assemble photos or drawings of furniture and rooms, displaying them on a bulletin board. In small groups, have students take turns describing the pictures.

www Internet Activities
Juegos

Practice

Re-enter / Recycle
Exs. 9–11: adjective agreement
from Chaps. 1 and 4
Ex. 9: direct object pronouns from
Chap. 6
Ex. 11: expressing likes and preferences from Chap. 4

Answers: Empecemos a conversar

8 ESTUDIANTE A
a. ¿Qué hay en el dormitorio de tu
casa (apartamento)?
b. . . . la sala . . .
c. . . . la sala de estar . . .
d. . . . el comedor . . .
ESTUDIANTE B
a.–d. A ver . . . hay . . . . *(Answers
will vary.)*

9 ESTUDIANTE A
a. La ventana está sucia.
b. La estufa está sucia.
c. La puerta está sucia.
d. El espejo está sucio.
ESTUDIANTE B
a. ¿Sucia? ¡Pero está limpia!
b. Tienes razón. La tengo que
limpiar.
c. Tienes razón. La tengo que
limpiar.
d. ¿Sucio? ¡Pero está limpio!

Empecemos a conversar

8 A —¿*Qué hay en la cocina de tu casa (apartamento)?*  la cocina
B —*A ver . . . hay una estufa y un refrigerador.*

Estudiante A
a. el dormitorio
b. la sala
c. la sala de estar
d. el comedor

Estudiante B

¡NO OLVIDES!

Remember that the
adjective agrees with
the noun in gender and
number and that a direct
object pronoun *(lo, la,
los, las)* has the same
gender and number as
the noun it is replacing.
La cocina está sucia.
tengo que limpiar.

9 A —*El refrigerador está sucio.*
B —*¿Sucio? ¡Pero está limpio!*
o: *Tienes razón. Lo tengo que limpiar.*

Estudiante A   **Estudiante B**

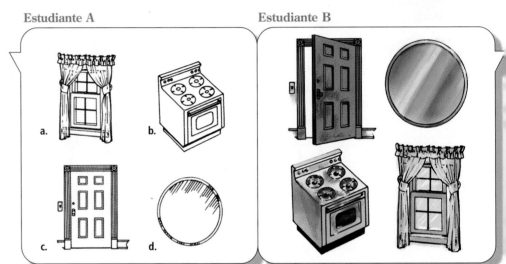

a.   b.   c.   d.

58   Capítulo 8

Options

Strategies for Reaching All Students

Students Needing Extra Help
Ex. 8: Use the Organizer along with
Overhead 43.
Ex. 9: Remind students of placement of
object pronouns and adjective agreement.
Model a feminine noun.

Exs. 9–10: Remind students that the
responses depicted in the art for *Estudiante
B* are not in sequential order and they must
choose the appropriate picture.
Ex. 11: Remind students of adjective agreement and that *Estudiante B* has to listen
carefully for his or her choices.

Enrichment
Ex. 8: To extend this dialogue, *Estudiante A*
can ask whether he or she likes the furniture
named and, once *Estudiante B* has
answered, ask for reasons for that answer.
Estudiante B's answer should include
descriptions of the furniture named.
Ex. 10: Extend this dialogue by having
Estudiante A ask where he or she plans to
buy the items named, and how much he or
she wants to pay.

8   Standards 1.1; 3.1

10

A —¿Qué vas a poner en <u>la sala</u>?

B —Voy a poner <u>un sofá muy cómodo</u>.

Estudiante A

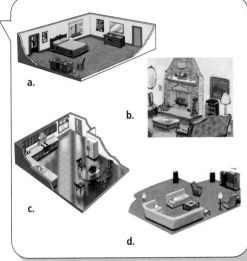

a.

b.

c.

d.

Estudiante B

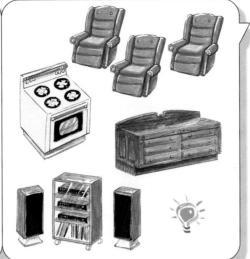

11

A —¿Prefieres <u>un escritorio de madera o de metal</u>?

B —Prefiero <u>un escritorio de metal</u>.

Estudiante A

Estudiante B

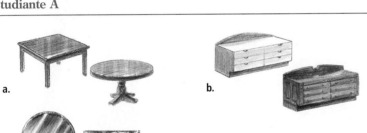

a.

b.

c.

d.

Vocabulario para conversar   259

10 ESTUDIANTE A

a. ¿Qué vas a poner en el dormitorio?

b. . . . la sala?

c. . . . la cocina?

d. . . . la sala de estar?

ESTUDIANTE B

Answers will vary. Look for logical responses.

a. Voy a poner una cómoda.

b. . . . tres sillones azules.

c. . . . una estufa blanca.

d. . . . un equipo de sonido.

11 ESTUDIANTE A

a. ¿Prefieres una mesa cuadrada o una mesa redonda?

b. . . . una cómoda moderna o una cómoda antigua?

c. . . . un espejo redondo o un espejo cuadrado?

d. Questions will vary.

ESTUDIANTE B

a.–d. Answers will vary depending on *Estudiante B*'s preferences.

Extended Written Practice/Homework

1. Write three sentences telling whether certain rooms in your house are usually clean or dirty.

2. Write three sentences telling why you need certain items in your house: *Necesitamos la lámpara para ver en la noche.*

3. Write three sentences of advice telling your classmates what chores they should do at home: *Debes limpiar el baño todos los días.*

Multiple Intelligences
Verbal/Linguistic
See Exs. 8–11.

Apply

Re-enter / Recycle

Ex. 12: numbers 0–31 from *El primer paso,* adjectives describing physical characteristics from Chap. 5, colors from Chap. 6

Answers: Empecemos a escribir y a leer

(In Exs. 12–13, give students the option of writing about a friend's house or an imaginary house.)

12–14 Answers will vary, but encourage students to use the full range of chapter vocabulary.

15 Drawings will vary, but should contain these features: The house has two stories with no basement. The first (ground) floor has a kitchen, a small bathroom, a large living room, a dining room, and a family room. The second floor has a bathroom and three bedrooms: two rather large ones and one very small one. The first floor also has a modern laundry room and a two-car garage.

 Practice Wkbk. 8-3, 8-4

 Audio Activity 8.2

 Writing Activity 8-C

 Pruebas 8-3, 8-4

Empecemos a escribir y a leer

Escribe tus respuestas en español.

12 Describe los muebles de un cuarto en tu casa. Di *(tell)* de qué colores son y si *(if)* son cómodos o incómodos. *En nuestra sala de estar hay dos sofás. Son . . .*

13 ¿Cómo es tu dormitorio? ¿Hay muchas ventanas? ¿Cuadros? ¿Qué más hay?

14 ¿Estás de acuerdo con que todos tienen que ayudar con los quehaceres de la casa? ¿Por qué?

15 Lee este párrafo y dibuja la casa descrita aquí.

Nuestra casa tiene dos pisos, pero no tiene sótano. En el primer piso hay una cocina, un baño pequeño, una sala grande, un comedor y una sala de estar. En el segundo piso hay otro baño y tres dormitorios: dos bastante grandes y uno muy pequeño. También tenemos en el primer piso un lavadero moderno y muy práctico y un garaje para dos coches. Los muebles que más me gustan son un sofá antiguo pero cómodo, y ¡la videocasetera!

MORE PRACTICE

- Más práctica y tarea, p. 530
- Practice Workbook 8–3, 8–4

En la sala de una casa en Rosario, Argentina

260 Capítulo 8

Options

Strategies for Reaching All Students

Spanish-Speaking Students

Ex. 12: Ask Spanish-speaking students: *¿En qué cuarto te gusta más estar? ¿Por qué? ¿Cómo te sientes ahí?*

 Un paso más Exs. 8-D, 8-E

Students Needing Extra Help

Ex. 12: Give students time to think through the exercise. You may wish to give a complete model. Have them use their Organizers and assign different rooms to groups or pairs.
Ex. 13: Give a model in which all the questions are answered.

Enrichment

Ex. 12: Students can also make a chart with three columns: *De metal, De madera,* and *De cuero.* Have them list items in their home that belong in each category.
For additional practice, students can also write a dialogue with *Estudiante A* saying that he or she wants to buy new furniture and *Estudiante B* asking why. After *Estudiante A* gives reasons, *Estudiante B* can say whether or not *Estudiante A* is right or wrong.

Usando el lavaplatos en Zaragoza, España

Cortando el césped en la Ciudad de México

También se dice...

el gavetero
el buró

el afiche
el póster

la refrigeradora   la nevera
el frigorífico   la heladera

la cocina

el armario   el clóset
el ropero   el placard

Vocabulario para conversar   261

Practice

Re-enter / Recycle
Ex. 1: time-telling from Chap. 2, places and buildings from Chap. 3
Ex. 2: direct object pronouns from Chap. 6

Answers:
¡Comuniquemos!

1 Dialogues will vary and may include: *el centro comercial, la playa, el parque de diversiones, el parque, la piscina, el gimnasio, cortar el césped, lavar la ropa, sacudir los muebles, arreglar el cuarto, lavar los platos, pasar la aspiradora.*

¡COMUN

1

Antes de *(before)* hacer planes con tus amigos, tienes que hacer otras cosas. Usa los dibujos y túrnate *(take turns)* con un(a) compañero(a) para hacer y aceptar invitaciones.

A —¿*Por qué no vamos al cine?*
B —¿*A qué hora? Tengo que limpiar el baño primero.*
A —¿*Puedes ir a las dos?*
B —*No, pero puedo ir a las cuatro.*

Estudiante A

Estudiante B

Options

Strategies for Reaching All Students

Spanish-Speaking Students

 Un paso más Ex. 8-F

Students Needing Extra Help
Ex. 1: Review time-telling and *al (a la)*, and show what changes in the dialogue.
Ex. 2: Have students use their Organizers. Have each pair choose four different things and make a chart listing "object" and "object location."
¿Qué sabes ahora?: Have students write out this section so they can check off what they have mastered.

Enrichment
Ex. 2: As an in-class assignment, have students describe the home in which they would like to live. Tell students to begin their descriptions: *Quisiera vivir en una casa (un apartamento) con . . . .* They could also begin: *En mi casa (apartamento) perfecta(o) hay . . . .*

¡QUEMOS!

Tu familia acaba de mudarse *(has just moved)* a una casa nueva. Con un(a) compañero(a), di dónde están los muebles y los aparatos *(appliances)* y dónde quieres ponerlos. Después, tu compañero(a) va a decir *(say)* si *(if)* está de acuerdo o no.

A —¿Dónde está la videocasetera?

B —Creo que está en el dormitorio de mamá.

A —Sí, aquí está. La pongo en la sala de estar.

B —No estoy de acuerdo. La debemos poner en el dormitorio.

¿Qué sabes ahora?

Can you:

► tell where you live?
—Vivo en un(a) ___ cerca de ___.

► name the rooms in your house?
—Mi casa tiene una cocina, ___,
___ y ___.

► describe some furnishings?
—Las sillas que están en el comedor son ___.

► name some household chores?
—Yo tengo que ___ y mis hermanos tienen que ___.

Vocabulario para conversar 263

2 Dialogues will vary. Suggested items include: *la videocasetera, el sofá (de cuero), el cartel, el cuadro, el sillón.*

Answers: ¿Qué sabes ahora?

- apartamento (casa) / *Answers will vary.*
- Answers will vary.
- Answers will vary. Look for correct adjective agreement.
- Answers will vary.

Audio Activity 8.3

Pasos vivos 1 CD-ROM
Slide Projector, Laboratorio de grabar

Cooperative Learning
Divide the class into groups of three or four students. Tell them they are to prepare an advertisement for a house for sale. The ad should feature a picture, a written description, the price, and possibly a floor plan. Assign tasks within each group: writer, artist, proofreader, presenter. Students should discuss the features of their house before work begins. Have presenters show and read the ads to the whole class. Display the ads on bulletin boards. Prior to assigning the exercise, you might want to have students clip ads from newspapers to use as models.

Multiple Intelligences
Interpersonal/Social
See Cooperative Learning and Exs. 1–2.
Intrapersonal/Introspective
See *¿Qué sabes ahora?*
Verbal/Linguistic
See Enrichment and Audio Activity 8.3.

Cultural Objective
• To compare and contrast the use of outdoor space in a home in Spain and in the U.S.

Teaching Suggestions
Have students compare the home here with the one shown in the photo on p. 250.

Multicultural Perspectives
In Granada, a *carmen* (from the Arabic word *karmat,* meaning garden) is a lush garden surrounded by walls. The same architectural concept was employed in the Spanish missions of the American Southwest and can still be seen today in the mission-style houses of California and other states in that region. Ask students if they know of architectural influences from other countries that have had a similar lasting impact.

Perspectiva cultural

Los patios

Un patio en Córdoba, España ▶

En España hay casas y apartamentos muy diferentes. También hay diversos tipos de patios.

What family members might use the part of the house pictured, and for what purpose? What might some people call it in English?

In the large cities of Spain, neighbors often visit each other's apartments in the same building. In small towns, you might see neighbors talking to each other through the windows that open onto the *patio.*

When you hear the English word "patio" you probably think of a small patch of concrete in a backyard. In Spanish, however, it can mean different things. For example, in a modern apartment building in a large city like Madrid, the *patio* is an air shaft in the center of the building. The kitchen may have a window that opens onto it.

However, in the south, in towns such as Sevilla and Córdoba, some *patios* are gardens with flowers, chairs, and perhaps caged birds. Some *patios* in Sevilla are in the front of the house and lead visitors in. More often, they are in the middle of the house, with big doors leading into the rooms. A *patio* in Sevilla is a place for friends and family to gather and talk.

Even though a *patio* in an apartment building in Madrid looks very different from a traditional one in Sevilla, they still have similar functions. A *patio* is a space that opens to the sky where friends and neighbors can spend time together chatting.

Una familia en su patio, Santiago de Chile

264 Capítulo 8

Options

Strategies for Reaching All Students

Spanish-Speaking Students
Ask Spanish-speaking students: *¿Qué actividades son comunes en los patios? ¿Tienes patio donde vives? ¿Es fácil o difícil encontrar casas con patios en tu comunidad?*

 Un paso más Ex. 8-G

Students Needing Extra Help
Discuss patios, decks, porches, outside entertainment areas, and so on.
Ex. 2: Explain that usually there is no roof on a *patio* in the middle of a house. Ask students if they would like this type of outdoor space.

Enrichment
Find photos of traditional homes in Spain or Latin America that have balconies and shuttered windows. After students have looked at these photos, conduct a brief class discussion. Ask: How are balconies and windows in these photos different from those you see in the U.S.?

La cultura desde tu perspectiva

1 Many houses in the United States have patios in back. They are usually made of concrete. In what ways is the design and function of a patio in the United States similar to and different from one in Spain?

2 In the United States, most open spaces are in front or in back of the house, while in Spain you might find them in the middle. What advantages do you see to having an open space in the middle of a house? If you were building a home, would you include a Spanish-style patio in your plans? Why or why not?

Cultural Activity www.pasoapaso.com

Pasos vivos 1 CD-ROM
Notas culturales, Maps

www Internet Activities
Perspectiva cultural

Cultural Notes ☀

Multiple Intelligences
Logical/Mathematical
Have students use a Venn diagram to illustrate comparisons and differences of Spanish homes (or apartments) and those in the U.S.
Naturalist
Have students compare how they use outdoor space of their own home to the information given in the text.

(p. 264, photo)
This family relaxes on their *patio* in Santiago, Chile. The *patio* has always been a special family place in Spanish-speaking countries, functioning as an "inner room outside" where the entire family can gather for refreshments, games, reading, and conversation.

(p. 265, photo)
This *patio* in Córdoba, Spain, clearly shows an Arabic influence in its layout and decoration. The *patio* is open from above, and can be entered or viewed from several rooms in the house. The archways, tile decoration on the floors and lower walls, and fountain are all distinctly Arabic, as is the tendency to decorate with an abundance of potted plants and shrubs.

Preview

Overhead 45

Answers

Answers will vary, but may include the family members, their home, etc.

A The word that follows determines whether *nuestra, nuestras,* or *nuestros* is used. *Nuestra* is used with *mamá* and *nuestro* is used with *papá.*

B In the phrase *sus hijos, sus* means "their" and refers to *los señores Ortiz.* In the phrase *su cama, su* means "her" and refers to Marcia.

Gramática en contexto

Look at this page from a teenager's sketchbook made during her term as an exchange student in San José, Costa Rica. What do you think she will remember as she looks back at these pictures?

Aquí estamos Marcia y yo con nuestra familia costarricense–los señores Ortiz, y sus hijos, Julia y Ramón. Viven en una casa cómoda cerca del Parque Central.

Hacemos nuestras camas todos los días. ¡A Marcia no le gusta hacer su cama! Pero nuestros quehaceres no son muchos porque todos nosotros ponemos y quitamos la mesa, lavamos los platos y sacamos la basura.

A In the captions you find the words *nuestra, nuestras,* and *nuestros.* What words determine which form of the adjective is used? Tell a partner which form you would use with the word *mamá.* And *papá?*

B You also find the phrases *sus hijos* and *su cama.* What does the word *su (s)* mean in each of those instances? To whom does *sus* refer in the first caption? To whom does *su* refer in the second caption?

266   Capítulo 8

Options

Strategies for Reaching All Students

Spanish-Speaking Students
Ex. 1: Have Spanish-speaking students write out this exercise.

Students Needing Extra Help
Have students begin their Organizers for the grammar portion.
Los verbos poner *y* hacer: Review *-er* verb endings from Chap. 4. Show students that these two verbs are presented together because of the *-go* in the *yo* form. Ask if they remember another verb that has *-go* in the *yo* form *(tengo).*
Ex. 1: Review compound subjects.

Extended Written Practice/Homework
1. Write two sentences telling how often you and another family member set the table. Refer to verb forms for *poner* on p. 267.
2. Write three sentences telling where you and your family put different things in your house: *Ponemos los calcetines en la cómoda.*
3. Write two sentences telling how often you and other family members make the bed.

266   Standards 1.2; 3.1; 4.1

Los verbos *poner* y *hacer*

The forms of *poner* ("to put, to place, to set") and *hacer* ("to make, to do") follow the pattern of other *-er* verbs in all except the *yo* forms, *pongo* and *hago*.

Here are all the present-tense forms of *poner* and *hacer*.

(yo)	pon**go** hag**o**	(nosotros) (nosotras)	pon**emos** hac**emos**
(tú)	pon**es** hac**es**	(vosotros) (vosotras)	pon**éis** hac**éis**
Ud. (él) (ella)	pon**e** hac**e**	Uds. (ellos) (ellas)	pon**en** hac**en**

1 Estas personas ayudan a una amiga a mudarse. Di en qué cuarto ponen las cosas.

Teresa pone el espejo en el baño.

  Teresa

a. Ud.

 b. Elena y tú

c. tú

d. yo

e. Roberto y Paco

f. Enrique y yo

Gramática en contexto   267

Cultural Notes

(p. 267, realia)
This Spanish-language moving guide from the U.S. Postal Service helps ensure a smooth *mudanza* both for people who are moving and for the postal service. Ask students: What are the topics covered in this guide? What do you think *sin percances* might mean? (Answer: without mishaps)

Present & Practice

Re-enter / Recycle

Ex. 2: school subjects from Chap. 2

Ex. 3: places and buildings from Chaps. 3 and 6

Answers

2 ESTUDIANTE A

a. ¿Qué tarea hace Felipe todos los días?

b. ...hacen Fabiola y tú ...

c. ...hacen Irene y Bárbara ...

d. ...hace Ud....

e. ...hacen Lupe y Raúl ...

f. ...haces tú ...

ESTUDIANTE B

a. Generalmente hace la tarea de ciencias.

b. ...hacemos ... español.

c. ...hacen ... ciencias de la salud.

d. ...hago ... inglés.

e. ...hacen ... ciencias sociales.

f. ...hago ... *(Answers will vary.)*

 Practice Wkbk. 8-5

 Writing Activity 8-D

 Prueba 8-5

 ¿Qué tareas tienen que hacer estos estudiantes todos los días?

A —*¿Qué tarea hacen Carlos y Javier todos los días?*

B —*Generalmente hacen la tarea de matemáticas.*

Carlos y Javier

a. Felipe	**b. Fabiola y tú**	**c. Irene y Bárbara**
d. Ud.	**e. Lupe y Raúl**	**f. tú**

Los verbos que terminan en -ir

You already know the pattern of endings of present-tense *-ar* and *-er* verbs. There is one other group of regular verbs, those that end in *-ir.* *Vivir* ("to live") is a regular *-ir* verb. Here are all its present-tense forms.

(yo)	vivo	(nosotros) (nosotras)	viv**imos**
(tú)	viv**es**	(vosotros) (vosotras)	viv**ís**
Ud. (él) (ella)	viv**e**	Uds. (ellos) (ellas)	viv**en**

• Notice that the pattern of endings for *-ir* verbs is identical to that of *-er* verbs, except for the *nosotros* and *vosotros* forms.

• Notice that *salir* is a regular *-ir* verb in the present tense except for its *yo* form: *(yo) salgo.*

268   Capítulo 8

Options

Strategies for Reaching All Students

Students Needing Extra Help

Ex. 2: Review compound subjects. *Los verbos que terminan en* -ir: Show similarities with *-er* and *-ir* endings. Tell students they practiced the *yo / tú* forms of *vivir* in Ex. 2 in the *Empecemos a conversar.* Ex. 3: Remind students that when a question is asked with the *Uds.* form, the answer will be in the *nosotros* form. Therefore, students should be looking for *nosotros* on the drawing.

Extended Written Practice/Homework

1. Write three sentences telling where you and your family live and where other people you know live. Use *cerca* and *lejos* in your sentences.

2. Write three sentences telling at what time you, your family, and your friends leave home. Use *salir de casa* in your sentences.

Multiple Intelligences

Verbal/Linguistic

See Exs. 2–3.

Visual/Spatial

See Practice Wkbk. 8-5 and 8-6 and Writing Activity 8-D.

3 Mira *(look at)* el dibujo de este pueblo *(town)*. Di a tu compañero(a) si estas personas viven cerca o lejos de ciertos lugares *(places)*.

A —¿Dónde viven David y Agustín?

B —*Viven cerca del centro comercial.*
  o: *Viven lejos de la escuela.*

David y Agustín

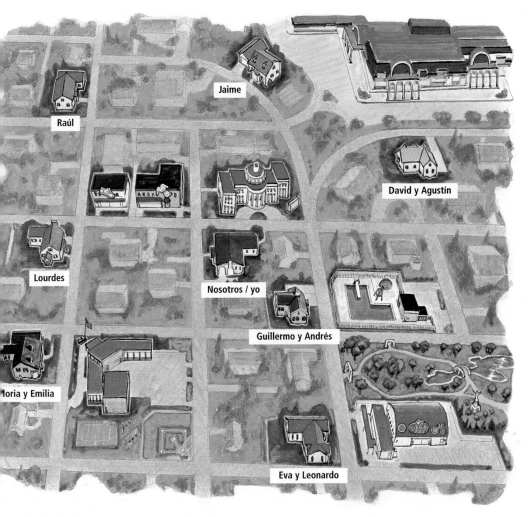

a. Gloria y Emilia
b. Uds.
c. Eva y Leonardo
d. Raúl
e. tú
f. Jaime
g. Lourdes
h. Guillermo y Andrés

Gramática en contexto   269

3 This exercise requires the contraction *del (de + el)*. Ask students to notice what happens to the definite article in the expression *cerca del centro comercial*, as contrasted with the expression *cerca de la escuela*. Remind them that items b. and e. refer to the same location.

ESTUDIANTE A
a. ¿Dónde viven Gloria y Emilia?
b. ... viven Uds.?
c. ... viven Eva y Leonardo?
d. ... vive Raúl?
e. ... vives tú?
f. ... vive Jaime?
g. ... vive Lourdes?
h. ... viven Guillermo y Andrés?

ESTUDIANTE B
Answers may vary depending on students' perception of distance.
a. Viven cerca de la escuela (lejos del centro comercial).
b. Vivimos cerca de (lejos de) ...
c. Viven cerca de (lejos de) ...
d. Vive cerca de (lejos de) ...
e. Vivo cerca de (lejos de) ...
f. Vive cerca de (lejos de) ...
g. Vive cerca de (lejos de) ...
h. Viven cerca de (lejos de) ...

 Practice Wkbk. 8-6

 Prueba 8-6

Present & Practice

Re-enter / Recycle
Ex. 4: activities from Chaps. 1 and 3, expressing likes and preferences from Chap. 4, family and friends from Chap. 5
Ex. 5: activities from Chaps. 1 and 3, adjective agreement from Chaps. 1 and 4

Answers

4 ESTUDIANTE A

a. ¿Qué prefiere tu abuelo, ir de pesca o ver la tele(visión)?
b. ¿Qué prefiere tu papá, cocinar o lavar los platos?
c. ¿Qué prefieren tus amigos(as), tomar el sol o nadar?
d. ¿Qué prefieren tus primos, ir de compras o pasar la aspiradora?
e. ¿Qué prefieren ustedes, ir a una fiesta o ir al cine?
f. ¿Qué prefiere tu amiga, leer o jugar videojuegos?

ESTUDIANTE B

Answers will vary.
a. Mi abuelo prefiere . . .
b. Mi papá prefiere . . .
c. Mis amigos(as) prefieren . . .
d. Mis primos prefieren . . .
e. Nosotros(as) preferimos . . .
f. Mi amiga prefiere . . .

El verbo *preferir*

Preferir ("to prefer") is an *e → ie* stem-changing verb, similar to *querer* and *pensar.* Here are all its present-tense forms.

(yo)	pref**ie**ro	(nosotros) (nosotras)	preferimos
(tú)	pref**ie**res	(vosotros) (vosotras)	preferís
Ud. (él) (ella)	pref**ie**re	Uds. (ellos) (ellas)	pref**ie**ren

• Notice that the endings of *preferir* follow the pattern of regular *-ir* verbs, like *vivir.*

4 Con un(a) compañero(a), túrnate para preguntar y contestar *(asking and answering)* sobre las preferencias de estas personas.

A —*¿Qué prefiere tu hermana, jugar fútbol o tenis?*
B —*Mi hermana prefiere jugar tenis.*

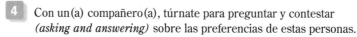
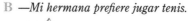

tu hermana

a. tu abuelo   b. tu papá   c. tus amigos(as)

d. tus primos   e. ustedes   f. tu amiga

Options

Strategies for Reaching All Students

Spanish-Speaking Students
Ex. 4: Ask Spanish-speaking students: *¿En qué actividades prefieres participar en el verano? ¿Durante el año escolar?*

Students Needing Extra Help
El verbo preferir: Review stem-changing verbs from Chap. 7. Remind students that they practiced the *yo / tú* forms in Ex. 11 in the *Empecemos a conversar.* Using the Organizer, brainstorm examples of *preferir, querer,* and *pensar* + inf.
Ex. 5: Have students use their Organizers from Chap. 1.
Los adjetivos posesivos: Have students review their Chap. 5 Organizers with *mi, tu,* and *su.*

Extended Written Practice/Homework
1. Write three sentences telling what different people prefer to eat at different meals.
2. Write three sentences telling where you and others prefer to do the following: *ir al cine, ir de compras, ir de vacaciones.*
3. Write three sentences telling where your relatives live: *Nuestra tía vive en Ohio.*

5 Di que las personas prefieren hacer estos pasatiempos y por qué.

A —¿Qué prefiere hacer Nicolás?
B —Prefiere jugar béisbol. Es muy deportista.

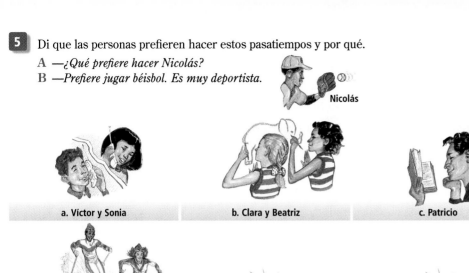

a. Víctor y Sonia   b. Clara y Beatriz   c. Patricio

d. Antonio y Claudia   e. tú   f. tú y tu familia

Los adjetivos posesivos: *Su* y *nuestro*

You already know that when we want to tell what belongs to someone and to show relationships, we can use *mi(s), tu(s),* and *su(s).* Here are the other possessive adjectives.

nuestro	primo	**nuestra**	prima
nuestros	primos	**nuestras**	primas
vuestro*	tío	**vuestra**	tía
vuestros	tíos	**vuestras**	tías
su	hermano	**su**	hermana
sus	hermanos	**sus**	hermanas

*Vuestro, -a, -os, -as is used mainly in Spain. We will use it occasionally and you should learn to recognize it.

- Like other adjectives, the possessive adjectives agree in number with the nouns that follow them. Only *nuestro* and *vuestro* have different masculine and feminine endings.

Gramática en contexto   271

Practice

Re-enter / Recycle

Exs. 6–7: adjectives describing physical characteristics from Chap. 5, colors from Chap. 6

Answers

6 Remind students that they may describe their own home or someone else's. If an item does not apply to their family situation, they may respond *No tenemos . . . .*
a. Nuestra mesa (no) es de metal.
b. Nuestras sillas (no) son de madera.
c. Nuestros sillones (no) son antiguos.
d. Nuestro sofá (no) es de cuero.
e. Nuestro equipo de sonido (no) es moderno.
f. Nuestros cuadros (no) son bonitos.
g. Nuestro garaje (no) es para dos coches.
h. Nuestra sala de estar (no) es cómoda.
i. Statements will vary.

7 a.–i. Statements will vary. Make sure students use correct possessive adjective forms.

---

6 Describe parte de tu casa o de otra casa. Usa las palabras *(words)* de abajo *(below).*

casa / azul
Nuestra casa (no) es azul.
dormitorios / grandes
Nuestros dormitorios (no) son grandes.

a. mesa / de metal
b. sillas / de madera
c. sillones / antiguos
d. sofá / de cuero
e. equipo de sonido / moderno
f. cuadros / bonitos
g. garaje / para dos coches
h. sala de estar / cómoda
i. 💡

7 Intercambia *(exchange)* tu hoja del Ejercicio 6 con un(a) compañero(a). Usa esta información para describir su casa a otro(a) estudiante.

La casa de los Johnson es azul. Sus dormitorios son muy grandes.

PASO CULTURAL Ushuaia, on the Argentine (east) side of the island of Tierra del Fuego, is the southernmost city in the world and the closest to Antarctica. The island's western side is owned by Chile. It is said that Tierra del Fuego (Land of Fire) was named by Ferdinand Magellan, the Portuguese explorer, who saw fires on its shore. These fires were used by the island's inhabitants to warm their houses and to keep invaders away. What are some advantages and disadvantages of living in such a remote location?

Una casa típica en Ushuaia, Tierra del Fuego, Argentina

272

Options

Strategies for Reaching All Students

Students Needing Extra Help
Ex. 6: Show students that they will use *es* or *son,* depending on how many objects are discussed.
Ex. 7: Remind students that *su(s)* does not reflect gender. Give examples.

Multiple Intelligences
Verbal/Linguistic
See Audio Activities 8.4 and 8.5.
Visual/Spatial
See Practice Wkbk. 8-8 and 8-9, Writing Activity 8-F, and Comm. Act. BLM 8-2.

Una casa cerca de San José, Costa Rica

Ahora lo sabes

Can you:

► tell where someone puts something?
—Generalmente (yo) ___ mis papeles en mi carpeta.

► say what someone makes or does?
—Ana María y yo ___ las camas todos los días.

► tell where a person lives?
—Mis abuelos ___ en Los Ángeles.

► tell what someone prefers?
—Mis hermanos y yo ___ ir al cine el sábado.

► describe possession using *su* and *nuestra*?
—___ mesa es redonda pero ___ mesa es cuadrada.

Una casa en Copacabana, Bolivia

MORE PRACTICE

Más práctica y tarea, pp. 530–532
Practice Workbook 8–5, 8–9

Gramática en contexto 273

Cultural Notes ☀

Paso cultural
Possible answers: Advantages would be that it's not crowded and its natural beauty is relatively intact. Disadvantages would be its physical isolation from the rest of the world.

(p. 272, photo)
Formerly little more than an outpost, Ushuaia (population 44,000) has become an important industrial and tourist center, with housing construction growing at a rapid pace. Visitors come to see the spectacular

scenery of Tierra del Fuego: lakes, streams, forests, mountains, and fjords. Other attractions include the Museo del fin del mundo (Museum at the End of the Earth) and the site of a famous prison that was built in 1902 because of Ushuaia's remote location.

(p. 273, top photo)
With its moderate climate, safe streets, and easy access to medical services, the area near San José, Costa Rica has become a desirable place to live for many elderly

Americans. Retirement colonies have brought jobs to the area, but they have also raised the cost of living. Ask students: Can you think of any other possible benefits or problems that these colonies might bring? (Answer: One problem is that native residents will not be able to afford to live there; one benefit is that these new residents will bring amenities and physical improvements to the area.)

Apply

Todo junto

Actividades

Una casa moderna en Cantel, Guatemala

1 Usando el dibujo de la página 269, escoge una casa e imagina que vives allí. Tu compañero(a) va a adivinar *(guess)* dónde vives con preguntas como las siguientes.

¿Vives cerca o lejos del centro comercial?
¿Es amarilla tu casa?

2 ¿Qué prefieren hacer tu compañero(a) y sus amigos cuando hace mucho calor o mucho frío? Pregunta y contesta y anota *(make a note of)* sus actividades preferidas. Después, en grupos de cuatro o cinco personas, haz *(make)* una lista de las actividades más populares de la clase.

3 Con un(a) compañero(a), haz una lista de algunos quehaceres. Pregunta y contesta cuáles tienen que hacer Uds. Después, haz un informe *(report)* para la clase. Tus compañeros van a preguntar cuáles son los quehaceres que prefieren Uds.

Options

Strategies for Reaching All Students

Spanish-Speaking Students
Ex. 3: Have Spanish-speaking students summarize : *Escucha bien lo que dicen en clase de los quehaceres. ¿Cuáles son los quehaceres más comunes para los estudiantes en tu clase? ¿Tienes tú estos mismos quehaceres u otros?*

Students Needing Extra Help
Ex. 1: Give students time to organize and formulate questions. Suggest that each pair formulate four or five questions.
Ex. 2: Review weather from Chap. 7. Have students use their Organizers from Chaps. 1, 3, and 7.
Ex. 3: Have students use their Organizers. Keep track of the information on a chart for reporting purposes.

Enrichment
Ex. 3: As a homework assignment, students can tell which family member does which household chore, how often or when, and whether or not that person likes doing the chore.

Cooperative Learning
Divide the class into groups of three or four students. Tell them that as owners of an apartment building, they are responsible for the upkeep and maintenance, with a budget

Conexiones

Las ciencias sociales

Casas diferentes

Las casas pueden variar mucho de una región del mundo a otra. Pero siempre reflejan la vida de la gente y lo que es importante para ella.

1. Haz una lista en español para describir el comedor japonés.

2. Haz otra lista para describir el comedor costarricense.

3. Con un(a) compañero(a), haz un diagrama de Venn para indicar en qué se parecen y en qué se diferencian los dos cuartos. Los tres segmentos del diagrama deben ser: Comedor japonés, Comedor costarricense y Los dos.

4. Con tu compañero(a), imagina cómo puede ser la vida de la gente que vive en estas dos casas.

Todo junto 275

Apply

Process Reading

For a description of process reading, see p. 48.

Answers
Antes de leer
Answers will vary.

Mira la lectura
Answers will vary.

¡Vamos a leer!

Antes de leer

STRATEGY ➤ **Using prior knowledge**

Remember the story of Cinderella? Did you ever wonder what it would be like to be in her shoes? In this reading, a young man is about to find out. Use the pictures and what you know about Cinderella to predict what this reading might be about.

Mira la lectura

STRATEGY ➤ **Skimming**

Skim through the story. Is it what you expected?

La historia de Esteban

Esteban es un muchacho de 18 años. Vive en una casa más o menos grande con su padre, su madrastra y un hermanastro y una hermanastra. Pero su padre está frecuentemente fuera del país. ¿Y quién hace todos los quehaceres de la casa? Esteban, ¡claro! Los hace, pero no está nada contento.

Madrastra: Tienes que lavar los platos y pasar la aspiradora... y cortar el césped.
Esteban: Pero . . .

UN DÍA . . .

TV: . . . La princesa Gabriela de Xilá está de visita aquí. Hay una gran fiesta en su honor.
Madrastra: ¡Claro que vamos a la fiesta!

Madrastra: Tú no puedes ir a la fiesta. Tienes que preparar nuestra ropa.

LA NOCHE DE LA FIESTA .
Hermanastro y Hermanast
Hasta luego, Esteban.

276 Capítulo 8

Options

Strategies for Reaching All Students

Spanish-Speaking Students
Have Spanish-speaking students rewrite the last four panels of the story.

 Un paso más Ex. 8-H

Students Needing Extra Help
Antes de leer: Ask for a volunteer to summarize the Cinderella story.
Infórmate 2: Review the term "turning point."

Enrichment
Explain that *Xilá* is a Nahuatl word that is actually the name of a princess in a Nicaraguan legend.
Aplicación: Have students work in pairs and propose a different solution to Esteban's situation. Ask: Instead of having the fairy godmother appear, what would you suggest Esteban do? How would you end the story?

Infórmate

STRATEGIES> **Using prior knowledge**
Recognizing word
families

Often you can use Spanish words you know to figure out the meaning of new words. For example: *madrastra, hermanastra,* and *hermanastro*. What names for family members do you recognize as parts of these words? Then think about the characters in Cinderella. Use this information to figure out the meaning of the three words. What do you think *madrina* means?

1 Compare the story with Cinderella. How are they alike and how are they different?

2 What is the turning point in the story? What happens?

3 Do you agree with the way the story ends? Why or why not?

Aplicación

What do you think *padrastro* means?

Madrina: Hola, Esteban. Soy la madrina de la Cenicienta. Y tú también vas a ir a la fiesta. A ver, ¿dónde están tu perro y la aspiradora? Los voy a convertir en un chófer y una limosina.

Pero ¿quién es? ¡Qué guapo! ¡Debe ser un príncipe! ¡Mira los zapatos de vidrio!

Hermanastra: Mamá . . . ¡Es Esteban!
Hermanastro: Pero ¿qué hace aquí?
Madrastra: No sé, hijo . . .

UNA SEMANA MÁS TARDE . . .
Esteban: Voy a ser el asistente personal de la princesa. Y ¡no voy a hacer nunca más los quehaceres!

¡Vamos a leer! 277

Infórmate
madre, hermana, and *hermano /* stepmother, stepsister, and step-brother / godmother

1 Answers will vary, but similarities may include the stepmother and the glass shoes. Differences may include the father and step-brother; a dog and vacuum cleaner (instead of mice and a pumpkin); and Esteban as the personal assistant at the end of the story.

2 The fairy godmother appears to change Esteban's life. He goes to the party and eventually becomes the personal assistant to the princess.

3 Answers will vary.

Aplicación
Students should be able to figure out the meaning (stepfather) from *padre.*

www Internet Activities

Multiple Intelligences
Verbal/Linguistic
Have students read the selection aloud.
Visual/Spatial and Bodily/Kinesthetic
1) When students have successfully completed 1, 2, and 3 of the *Infórmate* section, write the eight scenes of the story on strips of paper and arrange them in random order on the board. Then write the numbers 1–8 to the side. Have students come up and place the strips in the correct sequential order.

2) You may also wish to divide students into eight groups. Assign each group one of the scenes in the story, have them write or redraw it, and then have them arrange each scene on the board in sequential order. Ask a member from each group to describe their scene and how it fits in the story.

Apply

Process Writing
For information regarding developing a writing portfolio, see p. 50.

Multicultural Perspectives
Mud is used to keep houses looking new and clean in some countries in Central America. The color of the soil used varies from region to region. In some areas it is gray; in others, peach-colored or white. The soil is mixed with water to form a paste and then applied to the walls to make them smooth and new. Ask students what they and their family members do for home maintenance and upkeep.

Using Photos
Ask: *Describe las casas en las fotos. ¿Te gustaría vivir en una de estas casas? ¿Por qué o por qué no?*

Pasos vivos 1 CD-ROM
Word Processor

¡Vamos a escribir!

En la zona de Chapultepec, Ciudad de México

Una casa al estilo de Gaudí en Los Ángeles

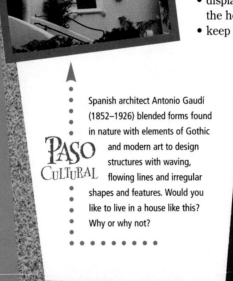

Everyone can picture an ideal home—the perfect dream house. How would you describe your dream house? Write an ad in Spanish for a dream house for sale.

1 First, think about the house plan and list the rooms. Is it a one- or two-story house? Name three or four special features.

2 Then write at least five sentences describing the house as if you were trying to sell it. You can start with the phrase *Se vende casa* (House for sale).

3 Show your description to a partner. Then revise and edit it. Recopy your corrected description. You might want to add a sketch of the floor plan with the rooms labeled.

4 Now you are ready to share your work. You can:
- collect all the ads into a book called *Se venden casas* and exchange books with another class
- display the ads on a bulletin board for each student to choose the house he or she would like to buy
- keep your ad in your writing portfolio

Una hacienda tradicional en San Antonio de Areco, Argentina

PASO CULTURAL
Spanish architect Antonio Gaudí (1852–1926) blended forms found in nature with elements of Gothic and modern art to design structures with waving, flowing lines and irregular shapes and features. Would you like to live in a house like this? Why or why not?

278 Capítulo 8

Options

Strategies for Reaching All Students

Students Needing Extra Help
Step 1: Students may not be familiar with the term "special features"; give them some examples.
Step 2: Have students use their Organizers, emphasizing adjectives. Brainstorm and model some sentences. You may wish to use real newspaper ads as a possible source.

Enrichment
Step 2: To give students ideas about sales pitches, bring in real estate magazines or newspaper sections in English and study the language used in them. The properties are often described as having qualities that go well with buyers' personalities, or as themselves having "personalities." Encourage students to write their ads along these lines (as well as listing house size, location, and price).

Follow-up activity: If students choose a house they would like to buy, have them state the reasons. This can then become another speaking or writing activity.

Multiple Intelligences
Musical/Rhythmic
Have students write a jingle to accompany their completed ads from *¡Vamos a escribir!*
Visual/Spatial
See steps 2–3.

¡Vamos a escribir! 279

Cultural Notes

Paso cultural
Answers will vary.

(p. 278, top photo)
House in Los Angeles, California, built in the unique Gaudí style. Gaudí spent most of his adult life in Barcelona, building residences for rich patrons and, most importantly, la Iglesia de la Sagrada Familia, which was left unfinished after his death.

(p. 278, bottom photo)
The Argentine *hacienda* or *estancia* developed in the eighteenth century, when wealthy ranchers consolidated their control over land, water, and cattle. The world of the *estancia* and *gaucho* (cowboy) continues to be a focus in Argentine movies, literature, and national identity. Ask students: Do you think that the U.S. cowboy culture is still a focus for Americans, as the *gaucho* culture is for Argentines? Explain.

(p. 279, photo)
This sprawling, luxurious house is in one of Mexico City's wealthiest residential areas, Las Lomas de Chapultepec. The stucco walls, tiled roof, arches, and grillwork are all in the traditional Spanish style. Within the walls of most of the homes in this neighborhood are such amenities as pools, tennis courts, and elaborate gardens.

Assess & Summarize

Test Preparation

You may want to assign parts of this section as written homework or as an in-class writing activity prior to administering the *Examen de habilidades.*

Answers

Listening: *Sí, puedes ir al cine con tu amiga, pero primero tienes que limpiar el refrigerador, sacar la basura, sacudir los muebles, lavar los platos y arreglar tu cuarto.* Answers will vary, but students should choose from among these chores to help Marina: clean the refrigerator, take out the garbage, dust the furniture, wash the dishes, and pick up her room. Answers will vary for the time it takes to perform two of the chores. When they finish, they'll go to the movies.

Reading: Answers will vary.

Writing: Writing samples will vary, but students should use chapter vocabulary.

Culture: Answers will vary. Students should make reference to the *Perspectiva cultural:* In Sevilla, a patio is more like a garden or courtyard in the middle of the house. In Madrid, it is an air shaft in an apartment building. Both let air and light in and offer a space for people to talk.

Repaso ¿Lo sabes bien?

This section will help you organize your studying for the proficiency test, where you will be asked to do similar, though not identical, tasks. There will not be any models on the test.

► Listening

Can you understand when people talk about their household chores? Listen as your teacher reads a sample similar to what you will hear on the test. This is a note from Marina's mother explaining what Marina has to do on Saturday. What could you do to help Marina? How long do you think it would take you to do two of these chores? What are you going to do when you finish?

► Reading

Can you understand a description of a dream house? Read the text that follows. Do you agree with some of the things María Elena wants?

"Quiero tener una casa no muy grande y amueblarla con cosas que me gustan—prácticas pero bonitas. Y me gusta vivir cómodamente. Quiero un equipo de sonido, una videocasetera, una piscina, una cancha de tenis, . . . ¡y otra persona para hacer todos los quehaceres!"

► Writing

Can you write a letter to a friend describing the new house or apartment you've just moved into? Here is a sample:

> Querido Ernesto:
> Vivo con mi madre en un apartamento de Manhattan. Tenemos dos dormitorios, un baño, una cocina y una sala. Nuestro apartamento es pequeño, pero tenemos muchos muebles. En la sala hay una mesa con ocho sillas, un sofá con dos sillones, tres mesitas, un escritorio, tres lámparas, diez cuadros y dos espejos. Menos mal que en mi cuarto no hay muchas cosas. Tengo sólo una cama y una cómoda. Me gusta donde vivo, pero quisiera tener una casa más grande.
>
> Tu amiga,
> Magdalena

► Culture

Can you describe a patio in Sevilla and in Madrid and its uses?

► Speaking

Can you talk about household chores? Create a dialogue with your partner. Do you and your friend like and dislike the same chores? Here is a sample dialogue:

A —*¿Tienes quehaceres de la casa para el sábado?*
B —*Sí. Por la mañana tengo que cortar el césped, lavar los platos y sacar la basura.*
A —*A mí no me gusta ni sacar la basura ni limpiar el baño, pero lo hago todos los sábados. Prefiero hacer las camas.*

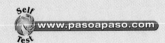

Self Test www.pasoapaso.com

280   Capítulo 8

Options

Strategies for Reaching All Students

Students Needing Extra Help
Listening: Model the answers to the questions.
Writing: Have students practice writing another letter. Tell them what you will be expecting from them in this exercise.

Culture: Review the *Perspectiva cultural.*
Speaking: Be sure that responses are appropriate to the questions. In both this and the writing section, give students time to prepare. You may want to give them the assignment in advance.

Resumen del vocabulario

Use the vocabulary from this chapter to help you:

► tell where you live

► describe your home

► name household chores

to talk about where someone lives
cerca (de)
lejos (de)
vivir: (yo) vivo
　　　 (tú) vives

to talk about houses or apartments
el apartamento
el baño
la casa (de . . . pisos)
el césped
la cocina
el comedor
el cuarto
el dormitorio
el garaje
el lavadero
el (primer) piso
la sala
la sala de estar
el sótano

to name household items
la cama
el cartel
el coche
la cómoda
las cosas
el cuadro
el equipo de sonido
el escritorio
el espejo

la estufa
el guardarropa
la lámpara
los muebles
la puerta
el refrigerador
la silla
el sillón, *pl.* los sillones
el sofá
la ventana
la videocasetera

to describe household items
antiguo, -a
bastante
cómodo, -a
cuadrado, -a
de cuero
de madera
de metal
incómodo, -a
limpio, -a
moderno, -a
redondo, -a
sucio, -a

to indicate possession
nuestro, -a
su, -s (here: *their*)

to name chores around a home
arreglar
cortar (el césped)
hacer: (yo) hago
　　　　 (tú) haces
hacer la cama
lavar la ropa / los platos
limpiar el baño
pasar la aspiradora
poner: (yo) pongo
　　　　 (tú) pones
poner / quitar la mesa
el quehacer (de la casa)
sacar la basura
sacudir los muebles

to indicate preferences
preferir (e → ie)

to indicate obligation
tener que + *inf.*

to indicate that someone is right or wrong
(no) tener razón

to indicate whether you agree with someone or something
(no) estar de acuerdo

other useful expressions
más (here: *else*)

Resumen 281

Assessment

 Prueba cumulativa

 Examen de habilidades

 Test Generator

Additional Assessment Options

 Comm. Act. BLMs

Small Group Activities
Situation Cards

 Pasos vivos 1 CD-ROM
Slide Presentation Maker, Video Presentation Maker, Word Processor, Spindle

 ¿Lo sabes bien? Video Quiz

www Internet Activities
Self-Test

CAPÍTULO 9

THEME: HEALTH

SCOPE AND SEQUENCE Pages 282–311

COMMUNICATION

Topics

Parts of the body

Health

Physical sensations

Objectives

To talk about health and health practices in the Spanish-speaking world

To name parts of the body

To ask or describe how someone is feeling

To name ways to maintain good health

To name medical professions

To indicate how long something has been going on

To express and ask for an opinion

To name places to go or things to do when you are sick

CULTURE

Health and health practices

GRAMMAR

El verbo dormir

El complemento indirecto: Los pronombres me, te, le

La expresión hace . . . que

La sustantivación de adjetivos

Ancillaries available for use with Chapter 9

Multisensory/Technology

 Overheads, 46–50

 Audio Tapes and CDs

 Vocabulary Art Blackline Masters for Hands-On Learning, pp. 48–52/CD-ROM

 Classroom Crossword

Video

 Pasos vivos 1 CD-ROM

 Internet Activities www.pasoapaso.com

Print

 Practice Workbook, pp. 94–103

 Writing, Audio & Video Activities, pp. 53–58, 117–119, 168–169

 Communicative Activity Blackline Masters

Pair and Small Group Activities, pp. 64–69

Situation Cards, p. 70

 Un paso más: Actividades para ampliar tu español, pp. 50–55

TPR Storytelling

Assessment

 Assessment Program

Pruebas, pp. 127–137

Examen de habilidades, pp. 138–141

 Test Generator

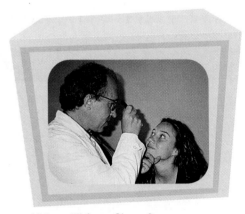

Video still from Chap. 9

Additional Technology

Planning Express, Teaching
Resources Library, and Clip Art
Library

 ¿Lo sabes bien?
Video Quiz

Cultural Overview

Health-Care Practices

Mexico addresses the medical needs of its rural populations through a compulsory service
program for medical students. Upon completion of medical school, interns and residents
must work for at least one year in the Instituto Mexicano de Seguro Social (IMSS) clinics in
rural areas. Local clinics have a permanent nursing staff in addition to the medical residents.
These clinics often have three or four beds for women in labor or for the very ill. In addition,
the IMSS system has a network of hospitals that support the clinics. Ambulances are available to transport people needing hospitalization from outlying clinics to hospitals in larger
towns.

Latin American doctors are more likely to practice from offices in their homes. Health care
can thus have a less institutionalized feeling. Physicians throughout Latin America, especially
in smaller cities and towns, may still make house calls.

Pharmacies are another important component of the health-care system. They are often
small, family-run businesses rather than large chain stores. When walking into a typical
large pharmacy in the U.S., the consumer is presented with aisle upon aisle of colorfully
packaged products. In contrast, a traditional *farmacia* will usually not carry the many items
we are accustomed to seeing. The only products available at a *farmacia* are medicinal drugs
and specific health-care related items. In a family-run pharmacy, the owner often greets customers at the door. Customers may purchase a single bandage or a single dose of a medicine. Prepackaged quantities are not as common as in the U.S.

Pharmacists play an important role in health care because they are legally able to dispense
many medications that are only available through a doctor's prescription in the U.S. Thus,
customers often rely on the pharmacist's medical expertise to recommend treatments
and medications when they are unable to visit a doctor or do not feel that such a visit is
necessary.

In addition to traditional modern medicine, *yerberos* are sometimes consulted for health
problems. These folk healers use the medicinal qualities of plants for healing. *Curanderos*
are also healers who treat both physical and spiritual ailments. Herb shops called *yerberías*
or *botánicas* sell a variety of products for both physical and spiritual healing.

Introduce

Re-entry of Concepts

The following list represents words, expressions, and grammar topics re-entered from *El primer paso* to Chap. 7.

El primer paso
Numbers 0–31
Calendar expressions

Chapter 1
Activities
Gustar expressions
Adjective agreement

Chapter 3
Activities
Places and buildings

Chapter 4
Foods

Chapter 6
Colors
Clothes
Direct object pronouns
Places and buildings

Chapter 7
Activities
Places and buildings

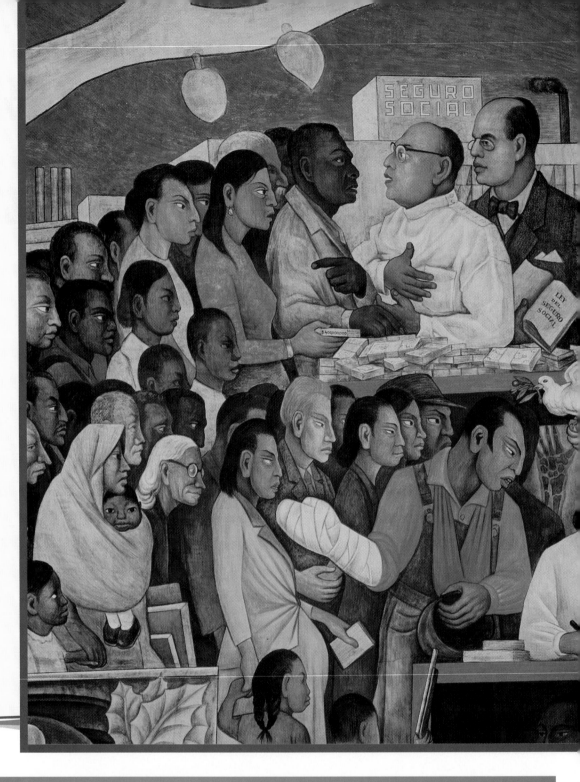

Planning

Cross-Curricular Connections

Art / Language Arts Connection (pp. 286–287)
Have each student secretly choose a well-known character or famous personality, write the person's name on a sheet of paper, and give it to you. For homework, each student prepares a drawing of the person chosen. On the bottom of the paper, they should write a short physical description and personality profile. To prepare for the next day, make copies of a list of all the names in alphabetical order with a blank next to each name. At the beginning of class, have students display the pictures and number them. Each student is then given a copy of the list and tries to match the names and numbers.

Health Connection (p. 308)
In small groups or pairs, have students prepare a poster advertising a new health product. Students should create a name, give a price, and a write a list that describes what the product does.

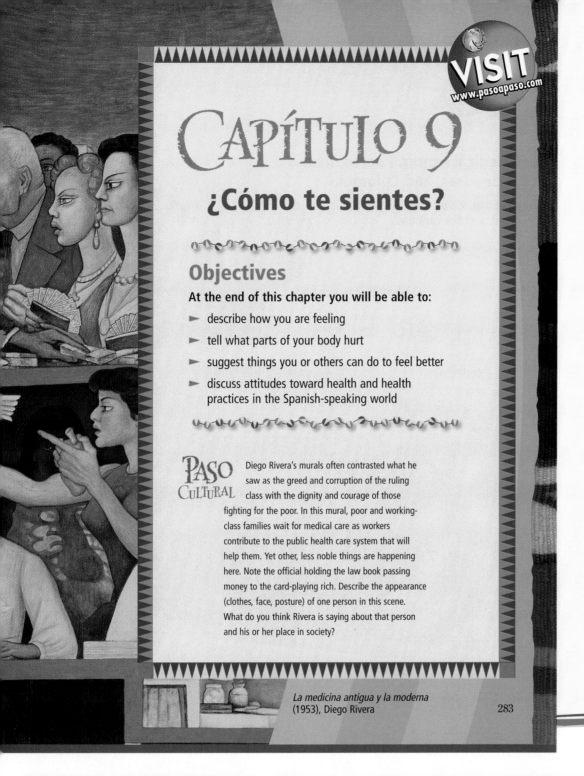

CAPÍTULO 9

¿Cómo te sientes?

Objectives

At the end of this chapter you will be able to:

► describe how you are feeling

► tell what parts of your body hurt

► suggest things you or others can do to feel better

► discuss attitudes toward health and health practices in the Spanish-speaking world

PASO CULTURAL

Diego Rivera's murals often contrasted what he saw as the greed and corruption of the ruling class with the dignity and courage of those fighting for the poor. In this mural, poor and working-class families wait for medical care as workers contribute to the public health care system that will help them. Yet other, less noble things are happening here. Note the official holding the law book passing money to the card-playing rich. Describe the appearance (clothes, face, posture) of one person in this scene. What do you think Rivera is saying about that person and his or her place in society?

La medicina antigua y la moderna (1953), Diego Rivera

283

Preview

Using the Video

This chapter's video focuses on health. Students will accompany one of our hosts in Madrid to the doctor's office and then to a class in flamenco dance.

To prepare students for the video, first ask them to predict what this chapter's tape will be about. Then have students watch the segment several times. After the first time, you may wish to have them brainstorm possible vocabulary and expressions they will need to talk about what they saw on the video. Ask students to identify: a) things they saw that were familiar to them, and b) things they saw that they probably would not see where they live.

Video segment 1: For more teaching suggestions, see the Video Teacher's Guide.

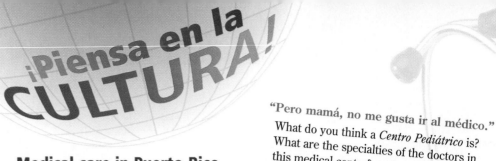

¡Piensa en la CULTURA!

Medical care in Puerto Rico, Honduras, and Colombia

Look at the pictures and read the captions.

Isla Verde, Puerto Rico

Medical personnel and facilities can be scarce in rural areas of Latin America. People may have to wait hours before they can be seen by visiting doctors.

"Pero mamá, no me gusta ir al médico."
What do you think a *Centro Pediátrico* is? What are the specialties of the doctors in this medical center?

Una clínica en Moramulca, Honduras

Moramulca, Honduras

284   Capítulo 9

Options

Strategies for Reaching All Students

Spanish-Speaking Students
Ask Spanish-speaking students to describe the photos in the chapter introduction. In addition, ask: *¿Qué haces tú cuando no te sientes bien?*

Students Needing Extra Help
Discuss some of the terminology we use in English to talk about health: fever, headache, and so on.

Multiple Intelligences
Visual/Spatial
See Using the Video and Critical Thinking: Synthesizing.

"Me lastimé el pie."

What do you think *Cruz Roja* means?
What do you think might have happened
to the boy? How might it have happened?

Cali, Colombia

Ayudando a un niño en Cali, Colombia

Cultural Exploration www.pasoapaso.com
Visit these countries on-line

¡Piensa en la cultura! 285

Cultural Notes

(p. 284, top photo)
This pediatric center in Isla Verde, a suburb of San Juan, is staffed by general pediatricians as well as a psychologist, a psychiatrist, and a podiatrist. Other *centros pediátricos* in Puerto Rico are exclusively for children with a life-threatening disease such as cancer or AIDS.

(p. 284, bottom photo)
U.S.-based mobile health clinics such as this one provide much-needed medical services in countries throughout Latin America. Contributing to these countries' public health problems are malnutrition, little or no provision for the sick who can't afford a

doctor, and a lack of clean water and proper sewerage systems. Decades of progress in the building of roads and hospitals in the Dominican Republic and Central America were wiped out after the deadly hurricane season of 1998.

Paso cultural
Answers will vary.

Present

Chapter Theme
Parts of the body and health

Communicative Objectives
- To name parts of the body
- To ask or describe how someone is feeling
- To name ways to maintain good health
- To name medical professions
- To indicate how long something has been going on
- To express and ask for an opinion
- To name places to go or things to do when you are sick

 Overheads 46–47

 Vocabulary Art BLMs/CD-ROM

 Pronunciation Tape 9-1

 Vocabulario para conversar A

Play

Using the Video
Video segment 2: See the Video Teacher's Guide.

 Video Activity B

Vocabulario para conversar

¡Ay! ¡Me duele el pie!

 **Chapter 9 Vocabulary**

Aquí tienes palabras y expresiones necesarias para hablar sobre las partes del cuerpo que te duelen y para sugerir *(suggest)* qué puedes hacer para sentirte mejor. Léelas varias veces y practícalas con un(a) compañero(a) en las páginas siguientes.

la garganta

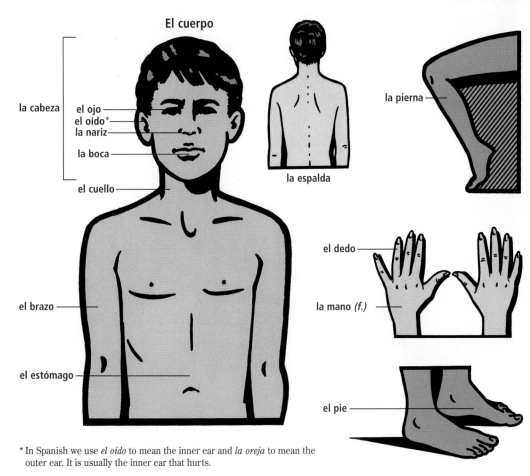

El cuerpo

la cabeza
el ojo
el oído*
la nariz
la boca
el cuello
el brazo
el estómago

la espalda

la pierna

el dedo
la mano *(f.)*
el pie

* In Spanish we use *el oído* to mean the inner ear and *la oreja* to mean the outer ear. It is usually the inner ear that hurts.

286   Capítulo 9

Options

Strategies for Reaching All Students

Spanish-Speaking Students

 Un paso más Exs. 9-A, 9-B, 9-C, 9-D

Students Needing Extra Help
Have students start their Organizers. Emphasize the difference between *médico(a)* and *doctor(a)*.
Show the connection between *doler, el dolor,* and *duele(n).*
If necessary, tell students that *hace* + time expression + *que* will be explained in the grammar section.

Emphasize the second footnote on p. 287. Since students see "my," "your," etc. in the translation, they will be tempted to use *mi, tu,* etc. They will probably need frequent reminders.

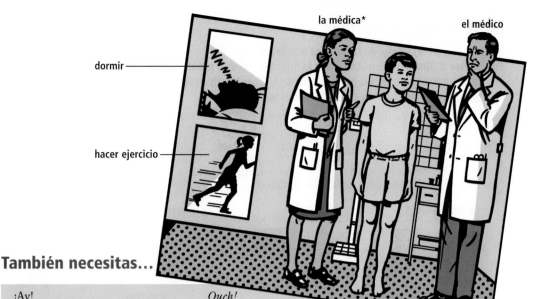

la médica*

el médico

dormir

hacer ejercicio

También necesitas...

¡Ay!	Ouch!
Me siento bien / mal.	I feel well / ill.
¿Qué pasa?	What's the matter?
doler (o → ue)	to hurt, to ache
¿Qué te duele?	Where does it hurt?
(A mí / ti) me / te duele(n)† ___.	My / your ___ hurts (hurt).
(No me duele) nada.	Nothing (hurts me).
derecho, -a	right
izquierdo, -a	left
¿Cuánto (tiempo) hace que ___?	How long has it been since ___? / (For) how long ___?
Hace + time expression + que ___.	It's been + time expression + since ___. / ___ for + time expression
(Yo) creo que ___.	I think that ___.
Debes quedarte en la cama.	You should stay in bed.
llamar	here: to call

¿Y qué quiere decir . . . ?

el dedo del pie
el dolor

---

* To refer to or address a physician, we use the term *doctor(a):* —*Doctor, me duele mucho la cabeza.*

† With expressions like *me / te duele(n)*, we usually use the definite article when talking about body parts: *Me duele el brazo.*

Vocabulario para conversar   287

Grammar Preview
Use of *me / te* with *doler* and the expression *hace . . . que* are presented lexically. Their explanation appears in the grammar section.

Teaching Suggestions
Preparing students to speak: Use one or two options from each of the categories of Comprehensible Input, Physical Response, or Limited Verbal Response. For a complete explanation of these categories and some sample activities, see pp. T22–T23.

Bring in one or more children's dolls for teaching the vocabulary in this section. In advance, prepare stick-on labels with the names of the parts of the body taught in this chapter.

Class Starter Review
On the day following initial presentation, you might begin the class with this activity:
Play *Simón dice* with you leading the class. Ask students to point to various parts of the body. Have students play the role of Simón on subsequent days.

www Internet Activities
Juegos

Learning Spanish Through Action
STAGING VOCABULARY: *Dibujen*
MATERIALS: large sheets of plain paper; colored pencils or markers
DIRECTIONS: Tell students that they are going to draw an extraterrestrial. Describe an alien creature using vocabulary for various parts of the body, colors, and sizes. (As an option, have individuals go to the chalkboard and draw one part of the body. Continue until you have completed the whole creature.)

Multiple Intelligences
Bodily/Kinesthetic
See Learning Spanish Through Action and Class Starter Review.
Verbal/Linguistic
See Pronunciation Tape 9-1.
Visual/Spatial
See Overheads 46–47, the Vocabulary Art BLMs/CD-ROM, and Using the Video.

Practice & Apply

Re-enter / Recycle
Ex. 3: calendar expressions from
El primer paso
Ex. 6: activities from Chaps. 1
and 3

Grammar Preview
Ex. 4 previews nominalization of
adjectives. The explanation of this
grammar point is on p. 303.

**Answers: Empecemos a
conversar**

1 ESTUDIANTE A
a. ¿Qué pasa? ¿Te duele el pie?
b. . . .¿Te duele el brazo?
c. . . .¿Te duele la pierna?
d. . . .¿Te duele la garganta?

ESTUDIANTE B
a.–d. No, me duele(n) . . . . *(Endings will vary, but may include:* la
mano, los dedos, los pies, el
cuello.)

2 ESTUDIANTE A
a. Hoy no puedo hacer ejercicio.
Me siento mal; me duele la
cabeza.
b. . . . la espalda.
c. . . . la garganta.
d. . . . el estómago.
e. . . . el cuello.

ESTUDIANTE B
a.–e. Creo que debes . . . .
*(Endings will vary. Remind stu-
dents to transpose* no *before*
debes *in the fourth and fifth possible responses for* Estudiante B.)

Empecemos a conversar

**Túrnate con un(a) compañero(a) para ser *Estudiante A* y
Estudiante B. Reemplacen las palabras subrayadas con palabras
representadas o escritas en los recuadros.** **quiere decir que
puedes escoger *(choose)* tu propia respuesta.**

1 A —¿Qué pasa? ¿Te duele <u>la cabeza</u>?
B —No, me duelen <u>los ojos</u>.
o: No, no me duele nada. Me siento bien.

Estudiante A   Estudiante B

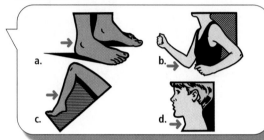 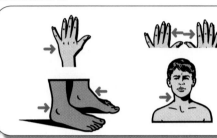

2 A —Hoy no puedo hacer ejercicio.
Me siento mal; me duele <u>el oído</u>.
B —Creo que debes <u>llamar al médico</u>.

Estudiante A   Estudiante B

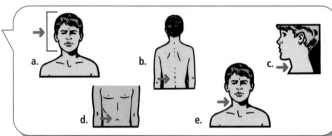

descansar
dormir
llamar al médico
no hacer ejercicio
no practicar deportes
quedarte en la cama

Options

Strategies for Reaching All Students

Spanish-Speaking Students
Ex. 5: Ask: *¿Qué debes hacer si estás enfer-
mo(a) y no puedes ir a la escuela?
Menciona tres cosas.*

 Un paso más Ex. 9-E

Students Needing Extra Help
Ex. 1: Allow students to use the second
response with *nada* only once.
Ex. 2: Encourage *Estudiante B* to use differ-
ent responses, not just one.
Ex. 6: Have students use their Organizers.
Ex. 7: Be specific if students have difficulty
answering. Ask questions such as: *¿Te
duele el brazo?* Have students refer back to
Ex. 1.

Enrichment
Ex. 2: To vary this dialogue, have pairs of
students take turns telling each other what
other activities they can't do because a certain part of their body hurts. Students
should give each other advice on how to get
rid of the pain. For example: *No puedo leer.
Me duelen los ojos. (Debes dormir) / No
puedo hablar. Me duele la garganta. (Debes
ir al médico.)*
Ex. 4: As a homework assignment, ask students to create a dialogue between two

3 A —¿Cuánto tiempo hace que te duele _la espalda_?

B —Hace _una semana_ que me duele.

Estudiante A   Estudiante B

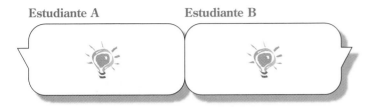

4 A —¿Qué pasa? ¿Te duele _el oído_?

B —Sí, _el derecho_.
  o: _No, no me duele._

Estudiante A   Estudiante B

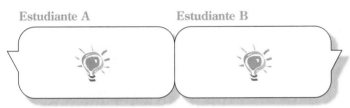

Empecemos a escribir

Escribe tus respuestas en español.

5 Dale _(give him / her)_ dos consejos _(pieces of advice)_ a un(a) amigo(a) que tiene dolor de garganta.

6 ¿Qué te duele cuando . . .

participas en un maratón? _Me duelen los pies._

a. estudias toda la noche para un examen?
b. comes demasiado?
c. lanzas la pelota _(pitch)_ en un partido de béisbol?
d. animas _(cheer)_ mucho en un partido de básquetbol?
e. tocas el piano por tres horas?

7 ¿Te duele algo? ¿Qué?

LAVESE LAS MANOS

ASOCIACION CHILENA DE SEGURIDAD ACHS
LIDER EN PREVENCION DE RIESGOS
02/90

Vocabulario para conversar 289

3 ESTUDIANTE A
¿Cuánto tiempo hace que te duele(n) ...? _(Questions will vary. Look for correct verb agreement.)_
ESTUDIANTE B
Hace ... que me duele(n). _(Answers will vary. Make sure students say_ hace, _even with plural time periods:_ Hace dos días ....)

4 ESTUDIANTE A
¿Qué pasa? ¿Te duele ...? _(Questions will vary.)_
ESTUDIANTE B
Sí, ... (No, no me duele.) _(Answers will vary, but see if students correctly omit the noun in their responses.)_

Answers: Empecemos a escribir
5–7 Answers will vary. Possible responses for Ex. 6:
a. Me duele(n) la cabeza (los ojos).
b. Me duele el estómago.
c. Me duele el brazo.
d. Me duele la garganta.
e. Me duelen los dedos (las manos).

 Practice Wkbk. 9-1, 9-2

 Audio Activity 9.1

 Writing Activities 9-A, 9-B

 Pruebas 9-1, 9-2

 Comm. Act. BLM 9-1

hypochondriacs in a doctor's waiting room who are asking each other what hurts and vying with one another to be the sicker one. The dialogue can progress from the more or less normal inquiries and responses to exaggerations. Encourage students to be creative and to use as much of their vocabulary as possible. For example: _¿Qué te duele? Me duele la mano. / Pues a mí me duele el brazo. / ¡Pues a mí me duelen los dos brazos!_

Extended Written Practice/Homework
1. Choose five body parts (pp. 286–287). For each, tell how often you feel pain there: _A veces me duele el cuello ._
2. Write three sentences saying that you cannot do different activities because parts of your body hurt.
3. Write three reasons that you might give for not going to school one day.
4. Write four questions or statements that a doctor might say to you.
5. Write two sentences telling how often you and another person exercise.

Multiple Intelligences
Interpersonal/Social
See Enrichment Ex. 4.
Verbal/Linguistic
See Exs. 1–4 and Audio Activity 9.1.
Visual/Spatial
See Practice Wkbk. 9-1 and 9-2, Writing Activities 9-A and 9-B, and Comm. Act. BLM 9-1.

Present

Chapter Theme
Health

Communicative Objectives
- To ask or describe how someone is feeling
- To name medical professions
- To indicate how long something has been going on
- To express and ask for an opinion
- To name places to go or things to do when you are sick

 Overheads 48–49

 Vocabulary Art BLMs/CD-ROM

 Pronunciation Tape 9-2

 Vocabulario para conversar B

Play

Step

Using the Video
Video segment 2: See the Video Teacher's Guide.

 Video Activity B

Vocabulario para conversar

¿Qué tienes?

 Chapter 9 Vocabulary

Aquí tienes el resto del vocabulario necesario para describir cómo te sientes.

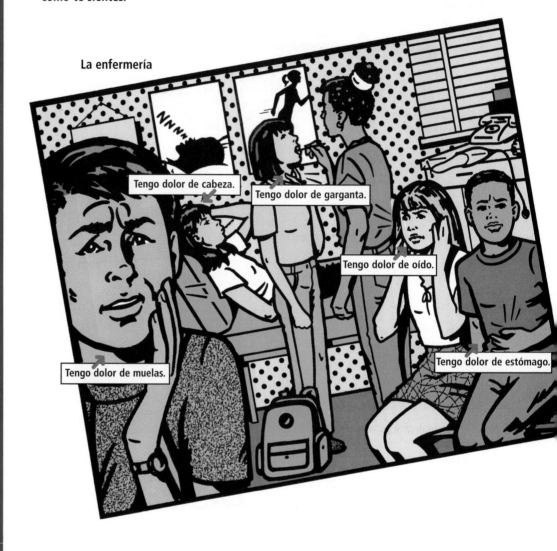

La enfermería

Tengo dolor de cabeza.

Tengo dolor de garganta.

Tengo dolor de oído.

Tengo dolor de muelas.

Tengo dolor de estómago.

290   Capítulo 9

Options

Strategies for Reaching All Students

Spanish-Speaking Students

 Un paso más Ex. 9-F

Students Needing Extra Help
También necesitas . . . : Practice *me lastimé* with other parts of the body.

Learning Spanish Through Action
STAGING VOCABULARY: *Finjan que tienen . . . .*
MATERIALS: none
DIRECTIONS: Ask students to act out ailments or illnesses from this vocabulary section. For example: *Finjan que tienen un resfriado.*

Tengo frío.*

Tengo gripe.

Tengo un resfriado.

Tengo sueño.

Tengo calor.

Tengo fiebre.

101°

la dentista

el dentista

el hospital

También necesitas...

¿Qué tienes?	*What's wrong?*	ahora	*now*
(Yo) me lastimé (la pierna).	*I hurt my (leg).*	todavía	*still*
¿Cómo te sientes?	*How do you feel?*	ya no	*no longer, not anymore*
mejor	*better*	¿no?	*don't you? aren't I? etc.*
peor	*worse*		

Debo quedarme en la cama.	*I should stay in bed.*
tomar	here: *to take*

¿Y qué quiere decir . . . ?
la clínica
la fiebre
terrible

* If we want to say "very," we use *mucho* with *sueño, frío,* and *calor,* but *mucha* with *hambre* and *sed: Tengo mucho sueño,* but *Tengo mucha sed.*

Vocabulario para conversar   291

Pasos vivos 1 CD-ROM
Clip Art Album

Teaching Suggestions
Preparing students to speak: Use one or two options from each of the categories of Comprehensible Input, Physical Response, or Limited Verbal Response. For a complete explanation of these categories and some sample activities, see pp. T22–T23.

Class Starter Review
On the day following initial presentation, you might begin the class with this activity:
Ask students: *¿Cómo te sientes hoy? (¿Qué tienes?) ¿Tienes dolor de . . .?* etc. Then have them turn to a partner and ask how he or she is feeling today.

www Internet Activities
Juegos

Extended Written Practice/Homework
1. Choose four types of illness (pp. 290–291) and write four sentences about different people who have them: *Mi hermana tiene dolor de garganta.*
2. Write four pairs of sentences saying that something is wrong with you and telling what you are going to do about it: *Tengo dolor de cabeza. Voy a dormir.*
3. Write three sentences telling when you go to these places: *la clínica, la enfermería, el hospital.*

Multiple Intelligences
Bodily/Kinesthetic
See Learning Spanish Through Action.
Intrapersonal/Introspective
Have students list three things they do when they are not feeling well: *Llamo al médico. Tomo aspirina. No como mucho.*
Verbal/Linguistic
See Pronunciation Tape 9-2 and Class Starter Review.
Visual/Spatial
See Overheads 48–49, the Vocabulary Art BLMs/CD-ROM, and Using the Video.

Practice & Apply

Re-enter / Recycle
Ex. 10: activities from Chaps. 1 and 3

Answers: Empecemos a conversar

8 ESTUDIANTE A
a. ¿Todavía tienes frío?
b. ...fiebre?
c. ...calor?
d. ...un resfriado?
e. Questions will vary.

ESTUDIANTE B
a.–e. Sí, todavía tengo.... (No, ya no tengo....) *(Answers will vary.)*

9 Explain to students that in talking about parts of the body, we usually use the definite article. The use of the possessive adjective in this exercise is an exception.

ESTUDIANTE A
a. ¿Cómo te sientes? ¿Está mejor tu oído?
b. ...pie?
c. ...espalda?
d. ...dolor de muelas?
e. ...cuello?
f. ...pierna?

ESTUDIANTE B
a.–f. No, ahora está peor. Creo que debo .... *(Endings may vary, depending on Estudiante B's choices.)*

Grammar Preview
Exs. 10 and 14 preview the use of *me* + *doler*. Its explanation appears in the grammar section on p. 300.

Empecemos a conversar

8 A —¿Todavía tienes <u>sueño</u>?
B —Sí, todavía tengo <u>sueño</u>.
   o: No, ya no tengo <u>sueño</u>.

Estudiante A   Estudiante B

9 A —¿Cómo te sientes? ¿Está mejor <u>tu brazo</u>?
B —No, ahora está peor.
   Creo que debo <u>ir a la enfermería</u>.

Estudiante A   Estudiante B

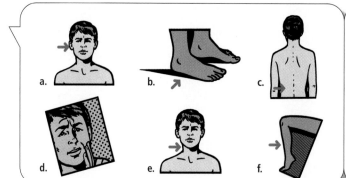

ir al hospital

ir a la enfermería / clínica

llamar al médico / al dentista

quedarme en la cama

tomar algo

descansar

292 Capítulo 9

Options

Strategies for Reaching All Students

Spanish-Speaking Students
Ex. 11: Ask: *¿Qué remedios recomiendan en tu familia si tienes un resfriado o gripe?*
Ex. 13: Ask: *¿Hay un remedio especial para el dolor de estómago? ¿Cuál es?*

 Un paso más Exs. 9-G, 9-H

Students Needing Extra Help
Ex. 10: If necessary, explain the difference between *me lastimé* and *¡qué lástima!* Brainstorm possible answers and have students use their Organizers.
Ex. 11: Have students use their Organizers.
Ex. 12: Refer students back to the *También necesitas...* on pp. 287 and 291.

Enrichment
Ex. 10: To expand this dialogue, have *Estudiante A* suggest a place for *Estudiante B* to go to get medical attention: *la enfermería, la clínica, el hospital, el (la) médico(a), el (la) dentista.*

10 A —*Vamos a <u>hacer ejercicio</u> el viernes, ¿no?*

B —*Lo siento, pero no puedo. Me lastimé <u>la pierna</u> y <u>me duele</u> mucho.*

A —*¡Qué lástima!*

Estudiante A

a. b. c. d.

Estudiante B

Empecemos a escribir y a leer

Escribe tus respuestas en español.

11 ¿Cómo te sientes?

12 Escribe otras dos formas diferentes para decir *¿Cómo te sientes?*

13 Cuando tienes dolor de estómago, ¿qué debes hacer?

14 Marta dice: "Carolina, lo siento, pero hoy no puedo ir al cine contigo. Me siento mal. Tengo mucho frío y me duele la garganta. Tengo un terrible dolor de cabeza también. Creo que debo quedarme en la cama."

a. ¿Qué crees que tiene Marta?
b. ¿Qué más debe hacer?
c. ¿Qué le dice Carolina a Marta?
d. ¿Qué va a hacer Carolina?

MORE PRACTICE

- Más práctica y tarea, p. 533
- Practice Workbook 9-3, 9-4

También se dice...

Tengo calentura.

Tengo gripa.

Tengo catarro.
Tengo resfrío.

---

10 ESTUDIANTE A
a. Vamos a ir de pesca el viernes, ¿no? / ¡Qué lástima!
b. ...jugar básquetbol .../...
c. ...ir de compras .../...
d. ...ir al cine .../...
ESTUDIANTE B
a.–d. Lo siento, pero no puedo. Me lastimé ... y me duele(n) mucho. *(Statements will vary.)*

Answers: Empecemos a escribir y a leer

11 Answers will vary.

12 ¿Cómo estás? ¿Qué tienes? ¿Te duele algo? ¿Qué pasa?

13 Answers will vary.

14 Answers will vary.
a. Marta tiene gripe (un resfriado).
b. Debe descansar (llamar al médico).
c. ¡Qué lástima!/Lo siento mucho./Sí, debes quedarte en la cama.
d. Va a ir al cine sola./Va a llamar a otra amiga./Va a quedarse en casa.

Practice Wkbk. 9-3, 9-4

Audio Activities 9.2, 9.3

Writing Activity 9-C

Pruebas 9-3, 9-4

Comm. Act. BLM 9-2

Extended Written Practice/Homework
1. Write three pairs of sentences telling how long ago you hurt parts of your body. Tell if these body parts are better now or if they still hurt.
2. Write three sentences telling in what places or situations you feel a certain way: *Siempre tengo sueño en la clase de inglés.*

Multiple Intelligences
Verbal/Linguistic
See Exs. 8–10 and Audio Activities 9.2 and 9.3.
Visual/Spatial
See Practice Wkbk. 9-3 and 9-4, Writing Activity 9-C, and Comm. Act. BLM 9-2.

Practice

Re-enter / Recycle

Exs. 2–3: activities from Chaps. 1, 3, and 7
Ex. 2: places and buildings from Chaps. 3, 6, and 7

Answers:
¡Comuniquemos!

1 ESTUDIANTE A

¿Cómo te sientes? ¿Todavía tienes sed?

. . . dolor de cabeza?

. . . hambre?

. . . dolor de oído?

. . . dolor de garganta?

. . . dolor de estómago?

ESTUDIANTE B

Ya no. Ahora tengo . . . . *(Answers will vary.)*

2 For the first three dialogues, the endings are not logical. Possible solutions will vary. Dialogue 4 is logical.

¡COMUNI

1

Tu amigo(a) no se siente bien. Cada vez *(each time)* que le preguntas le duele algo diferente. Túrnate con un(a) compañero(a) para preguntar y contestar.

A —*¿Cómo te sientes? ¿Todavía tienes fiebre?*

B —*Ya no. Ahora tengo dolor de cabeza.*

2

¿Es lógica la tercera línea? Si no, escribe una solución lógica. Después, escribe un diálogo semejante *(similar)*. Un(a) compañero(a) va a escribir una buena solución.

A —*¿Por qué no quieres ir a nadar?*

B —*Porque llueve.*

A —*Ah, podemos ir a tomar el sol.*

A —*¿Por qué no vamos al cine?*

B —*Porque me duelen mucho los ojos.*

A —*Pues, podemos ver la tele aquí en tu casa.*

A —*¿Por qué no vamos al gimnasio?*

B —*Porque me lastimé la espalda.*

A —*¿Prefieres jugar golf?*

A —*¿Por qué no comes algo?*

B —*Todavía tengo este terrible dolor de estóm*

A —*Yo creo que debes llamar al médico.*

Options

Strategies for Reaching All Students

Spanish-Speaking Students

Have students work in pairs to write an original dialogue modeled on the ones in Ex. 2, with either a logical or an illogical ending. Ask for volunteers to "perform" their dialogues for the class. After each performance, ask class members to determine whether the ending was logical or illogical.

Students Needing Extra Help

Ex. 1: Review *tener hambre / tener sed.*
Ex. 2: Guide students through this exercise. Model a possible response. You may wish to act out the dialogues for the class.
Ex. 3: Have students use their Organizers. Point out the difference in the grammar structure in the choices *(me duelen* and *tengo).*
¿Qué sabes ahora?: Have students write out this section so they can track their progress.

Cooperative Learning

Have groups of three or four students jointly create drawings of the human body. One student names a part of the body while another draws it and passes the drawing to the person on his or her right, allowing everyone an opportunity to name a part of the body. The group continues until the drawing is complete. Tell students that parts do not have to be named in any particular order. When completed, one member from each group describes the drawing.

Túrnate con un(a) compañero(a) para representar a una turista entusiasta y a su amiga que nunca se siente bien.

A —¡Qué bonito está el día! ¿Quieres ir a hacer ejercicio?

B —Lo siento, pero me duelen mucho las piernas.
o: Pues, no. Tengo un terrible dolor de cabeza.

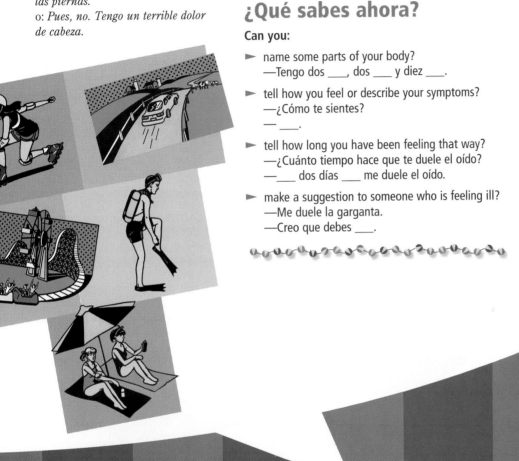

¿Qué sabes ahora?

Can you:

► name some parts of your body?
—Tengo dos ___, dos ___ y diez ___.

► tell how you feel or describe your symptoms?
—¿Cómo te sientes?
— ___.

► tell how long you have been feeling that way?
—¿Cuánto tiempo hace que te duele el oído?
— ___ dos días ___ me duele el oído.

► make a suggestion to someone who is feeling ill?
—Me duele la garganta.
—Creo que debes ___.

Vocabulario para conversar 295

3 If students ask: Explain that we sometimes use a form of *estar* instead of *ser* to express a condition.

ESTUDIANTE A
¡Qué bonito está el día! ¿Quieres ir ...? (*Suggested activities include:* a patinar, a bucear, al campo, a tomar el sol (a la playa), al parque de diversiones.)

ESTUDIANTE B
Answers will vary.

Answers: ¿Qué sabes ahora?

• *Possible answers:* (dos) brazos, manos, ojos, orejas, piernas, pies / (diez) dedos, dedos del pie
• Answers will vary.
• Hace / que
• Answers will vary.

 Audio Activity 9.4

 Writing Activities 9-D, 9-E

Pasos vivos 1 CD-ROM
Slide Projector, Laboratorio de grabar

Multiple Intelligences
Intrapersonal/Introspective
See *¿Qué sabes ahora?*
Logical/Mathematical
Have students in groups or pairs create a survey to determine what one could do to avoid catching a cold. Example: *Comer comidas buenas. Hacer ejercicio. Dormir mucho.* Place this in a chart or graph form and display it in the room.

Naturalist
Have students discuss how the weather affects their daily temperament. Ask them how they feel on cloudy, rainy days and then on sunny, warm days.
Verbal/Linguistic
See Audio Activity 9.4.
Visual/Spatial
See Writing Activities 9-D and 9-E.

Present & Apply

Cultural Objective

- To discuss attitudes toward health and health practices in the Spanish-speaking world

Teaching Suggestions

Prior to assigning the *Perspectiva cultural,* gather additional information and photographs about folk healers and remedies in Spanish-speaking countries to share with students after they have read the material.

Critical Thinking: Synthesizing

Have small groups of students prepare lists of adjectives that could be used to describe what they consider to be the ideal doctor or other health-care giver. Examples: *inteligente, simpático(a), paciente.* Afterward, the same groups could compile lists of adjectives that describe attributes they would *not* want their ideal health-care giver to have. For example: *cansado(a), impaciente, perezoso(a).* Record students' lists on the chalkboard and compare the results.

Perspectiva cultural

La salud

Las hierbas medicinales son importantes en la medicina moderna.

Algunas veces, cuando no me siento bien, voy a la farmacia para comprar una medicina. Otras veces tomo algunas hierbas medicinales.

Why do you think these two photos are shown? Why might someone who is sick choose to go sometimes to one of these two places and sometimes to the other?

Imagine this. You aren't feeling well. Your mother talks to some friends, but they can't agree on what your illness is or how to treat it. There is a woman in your community who is not a doctor, but who is known to be able to help people who are sick. You go to see her. She asks about your recent activities. After a while she decides which of her remedies is best for your situation.

In many Hispanic communities, folk remedies have been passed down from generation to generation, largely due to the availability of plants with medicinal value. For example, a tea made from mint (known in Mexico as *yerbabuena*) may be given to someone with a stomachache. A little piece of camphor *(alcanfor)* or the herb rue *(ruda)* wrapped in cotton and put in the ear is said to cure an earache. Other home remedies, such as quinine, have found their way into modern medicine.

Members of many ethnic groups treat an illness in this way. They may consult a doctor, or they may decide the illness can be more easily cured by a long-used folk remedy.

Today scientists are investigating new sources of medicine by consulting ethnic groups that have traditionally used remedies made from local plants.

296   Capítulo 9

Una farmacia en Chetumal, México ▶

Options

Strategies for Reaching All Students

Spanish-Speaking Students
Ask Spanish-speaking students: *¿Hay curanderos(as) en tu comunidad? ¿Va mucha gente a consultarlos(las)? ¿A quién prefieres ver cuando te sientes mal, a un(a) médico(a) o a un(a) curandero(a)? ¿Por qué?*

 Un paso más Ex. 9-I

Students Needing Extra Help
Ask students if their parents, grandparents, or other relatives have a home remedy that they use. Remind them of popular home remedy books with which they may be familiar because of television advertisements.

Enrichment
This rhyme is used to comfort a child when he or she is hurt: *Sana, sana, colita de rana / Si no sana hoy, sanará mañana.* It is used for scrapes and bruises, and the person reciting it waves a hand over the injury or caresses it. Although the rhyme makes little sense and has no real healing power, it often stops the child's crying by getting him or her to stop thinking of the pain. Discuss the power of positive thinking and its role in folk healing and standard medicine.

La cultura desde tu perspectiva

1 What folk remedies are you familiar with? Why might someone choose to go to a folk healer instead of a doctor?

2 If you were living in a different country and your friends and neighbors went to folk healers, would you do the same? Why or why not?

Cultural Notes ☀

(p. 296, top photo)
Medicinal herbs at a market in Tenancingo, Mexico. Traditional indigenous methods of healing, which often employ herbs in combination with special prayers, are still practiced throughout Latin America. So established and respected are the *curanderos(as)* that every year they meet for several days in Catemaco, Veracruz, to share their knowledge.
(p. 296, bottom photo) If students ask, tell them that the plant pictured at the bottom of the page is a spray of mint.

(p. 297, photo)
Pharmacy clerk in Chetumal, capital of the state of Quintana Roo, Mexico. As in the U.S., the fields of nursing and teaching in Mexico have traditionally been dominated by women, with medical and legal careers more often pursued by men. A notable difference between the two countries, however, is that in Mexico, pharmaceutical careers attract many more women than men.

Preview

 Overhead 50

Answers

Answers will vary, but may include a description of the illness, how to detect the illness, possible remedies, advice on treatment, etc.

A *Le* is used because it refers to a person other than the speaker. In this case it refers to *su hijo.*

B *Duele* is used when the object to which it refers is singular; *duelen,* when the object is plural. The other verb is *gustan.*

C It tells how long something has been going on (a week).

Gramática en contexto

Look at this article from a health magazine that tells parents how to detect an illness in their children. What kind of information would you expect to find?

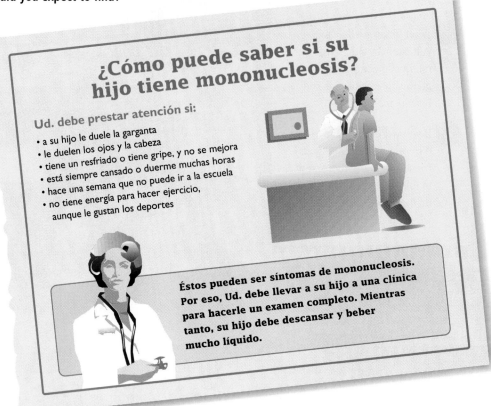

¿Cómo puede saber si su hijo tiene mononucleosis?

Ud. debe prestar atención si:

- a su hijo le duele la garganta
- le duelen los ojos y la cabeza
- tiene un resfriado o tiene gripe, y no se mejora
- está siempre cansado o duerme muchas horas
- hace una semana que no puede ir a la escuela
- no tiene energía para hacer ejercicio, aunque le gustan los deportes

Éstos pueden ser síntomas de mononucleosis. Por eso, Ud. debe llevar a su hijo a una clínica para hacerle un examen completo. Mientras tanto, su hijo debe descansar y beber mucho líquido.

A In the article, find the expressions *le duele(n)* and *le gusta(n).* Why do you think *le* is used instead of *me?*

B Compare the two sentences that use *duele* and *duelen.* When do we use each of these? Find another verb in the article that follows this pattern.

C Look at the sentence *Hace una semana que no puede ir a la escuela. Que* connects two parts of this sentence. The second part tells what the person cannot do. What information does the first part of the sentence give?

Options

Strategies for Reaching All Students

Students Needing Extra Help
A: Students may understand this concept but they might not be able to express it. Assist as needed.
C: Write the sentence on the chalkboard. Highlight it and separate the parts.
Have students start to fill in the grammar portion of their Organizers.
El verbo dormir: Emphasize the *nosotros* ending, since *dormir* is an *-ir* verb. Review *poder* and its verb forms.
Ex. 1: Review *-ir* verb endings.

Extended Written Practice/Homework
Write four sentences telling when different people sleep or don't sleep well: *Mi hermana y yo no dormimos bien cuando hace mucho calor.*

Multiple Intelligences
Bodily/Kinesthetic
Use the cube made of plastic foam to practice the present-tense forms of the verb *dormir.*
Verbal/Linguistic
See Ex. 1.
Visual/Spatial
See Overhead 50, Exs. A–C, and Practice Wkbk. 9-5.

El verbo *dormir*

Like *poder*, *dormir* is an *o → ue* stem-changing verb. Here are all its present-tense forms:

(yo)	d**ue**rmo	(nosotros) (nosotras)	dormimos
(tú)	d**ue**rmes	(vosotros) (vosotras)	dormís
Ud. (él) (ella)	d**ue**rme	Uds. (ellos) (ellas)	d**ue**rmen

¡NO OLVIDES!

Here are all of the other *o → ue* stem-changing verbs that you know: *costar, doler, poder.*

1 Pregunta a un(a) compañero(a) si estas personas duermen bien.

A —*¿Duerme bien Marta?*

B —*No, duerme mal porque todavía tiene dolor de oído.*

Marta

| a. Antonio y Pedro | b. Rosita | c. Juanito y Miguel | d. tú | e. Uds. |

¿Y cómo duermes tú? ¿Por qué?

Gramática en contexto   299

Present & Practice

Class Starter Review

For the day after the presentation of *dormir*, have pairs of students ask and answer how long they sleep on weekdays or weekends. Ask volunteers to report to the class on the information they found out.

Answers

1 ESTUDIANTE A

a. ¿Duermen bien Antonio y Pedro?

b. ¿Duerme bien Rosita?

c. ¿Duermen bien Juanito y Miguel?

d. ¿Duermes bien?

e. ¿Duermen bien Uds.?

ESTUDIANTE B

a. No, duermen mal porque todavía tienen fiebre.

b. No, duerme mal porque todavía tiene gripe.

c. No, duermen mal porque todavía tienen dolor de estómago.

d. No, duermo mal porque todavía tengo dolor de muelas.

e. No, dormimos mal porque todavía tenemos un resfriado.

Answers will vary.

Practice Wkbk. 9-5

¿? Prueba 9-5

Cultural Notes

(p. 299, realia)
If students ask, tell them that Tabcin is the brand name of these effervescent cold/decongestant tablets that are found throughout Latin America.

Present & Practice

Re-enter / Recycle
Ex. 5: *gustar* expressions from Chap. 1, foods from Chap. 4

Reteach / Review: Verbs like *gustar*
Ex. 3: Remind students that *duele(n)* is used the same way as *gusta(n)*, *encanta(n)*, and *queda(n)*.

Answers
2 a. la cabeza
b. las papas fritas
c. el jugo de naranja, hacer ejercicio
d. las piernas, los dedos
e. el jugo de naranja, hacer ejercicio
f. las piernas, los dedos

3 ESTUDIANTE A
¿Qué te duele?
ESTUDIANTE B
Answers will vary.

El complemento indirecto: Los pronombres *me, te, le*

Indirect object pronouns replace indirect object nouns. We use indirect object pronouns with *doler (o → ue)*.

- In Spanish, the part of the body that hurts is the subject of the sentence and the verb agrees with it. The indirect object pronoun tells who hurts:

Me duele **la pierna.** / **Me** duele**n las piernas.**

(yo)	**me**	(tú)	**te**	(Ud.) (él) (ella)	**le**

- We also use indirect object pronouns with *gustar* and *encantar*:

  Le encanta tocar la guitarra.

- Sometimes we use *a* + a pronoun or a person's name for emphasis or to make it clear who we are referring to.

  Me duelen los pies. Y **a ti,** ¿qué **te** duele?
  A Pablo le duelen los pies.
  A Ud. le duelen los pies, ¿no?

2 ¿Qué palabras de la columna de la derecha puedes usar con cada expresión de la columna de la izquierda? Puedes usar las palabras más de una vez.

a. me duele   las piernas
b. me encantan   la cabeza
c. le encanta   las papas fritas
d. le duelen   los dedos
e. te gusta   el jugo de naranja
f. te duelen   hacer ejercicio

3 Después de hacer ejercicio durante mucho tiempo, te duele todo el cuerpo. Túrnate con un(a) compañero(a) para preguntar y decir qué te duele.

A —¿Qué te duele?
B —Me duele el cuello.

300   Capítulo 9

Options

Strategies for Reaching All Students

Spanish-Speaking Students
Ex. 5: Ask Spanish-speaking students: *¿Qué comidas te encantan a ti? ¿Cuáles no te gustan nada?*

Students Needing Extra Help
Ex. 3: To simplify the use of *duele(n)*, tell students that when one thing hurts, use *duele*. When two (or more) things hurt, use *duelen*.
Ex. 4: Emphasize the necessary change of *cansado* to *cansada* in some items.

Ask what will happen to *cansado* with *Maricarmen,* as students may see it as two names.
Remind students to use *duelen* when two things hurt.
Ex. 5: Have students use their Organizers from Chap. 4.

4 Después de un examen difícil de historia estos estudiantes están cansados. Habla con un(a) compañero(a) y di cómo se sienten.

A —*Veo que José está cansado.*

B —*Sí, y también le duele mucho la cabeza.*

José

a. Felipe

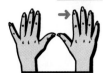
b. Maricarmen

c. Tomás

d. Fernando

e. Pepe

f. Sarita

5 Pregunta a tus compañeros de clase qué comidas les gustan o no les gustan.

A —*¿A ti te gustan las uvas?*

B —*Sí, a mí me gustan.*
   o: Sí, a mí me encantan.
   o: No, a mí no me gustan.

Ahora di qué comidas les gustan o no les gustan a tus compañeros de clase.

A Verónica le encantan las uvas.

La expresión *hace . . . que*

To tell how long something has been going on, we use *Hace* + period of time + *que* + present-tense verb.

Hace tres días **que estoy** enfermo.

If we want to ask how long something has been going on, we can use *¿Cuánto (tiempo) hace que* + present-tense verb?

¿Cuánto tiempo hace que Elena **está** enferma?

Gramática en contexto   301

Reteach / Review:
También and *tampoco*
Ex. 5: To practice *también / tampoco,* have students extend this dialogue by having *Estudiante A* agree with *Estudiante B*'s tastes.

Class Starter Review
For the day after the presentation of *hace . . . que,* ask students *¿Cuánto tiempo hace que ___?* Possible expressions: *estudiar español, practicar deportes, tener un resfriado,* etc.

Answers
4 ESTUDIANTE A
a. Veo que Felipe está cansado.
b. . . . Maricarmen está cansada.
c. . . . Tomás está cansado.
d. . . . Fernando está cansado.
e. . . . Pepe está cansado.
f. . . . Sarita está cansada.
ESTUDIANTE B
a. Sí, y también le duelen mucho los ojos.
b. . . . le duele mucho el dedo.
c. . . . le duele mucho la espalda.
d. . . . le duelen mucho las manos.
e. . . . le duele mucho el cuello.
f. . . . le duele mucho el brazo derecho.

5 Questions and answers will vary, but encourage students to use previously learned vocabulary.

Practice Wkbk. 9-6, 9-7

Prueba 9-6

Extended Written Practice/Homework
1. Write four sentences telling when different people have aches: *A mi mamá le duele la espalda cuando lava la ropa.*
2. Write four questions you can ask classmates to find out if they have aches in different parts of their body.
3. Write four sentences telling what types of food your friends and family love.

Multiple Intelligences
Verbal/Linguistic
See Exs. 3–5 and Class Starter Review.
Visual/Spatial
See Practice Wkbk. 9-6 and 9-7.

Cultural Notes

(p. 300, realia)
Reasons to say *no* to drugs abound, according to this ad from Spain's *Fundación de Ayuda contra la Drogadicción.* These reasons include both traditional and contemporary elements of teen life in Spain: *mi amiga, mi perro, los tebeos* (comic strips), Bart Simpson . . .

Present & Practice

Re-enter / Recycle
Ex. 6: numbers 0–31 from *El primer paso,* calendar expressions from Chap. 1

Answers

6 ESTUDIANTE A

a. ¿Cuánto tiempo hace que María tiene dolor de oído?

b. ... Susana tiene gripe?

c. ... Alejandra tiene dolor de garganta?

d. ... José tiene un resfriado?

e. ... Andrés tiene dolor de estómago?

f. ... Cecilia tiene fiebre?

ESTUDIANTE B

a. Pues, hace dos días que tiene dolor de oído.

b. ... una semana que tiene gripe.

c. ... tres días que tiene dolor de garganta.

d. ... cuatro días que tiene un resfriado.

e. ... dos días que tiene dolor de estómago.

f. ... cinco días que tiene fiebre.

7 Dialogues will vary, but look for the phrases *¿Cuánto tiempo hace que . . . ?* and *Hace . . . (que . . .).*

8 Statements will vary.

---

6 Pregunta a un(a) compañero(a) cuánto tiempo hace que estas personas están enfermas.

A —*¿Cuánto tiempo hace que Rodolfo tiene dolor de muelas?*

B —*Pues, hace seis días que tiene dolor de muelas.*

Rodolfo / 6 días

a. María / 2 días

b. Susana / 1 semana

c. Alejandra / 3 días

d. José / 4 días

e. Andrés / 2 días

f. Cecilia / 5 días

7 Escribe cinco actividades que te gusta hacer o cinco cosas que tienes. Lee tus frases a un(a) compañero(a). Tu compañero(a) debe averiguar *(find out)* cuánto tiempo hace que haces esas actividades o que tienes esas cosas.

A —*A mí me gusta patinar.*
o: *Yo patino.*

B —*¿Cuánto tiempo hace que patinas?*

A —*Hace seis años (que patino).*

8 Dile a un(a) compañero(a) lo que aprendiste en el Ejercicio 7 de las actividades y las cosas del (de la) primer(a) compañero(a).

A Patricia le gusta patinar. Hace seis años que patina.

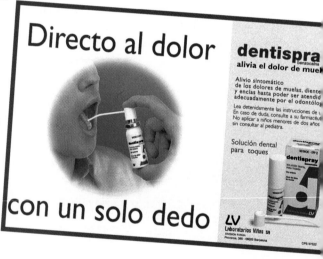

302   Capítulo 9

Options

Strategies for Reaching All Students

Students Needing Extra Help
Ex. 6: Give other examples of time: hours, weeks, months, years.
Have students use their Organizers and point out that this exercise requires the use of *tener* expressions.
Sustantivación de adjetivos: Give students further examples. Show how *clase* and *tarea* are removed, but *la de* + subject remain in the examples given.
Ahora lo sabes: Have students write out this section so they can track their progress.

Enrichment
Ex. 6: As a homework assignment, have students create other dialogues in which *Estudiante A* asks *Estudiante B* how long someone has been doing an activity. Encourage them to use plural as well as singular subjects. For example: *¿Cuánto hace que los muchachos patinan? Hace cuarenta y cinco minutos que patinan.*

Extended Written Practice/Homework
1. Write two sentences telling how long you or another person has been sick or had an ache.
2. Write a sentence telling how long you and your family have lived in your present location. Write a similar sentence about another person.

La sustantivación de adjetivos

Look at how we can avoid repeating the noun in these instances:

¿Te duele **la pierna derecha** o **la izquierda?**

¿Qué prefieres, **un gorro azul** o **uno amarillo?**

To avoid repetition we drop the noun in the second part of the sentence and put the definite or indefinite article right before the second adjective. Note that the adjective must agree in gender and number just as if the noun were still there. Also note that *un* becomes *uno(a)* when it is not followed by a noun.

We can do the same thing with what we call a "prepositional phrase," or a description that begins with *de*.

¿Qué haces, **la tarea de matemáticas** o **la de ciencias?**

¿Necesitas marcadores para **la clase de inglés** o para **la de arte?**

9 Con un(a) compañero(a), pregunta y contesta. En vez de *(instead of)* repetir el sustantivo, usa el adjetivo como sustantivo.

a. ¿Prefieres los muebles modernos o los muebles antiguos?
b. En tu baño, ¿tienes un espejo redondo o un espejo cuadrado?
c. En tu sala, ¿hay un sofá incómodo o un sofá cómodo?
d. ¿Prefieres un escritorio de madera o un escritorio de metal?
e. ¿Vives en una casa grande o en una casa pequeña?
f. ¿Te gustaría una silla roja o una silla azul?

Ahora, escribe tres preguntas semejantes *(similar)* que puedes preguntarle a tu compañero(a).

Ahora lo sabes

Can you:

► recommend a way to maintain good health?
—Debes dormir más. Estás enfermo porque no ___ bien.

► say that a part of the body hurts?
—___ María ___ la mano derecha.

► tell how long something has been going on?
—___ tres días ___ Rafael tiene un resfriado.

► avoid repeating a noun?
—¿Te duele el oído derecho o ___?

> ### MORE PRACTICE
>
> Más práctica y tarea, pp. 533–535
> Practice Workbook 9–5, 9–9

Gramática en contexto 303

---

3. Write two pairs of sentences naming colors of clothing that you have. In the second sentence, tell which you prefer: *Tengo una sudadera roja y otra azul. Me gusta más la roja.*

Multiple Intelligences
Verbal/Linguistic
See Exs. 6–7, Enrichment, and Audio Activity 9.5.
Visual/Spatial
See Practice Wkbk. 9-8 and 9-9 and Writing Activities 9-F, 9-G, and 9-H.

Cultural Notes

(p. 302, realia)
Have students read this ad, indicating whether or not they've gotten the gist of the text. Ask them to use context clues to decode words such as *encías* and *odontólogo* and any other words they don't understand.

Apply

 Pronunciation Tape 9-3

 **Todo junto A**

Play

Todo junto B

Play

Using the Video
Video segment 3: See the Video Teacher's Guide.

 Video Activity C

 Pasos vivos 1 CD-ROM

Video Monitor, Video Presentation Maker

Re-enter / Recycle
Ex. 1: colors, clothes, and direct object pronouns from Chap. 6

Answers: Actividades
1 Dialogues will vary, but should include correct agreement of adjective (color) and article.

2 Statements will vary, but look for correct use of *duele(n).*

Todo Junto

Actividades

1 Trae *(Bring)* a la sala de clases dos cosas iguales *(alike)* pero de color diferente; por ejemplo, una camisa roja y otra amarilla. Con un(a) compañero(a), inventa un diálogo con un(a) vendedor(a) *(salesperson)* y su cliente.

2 Cada estudiante debe escribir un problema de salud en una hoja de papel. El (La) profesor(a) recogerá *(will collect)* los papeles y le dará *(will give)* uno a cada estudiante. Ahora representa *(act out)* el problema que tú recibes. La clase debe identificar el problema y hacer una recomendación médica.

304   Capítulo 9

Options

Strategies for Reaching All Students

Students Needing Extra Help
Ex. 1: Bring in extra items in case some students forget to bring theirs. Review *ni. . . ni.*
Ex. 2: Brainstorm responses. Have students use their Organizers.

Enrichment
As an in-class writing assignment, have students create a dialogue between an overworked, sleepy doctor and a patient. Tell students that the basic situation to be dramatized here is a reversal of roles between doctor and patient, with the patient gradually realizing that the doctor needs care and advice.

Cooperative Learning
In groups of three or four, have students brainstorm and compile a list of activities that they all do. Have them then list how long they have been doing these activities. Give them a time limit of approximately five minutes, and then ask one member from each group to summarize their information.

304   **Standards** 1.1; 1.2; 2.1; 2.2; 3.1

Conexiones

El arte

Las meninas

En 1656, Diego Velázquez, un artista de la corte del Rey Felipe IV, pintó *Las meninas*. Trescientos un años después, Pablo Picasso creó su propia versión del cuadro famoso. Compara los cuadros. Menciona por lo menos:

• la infanta (princesa) Margarita, hija del rey, que está en el centro

• las meninas *(ladies-in-waiting)*, incluso la enana *(dwarf)*

• el artista

• el perro

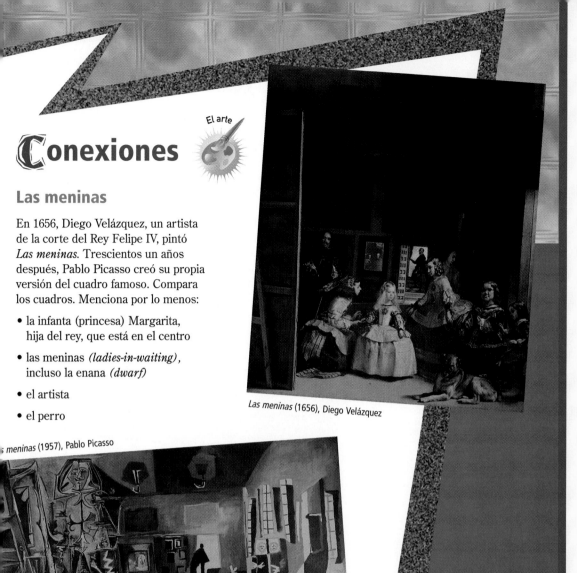

Las meninas (1656), Diego Velázquez

...s meninas (1957), Pablo Picasso

Todo junto   305

Cultural Notes

Multiple Intelligences
Bodily/Kinesthetic
See Enrichment and *Actividades* 1–2.
Interpersonal/Social
See Cooperative Learning.
Verbal/Linguistic
See Pronunciation Tape 9-3.
Visual/Spatial
See Using the Video; Comm. Act. BLMs 9-3, 9-4, and 9-5; and Enrichment.

(p. 305, top photo)
In this masterpiece Diego Velázquez shows the splendor and complexity of the royal court. The point of view of the painting is that of the king and queen, who are shown reflected in the mirror on the rear wall and who seem to be the source of light in the foreground of the painting. Their daughter, the Infanta Margarita, forms the top of a triangle of light, dominating the scene. Velázquez himself is shown as he works before the canvas.

(p. 305, bottom photo)
In his version of *Las meninas,* Pablo Picasso shatters the world of Velázquez's painting. The point of view of the painting is fractured and scattered and the king and queen no longer illuminate the scene. The Infanta and her entourage are scarcely recognizable. Ask students: Why do you think Picasso makes these changes to Velázquez's work?

Standards 1.1; 1.3; 2.1; 3.1   **305**

Apply

Process Reading

For a description of process reading, see p. 48.

Teaching Suggestions

Remind students of some of the reading strategies that they have already practiced and that they can now apply to everything they read to help their comprehension: for example, prediction, skimming, scanning, using context clues, using prior knowledge, and identifying the main idea.

¡Vamos a leer!

www.pasoapaso.com

Antes de leer

STRATEGY ▶ **Using prior knowledge**

Look at the pictures. What do you think this article will be about? In two or three sentences, try to summarize what you know about the topic. What new information do you think you might find out?

Mira la lectura

STRATEGY ▶ **Using titles and photos to predict**

Find the title and the name of the section in the magazine where it appears. Look at the photo and the caption, and read the boldface headings. What cause of headaches do you think will be discussed?

TU SALUD

CAUSAS DEL DOLOR DE CABEZA

El dolor de cabeza tiene diferentes causas. La mala postura puede ser una de ellas. Diversos doctores y terapistas han hablado sobre la importancia de comprobar la postura de nuestro cuerpo cada vez que nos sentamos. Para eso, hay que considerar varios aspectos:

- **Los pies** deben apoyarse totalmente sobre el suelo mientras estamos sentados.

- **La espalda baja** debe apoyarse contra el respaldo de la silla.

- **La cabeza** debe estar colocada correctamente sobre los hombros.

- **Los hombros** no deben estar tensos.

Sin duda, una buena postura puede evitar que nos duela la espalda, el cuello, los hombros y, por supuesto, la cabeza.

Siéntate derecho y di adiós al dolor de cabeza.

306 Capítulo 9

Options

Strategies for Reaching All Students

Students Needing Extra Help
Infórmate: Have students write a list of the cognates in the article.

Enrichment
Extended activity: Think of another common health problem and recommend several things you can do to avoid it.

Infórmate

STRATEGY ▷ **Coping with unknown words**

Remember that you should keep reading when you come across an unknown word. You may find that you do not need to know its meaning, that you can use the surrounding words to figure it out, or that you may have to look it up or ask someone the meaning.

1 Read the entire article several times, without stopping to puzzle over words you do not know. What general body behavior does the author recommend to avoid headaches?

2 Now read the article carefully, paying attention to words you don't know. Can you identify instances where the exact meaning of unknown words isn't important for getting the gist of the sentence?

Use context clues and the diagram to figure out the meaning of each underlined word.

> hombros . . . estar <u>tensos</u>
>
> pies . . . sobre *(on)* el <u>suelo</u>
>
> cabeza . . . está <u>colocada</u> . . . sobre <u>los hombros</u>

Aplicación

Look at yourself and your classmates right now. Are you following the article's recommendations? If not, try doing the four things that the author advises. Do they feel comfortable or uncomfortable, natural or unnatural? Evaluate the article's recommendations on a scale of 1 to 5 (1 = not at all useful; 5 = extremely useful).

Para no tener dolor de cabeza, visita al dentista regularmente

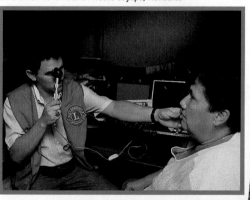

Un examen de la vista en Nueva Suyapa, Honduras

¡Vamos a leer!   307

Answers
Antes de leer
Answers will vary, but may include posture, stress, headaches, etc., and how to avoid them.

Mira la lectura
Bad posture as a cause of headaches will be discussed.

Infórmate
1 sitting up straight

2 Answers will vary. / tense / floor / set (placed), the shoulders

Aplicación
Answers will vary. Encourage student discussion.

 **Internet Activities**

Cultural Notes ☼

(p. 307, photo)
Inspired by Helen Keller, the Lions Club International Foundation has become a leader in blindness prevention services worldwide. Each year the Lions Club Sight First program sends hundreds of optometrists and ophthalmologists to Latin American countries to provide vision care to those who can't afford it. The Lions Club also collects glasses for distribution in these countries and funds ophthalmic education and eye clinics.

Process Writing
For information regarding developing a writing portfolio, see p. 50.

Multicultural Perspectives
In many Latin American countries, government health agencies use educational radio programs to transmit health information to the people in rural areas. Poster campaigns to encourage vaccination of children are common. Traveling nurses and other health practitioners make rounds to remote areas that don't have clinics or hospitals. Discuss health-related advertisements, public service announcements, and / or commercials that students have seen or heard in Spanish. Could they figure out what messages these ads and announcements were trying to get across?

Answers: ¡Vamos a escribir!
Look for correct use of adjectives and verbs, and encourage students to use the chapter vocabulary.

Pasos vivos 1 CD-ROM
Word Processor

¡Vamos a escribir!

Cartel en una clínica rural ▶
cerca de Torreón, México

Make a poster in Spanish that might be displayed in a nurse's office or other medical facility. The poster should give information about how to prevent illness or how to take care of yourself when you are sick.

1 First, decide on your theme. Do you want to give suggestions for staying healthy *(Ideas para mantener la salud),* such as eating healthful foods, exercising, and getting enough sleep? Or do you want to make suggestions for someone who isn't feeling well *(Ideas para sentirte mejor),* such as staying in bed, drinking a lot of water, and resting?

2 Write the suggestions that you will put on your poster. You may want to use the verbs *debes* or *necesitas.*

3 Show the text of your poster to a partner. Then revise and edit it. Recopy the corrected sentences on your poster. You may want to add a drawing or a picture from a magazine to illustrate your suggestions.

4 Now you are ready to share your work. Here are some ways you can do this:

- Display your posters in the classroom, the hallway, or the nurse's office.
- With your teacher's help, organize a school health fair, and make your posters the main display.
- With your teacher's help, find out if some nearby elementary school or health facility would like to display your posters.

308 Capítulo 9

Options

Strategies for Reaching All Students

Spanish-Speaking Students

Un paso más Ex. 9-J

Students Needing Extra Help
Step 1: Emphasize that you are asking students to make a choice between two poster themes: maintaining health or taking care of yourself when you are sick. Brainstorm ideas with the class. Have students use their Organizers from other chapters.

(p. 309, realia)
This poster from a rural clinic in Mexico's
Lake District urges women who are planning
to have children to get vaccinated against
tetanus, a potentially deadly disease.
Discuss with students the ways in which
this poster has been made appealing and
appropriate to the rural women who are its
target audience.

Assess & Summarize

Test Preparation

You may want to assign parts of this section as written homework or as an in-class writing activity prior to administering the *Examen de habilidades.*

Answers

Listening:
—*Señor Donoso, tengo un terrible dolor de cabeza. Tengo un resfriado, tengo fiebre y me duele la garganta. Debo quedarme en la cama. Si necesita hablar conmigo, puede llamar a mi casa.*
—*Pero, Justino, hace una semana que te sientes mal. ¡Debes llamar al médico!*
Justino is feeling bad. Justino's problems include: He has a terrible headache, a cold, a fever, and a sore throat. His boss suggests that he call the doctor.

Reading: The prescription is probably for a toothache. / No, it should be taken with food or milk.

Writing: Encourage students to use the chapter vocabulary. Look for logical sentences.

Culture: Answers will vary. Students may include references to the *Perspectiva cultural,* such as taking *yerbabuena* or consulting a doctor.

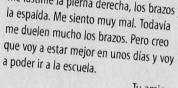
This section will help you organize your studying for the proficiency test, where you will be asked to do similar, though not identical, tasks. There will not be any models on the test.

► Listening

Can you understand this telephone conversation between Justino and his boss, Señor Donoso? Listen as your teacher reads a sample similar to what you will hear on the test. How is Justino feeling? Mention at least two problems he has. What does his boss suggest?

► Reading

Can you read the label on this prescription bottle and use cognates, context, or any other strategy to understand the gist of it? What is the prescription for? Should this medicine be taken on an empty stomach?

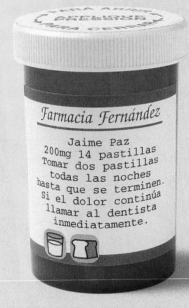

Farmacia Fernández

Jaime Paz
200mg 14 pastillas
Tomar dos pastillas
todas las noches
hasta que se terminen.
Si el dolor continúa
llamar al dentista
inmediatamente.

► Writing

Can you write a letter to a friend explaining how you are feeling after an accident you have just had? Here is a sample:

Querida María Marta:

Hace una semana que estoy en la cama. Me lastimé la pierna derecha, los brazos y la espalda. Me siento muy mal. Todavía me duelen mucho los brazos. Pero creo que voy a estar mejor en unos días y voy a poder ir a la escuela.

Tu amiga,
Maribel

► Culture

Can you explain some options for what you could do if you had a stomachache while visiting México?

► Speaking

Can you work with a partner to play the roles of a doctor and a patient? Here is a sample dialogue:

A —*Doctor, me siento muy mal. Me duele mucho el estómago.*

B —*¿Cuánto tiempo hace que te duele el estómago?*

A —*Hace sólo unas horas, doctor.*

B —*Pues, creo que comes mucho. Pero, ahora debes ir a tu casa, quedarte en la cama y no comer nada esta noche.*

Self Test www.pasoapaso.com

Options

Strategies for Reaching All Students

Students Needing Extra Help
Listening: Make a three-column chart with headings "feelings," "problems," and "suggestions."
To indicate two people speaking, put on a hat, move to a new spot, alter your voice, etc.
Writing: Brainstorm other possibilities, such as a specific number of days until you are better, other activities you might be returning

to such as skating, playing the guitar, and so on. Go sentence by sentence. Have students use their Organizers from this and other chapters.
Culture: Review the *Perspectiva cultural.*
Speaking: Make up some other possibilities. Have students use their Organizers.

Enrichment
Writing: Students can also write instructions for a pet-sitter taking care of a sick dog or cat. Remind students to name or describe the ailment and its symptoms as well as to list instructions for giving the animal what it needs to get better (food, water, rest, etc.).

Resumen del vocabulario

Speaking: Dialogues will vary, but students should use chapter vocabulary. Look for correct use of *me / te duele(n)* and *hace +* time expression + *que*. Encourage use of vocabulary from previous chapters.

Use the vocabulary from this chapter to help you:

► describe how you are feeling

► tell what parts of your body hurt

► suggest things you or others can do to feel better

to name parts of the body
la boca
el brazo
la cabeza
el cuello
el cuerpo
el dedo
el dedo del pie
derecho, -a
la espalda
el estómago
la garganta
izquierdo, -a
la mano *(f.)*
la nariz
el oído
el ojo
el pie
la pierna

to ask how someone is feeling
¿Cómo te sientes?
¿Qué pasa?
¿Qué te duele?
¿Qué tienes?

to describe how someone is feeling
¡Ay!
el dolor
doler (o → ue)
(A mí / ti) me / te duele(n) ___.

(No me duele) nada.
la fiebre
Me siento bien / mal.
Tengo dolor de cabeza.
     estómago.
     garganta.
     muelas.
     oído.
Tengo calor.
     fiebre.
     frío.
     gripe.
     sueño.
     un resfriado.
(Yo) me lastimé ___.
mejor
peor
terrible

to name places to go or things to do when you are sick
la clínica
la enfermería
el hospital
Debo quedarme en la cama.
Debes quedarte en la cama.
llamar
tomar

to name ways to maintain good health
dormir (o → ue)
hacer ejercicio

to name medical professions
el / la dentista
el médico, la médica

to indicate how long something has been going on
¿Cuánto (tiempo) hace que
   ___?
Hace + *time expression* + que
   ___.
ahora
todavía
ya no

to express and ask for an opinion
(Yo) creo que ___.
¿no?

Resumen 311

Assessment

 Prueba cumulativa

 Examen de habilidades

 Test Generator

Additional Assessment Options

 Comm. Act. BLMs
Small Group Activities
Situation Cards

 Pasos vivos 1 CD-ROM
Slide Presentation Maker, Video Presentation Maker, Word Processor, Spindle

 ¿Lo sabes bien? Video Quiz

Internet Activities
Self-Test

Multiple Intelligences
Visual/Spatial
See Enrichment.

CAPÍTULO 10

THEME: COMMUNITY

SCOPE AND SEQUENCE   Pages 312–345

COMMUNICATION

Topics

Places in the community

Activities and errands

Transportation

Numbers 200–1,000

Objectives

To talk about Hispanic communities in the U.S.

To talk about places

To talk about activities or errands in a community

To talk about things you buy

To talk about money

To talk about mailing things

To ask and give directions

To talk about transportation

To talk about past activities

To indicate when an event occurred

To say you don't / didn't know something

CULTURE

Hispanic communities in the U.S.

GRAMMAR

La preposición de + el

El pretérito de los verbos que terminan en -ar

El pretérito del verbo ir

Ancillaries available for use with Chapter 10

Multisensory/Technology

 Overheads, 51–55

 Audio Tapes and CDs

 Vocabulary Art Blackline Masters for Hands-On Learning, pp. 53–57/CD-ROM

 Classroom Crossword

 Video

 Pasos vivos 1 CD-ROM

 Internet Activities www.pasoapaso.com

Print

 Practice Workbook, pp. 104–113

 Writing, Audio & Video Activities, pp. 59–64, 120–122, 170–171

 Communicative Activity Blackline Masters

Pair and Small Group Activities, pp. 71–76

Situation Cards, p. 77

Un paso más: Actividades para ampliar tu español, pp. 56–61

TPR Storytelling

Assessment

 Assessment Program

Pruebas, pp. 143–153

Examen de habilidades, pp. 154–157

 Test Generator

Video still from Chap. 10

311A

Planning Express, Teaching
Resources Library, and Clip Art
Library

¿Lo sabes bien?
Video Quiz

Cultural Overview

Hispanic Communities in the U.S.

Hispanic culture is evident in most parts of the U.S. But who are Hispanic Americans?

The meaning of the word Hispanic is somewhat elusive. Contrary to popular notions, not all U.S. Hispanics speak Spanish, are Roman Catholics, or are recent immigrants, even though these characteristics do describe many Hispanics. Virtually all, however, can trace their lineage to Latin America or to Spain. The most common places of origin are Mexico, Puerto Rico, and Cuba.

Much of the southwestern U.S. was Mexican territory before the Mexican-American War (1846–1848), and many Mexican American families have resided in the region for generations. In this century, immigration from Mexico to the U.S. was spurred by the revolution of 1910–1917. This northward migration established large Mexican communities in such places as Kansas City and Chicago.

During the 1940s, Puerto Rican immigration to the U.S. mainland increased. Fueled by an expanding job market, as well as the availability of regular airline flights between San Juan and New York City, large Puerto Rican communities were established in New York, Connecticut, Rhode Island, and Illinois. Since the passage of the 1917 Jones Act, Puerto Ricans have been U.S. citizens by birth. This status facilitates their movement between the mainland and the island. Puerto Rican migration has been described as a "revolving door," as there is frequent travel back and forth, often for long periods of time. This provides a regular infusion of Puerto Rican culture in the U.S. and of U.S. culture in the island.

Economic, social, and political conditions have sparked four large waves of immigration from Cuba to the U.S. in the last 40 years. The first wave began in 1959, shortly after Fidel Castro gained power; the second one in 1965. The third, one in which approximately 125,000 Cubans arrived in the U.S. during the Mariel boat lift, occurred during a five-month period in 1980. In 1994 thousands of Cubans once again sought refuge in the U.S. Because of a U.S. policy limiting Cuban visas to about 2,700 a year, however, most were taken to refugee camps in Guantánamo Bay. There they awaited results of negotiations between the U.S. and Cuban governments that would tell them if they would be allowed to immigrate to the U.S. or be forced to return to Cuba. Many Cuban immigrants have now settled in the Miami area. However, smaller, but vital communities also exist in New Jersey, Illinois, and elsewhere.

Introduce

Re-entry of Concepts

The following list represents words, expressions, and grammar topics re-entered from *El primer paso* to Chap. 9:

El primer paso
Numbers 0–31
Calendar expressions

Chapter 1
Activities

Chapter 2
Time-telling
School supplies
School subjects

Chapter 3
Leisure-time activities
Places and buildings
Ir a + infinitive

Chapter 4
Food
Expressing likes and preferences

Chapter 6
Places and buildings
Direct object pronouns
Clothing

Chapter 7
Vacation activities
Para + inf.

Chapter 8
Household chores

Chapter 9
Places and buildings
Hace . . . que

Planning

Cross-Curricular Connections

Geography Connection *(pp. 316–317)*
Have students choose a Spanish-speaking country and create a stamp or monetary note. This might feature a famous historical figure, landmark, or place. They should draw it large enough for the whole class to see.

Math Connection *(pp. 328–329)*
Using census data for your community, have students make a bar graph to illustrate the distribution of ethnic communities in your city, town, or state.

Spanish in Your Community
Have students investigate where in their community they could go to exchange U.S. money for foreign currency. Have them determine how much money can be exchanged and what foreign currencies are available. Ask them to find the exchange rate tables in the newspaper.

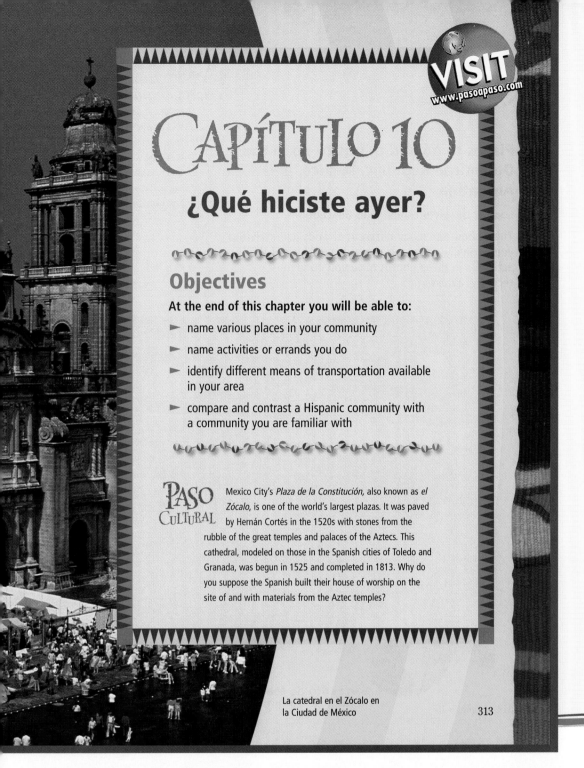

CAPÍTULO 10

¿Qué hiciste ayer?

Objectives

At the end of this chapter you will be able to:

► name various places in your community

► name activities or errands you do

► identify different means of transportation available in your area

► compare and contrast a Hispanic community with a community you are familiar with

PASO CULTURAL Mexico City's *Plaza de la Constitución*, also known as *el Zócalo*, is one of the world's largest plazas. It was paved by Hernán Cortés in the 1520s with stones from the rubble of the great temples and palaces of the Aztecs. This cathedral, modeled on those in the Spanish cities of Toledo and Granada, was begun in 1525 and completed in 1813. Why do you suppose the Spanish built their house of worship on the site of and with materials from the Aztec temples?

La catedral en el Zócalo en la Ciudad de México

313

Cultural Notes ☼

Paso cultural
Possible answers: The Spaniards did not want the Aztecs to continue worshipping their own gods./Taking the site and materials of the Aztec temples to build Roman Catholic cathedrals was a physical way of making the Aztecs substitute the new faith for their old beliefs.

(pp. 312–313, photo)
As in most Spanish colonial cities, Mexico City's main *plaza* was surrounded by government and commercial buildings, the houses of leading citizens, and the cathedral shown here. Today the *Zócalo* (from the Aztec word meaning stone base) is the site of presidential inaugurations, national celebrations and, every day, dozens of political demonstrations by groups from all over Mexico.

Cultural Objective
• To compare errands and activities in Spanish-speaking countries with those in the U.S.

 **¡Piénsalo bien!**

Play

 Video Activity A

Using the Video
This chapter's video focuses on community. Our host takes students on a tour of the area of Miami known as Little Havana. To prepare students for the video, first ask them to predict what this chapter's tape will be about. Then have students watch the segment several times. After the first time, you may wish to have them brainstorm possible vocabulary and expressions they will need to talk about what they saw on the video. Ask students to identify: a) things they saw that were familiar to them, and b) things they saw that they probably would not see where they live.
Video segment 1: For more teaching suggestions, see the Video Teacher's Guide.

Places to go and things to do in the Dominican Republic, Mexico, and Argentina

Look at the pictures and read the captions.

Think about the many different errands and activities you normally do in your community. Which of the activities in these photos have you done most recently? When?

PASO CULTURAL Baseball is a year-round sport in the Caribbean. The Dominican Republic, Puerto Rico, Mexico, and Venezuela all have winter leagues, in which many U.S. major league baseball stars play. In February, professional teams from these countries and Cuba compete in *la Serie del Caribe,* the winter season championship. Many Caribbean players play or have played in the U.S. majors. Can you name three, present or past, who have had outstanding careers?

San Pedro de Macorís, República Dominicana

"Yo fui a ver un partido de béisbol."
What do you suppose *un partido* means

314 Capítulo 10

Options

Strategies for Reaching All Students

Spanish-Speaking Students
Ask: *¿Haces las mismas cosas que las personas en las fotos? ¿Cuándo fue la última vez que fuiste a la biblioteca, que fuiste al museo o que fuiste a un partido? ¿Te gusta el béisbol? ¿Lo juegas? ¿Qué posición juegas? Si no lo juegas, ¿te gusta verlo? ¿Qué deportes juegas?*

 Un paso más Exs. 10-A, 10-B

Enrichment
(p. 314, photo): Ask students if they know of any Hispanic players in other sports. (Mary Jo Fernández, Aranxta Sánchez-Vicario, and Carlos Moya, tennis; Julio César Chavez and Oscar De La Hoya, boxing; Nancy López and Seve Ballesteros, golf; Jorge Campos and Tab Ramos, soccer)

Multiple Intelligences
Bodily/Kinesthetic and Interpersonal/Social
Have students make a collage of Hispanic athletes to be displayed in the room.
Visual/Spatial
See Using the Video.

"Fui a la librería para comprar un libro sobre la historia de México."

Librería is a false cognate. Based on the photograph, what do you suppose it means?

Mérida, México

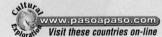

San Carlos de Bariloche, Argentina

"Fuimos al Centro Cívico y después al Museo de La Patagonia."

PASO CULTURAL

Located at the foot of the Andes near the Chilean border, San Carlos de Bariloche is one of Argentina's most popular winter resort towns. Its steep streets and stone and wood chalets have earned it the name, "the Switzerland of South America." The clock tower in the town's *Centro Cívico* is a popular attraction at noon, when four wooden figures emerge and move in rotation. The figures represent the four groups of people who have inhabited and shaped the region's history: indigenous, conquistador, colonial, and missionary. What groups of people have lived in your area? What impact did they have on regional history?

www.pasoapaso.com
Visit these countries on-line

¡Piensa en la cultura! 315

Cultural Notes

(p. 314, photo)
Like many young people in the U.S., many Dominican teens dream of becoming U.S. major-league baseball players. Every year U.S. and Japanese professional baseball teams seek out potential players in the Dominican Republic.

(p. 315, top photo)
Mexican bookstores offer how-to books, bestsellers, and classics, and, most often, translated U.S. and European bestsellers. Mexico is one of the most important literary and publishing centers in the Spanish-speaking world, and Mexican authors regularly win honors in international competitions. Ask students: What Mexican author won the Nobel Prize for Literature in 1990? (Octavio Paz) What other Mexican authors do you know of?

(p. 315, bottom photo)
The architectural style of the buildings around Bariloche's central *plaza* reflects the influence of Swiss-German immigration to the region. Like the U.S., Argentina saw a huge influx of European immigrants during the 1800s and early 1900s. More recently, immigrants have come from Syria, Lebanon, Japan, and Korea. Ask students to compare the patterns of immigration in Argentine history with those in U.S. history.

Communicative Objectives
- To talk about places
- To talk about activities or errands in a community
- To talk about money
- To talk about mailing things
- To talk about past activities
- To indicate when an event occurred
- To say you didn't know something
- To express a condition

 Overheads 51–52

 Vocabulary Art BLMs/CD-ROM

 Pronunciation Tape 10-1

 Vocabulario para conversar A

Play

Using the Video
Video segment 2: See the Video Teacher's Guide.

 Video Activity B

Vocabulario para conversar

 Chapter 10
Vocabulary

¿Adónde vas?

Aquí tienes palabras y expresiones necesarias para hablar de las cosas que puedes hacer en tu comunidad. Léelas varias veces y practícalas con un(a) compañero(a) en las páginas siguientes.

el supermercado

la librería

la biblioteca

los comestibles

la tarjeta de cumpleaños

devolver (o → ue) un libro

las pastillas (para la garganta)

el regalo

la farmacia

el champú

el jabón

la pasta dentífrica

la tienda de r

ir a pasear

ver un partido de béisbol

316   Capítulo 10

Options

Strategies for Reaching All Students

Students Needing Extra Help
Have students begin to fill in their Organizers.
También necesitas . . . : Some of these words can be taught as opposites. For example: *abrir* and *cerrar, sacar* and *devolver, temprano* and *tarde.*
Teach the preterite verbs as vocabulary, not grammar.
Write out the complete present-tense verb chart for *cerrar.*

Learning Spanish Through Action
STAGING VOCABULARY: *Borren, Escriban, Pasen*
MATERIALS: a dozen index cards, with any number from 200 to 1,000 written on each one
DIRECTIONS: Call on a group of three or four students to go to the chalkboard. Select a card and show it to the class but not to the group at the board. Now read the num-

ber and have students at the board write out the number. Continue with new groups until all numbers have been written. For extra practice, call out selected numbers from the board, having volunteers erase them as you call them out.

la tarjeta postal

el sello

enviar una carta

carta

el correo

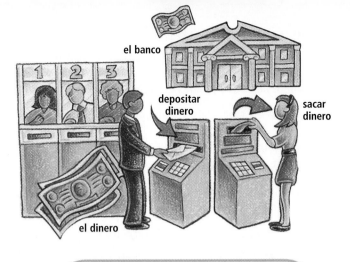

el banco

depositar dinero

sacar dinero

el dinero

200	doscientos*	700	setecientos
300	trescientos	800	ochocientos
400	cuatrocientos	900	novecientos
500	quinientos	1000	mil
600	seiscientos		

También necesitas...

abrir	*to open*
cerrar (e → ie)	*to close*
llegar	*to arrive, to get to*
devolver:	*to return (an object):*
(yo) devolví	*I returned*
(tú) devolviste	*you returned*
enviar: (yo) envié	*to send: I sent*
hacer:	*to do, to make:*
(yo) hice	*I did / made*
(tú) hiciste	*you did / made*
sacar: (yo) saqué	*to take out: I took out*
ver: (yo) vi	*to see: I saw*
(tú) viste	*you saw*

anoche	*last night*
ayer	*yesterday*
luego	*afterward, later, then*
temprano	*early*
tarde†	*late*
ya	*already*
(Yo) no lo sabía.	*I didn't know that.*
si	*if, whether*

¿Y qué quiere decir . . . ?

¿Me compras ___?
(yo) deposité

---

* Note that when a number ending in *-ientos* is followed by a feminine noun, we use *-ientas* instead: *doscientas personas, trescientas cincuenta cartas.*

† Remember that *la tarde* means "afternoon" or "evening."

Vocabulario para conversar   317

Grammar Preview
Envié and *saqué* are presented lexically. The explanation of the preterite of *-ar* verbs appears in the grammar section on p. 333.

Teaching Suggestions
Preparing students to speak: Use one or two options from each of the categories of Comprehensible Input, Physical Response, or Limited Verbal Response. For a complete explanation of these categories and some sample activities, see pp. T22–T23.

Point out that *mil* is a false cognate (often referred to as an *amigo falso*). It means "thousand," but it may be confused with "million." A million is *un millón*.

Class Starter Review
On the day following initial vocabulary presentation, you might begin the class with one of these activities:
1) Call out specific activities related to places shown in the *Vocabulario para conversar.* Have students name the places. Then reverse the activity.
2) Have students name three places where they might run errands.

Internet Activities
Juegos

Extended Written Practice/Homework
1. Refer to the vocabulary on pp. 316–317 and write four sentences telling if you live near or far from different places.
2. Write four sentences telling what you have to do and where: *Tengo que depositar dinero en el banco mañana.*
3. Refer to the vocabulary on pp. 316–317 and write four sentences telling when you bought different items.

Multiple Intelligences
Bodily/Kinesthetic
See Learning Spanish Through Action.
Verbal/Linguistic
See Pronunciation Tape 10-1 and Class Starter Review.
Visual/Spatial
See Overheads 51–52, the Vocabulary Art BLMs/CD-ROM, and Using the Video.

Practice

Reteach / Review: ¿Por qué? / porque
Ex. 1: To extend this dialogue, *Estudiante A* can ask *Estudiante B* why he or she has to go to the second place mentioned.

Re-enter / Recycle
Ex. 1: places and buildings from Chaps. 3 and 6
Ex. 2: school supplies from Chap. 2, places and buildings from Chap. 3, food from Chap. 4, direct object pronouns from Chap. 6
Ex. 3: places and buildings from Chap. 3
Ex. 4: calendar expressions from *El primer paso*, time-telling from Chap. 2

Answers: Empecemos a conversar

1 ESTUDIANTE A
a. ¿Adónde vas? ¿A la biblioteca?
b. . . .¿Al supermercado?
c. . . .¿Al correo?
d. . . .¿Al parque?
e. . . .¿A la tienda de regalos?

ESTUDIANTE B
a. Sí, y luego tengo que ir a la farmacia.
b. . . .al gimnasio.
c. . . .al almacén.
d. . . .a la piscina.
e. . . .a la tienda de descuentos.

Empecemos a conversar

Túrnate con un(a) compañero(a) para ser *Estudiante A* y *Estudiante B*. Reemplacen las palabras subrayadas con palabras representadas o escritas en los recuadros.
💡 quiere decir que puedes escoger *(choose)* tu propia respuesta.

1 A —¿Adónde vas? ¿Al banco?
B —Sí, y luego tengo que ir al parque.

Estudiante A · Estudiante B

2 A —Si vas a la farmacia, ¿me compras pastillas para la garganta?
B —Pero ya las compré ayer.
A —¡Ah! No lo sabía.

Estudiante A · Estudiante B

¡NO OLVIDES!
Remember that the direct object pronouns are *lo, la, los,* and *las.*

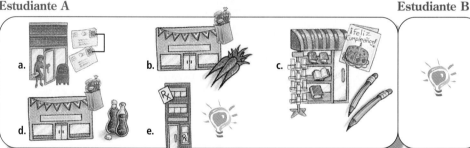

318 Capítulo 10

Options

Strategies for Reaching All Students

Spanish-Speaking Students
Exs. 1–4: Pair bilingual and non-bilingual students whenever possible.

 Un paso más Exs. 10-C, 10-D

Students Needing Extra Help
Ex. 1: Review *al* and *a la* from Chap. 3.
Ex. 2: Show students how *pastillas para la garganta* becomes *las* in the response. Write it on the chalkboard and then do another example.
Ex. 3: Write *fui, fuiste, llevé, compré, pagué, envié,* and other preterite forms on the chalkboard for possible responses.

Otherwise students may be tempted to use just one response. Show students that the places and associated activities from p. 316 are grouped together. They will need to know this to do the activity.
Ex. 4: Review *tarde* and *temprano*. Review time-telling from Chap. 2.

318 Standards 1.1; 3.2

3

A —¿Qué hiciste ayer? ¿Fuiste <u>al banco</u>?

B —Sí, fui y saqué (deposité) dinero (doscientos dólares).
    o: No, fui <u>al parque de diversiones</u>.

Estudiante A   **Estudiante B**

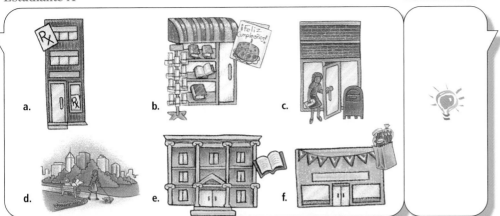

a.   b.   c.

d.   e.   f.

4

A —¿<u>La biblioteca</u> abre tarde los sábados?

B —Sí, abre a las diez y cierra temprano por la noche.
    o: No, abre temprano y cierra temprano por la tarde.

Estudiante A   **Estudiante B**

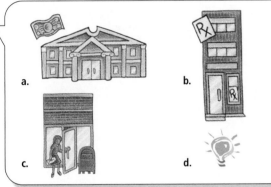

a.   b.

c.   d.

2 ESTUDIANTE A

a. Si vas al correo, ¿me compras sellos? / ¡Ah! No lo sabía.
b. ...al supermercado, ...zanahorias? / ...
c. ...a la librería, ...lápices? /...
d. ...al supermercado, ...refrescos? / ...
e. ...a la farmacia, ... *(Endings will vary.)*

ESTUDIANTE B

a. Pero ya los compré ayer.
b. ...las ...
c. ...los ...
d. ...los ...
e. Answers will vary. Look for correct use of direct object pronouns.

3 ESTUDIANTE A

a. ¿Qué hiciste ayer? ¿Fuiste a la farmacia?
b. ...a la librería?
c. ...al correo?
d. ...al parque?
e. ...a la biblioteca?
f. ...al supermercado?

ESTUDIANTE B

a.–f. Answers will vary. Encourage students to use vocabulary from previous chapters.

4 ESTUDIANTE A

a. ¿El banco abre tarde los sábados?
b. ¿La farmacia ...
c. ¿El correo ...
d. Questions will vary.

ESTUDIANTE B

a.–d. Answers will vary.

Enrichment

Ex. 3: This exercise can be done with the entire class with you playing the role of *Estudiante A* and eliciting various answers for each place named. Vary the initial question. Examples: *Y tú, ¿qué hiciste ayer? Y tú, ¿fuiste al banco también? Y tú, ¿adónde fuiste ayer?*

Extended Written Practice/Homework

1. Write three sentences telling at what time different places open and close.
2. Write four sentences telling about four different places you went to last week.
3. Choose from *vi, devolví, envié, deposité,* and *saqué* to write four sentences telling when you did different things.

Multiple Intelligences

Naturalist

Have students take note of the buildings/stores in their community and see what, if any, impact they have caused on the surrounding environment.

Verbal/Linguistic

See Exs. 1–4 and Enrichment.

Apply

Re-enter / Recycle

Ex. 5: places and buildings from Chaps. 3 and 6, expressing likes and preferences from Chap. 4
Ex. 6: direct object pronouns from Chap. 6
Ex. 8: *ir a* + inf. from Chap. 3

Answers: Empecemos a escribir

5 Answers will vary, but look for *prefiero* + inf. and use of the contraction *al.*

6 Answers will vary, but look for use of *hice / hago* and the pronoun *las.*

7 Answers will vary, but make sure students use the preterite form. Encourage use of new vocabulary.

8 Answers will vary, but look for *ir a* + inf.

Empecemos a escribir

Escribe tus respuestas en español.

5 ¿Prefieres llegar tarde o temprano a una fiesta? ¿A un partido? ¿Al cine?

6 ¿Ya hiciste todas las tareas para hoy? ¿Las hiciste anoche? Generalmente, ¿las haces por la tarde o por la noche?

7 ¿Adónde fuiste ayer? ¿Y el fin de semana pasado? ¿A quién viste?

8 ¿Qué vas a hacer si recibes *(receive)* mil dólares? ¿Vas a depositarlos en el banco o vas a comprar cosas? ¿Qué vas a comprar?

PASO CULTURAL Madrid's streets are rarely empty, even at night. Landmarks and cultural attractions fill up with visitors into the night, as do stores, cafés, and *tapas* restaurants. The eighteenth-century Cibeles statue and fountain are the city's symbol and a popular gathering place for special events. Most major cities have landmarks—statues, city squares, buildings, or other structures—that have become their symbols. Name three cities anywhere in the world and the landmarks that you associate with them.

La Plaza de la Cibeles en Madrid

Options

Strategies for Reaching All Students

Spanish-Speaking Students
Have Spanish-speaking students write a paragraph about the last time they went shopping for a gift. *Escribe sobre la última vez que saliste a comprar un regalo. ¿Adónde fuiste? ¿Qué compraste? ¿Para quién lo compraste? ¿Por qué le compraste un regalo? ¿Fue fácil encontrar lo que querías?*

Students Needing Extra Help
Ex. 7: Have students make a chart before writing sentences if this exercise is done in groups. Remind students of the *a personal.*
Ex. 8: Have students make a columned chart to help them get organized.

Enrichment
Empecemos a escribir: Additional writing assignments: 1) Students can write a sentence telling three things they saw on their last vacation. 2) Students can tell when and where they last bought three school supplies or items of clothing.

Multiple Intelligences
Intrapersonal/Introspective
See *Empecemos a escribir* Exs. 5–8 and Enrichment.
Verbal/Linguistic
See Audio Activity 10.1.
Visual/Spatial
See Practice Wkbk. 10-1 and 10-2 and Writing Activities 10-A and 10-B.

Delante del Palacio de Comunicaciones, el correo central de Madrid

La estación de trenes Atocha, en Madrid

También se dice...

la estampilla
el timbre

la postal

el hipermercado

los correos
la oficina de correos

la botica
la droguería

Vocabulario para conversar   321

 Practice Wkbk.
10-1, 10-2

 Audio Activity 10.1

 Writing Activities
10-A, 10-B

 Pruebas 10-1, 10-2

Cultural Notes ☀

Paso cultural
Possible answers: Paris, the Eiffel Tower; London, Big Ben; Rome, the Coliseum; New York, the Statue of Liberty, the Empire State Building; San Francisco, the Golden Gate Bridge; Chicago, the Sears Tower; St. Louis, the Gateway Arch.

(p. 320, photo; p. 321, top photo)
The Cibeles fountain dates from the 1700s and represents Cibeles (Cybele), the Greek goddess of fertility, riding her chariot amid cascading water. The fountain stands in the center of a major traffic circle, la Plaza de la Cibeles. The building in the background is the city's main post office, el Palacio de Comunicaciones, built in the early 1900s.

(p. 321, bottom photo)
The Spanish government owns and operates Spain's rail network, RENFE *(Red Nacional de los Ferrocarriles Españoles)*. In 1992, Spain improved its already efficient service by launching its first high-speed train, the AVE *(Alta Velocidad Española)*, to make the run between Madrid and Expo '92 in Sevilla. Traveling at speeds of up to 186 miles per hour, the AVE cuts the travel time between these two cities from six hours to two hours and forty-five minutes.

Present

Chapter Theme
Transportation

Communicative Objectives
- To talk about places
- To ask and give directions
- To talk about transportation
- To express agreement
- To say you don't know something

 Overheads 53–54

 Vocabulary Art BLMs/CD-ROM

 Pronunciation Tape 10-2

 Vocabulario para conversar B

Play

Step

Using the Video
Video segment 2: See the Video Teacher's Guide.

 Video Activity B

Vocabulario para conversar

 **Chapter 10 Vocabulary**

¿Dónde queda el banco?

Aquí tienes el resto del vocabulario necesario para hablar de tu comunidad.

322 Capítulo 10

Options

Strategies for Reaching All Students

Students Needing Extra Help
Tambien necesitas . . . : Illustrate the location words with hand and / or body motions. Explain *en* + vehicle by giving examples using the new vocabulary.

Enrichment
También necesitas . . . : Review *lejos de / cerca de* and practice the new prepositions by asking questions about the location of classroom objects and where students are sitting. You may want to preview *del* with *lejos de / cerca de* and the new prepositions by modeling a complete sentence: *El bolígrafo está cerca (a la izquierda) del cuaderno.*

Learning Spanish Through Action
STAGING VOCABULARY: *Señalen, Toquen*
MATERIALS: photocopies or printouts of this vocabulary section from the Vocabulary Art BLMs/CD-ROM
DIRECTIONS: Tell students where you went last week. Have them touch or point to the locations on the map. Ask follow-up questions such as: *¿Dónde está el (la) ____?* *¿Está a la derecha (izquierda) del (de la) ____?*

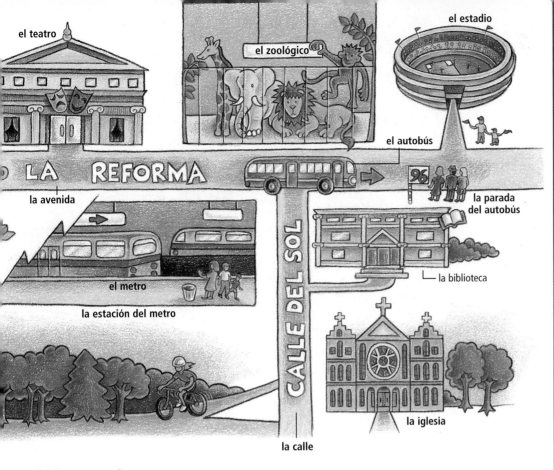

el teatro

el zoológico

el estadio

LA REFORMA

la avenida

el autobús

la parada del autobús

CALLE DEL SOL

el metro

la estación del metro

la biblioteca

la iglesia

la calle

También necesitas...

trabajar	*to work*
¿A cuántas cuadras (de ___)?	*How many blocks (from ___)?*
A (cinco) cuadras (de ___).	*(Five) blocks (from ___).*
queda(n)	*is (are) located*
a la derecha (de)	*to the right (of)*
a la izquierda (de)	*to the left (of)*
al lado (de)	*next to, beside*
detrás (de)	*behind*

enfrente (de)	*facing, opposite, in front (of)*
entre	*between, among*
en + *vehicle*	*by* + vehicle
Bueno	*here: OK, fine, all right*

¿Y qué quiere decir...?
la comunidad
el templo
(Yo) no sé.

 Pasos vivos 1 CD-ROM
Clip Art Album

Grammar Preview
Del appears here lexically. The explanation of the preposition *de + el* appears in the grammar section on p. 331.

Teaching Suggestions
Preparing students to speak: Use one or two options from each of the categories of Comprehensible Input, Physical Response, or Limited Verbal Response. For a complete explanation of these categories and some sample activities, see pp. T22–T23.

Note: Only boldface labels are new vocabulary items. The others were introduced earlier in this chapter.

Class Starter Review
Following initial vocabulary presentation, you might begin the class with this activity:
Mark a specific spot on the overhead of the town. Ask pairs of students to write down as many ways as they can to say where that place is. Provide a time limit. Do one place per day for several days. (As an alternative, bring in authentic city maps of your area or one from a Spanish-speaking country so students can practice asking for and giving directions.)

www Internet Activities
Juegos

Multiple Intelligences
Bodily/Kinesthetic
See Learning Spanish Through Action.
Verbal/Linguistic
See Pronunciation Tape 10-2 and Enrichment.
Visual/Spatial
See Overheads 53–54, the Vocabulary Art BLMs/CD-ROM, Using the Video, and Class Starter Review.

Practice & Apply

Re-enter / Recycle
Ex. 14: numbers 0–31 from *El primer paso*

Answers: Empecemos a conversar

9 ESTUDIANTE A

a. ¿Cómo vamos al zoológico? / Bueno.

b. ...al hotel? / ...

c. ...al restaurante? / ...

d. ...al estadio? / ...

e. ...a la iglesia? / ...

ESTUDIANTE B

a. Pues, no sé. ¿Por qué no vamos a pie?

b. ...en taxi?

c. ...en metro?

d. ...en autobús?

e. Answers will vary.

10 ESTUDIANTE A

a. Perdón, señora (señor / joven / señorita). ¿Dónde queda la estación de policía?

b ...el zoológico?

c. ...la estación del metro?

d. ...la estación de servicio?

e. ...el correo?

f. ...la plaza?

ESTUDIANTE B

a.–f. Answers will vary.

Empecemos a conversar

Para los ejercicios 10–11, usa el mapa en las páginas 322–323.

9

A —¿Cómo vamos *al teatro*?

B —Pues, no sé. ¿Por qué no vamos *en coche*?

A —Bueno.

Estudiante A   Estudiante B

10

A —Perdón, señora (señor / joven / señorita). ¿Dónde queda *el banco*?

B —Está en la *calle Rivera, entre el restaurante y la estación de servicio*.

Estudiante A   Estudiante B

324   Capítulo 10

Options

Strategies for Reaching All Students

Spanish-Speaking Students
Exs. 9–10: Pair bilingual with non-bilingual students whenever possible.
Ex. 14: After this exercise, ask Spanish-speaking students: *¿Cómo se llega a tu casa o apartamento desde la escuela? Escribe direcciones específicas.*
Ex. 15: Have students create a similar letter and ask non-bilingual students to help find the sentences that don't make sense.

Students Needing Extra Help
Ex. 10: Remind students to use the map. Have students repeat the activity using location words in preparation for Ex. 11.
Ex. 11: Point out the entrances to the buildings on the map.
Ex. 12: Have students use their Organizers. Brainstorm possible responses by using the map. Start with a list of location words.
Ex. 14: Students in rural areas may not be familiar with the term "block." Provide an example.

Enrichment
Ex. 10: Encourage students to give a variety of answers. For instance, *el banco queda al lado del restaurante.*
Ex. 12: To extend this assignment, students can make and label a map of their neighborhood that includes as many of the places as possible from both vocabulary sections.
Ex. 15: In pairs, have students create their own illogical letters. Post the letters and have them select the funniest ones.

11 A —¿Qué hay *cerca de la biblioteca*?

B —*A ver . . . está la iglesia.*

 cerca de

Estudiante A

a. al lado del

b. detrás de la

c. enfrente de la

d. a la izquierda del

e. a la derecha del

Estudiante B

Empecemos a escribir y a leer

Escribe tus respuestas en español.

12 ¿Qué hay en tu comunidad? Por ejemplo:

En mi comunidad hay un monumento en una plaza, un templo, una iglesia, dos bancos, . . .

13 ¿Dónde trabajan tus padres? ¿Trabajan en tu comunidad o en otra comunidad? ¿Y los padres de tu compañero(a)?

14 ¿Dónde queda la estación de policía de tu comunidad? ¿Queda cerca o lejos de tu casa? ¿A cuántas cuadras?

15 Lee la carta y luego cambia *(change)* las palabras *(words)* o frases que no tienen sentido *(make sense)*.

> **Querida mamá:**
> Ayer estuve muy ocupada todo el día. Primero fui al correo y compré unas pastillas para la garganta. Luego fui al teatro y vi un partido de vóleibol. Por la tarde fui al supermercado, donde compré unas tarjetas postales deliciosas. Luego, fui al zoológico para comprar zapatos nuevos. Hoy tengo que ir a la biblioteca porque necesito comprar un regalo para papá.
>
> Tu hija,
> Teresa

También se dice...

la gasolinera

el subterráneo (el subte)

el bus   la guagua
el camión   el micro
el colectivo   el
ómnibus

 www.pasoapaso.com

MORE PRACTICE

- Más práctica y tarea, p. 536
- Practice Workbook 10–3, 10–5

Extended Written Practice/Homework

1. Write four sentences telling how you prefer to go to different places: *Prefiero ir al correo en autobús.*
2. Choose three places in your community and write sentences telling what they are like.
3. Write three sentences telling on what streets or avenues different places in your community are located.

Multiple Intelligences

Verbal/Linguistic

See Exs. 9–11 and Audio Activity 10.2.

Visual/Spatial

See Enrichment Ex. 12; Ex. 15; Practice Wkbk. 10-3, 10-4, and 10-5; Writing Activities 10-C and 10-D; and Comm. Act. BLM 10-1.

Practice

Re-enter / Recycle
Ex. 1: school supplies from Chap. 2, food from Chap. 4, clothing from Chap. 6, vacation items from Chap. 7
Ex. 3: school subjects and numbers 32–59 from Chap. 2, numbers 60–100 from Chap. 5

Answers:
¡Comuniquemos!

1 ESTUDIANTE A
¿Adónde vas?/¿Por qué?
ESTUDIANTE B
Statements will vary, but may include the following destinations: *al banco, al restaurante, a la tienda de regalos, a la biblioteca, a la zapatería, al gimnasio, a la librería, al correo, al centro comercial, a la farmacia, a la tienda de ropa, al supermercado./* Statements will vary, but look for logical responses.

2 ESTUDIANTE A
Questions will vary, but look for correct verb forms: *fuiste, viste, escuchaste, hiciste, compraste.*
ESTUDIANTE B
Answers will vary.

¡COMUNI

1 Con un(a) compañero(a), imagina que tienes muchos quehaceres hoy. Por ejemplo:

A —*¿Adónde vas?*
B —*Primero tengo que ir a la biblioteca y luego a la farmacia.*
A —*¿Por qué?*
B —*Porque quiero devolver un libro y comprar champú.*

2 Averigua cuatro cosas que tu compañero(a) hizo ayer. Usa expresiones de la lista.

A —*¿Fuiste al gimnasio ayer?*
B —*Sí, fui al gimnasio para jugar básquetbol.*
  o: *No, no fui al gimnasio.*

ir a la (al) ___   hacer ejercicio
ver la tele   ir de compras
ver un partido de ___   comprar algo
escuchar ___   comprar algo en
hacer la tarea de ___   el supermercado

326   Capítulo 10

Options

Strategies for Reaching All Students

Spanish-Speaking Students
Exs: 1–2: Have Spanish-speaking students work together and present one of these exercises to the whole class.

 Un paso más Ex. 10-E

Students Needing Extra Help
Ex. 1: Model possible final responses for *Estudiante B,* and give examples of items which might be bought and activities which occur at the various destinations.
¿Qué sabes ahora?: Have students write out this section so that they can check off what they have mastered.

Cooperative Learning
Divide the class into groups of three or four. Using the map on pp. 322–323 of their texts, have students write clear instructions in how to get from one place to another. Assign each group a different set of start and end points. After they have written their sentences, call on individuals to read them, but without revealing the destination. Have other groups try to guess the final destination.

PASO CULTURAL

Plaza Morazán is the main square in Honduras's capital, Tegucigalpa. It is named after the great national hero, Francisco Morazán (1792–1842), whose statue appears in this painting. An able, progressive leader, Morazán tried unsuccessfully to bring under one government the area that today includes the countries of Guatemala, El Salvador, Honduras, Nicaragua, and Costa Rica. What do you see in this plaza that is similar to what you might expect to see in a public square in the U.S.?

Plaza Morazán en Tegucigalpa (1969), José Antonio Velásquez

¿Qué sabes ahora?

Can you:

► name places in your community
—En mi comunidad hay ___.

► ask about and give the location of a place?
—¿Dónde ___ la estación de policía?
—Está ___ la librería.

► tell where you go to run errands?
—Voy ___ para enviar unas cartas.

8

Los padres van a visitar tu escuela esta noche y tú tienes que trabajar de guía *(guide)*. Con un(a) compañero(a), ayuda a los padres a llegar a los lugares correctos.

A —¿Quién es tu profesor(a) de ___?

B —Es el señor / la señora ___.

A —¿Dónde queda su sala de clases?

B —Queda cerca de ___. Es la sala número ___.

3 Dialogues will vary.

Answers: ¿Qué sabes ahora?
• Answers will vary.
• *está, queda;* Answers will vary, but look for a variety of prepositions.
• al correo

Multicultural Perspectives

Ancient civilizations such as those of the Mayas in Central America and the Incas in South America organized their cities around a *plaza*. The site was selected for religious or for practical reasons, such as its being a source of water. Temples and palaces were built around the *plaza*. Ask students to think about how towns and cities are designed and organized. Ask them what the central area or areas of their own towns are. How do they attract people?

 Audio Activity 10.3

 Pasos vivos 1 CD-ROM
Slide Projector, Laboratorio de grabar

Cultural Notes ☀

Extended Written Practice/Homework
1. Write three sentences telling where friends and family members work.
2. Write three sentences telling how far away your house is from different places: *Nuestra casa queda a tres cuadras de un banco.*
3. Write three sentences about places in your community that are located between other places: *La farmacia queda entre la tienda de ropa y la librería.*

(p. 326) If students ask, inform them that the man in the photo is a traffic patrolman in Argentina.

Paso cultural
Possible answers: gardens, walkways, and benches; the layout of the square; the fact that it has a focal point (in this case, the statue); the activities of the people (taking pictures, resting, talking, reading newspapers, strolling).

(p. 327, photo)
The Honduran artist, José Antonio Velásquez (1906–1983), was born in La Caridad. He worked as a telegraph operator and barber before devoting himself to his art in 1930. Today he is considered one of the most renowned painters from Latin America.

Critical Thinking: Identifying Stereotypes

Help students understand that Hispanics are not the only group that has established neighborhoods such as Pilsen. Discuss immigrant groups, past and present, that have developed similar neighborhoods in towns and cities throughout the country. Ask students why they believe people decide to move to areas that are heavily populated with people of their own ethnicity or cultural background. Identify and discuss stereotypes that sometimes cloud people's perceptions of ethnic neighborhoods and why people choose to live in them.

Perspectiva cultural

Las comunidades hispanas en los Estados Unidos

En esta ciudad hay muchos productos hispanos y servicios en español.

Do you think these photographs were taken in the United States? Why do you think so? Looking at the signs, which language do you think predominates? Why? What do the signs tell you about the community and the people who live there?

Yrma is fourteen and lives in Chicago with her family. When she wants to see a Spanish-language movie at a local theater, she can find the information she needs in any of several Spanish-language papers published in the city. These are the papers that almost one million Hispanic residents in Chicago can read to keep informed, look for a job, or find weekly sales on groceries.

Yrma's neighborhood is called Pilsen. It's one of several large Hispanic communities in Chicago. Most residents of Pilsen are Mexican American. The Pilsen community offers its residents and the rest of the city a large variety of products and services. Within walking distance of Yrma's home, you can find several small tortilla factories; offices of bilingual doctors, lawyers, and dentists; grocery stores with products from the United States and Mexico; bookstores and record stores with Spanish-language titles; restaurants; and several travel agencies.

Tienda de productos latinoamericanos en Nueva Jersey

Options

Strategies for Reaching All Students

Spanish-Speaking Students
Ask: *¿Hay muchos hispanos en tu comunidad? ¿Puedes comprar periódicos y revistas en español? ¿Hay tiendas y comidas especiales? ¿Qué otros idiomas se hablan donde vives? ¿Has visitado otras partes de tu pueblo o ciudad donde viven personas de otras partes del mundo? ¿Qué puedes ver o hacer allí?*

 Un paso más Ex. 10-F

Students Needing Extra Help
Have students take notes on important information to use as a review later in *¿Lo sabes bien?*
Discuss the Spanish-speaking community in your area if there is one. Ask students which Spanish-speaking culture predominates.
Exs. 1–2: Be aware that some students may not be familiar with any culture other than their own.

Enrichment
Tell students that the Mexican Fine Arts Center Museum in Chicago is the largest facility of its kind in the country. It not only presents exhibits on the visual arts, but also offers film, theater, music festivals, and art education programs and materials. Among other goods and services in Pilsen are newspapers and magazines from Mexico and clothing stores featuring Western or *vaquero* fashions.

A few blocks from Yrma's home is the Mexican Fine Arts Center Museum, where works by Mexican and Mexican American artists are always on view.

People from other areas of Chicago come to Pilsen looking for the special products and services it offers. Where else would you buy the freshest tortillas in town? Or the latest pop hits from Mexico?

Yrma's neighborhood is a good example of how the many Hispanic communities throughout the United States provide unique goods and services to the entire population of the city. Pilsen is part of the diverse mosaic of cultures that make the United States a multicultural society.

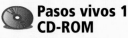
www.pasoapaso.com

Del Centro Museo de Bellas Artes Mexicanas en Chicago: tapiz de madera hecho por una joven mexicana; árbol de la vida en la tienda de regalos.

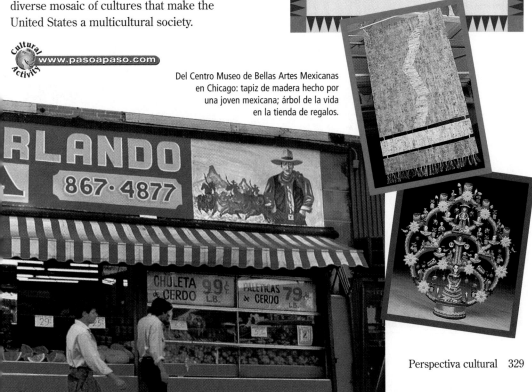

Perspectiva cultural   329

Answers
Answers will vary. Students may say that the photo was taken in a Spanish-speaking country, because Spanish predominates in the signs. However, if they look closely at the signs on the right, they will see the abbreviation for pound and the monetary symbol for cents, thus indicating that the photo was taken somewhere in the U.S. / Answers will vary. The use of Spanish in the signs probably indicates that this store caters to a Spanish-speaking community.

Answers: La cultura desde tu perspectiva
1–2 Answers will vary.

Pasos vivos 1 CD-ROM
Notas culturales, Maps

Internet Activities
Perspectiva cultural

Cultural Notes
(p. 328, realia)
Corn tostadas from the Pilsen neighborhood in Chicago. Ask students why they think both Spanish and English are used on the package.

Cultural Notes

(p. 328, realia)
This clipping from the Chicago Spanish-language newspaper *Éxito* (success), announces *¡Viva! Chicago,* an annual music festival. The festival features music from throughout Latin America, reflecting the ethnic makeup of Chicago's Latino community. Chicago has large Mexican and Puerto Rican populations, and smaller groups from other South and Central American countries.

(pp. 328–329, photo)
Stores like this one in Union City, New Jersey, cater to large communities of Hispanics. They carry products that can be found in American grocery stores, in addition to foods, spices, newspapers, and magazines from Latin America. The sign in the window, *Paleticas de cerdo* (ham hocks), uses the Cuban form of the diminutive for *paletas (-icas* instead of *-itas),* indicating that it is either Cuban-owned or serves a primarily Cuban clientele.

(p. 329, right photos)
The Mexican Fine Arts Center Museum (founded in 1982) is located in Pilsen, a Chicago neighborhood that has been predominantly Mexican for several decades. It is the Midwest's first Mexican cultural center and the largest of its kind in the U.S. Every year more than 75,000 visitors view its exhibits or enjoy performing arts events.

Preview

 Overhead 55

Answers

A *Llegaron* means "they arrived"; *llevaron* "they took"; *enviaron,* "they mailed (sent)"; and *regresaron,* "they returned."

B *Escuchó* means "he listened"; *habló,* "he talked."

C *Fueron / fue*

Gramática en contexto

Read this story about a reporter and some visiting aliens.

Hoy dos individuos muy extraños llegaron a nuestra ciudad. Creemos que son agentes secretos de otro planeta.

Los dos agentes fueron a diferentes partes de la ciudad. Uno de ellos fue a ver un desfile y sacó fotos.

El otro agente fue al estadio a escuchar un concierto del grupo Los Tigres. El agente escuchó la música rock y grabó el concierto. También habló con varias personas.

LOS TIGRES

330 Capítulo 10

Options

Strategies for Reaching All Students

Students Needing Extra Help
C: Have students start filling in the grammar portion of their Organizers. Have them refer to the verb chart on p. 336 if necessary.

Extended Written Practice/Homework
(Have students do this activity after you present *de + el*). Choose a street in your community and write five sentences telling what places are there. Tell where they are in relationship to other places: *En la Avenida 3, la biblioteca queda al lado del correo.*

Multiple Intelligences
Verbal/Linguistic
Have students in pairs take turns reading segments of the story to each other.
Visual/Spatial
See Overhead 55.

Creemos que los agentes llevaron las fotos y otras cosas a su nave espacial y las enviaron a su líder.

No sabemos dónde están en este momento, pero creemos que los agentes ya regresaron a su planeta.

A In the story, the verb forms *llegaron, llevaron, enviaron,* and *regresaron* are used. What do you think they mean? (Remember you already know the meaning of *llegar, llevar, enviar,* and *regresar.*)

B The verbs *escuchó* and *habló* are used to talk about what one of the secret agents did. Can you figure out what these words mean?

C In the second paragraph, find two verb forms that tell where both secret agents went and then where one secret agent went.

La preposición *de + el*

When we use the preposition *a + el*, we form the contraction *al*. In the same way, when we use the preposition *de + el*, we form the contraction *del* ("of the," "from the").

Luisa está enfrente **del** cine.

Gramática en contexto   331

Present
Teaching Suggestions
Remind students how contractions are formed in English: did not → didn't, I am → I'm. Spanish contractions are formed the same way, but without the apostrophe.

Answers

1 Answers will vary, but should be based on the accompanying map. Look for contractions *al* and *del.*

 Practice Wkbk. 10-6

 Prueba 10-5

1 Mira el mapa de abajo. Imagina que buscas varios lugares y tu compañero(a) es un(a) agente de policía. Pregunta y contesta según *(according to)* el modelo. Puedes usar las palabras *(words)* de la lista a la derecha.

A —¿Dónde está la farmacia? ¿Queda lejos?

B —No, no queda lejos. Está al lado del hotel.

A —¿A cuántas cuadras de aquí?

B —Pues, queda a una (dos) cuadra(s) de aquí.

cerca (de)
lejos (de)
a la izquierda (de)
a la derecha (de)
detrás (de)
enfrente (de)
al lado (de)
entre

ESTÁS AQUÍ

Options

Strategies for Reaching All Students

Spanish-Speaking Students
Exs. 1–11: For this grammar section, have Spanish-speaking students work together when possible.

Students Needing Extra Help
Ex. 1: Review *a + el* with examples from earlier chapters, using all forms *(al, a la, a los, a las).*
Point out that *entre* is the only preposition in the list that does not require *de.*
Generate a list of places; students have only a list of location words.
El pretérito de los verbos que terminan en -ar: First review the present-tense endings with a chart. Then use preterite endings. Emphasize the need for the accent *(o* without the accent is the present-tense *yo* form; with the accent it's the preterite tense *Ud. / él / ella* form). Practice pronunciation with examples.
Write out a complete chart for all the spelling-changing and stem-changing verbs, color-coding or highlighting the stem-changing or irregular parts.
Show *cerrar* in both tenses to illustrate that there is no stem change in the preterite.

El pretérito de los verbos que terminan en *-ar*

Up to now you have seen verbs in the present tense and a few in the past tense. This past tense is called the preterite. Here are all the forms of *comprar* in the preterite.

(yo)	compré	(nosotros) (nosotras)	compr**amos**
(tú)	compr**aste**	(vosotros) (vosotras)	compr**asteis**
Ud. (él) (ella)	compr**ó**	Uds. (ellos) (ellas)	compr**aron**

- You have already learned that the verb endings tell you who does an action. They also tell you when an action is done (in the present, in the past, or in the future). In the same way that *-o, -as, -a, -amos, -áis, -an* tell you that the action takes place in the present, *-é, -aste, -ó, -amos, -asteis, -aron,* tell you that the action took place in the past.

- Notice the accent marks on the endings *-é* and *-ó.* Also notice that the *nosotros* form is the same in the present tense and the preterite.

- Verbs whose infinitive ends in *-gar,* like *pagar, jugar,* and *llegar,* end in *-gué* in the *yo* form of the preterite. For example:

  Lle**gué** al teatro a las ocho. ¿Cuándo lle**gaste** tú?

- Verbs whose infinitive ends in *-car,* like *buscar, tocar,* and *sacar,* end in *-qué* in the *yo* form of the preterite. For example:

  Sa**qué** dos libros de la biblioteca. ¿Cuántos sa**caste** tú?

- Verbs that have a stem change in the present do *not* have a stem change in the preterite. For example:

  Generalmente el museo **cierra** a las cinco.
  Anoche **cerró** a las nueve.

2 Con un(a) compañero(a), decide cuál es el infinitivo de estos verbos.

a. busqué   c. llegué   e. toqué   g. saqué
b. practiqué   d. pagué   f. jugué   h. apagué

Gramática en contexto   333

PASO CULTURAL   Mexico City's reliable and inexpensive *metro* serves five million passengers a day. Many stops, like this one, feature murals on Mexican culture and history. Others, like the Pino Suárez stop, display archaeological treasures unearthed at that location as the *metro* was being built. What is the mass transportation system like in the largest city in your state? Are there cultural attractions in the stations?

La estación del metro Universidad, Ciudad de México

Cultural Notes

Enrichment
El pretérito de los verbos que terminan en -ar: To prepare for the exercises in this section, have students work in pairs to ask and answer questions that use all of the preterite verb forms of *pagar, jugar, llegar* and *buscar, tocar, sacar.*

Extended Written Practice/Homework
1. Write two sentences telling when you and a member of your family arrived home yesterday.

2. Write three sentences telling which students in your school played different sports last year.
3. Write three sentences telling how long ago your family and friends bought different things.

Multiple Intelligences
Visual/Spatial
See Ex. 1 and Practice Wkbk. 10-6.

Paso cultural
Answers will vary.

Practice

Re-enter / Recycle

Ex. 4: time-telling from Chap. 2
Ex. 6: activities from Chap. 1,
leisure-time activities from
Chap. 3, vacation activities from
Chap. 7

Answers

3 anoche-a.,b.,d.,h.,j.
los lunes-c.,e.,f.,i.,l.
las dos-g.,k.

4 ESTUDIANTE A
a. ¿A qué hora llegaron Alejandro y Carmen al banco?
b. . . . llegó Catalina . . .
c. . . . llegó Agustín . . .
d. . . . llegaron Soledad y Victoria . . .
e. . . . llegaste tú . . .
f. Questions will vary.

ESTUDIANTE B
a. Llegaron temprano: a las ocho y treinta y cinco.
b. Llegó muy tarde: a las nueve y treinta y cinco.
c. Llegó muy tarde: a las nueve y cuarenta y cinco.
d. Llegaron temprano: a las ocho y cuarenta y cinco.
e. Llegué temprano: a las ocho y media (treinta).
f. Answers will vary.

---

3 Dile a tu compañero(a) cuáles de estas formas se pueden usar con la expresión *anoche*, cuáles se pueden usar con la expresión *los lunes* y cuáles se pueden usar con las dos. Después, haz frases usando seis de estas formas.

a. deposité	d. pensaron	g. estudiamos	j. sacó
b. cerraste	e. cortan	h. cerré	k. enviamos
c. cierras	f. compras	i. llego	l. trabajan

4 Los empleados de este banco tienen que llegar a las 9:00 de la mañana. ¿A qué hora llegaron ayer?

A —¿A qué hora llegó Carlos al banco?
B —Llegó muy tarde: a las nueve y veinticinco.

 Carlos

Cádiz, España

 a. Alejandro y Carmen

 b. Catalina

c. Agustín

d. Soledad y Victoria

e. tú

 f.

5 Dile a tu compañero(a) a qué hora llegaste a estos lugares ayer o el viernes pasado. Dile también si llegaste temprano o tarde.

- a la escuela
- a la clase de español
- a casa después de las clases

Una estación del metro en Caracas, Venezuela

Options

Strategies for Reaching All Students

Students Needing Extra Help
Ex. 4: Review time-telling.
Point out that early and late are based on a 9:00 A.M. opening.
Write a *llegar* verb chart (in the preterite) on the chalkboard.

Ex. 6: Review *hace* + time period.
Have students make three columns, indicating *what* you did, *when* you did it, and *with whom* you did it.
Review the *yo* and *tú* forms of each of the possible verb choices.

Extended Written Practice/Homework
1. Refer to the *-ar* verbs on pp. 316–317. Write three sentences telling what different people did in your community.
2. Refer to the *-ar* verbs on p. 253. Write three sentences telling who did different chores in your home recently.
3. Refer to the *-ar* verbs on pp. 73, 220, and 221. Tell what different people did on their vacations: *El año pasado mis padres bucearon en el mar en Cozumel.*

6 Escoge *(choose)* cinco de las actividades y di cuándo las hiciste la última vez *(last time)*. Tu compañero(a) va a preguntar con quién las hiciste.

A —*Hace dos días que escuché música.*

B —*¿Con quién escuchaste música?*

A —*Con mi amiga Isabel.*
    o: *Lo hice solo(a).*

¡NO OLVIDES!

You know how to use *hace* + time expression to say "ago."

7 Piensa en cuatro personas de tu clase y escribe sus nombres en una hoja de papel. Luego escribe las actividades del Ejercicio 6 que piensas que ellos hicieron y cuándo. Por ejemplo:

¿Quién?	¿Qué?	¿Cuándo?
Marcos	sacó fotos	el domingo pasado
Luz y Juana	esquiaron	ayer

Luego, hazles preguntas a esas personas para averiguar si tienes razón.

A —*Marcos, ¿sacaste fotos el domingo pasado?*

B —. . .

8 Escoge dos de las actividades del Ejercicio 6 y averigua si tu profesor(a) las hizo el fin de semana pasado.

Gramática en contexto 335

 5 Statements will vary, but look for use of the verb form *llegué.*

 6 Dialogues will vary. Possible exchanges may include these verb forms: *escuché (escuchaste) música, practiqué (practicaste) deportes, saqué (sacaste) fotos, paseé (paseaste) en bote, lavé (lavaste) el coche, jugué (jugaste) tenis, dibujé (dibujaste), esquié (esquiaste), toqué (tocaste) la guitarra.*

 7 Responses will vary, but will include these verb forms: *escuchó/escucharon, practicó/practicaron, sacó/sacaron, paseó/pasearon, lavó/lavaron, jugó/jugaron, dibujó/dibujaron, esquió/esquiaron, tocó/tocaron.*

 8 Dialogues will vary. If the formal *(Ud.)* address is used with the teacher, verb forms from Ex. 6 would change to *escuchó música, practicó deportes, sacó fotos, paseó en bote, lavó el coche, jugó tenis, dibujó, esquió,* and *tocó la guitarra.*

Practice Wkbk. 10-7, 10-8

Writing Activity 10-E

Pruebas 10-6, 10-7

Comm. Act. BLM 10-2

Cultural Notes

Multiple Intelligences
Interpersonal/Social
See Ex. 5.
Verbal/Linguistic
See Exs. 3–4 and 6–8.
Visual/Spatial
See Practice Wkbk. 10-7 and 10-8, Writing Activity 10-E, and Comm. Act. BLM 10-2.

(p. 334, top photo)
Cádiz is believed to have been founded by Phoenician traders as early as 1100 B.C. and was later occupied by Rome. From the late 1400s to the early 1800s, Cádiz was the headquarters of the Spanish treasure fleets. Construction of the *ayuntamiento* building shown here was begun in 1799, during the height of Cádiz's prosperity, but the city never recovered from the loss of Spain's overseas colonies in later decades.

(p. 334, bottom photo)
Caracas opened its *metro* system in 1983, hoping to relieve a growing traffic problem. There are currently three lines with a proposed fourth one expected to open after the year 2000. Extensive train systems also exist in Mexico City, Santiago, and Buenos Aires, but all of these Latin American cities continue to suffer from pollution and congestion caused by intense auto traffic.

After the initial presentation of the preterite of *ir,* you might begin the class with this activity:
Hang signs labeled with the countries from *El primer paso.* Have volunteers (individually or in pairs) stand beneath the signs. Ask students where their classmates went: *¿Adónde fue Miguel? (Fue a Bolivia.) ¿Adónde fueron Ana y Alex? (Fueron a España.)* Continue until all preterite forms of *ir* have been used.

Re-enter / Recycle

Ex. 9: places and buildings from Chap. 3
Ex. 11: activities from Chap. 1, leisure-time activities from Chap. 3, vacation activities from Chap. 7, places and buildings from Chaps. 3 and 6

Answers

9 ESTUDIANTE A
a. ¿Adónde fue Jorge? / ¿Cómo fue?
b. ¿Adónde fueron los Sánchez? / ¿Cómo fueron?
c. ¿Adónde fueron Adela y Nicolás? / ¿Cómo fueron?
d. ¿Adónde fue la Sra. Ochoa? / ¿Cómo fue?
e. ¿Adónde fue Pilar? / ¿Cómo fue?
f. ¿Adónde fueron tú y . . .?/ ¿Cómo fueron?

El pretérito del verbo *ir*

You know that we use *fui* and *fuiste* to say that "I went" and "you went" somewhere. They are preterite-tense forms of *ir.* Here are all the forms of *ir* in the preterite.

(yo)	**fui**	(nosotros) (nosotras)	**fuimos**
(tú)	**fuiste**	(vosotros) (vosotras)	**fuisteis**
Ud. (él) (ella)	**fue**	Uds. (ellos) (ellas)	**fueron**

Notice that, unlike regular *-ar* verbs in the preterite, the forms of *ir* do not have accent marks.

Plano de los transportes del Centro de Madrid

9 Con un(a) compañero(a), di adónde y cómo fueron estas personas.

A —*¿Adónde fueron Federico y Esteban?*
B —*Fueron al centro comercial.*
A —*¿Cómo fueron?*
B —*En taxi.*

Federico y Esteban

a. Jorge

b. los Sánchez

c. Adela y Nicolás

d. la Sra. Ochoa

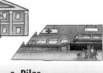

e. Pilar

f. tú y (nombre de un amigo)

336   Capítulo 10

Options

Strategies for Reaching All Students

Students Needing Extra Help
El pretérito del verbo ir: Remind students that *fui* and *fuiste* were taught in Chap. 7.
Ex. 11: Allow students enough time to make their lists of destinations, talk with their classmates, and record their answers.
To organize their responses, have students make a three-column "T" chart with these headings: *adónde/cuándo/qué.*
Ahora lo sabes: Have students write out this section so that they can check off what they have mastered.

Extended Written Practice/Homework
1. Write three sentences telling where you and your family or you and your friends went yesterday.
2. Write a sentence for each of these expressions telling who did which activity and when: *ir de compras, ir a una fiesta, ir de pesca, ir de vacaciones, ir a pasear.*

Multiple Intelligences
Bodily/Kinesthetic
See Class Starter Review.
Verbal/Linguistic
See Ex. 9 and Audio Activity 10.4.
Visual/Spatial
See Practice Wkbk. 10-9, Writing Activity 10-F, and Comm. Act. BLM 10-3.

10 Escoge la respuesta de la derecha que mejor responde a cada pregunta de la izquierda.

a. ¿Con quién fuiste al partido de fútbol?
b. ¿Con quién fueron Ana y tú al partido de básquetbol?
c. ¿Con quién fue Nicolás?
d. ¿Con quién fueron Jaime y Tomás al partido de fútbol americano?

Fuimos con Felipe.
Fue con Gloria.
Fueron con Gregorio.
Fui con mi hermano.

11 Di adónde fueron tú y otras personas, cuándo fueron y qué hicieron *(what you/they did)* allí. Usa verbos de la lista.

Mis amigos y yo fuimos al parque ayer y jugamos básquetbol.
a. mis amigos y yo
b. mis padres
c. yo
d. (nombre de un amigo)
e. (nombres de dos amigos)

arreglar	lavar
ayudar	limpiar
bucear	llamar
buscar	llegar
cerrar	llevar
cocinar	nadar
comprar	pagar
cortar	pasar
depositar	pasear
descansar	patinar
dibujar	pensar
empezar	practicar
enseñar	regresar
enviar	sacar
escuchar	terminar
esquiar	tocar
explorar	tomar
hablar	trabajar
jugar	visitar

Ahora lo sabes

Can you:

► indicate where one person or place is in relation to another?
—El restaurante está al lado ___ hotel. Está ___ la biblioteca.

► talk about an errand someone ran?
—Mi mamá ___ al banco para ___ dinero.

► tell where someone went?
—Anoche mis hermanos ___ a la farmacia y nosotros ___ al supermercado.

MORE PRACTICE

Más práctica y tarea, pp. 536–538
Practice Workbook 10–6, 10–9

ESTUDIANTE B
a. Fue al estadio. / A pie.
b. Fueron a la farmacia. / En autobús.
c. Fueron al parque de diversiones. / En coche.
d. Fue a la estación de policía. / En taxi.
e. Fue al banco. / En metro.
f. Fuimos . . . *(Answers will vary.)*

10 a. Fui con mi hermano.
b. Fuimos con Felipe.
c. Fue con Gloria.
d. Fueron con Gregorio.

11 Answers will vary. Look for the correct form of *ir* and of the *-ar* verbs in the preterite. Make sure that there is logic in the sentences.

Answers: Ahora lo sabes
• del / *Answers will vary.*
• fue / depositar (sacar)
• fueron / fuimos

 Practice Wkbk. 10-9

 Audio Activity 10.4

 Writing Activity 10-F

 Prueba 10-8

 Comm. Act. BLM 10-3

 Pasos vivos 1 CD-ROM
Bulletin Board, Slide Presentation Maker, Spindle, Treadmill

Cultural Notes ☀

(p. 336, realia)
Published by Madrid's Empresa Municipal de Transportes, this *Plano de los transportes* is geared toward an international audience. Note the use of "universal" icons along the right edge of the map cover, which do not require any knowledge of Spanish. Ask students: Have you seen these or similar icons used in the U.S.? Where?

Todo junto

Actividades

La escuela de madera más antigua de los Estados Unidos, en San Agustín, Florida

1 En una hoja de papel, cada estudiante debe escribir tres cosas que él (ella) hizo el mes pasado. Por ejemplo:

Compré champú y pasta dentífrica.

Junten *(put together)* las hojas de papel. Luego deben sacar los papeles y preguntar quién hizo cada cosa.

¿Quién compró champú y pasta dentífrica?

¿Cuántas personas hicieron la misma *(same)* cosa? ¿Qué actividades hizo la mayoría de las personas?

2 En una tarjeta, escribe una frase sobre cuándo y adónde fueron de vacaciones tú y tu familia. (Si prefieres, puedes escoger un lugar que te gustaría visitar.)

Hace tres años que mi familia y yo fuimos a San Agustín, Florida.

Intercambia *(exchange)* tarjetas con tu compañero(a). En una hoja de papel, escribe cinco preguntas sobre lo que hicieron tu compañero(a) y su familia. Hazle las preguntas.

Después, di a un grupo de tres o cuatro estudiantes lo que hicieron tu compañero(a) y su familia cuando fueron de vacaciones.

La Casa González-Álvarez, la casa más antigua de San Agustín

338 Capítulo 10

Conexiones

La historia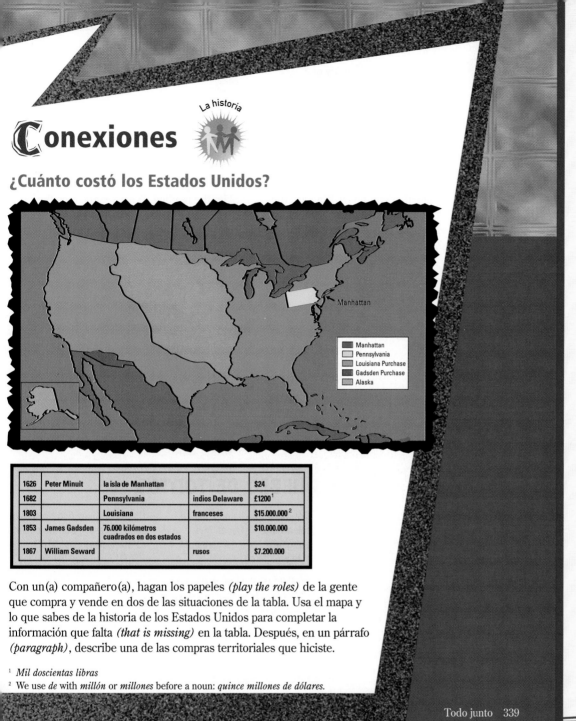

¿Cuánto costó los Estados Unidos?

Manhattan

Legend:
- Manhattan
- Pennsylvania
- Louisiana Purchase
- Gadsden Purchase
- Alaska

1626	Peter Minuit	la isla de Manhattan		$24
1682		Pennsylvania	indios Delaware	£1200 [1]
1803		Louisiana	franceses	$15.000.000 [2]
1853	James Gadsden	76.000 kilómetros cuadrados en dos estados		$10.000.000
1867	William Seward		rusos	$7.200.000

Con un(a) compañero(a), hagan los papeles *(play the roles)* de la gente que compra y vende en dos de las situaciones de la tabla. Usa el mapa y lo que sabes de la historia de los Estados Unidos para completar la información que falta *(that is missing)* en la tabla. Después, en un párrafo *(paragraph)*, describe una de las compras territoriales que hiciste.

[1] *Mil doscientas libras*
[2] *We use de with millón or millones before a noun: quince millones de dólares.*

Re-enter / Recycle
Ex. 2: *hace . . . que* from Chap. 9

Answers: Actividades
1 Answers will vary. Look for the correct forms of the preterite: *Fui al cine; nadé; saqué fotos (¿Quién fue al cine? ¿Quién nadó? ¿Quién sacó fotos?)*

2 Answers will vary. Students should answer the first part in the following manner:
Hace + time expression + *que* + *mi familia y yo fuimos a* + place.
Or: *Mi familia y yo fuimos a* + place + *hace* + time expression.

Answers: Conexiones
1. Minuit bought Manhattan from the Algonquin Indians.
2. William Penn bought Pennsylvania from the Delaware Indians.
3. Thomas Jefferson bought the Louisiana Purchase from France.
4. Gadsden bought parts of two states from Mexico.
5. Seward bought Alaska from Russia.

Paragraphs will vary depending on students' purchases.

 Writing Activities 10-G, 10-H

 Comm. Act. BLMs 10-4, 10-5

 Pasos vivos 1 CD-ROM
A Jugar, Boom Box, Laboratorio de grabar, Maps, Spindle

Cooperative Learning
Divide the class into groups of three. Have each student write a preterite-tense form of *ir.* Papers are passed to the right and students then write a destination (place). Papers are passed to the right once again, with students writing a reason *(para* + inf.) for going somewhere. Ask one member of each group to read the three sentences. Poll the class to see if they make sense. If the sentences seem illogical, ask what changes should be made to make them logical.

Multiple Intelligences
Bodily/Kinesthetic
See Cooperative Learning.
Interpersonal/Social
See Critical Thinking: Synthesizing, and Cooperative Learning.
Verbal/Linguistic
See Pronunciation Tape 10-3.
Visual/Spatial
See Using the Video, Writing Activities 10-G and 10-H, and Comm. Act. BLMs 10-4 and 10-5.

Cultural Notes

(p. 338, photos)
Historic buildings in San Agustín, Florida. Spanish explorer Juan Ponce de León first saw the North American continent in 1513, and called it *La Florida,* "flowered land." San Agustín, founded in 1565—55 years before Plymouth, Massachusetts—is the oldest permanent European settlement in the U.S.

Apply

Process Reading

For a description of process reading, see p. 48.

Answers

Antes de leer

Answers will vary. / Explain that folk tales are stories circulated by word of mouth. They tend to be traditional in theme, and may be anonymous, timeless, and even without a place.

Mira la lectura

They are never able to finish filling the holes in their town.

¡Vamos a leer!

 www.pasoapaso.com

Antes de leer

STRATEGY ▶ **Using prior knowledge**

Think of a folktale that you know. Who are the characters? What problem do they have? How is it resolved? How are folktales different from other stories?

Mira la lectura

STRATEGY ▶ **Skimming**

Skim the reading. What seems to be the problem facing the Tolencianos?

EL PUEBLO DE TONTOS

Hay muchos tontos en la Tierra, pero en el pueblo de Tolencia todos son tontos. Un día don Hortensio Hortalecio, el alcalde de Tolencia, fue a su oficina y vio un hoyo enorme en el camino. "¿Qué pasa?" dijo don Hortensio. "¡Vamos a arreglar este hoyo ahora!"

Don Hortensio llamó a los tolencianos. "¡Tienen que arreglar el hoyo del camino!" Y lo arreglaron.

Después de trabajar don Hortensio fue a su casa. ¿Qué vio en el camino? ¡Otro hoyo! Llamó a los tolencianos y ellos arreglaron ese hoyo también.

Un día después don Hortensio salió de casa. ¿Qué vio delante de su puerta? ¡Sí! ¡OTRO HOYO! El alcalde llamó a los tolencianos y ellos arreglaron ese hoyo también. "¡Ya estamos cansados de arreglar hoyos!" dijeron. Pero esta cosa de los hoyos ocurría todos los días. Estaban enfrente de la

340   Capítulo 10

Options

Strategies for Reaching All Students

Students Needing Extra Help

Antes de leer: Explain what a folk tale is and elicit some examples. You may want to check with the English department in your school to find out what kinds of literature students are familiar with.

Infórmate: Students may be discouraged if they can't find the words as they are spelled here. Help them come up with the dictionary forms before they start to look for them.

Aplicación: Have the class brainstorm possible endings and use the Organizer to rewrite the ending. Show the exact place in the text where the new ending would begin. Give students a definite minimum or maximum number of words or sentences that you expect them to write for the new ending.

Infórmate

  STRATEGIES ➤ **Using the dictionary**
Scanning

In a dictionary, adjectives and nouns that have masculine and feminine forms are listed under the masculine singular form. Verbs are listed in the infinitive form. Look up these words: *tontos, tierra, alcalde, hoyo, camino, cavaron,* and *llenaron.*

Now read the story thoroughly. How did looking up the words help you?

1 How did the Tolencianos' problem worsen?

2 How was it solved?

3 Do you think the Tolencianos learned from their mistake?

Aplicación

If you had written this folktale, how would your ending have differed? Get together with a partner and write your own ending for this tale.

escuela, a la izquierda del banco, a la derecha de la biblioteca, ¡en todas partes!

¿Cómo arreglaron los tolencianos los hoyos? Fueron un poco lejos del hoyo y cavaron tierra. Cavaron y cavaron . . . ¡e hicieron otro hoyo! Después llevaron la tierra al primer hoyo y lo llenaron con la tierra.

Bueno . . . la gente del otro pueblo, al lado, vio los hoyos y el trabajo tonto de los tolencianos. Una noche esa gente fue a Tolencia y llenó los hoyos con cosas viejas: guitarras, teléfonos, radios y equipos de sonido . . . y un niño los llenó con zanahorias y guisantes. ¡Ya no había más hoyos!

Esa mañana don Hortensio Hortalecio salió de su casa. ¡Y no vio hoyos! Todos los tolencianos y él estaban muy contentos.

Infórmate

tontos: silly, dumb, foolish; *tierra:* earth; *alcalde:* mayor; *hoyo:* hole; *camino:* path; *cavaron:* they dug; *llenaron:* they filled / Remind students that they should look up the masculine, singular form *tonto,* and the infinitives *cavar* and *llenar.* / Answers will vary.

1. They kept digging new holes to fill the old ones.

2. People from another town filled the holes with old things.

3. Answers will vary.

Aplicación
Story endings will vary.

www **Internet Activities**

Apply

Process Writing
For information regarding developing a writing portfolio, see p. 50.

Multicultural Perspectives

The growth of settlements on the outskirts of many Latin American cities is attributed in large part to people moving from rural to urban areas in search of jobs. These settlements, known as *barrios,* or *pueblos jóvenes,* are common in many large cities in Latin America. The houses of these *pueblos jóvenes* are usually made of cardboard, adobe, or any material people can find. Some of the older *pueblos* have formed committees to obtain water and electrical services and to start schools. Have students compile a list of reasons that people migrate from rural areas to urban ones.

Pasos vivos 1 CD-ROM

Word Processor

¡Vamos a escribir!

Jóvenes guatemaltecos hacer trabajo comunitario. ►

Every community has places or programs that depend on volunteers. Think about the programs in your community. What kinds of help do they need, and who can help? Make a poster that encourages people to volunteer. Follow these steps.

1 First, think about why community service is important. *(¿Por qué es importante trabajar como voluntario?)* List three reasons. Who can help? *(¿Quién puede ayudar?)*

2 Use your list and the answers to the questions to design your poster.

3 Show the draft of your poster to a partner. Then revise, edit, and make a final copy.

4 Now you are ready to show your poster. In addition to sending it to a Spanish-language newspaper or magazine, you can:

- post your work in the classroom
- submit it to your school newspaper
- include it in a newsletter or other publication that the school sends home
- add it to your writing portfolio

¿Puedes ayudarnos? ¡La Casa de los Amigos necesita tu ayuda!

¿Qué puedes hacer?
- Ayudar a otros jóvenes
- Jugar con los niños
- Cortar el césped de los patios

¿Adónde hay que ir?
¡A la calle 23!
¿A qué número hay que llamar?
Al 555-1212

342   Capítulo 10

PASO CULTURAL
Young people such as these in Guatemala and Honduras are key to community improvement efforts throughout Latin America. Local governments and organizations often help to organize volunteers for projects that beautify public areas, conserve the environment, and improve public health and education. What similar volunteer projects are going on in your school or community? How can you benefit from volunteering for these kinds of projects?

Options

Strategies for Reaching All Students

Spanish-Speaking Students
Step 1: Ask Spanish-speaking students: *¿Benefician al (a la) voluntario(a) los servicios a la comunidad?*

Un paso más Exs. 10-G, 10-H

Students Needing Extra Help
Brainstorm places, help needed, who can help, and the benefits. The local newspaper might be a good resource.

"¡Hola! Soy Jorge y trabajo en un proyecto escolar en Tegucigalpa."

¡Vamos a escribir! 343

Cultural Notes

Paso cultural
Possible answers: Volunteer projects in schools and communities vary.
Volunteers can meet different people, learn skills and obtain knowledge that will be useful in getting jobs, and feel satisfied that they are improving their community.

Assess & Summarize

Test Preparation

You may want to assign parts of this section as written homework or as an in-class writing activity prior to administering the *Examen de habilidades*.

Answers

Listening: *Ayer por la tarde fui al banco y deposité dinero. Luego fui al correo que está al lado del banco y envié una carta a mis tíos. También compré una tarjeta postal.*

The person speaking went to the bank and then to the post office.

Reading: Remind students to look up the infinitive form of verbs and the masculine, singular form of adjectives.

Culture: Answers will vary. Students may include references to the *Perspectiva cultural*. For example: grocery stores, theaters, doctor's offices, newspapers, books, etc.

Writing: Encourage students to use most of the vocabulary from this chapter and from Chaps. 1 and 3.

Speaking: Answers will vary. Students may use actual places in their community, or they may refer to the map on pp. 322–323.

Repaso ¿Lo sabes bien?

This section will help you organize your studying for the proficiency test, where you will be asked to do similar, though not identical, tasks. There will not be any models on the test.

► Listening

Can you understand when someone talks about what he or she did in different places in the community? Listen as your teacher reads a sample similar to what you will hear on the test. Can you mention two places the person making the statement went to run these errands?

► Reading

Can you read a passage and know how to look up unknown words in the dictionary?

Ayer vi a Ana en el centro. Ella fue al banco y después a la biblioteca, donde sacó varios libros. Después tomó el autobús y la vi luego cerca del estadio. Por la tarde la vi en una tienda de regalos. Entonces recordé que va a ser el cumpleaños de su esposo dentro de dos semanas. Me gustaría saber qué le compró…

► Culture

Can you name some services or products especially offered to meet the needs of the Hispanic community?

► Writing

Can you write a letter about various places in your community and the activities that you did there? For example:

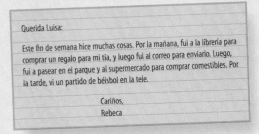

Querida Luisa:

Este fin de semana hice muchas cosas. Por la mañana, fui a la librería para comprar un regalo para mi tía, y luego fui al correo para enviarlo. Luego, fui a pasear en el parque y al supermercado para comprar comestibles. Por la tarde, vi un partido de béisbol en la tele.

Cariños,
Rebeca

► Speaking

Can you tell someone the location of a place? Here is a sample:

—*Ud. tiene que tomar el metro porque el correo no está muy cerca de aquí. Queda cerca de la farmacia, en la esquina de la Calle Ocho y Valencia. Enfrente del correo hay un banco y una tienda de ropa. Debe ir rápido; es tarde. El correo cierra a las dos y ya es la una y media.*

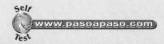

Self Test
www.pasoapaso.com

Una tienda hispana en San Francisco

Options

Strategies for Reaching All Students

Students Needing Extra Help
Have students write out this section so that they can check off what they have mastered.
Listening: Have students first review their Organizers for possible words they will hear in the sample.
Reading: Remind students how to look up unknown words in a dictionary.
Culture: Have students review any notes they might have taken during their reading of the *Perspectiva cultural*.

Writing: Have students use their Organizers. Give some guidelines as to the number of places and activities you want included.
Speaking: Give this assignment a few days ahead of time so students can prepare. Have students use their Organizers. Emphasize what needs to be included: a place, transportation, and a landmark. Show students how *no está muy cerca de aquí* is the same as *está lejos de aquí*.

The principal's office might be a good place for which to provide directions.
Give students a visual, such as a map, to use while speaking.

Resumen del vocabulario

Use the vocabulary from this chapter to help you:

➤ name various places in your community

➤ name activities or errands you do

➤ identify different means of transportation available in your area

to talk about places
la avenida
el banco
la biblioteca
la calle
el correo
la cuadra
la esquina
la estación (de policía / etc.)
el estadio
la farmacia
el hotel
la iglesia
la librería
el monumento
la parada del autobús
la plaza
el restaurante
el supermercado
el teatro
el templo
la tienda de regalos
el zoológico

to talk about activities or errands in a community
abrir
cerrar
la comunidad
el partido

devolver (o → ue) un libro
ir a pasear
llegar
sacar un libro
trabajar

to talk about things you buy
¿Me compras ___?
los comestibles
el champú
el jabón
la pasta dentífrica
las pastillas (para la garganta)
el regalo

to talk about money
el dinero: depositar / sacar
doscientos . . .
quinientos . . .
setecientos . . .
novecientos
mil

to talk about mailing things
la carta
enviar
el sello
la tarjeta de cumpleaños
la tarjeta postal

to ask and give directions
¿A cuántas cuadras (de ___)?
A (cinco) cuadras (de ___).
queda(n)
del
a la derecha / izquierda (de)
al lado (de) / detrás (de) / enfrente (de)
entre

to talk about transportation
el autobús   a pie
el metro   en + *vehicle*
el taxi

to talk about past activities
(yo) devolví, (tú) devolviste
(yo) hice, (tú) hiciste
(yo) vi, (tú) viste

to indicate when an event occurred
anoche / ayer
luego
temprano / tarde
ya

to say you don't / didn't know something
(Yo) no sé. / (Yo) no lo sabía.

to express a condition
si

to express agreement
Bueno.

Assessment

 Prueba cumulativa

 Examen de habilidades

 Test Generator

Additional Assessment Options

 Comm. Act. BLMs
Small Group Activities
Situation Cards

 Pasos vivos 1 CD-ROM
Slide Presentation Maker, Video Presentation Maker, Word Processor, Spindle

 ¿Lo sabes bien? Video Quiz

Internet Activities
Self-Test

Cultural Notes

(p. 344, photo)
The sign on this market in San Francisco's Mission District reflects the presence of Central and South American immigrants to this established Mexican American community. A well-organized network of agencies exists there to help newly arrived people adapt to ways of life in the U.S.

CAPÍTULO 11
THEME: MOVIES AND TV SHOWS

SCOPE AND SEQUENCE Pages 346–379

COMMUNICATION

Topics
TV shows
Movies

Objectives
To discuss television in the Spanish-speaking world

To name types of movies

To talk about TV and TV shows

To describe a movie or TV show

To indicate time or duration

To express opinions or reactions

To indicate a reason

CULTURE
Spanish-language television

GRAMMAR
Los comparativos y los superlativos

Los pronombres y el infinitivo

El pretérito del verbo ver

Los pronombres nos *y* les

Ancillaries available for use with Chapter 11

Multisensory/Technology

 Overheads 56–60

 Audio Tapes and CDs

 Vocabulary Art Blackline Masters for Hands-On Learning, pp. 58–62/CD-ROM

 Classroom Crossword

 Video

 Pasos vivos 1 CD-ROM

Internet Activities www.pasoapaso.com

Print

 Practice Workbook, pp. 114–124

 Writing, Audio & Video Activities, pp. 65–70, 123–125, 172–173

 Communicative Activity Blackline Masters
  Pair and Small Group Activities, pp. 78–83
  Situation Cards, p. 84

 Un paso más: Actividades para ampliar tu español, pp. 62–67

TPR Storytelling

Assessment

 Assessment Program
  Pruebas, pp. 159–170
  Examen de habilidades, pp. 171–174

 Test Generator

Video still from Chap. 11

345A

Planning Express, Teaching
Resources Library, and Clip Art
Library

¿Lo sabes bien?
Video Quiz

Cultural Overview

Spanish-Language Television

Spanish-language television was first broadcast in San Antonio and New York in the mid-1940s. Programs were aired in time slots purchased from English-language stations. In 1955, the first Spanish-language station, KCOR-TV in San Antonio, was born. One early program was called *Buscando estrellas,* a talent search and entertainment show that brought young entertainers from Mexico to Texas.

In the early 1970s the Spanish International Communications Corporation (SICC) was formed by U.S. and Mexican partners. This corporation was organized to provide programming to stations around the country. Many of the programs distributed through SICC were produced by Telesistema (now Televisa) in Mexico.

Today there is a well-established audience for Spanish-language broadcasting. Viewers can enjoy *telenovelas* and other entertainment shows from Mexico, Argentina, Venezuela, and Spain. International sports events are beamed from around the globe, accompanied by commentary and play-by-play coverage in Spanish.

Because Hispanic populations in the U.S. represent many different cultures, one challenge has been to create programs that appeal to the very diverse market. One major success was a *telenovela* entitled *Angélica, mi vida,* produced in Puerto Rico in the 1980s. The subplots dealt with love, tragedy, passion, and power struggles involving families of Puerto Rican, Cuban, and Mexican origin.

Popular programs today include the most-watched talk show in the world, *Cristina,* hosted by Cuban-born Cristina Saralegui, and the longest-running show on Spanish-language television, *Sábado gigante.* Cristina engages her guests and audiences in debates on lively topics. *Sábado gigante* features celebrity guest appearances, contests, games, and comedy. Other shows originating outside the U.S. include *El show de Chespirito* (Mexico), *Informe semanal* (Spain), and *Sábados felices* (Colombia).

English-language programs are also available on Spanish-language TV channels, usually with a Spanish soundtrack. The translation of a newer show's title may have variants—*The X-Files,* for example, can be found listed as *Expediente X, Los expedientes secretos X, Episodios X-Files,* and *Los X-Files.* Longer-running programs such as the cartoon series *The Pink Panther* and *Spiderman (La pantera rosa* and *El hombre araña)* have more established Spanish names.

Introduce

Re-entry of Concepts

The following list represents words, expressions, and grammar points re-entered from *El primer paso* to Chap. 8:

El primer paso
Calendar expressions

Chapter 1
Activities
Gustar expressions
Adjectives describing personality

Chapter 2
Time-telling

Chapter 3
Gustar expressions
Ir a + inf.
Leisure-time activities

Chapter 4
Foods
Expressing likes and preferences

Chapter 5
Adjectives describing physical
  characteristics

Chapter 6
Demonstrative adjectives

Chapter 8
Household chores
Tener que + inf.

Planning

Cross-Curricular Connections

Journalism Connection *(pp. 350–351)*
Have pairs of students write or orally present a critique of their favorite TV show from the current week. They should describe the key elements of the plot and give it a rating of 1–5 *estrellas.* Have them tell why they gave that rating.

Speech and Debate Connection
(pp. 366–367)
Divide the class in half. Name two TV programs, movies, or songs. Then have both groups discuss which one is better and why. A spokesperson from each group can then present the views to the class.

Drama Connection *(pp. 372–373)*
In groups of three or four, have students plan and act out a simple scene which they remember from a TV program or movie. Have them use learned vocabulary when possible, but otherwise they may pantomime.

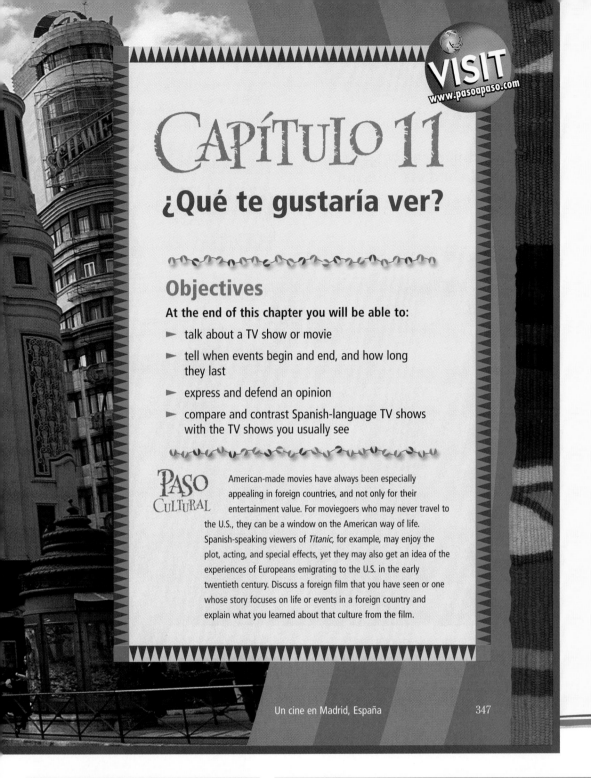

CAPÍTULO 11

¿Qué te gustaría ver?

Objectives

At the end of this chapter you will be able to:

► talk about a TV show or movie

► tell when events begin and end, and how long they last

► express and defend an opinion

► compare and contrast Spanish-language TV shows with the TV shows you usually see

PASO CULTURAL

American-made movies have always been especially appealing in foreign countries, and not only for their entertainment value. For moviegoers who may never travel to the U.S., they can be a window on the American way of life. Spanish-speaking viewers of *Titanic*, for example, may enjoy the plot, acting, and special effects, yet they may also get an idea of the experiences of Europeans emigrating to the U.S. in the early twentieth century. Discuss a foreign film that you have seen or one whose story focuses on life or events in a foreign country and explain what you learned about that culture from the film.

Un cine en Madrid, España   347

Cultural Notes

Spanish in Your Community
Have students look at television guides or visit a video store to find out what types of Spanish-language movies, if any, are available in their community. Have them write down the titles of three movies they find and guess what type of movie each one is. (See pp. 354–355 for categories.) When sharing their findings, students should explain why they guessed as they did.

Paso cultural
Responses will vary.

(pp. 346–347, photo)
Spain and Latin America are important markets for Hollywood productions, but many of these movies are also being shot in Latin America. Much of the production of Titanic, for example, was based in Rosarito, a coastal town just south of the U.S.-Mexican border. Other parts of the movie were filmed in Halifax, Nova Scotia, as well as in U.S. locations.

Preview

Cultural Objective
• To talk about Spanish-language television shows and movies

 ¡Piénsalo bien!

Play

 Video Activity A

Using the Video
This chapter's video focuses on communication and entertainment. Host Alexander Ruiz and his friends go to a movie at CocoWalk Mall in Miami and discuss their opinions. Afterwards Alexander interviews moviegoers about their own entertainment preferences. To prepare students for the video, ask them to predict what this chapter's tape will be about. Then have students watch the segment several times. Ask them to identify: a) how the movie theater in Little Havana resembles their favorite theater, and b) what was new to them about the Little Havana theater.
Video segment 1: For more teaching suggestions, see the Video Teacher's Guide.

¡Piensa en la CULTURA!

"¿Cuántos programas deportivos da este canal esta noche? ¿Cuál te gustaría ver?"

Entertainment in Spain and Florida and via Internet

Look at the photos and read the captions.

"Dos entradas, por favor."
Does this movie theater look like the ones you go to? What kind of information do you think appears on the window?

Barcelona, España

348   Capítulo 11

Options

Strategies for Reaching All Students

Spanish-Speaking Students
Ask: ¿Ves películas en español? ¿Dónde? ¿Qué te gusta más, ver la tele(visión) o ir al cine? ¿Qué clase de programa te gusta ver en la tele(visión)?

 Un paso más Ex. 11-A

Multiple Intelligences
Musical/Rhythmic
Locate one of Gloria Estefan's Spanish albums, such as *Mi Tierra* or *Abriendo Puertas,* and play a song for the class. Choose one of the slower, simpler songs, such as *Más allá* from *Abriendo Puertas,* and teach a part of it to the students.

"Me encantan los conciertos de Gloria Estefan. ¡Nadie canta mejor que ella!"

Gloria Estefan brought Spanish to the world of top-selling U.S. pop music with her two Grammy-award-winning CDs, *Mi Tierra* and *Abriendo Puertas*. *Mi Tierra* is a collection of Cuban music representing Estefan's own cultural roots, and *Abriendo Puertas* is a mix of dance music styles from Cuba, Colombia, Panama, and the Dominican Republic. Think about the titles of these two CDs. What feelings do you think Estefan is trying to communicate or share with her listeners through these two titles?

PASO CULTURAL

Miami, Florida

www.pasoapaso.com
Visit these countries on-line

Cultural Exploration

¡Piensa en la cultura! 349

Multicultural Perspectives

Mexican movies—from the comedies of Cantinflas to the dramas of Jorge Negrete—continue to be favorites with Spanish-speaking communities in the U.S. and throughout Latin America. Cantinflas (1911–1993) has been compared to Charlie Chaplin. His characters poked fun at distinguished members of society. Invite students familiar with other cultures to share their knowledge of popular film and television personalities.

Answers:
¡Piensa en la cultura!
(p. 348, photo) Answers will vary. / Ticket prices are listed.

Cultural Notes

(p. 348, photo)
The Spanish film industry suffered severe censorship during the 36-year rule of Francisco Franco. Since Franco's death in 1975, however, a new Spanish cinema has flourished. Much of the credit for this success can be given to the Ministry of Culture, which was founded in 1977. This governmental agency provides subsidies for films showing artistic merit.

(p. 348, realia)
Founded in 1979, Galavisión was the first Spanish-language cable TV network in the U.S. It is based in New York and is a division of Univisión. To appeal to the growing number of U.S. viewers who speak both English and Spanish, Galavisión's programming now includes three bilingual comedy shows. In addition, as seen in this screen shot from their Web site, viewers or "surfers" can browse in either language.

Paso cultural
Answers will vary. Students may mention: nostalgia for her homeland for *Mi Tierra,* and her audience being exposed to different dance music in *Abriendo Puertas.*

Present

Chapter Theme
Television

Communicative Objectives
• To talk about TV and TV shows
• To describe a movie or TV show
• To express opinions or reactions
• To indicate a reason

 Overheads 56–57

 Vocabulary Art BLMs/CD-ROM

 Pronunciation Tape 11-1

 Vocabulario para conversar A

Play

Using the Video
Video segment 2: See the Video Teacher's Guide.

 Video Activity B

Grammar Preview
El / la / los / las mejor(es) / peor(es) are presented lexically. The explanation of superlatives is in the grammar section on p. 366.

Vocabulario para conversar

¿Cuál es tu programa favorito?

At Home VIDEO Chapter 11 Vocabulary

Aquí tienes palabras y expresiones necesarias para hablar sobre la televisión y para expresar o defender una opinión. Léelas varias veces y practícalas con un(a) compañero(a) en las páginas siguientes.

el canal

un concierto

cómico, -a

el programa de detectives

el programa musical

la comedia

la actriz
el actor

la telenovela

el anuncio

el programa deportivo

interesante

el programa educativo

las noticias

350   Capítulo 11

Options

Strategies for Reaching All Students

Students Needing Extra Help
Have students begin to fill in the Organizer. *También necesitas . . . :* Explain how the word "here" is not part of the definition, but means "in this chapter."
Emphasize that the asterisk for *aburrir, dar miedo, fascinar,* and *interesar* is not part of the spelling. Give examples.

Give examples of *dar* + movie or TV program. Write out *¿cuál?* and *¿cuáles?* Students may have difficulty with the parentheses and fail to see these as two different questions.
Remind students that they already know *pensar* (Chap. 7). Review the forms and explain the slight change in meaning when *que* is added.

Learning Spanish Through Action
STAGING VOCABULARY: *Apunten, Marquen, Señalen*
MATERIALS: *Vocabulario para conversar* transparency or Vocabulary Art BLMs/CD-ROM
DIRECTIONS: Direct students to mark appropriate shows using plus (+) and minus (−) as you give your opinion. For example: *Los dibujos animados son muy divertidos.* (plus) / *Los programas de entrevistas son aburridos.* (minus)

divertido, -a

realista

el programa de hechos
de la vida real

los dibujos animados

el programa de
entrevistas

aburrido, -a

el pronóstico del tiempo

el documental

También necesitas...

dar + *movie or TV program*	*to show*	más	here: *more*
la clase (de)	here: *kind / type (of)*	el / la / los / las mejor(es)	here: *best*
sobre	*about*	el / la / los / las peor(es)	here: *worst*
pensar (e → ie) (que)	here: *to think (that)*	aburrir*	*to bore*
por eso	*that's why, for that reason, therefore*	dar miedo*	*to scare*
¿Cuál(es)?	*What? Which? Which one(s)?*	fascinar*	*to fascinate*
demasiado	*too*	interesar*	*to interest*
aburrido, -a	*boring*		
emocionante	*exciting, touching*	**¿Y qué quiere decir . . . ?**	
tonto, -a	*silly, dumb*	en blanco y negro	
triste	*sad*	en colores	
		fascinante	

* With the verbs *aburrir, dar miedo, fascinar,* and *interesar* we use the indirect object pronouns *me, te,* and *le,* as we do with *gustar* and *encantar:* **Me fascinan** *los programas de detectives.*

Vocabulario para conversar   351

Practice & Apply

Re-enter / Recycle

Ex. 1: *gustar* expressions from Chap. 3, demonstrative adjectives from Chap. 6

Ex. 3: demonstrative adjectives from Chap. 6

Ex. 7: calendar expressions from *El primer paso*, time-telling from Chap. 2

Answers: Empecemos a conversar

1 ESTUDIANTE A

a. ¿Te gustaría ver un programa educativo?

b. ...un programa musical?

c. ...un documental?

d. Questions will vary.

ESTUDIANTE B

a.–d. Answers will vary.

2 ESTUDIANTE A

a. ¿Quién es el mejor actor de televisión?

b. ...la mejor actriz de televisión?

c. ...el peor actor de televisión?

d. ...la peor actriz de televisión?

ESTUDIANTE B

a.–d. Answers will vary. Look for correct use of superlatives.

Empecemos a conversar

Túrnate con un(a) compañero(a) para ser *Estudiante A* y *Estudiante B*. Reemplacen las palabras subrayadas con palabras representadas o escritas en los recuadros. 💡 quiere decir que puedes escoger tu propia respuesta.

1 A —¿Te gustaría ver <u>un programa de entrevistas</u>?

B —<u>Sí, me gustaría mucho</u>.

   o: No, <u>esa clase de programas me aburre</u>.

Estudiante A   Estudiante B

a.   b.   c.   d.

2 A —¿Quién es <u>la mejor actriz de televisión</u>?

B —<u>Para mí, (nombre) es la mejor. Me fascina</u>.

| la mejor actriz de televisión |

Estudiante A   Estudiante B

a. el mejor actor de televisión   c. el peor actor de televisión

b. la mejor actriz de televisión   d. la peor actriz de televisión

Options

Strategies for Reaching All Students

Spanish-Speaking Students

Exs: 1–3: Pair bilingual with non-bilingual students if possible.

Ex. 7: After this exercise, ask Spanish-speaking students: *¿Cuál es tu telenovela favorita? ¿De qué se trata?*

 Un paso más Exs. 11-B, 11-C, 11-D

Students Needing Extra Help

Ex. 1: Review *Me dan miedo.* Brainstorm other possibilities using *aburrir, fascinar,* and *interesar.* Regardless of whether *Estudiante B* answers in the negative or the affirmative, have him or her give a reason.

Ex. 6: Explain that *¿por qué?* refers to each question.

Exs. 6–7: Encourage complete sentences.

Extended Written Practice/Homework

1. Write five sentences using *me gusta(n), me encanta(n), me fascina(n), me aburre(n)* and *me interesa(n)* to talk about what you like/dislike on TV.

2. Write three sentences each about what you consider to be the best and the worst programs on TV: The X-Files *es el mejor programa de detectives.*

3

A —*Pienso que deben dar* <u>*más (menos)*</u> <u>*programas de detectives.*</u> *Y tú,* *¿qué piensas?*

B —<u>*(No) Estoy de acuerdo.*</u> *Esos programas* <u>*(no)*</u> *son muy interesantes.*

Estudiante A

Estudiante B

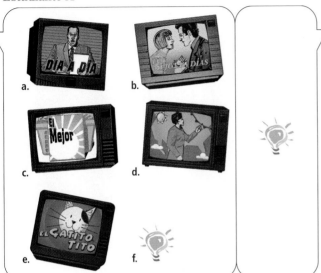

a.

b.

c.

d.

e.

f.

Empecemos a escribir

Escribe tus respuestas en español.

4 ¿Ves la televisión después de la escuela? ¿Qué programas de televisión te interesan? ¿Por qué?

5 ¿Qué piensas tú? ¿Crees que deben dar más o menos programas de hechos de la vida real en la tele? ¿Más o menos programas de entrevistas? ¿Por qué?

6 ¿Te interesan las noticias o te aburren? ¿Y los dibujos animados? ¿Y las telenovelas? ¿Por qué?

7 ¿Cuál es tu programa favorito? ¿A qué hora empieza? ¿Qué día de la semana lo dan? ¿En qué canal?

También se dice...

la artista   el artista

el programa policial
el programa policíaco
el programa de misterio

el comercial
la propaganda

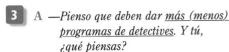

el noticiero
el informativo

MORE PRACTICE

• Más práctica y tarea, p. 538
• Practice Workbook 11–1, 11–2

Vocabulario para conversar   353

3 ESTUDIANTE A

a. Pienso que deben dar más (menos) noticias. Y tú, ¿qué piensas?

b. ...telenovelas ...

c. ...anuncios ...

d. ...pronósticos del tiempo ...

e. ...dibujos animados ...

f. Questions will vary.

ESTUDIANTE B

a.–f. Answers will vary.

Answers: Empecemos a escribir

4 Answers will vary.

5 Answers will vary, but should begin with *Deben dar más (menos) programas... porque ....*

6 Answers will vary and may include *Me interesan (Me aburren)... porque ....*

7 Answers will vary.

Practice Wkbk. 11-1, 11-2

Audio Activity 11.1

Writing Activity 11-A

Pruebas 11-1, 11-2

Multiple Intelligences

Interpersonal/Social
See Exs. 1–3.

Intrapersonal/Introspective
See Exs. 4–7.

Verbal/Linguistic
See Audio Activity 11.1.

Visual/Spatial
See Practice Wkbk. 11-1 and 11-2 and Writing Activity 11-A.

Present

Chapter Theme
Movies

Communicative Objectives
• To name types of movies
• To indicate time or duration

 Overheads 58–59

 Vocabulary Art BLMs/CD-ROM

 Pronunciation Tape 11-2

 Vocabulario para conversar B

Play

Step

Using the Video
Video segment 2: See the Video Teacher's Guide.

 Video Activity B

Grammar Preview
Más is presented here lexically. The explanation of comparatives is in the grammar section on p. 363.

Vocabulario para conversar

 At Home VIDEO Chapter 11 Vocabulary

¿Quién es la mejor actriz de cine?

Aquí tienes el resto del vocabulario necesario para hablar sobre el cine y para decir cuándo algo empieza y termina, y cuánto dura.

la película romántica

la película de terror

la película de ciencia ficción

la película del oeste

354   Capítulo 11

Options

Strategies for Reaching All Students

Students Needing Extra Help
Vocabulario para conversar: Have students continue to fill in their Organizers.
Have them review their Organizers for Chap. 2 (time-telling).
Write several times of the day on the chalkboard. Ask: *¿Qué hora es?* or *¿Son las . . . ?* Encourage them to use *en punto, casi,* and *todavía no.*

Enrichment
Help students expand their use of new vocabulary by pointing out that they can apply the same descriptive words to both movies and TV programs. For example, talk about *películas de dibujos animados, películas musicales, películas cómicas,* and ask students to name movies that fit in those categories. Include *programas de ciencia ficción, programas del oeste,* and *programas románticos* and ask students to name TV shows of those kinds.

Learning Spanish Through Action
STAGING VOCABULARY: *Dibujen, Muestren*
MATERIALS: sheets of paper with blank clock faces or individual toy clocks
DIRECTIONS: Ask students to draw or move the clock hands to the times you announce. Remember to include *en punto* and *de la mañana (tarde, noche).* If you elect to have your students draw, have them also put in a sun *(el sol)* or a moon *(la luna)* to show morning, afternoon, or evening.

la película de aventuras

la película musical

También necesitas...

en punto	*sharp, on the dot*	el tiempo	here: *time*
de la mañana	*in the morning, A.M.*	un poco	*a little*
de la tarde	*in the afternoon, early evening; P.M.*	largo, -a	here: *long* (duration)
		corto, -a	here: *short* (duration)
de la noche	*in the evening, at night; P.M.*	más tarde	*later*
la medianoche	*midnight*	más temprano	*earlier*
el mediodía	*noon*		
casi	*almost*	**¿Y qué quiere decir . . . ?**	
durar	*to last*	media hora	
hasta	*until*	el minuto	
		puntualmente	
		todavía no	

Vocabulario para conversar 355

**Pasos vivos 1
CD-ROM**
Clip Art Album

Teaching Suggestions
Preparing students to speak: Use one or two options from each of the categories of Comprehensible Input, Physical Response, or Limited Verbal Response. For a complete explanation of these categories and some sample activities, see pp. T22–T23.

También necesitas . . . : Explain that *de la tarde* is usually used until 6:00 P.M. *(las seis de la tarde).* From 7:00 P.M. on, *de la noche (las siete de la noche)* is used, although in certain regions of the Spanish-speaking world 7:00 P.M. is still considered *la tarde* and 8:00 P.M. is the start of *la noche.*

Class Starter Review
On the day following initial vocabulary presentation, you might begin the class with this activity: Ask students to name their favorite movie (in English) or one they've recently seen. Ask them what kind of movie it is and who the actors are.

www Internet Activities
Juegos

Extended Written Practice/Homework
1. Choose four types of movies from pp. 354–355 and write sentences naming a movie for each type: Montañas peligrosas *es una película de aventuras.*
2. Refer to the lists on p. 351 and the words on pp. 354–355 and write four sentences telling how you react to different types of movies: *Me aburren las películas del oeste.*
3. Choose three movies and tell if they are long or short. Tell how long each lasts.

Multiple Intelligences
Bodily/Kinesthetic
See Learning Spanish Through Action.
Verbal/Linguistic
See Pronunciation Tape 11-2.
Visual/Spatial
See Overheads 58–59, the Vocabulary Art BLMs/CD-ROM, and Using the Video.

Practice & Apply

Re-enter / Recycle

Ex. 8: *gustar* expressions from Chap. 1

Exs. 9–10, 12: time-telling from Chap. 2

Ex. 13: expressing likes and preferences from Chap. 4

Ex. 14: calendar expressions from *El primer paso*, time-telling from Chap. 2

Answers: Empecemos a conversar

8 ESTUDIANTE A

a. ¿Qué piensas sobre las películas de terror?

b. . . . las películas de aventuras?

c. . . . las películas del oeste?

d. . . . las películas románticas?

ESTUDIANTE B

a.–d. Answers will vary.

9 ESTUDIANTE A

a. ¿Hoy dan una película de ciencia ficción en el cine?

b. . . . una comedia . . .

c. . . . una película musical . . .

d. . . . una película de aventuras . . .

e. Questions will vary.

ESTUDIANTE B

a. Sí, pero empezó a las cinco y ya son casi las seis.

b. . . . a las diez . . . las diez y media.

c. . . . a las siete y media (. . . a las siete y treinta) . . . las ocho.

d. . . . a las seis . . . las siete.

e. Answers will vary.

Empecemos a conversar

8 A —¿Qué piensas sobre las películas *de ciencia ficción*?

B —Pienso que son *interesantes y divertidas.* Por eso *me gustan.*

Estudiante A

a. b. c. d.

Estudiante B

9 A —¿Hoy dan *una película de terror* en el cine?

B —Sí, pero empezó a *las nueve* y ya son casi *las nueve y media*.

¡NO OLVIDES!

You know the word *empezar*. It is an e → *ie* verb.

Estudiante A

a. b. c.

d. e.

Estudiante B

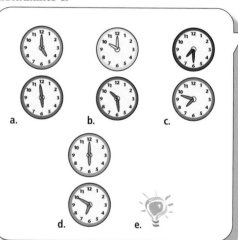

a. b. c.

d. e.

356   Capítulo 11

Options

Strategies for Reaching All Students

Spanish-Speaking Students
Exs. 8–10: Pair bilingual with non-bilingual students if possible.

 Un paso más Ex. 11-E

Students Needing Extra Help
Ex. 10: Do the last response (*Solamente dura . . .*) on the chalkboard.

Enrichment
Ex. 9: As a homework assignment, have students do this exercise twice: first, using the *menos* form of telling time, and then using the digital way: *doce y cincuenta y cinco, diez y cuarenta y cinco,* and so on.
Empecemos a escribir y a leer: Additional topics to write and read about:
1) Ask students to list three of their favorite movies or TV programs and to tell why they like them. Remind them that they can name

10 A —¿*Va a ser largo el documento?*

B —*Sí. Dura una hora y media.*

o: *No, es corto. Solamente dura . . .*

Estudiante A   **Estudiante B**

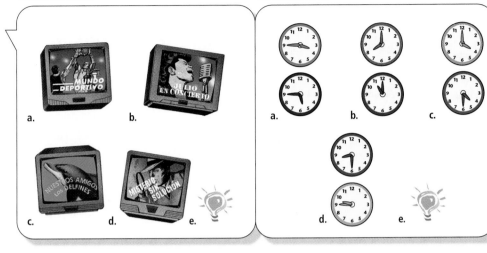

a.   b.

c.   d.   e.

a.   b.   c.

d.   e.

Empecemos a escribir y a leer

Escribe tus respuestas en español.

11 ¿Qué clases de películas te interesan? ¿Por qué? ¿Cómo se llama tu película favorita?

12 ¿Cuánto tiempo dura tu programa favorito? ¿Lo dan tarde o temprano? ¿De qué hora a qué hora?

13 ¿Qué prefieres, las películas en blanco y negro o en colores? ¿Por qué?

14 Mariana dice: "El domingo, a las nueve de la noche, dan una presentación especial en el cine Elíseos. Dura tres horas y media. Quiero llegar puntualmente. ¿Quieres venir conmigo?"

¿Termina la película antes de la medianoche?

MORE PRACTICE

- Más práctica y tarea, p. 539
- Practice Workbook 11–3, 11–4

También se dice...

la película de vaqueros

www.pasoapaso.com

Vocabulario para conversar   357

Practice

Re-enter / Recycle
Ex. 1: calendar expressions from *El primer paso,* time-telling from Chap. 2
Ex. 2: time-telling from Chap. 2
Ex. 3: adjectives describing personality from Chap. 1, adjectives describing physical characteristics from Chap. 5

Answers:
¡Comuniquemos!

1 a. A —Ya son las ocho. ¿Qué podemos hacer? / *(Answers will vary for* Estudiante A*'s second response.)*
    B —En media hora hay un concierto de música folklórica. ¿Quieres ir?

b. A —Ya son las tres y cuarto ...
    B —... hay un partido de fútbol ... (... hay una película de aventuras ...)

c. A —Ya son las nueve ...
    B —... hay un concierto de la orquesta nacional ...

d. A —Ya son las cuatro y media ...
    B —... hay un partido de béisbol ... (... hay un concierto de Paco Argollas ... /... hay una exposición internacional ...)

¡COMUNI

1

Tu amigo(a) y tú están aburridos. Uds. buscan actividades que les gustaría hacer media hora después de la hora indicada *(given)*. Deben usar el calendario de la derecha.

7:20

A —*Ya son las siete y veinte. ¿Qué podemos hacer?*

B —*En media hora hay una película de ciencia ficción. ¿Quieres ir?*

A —*Sí, vamos.*
    o: *Hoy no. A mí me aburre esa clase de películas.*

a. 8:00   d. 4:30
b. 3:15   e. 7:20
c. 9:00   f. 3:30

Este sábado en nuestra comunidad

Deportes
Béisbol: Tigres contra Leones
Fútbol: Cachorros contra Medias Blancas   5:00   3:45

Cine
El detective perezoso
La conquista del Sol   4:00 y 7:50
Aventura en la selva   7:50   3:45

Teatro
Festival nacional de teatro
La casa de Teresa   7:45   4:15 y 8:45

Conciertos
La guitarra de Paco Argollas   5:00
Orquesta Nacional   9:30
Música folklórica   8:30

Museos
Exposición internacional   4:00 y 5:00
Impresionismo mexicano   7:15

2

Con un(a) compañero(a) haz *(make)* planes para ver una película este sábado. Luego, dile a un grupo pequeño lo que Uds. piensan hacer.

3

En una hoja de papel, escribe una descripción corta de tu actor o actriz favorito(a). ¿Es alto(a)? / ¿Bajo(a)? ¿Es joven? / ¿Viejo(a)? ¿Cuál es el nombre de una película o del programa de televisión en el que aparece? No escribas su nombre. En grupos de cuatro, cada *(each)* estudiante lee su descripción. El resto del grupo debe adivinar *(guess)* quién es.

Options

Strategies for Reaching All Students

Spanish-Speaking Students
Exs. 2–3: Have Spanish-speaking students write out these exercises.

Students Needing Extra Help
Ex. 1: Encourage students playing *Estudiante A* to vary the reasons they give whenever they disagree with *Estudiante B*'s suggestion.

Ex. 3: To prepare for this exercise, you may want to have students do a written homework assignment the night before in which they describe their favorite actor or actress (both their personality and physical appearance). Have them use their Organizers.
¿Qué sabes ahora?: Have students write out this section so they can check off what they have mastered.

Cooperative Learning
Divide students into groups of three or four. Prepare or have students prepare index cards with the names (in English) of popular movies or television shows. Students then select a card and, in Spanish, give the category to which it corresponds. Compile complete lists and see which group has the most categories.

¿QUEMOS!

e. A —Ya son las siete y veinte . . .
   B —. . . hay una película de
detectives (de ciencia ficción) . . .

f. A —Ya son las tres y media . . .
   B —. . . hay una película de
detectives . . . (. . . hay una exposición internacional . . .)

2–3 Answers will vary.

Answers: ¿Qué sabes ahora?

• Answers will vary / *interesan*
• Answers will vary.
• Answers will vary.

 Audio Activity 11.4

 Pasos vivos 1 CD-ROM
Slide Projector, Laboratorio de grabar

¿Qué sabes ahora?

Can you:

► tell what kind of television programs and movies you are interested in?
—Los programas ____ me ____.

► say why you like or dislike certain programs or movies?
—Las telenovelas (no) me gustan porque ____.

► tell how long something lasts?
—Este programa dura ____; de la(s) ____ hasta la(s) ____ de la ____.

PASO CULTURAL

Univisión is the largest Spanish-language television network in the U.S. More than 90 percent of Spanish-speaking households in the U.S. tune in to Univisión regularly. What daytime shows on English-speaking networks are similar to the show in this ad?

Univisión Despierta Su Apetito Con Un Programa Que Cae Bien.

Igual que una buena sopa, "Al Mediodía" es el nuevo programa de televisión que cae bien a la hora de almuerzo.
María Antonieta Collins y Mauricio Zeilic con Cristina Aceves y Ambrosio Hernández les traen lo mejor en noticias locales e inter-

nacionales, lo último en medicina y salud, entrevistas con sus artistas favoritos, segmentos de viajes, moda, cocina y mucho más.
"Al Mediodía" contiene todos los ingredientes para convertirse en su programa favorito.

Lunes a viernes 12 pm/11 am Centro.

✤ Univisión

Vocabulario para conversar **359**

Multiple Intelligences
Interpersonal/Social
See Exs. 1–3 and Cooperative Learning.
Intrapersonal/Introspective
See *¿Qué sabes ahora?*
Verbal/Linguistic
See Audio Activity 11.4.

Cultural Notes ☀

(p. 359, realia)
Al mediodía is the name of the noontime program advertised here by Los Angeles-based Univisión, the largest Spanish-language television network in the U.S. The ad claims that the new program "goes down well" *(cae bien),* like a good bowl of alphabet soup.

Paso cultural
Answers will vary.

Present & Apply

Cultural Objective
- To compare and contrast Spanish-language TV shows with the TV shows you usually watch

Critical Thinking: Drawing Conclusions
After reading the *Perspectiva cultural,* have students identify valid and invalid conclusions. Write these sentences on the chalkboard:
1) All Venezuelan teenagers like soap operas.
2) Most Venezuelan teenagers do not have TVs in their bedrooms. (Sentence 2 is valid.) Formulate additional statements if time permits.

Using Realia
Ask students to look at the *Venevisión* section of the TV guide. Using their knowledge of Spanish and certain clues, such as the program's time, have them choose a program they think they would like to watch and explain why.

Perspectiva cultural

En un estudio de televisión en San José, Costa Rica

Los programas de televisión en los países hispanos

En estos canales dan programas divertidos. ¿Qué clases de programas son más populares en América del Sur? ¿Son como los que ven tus amigos y tú?

Look at the picture of a Venezuelan household. What does the information in the photo tell you about what room the TV is usually located in and who you would find watching it?

Imagine this: You're an exchange student living in Caracas. You're staying with a family that has two children: Jaime, who is fourteen, and Mariana, sixteen. On your first night there, you sit down with them to watch television and . . . surprise! Bill Cosby pops up speaking perfect Spanish!

What you're watching is the dubbed version *El Show de Bill Cosby.*

Although Jaime and Mariana can also watch other dubbed imports from the United States, those programs are the exception. Venezuela has one of the largest television industries in Latin America.

Some weekend variety shows in Venezuela last several hours. For instance, *Super Sábado Sensacional.* It features performers from all over the world, combining entertainment with mini-interviews. *Super Sábado Sensacional* competes with similar shows from other countries that are also shown in Venezuela, such as *Sábado gigante,* produced by a Spanish-language station in Miami.

In most of the Spanish-speaking world, teenagers rarely have their own TV, even if the family can afford it. So at night, Jaime and Mariana sit down with the rest of the

Options

Strategies for Reaching All Students

Spanish-Speaking Students
Ask Spanish-speaking students: *¿Has visto Cristina o Sábado gigante? ¿Qué te gusta más de estos programas? ¿Prefieres ver los programas de televisión en inglés o en español? Por qué?*

 Un paso más Ex. 11-F

Students Needing Extra Help
Discuss the Spanish TV stations in your viewing area if there are any. Assign students to watch a program or find a listing in the paper.

Multiple Intelligences
Logical/Mathematical
Have students conduct a survey to determine which TV shows, movies, and actors/actresses are most popular among their classmates. Results can be displayed in the room on a bar graph or chart.
Naturalist
If possible, have students watch a Spanish-language television program that addresses environmental issues.
Visual/Spatial
See Using Realia and Critical Thinking: Drawing Conclusions.

family to watch TV in the living room. They usually tune in to one of several *culebras.* The word means "snake," which is how Venezuelans jokingly refer to their soap operas, because they're long and winding. Venezuela, Mexico, Argentina, and Spain produce many popular soap operas. They usually last several months, then new shows begin, with new characters.

If Jaime and Mariana could watch Spanish-language TV in other countries, they would be surprised to see how many shows from Venezuela are broadcast there. This would give them a sense of how Venezuelan television plays an important role in world communications.

"*Me gusta ver la televisión con mi familia.*"

La cultura desde tu perspectiva

 If there is a Spanish-language TV channel in your area, watch a program for at least ten minutes. Make sure you see a commercial break. Write down everything you understood. Which was easier to understand, the program or the commercials? How might watching TV in Spanish benefit you beyond learning the language?

 If you don't have access to a Spanish-language broadcast, imagine that you are living in Venezuela for an extended period of time. What would be the advantages of watching TV? What could you learn from a Venezuelan program that you could not learn from a dubbed imported program? How might you benefit from watching a dubbed imported program?

Perspectiva cultural   361

Answers
Answers will vary for inductive questions, but may include *las telenovelas* or *los programas importados de los Estados Unidos.* / The room is a living room or family room. All family members from different generations might be watching TV.

Answers: La cultura desde tu perspectiva

1 Answers will vary, but students may say that the commercials were easier to understand because of their familiarity with the English commercial for the same product. Watching TV in Spanish would expose them to such things as body language, pronunciation, and culture. In addition, the information and perspectives presented in Spanish-language programs could expand their knowledge and way of thinking. All these things would help them communicate more effectively with Spanish speakers.

2 Answers will vary, but may include some of the items mentioned in No. 1.

Pasos vivos 1 CD-ROM
Notas culturales, Maps

www Internet Activities
Perspectiva cultural

Cultural Notes ☼

(p. 360, realia)
Mexican *telenovelas* have attracted a passionate following throughout Latin America. This Venezuelan TV guide features a brief article on Mexican *telenovela* star José Ángel Llamas. Ask students to paraphrase the content of the article. Also have students read the listings and ask if they can recognize programs from the U.S.

(p. 360, photo)
With its long-standing commitment to democracy, Costa Rica has a vigorous national press, a host of FM stations, and six local television stations. Multinational cable news networks such as TeleNoticias are relative newcomers. Purchased in 1997 by CBS, TeleNoticias operates in 22 countries.

(p. 361, photo)
Since 1980, television programs in Venezuela are subject to government approval. Private and government-run stations must submit their programs to the Ministry of Communications 48 hours before airtime to ensure that their content meets educational and/or cultural standards.

Preview

Critical Thinking: Distinguishing Between Fact and Opinion

Advertisements often rely upon opinions rather than facts to try to sell products. Have students read the entire advertisement once again. Ask: What are some of the adjectives that are used to describe the food? *(deliciosa, sabrosas, etc.)* Are these descriptions based on facts or are they just the opinions of the restaurant's owners?

Answers

Answers will vary. Students may say they are showing customers' testimonies, the commercial is trying to reach a large audience, etc.

A The expressions are: *nos gustan* and *les encanta. Nos* refers to us and *les,* to them *(a nuestros hijos).*

B The foods being compared are *pollo al horno* and *las ensaladas.* The words that make the comparison are *menos, más,* and *que.* The two comparisons have the word *que* in common.

Gramática en contexto

Look at the story boards for this TV commercial for a restaurant delivery service. How is the restaurant using TV to advertise?

Ahora Uds. pueden disfrutar la comida del mejor restaurante de la ciudad sin salir de casa y ¡sin tener que preparar nada!

El Restaurante Taxi

les lleva a sus casas una cena deliciosa. Aquí tienen Uds. los comentarios de algunos de nuestros clientes:

A nosotros nos gustan mucho las enchiladas. Por eso, siempre llamamos al Restaurante Taxi, donde hacen las más sabrosas enchiladas.

Las ensaladas del Restaurante Taxi son más sabrosas y baratas que las ensaladas de otros restaurantes.

El pollo al horno del Restaurante Taxi tiene menos grasa que el pollo frito de los otros restaurantes. A nuestros hijos les encanta.

A You know that we use *me gusta(n)* and *me encanta(n)* when we talk about things we "like" or "love." In the ad, there are similar expressions, but *nos* and *les* are used instead of *me.* Find these expressions. To whom do you think *nos* refers? To whom do you think *les* refers?

B Find the sentence that begins *El pollo al horno del Restaurante Taxi tiene . . .* and the one that begins *Las ensaladas del Restaurante Taxi son . . . .* In each sentence, what foods are being compared? Which words make the comparison? What word do the two comparisons have in common?

362   Capítulo 11

Options

Strategies for Reaching All Students

Students Needing Extra Help

A: Students might have trouble with the pronoun "we" associated with just one thing. Make a chart that indicates to students that one person can like one thing, one person can like two things, two people can like one thing, and two people can like two things. Model with several sentences.
B: If students have difficulty, remind them of their first introduction to *más* in *Me gusta más . . .* and build from there.

Los comparativos: Write the formula on the chalkboard.
Show students how the adjectives agree. The irregular forms can be difficult for some students. Comparing to the English "good, better, best" helps them understand the irregular forms in Spanish. Give some examples, both with regular and irregular forms.

Enrichment

A–B: To help students answer these questions, you may want to first have individuals take turns reading this passage aloud. (This will also give you a chance to check pronunciation and overall comprehension.) Have students look at the expressions *gusta(n)* and *encanta(n).* Then ask: Which nouns determine whether the singular or plural form is used in these expressions? Which noun determines the form of the verb: the person who likes the food or the food itself?

Los comparativos

You have learned *más* and *menos* in certain expressions.

> Me gusta el tenis pero me gusta **más** el fútbol.
> ¿Te gustan las manzanas? Sí, **más o menos**.

- We also use *más / menos* + adjective + *que* ("than") to make comparisons.

    > Las películas de aventuras son **más emocionantes que** las películas del oeste.
    > Una telenovela es **menos realista que** un programa de hechos de la vida real.

- The adjectives agree with the nouns they refer to.

- The adjectives *bueno, -a, malo, -a, viejo, -a,* and *joven* have irregular comparative forms. We do not use *más* with them.

ADJETIVO	COMPARATIVO
bueno, -a	**mejor (que)**
malo, -a	**peor (que)**
viejo, -a	**mayor (que)**
joven	**menor (que)**

- *Mejor, peor, mayor,* and *menor* have plural forms ending in *-es.* However, they don't have a different feminine form:

    > **Las hermanas** de Pedro son **menores** que las de Juan.

- *Mejor* ("better") is also the comparative form of *bien* ("well"), and *peor* ("worse") is also the comparative form of *mal* ("badly"). When used in this sense, *mejor* and *peor* have only one form.

    > Graciela y Fabián son **mejores que** Susana y Gustavo en tenis.
    > Graciela y Fabián juegan tenis **mejor que** Susana y Gustavo.

Nace la
Televisión Personal.

En
Septiembre.

La manera más completa y sencilla de poder elegir el tema que usted prefiera, en el momento que usted prefiera.

VÍA
DIGITAL

La televisión personal

Gramática en contexto   363

Present

Class Starter Review
On the day following the presentation of comparatives, you might begin the class with this activity: Arrange pictures of three famous people on the chalkboard. Students then give a comparative sentence saying who is more or less intelligent, beautiful, interesting, etc.

Cultural Notes
(p. 363, realia)
Digital television uses computer technology to create crystal-clear reception. It also allows consumers access to a greater range of channels. Digital television decoders are expensive, however, and in most countries digital television is available only by subscription or pay-per-view. Ask students: How does this ad try to sell Vía Digital to viewers?

Los comparativos: Have students work in pairs to create more sets of sentences such as that at the bottom of the box: *Graciela y Fabián son <u>mejores</u> que Susana y Gustavo en tenis. Graciela y Fabián juegan tenis <u>mejor</u> que Susana y Gustavo.* Make sure students understand that in each set one sentence has *mejor* or *peor* referring to nouns, and therefore changing (in number only) as required, and the other sentence has *mejor* or *peor* referring to verbs and remaining unchanged.

Extended Written Practice/Homework
1. Choose three pairs of TV programs or movies. Compare them and write a sentence for each pair: *Las películas de terror son más emocionantes que las películas musicales.*
2. Choose three pairs of actors and actresses. Compare them and write a sentence for each pair: *Isabel Montoya es más atractiva que Clara Fernández.*

Multiple Intelligences
Verbal/Linguistic
See Enrichment A–B and Class Starter Review.
Visual/Spatial
See Overhead 60, Critical Thinking, Exs. A–B, and Students Needing Extra Help *(Los comparativos).*

Practice

Re-enter / Recycle

Exs. 4–5: adjectives describing physical characteristics from Chap. 5
Ex. 5: adjectives describing personality from Chap. 1

Answers

1 a. falso
b. falso
c. verdad
d. falso
e. falso

2 Adjective choice will vary, but look for logical responses and agreement in gender and number.
a. Las comedias son más emocionantes que los programas de entrevistas. (Los programas de entrevistas son menos emocionantes que las comedias.)
b. Los programas de entrevistas son más . . . que los programas musicales. (Los programas musicales son menos . . . que los programas de entrevistas.)
c. Los programas educativos son más . . . que los programas musicales. (Los programas musicales son menos . . . que los programas educativos.)
d. Las comedias son más . . . que las telenovelas. (Las telenovelas son menos . . . que las comedias.)
e. Las películas de ciencia ficción son más . . . que las películas del oeste. (Las películas del oeste son menos . . . que las películas de ciencia ficción.)

---

1 En una hoja de papel escribe V *(verdad)* o F *(falso)* para cada frase.

a. Una nota de B es mejor que una nota de A.
b. Dormir ocho horas es peor para la salud que dormir seis horas.
c. Los refrescos son peores para la salud que la leche.
d. Jugar videojuegos es mejor para la salud que practicar deportes.
e. Generalmente los estudiantes de séptimo grado son mayores que los de octavo grado.

2 Túrnate con un(a) compañero(a) para comparar estos programas y películas. Usa estos adjetivos.

| aburrido, -a | divertido, -a | interesante | triste |
| cómico, -a | emocionante | realista | |

Los dibujos animados son más divertidos que las noticias.
o: *Las noticias son menos divertidas que los dibujos animados.*

a.   b.

c.   d.

e.   f.

364   Capítulo 11

Options

Strategies for Reaching All Students

Spanish-Speaking Students
Ex. 2: Have Spanish-speaking students write out this exercise.
Ex. 3: Pair Spanish-speaking students if possible.

Enrichment
Ex. 3: You may want to extend the practice of *mejor* and *peor* by having students compare movies and TV programs: *Pienso que Aladino es mejor (peor) que . . . ,* etc.

Cooperative Learning
Have students work in groups of three. *Estudiante A* begins a sentence by choosing a category from pp. 350–351 or 354–355. *Estudiante B* adds the *más* or *menos* comparative phrase, and *Estudiante C* chooses a second program category:
A—Las películas de terror . . .
B—son menos divertidas . . .
C—que los dibujos animados.
Have the group make similar statements, then switch parts.

3 Haz una lista de tus actores y atletas favoritos y escribe una frase sobre cada uno. Túrnate con un(a) compañero(a) para comparar a las personas de tu lista con las de su lista.

A —*Michael Jordan juega béisbol mejor que Sammy Sosa.*
　o: *Sammy Sosa es peor atleta que Leonardo DiCaprio.*

B —*Tienes razón.*
　o: *¡No lo creo!*
　　　(No) Estoy de acuerdo.

4 Con un(a) compañero(a), compara la edad de estos personajes.

A —*¿Crees que Donald Duck es mayor que Mickey Mouse?*

B — *Creo que Donald Duck es menor.*
　o: *Creo que Mickey Mouse es mayor.*

a. Batman y Robin
b. Superman y Lois Lane
c. Bert y Ernie
d. Kermit y Miss Piggy
e. Seinfeld y Frasier
f.

5 Con un(a) compañero(a), usa unos adjetivos de la lista para comparar a los personajes del Ejercicio 4.

alto, -a	inteligente
amable	ordenado, -a
atrevido, -a	pequeño, -a
bonito, -a	perezoso, -a
deportista	simpático, -a
guapo, -a	trabajador, -a

7 NOMINACIONES A LOS OSCAR
INCLUIDAS
MEJOR PELICULA | MEJOR ACTOR *Jack Nicholson* | MEJOR ACTRIZ *Helen Hunt* | MEJOR ACTOR SECUNDARIO *Greg Kinnear*

PREPÁRATE PARA CONOCER A MELVIN

GANADORA DE
3 GLOBOS DE ORO
MEJOR PELICULA
COMEDIA
MEJOR ACTOR *JACK NICHOLSON* | MEJOR ACTRIZ *HELEN HUNT*

ESTRENO **27** FEBRERO

JACK NICHOLSON
HELEN HUNT　GREG KINNEAR

MEJOR... IMPOSIBLE

Una comedia del corazón que no tiene pelos en la lengua.

MoviStar **CON EL CINE**

Gramática en contexto　365

Extended Written Practice/Homework
1. Choose three pairs of foods and write a sentence for each telling which is better or worse for your health: *El cereal es mejor para la salud que los huevos.*
2. Write four sentences telling which people among your friends and family are older or younger than others.

Multiple Intelligences
Verbal/Linguistic
See Exs. 2–5.
Visual/Spatial
See Practice Wkbk. 11-5 and Writing Activity 11-D.

---

f. Los programas de detectives son más . . . que las películas románticas. (Las películas románticas son menos . . . que los programas de detectives.)

3 Lists and dialogues will vary. Look for logical responses from *Estudiante B*.

4 ESTUDIANTE A
a. ¿Crees que Batman es mayor que Robin?
b. . . . Superman . . . Lois Lane?
c. . . . Bert . . . Ernie?
d. . . . Kermit . . . Miss Piggy?
e. . . . Seinfeld . . . Frasier?
f. Questions will vary.
ESTUDIANTE B
a.–f. Answers will vary.

5 Questions and answers will vary, but look for adjective agreement. For example:
¿Crees que Batman es más guapo que Robin?

Practice Wkbk. 11-5

Writing Activity 11-D

Prueba 11-5

Cultural Notes ☀

(p. 365, realia)
In this poster the movie title *As Good as It Gets* has been rendered as *Mejor... Imposible.* Go through the text of the poster with students, asking them to tell you what they can understand. Pay special attention to *que no tiene pelos en la lengua,* explaining to students that this is an expression meaning "not mincing words." Also ask: Can you think of other English movie titles that would be difficult to translate into Spanish?

Present & Practice

Los superlativos

- To say that someone or something is "the most" of a group, we use the definite article + (noun) + *más* + adjective.

  Para mí, *Los tres perezosos* es **el programa más divertido.**

- To say that someone or something is "the best" or "the worst," we use *el / la mejor* and *el / la peor.* These come before the noun.

  Pienso que Gonzalo Ochoa es **el mejor actor.**

- When we say that someone or something is "the most," "the best," or "the worst" in a group or category, we use *de.*

  Para mí, *El día del terror* es **la peor película de todas.**

  Mis amigos los perros es **el mejor programa del domingo.**

  Clara Vega es **la mejor actriz de las telenovelas.**

6 Con un(a) compañero(a), contesta las preguntas.

interesante

A —*¿Cuál es el programa más interesante?*

B —*El programa más interesante es . . .*

a. aburrido
b. divertido
c. emocionante
d. tonto
e. 💡

7 En grupos de cinco o seis, hagan una encuesta *(survey)* para averiguar *(find out)* el/la mejor y el/la peor de estas categorías y por qué. Luego, escribe los resultados de la encuesta.

mes del año

A —*Para ti, ¿cuál es el mejor mes del año?*

B —*Creo que el mejor mes del año es . . . porque . . .*

A —*¿Y cuál es el peor mes del año?*

B —*El peor mes del año es . . . porque . . .*

a. programa de televisión
b. anuncio de televisión
c. grupo musical
d. película del año
e. restaurante de la ciudad
f. tienda de la ciudad

Ahora, informa a la clase sobre los resultados de la encuesta.

Tres personas creen que . . . es el mejor mes del año porque . . .

Cuatro estudiantes creen que . . . es el peor mes del año porque . . .

Options

Strategies for Reaching All Students

El complemento directo: Los pronombres y el infinitivo

You know that we use direct object pronouns (*lo, la, los, las*) to avoid repeating a noun.

- When we use direct object pronouns with infinitives, we can either put them before the verb or attach them to the end of the infinitive. For example:
  —¿Vas a ver **las noticias**?
  —Sí, **las** voy a ver.
    o: Sí, voy a ver**las**.

8 Empareja *(match up)* cada expresión de la derecha con dos frases de la izquierda. Dos frases sobrarán *(will be left over)*.

a. Debo llamarlos.   mis amigos
b. Lo voy a enviar.   estos zapatos
c. No podemos llevarlos. mi tarea
d. La necesito hacer.
e. Pienso verlo.
f. Los voy a comprar.
g. Los quiero visitar.
h. Tengo que hacerla.

9 Escribe los nombres de cinco películas o programas de televisión y de qué clase es cada uno de ellos. Después, pregunta a otros(as) compañeros(as) si quieren verlos y por qué.

A —¿*Quieres ver la comedia (nombre)?*

B —*Sí, me gustaría verla.*
   o: *No, no quiero verla.*

A —¿*Por qué?*

B —*Porque me encantan las comedias.*
   o: *Porque a mí me aburren las comedias.*

Gramática en contexto   367

HÉROES DE PLASTILINA

Wallace y Gromit ya están en España. Gracias a BMG Vídeo podremos disfrutar en casa de las disparatadas aventuras de estos maravillosos personajes realizados en plastilina por Nick Park. Con su inigualable animación, exquisito humor e inolvidables personajes, Wallace y Gromit enamorarán tanto a niños como adultos. Los dos primeros títulos en venta directa son *Los Tecnopantalones*, que ganó el Oscar al mejor corto de animación en 1994, y *La gran excursión*, candidata al mismo premio. Para celebrar este lanzamiento, sorteamos 25 camisetas de Wallace y Gromit. Para conseguirla, envíe una carta con sus datos personales antes del 24 de noviembre a Club METRÓPOLI, Sorteo Wallace y Gromit, c/ Pradillo 42, 28002 Madrid, y díganos qué profesión tiene Wallace.

Sección coordinada por BEATRIZ TORRES

Answers

8 a. mis amigos
b. *no match*
c. estos zapatos
d. mi tarea
e. *no match*
f. estos zapatos
g. mis amigos
h. mi tarea

9 Questions and answers will vary.

Cultural Notes
(p. 366, realia)
From the earliest days of Hollywood, U.S. movie stars have always attracted an enormous following throughout the Spanish-speaking world. This poster makes Julia Roberts the most important selling point for *La boda de mi mejor amigo,* assuming that moviegoers are already familiar with her role in *Pretty Woman.* Ask students: What Hispanic actors have become Hollywood stars? What movies have they been in?

Using Realia
(p. 367) See if students can get the gist of this article by scanning it. Tell them to look for cognates and word families throughout the text.

Enrichment
Ex. 7: As an in-class assignment, have students work in pairs or groups to survey all of their classmates on just one of the items in a.–f. In that way, information about the opinions of the entire class on a given topic can be gathered and presented later.
El complemento directo: Los pronombres y el infinitivo: Do a quick review with students in which they answer these questions in one or another of the ways indicated in the example in the box: ¿*Vas a hacer la tarea?* ¿*Vas a visitar a tus primas?* ¿*Vas a comprar estos libros?* ¿*Vas a comer ese flan?*

Extended Written Practice/Homework
1. Create four categories *(la clase más difícil, la ropa más cara)* and write a sentence for each telling what or who is at the top of the list: *Matemáticas es la clase más difícil.*
2. Refer to pp. 220–221 and write three sentences describing ideal vacation spots: *La selva tropical más bonita está en Costa Rica.*
3. Write sentences telling what is the best or worst of these categories: *quehaceres de la casa, formas de ejercicio, regalos, telenovelas.*

Multiple Intelligences
Interpersonal/Social
See Enrichment and Exs. 6–7 and 9.
Visual/Spatial
See Practice Wkbk. 11-6, Writing Activity 11-E, and Comm. Act. BLM 11-2.

Standards 1.1; 1.2 **367**

Present & Practice

Re-enter / Recycle
Ex. 10: household chores and *tener que* + inf. from Chap. 8

Answers

10 ESTUDIANTE A

a. ¿Tengo que arreglar el cuarto?

b. . . . sacudir los muebles?

c. . . . cortar el césped?

d. . . . limpiar el baño?

e. . . . hacer la cama?

f. . . . poner la mesa?

ESTUDIANTE B

a. Sí, tienes que arreglarlo. Hay ropa en la cama, en la silla y en el escritorio.

b. . . . sacudirlos. Puedes empezar con la sala.

c. . . . cortarlo. El césped está demasiado alto.

d. . . . limpiarlo. Está sucio.

e. . . . hacerla. ¡Ya son las once y no vas a dormir más!

f. . . . ponerla. Vamos a comer en cinco minutos.

 Practice Wkbk. 11-7

 Prueba 11-7

---

10 Pregúntale a un(a) compañero(a) si tienes que hacer estos quehaceres en la casa y por qué.

A —¿Tengo que lavar la ropa?

B —Sí, tienes que lavarla. Está sucia.

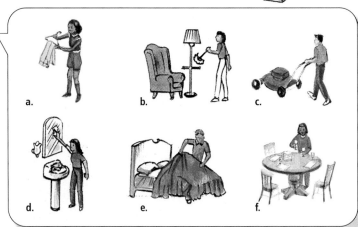

a.

b.

c.

d.

e.

f.

El césped está demasiado alto.

Vamos a comer en cinco minutos.

Hay ropa en la cama, en la silla y en el escritorio.

¡Ya son las once y no vas a dormir más!

Puedes empezar con la sala.

Está sucio.

El pretérito del verbo *ver*

We use *vi* and *viste* to talk about things that we saw. Here are all of the preterite-tense forms of the verb *ver*.

(yo)	**vi**	(nosotros) (nosotras)	**vimos**
(tú)	**viste**	(vosotros) (vosotras)	**visteis**
Ud. (él) (ella)	**vio**	Uds. (ellos) (ellas)	**vieron**

Recuerdos de un viaje a Bogotá, Colombia

368   Capítulo 11

Options

Strategies for Reaching All Students

Students Needing Extra Help
Ex. 10: Remind students to attach the *lo, la, los,* or *las* to the first part of *Estudiante B's* answer before choosing the second part from the list on the right.
El pretérito del verbo ver: Remind students that preterite means "past" and of the clue words *ayer, anoche, la semana pasada,* etc.
Ex. 12: Make a chart with columns for "movie" and "place." Do the exercise using TV programs if students haven't seen a movie recently. Remind them to use the third person when reporting.

Enrichment
Ex. 12: As a homework assignment, students can tell which they like better—seeing movies at the theater or on a VCR at home. Have them give reasons for their preferences and name the advantages and disadvantages of each kind of viewing.

Extended Written Practice/Homework
1. Write two pairs of sentences identifying new movies and saying whether you want to see them: Amor en la ciudad *es una película romántica nueva. No quiero verla.*
2. Write two pairs of sentences naming items of clothing you need and telling when you would like to buy them: *Necesito calcetines nuevos. Me gustaría comprarlos esta semana.*

11 En grupos de cuatro, pregunta quiénes vieron una de estas clases de programas anoche. Después, dile a la clase quiénes las vieron.

A —¿*Viste un documental anoche?*

B —*No. No vi un documental anoche.*
   o: *Sí, vi uno.*

Nadie vio un documental anoche.

o: *(Nombre/nombres/nombre y yo) vio/vieron/vimos un documental anoche.*

12 ¿Qué películas vieron tus compañeros(as) el mes pasado? ¿Dónde? Haz una encuesta para averiguarlo. Escribe la información y comparte *(share)* tus resultados con la clase.

A —¿*Qué películas viste el mes pasado?*

B —*Vi (título).*

A —¿*Dónde la viste?*

B —*La vi en mi casa (en el cine).*

Gramática en contexto 369

Present & Practice

Re-enter / Recycle
Exs. 13–14: *gustar* expressions from Chap. 1

Answers
13 Dialogues will vary, but look for the use of the full range of chapter vocabulary and correct use of indirect object pronouns.

14 a. A mi amigo (nombre) (no) le gustan . . .
b. A mis compañeras (nombres) (no) les gustan . . .
c. A mi profesor(a) de español (no) le gustan . . .
d. A nosotros(as) (no) nos gustan . . .
e. A mis padres/hermanos(as) (no) les gustan . . .
f. Answers will vary.

El complemento indirecto: Los pronombres *nos* y *les*

We use the indirect object pronouns *me, te,* and *le* with verbs like *dar, doler, encantar, fascinar, gustar,* and *interesar.* Here are all of the indirect object pronouns.

me	(to / for) me	**nos**	(to / for) us
te	(to / for) you	**os***	(to / for) you
le	(to / for) you him her it	**les**	(to / for) you them

* The pronoun *os* is used mainly in Spain. We will use it occasionally and you should learn to recognize it.

 ¡NO OLVIDES!

Sometimes we use *a* + noun or name to clarify who the indirect object pronoun refers to.
A mis padres les encantan los programas musicales.

13 Pregúntales a unos compañeros qué clases de programas de televisión les gustan. Despúes, dile a la clase qué programas les gustan (o no) a tus compañeros y a ti.

A —¿*Te gustan los documentales?*
B —*Sí, me fascinan.*
   o: *No, no me interesan.*

A (*nombre/nombres*) *le/les fascinan los documentales.*
o: *A (nombre y a mí) no nos interesan los documentales.*

14 Averigua qué piensan estas personas de las varias clases de películas. Luego, diles a tus compañeros en grupo lo que aprendiste.

A mi amiga (nombre) no le gustan nada las películas de ciencia ficción. Piensa que son aburridas.

a. (nombre de un amigo)
b. (nombre de dos compañeras)
c. tu profesor(a) de español
d. tu compañero(a) y tú
e. tus padres o hermanos(as)
f. 💡

Options

Strategies for Reaching All Students

Students Needing Extra Help
Ahora lo sabes: Have students write out this section so they can check off what they have mastered.

Extended Written Practice/Homework
1. Choose three of these groups of people (*amigos, padres, hermanos, primos, profesores, compañeros*) and write a sentence for each telling what types of movies or TV programs they like.
2. Write four sentences using *fascinar, gustar, interesar,* and *encantar* to tell what activities you and your friends like best.

Multiple Intelligences
Bodily/Kinesthetic
Write the indirect object pronouns on index cards and place them on the chalkboard ledge. Have students come up and select the correct pronoun for each of the sentences in Ex. 14.
Interpersonal/Social
See Exs. 13–14.

Answers: Ahora lo sabes
- más (menos) / que
- el mejor (peor)
- verla
- vimos
- nos interesan

 Practice Wkbk. 11-9

 Audio Activity 11.5

 Writing Activity 11-G

 Prueba 11-9

 Pasos vivos 1 CD-ROM

Phone Task, Slide Presentation Maker, Spindle, Treadmill

Ahora lo sabes

Can you:

► compare people and things?
—Las películas de aventuras son ___ emocionantes ___ las románticas.

► tell what is the best or worst in a group or category?
—(No) me gusta ese programa. Es _____ programa de televisión.

► avoid repeating a noun?
—¿Cuándo vas a ver la película? Voy a ___ esta tarde.

► tell what you saw?
—La semana pasada, mis hermanos y yo ___ una película del oeste.

► tell what you and others are interested in?
—A nosotros _____ las ciencias.

MORE PRACTICE

Más práctica y tarea, pp. 539–540
Practice Workbook 11–5, 11–9

Gramática en contexto 371

Cultural Notes ☀

Verbal/Linguistic
See Audio Activity 11.5.
Visual/Spatial
See Practice Wkbk. 11-9 and Writing Activity 11-G.

(p. 371, realia)
Baloncesto and *fútbol americano* are attracting an ever-growing audience in Spain, although the country does not have any important teams of its own. Spanish athletes have been far more successful in sports such as rugby, tennis, and especially soccer, which gets top billing in this television ad. Read the descriptions of the various programs with students, checking for comprehension.

Todo Junto

Actividades

1 ¿Qué programas de televisión te interesan más? Para esta actividad, diferentes lugares de la clase representan clases de programas diferentes. Tu profesor(a) te va a decir el lugar adonde debes ir. En grupo, digan *(tell)* a la clase:

- qué clase de programa les gusta y por qué
- cuál es el mejor ejemplo de esta clase de programa
- cuándo lo vieron

2 Prepara una crítica *(review)* de una película. En tu crítica puedes hablar sobre:

- qué película viste y cuándo
- qué clase de película es
- quiénes son los actores y qué piensas de ellos
- algo que uno de los actores hizo *(did)* en la película
- qué piensas de la película

3 Para esta actividad, necesitas la sección de pasatiempos del periódico. Haz planes con otro(a) estudiante para ir al cine este fin de semana. Tienes que:

- averiguar qué clase de películas le gusta a tu compañero(a)
- buscar en el periódico una película que le va a interesar
- invitarle a ir al cine
- decidir qué día van a ir y a qué hora
- decidir cómo van a ir

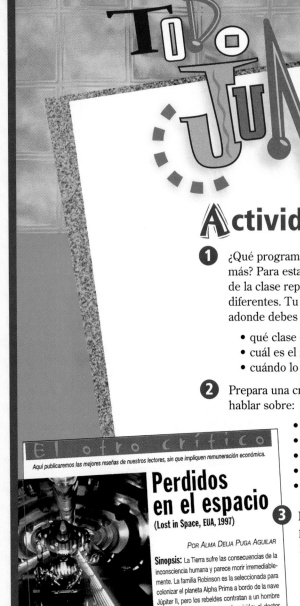

El otro crítico

Aquí publicaremos las mejores reseñas de nuestros lectores, sin que impliquen remuneración económica.

Perdidos en el espacio
(Lost in Space, EUA, 1997)

POR ALMA DELIA PUGA AGUILAR

Sinopsis: La Tierra sufre las consecuencias de la inconsciencia humana y parece morir irremediablemente. La familia Robinson es la seleccionada para colonizar el planeta Alpha Prima a bordo de la nave Júpiter II, pero los rebeldes contratan a un hombre sin escrúpulos para sabotear la misión: el doctor Zachary Smith (Gary Oldman). Así, él y la familia Robinson se ven involucrados en una gran aventura cuya meta es encontrar el camino a casa.

Reseña: Vuelve a la pantalla grande una serie más de nuestra infancia, la cual –sin duda alguna– nos mantenía sentados frente al televisor. Una película que respeta la idea original de la serie, sin cambios innecesarios, pero con una novedad excelente: los efectos especiales. Además, destaca el cínico y malévolo doctor Smith, a quien el director Stephen Hopkins quitó la personalidad caricaturesca de la serie, dándole un toque que contrasta con el resto de los personajes. Si tú eres de los que piensa que los tiempos pasados fueron mejores, no te puedes perder esta película. Y si piensas que las series de ficción son inmortales, entonces, ¡definitivamente tienes que verla!

Options

Strategies for Reaching All Students

Students Needing Extra Help
Ex. 1: Designate one corner of the room as *programas de terror,* another corner as *programas musicales,* another as *programas educativos,* and so on.

Enrichment
Ex. 1: This activity allows students to express and defend opinions about TV programs. Encourage them to agree or disagree with other groups' comments. To generate discussion, you might repeat the opinions of one group and then ask what others think of these opinions: *A ellos les interesan los programas de detectives. ¿Qué piensan Uds.?*

Ex. 2: Students may benefit from hearing you model a movie review. They can then prepare their reviews orally or in writing. They can present orally in front of the entire class or in small groups. If presentations are done in small groups, students can respond by saying whether they also saw the movie, what they think of it, what movies are comparable, and so on.

Conexiones

 La salud

¡Cuidado con el televisor!

Este artículo se trata de la relación entre el nivel de colesterol y la cantidad de tiempo que los jóvenes pasan frente al televisor. Antes de leerlo, lee de nuevo *(again)* el título de esta actividad. ¿Cuáles de estas ideas crees que van a aparecer en el artículo? Escribe las letras en una hoja de papel.

a. El nivel de colesterol de los jóvenes que ven mucha televisión es más alto que el nivel de los que no ven mucha televisión.

b. Los jóvenes que ven mucha televisión generalmente no practican deportes.

c. No hay ninguna relación entre el nivel de colesterol de una persona y la cantidad de tiempo que ve la televisión.

d. El nivel de colesterol no es muy importante.

¿Aparecieron en el artículo las ideas que tú marcaste?

En Chile, una persona que ve mucha televisión se llama *un(a) tevito(a)*. Escribe un párrafo para persuadir a *un(a) tevito(a)* a ir a pasear contigo. Puedes usar información del artículo y también otros argumentos.

WASHINGTON, (EFE).—Los niños que ven de dos a cuatro horas diarias de televisión tienen mayor riesgo de acumular altos índices de colesterol que aquéllos que se sientan frente a la pequeña pantalla menos de dos horas, según un estudio.

Una investigación dirigida por expertos de las universidades de California y Loma Linda entre 550 varones y 531 hembras, de dos a 20 años, encontró una mayor concentración de colesterol entre los que se sientan más horas frente al televisor.

El 53 por ciento de los niños y jóvenes observados entre los que veían más de dos horas la TV registró niveles de más de 200 miligramos de colesterol por cada decilitro.

El mismo estudio determinó que aquéllos que son propensos a sentarse por más tiempo frente al aparato de televisión tienen poca predisposición para participar en las actividades deportivas.

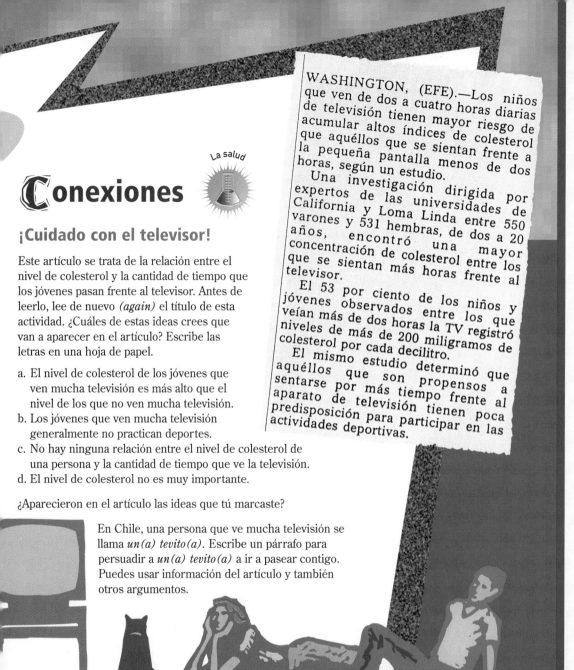

Todo junto 373

Critical Thinking: Synthesizing

Tell groups of three or four students to imagine that they are television producers developing a new half-hour show. Have each group prepare a newspaper advertisement for the show that will include: type of show (comedy, drama, talk show, sports, etc.), main characters (with a brief description of each), and when it can be seen (channel, time, day).

Answers: Conexiones

Statements a and b are ideas that appear in the article. Before telling students the answer, have them check their own predictions by reading the article./Paragraphs will vary.

 Practice Wkbk.
11-10

 Writing Activities
11-H, 11-I

 Comm. Act. BLMs
11-3, 11-4, 11-5

 Paso vivos 1
CD-ROM

A Jugar, Boom Box, Laboratorio de grabar, Maps, Spindle

Using Realia

(p. 372) Ask students if the reviewer gave the movie a positive review (yes). Where does she say so? (in the last two sentences)

Cooperative Learning
Tell students that they are going to develop a show similar to the People's Choice Awards. Help the class develop categories for awards and then assign a specific category, such as sports, television, music, etc., to each group. Instruct each group to develop four questions, using comparatives / superlatives, and a tally sheet for their category. Collect the questions to compile a whole-class list.

Multiple Intelligences
Interpersonal/Social
See Critical Thinking: Synthesizing and Exs. 1 and 3.
Interpersonal/Social and Logical/Mathematical
See Cooperative Learning.
Verbal/Linguistic
See Pronunciation Tape 11-3 and Enrichment Ex. 2.

Visual/Spatial
See Using the Video, Practice Wkbk. 11-10, Writing Activities 11-H and 11-I, and Comm. Act. BLMs 11-3, 11-4, and 11-5.

Apply

Process Reading
For a description of process reading, see p. 48.

Multicultural Perspectives
A wide variety of children's television programs are available in Puerto Rico. One of the most popular is *El show de Don Pacheco.* Children in Puerto Rico dream of having their birthday acknowledged or of winning a contest on this after-school program that features games, contests, and *muñequitos*. Dressed in a suit, a bow tie, and a Panama straw hat (his trademark) Don Pacheco has been entertaining children for years with his comforting voice and grandfatherly image. Invite students to share information about programs that they watched when they were children. Encourage comparisons with children's programs that younger brothers or sisters watch today.

Answers
Antes de leer
Answers will vary, but may include: the name of the movie; where it is shown and when; a review or description of the movies; etc. / Answers will vary. / Students' movie listings will vary.

¡Vamos a leer!

Antes de leer

STRATEGY ➤ **Using prior knowledge**

What kind of information would you expect to find in a page of movie listings? How would you expect it to be presented? Think of a movie you know well and write a movie listing for it.

Mira la lectura

STRATEGY ➤ **Skimming**

Look at this selection from the Puerto Rican magazine *Vea*. What is the topic of this page? How is the information organized? (Alphabetically? By time sequence? By location?)

374   Capítulo 11

Options

Strategies for Reaching All Students

Spanish-Speaking Students

Un paso más Exs. 11-G, 11-H

Students Needing Extra Help
Infórmate 1: Make a chart with columns to help students organize the information.
Infórmate 3: Have students pick words that tell what is important.
Show how adding a negative or *más / menos* could easily change the description.
Aplicación: Ex. 1: Have students use their Organizers from previous chapters.

Enrichment
Aplicación: As a homework assignment, students can pretend that they have seen two of the movies listed and tell what happened, using the brief description from the movie listings. Remind students that to recount the action in the past, they must use the preterite.

Infórmate

STRATEGY ➤ Using cognates

One of the most useful strategies for dealing with unfamiliar words is using cognates. Here are some patterns that might help you recognize them.

- Frequently a double consonant in an English word is represented by a single consonant in the Spanish cognate: *clase, inocente, aceptar.*
- Often words ending in *-y* in English end in *-ia* or *-ía* in Spanish: *historia, geografía, infancia.*
- Many English adjectives ending in *-ed* end in *-ado(a)* or *-ido(a)* in Spanish: *aceptado, -a; permitidos, -as.*

Look at the bold-faced headings in the reading.

- When are the most movies shown, in the morning, afternoon, or evening?
- How many channels show movies?
- Read the titles, then classify the movies according to type. Which category seems to be the most popular?

película de detectives
comedia
película musical
película del oeste
película romántica
película de aventuras
dibujos animados

"Titanic es una película muy emocionante."

2 Choose a movie that sounds interesting and read its description several times to get an idea about the plot. Pick out a few cognates that help you understand the description.

3 After reading the description, do you still think the movie belongs to the category suggested by its title? If you have already seen the movie, do you think the description tells what is most important about the plot? Would you change the description? How?

Aplicación

1 Which of these movies would you prefer to see? Why?

2 On a piece of paper, list at least ten new words that you learned from this reading selection and ten cognates that you found.

Mira la lectura

The topic of the page is listings of movies on TV. The information is organized by day and time.

Infórmate

1 Most movies are shown in the evening. / Eight channels show movies: 2, 4, 5, 7, 9, 11, 12, 22. / *película de detectives:* Black Magic, V.I. Warshawski, The Kansas City Massacre; *comedia:* Father of the Bride; *película romántica:* Oscar; *película de aventuras:* First Blood, The Towering Inferno, Romancing the Stone, Teenage Mutant Ninja Turtles, Things Change; *dibujos animados:* Alice in Wonderland. The category *película de aventuras* has the most titles.

2–3 Answers will vary.

Aplicación

1 Answers will vary.

2 New words that students have learned will vary. Possible cognates found may include: *versión, clásico, famosa, mágico, veterano, escapa,* etc.

www Internet Activities

Cultural Notes ☼

Multiple Intelligences
Intrapersonal/Introspective
See *Aplicación.*
Visual/Spatial
See Enrichment and Exs. 1–2 in *Infórmate.*

(p. 374, realia)
The strong U.S. influence on Puerto Rican culture is clear in the many listings of films in this television guide. Although many of these films may be dubbed or subtitled in Spanish, English is widely used, as it is a required subject in all school grades. About 97 percent of Puerto Rican homes have a TV set, with approximately one out of four having a VCR.

Answers: ¡Vamos a escribir!
Students' reviews will vary.

**Pasos vivos 1
CD-ROM**
Word Processor

¡Vamos a escribir!

Choose a recent TV show that you enjoyed and write a review of it.

1 First, write out the answers to these questions about the program.

- ¿Cómo se llama el programa?
- ¿Qué clase de programa es?
- ¿Qué día viste el programa?
  ¿En qué canal?
  ¿Cuánto tiempo duró?
- ¿Qué artistas participaron?
  ¿Cómo son?
- ¿Te gustó el programa?
  ¿Por qué?
- ¿Lo recomiendas?
  ¿A quién lo recomiendas? (a los niños, a los jóvenes ...)

2 Now write the review using your answers to the preceding questions as a guide. Show your review to a partner. Ask if there is any other information he or she would want to have or if you should change or rearrange any of your information to make it more helpful to the reader.

3 Decide about the changes you might like to make, and rewrite your review.

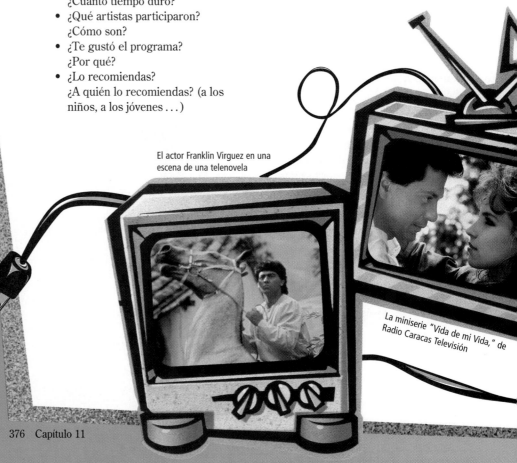

El actor Franklin Virguez en una escena de una telenovela

La miniserie "Vida de mi Vida," de Radio Caracas Televisión

376 Capítulo 11

Options

Strategies for Reaching All Students

Students Needing Extra Help
Have students use their Organizers.
Step 1: Tell students to first answer with phrases, then put in complete sentences.

Enrichment
For an alternate writing assignment, students can pretend to be television or movie writers trying to sell their new show or movie to entertainment industry executives. Students should describe their TV show or movie by giving its title, genre, length, and intended audience. They can also suggest actors to play the roles and, if their creation is a TV show, the best time slot.

Multiple Intelligences
Intrapersonal/Introspective
See Enrichment and step 1.

4 Check for spelling and accents. Did you use the correct forms of the verbs and adjectives? If necessary, rewrite your review.

5 Now you are ready to share your work. You can:
- collect all the reviews into a class program guide called *Guía de televisión: Los mejores programas,* or
- include it in your writing portfolio

La actriz Marlene Mesada

La comedia "Corte Tropical"

"Kassandra," una telenovela popular

377

Cultural Notes

(pp. 376–377, photos)
The situation comedy *Corte Tropical* is broadcast by Univisión, one of the leading Spanish networks in the U.S. Univisión, which is headquartered in Dade County, Florida, also carries the variety game show *Sábado gigante,* which is popular in the U.S. and throughout Latin America. Miniseries from Venezuela, such as *Vida de mi vida,* are favorites with family viewers.

Telenovelas such as *Kassandra* also enjoy a wide viewership in the U.S. and Latin America. Many are filmed in Caracas; others come mainly from Mexico, Argentina, and Puerto Rico. Several *telenovelas,* such as *El Magnate,* are filmed in the U.S. with Miami as their setting.

Assess & Summarize

Test Preparation
You may want to assign parts of this section as written homework or as an in-class writing activity prior to administering the *Examen de habilidades.*

Answers
Listening: *Esta noche dan una comedia divertida en el canal doce. En la comedia van a estar los mejores actores de cine de Puerto Rico. La comedia empieza a las ocho y media y termina a las diez.* More than one hour. The person would be watching at home.

Reading: By using cognates and phrases such as the title of the movie *(Tren expreso), no hay ni fantasmas ni vampiros ni monstruos,* and *el robo de un banco,* we can tell it's an adventure film.

Writing: Movie descriptions will vary.

Culture: Answers will vary. Students may cite some variety shows, such as *Sábado sensacional* or *Sábado gigante.* Other programming includes soap operas and dubbed imports from the U.S. / Answers will vary for program choices.

Speaking: Answers will vary.

This section will help you organize your studying for the proficiency test, where you will be asked to do similar, though not identical, tasks. There will not be any models on the test.

► Listening
Can you understand when someone talks about how long an event will last? Listen as your teacher reads a sample similar to what you will hear on the test. According to the person making the statement, how much time would someone spend watching this, one hour or more than an hour? Would the person watching be at home or at a movie theater?

► Reading
Can you read this movie review and use the cognates that appear in it to find out what kind of movie it is?

Tren expreso
Con *Tren expreso,* Ud. no puede aburrirse. *Tren expreso* es una película divertida, con mucho humor, donde no hay ni fantasmas ni vampiros ni monstruos. Todo es real. Es una emocionante aventura que empieza con el robo de un banco. Los críticos dicen que es la mejor película del año. Véala en el Cine Acuario.

378 Capítulo 11

► Writing
Can you write a letter describing a movie you saw recently? Here is a sample letter:

Hola, Carmelo:

La semana pasada, mi hermano y yo vimos una película bastante buena. Es muy realista. Nos fascinó. En la película hay una familia que no tiene dinero: el padre no tiene trabajo y la hija está enferma. Una persona generosa los ayuda. No es la mejor película del verano, pero es muy interesante.

Saludos, Ana

► Culture
Can you explain what is shown on TV in Venezuela, what programs you would choose to watch, and why?

El programa de entrevistas *Cristina*

► Speaking
Can you express and defend an opinion about a television program?

—*Para mí, el mejor programa del canal 9 es el programa educativo,* Ambiente. *Es un programa fascinante. Los dibujos animados son demasiado tontos y aburridos. No me interesan. Yo creo que deben dar más programas educativos.*

Self Test www.pasoapaso.com

Options

Strategies for Reaching All Students

Students Needing Extra Help
Have students write out this section so they can check off what they have mastered.
Listening: Ask students what words they should be listening for, given the topic (numbers, time expressions).
Reading: Ask students for words that might be found in a description of different types of movies. Put them in columns.

Remind students to watch for these words. Remind them that a negative word changes the meaning of the phrase.
Writing: Break this into parts. What information is given in each sentence? Have them write a letter as a class.
Culture: Have students review any notes they took earlier.

Resumen del vocabulario

Use the vocabulary from this chapter to help you:

► talk about a TV show or movie
► tell when events begin and end, and how long they last
► express and defend an opinion

to name types of movies
la clase (de)
la película de aventuras
la película de ciencia ficción
la película musical
la película del oeste
la película romántica
la película de terror

to talk about TV and TV shows
el actor
la actriz, *pl.* las actrices
el anuncio (de televisión)
el canal
la comedia
el concierto
dar + *movie or TV program*
los dibujos animados
el documental
las noticias
el programa deportivo
el programa de detectives
el programa educativo
el programa de entrevistas
el programa de hechos de la vida real
el programa musical
el pronóstico del tiempo
la telenovela

to describe a movie or TV show
aburrido, -a
cómico, -a
¿Cuál(es)?
demasiado
divertido, -a
emocionante
en blanco y negro
en colores
fascinante
interesante
más (here: *more*)
el / la / los / las mejor(es) (here: *best)*
el / la / los / las peor(es) (here: *worst)*
realista
tonto, -a
triste
un poco

to indicate time or duration
casi
corto, -a
de la mañana
de la noche
de la tarde
durar
en punto
hasta
largo, -a
más tarde
más temprano
media hora *(f.)*
el mediodía
la medianoche
el minuto
puntualmente
el tiempo
todavía no

to express opinions or reactions
aburrir
dar miedo
fascinar
interesar
pensar (e → ie) (que)
sobre

to indicate a reason
por eso

Resumen 379

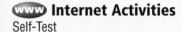
Cultural Notes

(p. 378, photo)
Cuban-born Cristina Saralegui hosts *El Show de Cristina*, the most-watched talk show in the world. The program is similar in style and content to English-language talk shows in the U.S., but the delivery is uniquely Hispanic.

CAPÍTULO 12

THEME: RESTAURANTS

COMMUNICATION

Topics

Restaurants

Mexican food

Table settings

Objectives

To discuss Mexican food and restaurants

To name and discuss foods

To talk about food

To describe table settings

To talk about eating out

To express needs

To indicate time or frequency

To indicate position

CULTURE

Mexican food and restaurants

GRAMMAR

Verbos con el cambio e → i

El verbo traer

El complemento indirecto: Los pronombres

El pretérito de los verbos que terminan en -er *e* -ir

Ancillaries available for use with Chapter 12

Multisensory/Technology

Overheads, 61–65

Audio Tapes and CDs

Vocabulary Art Blackline Masters for Hands-On Learning, pp. 63–67/CD-ROM

Classroom Crossword

Video

Pasos vivos 1 CD-ROM

www Internet Activities www.pasoapaso.com

Print

Practice Workbook, pp. 125–135

Writing, Audio & Video Activities, pp. 71–76, 126–128, 174–175

Communicative Activity Blackline Masters
  Pair and Small Group Activities, pp. 85–90
  Situation Cards, p. 91

Un paso más: Actividades para ampliar tu español, pp. 68–73

TPR Storytelling

Assessment

Assessment Program
  Pruebas, pp. 175–185
  Examen de habilidades, pp. 186–189

Test Generator

Video still from Chap. 12

Additional Technology

Planning Express, Teaching
Resources Library, and Clip Art
Library

¿Lo sabes bien?
Video Quiz

Cultural Overview ☼

The Versatile Tortilla

When the Spaniards first arrived in Tenochtitlán, the site that is now Mexico City, they arrived with barrels of wheat. Within 25 years, according to some sources, Mexican bakers could produce bread as well as any baker in Spain. This legacy continues.

In spite of the popularity of bread, tortillas are considered staples in Mexican cooking. They are used to prepare such dishes as *tacos, enchiladas, tostadas, chilaquiles,* and *sopa de tortilla.* They serve as thickeners in soups, *moles,* and stews and are used to scoop beans, eggs, and salsas.

Tortillas can be found throughout Mexico, and preparation techniques vary little from region to region. They can be made by hand at home or by mechanized press and conveyor belt in a *tortillería.* Corn tortillas *(tortillas de maíz)* are prepared the same way as they were in the days of the Aztec empire. Flour tortillas *(tortillas de harina)* are an innovation developed after the Spaniards introduced wheat to the American continent.

Corn tortillas are made with white corn, slaked lime (a white powder obtained by exposing calcium hydroxide to moist air or water), and water. The washed corn is boiled in water with dissolved lime for about five minutes. After standing for several hours, it is rinsed, ground, and kneaded into dough *(masa).* (Prepackaged *masa* mixes are now available in supermarkets.) Then the tortillas are shaped.

To shape a tortilla by hand, a small ball of *masa* is clapped back and forth from hand to hand to form a thin, flat circle. (When making tortillas at home, many people use a special press that flattens the dough to a uniform thickness and diameter.) After the tortilla has been formed, it is baked on a griddle until it puffs in the center and acquires a golden brown color.

Flour tortillas are prepared with flour, lard or vegetable shortening, salt, and water. The shortening produces a slightly more elastic tortilla with a chewy texture. As with corn tortillas, a small ball of *masa* is pinched off. Flour tortillas, on the other hand, when prepared at home, are usually rolled out with a lightly floured rolling pin and then baked over a low flame on a griddle for a only few seconds.

Introduce

Planning

Cross-Curricular Connections

Health Connection *(pp. 384–385)*
Tell students that, as nutrition consultants, they are to plan a lunch for the following clients:
1) A group of vegetarians
2) A sports team that needs to maintain their weight
3) A weight-loss group

Math Connection *(pp. 388–389)*
Assign prices to the food items in the *Vocabulario para conversar* on pp. 384–385. Have students order a meal, complete with beverage and dessert. Have them add up the bill and then calculate a 20 percent tip for the waiter.

Visual Arts Connection *(pp. 388–389)*
Have students create a poster for a place setting of a restaurant of their choice. Students should pay attention to balance and scale, color, texture, and pattern. They might use a sheet of colored construction paper as the tablecloth and then add cutouts to represent the silverware, glassware, plates, and condiments. Then have them label the components of their place setting. Display the posters around the classroom.

CAPÍTULO 12

¡Vamos a un restaurante mexicano!

Objectives

At the end of this chapter, you will be able to:

► ask politely to have something brought to you

► order a meal

► say what you ate or drank

► compare family dinners in the Spanish-speaking world and in the United States

PASO CULTURAL The corn tortilla has been a staple food for thousands of years in Mexico and Central America. The flour tortilla is a much more recent creation, dating to when the Spaniards introduced wheat to Tenochtitlán (now Mexico City) in the 16th century. Whenever cultures mix, one of the first areas affected is food. What foods popular in the United States represent a mixing of cultures?

Haciendo tortillas en el mercado de Chichicastenango, Guatemala

381

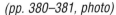

Cultural Notes

Spanish in Your Community
Have students visit a local Mexican restaurant where the waiters speak Spanish. Have the students order in Spanish. If this is not possible, have them visit a Mexican fast-food restaurant. They might want to follow up their visit by writing a review of the establishment in the style used by restaurant critics.

(pp. 380–381, photo)
Corn meal tortillas have been a staple at mealtimes in Mexico and Central America since ancient times. Today, some people continue to make tortillas the traditional way—by hand—as this woman is doing at the Sunday market in Chichicastenango, Guatemala. Others, however, now save themselves several hours of work by taking their corn to the *tortillería,* where it is ground and then made into tortillas by machine.

Paso cultural
Possible answers: Almost all U.S. foods represent a mixing of cultures, because immigrants adapt their food to local tastes and ingredients. Some specific examples are hamburgers, chop suey, chow mein, taco salad, burritos, and deep-dish pizza.

¡Piensa en la CULTURA!

"¿Y qué van a pedir?"

El restaurante El Set en la Playa Conchas Chinas en Puerto Vallarta, México

Restaurants in Mexico

Look at the photos and read the captions.

Think about the Mexican restaurants you know. What are their names? What are they like? Which of these restaurants is most similar to those in your community?

"Creo que voy a pedir lo mismo que esa muchacha."

Puerto Vallarta, México

En Pátzcuaro, México

PASO CULTURAL

Pescado blanco is the specialty of Pátzcuaro, a small fishing town on *el Lago de Pátzcuaro* in western Mexico. Other kinds of fish are also plentiful in the local restaurants, whose offerings reflect the traditional diet of the region's Tarascan Indians. Menus feature *trucha* (trout), *caldo de pescado* (fish broth), and two kinds of tiny fish—*charales* (sardines) and *boquerones* (smelts)—which are fried plain or *a la mexicana*, with onions, tomatoes, and chiles. Another traditional dish is *sopa tarasca*, made with toasted tortillas, tomatoes, cream, cheese, and a bitter chile called *pasilla*. What are some *especialidades regionales* where you live? Why did they become regional specialties?

Pátzcuaro, México

382   Capítulo 12

Options

Strategies for Reaching All Students

The people of Mexico eat as wide
a variety of foods as we do.

Ciudad de México

"¿Pedimos la cuenta, o van a querer
algo más?"

Este restaurante Sanborn's está en la Casa de los Azulejos,
un palacio del siglo XVI.

Cultural
Exploration
www.pasoapaso.com
Visit these countries on-line

¡Piensa en la cultura! 383

Multicultural Perspectives

In Mexico many people begin the
day with a *desayuno* consisting of
café and *pan dulce.* In some
regions, people might have a second breakfast in mid-morning.
This might include eggs, beans,
tortillas, and a beverage. The
comida, usually the heaviest and
most important meal of the day,
often occurs in early afternoon.
Later in the day, some people have
a *merienda* of fruit or something
sweet. Ask students to share their
meal patterns. Can they describe
the meal patterns of any other
cultures?

Cultural Notes
Paso cultural
Answers will vary.

(p. 383, top photo)
Tamales, such as these pictured
here, can come in all kinds of vari-
eties, but they all have a common
ingredient: corn.

(p. 383, bottom photo)
Built in 1596 and decorated with
tiles from the city of Puebla, the
Casa de los Azulejos in downtown
Mexico City was the home of a
noble family until the nineteenth
century. Today the building is
occupied by Sanborn's Restaurant,
which has restored the central
patio's murals and Moorish-style
architecture for its main dining
room. Ask students to identify
some of the features of Moorish-
style architecture in this photo.

Cultural Notes

(p. 382, top photo)
Although the present site of Puerto Vallarta,
Mexico, was mentioned by Spanish explorers in the sixteenth century, it was not per-
manently settled by Europeans until the
1850s. In 1963 the town was made famous
by the filming of John Huston's *Night of the
Iguana,* and it soon became a favorite destination for Hollywood celebrities. It is now
one of Mexico's most popular international
resorts.

(p. 382, bottom photo)
Isolated by high mountains, Pátzcuaro was
the center of the ancient Tarascan civilization. In the twentieth century, the Tarascan
Indians have fought to preserve their culture, lands, and the fragile lake ecosystem
they all depend on. The Tarascan Indians'
craft traditions and Pátzcuaro's spectacular
scenery attract thousands of international
tourists to the region each year.

(p. 382, realia)
Mariachi figure from Oaxaca. Mariachi
music developed in northern Mexico, primarily in the state of Jalisco. Its popularity
rose sharply through its use in Mexican
cowboy movies in the 1940s and 1950s. A
Mariachi band originally consisted of a harp,
two violins, and a guitar. Over time, the harp
has disappeared, and more violins, two
trumpets, a *vihuela* (a guitarlike instrument),
and a *guitarrón* (Mexican bass guitar) have
been added.

Present

Chapter Theme
Mexican food: Ingredients

Communicative Objectives
- To name and discuss foods
- To talk about food
- To indicate time or frequency

 Overheads 61–62

 Vocabulary Art BLMs/CD-ROM

 Pronunciation Tape 12-1

 Vocabulario para conversar A

Play

Using the Video
Video segment 2: See the Video Teacher's Guide.

 Video Activity B

Grammar Preview
Pedir is presented here lexically. The complete paradigm is in the grammar section on p. 397.

Vocabulario para conversar

¿Con qué se hacen las enchiladas?  Chapter 12 Vocabulary

Aquí tienes palabras y expresiones necesarias para hablar sobre algunas comidas mexicanas y con qué se hacen. Léelas varias veces y practícalas con un(a) compañero(a) en las páginas siguientes.

la tortilla de harina

la carne de res

las salsas

el chile

la tortilla de maíz

el aguacate

los frijoles refritos

las enchiladas

los tacos

el guacamole

el chile con carne

los burritos

las quesadillas

los chiles rellenos

Platos principales

384 Capítulo 12

Options

Strategies for Reaching All Students

Students Needing Extra Help
Vocabulario para conversar: Have students start their Organizers.
También necesitas . . . : Give examples of *¿con qué se hace(n) ___?* and *se hace(n) con ___.*
Model *probar* if necessary.

Learning Spanish Through Action
STAGING VOCABULARY: *Tráiganme*
MATERIALS: index cards with pictures of the food items from the Vocabulary Art BLMs/CD-ROM or cut out of magazines
DIRECTIONS: Distribute the index cards at random. Tell students you are going to pre-

pare a main dish from the vocabulary list: *Voy a preparar quesadillas. Tráiganme el queso y las tortillas.* The students with the corresponding cards should then pass them to you and say *Aquí está(n).* Redistribute the cards and continue until all main dishes have been covered.

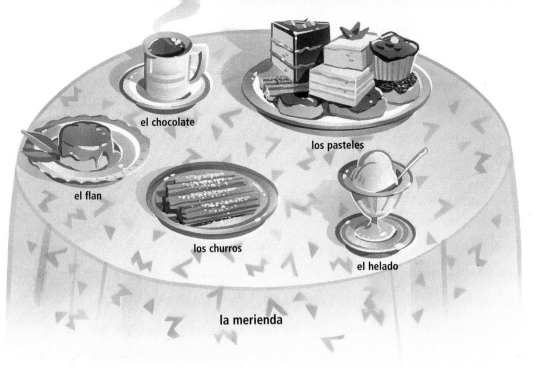

el chocolate

los pasteles

el flan

los churros

el helado

la merienda

También necesitas...

¿Con qué se hace(n) ___?	What is / are ___ made with?	de postre	for dessert
Se hace(n) con ___.	It's (they're) made with . . .	picante	spicy, peppery, hot (flavor)
pedir (e → i)	to ask for; to order	no picante	mild (flavor)
probar (o → ue)	to try; to taste	a menudo	often
¿Has probado ___?	Have you tried ___?	vender	to sell
he probado	I've tried	la comida	food
una vez	once		
alguna vez	ever	**¿Y qué quiere decir . . . ?**	
¿Algo más?	here: Anything else?	de merienda	
el postre*	dessert	muchas veces	
		servir (e → i)	

* It's not typical in Spanish-speaking countries to have ice cream or cake for dessert. When dining at home, the usual dessert is *queso y fruta*. For your late-afternoon *merienda* you might have sandwiches, pastries, rolls, and *té* or *café con leche*, or *chocolate con churros*.

Re-enter / Recycle

Ex. 1: foods from Chap. 4
Ex. 2: *gustar* expressions from Chap. 1
Ex. 3: *gustar* expressions from Chap. 1, *ir a* + inf. from Chap. 3, *querer* + inf. from Chap. 7
Ex. 5: *gustar* expressions from Chap. 1
Ex. 6: expressing likes and preferences from Chap. 4
Ex. 8: foods from Chap. 4

Answers: Empecemos a conversar

1 ESTUDIANTE A
a. ¿Qué vas a pedir de postre?
b. . . . de merienda?
c. . . . para el almuerzo?
d. . . . para la cena?

ESTUDIANTE B
a.–d. Answers will vary, but encourage a wide selection of foods.

2 ESTUDIANTE A
a. ¿Has probado aguacate alguna vez?
b. . . . frijoles refritos. . .
c. . . . churros. . .
d. . . . sopa de tomate. . .
e. Questions will vary.

ESTUDIANTE B
a.–e. Answers will vary, but look for the correct use of *gustar*.

Empecemos a conversar

Túrnate con un(a) compañero(a) para ser *Estudiante A* y *Estudiante B*. Reemplacen las palabras subrayadas con palabras representadas o escritas en los recuadros. ⬤ quiere decir que puedes escoger *(choose)* tu propia respuesta.

1 A —¿Qué vas a pedir <u>de plato principal</u>?
B —Quisiera probar <u>las quesadillas</u>.

plato principal

Estudiante A   **Estudiante B**

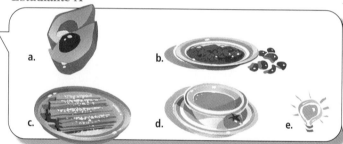

a. de postre   c. para el almuerzo

b. de merienda   d. para la cena

El menú de un restaurante en Panajachel, Guatemala

2 A —¿Has probado <u>chiles rellenos</u> alguna vez?
B —<u>Sí, una vez.</u> (<u>Sí, muchas veces.</u>)
   o: No, nunca. (No me gustan los chiles rellenos.)

Estudiante A   **Estudiante B**

a.   b.   c.   d.   e.

386   Capítulo 12

Options

Strategies for Reaching All Students

3

A —¿Quieres probar _el flan_?

B —_Sí, voy a pedirlo._
  o: _No, no me gusta._

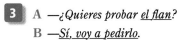

Estudiante A

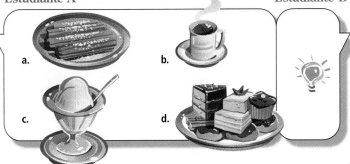

a.

b.

c.

d.

Estudiante B

¡NO OLVIDES!

Remember that you can attach the pronouns _lo, la, los,_ or _las_ to an infinitive.

4

A —¿Con qué se hacen _las enchiladas_?

B —Con _tortillas de maíz y pollo o carne de res._

Estudiante A   Estudiante B

Empecemos a escribir

Escribe tus respuestas en español.

5 ¿Cuáles de las comidas de la página 384 has probado? ¿Cuáles te gustaron? ¿Dónde las probaste?

6 ¿Prefieres la comida picante o no picante? ¿Qué restaurantes de tu comunidad sirven comida picante?

7 ¿Cuál es tu comida mexicana favorita? ¿Con qué se hace? ¿Puedes comprar los ingredientes necesarios en el supermercado donde tú vas de compras?

8 ¿Qué comes de postre más a menudo? ¿Pasteles, helado o frutas? ¿Cuál es tu favorito?

MORE PRACTICE

- Más práctica y tarea, p. 541
- Practice Workbook 12–1, 12–2

También se dice...

las masas

el ají

los porotos

la palta

Vocabulario para conversar   387

---

3 ESTUDIANTE A

a. ¿Quieres probar los churros?

b. ...el chocolate?

c. ...el helado?

d. ...los pasteles?

ESTUDIANTE B

a.–d. Answers will vary, but look for correct use of pronouns.

4 Dialogues will vary.

Answers: Empecemos a escribir

5 Answers will vary, but look for _He probado, Me gustó (gustaron),_ and _lo, la, los, las + probé._

6–8 Answers will vary.

 Practice Wkbk. 12-1, 12-2

 Audio Activity 12.1

 Writing Activities 12-A, 12-B

 Pruebas 12-1, 12-2

Extended Written Practice/Homework

1. Write two pairs of sentences naming foods that are or are not usually spicy. Tell whether or not you like these foods.

2. Write three sentences telling where different foods pictured on pp. 384–385 are sold in your community.

3. Write two sentences telling what you prefer to eat as an afternoon snack and for dessert.

Multiple Intelligences

Intrapersonal/Introspective and Visual/Spatial
See Exs. 5–8.

Verbal/Linguistic
See Exs. 1–4 and Audio Activity 12.1.

Visual/Spatial
See Practice Wkbk. 12-1 and 12-2 and Writing Activities 12-A and 12-B.

Cultural Notes

(p. 386, realia)
Serving full meals as well as _refacciones_ (snacks), this restaurant advertises many of the basic _comidas típicas_ of Guatemala. Most Guatemalan food is quite similar to Mexican food, although it is generally less spicy. _Churrasco,_ charcoal-grilled steak, is a local specialty and is often served with _chirmol,_ a sauce of tomato, onion, and mint. _Aguas frías_ are tropical fruit juices mixed with water.

Present

Chapter Theme
Restaurants: Eating out

Communicative Objectives
- To describe table settings
- To talk about food
- To talk about eating out
- To express needs
- To indicate position

 Overheads 63–64

 Vocabulary Art BLMs/CD-ROM

 Pronunciation Tape 12-2

 Vocabulario para conversar B

Play

Step

Using the Video
Video segment 2: See the Video Teacher's Guide.

 Video Activity B

 Pasos vivos 1 CD-ROM

Clip Art Album

Vocabulario para conversar

¡Me falta una cuchara!

 **At Home VIDEO** Chapter 12 Vocabulary

Aquí tienes el resto del vocabulario necesario para pedir algo, para pedir una comida y para decir lo que comiste o bebiste.

el camarero — la camarera —

el menú

la cuenta

el plato

el vaso

la taza
el platillo — la mantequilla — el tazón

la sal

el tenedor

el cuchillo
el azúcar — la pimienta

la cuchara — la servilleta

el mantel

388 Capítulo 12

Options

Strategies for Reaching All Students

Students Needing Extra Help
Vocabulario para conversar: Bring in some old dishes and silverware, paper / plastic plates, etc. from home. When students have learned the vocabulary, have them set the table, naming each item as they go along. *También necesitas . . . :* Give examples of *me falta, me faltan, me pasas, me trae,* and *lo mismo.* To review *la merienda,* refer to p. 385.

Learning Spanish Through Action
STAGING VOCABULARY: ¿Me trae ___?
MATERIALS: paper goods (paper cups, plates, etc.) for table settings, index cards with pictures of food items from the Vocabulary Art BLMs/CD-ROM or cut out from magazines

DIRECTIONS: Pass out the materials to groups of students. Sit at a table set for dinner. State that an item is missing. Ask a student to bring it to you. Repeat two or three times. Then pretend to get your food. State that you ordered an item and do not have it. Ask if a student will bring it to you. This can be continued until asking for the check.

encima de

detrás de

debajo de

delante de

También necesitas...

Me falta(n)	*I need; I am lacking*	pedir: (yo) pedí	*to order: I ordered*
¿Me pasas ___?	*Will you pass me ___?*	(tú) pediste	*you ordered*
traer	*to bring*	lo mismo	*the same thing*
¿Me trae ___?	*Will you bring me ___?*	en seguida	*right away*
(Le) traigo	*I'm bringing (you)*		
beber: (yo) bebí	*to drink: I drank*	**¿Y qué quiere decir . . . ?**	
(tú) bebiste	*you drank*	a la carta	
comer: (yo) comí	*to eat: I ate*	la especialidad de la casa	
(tú) comiste	*you ate*	el plato del día	

Grammar Preview
Traigo / trae are presented lexically. The complete paradigm is on p. 398. *Bebí / bebiste, comí / comiste,* and *pedí / pediste* are presented lexically. The explanation of the preterite of *-er* and *-ir* verbs is on p. 403.

Teaching Suggestions
Preparing students to speak: Use one or two options from each of the categories of Comprehensible Input, Physical Response, or Limited Verbal Response. For a complete explanation of these categories and some sample activities, see pp. T22–T23.

Note: Only boldface labels are new vocabulary items. The others were introduced in earlier chapters.

Class Starter Review
On the day following initial vocabulary presentation, you might begin the class with this activity: Arrange table settings on a table in the classroom. Have students close their eyes as you hide one or two items. When students open their eyes, ask: *¿Qué te (nos) falta?*
As an alternate activity, have students place the items on a table, telling you where each item goes as they set the table.

www Internet Activities
Juegos

Multiple Intelligences
Bodily/Kinesthetic
See Learning Spanish Through Action and Class Starter Review.
Verbal/Linguistic
See Pronunciation Tape 12-2.
Visual/Spatial
See Overheads 63–64, the Vocabulary Art BLMs/CD-ROM, and Using the Video.

Standards 1.1; 1.2; 1.3; 4.1; 5.1   **389**

Re-enter / Recycle

Ex. 11: direct object pronouns from Chap. 6
Exs. 11–12: foods from Chap. 4
Ex. 13: expressing likes and preferences from Chap. 4

Answers: Empecemos a conversar

9 ESTUDIANTE A

a. Camarero, me falta una taza. ¿Me trae una, por favor?
b. ...un menú. ...uno...
c. ...un tazón. ...uno...
d. ...una servilleta. ...una...
e. ...un tenedor. ...uno...
f. Questions will vary, but look for correct use of *uno(a)*.

ESTUDIANTE B

a. Sí, le traigo una taza en seguida.
b. ...un menú...
c. ...un tazón...
d. ...una servilleta...
e. ...un tenedor...
f. Answers will vary, but look for correct use of indefinite articles.

10 ESTUDIANTE A

a. No veo el vaso. ¿Dónde está?
b. ...la sal. ...está?
c. ...el azúcar. ...está?
d. ...los platos. ...están?
e. ...las servilletas. ...están?
f. ...la cuenta. ...está?

Empecemos a conversar

9 A —*Camarero, me falta un vaso. ¿Me trae uno, por favor?*
B —*Sí, le traigo un vaso en seguida.*

Estudiante A

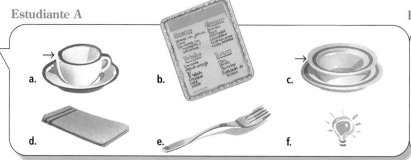

Estudiante B

10 A —*No veo la(s) cuchara(s). ¿Dónde está(n)?*
B —*Está(n) delante de los vasos.*

Estudiante A   Estudiante B

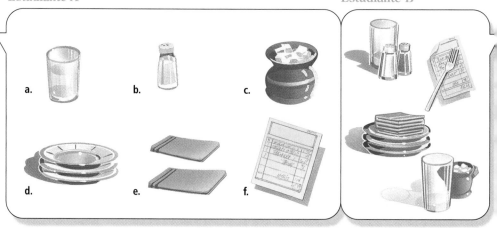

Options

Strategies for Reaching All Students

Spanish-Speaking Students
Ex. 12: Add: *¿Por qué es bueno desayunar todos los días?*

Students Needing Extra Help
Ex. 9: Remind students that *una* refers to feminine nouns.
Ex. 10: Review prepositions of place from Chap. 10.
Write a singular and a plural example separately on the chalkboard. Students might find the parentheses confusing.

Ex. 11: Review direct object pronouns *lo, la, los,* and *las.*
Exs. 12–13: Have students use their Organizers from Chap. 4.
Ex. 14: Allow students ample time to read the entire section before beginning the exercise. You may wish to do the first two items with students.

11 A —¿Me pasas <u>la sal</u>, por favor?

B —Sí, aquí <u>la</u> tienes. ¿Necesitas algo más?

A —Ahora no, gracias.

Estudiante A

Estudiante B

Empecemos a escribir y a leer

Escribe tus respuestas en español.

12 ¿Qué comiste y bebiste en el desayuno esta mañana?

13 ¿Te gustó el plato del día de la cafetería ayer? ¿Qué platos de la cafetería te gustan más? ¿Cuáles no te gustan nada?

14 Un miembro de tu familia está enfermo y tú tienes que servirle estas comidas. ¿Qué utensilios necesitas? Una comida va a sobrar *(will be left over)*.

1. sopa de pollo, un sandwich de queso y té
2. sopa de verduras, arroz con pollo, ensalada de lechuga y, de postre, fruta
3. jugo de tomate, huevos, jamón, pan tostado con mantequilla y leche
4. pescado, zanahorias, guisantes y té helado
5. chile relleno y limonada
6. jugo de naranja y cereal
7. bistec, papas al horno, ensalada de tomate y agua mineral

a. dos vasos, un plato grande y un plato pequeño
b. un tazón, un plato grande y dos platos pequeños
c. un plato grande, un plato pequeño y un vaso
d. un tazón, un plato pequeño y una taza y un platillo
e. un vaso y un tazón
f. un vaso y un plato grande

15 Escoge una de esas comidas y escribe las otras cosas que vas a necesitar para poner la mesa.

MORE PRACTICE

- Más práctica y tarea, p. 541
- Practice Workbook 12–3, 12–4

www.pasoapaso.com

¡NO OLVIDES!

Remember that the pronouns *lo, la, los,* and *las* are placed before the conjugated verb.

También se dice...

el mesero, el mozo

la mesera, la moza

la carta
la minuta
la lista

Vocabulario para conversar 391

Enrichment
Ex. 10: To extend this exercise, have pairs of students find other ways of giving the locations of objects by using location words from Chap. 10: *entre, a la izquierda (de), a la derecha (de), al lado (de).*

Extended Written Practice/Homework
1. Write four sentences telling what you cannot eat because of something you are lacking: *No puedo comer la sopa porque me falta una cuchara.*
2. Write three questions asking a server to bring you something: *Camarero, ¿me trae más pan, por favor?*
3. Write three questions you can ask classmates in order to find out what they ate or drank at different meals.

Multiple Intelligences
Interpersonal/Social
See Exs. 9–11.
Intrapersonal/Introspective
See Exs. 12–15.
Verbal/Linguistic
See Audio Activity 12.2.
Visual/Spatial
See Practice Wkbk. 12-3 and 12-4, Writing Activity 12-C, and Comm. Act. BLM 12-1.

Practice

Re-enter / Recycle
Ex. 1: *ir a* + inf. from Chap. 3, foods from Chap. 4
Ex. 2: foods from Chap. 4, *querer* + inf. from Chap. 7

Reteach / Review:
Vocabulary
Ex. 3: Before doing this exercise, review location words from Chap. 10. Ask the location of students and classroom objects, encouraging as many answers as possible to describe a location.

Answers:
¡Comuniquemos!

1 Dialogues will vary.

2 Questions may vary:
a. ¿Me trae una cuchara, por favor?
b. ¿Con qué se hace el guacamole...
c. ¿Me trae la mantequilla, ...
d. ¿Me trae más agua, ...
e. ¿Me trae otro tenedor, ...
f. ¿Me trae la cuenta, ...
g. ¿Me trae algo para beber, ...

¡COMUNI

1

Usa el menú para pedir una comida completa. Con tu compañero(a) representen *(play the role)* al (a la) camarero(a) y al (a la) cliente.

A —*¿Qué desea, señor?*
   o: *¿Qué va a comer?*
   (*¿Y para beber? ¿Y de postre?*)
B —*Pan tostado con mantequilla y mermelada.*

2

¿Qué dirías *(would you say)* en estas situaciones?

Pediste el bistec pero sólo tienes un tenedor y una cuchara.

¿Me trae un cuchillo, por favor?

a. Pediste sopa pero sólo tienes un tenedor y un cuchillo.
b. Te gustaría pedir guacamole pero no sabes con qué se hace.
c. Hay pan pero no hay nada más en la mesa.
d. Pediste agua pero ya la bebiste.
e. Tu tenedor está sucio.
f. Quieres salir del restaurante pero no sabes cuánto tienes que pagar.
g. Las enchiladas que comes están demasiado picantes. Necesitas beber algo.

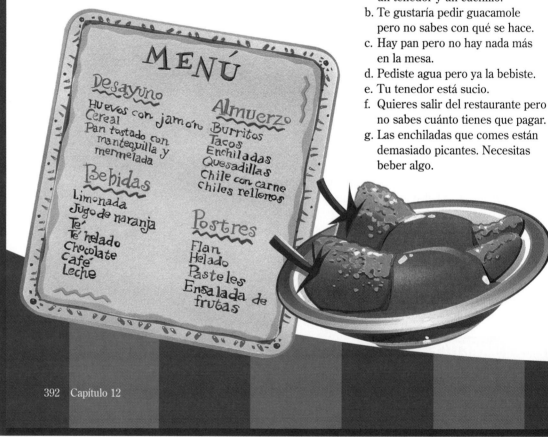

MENÚ

Desayuno
Huevos con jamón
Cereal
Pan tostado con mantequilla y mermelada

Bebidas
Limonada
Jugo de naranja
Té
Té helado
Chocolate
Café
Leche

Almuerzo
Burritos
Tacos
Enchiladas
Quesadillas
Chile con carne
Chiles rellenos

Postres
Flan
Helado
Pasteles
Ensalada de frutas

392   Capítulo 12

Options

Strategies for Reaching All Students

Spanish-Speaking Students

 Un paso más Exs. 12-D, 12-E, 12-F

Students Needing Extra Help
Ex. 1: Tell students if they will be ordering breakfast or lunch.
Remind them that they must address each other as *señor* or *señorita*.
Ex. 2: Have students brainstorm as many ways as possible to answer: *necesito, no tengo, me falta(n), quisiera, ¿me trae?*, etc.

Ex. 3: Review food from Chap. 4 and prepositions of place from Chap. 10.
¿Qué sabes ahora?: Have students write out this section so they can check off what they have mastered.

En este dibujo hay siete errores. ¿Cuántos puedes encontrar? Trabaja en grupos pequeños para encontrarlos. Después, compartan *(share)* con otros grupos los errores que encontraron.

⚭⚭⚭⚭⚭⚭⚭⚭⚭⚭⚭⚭⚭⚭⚭⚭⚭

¿Qué sabes ahora?

Can you:

► describe the ingredients in certain dishes?
—Los burritos se hacen con ___ y con ___.

► make polite requests to have something brought or passed to you?
¿ ___ la salsa, por favor?

► order a meal?
—Voy a comer ___, y de ___ quisiera un helado.

► tell what you ate or drank?
—Ayer yo ___ chile con carne y ___ una limonada.

⚭⚭⚭⚭⚭⚭⚭⚭⚭⚭⚭⚭⚭⚭⚭⚭⚭

Vocabulario para conversar   393

3 *(Answers will vary.)* Las frutas están encima del tazón. La cuchara está debajo del plato. El plato está encima del vaso. La zanahoria está debajo del vaso. El sandwich está en el (encima del) tazón. La ensalada está en (sobre) la mesa. El tomate está en el vaso.

Answers: ¿Qué sabes ahora?

- tortillas de harina / frijoles refritos o carne de res
- Me trae
- *Answers will vary.* / postre
- comí / bebí

 Audio Activity 12.3

 Pasos vivos 1 CD-ROM
Slide Projector, Laboratorio de grabar

Cooperative Learning
Divide the class into groups of three. Prepare copies of the Vocabulary Art BLMs/CD-ROM from the second *Vocabulario para conversar* (p. 388) for each group, with different table items "missing" from each table setting. Have one person in each group be responsible for recording what's missing. Have another person report the findings to the class.

Extended Written Practice/Homework
1. Write two sentences telling what the house specialty is in two restaurants you like.
2. Write two pairs of sentences naming something you recently ordered in a restaurant. Tell whether or not you liked the item.
3. Write three pairs of sentences naming items on a table, desk, and dresser. Tell where the items are in relation to other things: *Hay unos libros encima de mi escritorio. La lámpara está detrás de los libros.*

Multiple Intelligences
Interpersonal/Social
See Cooperative Learning.
Verbal/Linguistic
See Exs. 1–2 and Audio Activity 12.3.
Visual/Spatial
See Ex. 3.

Present & Apply

Cultural Objective

- To compare family dinners in Spanish-speaking countries and in the U.S.

Critical Thinking: Identifying Stereotypes

Clear up any misconceptions students may still have about what is considered Mexican food. (e.g.: *Nachos* and *burritos* are really "Tex-Mex" food.) Stress that cuisine varies tremendously from region to region, as it does in the U.S.

Perspectiva cultural

La cena en un restaurante mexicano

Un plato típico mexicano: camarones rancheros, arroz, frijoles, guacamole y salsa

¿Vas a restaurantes con frecuencia? ¿Te gusta ir con tu familia? ¿Con tus amigos? Generalmente, ¿con quién vas?

What words would you use to describe this restaurant and the people in it? How often do you eat the foods shown on the plate?

The large photo gives you a glimpse of what a family dinner might be like in a restaurant in Mexico. If you lived there, you'd probably be looking forward to seeing your favorite aunt and uncle because a restaurant meal usually implies a Sunday afternoon dinner, which is an important family event. It is generally a long, leisurely meal that can last for two or three hours. It is an occasion for the whole extended family to get together: brothers, sisters, parents, aunts, uncles, and godparents. Unlike in the United States, where children are often left at home with a baby-sitter, in Mexico even infants are an important presence during a family dinner.

A restaurant dinner can also take place very late at night, especially in a bustling metropolis such as Mexico City. It is common to see an entire family arrive at a restaurant at 10 or 11 in the evening. On Friday and Saturday nights, restaurants often stay open until 2 or 3 in the morning. Some restaurants have entertainment, such as a band.

Many late-night restaurants are inexpensive and the food is very good. They attract people from all walks of life. A man in a work shirt might end up having dinner with his family next to a table of people dressed in suits and expensive fur coats who have just come from the theater.

La cultura desde tu perspectiva

1. What are the similarities and differences between dining out in Mexico and in the United States?

2. You have read about a typical Saturday night and Sunday afternoon in a Mexican restaurant. What values do you think these customs reflect?

394   Capítulo 12

Options

Strategies for Reaching All Students

Spanish-Speaking Students
Ask Spanish-speaking students: *¿Te gusta la comida típica mexicana como las tortillas, los chiles y los frijoles? ¿Qué clase de comida se prepara en tu casa? ¿Es como los platos que se describen aquí o es diferente?*

 Un paso más Ex. 12-G

Enrichment
Have students bring in various food items for a class *fiesta*. Ask Spanish-speaking students to bring in a dish that they frequently prepare at home.

Multiple Intelligences
Bodily/Kinesthetic
See Enrichment.

Cenando en la Ciudad de México

Answers

Answers will vary for inductive questions.

Answers: La cultura desde tu perspectiva

1 Answers will vary. Similarities may include live entertainment, while differences include the length and time of the meal and the presence of the entire family.

2 Answers will vary, but students may mention that family values are important.

 Pasos vivos 1 CD-ROM
Notas culturales, Maps

 Internet Activities
Perspectiva cultural

Cultural Notes ☀

(p. 395, left photo)
This dish of *camarones rancheros* (jumbo prawns sautéed in tomato sauce) illustrates the blend of indigenous and Spanish foods that characterizes Mexican cuisine. Shown here is a version of beans, rice, and guacamole.

(p. 395, right photo)
Mexico City's Sanborn's restaurants serve inexpensive Mexican and international food. They are most often located within department stores of the same name. The most famous Sanborn's restaurant is housed in the glass-roofed courtyard of a sixteenth-century mansion known as the *Casa de los azulejos,* so named because of the beautiful tile work on its outer walls.

Teaching Suggestions
Remind students that *-ir* verbs use the present-tense ending *-imos* for *nosotros*. Ask whether the present-tense ending is different from or the same as the preterite-tense ending.

Answers
A *subieron;* this ends in *-ron* like the ending for *-ar* verbs; it uses *e* rather than *a* before the *-ron.*

B *describió:* he described; *vendió:* he sold / Both verbs are third-person singular and end in *-ió.*

C The guide described the plan of the city to us. / *nos*

Gramática en contexto

Look at this page from a student's travel album and read the captions that she wrote.

En Guatemala, fuimos a visitar las ruinas mayas de Tikal.

Nuestro guía nos describió la ciudad antigua. Mis amigos subieron el Templo de las Máscaras. ¡Yo no! Las alturas me dan miedo. Yo les saqué esta foto a mis amigos.

Cuando bajaron, un vendedor nos vendió recuerdos de nuestra visita.

A You know that *-aron* is the ending for the *ellos/Uds.* form of *-ar* verbs in the preterite. In the captions, find an *-ir* verb that has the *ellos/Uds.* ending in the preterite. How is it similar to the ending for *-ar* verbs? How is it different?

B There are two verbs used in the caption that may be new to you: *describió* and *vendió.* Can you guess their meanings? What do these preterite verb forms have in common?

C Find the sentence that begins *Nuestro guía....* To whom did the guide describe the plan of the city? What word gives you this information?

396 Capítulo 12

Options

Strategies for Reaching All Students

Students Needing Extra Help
B: Remind students of cognates.
C: Give more examples of indirect object pronouns in the selection: 1) In the sentence that begins *Yo les saqué . . . ,* whose picture did the girl take? (her friends') What words give you this information? *(les . . . a mis amigos)* 2) In the sentence that begins *Cuando bajaron . . . ,* to whom did the vendor sell souvenirs? (to us) What words give you this information? *(nos . . . nuestra)*

Verbos con el cambio e → i: To review *pensar* and *poder,* refer students to the Chap. 7 Organizer.
Remind them of the "boot" verb construction.
Ex. 1: Remind students of the stem change in *pedir.*

Enrichment
Ex. 1: Personalize the model dialogue by telling students what you actually order. Encourage students to use appropriate expressions of frequency in the *Estudiante B* response.

Verbos con el cambio e → i

You know two types of stem-changing verbs: those like *poder (o → ue)* and those like *pensar (e → ie)*. There is a third type in which the *e* in the stem changes to *i* in some of the present-tense forms. *Pedir* is an example of this type.

(yo)	pido	(nosotros) (nosotras)	pedimos
(tú)	pides	(vosotros) (vosotras)	pedís
Ud. (él) (ella)	pide	Uds. (ellos) (ellas)	piden

- The infinitives of all *e → i* verbs end in *-ir.* Notice that the endings follow the pattern of regular *-ir* verbs.

- Another verb of this type that you know is *servir.*

  En ese restaurante siempre **sirven** arroz con pollo.
  Mi mamá y yo **servimos** jamón y huevos los domingos.

1 Dile a un(a) compañero(a) qué piden de postre o de merienda las siguientes personas en un restaurante.

A —*En un restaurante, ¿qué pide de postre tu profesor?* **tu profesor**

B —*Generalmente pide flan.*

a. tú
b. (nombre de una amiga)
c. tú y tus amigos
d. tu hermano(a)
e. (nombre de dos amigos)
f. tu profesor(a)

¡NO OLVIDES!

Here are the *o → ue* stem-changing verbs that you know:

costar	llover
doler	poder
dormir	probar

These are the *e → ie* stem-changing verbs that you know:

cerrar	pensar
empezar	preferir
nevar	querer

Two of these twelve verbs have only one present-tense and one preterite form. Which ones are they?

En la Zona Rosa, Ciudad de México

Present & Practice

Re-enter / Recycle

Ex. 1: family members from Chap. 5

Answers

1 Dialogues will vary, but should include the correct forms of *pedir.*

ESTUDIANTE A

a. En un restaurante, ¿qué pides de merienda (postre) tú?
b. . . . pide . . . (nombre de una amiga)?
c. . . . piden . . . tú y tus amigos?
d. . . . pide . . . tu hermano(a)?
e. . . . piden . . . (nombre de dos amigos)?
f. . . . pide . . . tu profesor(a)?

ESTUDIANTE B

a. Generalmente pido . . .
b. . . . pide . . .
c. . . . pedimos . . .
d. . . . pide . . .
e. . . . piden . . .
f. . . . pide . . .

¡No olvides!: llover and *nevar*

Cultural Notes ☼

Multiple Intelligences

Bodily/Kinesthetic
Use the cube made of plastic foam to have students practice the present-tense forms of the verb *pedir.*

Interpersonal/Social
See Ex. 1.

Verbal/Linguistic
Have students in pairs practice reading aloud the travel album on p. 396.

Visual/Spatial
See Overhead 65.

(p. 396, photos)
Located in present-day northern Guatemala, the Mayan center of Tikal was one of the most important cities of the ancient Americas. At its height between A.D. 600 and 800, Tikal had a population of more than 10,000 people and boasted ornate palaces, temples, and pyramids. By the tenth century Tikal was abandoned for reasons that remain a mystery. Ask students: Why do you think Tikal was abandoned?

(p. 397, photo)
A café in Mexico City's Zona Rosa, whose streets are lined with art galleries, shops, discotheques, and restaurants. Although many visitors and residents now prefer to do their shopping in malls, la Zona Rosa continues to thrive as a shopping and entertainment center.

Paso cultural
Answers: Geneva, Hamburg, London, Prague, Warsaw.

Present & Practice

After the initial presentation of present-tense *traer,* you might begin the class with this activity: Have students write a sentence listing five things they bring to school every day.

Re-enter / Recycle

Ex. 2: calendar expressions from *El primer paso,* seasons from Chap. 3, family from Chap. 5
Ex. 4: foods from Chap. 4, items brought on vacation from Chap. 7

Answers

2 Answers will vary, but should include the correct forms of *servir.*
a. Mis amigos sirven . . .
b. Mi restaurante favorito sirve . . .
c. Mi mamá (papá) sirve . . .
d. (Yo) sirvo . . .
e. Mis amigos y yo servimos . . .
f. La cafetería de la escuela sirve . . .

3 Answers will vary, but look for correct verb forms and the use of chapter vocabulary.

 Practice Wkbk. 12-5

 Prueba 12-5

---

2 Escribe frases para decir qué comida sirven en diferentes ocasiones.

Mis amigos y yo servimos sandwiches y guacamole en la cena.

a. mis amigos	en el verano
b. mi restaurante favorito	en el invierno
	los domingos
c. mi mamá / mi papá	los fines de semana
d. (yo)	en las fiestas
e. mis amigos y yo	todos los días
f. la cafetería de la escuela	en la cena
	de postre
	el 4 de julio

3 ¿Cuál es tu restaurante favorito? ¿Puedes describirlo? Dile a un grupo pequeño:

• dónde está
• si el restaurante es caro o barato
• la clase de comida que sirven allí
• qué pides generalmente cuando vas allí
• qué piden generalmente las personas que van allí contigo

El verbo *traer*

Here are all of the present-tense forms of *traer* ("to bring").

(yo)	traigo	(nosotros) (nosotras)	traemos
(tú)	traes	(vosotros) (vosotras)	traéis
Ud. (él) (ella)	trae	Uds. (ellos) (ellas)	traen

• Like *poner* and *hacer, traer* has only one irregular present-tense form: *traigo.* All other forms follow the pattern of regular *-er* verbs.

398   Capítulo 12

Options

Strategies for Reaching All Students

Students Needing Extra Help
Ex. 2: Remind students that they are to formulate their answers in the present tense. *El verbo* traer: Do a quick review of *poner* and *hacer* for the *yo* form ending *(-go).* Or present *traer* and then ask students for other words they know that have a similar *yo* form.
Ex. 4: Remind students of how *Uds.* changes to *nosotros* in the answer. Give more examples so that students can see that *creo que* does not change.

Extended Written Practice/Homework
1. Write four sentences telling what you and other people usually order at different restaurants.
2. Write three sentences telling what tasty items are served at different restaurants you know: *En La Mariposa sirven unos chiles rellenos muy sabrosos.*
3. Imagine that your class is going to make a Mexican dinner. Write four sentences telling what you and other people are bringing.

Multiple Intelligences
Verbal/Linguistic and Bodily/Kinesthetic
Have students stand at their desks and show and tell the class five things they bring to school every day.
Visual/Spatial
See Class Starter Review; Practice Wkbk. 12-5, 12-6, and 12-7; and Comm. Act. BLM 12-2.

4 Estás en la playa con un(a) amigo(a). Pregúntale a tu amigo(a) qué trae al picnic cada una de estas personas.

A —¿Qué trae Marta?

B —Creo que trae los platos y los vasos.

Marta

a. Alejandro y Federico **b. Uds.**

 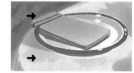

c. Paquita **d. Elena y Joaquín**

e. tú **f. Diego**

5 ¿Qué traen a la escuela estas personas todos los días? ¿Y qué traen sólo una vez o dos veces por semana?

Sara trae su mochila todos los días.

a. los profesores
b. (nombre de) un(a) estudiante trabajador(a)
c. (nombre de) un(a) estudiante deportista
d. tu mejor amigo(a)
e. tú y tus compañeros de la clase de español

Túrnate con un(a) compañero(a) para hablar de lo que traen Uds. a la escuela.

¿Qué traes tú . . . ?
Traigo . . .

En Ponce, Puerto Rico

Gramática en contexto 399

Cultural Notes

(p. 398, realia)
Guava/guayaba and tamarind sodas. These Mexican soft drinks are exported to the U.S. and Central America. Due to the abundance of tropical fruits in Latin America, sodas and juices are available in unusual (to most U.S. inhabitants) flavors to appeal to local tastes.

(p. 399, photo)
Outdoor grilling is popular in many parts of Latin America. Popular grilled items include the numerous variations of beef found in Argentina and Uruguay, *anticuchos* (marinated beef heart) in the Andean countries, and *arrachera* (marinated thin steaks) in Mexico. This Puerto Rican woman is about to savor grilled shish kebab.

El complemento indirecto: Los pronombres

An indirect object tells to whom or for whom an action is performed. You already know the indirect object pronouns *me, te, le, nos,* and *les.* They are used to replace an indirect object noun.

El camarero **nos** sirve enchiladas de queso.	*The waiter serves **us** cheese enchiladas.*
Me trae un refresco.	*He's bringing **me** a soft drink.*
¿**Te** trae el postre ahora?	*Is he bringing **you** dessert now?*

• Because *le* and *les* can have more than one meaning, we can make the meaning clear by adding *a* + pronoun.

Rafael **le** trae el postre **a ella**.	*Rafael is bringing dessert **to her**.*
Les servimos tacos **a ellos**.	*We serve **them** tacos.*

• When we use an indirect object noun, we usually use the indirect object pronoun too.

Le compro naranjas **a mi mamá**.	*I'm buying oranges **for my mom**.*
Les sirvo burritos **a mis amigos**.	*I serve burritos **to my friends**.*

• We can attach an indirect object pronoun to an infinitive or put it before the main verb.

Voy a traer**les** guacamole.	*I'm going to bring **them** guacamole.*
Les voy a traer guacamole.	

¡NO OLVIDES!

Remember that we always use indirect object pronouns with *doler, encantar, faltar, fascinar, gustar,* and *interesar.*

400   Capítulo 12

Options

Strategies for Reaching All Students

Students Needing Extra Help
El complemento indirecto: Los pronombres:
Students may look for the "to" because of the "to whom, for whom" explanation. Show them how in English we drop the "to": We say "bring me" rather than "bring to me." Explain why we can attach the pronoun to the infinitive, but give students the option of using whichever way is more comfortable to them.

Give examples using *duele(n)* and other verbs listed here.
Ex. 6: Have students refer to the first vocabulary section to identify which ingredients are in each dish.
Explain that flan is a baked custard dessert. Have students take note of the change in verb form from question to answer and the change in the pronoun.

Ex. 7: Make a chart of corresponding subject pronouns and object pronouns: *yo (me), tú (te),* and so on.
Show that *pedir* and the object pronoun change; the *servir* verb form does not. Categorize main meal, vegetables, and desserts so that students will use related foods.

 **6** Tu compañero(a) y tú van a preparar las siguientes comidas. Pídele algo que necesitas. Luego continúa la conversación.

A —*Quiero hacer guacamole. ¿Me traes una cebolla?*

B —*Sí, ¿y te traigo tomates también?*

A —*Sí, por favor.*
  o: *No, gracias.*

a.　　　　　b.　　　　　c.

d.　　　　　e.　　　　　f.　　　　　g.

7 El camarero nunca les sirve a Uds. lo que *(what)* piden. Explica la situación con un(a) compañero(a).

Cuando ella pide pollo, el camarero le sirve pescado.

a.　　　　b.

c.　　　　d.

e.　　　　f.

Gramática en contexto   401

Present & Practice

Re-enter / Recycle
Ex. 8: places in a community, clothing from Chap. 6 and Chap. 10, health-care items from Chap. 9

Ex. 9: foods from Chap. 4, family members from Chap. 5

Reteach / Review:
Para + inf.
Ex. 8: Encourage students to use *para + inf.* with the indirect object pronoun attached to tell why they are going to the place named: *Para comprarle un regalo a mi mamá.*

Answers

8 ESTUDIANTE A
a. ¿Por qué vas a la librería?
b. . . . al correo?
c. . . . al supermercado?
d. . . . a la tienda de ropa?
e. . . . al almacén?
f. . . . a la farmacía?
g. Questions will vary.

ESTUDIANTE B
a.–g. Answers will vary, but look for logical responses and the correct use of indirect object pronouns.

9 ESTUDIANTE A
a. ¿Qué vas a servirle a tu mejor amigo(a)?
b. . . . servirles a tus primos?
c. . . . servirle al Presidente de los Estados Unidos?

---

8 Vas a ir de compras. Tu compañero(a) te pregunta por qué vas a estos lugares.

A —*¿Por qué vas a la tienda de regalos?*
B —*Necesito comprarle un regalo a mi mamá.*

Estudiante A   **Estudiante B**

a mis amigos

a mi amigo(a)

a mi mamá / papá

a mis padres

a (nombre de una amiga)

9 Vas a invitar a estas personas a tu casa. Dile a tu compañero(a) qué vas a servirles.

tus abuelos

A —*¿Qué vas a servirles a tus abuelos?*
B —*Voy a servirles arroz con pollo, ensalada, zanahorias y pan.*

a. tu mejor amigo(a)
b. tus primos
c. el Presidente de los Estados Unidos
d. tu profesor(a) de español
e. (nombre de un actor o una actriz)
f. (nombre de un grupo musical)

402   Capítulo 12

Options

Strategies for Reaching All Students

Students Needing Extra Help
Ex. 8: Remind students that *le* can mean a variety of things. Give them a minute to associate stamps with post office, lozenges with pharmacy, and so on.
Ex. 9: Have students use their Organizers from this chapter and Chap. 4.
Before starting Ex. 7, ask students if they can figure out what *mejor amigo(a)* in item *a* means.

El pretérito de los verbos que terminan en -er e -ir: Model an *-ar* verb in the preterite. Then, when the *-er* and *-ir* verb endings are presented, students can see similarities with what they have already learned.
¡No olvides!: Write out *ver* in chart form.

Multiple Intelligences
Verbal/Linguistic
Have students use the correct preterite forms of the verb *comer* by stating what they ate this morning, last night, and yesterday.
Visual/Spatial
See Practice Wkbk. 12-8 and Writing Activities 12-D and 12-E.

10 ¿Qué les sirve tu mamá a estas personas en estas ocasiones? Habla con un(a) compañero(a).

cuando tú y tus amigos tienen mucho frío

A —¿Qué les sirve tu mamá a ti y a tus amigos(as) cuando tienen mucho frío?

B —Nos sirve chocolate.

a. cuando tienes dolor de estómago
b. cuando tú y tus hermanos(as) tienen gripe
c. cuando tú y tus amigos(as) tienen mucho calor
d. cuando tienes fiebre
e. para tu cumpleaños
f.

El pretérito de los verbos que terminan en *-er* e *-ir*

As you know, we use the preterite tense to tell what happened in the past. For *-ar* verbs, we use this pattern of endings: *-é, -aste, -ó, -amos, -asteis, -aron*. The preterite endings for regular *-er* and *-ir* verbs are alike: *-í, -iste, -ió, -imos, -isteis, -ieron*.

Here are all of the preterite forms of *comer* and *salir*:

(yo)	comí salí	(nosotros) (nosotras)	comimos salimos
(tú)	comiste saliste	(vosotros) (vosotras)	comisteis salisteis
Ud. (él) (ella)	comió salió	Uds. (ellos) (ellas)	comieron salieron

Notice the accent marks on the endings *-í* and *-ió*. These must be included as a part of the spelling.

¡NO OLVIDES!

Remember that *ver* does not have accent marks on any of its preterite forms: *vi, viste, vio; vimos, visteis, vieron.*

Un cartel en un restaurante chino en Santiago, Chile

红棉酒家 经营中国名菜 驰誉北京烤鸭
RESTAURANT HONG MIAN
Comida China especial, sabrosa y económica. Platos preparados para llevar

Gramática en contexto   403

---

d. . . . servirle a tu profesor(a) de español?
e.–f. *(Questions will vary.)*
. . . servirle a ___?
ESTUDIANTE B
Answers will vary according to students' choices.
a. Voy a servirle. . .
b. Voy a servirles. . .
c. Voy a servirle. . .
d. Voy a servirle. . .
e. Voy a servirle. . .
f. Voy a servirle(s). . .

10 ESTUDIANTE A
a. ¿Qué te sirve tu mamá a ti cuando tienes dolor de estómago?
b. ¿Qué les sirve tu mamá a ti y a tus hermanos(as) cuando tienen gripe?
c. ¿Qué les sirve tu mamá a ti y a tus amigos(as) cuando tienen mucho calor?
d. ¿Qué te sirve tu mamá a ti cuando tienes fiebre?
e. ¿Qué te sirve tu mamá a ti para tu cumpleaños?
f. Questions will vary.
ESTUDIANTE B
a. Me sirve . . .
b. Nos sirve . . .
c. Nos sirve . . .
d. Me sirve . . .
e. Me sirve . . .
f. Answers will vary.

Practice Wkbk. 12-8

Writing Activities 12-D, 12-E

Prueba 12-7

Cultural Notes

(p. 403, realia)
In the mid-nineteenth century hundreds of thousands of Chinese immigrated to Latin America, working in mines, plantations, and railroads and helping establish trading networks in many outlying areas. Latin Americans of Chinese descent faced widespread discrimination, but they remain an important presence in many parts of Latin America. Ask students: What role did Chinese immigrants play in the U.S.?

Practice

Re-enter / Recycle
Ex. 11: time-telling from Chap. 2
Ex. 12: foods from Chap. 4

Answers

11 ESTUDIANTE A

a. ¿A qué hora comieron Eduardo y Santiago? / ¿Y luego salieron?
b. ... comió Benjamín? / ... salió?
c. ... comieron Uds.? / ... salieron?
d. ... comieron Claudia y Soledad? / ... salieron?
e. ... comió María Eugenia? / ... salió?
f. ... comiste tú? / ... saliste?

ESTUDIANTE B

a. Comieron a las siete y cuarto (quince). / Sí, salieron a las siete y cuarenta y cinco (a las ocho menos cuarto / quince).
b. Comió a las ocho y veinte. / ... salió a las ocho y cincuenta (nueve menos diez).
c. Comimos a las ocho y cuarenta y cinco (nueve menos cuarto / quince). / ... salimos a las nueve y cuarto (quince).
d. Comieron a las seis y cuarenta (siete menos veinte). / ... salieron a las siete y diez.
e. Comió a las siete y media. / ... salió a las ocho.
f. *Answers will vary, but should include:* Comí a la(s) ... *and* Salí a la(s) ....

---

11 Estas personas salieron de sus casas treinta minutos después de comer. Dile a tu compañero(a) a qué hora comieron y a qué hora salieron.

Pablo / 6:30

A —*¿A qué hora comió Pablo?*
B —*Comió a las seis y media.*
A —*¿Y luego salió?*
B —*Sí, salió a las siete.*

a. Eduardo y Santiago / 7:15
b. Benjamín / 8:20
c. Uds. / 8:45
d. Claudia y Soledad / 6:40
e. María Eugenia / 7:30
f. tú / 💡

12 En cuatro hojas de papel escribe cuatro cosas diferentes que comiste o bebiste la semana pasada. Mezcla *(mix)* tus papeles con los de otros(as) tres compañeros(as). Una persona del grupo va a escoger un papel y preguntar quién comió o bebió esas cosas.

A —*¿Quién comió tacos la semana pasada?*
B —*Yo comí tacos.*
C —*Yo también.*

Lleva un registro *(keep a tally)* de las respuestas de tus compañeros(as) para informar a la clase qué comieron y bebieron las personas de tu grupo.

Miguel y yo comimos tacos la semana pasada.
o: *Miguel y Sara comieron tacos la semana pasada.*
o: *Ricardo no comió tacos la semana pasada.*

13 En grupos, hagan una encuesta para averiguar a qué hora los estudiantes de la clase salieron de su casa para ir a la escuela esta mañana. ¿A qué hora salió la mayoría de los estudiantes? ¿A qué hora saliste tú? Después, combinen los resultados en una gráfica en la pizarra.

404 Capítulo 12

Options

Strategies for Reaching All Students

Spanish-Speaking Students
Ex. 12: Have Spanish-speaking students write sentences: *Escribe oraciones que dicen qué comieron y bebieron tus compañeros(as).*

Students Needing Extra Help
Ex. 11: Review time-telling from Chap. 2. Go through the exercise, having students add the half hour to each example beforehand so they can concentrate their efforts on forming the preterite.
Ahora lo sabes: Have students write out this section so they can check off what they have mastered.

Extended Written Practice/Homework
1. Write four sentences telling what you and other people ate or drank yesterday.
2. Write four sentences telling how often different people ate at these places last month: *un restaurante mexicano, un restaurante de comida rápida* (a fast-food restaurant), *la cafetería de la escuela, la casa de un amigo.*
3. Write three sentences telling at what time people left different places *(salir de casa, salir de la escuela, salir de la ciudad,* etc.).

Ahora lo sabes

Can you:

► tell what people order and serve?
—Mis padres siempre ___ pescado cuando van al restaurante.
—La cafetería de mi escuela ___ hamburguesas a menudo.

► tell what someone brings to a place or to another person?
—(Yo) le ___ una cuchara a mi hermana.

► tell what someone does or did for you or for someone else?
—Mis padres no tienen servilletas. Por eso, la camarera ___ trae servilletas.

► tell what someone ate?
—Federico ___ chile con carne anoche.

MORE PRACTICE

Más práctica y tarea, pp. 542–543
Practice Workbook 12–5, 12–10

Con la familia a la hora de la cena en Madrid

Gramática en contexto   405

---

12 Answers will vary, but encourage students to use chapter vocabulary. Look for correct use of *comer* and *beber* in the preterite.

13 Answers and graphs will vary, but look for correct preterite forms of *salir*.

Answers: Ahora lo sabes
• piden / sirve
• traigo
• les
• comió

Using Photos
(p. 405) Ask: ¿Qué hay en la mesa? Describe la foto.

 **Practice Wkbk.
12-9, 12-10**

 **Audio Activities
12.4, 12.5**

 **Writing Activity
12-F**

 Prueba 12-8

 **Pasos vivos 1
CD-ROM**
Fax Task, Slide Presentation Maker, Spindle, Treadmill

Cultural Notes

Multiple Intelligences
Bodily/Kinesthetic
See Ex. 12.
Verbal/Linguistic
See Ex. 11 and Audio Activities 12.4 and 12.5.
Visual/Spatial
See Practice Wkbk. 12-9 and 12-10 and Writing Activity 12-F.

(p. 404, realia)
This ad encourages Mexican consumers to buy products with the CONPAPA seal, which indicates that they contain potatoes grown in Mexico. Have students discuss this kind of ad that encourages consumers to buy from their own country. Ask students: What prompts ads like this? Do you think that this kind of ad works? Have you seen it here in the U.S.? For which products?

(p. 405, photo)
In Spain, the supper hour is much later than in the U.S., usually between 9:00 and 11:00 P.M. Supper is a light meal and a chance for socializing and sharing time with family at the end of the day. Lunch is the main meal, and takes place between 1:00 and 3:00 in the afternoon.

**Pronunciation Tape
12-3**

Todo junto A

Play

Todo junto B

Play

Using the Video
Video segment 3: See the Video
Teacher's Guide.

 Video Activity C

 **Pasos vivos 1
CD-ROM**
Video Monitor, Video
Presentation Maker

**Critical Thinking:
Synthesizing Information**
Have students make columns with
the headings *siempre, nunca,* and
a veces to generate a list of how
often they eat the foods shown in
this chapter's vocabulary. Tally the
lists and post the results.

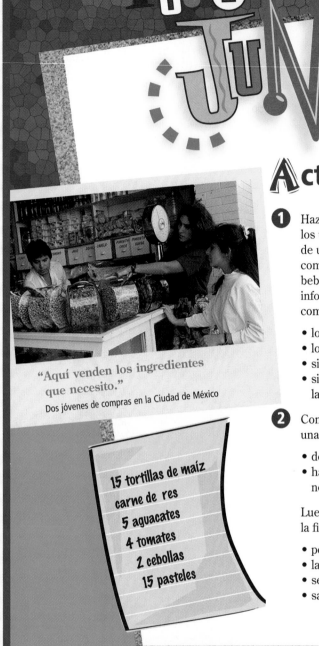

"Aquí venden los ingredientes
que necesito."
Dos jóvenes de compras en la Ciudad de México

15 tortillas de maíz
carne de res
5 aguacates
4 tomates
2 cebollas
15 pasteles

Actividades

1 Haz una lista de lo que comiste y bebiste durante
los últimos tres días. Si comiste o bebiste algo más
de una vez, indica cuántas veces. Con un(a)
compañero(a) habla de lo que Uds. comieron y
bebieron y escríbanlo en una hoja de papel. Luego
informen a la clase o a otro grupo sobre lo que
comieron. Pueden hablar sobre:

• lo que comiste y bebiste y cuántas veces
• lo que tu compañero(a) comió y bebió
• si sus dietas tienen algo en común o no
• si comieron y bebieron cosas buenas o malas para
la salud

2 Con un(a) compañero(a) prepara una comida para
una fiesta de la escuela. Deben:

• decidir qué comida van a preparar
• hacer una lista de los ingredientes que van a
necesitar y cuánto van a necesitar de cada uno

Luego, digan a la clase qué comida piensan traer a
la fiesta. También pueden decidir quiénes van a:

• poner la mesa
• lavar los platos
• ser los camareros y las camareras
• sacar la basura

406   Capítulo 12

Options

Strategies for Reaching All Students

Spanish-Speaking Students
Ex. 2: After completing this exercise, have
Spanish-speaking students write a letter to a
friend who missed the party. *Escríbele una
carta a un(a) amigo(a) que se perdió la fiesta. Dile cómo estuvo la fiesta, quiénes
fueron, qué comieron, etc.*
Have students give a demonstration on how
to make a dish which can be easily prepared
in the classroom.

Students Needing Extra Help
Exs. 1–2: Have students use their
Organizers to help them develop statements.
Remind students to change the verb form
when reporting to the class.

Enrichment
Have students design posters about their
favorite restaurants. The description of a
favorite restaurant can be written as a short
composition and included on the poster.
They can then give a presentation about

their favorite restaurant, using the poster as
an aid. Encourage other students to follow
up each presentation with questions and
comments.
Ex. 2: Additional topics pairs of students
might discuss: 1) how much to expect to
spend on ingredients; 2) how long the dish
will take to make (students may discuss
what time to start preparing the dish and
what can be prepared ahead of time);
3) where to keep the dish at school.

Conexiones

Más helado, por favor

Sin mirar *(without looking at)* la tabla, adivina en qué países del mundo se come más helado. Menciona tres países.

Busca en un mapa del mundo los tres países que escogiste. Localiza *(Locate)* el ecuador. Usa la clave *(key)* del mapa para determinar la distancia aproximada de estos países al ecuador.

Ahora, mira la tabla de abajo. ¿Coinciden los datos con tu predicción? Mira la tabla otra vez. Los países en los que se come más helado tienen algo en común. Sigue los pasos siguientes para descubrir este elemento común.

- Busca en tu mapa los países de la tabla. Averigua la distancia aproximada de cada uno de ellos al ecuador. Organiza la lista de acuerdo a la proximidad de los países al ecuador.

- En los países que están *cerca del ecuador,* hace mucho ___ en el verano y no hace mucho ___ en el invierno. En los países que están *lejos del ecuador,* hace mucho ___ en el invierno.

- ¿Qué tienen en común los países de la tabla?

Source: *The Top Ten of Everything* by Russell Ash (DK Publishing, 1997)

Estados Unidos	47.04 pintas por persona
Nueva Zelanda	37.70
Dinamarca	36.02
Australia	32.64
Bélgica/Luxemburgo	31.50
Suecia	30.09
Canadá	27.02
Noruega	25.65
Irlanda	19.32
Suiza	15.79

Basándote en esta información, ¿en qué región de los Estados Unidos piensas que se come más helado por persona?

Todo junto   407

Answers: Actividades

1 Answers will vary, but look for correct use of *comer* and *beber* in the preterite and encourage a wide range of food choices.

2 Answers will vary, but look for a wide selection of food choices and the correct use of *ir a* + inf.

Answers: Conexiones

- Based on closest point to the equator: *Australia, Estados Unidos, Nueva Zelanda, Canadá, Suiza, Bélgica/Luxemburgo, Irlanda, Dinamarca, Suecia,* and *Noruega.*
- calor/frío/frío
- Most of the countries are industrialized. All the countries are either in Europe or inhabited mostly by people of European descent. None of the countries (except for northern Australia) is tropical or equatorial.

Research indicates that ice cream consumption is highest in the north central states.

Writing Activities 12-G, 12-H

Comm. Act. BLMs 12-3, 12-4, 12-5

Pasos vivos 1 CD-ROM
A Jugar, Boom Box, Laboratorio de grabar, Maps, Spindle

Cooperative Learning
Divide the class into groups of three. Tell students that, as owners of a Mexican restaurant, they are to design a menu. Each person in every group will be responsible for creating one of these categories: *carne, postres,* and *bebidas.* The menus should include food items, prices, name and location of the restaurant, etc. When completed, have the class pass around their menus to see which one represents the most popular restaurant.

Multiple Intelligences
Bodily/Kinesthetic
See Cooperative Learning.
Interpersonal/Social
See Ex. 2.
Intrapersonal/Introspective
See Ex. 1.
Verbal/Linguistic
See Pronunciation Tape 12-3.
Visual/Spatial
See Using the Video, *Conexiones,* Writing Activities 12-G and 12-H, and Comm. Act. BLMs 12-3, 12-4, and 12-5.

Cultural Notes

(p. 406, photo)
Although modern supermarkets are now common in Mexico's large cities, small neighborhood grocery stores such as this continue to attract customers. In these establishments most of the food products are stored behind a counter. Grocers weigh and price customers' purchases individually.

Process Reading

For a description of process reading, see p. 48.

Multicultural Perspectives

Mole, which is a thick sauce commonly served with poultry, was created by the Aztecs well before the arrival of the Spanish. *Mole* comes from the Nahuatl word *molli,* meaning "mixture." The Spanish then adapted the sauce with ingredients from Europe. In addition to various blends of herbs and spices, many *moles* include poultry broth, tomatoes or tomatillos, chiles, pumpkin seeds or sesame seeds, and ground tortillas. In some *moles,* chocolate is a key ingredient. Students familiar with other cultures can share information about other traditional dishes.

Answers

Antes de leer

Answers will vary, but students may say that the menu in a restaurant in Mexico might be more varied and feature more authentic food.

Mira la lectura

Veracruz, Jalisco, and Nuevo León / Most students would say yes, that American cooking also varies from one region to another.

¡Vamos a leer!

www.pasoapaso.com

Antes de leer

STRATEGY ➤ **Using prior knowledge**

How familiar are you with Mexican food? Do you suppose the menu in a restaurant in Mexico might be different from one found in a Mexican restaurant in the United States? How do you think it might be different?

EN LA VARIEDAD ESTÁ EL GUSTO

¿Con qué frecuencia comes en restaurantes mexicanos? ¿Te gustan los burritos o el chile con carne? ¿Crees que estas comidas son auténticas? La comida mexicana en los Estados Unidos es diferente a la que se come en México. Los inmigrantes y los mexico-americanos han creado un nuevo mundo de la cocina mexicana. Los burritos y el chile con carne son populares en las ciudades norteamericanas, pero en México son casi desconocidos.

La comida de México es más variada y sustancial. Tiene sus orígenes en las diferentes culturas precolombinas y en España. El chile, el maíz y el tomate son de origen americano, pero la pimienta, la cebolla y el trigo fueron traídos por los españoles. La comida mexicana de hoy usa todos estos ingredientes.

En cada región de México se pueden encontrar diferentes tipos de comidas o platillos. Imagina que haces un viaje por tres estados de México y que en cada estado comes algo distinto. Mira los menús a la derecha.

Mira la lectura

STRATEGY ➤ **Scanning**

This article compares Mexican food found in Mexico with that found in the United States. It also points out the variety of dishes in three different states in Mexico. What states do the menus come from? Does American cooking vary from one region to another?

PLATILLOS DE VERACRU
EN EL SURESTE DE MÉXI

ensalada tropical
pescado a la veracruza
arroz verde
dulce de guayaba
café

Options

Strategies for Reaching All Students

Students Needing Extra Help

Mira la lectura: Students may not be aware that there are states in Mexico. Show them a map that has all the states clearly labeled. *Infórmate:* In No. 1, tell students that certain beverages can also be food ingredients; as in this case, *leche.* In No. 3, have students list the similarities and differences.

Infórmate

STRATEGY **Using illustrations to guess the meaning of unknown words**

1 Were you able to figure out some of the items in each menu by looking at the pictures? What drinks are offered with each meal?

2 Are there any ingredients you did not expect to find in a Mexican dish? What are they?

3 After reading these menus, explain how the food served in Mexico compares with that served in the United States.

PLATILLOS DE JALISCO, EN EL CENTRO DEL PAÍS

ensalada de nopales
carne asada
arroz con leche
agua de horchata

Aplicación

A Mexican exchange student in your class wants to eat at a Mexican restaurant this weekend. What would you tell him about the Mexican food found in the United States? What do you think will surprise him the most?

PLATILLOS DE NUEVO LEÓN, AL NORTE DE MÉXICO

guacamole con enchiladas
huevos con carne de res
dulce de leche
té helado

¿Te gustaría probar alguna de estas tres variedades de comida? ¿Cuál te parece más interesante? ¡Las tres son deliciosas!

Infórmate

1 Answers will vary. / coffee (Veracruz), a type of rice drink (Jalisco), iced tea (Nuevo León)

2 Answers will vary, but students may say eggs with beef.

3 Answers will vary, but students may say that some foods, such as guacamole and enchiladas, are also served in the U.S.

Aplicación

Answers will vary, but students may say that the Mexican food found in the U.S. will probably be different from that found in Mexico. The exchange student would probably be surprised to find that *chile con carne* is not what the name implies, or that food he or she has never heard of is considered Mexican food in the U.S.

www Internet Activities

Apply

Process Writing
For information regarding developing a writing portfolio, see p. 50.

**Pasos vivos 1
CD-ROM**
Word Processor

¡Vamos a escribir!

Everyone enjoys going out to eat, but it's not alw easy to decide where to go. Write a review of a restaurant that you would recommend to your classmates.

1 Think about a restaurant you go to. It can be a fast-fo restaurant, a coffee shop, or even the school cafeteri

- ¿Cómo se llama el restaurante?
- ¿Dónde está?
- ¿A qué hora abre y a qué hora cierra?
- ¿Qué clase de comida sirve?
- ¿Cuáles son sus platos especiales?
- ¿Qué plato te gusta más? ¿Por qué?
- ¿Es caro o barato? ¿Aceptan tarjetas de crédito?
- ¿Es accesible para personas incapacitadas?

2 Use the answers to the questions to write a review of restaurant. Show your review to a partner. Does he o she think you should change anything? Is there som other information your partner would suggest adding

3 Rewrite your review, taking into consideration the changes suggested by your partner and any others y might like to make. Check for spelling, accents, verb forms, and adjective agreement. If necessary, write y review again.

4 Now your review is ready to be published. You can:
- submit it to the school paper or Spanish club
- include it in a pamphlet about local restaurant called *Buenos restaurantes*
- add it to your writing portfolio

Buenos Restaurantes

En la Fonda Refugio se cocina la mejor comida mexicana de la ciudad. Allí puede probar la especialidad de la casa: chiles con queso. Son sabrosos, nutritivos y no son muy picantes. Además, en la Fonda Refugio hay una variedad de enchiladas, tacos, quesadillas y burritos.

El restaurante está en la calle Independencia, 4. Abren de 11:00 de la mañana a 11:00 de la noche. ¡Debe visitarlo!

"Y para la merienda, ¿te gust pedir unos pasteles?"

Café al aire libre en la Ciudad de México ►

410   Capítulo 12

Options

Strategies for Reaching All Students

Students Needing Extra Help
Show the class a typical review from a newspaper or magazine.
Have students use their Organizers.

FONDA 'Los...

Bigotes de Villa'

Cultural Notes

(p. 411, photo)
This outdoor café is located in Coyoacán, a district of Mexico City, where some of the city's most beautiful colonial mansions are located. Many of them house art and antique dealers, galleries, and museums.

Assess & Summarize

Test Preparation

You may want to assign parts of this section as written homework or as an in-class writing activity prior to administering the *Examen de habilidades*.

Answers

Listening: *Después de comer un chile relleno y dos enchiladas con salsa picante, voy a pedir un flan. ¡Nunca lo he probado!* The speaker is planning to eat a main meal with dessert.

Reading: This dish is prepared by grilling skirt steak over a charcoal grill. *Asar* means to grill. The dish is called *carne al carbón* because of the way it's cooked over coals.

Writing: Letters will vary.

Speaking: Dialogues will vary.

Culture: Answers will vary. Similarities may include conversation and live entertainment. Differences may include the length and time of the meal and the participation of the entire family.

This section will help you organize your studying for the proficiency test, where you will be asked to do similar, though not identical, tasks. There will not be any models on the test.

► Listening

Can you understand when someone talks about a meal? Listen as your teacher reads a sample similar to what you will hear on the test. Is the person planning to eat a snack, a main meal, or a dessert?

► Reading

Using the illustration on this recipe, can you figure out how to prepare this dish? What do you think *asar* means? Why is the dish called *carne al carbón*?

Carne al carbón

Ingredientes:

**carne de res
1 limón verde
sal y pimienta**

Diez minutos antes de servirla, pon el jugo de limón verde, la sal y la pimienta sobre la carne. Debes asar la carne tres minutos por cada lado.

► Writing

Can you write a letter to a friend describing a meal you ate recently? Here is a sample letter:

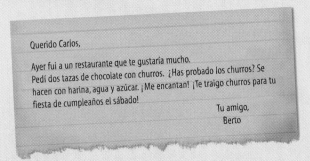

Querido Carlos,

Ayer fui a un restaurante que te gustaría mucho. Pedí dos tazas de chocolate con churros. ¿Has probado los churros? Se hacen con harina, agua y azúcar. ¡Me encantan! ¡Te traigo churros para tu fiesta de cumpleaños el sábado!

Tu amigo,
Berto

► Speaking

Can you and a partner play the roles of a waiter and a customer?

A —*Aquí le traigo el menú.*

B —*Gracias. ¿Cuál es el plato del día?*

A —*Enchiladas de pollo, pero no son muy picantes.*

B —*¡Genial! Pero, camarero, me faltan una servilleta y un tenedor.*

A —*¿De veras? ¡Los traigo en seguida!*

► Culture

Can you name two similarities and two differences between dining out in Mexico and in the United States.

Self Test www.pasoapaso.com

"El domingo voy al restaurante con mi familia."

412   Capítulo 12

Options

Strategies for Reaching All Students

Students Needing Extra Help

Have students write out this section so they can check off what they have mastered. Reading: Remind students to use picture and word clues to help them read the recipe.

Resumen del vocabulario

Use the vocabulary from this chapter to help you:

➤ ask politely to have something brought to you

➤ order a meal

➤ say what you ate or drank

to name and discuss foods
el aguacate
el azúcar
los burritos
la carne de res
el chile
el chile con carne
los chiles rellenos
el chocolate
los churros
las enchiladas
el flan
los frijoles refritos
el guacamole
el helado
la mantequilla
los pasteles
la pimienta
las quesadillas
la sal
las salsas
los tacos
la tortilla de harina / de maíz

to talk about food
a la carta
la especialidad de la casa
la merienda
de merienda
(no) picante
el plato del día
los platos principales

el postre
de postre
beber: (yo) bebí
(tú) bebiste
comer: (yo) comí
(tú) comiste
¿Con qué se hace(n) ___?
Se hace(n) con ___.
pedir (e → i)
probar (o → ue):
(yo) he probado
(tú) has probado
servir (e → i)
vender

to describe table settings
la cuchara
el cuchillo
el mantel
el platillo
el plato
la servilleta
la taza
el tazón
el tenedor
el vaso

to talk about eating out
el camarero, la camarera
la cuenta
el menú

to express needs
Me falta(n) ___.
¿Me pasas ___?
¿Me trae ___?
Le traigo ___.
traer: (yo) traigo
(tú) traes

to indicate time or frequency
alguna vez
a menudo
en seguida
muchas veces
una vez

to indicate position
debajo de
delante de
encima de

other useful expressions
¿Algo más?
lo mismo

Resumen 413

CAPÍTULO 13

THEME: THE ENVIRONMENT

SCOPE AND SEQUENCE Pages 414–445

COMMUNICATION

Topics

Environmental conservation

Environmental dangers

Endangered species

Objectives

To discuss endangered species in the U.S. and the Spanish-speaking world

To talk about conservation

To name items that can be recycled

To talk about animals

To talk about nature and the environment

To describe environmental dangers

To talk about transportation

To talk about everyday activities

To give an opinion

CULTURE

Endangered species in the Spanish-speaking world

GRAMMAR

El verbo decir

El mandato afirmativo (tú)

El verbo saber

Ancillaries available for use with Chapter 13

Multisensory/Technology

 Overheads, 66–70

 Audio Tapes and CDs

 Vocabulary Art Blackline Masters for Hands-On Learning, pp. 68–72/CD-ROM

 Classroom Crossword

Video

Pasos vivos 1 CD-ROM

 Internet Activities www.pasoapaso.com

Print

 Practice Workbook, pp. 136–146

 Writing, Audio & Video Activities, pp. 77–82, 129–131, 176–177

 Communicative Activity Blackline Masters

   Pair and Small Group Activities, pp. 92–97

   Situation Cards, p. 98

 Un paso más: Actividades para ampliar tu español, pp. 74–79

TPR Storytelling

Assessment

 Assessment Program

   Pruebas, pp. 191–200

   Examen de habilidades, pp. 201–204

 Test Generator

Video still from Chap. 13

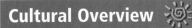

Planning Express, Teaching
Resources Library, and Clip Art
Library

¿Lo sabes bien?
Video Quiz

Cultural Overview

Environmental Problems and Solutions

Population growth coupled with efficient transportation have contributed to an extraordinary migration in the latter half of the twentieth century. In Latin America, as in much of the world, urban locales have become the destination for millions of people. Mexico City's metropolitan-area population grew from 2.9 million in 1950 to 16.4 million in 1995. In Peru, the Lima-Callao area has grown from 1 million in 1950 to 6.1 million in 1995.

Such rapid growth inevitably places a strain on the availability of resources and the quality of the environment. Mexico City, for example, lacks an adequate supply of drinking water. To fill its needs, the metropolis draws water from surrounding areas which, in turn, experience water shortages. Many areas of Mexico City lack a developed infrastructure of services and utilities. The Netzahualcóyotl landfill, for example, presents a problem because it is growing too rapidly. Although entrepreneurs collect and sell recyclable items from the landfill, they cannot keep up with the steadily increasing volume of material.

The destruction of Latin America's rain forests has captured the attention of many people in the U.S. In Central American countries and in the Amazon Basin of South America, rain forests have been destroyed for grazing land, farms, and roads. They have also been cut down for the tropical hardwoods that are sold at high prices in the world market. In addition, forested lands are sometimes destroyed as the by-product of other projects, such as hydroelectric dams, which can flood hundreds of thousands of forested acres. Often the trees are not cut down before flooding, and as the vegetation decomposes in the water, it emits a toxic hydrogen sulfide gas.

Environmentalists are searching for solutions to these problems. Mexico City has devised a system of "non-driving" days *(días de "no circula")* for motorists. License plates are color-coded to indicate one day a week on which that car may not be driven within the city, and anyone who breaks the law is issued a stiff fine. This system has helped somewhat to reduce traffic congestion and air pollution.

Introduce

Planning

Cross-Curricular Connections

Math Connection *(p. 413B)*
Provide students with census data on the size of major cities in Latin America in 1950 and today (see p. 4). Have them compute the percentage of growth which has taken place in the intervening decades, and compare the rate of growth for these cities.

Science Connection *(pp. 434–435)*
Have pairs of students write and present a recycling plan, using commands, that the school can use on a class-by-class basis. Tell students to illustrate their ideas with drawings or pictures.

**Communications Connection
*(pp. 438–439)***
Have pairs of students create and perform a public service ad in which they assume the roles of endangered plants or animals. They may enhance their presentations with posters or by wearing costumes. Some students might like to videotape their ad.

CAPÍTULO 13

Para proteger la Tierra

Objectives

At the end of this chapter, you will be able to:

► describe the natural environment

► list actions to protect the environment

► discuss environmental dangers

► name species in danger of extinction in the United States and the Spanish-speaking world and say what can be done to protect them

PASO CULTURAL In the early 1900s, the area of *las cataratas de Iguazú* was made an Argentinian national park. Three countries—Brazil, Argentina, and Paraguay—meet at these spectacular falls, which are four times the width of Niagara Falls and 50 percent higher. Hundreds of species of insects, birds, and mammals are found in the area—pumas, jaguars, toucans, and at least 500 species of butterflies. As many as 15,000 tourists a day visit the falls, a worrisome number for environmentalist groups, who continue to lobby against nearby hotel construction projects. What natural phenomena are in the part of the country where you live? What efforts are being made to preserve or restore them?

Las cataratas de Iguazú, Argentina

415

Spanish in Your Community
Help students contact local utilities or waste disposal companies to obtain energy conservation or recycling information in Spanish. Ask them to share the brochures and other information with the class.

Paso cultural
Answers will vary.

Preview

Cultural Objective
• To discuss conservation efforts in Spanish-speaking countries and in the U.S.

¡Piénsalo bien!

Play

 Video Activity A

Using the Video
This chapter's video focuses on the environment. Host Karina Romera visits a recycling center to see how Guadalajarans are working to clean up the environment. She also visits the Guadalajara Zoo, where she learns about endangered species.

To prepare students for the video, first ask them to predict what this chapter's tape will be about. Then have students watch the segment several times. After the first viewing, have them brainstorm possible vocabulary words and phrases they will need to discuss environmental issues in Spanish. After subsequent viewings, ask students to identify: a) ways in which residents of Guadalajara help keep the environment clean and safe, and

¡Piensa en la CULTURA!

"Es importante reciclar para proteger la Tierra."
Jóvenes en un centro de reciclaje en Puerto Rico

Environmental protection in Puerto Rico, Chile, Costa Rica, and Equatorial Guinea

Look at this photograph. What do you see that is similar to the environmental efforts in your community?

San Juan, Puerto Rico

What do you think the words *reciclar* and *proteger* mean?
What does *centro de reciclaje* mean?

416   Capítulo 13

Options

Strategies for Reaching All Students

Spanish-Speaking Students
Ask: *¿Por qué es importante reciclar? ¿Qué reciclan tú y tus amigos(as)? ¿Qué podemos hacer para proteger la Tierra? ¿Qué haces tú?*

 Un paso más Ex. 13-A

Students Needing Extra Help
Check with the science department of your school for pictures and information about endangered species.

Multiple Intelligences
Naturalist
Have a group of students make a video of the outdoor environment around their school. Have them prepare a simple narration in Spanish to use when the video is shown to the class.
Visual/Spatial
See Using the Video.

En América Central el jaguar está en peligro de extinción.

América Central

PASO CULTURAL

These conservation stamps were issued by Equatorial Guinea, a West African nation about the size of the state of Maryland, densely covered with tropical rain forests. The country was once ruled by Spain, and Spanish continues to be its official language alongside a dozen or more African languages. This series of stamps features birds from Asia and parts of Africa. Why do you think these images were used on these stamps? What three things would you choose to show on a series of stamps commemorating the environment?

What other animals do you know of that are endangered?

Cultural Exploration
www.pasoapaso.com
Visit these countries on-line

Guinea Ecuatorial

¡Piensa en la cultura! 417

b) ways in which they can work to protect the environment where they live.

Video segment 1: For more teaching suggestions, see the Video Teacher's Guide.

Multicultural Perspectives

The *quetzal,* the national bird of Guatemala, is an exotic animal in danger of extinction. The male has green feathers, a red breast, and white tail feathers as long as 60 centimeters (24 in.). Legend tells how the *quetzal* was the spiritual protector of the Maya. When Pedro de Alvarado, the Spanish *conquistador,* defeated Tecún Umán, the Mayan chief, the *quetzal* fell on the chest of Umán. The bird watched over the body, and when it flew away, its breast was covered with blood. This is why the *quetzal* has a blood-red breast. Ask students to share any animal legends or myths from other cultures that they might know.

Answers: ¡Piensa en la cultura!

(p. 416, photo) Answers will vary, but students may mention recycling efforts. / *Reciclar:* to recycle; *proteger:* to protect; *centro de reciclaje:* recycling center

(p. 417) Answers will vary, but may include the California condor, American crocodile, red wolf, black-footed ferret, and panda.

Cultural Notes

(p. 416, photo)
The work of these teenagers at a recycling center in San Juan reflects an island-wide concern with environmental problems directly linked to Puerto Rico's growing population, estimated in 1991 at 3,551,000, and expected to reach 1,200 people per square mile in the near future.

(p. 417, top photo)
The jaguar, native to tropical forests in the Americas, is now one of many animals that have become endangered through hunting or destruction of their habitat. In Guatemala, destruction of the forests—the jaguar's home—has proceeded at a devastating rate: great areas of the country's original forest cover have been destroyed over the last three to four decades.

Paso cultural
Answers will vary, but may include: to celebrate the region's natural resources; to encourage conservation./Answers will vary.

Present

Chapter Theme
Environmental conservation

Communicative Objectives
- To talk about conservation
- To name items that can be recycled
- To talk about transportation
- To give an opinion
- To talk about everyday activities

 Overheads 66–67

 Vocabulary Art BLMs/CD-ROM

 Pronunciation Tape 13-1

 Vocabulario para conversar A

Play

Using the Video
Video segment 2: See the Video Teacher's Guide.

 Video Activity B

Grammar Preview
Saber is presented here lexically. The complete present-tense paradigm is on p. 436.

Vocabulario para conversar

¿Cómo podemos conservar energía?

Aquí tienes palabras y expresiones necesarias para discutir peligros del medio ambiente y para hablar sobre qué podemos hacer para protegerlo. Léelas varias veces y practícalas con un(a) compañero(a) en las páginas siguientes.

At Home VIDEO Chapter 13 Vocabulary

la luz, *pl.* las luces

la botella

la madera

el plástico

la piel

el cartón

el vidrio

la lata* el aluminio

418 Capítulo 13

Options

Strategies for Reaching All Students

Spanish-Speaking Students

 Un paso más Exs. 13-B, 13-C, 13-D

Students Needing Extra Help
Remind students that they saw *de* + material (*de madera* and *de metal*) in Chap. 8. Likewise, they can also say *de aluminio, de plástico,* and *de vidrio* to describe something: *una lata de aluminio, un vaso de plástico, una botella de vidrio.*
También necesitas . . . : Give examples of *hay que* and *no hay que.* Explain *vale la pena* and *no vale la pena.*

Learning Spanish Through Action
STAGING VOCABULARY: *Pon*
MATERIALS: Vocabulary Art BLMs/CD-ROM or magazine cutouts, index cards
DIRECTIONS: Mount photocopies of the following pictures on index cards: *hoja de papel* (El primer paso), *vaso* (Chap. 12), and recyclable items from this chapter. On sepa-

montar en bicicleta

la bicicleta

la revista

el periódico

la guía telefónica

Teaching Suggestions
Preparing students to speak: Use one or two options from each of the categories of Comprehensible Input, Physical Response, or Limited Verbal Response. For a complete explanation of these categories and some sample activities, see pp. T22–T23.

Class Starter Review
On the day following initial vocabulary presentation, you might begin the class by asking students to list four or five recyclable products.

www Internet Activities
Juegos

También necesitas...

apagar	*to turn off*	(No) vale la pena.	*It's (not) worth it.*
proteger*	*to protect*	a la vez	*at the same time*
recoger*	*to pick up*		
la gente	*people*	**¿Y qué quiere decir . . . ?**	
saber: (yo) sé	*to know: I know*	conservar	reducir†
(tú) sabes	*you know*	la energía	separar
(No) hay que ___ .	*It's (not) necessary to___.*	reciclar	usar

* Note that to talk about a tin can, a glass bottle, a cardboard folder, a metal table, etc., we use noun + *de* + material.
  For example: *lata de aluminio, botella de vidrio.*
* *Proteger* and *recoger* are regular *-er* verbs with a spelling change in the *yo* form of the present tense: *protejo, recojo.*
† *Reducir* is a regular *-ir* verb in the present tense, except for the *yo* form: *reduzco.*

rate index cards, mount pictures of glass, paper, plastic, and aluminum, and post them in a row on the chalkboard. (Use real items, if possible.) Distribute the first set of index cards. Ask: *¿Quién tiene el vaso? Ponlo en la categoría correcta, por favor.* Continue in this manner until all items have been sorted under the proper category.

Extended Written Practice/Homework
1. Refer to the materials on p. 418 and write four sentences naming things you have or use in your home and community that are made out of these materials: *Tenemos muchas botellas de vidrio en el garaje.*
2. Write three sentences telling what you usually recycle in your home, school, and community.
3. Write three sentences about things to do to help the environment: *Hay que …*

Multiple Intelligences
Bodily/Kinesthetic
See Learning Spanish Through Action.
Verbal/Linguistic
See Pronunciation Tape 13-1 and Class Starter Review.
Visual/Spatial
See Overheads 66–67, the Vocabulary Art BLMs/CD-ROM, and Using the Video.

Practice & Apply

Re-enter / Recycle

Ex. 2: household chores from Chap. 8

Ex. 3: direct object pronouns from Chap. 6, *tener que* + inf. from Chap. 8

Answers: Empecemos a conversar

1 ESTUDIANTE A

a. ¿Vale la pena reciclar el plástico?

b. ...el vidrio?

c. ...el cartón?

d. ...el periódico (el papel)?

e. ...la madera?

ESTUDIANTE B

a.–e. Answers will vary.

2 ESTUDIANTE A

a. ¿Cómo puedo reducir la basura?

b. ...conservar agua?

c. ...proteger mi comunidad?

d. Questions will vary.

ESTUDIANTE B

a.–d. Answers will vary, but look for a logical response that follows this format: *Puedes* + inf. phrase.

3 ESTUDIANTE A

a. ¿Sabes si tenemos que reciclar las latas?

b. ...las guías telefónicas?

c. ...el periódico (el papel)?

d. ...las revistas?

e. ...las botellas?

f. Questions will vary.

Empecemos a conversar

Túrnate con un(a) compañero(a) para ser *Estudiante A* y *Estudiante B*. Reemplacen las palabras subrayadas con palabras representadas o escritas en los recuadros.
 quiere decir que puedes escoger *(choose)* tu propia respuesta.

¡NO OLVIDES!

In *El primer paso* you learned *hoja de papel* for "a sheet of paper." *Papel* is the term for "paper" in general.

1 A —¿Vale la pena reciclar <u>el aluminio</u>?

   B —¡Claro que sí (o: no)!

Estudiante A   Estudiante B

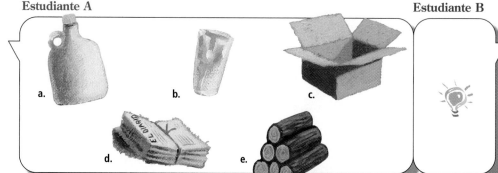

2 A —¿Cómo puedo <u>conservar energía</u>?   conservar energía

   B —Puedes <u>usar menos luz</u>.

Estudiante A

a. reducir la basura

b. conservar agua

c. proteger mi comunidad

d.

Estudiante B

reciclar latas y botellas

montar más en bicicleta

usar menos agua en el baño

lavar mucha ropa a la vez

lavar muchos platos a la vez

usar menos el coche

apagar las luces

420   Capítulo 13

Options

Strategies for Reaching All Students

Spanish-Speaking Students

Ex. 7: Add: *¿Cómo podemos tener comida y productos como el cuero que necesitamos y, a la vez, proteger a los animales de la Tierra?*

 Un paso más Exs. 13-E, 13-F, 13-G

Students Needing Extra Help

Ex. 2: Remind students of the spelling change from *luz* to *luces*.

Ex. 3: Point out how the object pronoun moves in *Estudiante B*'s answer. Refer to the grammar section in Chap. 12. Remind students that the object pronoun may be *lo, la, los,* or *las*.

Ex. 6: Ask the same question with regard to your school.

Enrichment

As a homework assignment, have students make lists with the following headings: *Cosas que puedo apagar, Cosas que puedo conservar,* and *Cosas que puedo reciclar*.

3

A —¿*Sabes si tenemos que reciclar*
las botellas de plástico?

B —*Sí, las tenemos que reciclar.*
o: No. No hay que reciclarlas.

Estudiante A

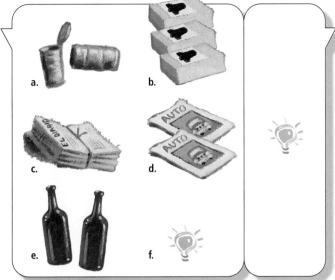

a.

b.

c.

d.

e.

f.

Empecemos a escribir

Escribe tus respuestas en español.

4 ¿Qué puedes hacer con libros que ya no usas? ¿Con ropa que ya no te queda bien?

5 ¿Cómo vas a la escuela? ¿En bicicleta? ¿En autobús? ¿A pie? ¿Por qué?

6 En tu comunidad, ¿qué pueden reciclar que no reciclan ahora?

7 ¿Piensas que la gente debe comprar abrigos u otra ropa de piel o no? ¿Por qué?

MORE PRACTICE

- Más práctica y tarea, p. 543
- Practice Workbook 13–1, 13–2

Estudiante B

¡NO OLVIDES!

When we use direct object pronouns with infinitives, we can either attach them to the end of the infinitive or put them before the main verb. When we use *hay que* they must be attached to the infinitive.

También se dice...

andar en bicicleta

el directorio
la guía de teléfonos
el listín

Vocabulario para conversar   421

ESTUDIANTE B

a. Sí, las tenemos que reciclar.
(No. No hay que reciclarlas.)
b. Sí, las ... (... reciclarlas.)
c. Sí, lo ... (... reciclarlo.)
d. Sí, las ... (... reciclarlas.)
e. Sí, las ... (... reciclarlas.)
f. Answers will vary.

Answers: Empecemos a escribir

4 Answers will vary, but will probably include the verb *reciclar*: *Puedo reciclarlos(la).*

5 Answers will vary, but should follow this pattern: *Voy a la escuela en* + mode of transportation, or *a pie.*

6 Answers will vary, but should follow this construction: *Podemos reciclar ... porque ....*

7 Answers will vary. Help students with additional vocabulary as necessary.

 Practice Wkbk. 13-1, 13-2

 Audio Activity 13.1

 Writing Activity 13-A

 Pruebas 13-1, 13-2

Comm. Act. BLM 13-1

Multiple Intelligences
Intrapersonal/Introspective
See Exs. 4–7 and Enrichment.
Naturalist
Have students work in pairs to draw a "perfect environment." Compare final products and present to the class.

Verbal/Linguistic
See Exs. 1–3 and Audio Activity 13.1.
Visual/Spatial
See Practice Wkbk. 13-1 and 13-2, Writing Activity 13-A, and Comm. Act. BLM 13-1.

Present

Chapter Theme
The natural environment

Communicative Objectives
- To talk about animals
- To talk about nature and the environment
- To talk about transportation
- To describe environmental dangers
- To talk about everyday activities

 Overheads 68–69

 Vocabulary Art BLMs/CD-ROM

 Pronunciation Tape 13-2

 Vocabulario para conversar B

Play

Step

Using the Video
Video segment 2: See the Video Teacher's Guide.

 Video Activity B

Vocabulario para conversar

¿La Tierra forma parte del medio ambiente?

At Home **VIDEO** Chapter 13 Vocabulary

Aquí tienes el resto del vocabulario necesario para hablar sobre el medio ambiente y sus peligros.

Los animales

el caballo

el jaguar

la vaca

el oso

el lobo

el gorila

la ballena

el océano

el elefante

la serpiente

el tigre

422 Capítulo 13

Options

Strategies for Reaching All Students

Students Needing Extra Help
También necesitas . . . : Some students may need to see the complete paradigm of *decir,* found on p. 433.

Learning Spanish Through Action
STAGING VOCABULARY: *Nombren, Señalen*
MATERIALS: transparency of the *Vocabulario para conversar*
DIRECTIONS: Project the transparency and direct students to point to animals as you describe them.

Extended Written Practice/Homework
1. Write three sentences saying what people should do to conserve energy: *La gente debe …*
2. Write a sentence telling if you and your family read a lot of magazines and newspapers. Write a second sentence telling whether or not you recycle those items.

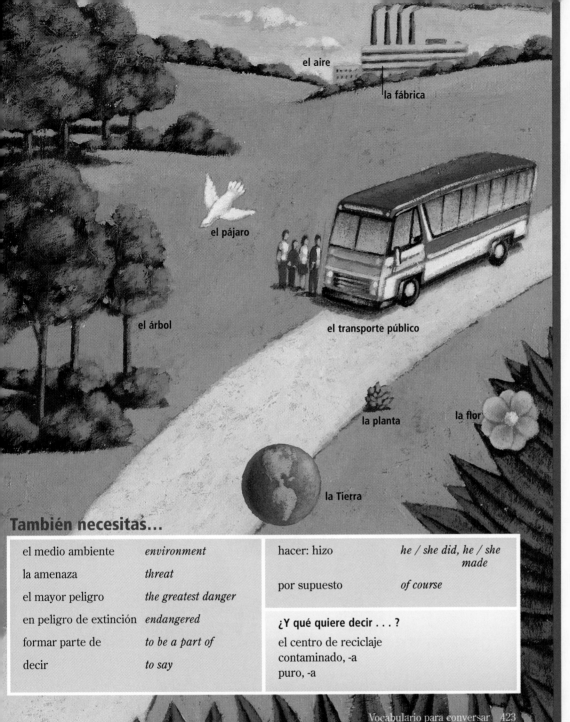

el aire

la fábrica

el pájaro

el árbol

el transporte público

la planta

la flor

la Tierra

También necesitas...

el medio ambiente	*environment*	hacer: hizo	*he / she did, he / she made*
la amenaza	*threat*	por supuesto	*of course*
el mayor peligro	*the greatest danger*		
en peligro de extinción	*endangered*	**¿Y qué quiere decir . . . ?**	
formar parte de	*to be a part of*	el centro de reciclaje	
decir	*to say*	contaminado, -a	
		puro, -a	

Vocabulario para conversar 423

Pasos vivos 1 CD-ROM
Clip Art Album

Grammar Preview
Decir is presented lexically. The complete present-tense paradigm is presented on p. 433.

Teaching Suggestions
Preparing students to speak: Use one or two options from each of the categories of Comprehensible Input, Physical Response, or Limited Verbal Response. For a complete explanation of these categories and some sample activities, see pp. T22–T23.

Class Starter Review
On the day following initial vocabulary presentation, you might begin the class with this activity: Write two categories on the board: *En peligro de extinción* and *No en peligro de extinción*. Have pairs of students put the animals listed in the chapter vocabulary into the categories. Compile a class consensus.

www Internet Activities
Juegos

Multiple Intelligences
Bodily/Kinesthetic
See Learning Spanish Through Action.
Naturalist
Have students write a journal entry about their own natural surroundings.
Verbal/Linguistic
See Pronunciation Tape 13-2.
Visual/Spatial
See Overheads 68–69, the Vocabulary Art BLMs/CD-ROM, and Using the Video.

Practice

Re-enter / Recycle

Ex. 8: direct object pronouns from Chap. 6

Ex. 9: sites from Chap. 7

Answers: Empecemos a conversar

8 Point out the structure of the answer in the model: direct object pronoun *(Las)*, verb *(hizo)*, subject *(la gente)*.

ESTUDIANTE A

a. ¿Los árboles forman parte del medio ambiente?

b. ¿El aire forma . . .

c. ¿Las flores forman . . .

d. ¿El océano forma . . .

e. ¿Los coches forman . . .

f. ¿La selva tropical forma . . .

ESTUDIANTE B

a.–d., f. Sí, claro que sí.

e. No. Los hizo la gente.

9 ESTUDIANTE A

a. ¿Qué es una amenaza para los animales?

b. . . . para los árboles?

c. . . . para la Tierra?

d. . . . para la selva tropical?

e. . . . para las ruinas?

ESTUDIANTE B

a.–e. Answers will vary and may include more than one option.

Empecemos a conversar

8 A —¿*La Tierra* forma parte del medio ambiente?

  B —*No, claro que no.*

   o:

  A —¿*Las fábricas* forman parte del medio ambiente?

  B —*No. Las hizo la gente.*

Estudiante A   Estudiante B

a.   b.   c.   d.   e.   f.

9 A —¿*Qué es una amenaza para el aire puro?*

  B —*Los coches.*

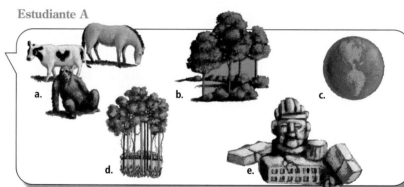

Estudiante A   Estudiante B

a.   b.   c.   d.   e.

las fábricas
las ciudades
la gente
el aire
  contaminado
el agua
  contaminada

Options

Strategies for Reaching All Students

Students Needing Extra Help

Ex. 9: Students may need some background information regarding the effects of the environment on ruins and the rain forest.

Extended Written Practice/Homework

1. For each of the following locations, write a sentence naming one or more animals that live there: *la selva, el campo, el mar.*

2. Write three sentences telling what you like about the countryside: *Me encantan las plantas en el campo.*

3. Write three sentences naming endangered animals that need our protection and telling why: *Debemos proteger los tigres porque . . .*

Multiple Intelligences

Naturalist

If possible, have students go on a nature hike and then talk and/or write about their reactions in Spanish.

Verbal/Linguistic and Interpersonal/Social

See Exs. 8–10.

10

A —¿Están en peligro de extinción <u>los jaguares</u>?

B —Creo que sí.
o: No, creo que no.

Estudiante A   Estudiante B

a.   b.   c.

d.   e.   f.   g.

. . . . ▶

PASO CULTURAL

Born in 1935 in Morelia, Mexico, Alfredo Arreguín is today one of the best-known painters in the U.S. His artistic talents were already evident by age eight, when his grandfather bought him paint and brushes and enrolled him in the local fine arts school. He moved to the U.S. in 1958 to attend the University of Washington. Today he is a resident of the Seattle area. How might moving to another country and culture affect an artist's work? Give an example from the life of a painter, writer, composer, or performer whose work you know.

El último retorno del salmón (1988), Alfredo Arreguín

Vocabulario para conversar   425

10 ESTUDIANTE A

a. ¿Están en peligro de extinción los lobos?
b. ...los osos?
c. ...los caballos?
d. ...los gorilas?
e. ...los perros?
f. ...las vacas?
g. Questions will vary, but should follow the same format.

ESTUDIANTE B

a.–g. Answers will vary.

Cultural Notes

(p. 425, photo)
El último retorno del salmón (The Last Salmon Run), a 1988 painting by Alfredo Arreguín. A Mexican American artist, sculptor, and educator, Arreguín is known for his realistic depictions of nature. Besides having his works displayed at many U.S. galleries, he has also designed greeting cards for UNICEF.

Paso cultural
Possible answers: The artist's feelings about the move (nostalgia, new energy, depression, etc.) could affect his or her artistic style or productivity; the new country could offer new subject matter, different weather/intensity of light, or different materials with which to create art; the community of artists in the new country, as well as the culture's overall approach to life, could give the artist new ideas./Responses will vary.

Practice & Apply

Re-enter / Recycle
Ex. 11: comparatives from
Chap. 11

**Answers: Empecemos a
conversar**

11 ESTUDIANTE A

a. ¿Qué es más importante para
la comunidad, el aire puro o las
fábricas?

b. ...los coches o el transporte
público?

c. ...las ciudades o la selva
tropical?

d. ...los parques o...?

(Questions will vary.)

ESTUDIANTE B

a.–d. Answers will vary, but look
for a logical choice. Encourage
class discussion.

Using Realia

Ricky el reciclador is a fictitious
character that informs people
about conservation. Ask students
if they can get the gist of the ad.
Have them identify the three
words used in the middle of the
ad. *(Corresponsabilidad, codependencia y coevolución)* By using
cognates, see if they can figure
out the meaning of these words
by removing the prefix *co-*.
*(Responsabilidad, dependencia y
evolución)*

11 A —¿*Qué es más importante para la comunidad,
los árboles o los centros comerciales?*

B —*Los árboles.*

o: *No sé. Las dos cosas son importantes.*

Estudiante A   Estudiante B

a.   b.

c.   d.

Ricky

Si mantienes presente estas tres palabras:

CORRESPONSABILIDAD, CODEPENDENCIA
Y COEVOLUCION

podrás conservar mejor nuestro medio ambiente
y nuestros recursos naturales. ¡Recuerda que tu
comportamiento es importante para que todos
vivan mejor!

"UNETE A LA CAMPAÑA DE:
RICKY EL RECICLADOR

426   Capítulo 13

Options

Strategies for Reaching All Students

Spanish-Speaking Students
Ex. 12: Add: *¿Qué podemos hacer para
mantenerlos limpios o limpiarlos?*

Students Needing Extra Help
Exs. 14–15: Have students use their
Organizers from Chaps. 3 and 10 for
places, location words, and means of
transportation.
Ex. 15: Ask: *¿Te gustaría usar el transporte
público?* if there is no public transportation
in your area.

Extended Written Practice/Homework
1. Write three sentences telling about different threats to our environment: *El aire contaminado es una amenaza para la gente de
las ciudades.*
2. Write three sentences telling how people
can conserve energy through different
means of transportation: *Para conservar
energía, podemos ...*

Empecemos a escribir y a leer

Escribe tus respuestas en español.

12 ¿Está contaminada el agua de tu comunidad? ¿Y el aire?

13 ¿Trabaja alguien que conoces en un centro de reciclaje? ¿Quién? ¿Qué hace?

14 ¿Cuántos parques con muchos árboles y flores hay en tu comunidad? ¿Dónde están?

15 En tu opinión, ¿hay suficiente transporte público en tu comunidad? ¿De qué clase? ¿Usa la gente de tu comunidad el transporte público?

16 Lee este párrafo ¿En qué recipiente debemos poner las botellas? ¿Y los periódicos?

Debemos reciclar latas, botellas, plásticos, revistas, periódicos, cartón, vidrio. No olvide que debe poner las revistas, los periódicos y el cartón en el recipiente amarillo. El aluminio, el vidrio y el plástico deben ponerse en el rojo.

También se dice...

la culebra
la víbora

Un madrileño reciclando botellas

www.pasoapaso.com

MORE PRACTICE

Más práctica y tarea, p. 544
Practice Workbook 13–3, 13–4

Vocabulario para conversar   427

Cultural Notes

Multiple Intelligences
Verbal/Linguistic
See Ex. 11 and Audio Activity 13.2.
Visual/Spatial
See Practice Wkbk. 13-3 and 13-4, Writing Activity 13-B, Using Realia, and Ex. 16.

(p. 427, left photo)
Recycling igloos, such as the one in the photo, have become a familiar sight in many Spanish cities. In Córdoba, in addition to recycling, households separate wet and dry garbage for curbside collection. The pre-sorted wet garbage is then turned into high-quality fertilizer and sold to farmers. Ask students: What kind of recycling program does your neighborhood have? How could it be improved?

Practice

Re-enter / Recycle
Ex. 1: obligation from Chap. 4
Ex. 3: demonstrative adjectives
and direct object pronouns from
Chap. 6, *pensar* + inf. from
Chap. 7

Answers:
¡Comuniquemos!

1 *(Answers will vary.)* La señora debe apagar las luces y la calculadora. Debe reciclar las cosas en la basura.

2 Statements will vary. Animals pictured include: *el elefante, el oso, la serpiente, el jaguar.*

¿Qué debe hacer la señora para proteger el medio ambiente? Observa bien este dibujo. Trabaja con un(a) compañero(a).

Debe reciclar las latas.

¿Están estos animales en peligro de extinción? Si lo están, di por qué. Tu compañero(a) debe decir qué podemos hacer para protegerlos.

A —*Las ballenas están en peligro de extinción porque los océanos están contaminados.*

B —*No debemos contaminar el agua de los océanos.*

Estudiante A   Estudiante B

a.   b.   c.   d.   e.

428   Capítulo 13

Options

Strategies for Reaching All Students

Spanish-Speaking Students
Ex. 1: Have Spanish-speaking students write out this exercise.

Students Needing Extra Help
Ex. 3: Students may have difficulty deciding which verb to use in the response. Brainstorm with them.
Review *este / ese* from the Chap. 6 Organizer.
Remind students of the direct object pronouns *lo, la, los,* and *las.*
¿Qué sabes ahora?: Have students write out this section so they can check off what they have mastered.

Cooperative Learning
Divide the class into groups of four. Tell students that they are going to develop some new home products made out of recycled materials: paper, wood, glass, and aluminum. Assign the four materials to each group and ask students to brainstorm ideas

¡UEMOS!

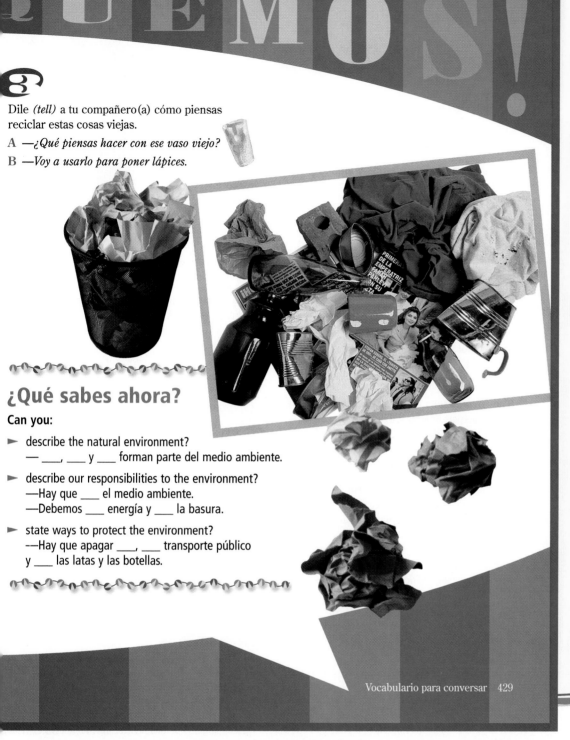

Dile *(tell)* a tu compañero(a) cómo piensas reciclar estas cosas viejas.

A —*¿Qué piensas hacer con ese vaso viejo?*

B —*Voy a usarlo para poner lápices.*

¿Qué sabes ahora?

Can you:

► describe the natural environment?
— ___, ___ y ___ forman parte del medio ambiente.

► describe our responsibilities to the environment?
—Hay que ___ el medio ambiente.
—Debemos ___ energía y ___ la basura.

► state ways to protect the environment?
—Hay que apagar ___, ___ transporte público
y ___ las latas y las botellas.

Vocabulario para conversar   429

---

3 **ESTUDIANTE A**
Questions will vary, and may include:
¿Qué piensas hacer con ese papel viejo?
...con esa revista vieja?
...con esa camiseta vieja?
...con esa taza vieja?
...con esa botella vieja?
...con esa lata vieja?

ESTUDIANTE B
(Answers will vary.)
Voy a usarlo para dibujar.
...usarla para hacer un cartel.
...usarla para sacudir los muebles.
...usarla para poner flores.
...usarla para (hacer) una lámpara.
...usarla para mi clase de arte.

Answers: ¿Qué sabes ahora?

• Answers will vary.
• proteger / conservar / separar (reducir)
• las luces / usar / reciclar

 Audio Activity 13.3

 Writing Activity 13-C

 Pasos vivos 1 CD-ROM
Slide Projector, Laboratorio de grabar

---

for the products. Set a time limit for the activity. After they have written down their ideas, you may want to have students create drawings of their products. Ask the groups to share their drawings and to explain them to the class. You may then wish to display the artwork on posterboard.

Multiple Intelligences
Bodily/Kinesthetic and Interpersonal/Social
See Cooperative Learning.
Interpersonal/Social
See Exs. 1–3.
Verbal/Linguistic
See Audio Activity 13.3.
Visual/Spatial
See Writing Activity 13-C.

• To discuss endangered species in Cuba and the U.S.

Multicultural Perspectives

Anthropologists, other scientists, and traditional healers are collaborating to collect and document species of plants from tropical rain forests throughout Latin America. Scientists are learning from traditional healers about the medicinal value of plants virtually unknown to the scientific community. Especially in light of the fact that the rain forests are disappearing at an alarming rate, documenting this valuable knowledge is extremely important. In Costa Rica alone, 1,500 species of orchids have been recorded. The possible existence of plants with curative properties is a major reason for the collaboration between scientists and traditional healers. Ask students to research information about plants from other areas of the world that are used for medicinal purposes.

Perspectiva cultural

Animales de Cuba que están en peligro de extinción

Almiquí cubano

Muchas especies de plantas y animales están en peligro de extinción. Otras ya han desaparecido.

Does anything seem unusual about the animals in these photographs? Explain. What clues do the captions give you about the part of the world they live in?

Can you imagine a three-foot-tall owl or a bird as small as a bee? The giant owl is long extinct, but the *zunzún,* the smallest bird in the world, still lives in Cuba, although it is endangered.

The *Greta cubana* is a very beautiful butterfly with transparent wings. Like the *zunzún,* it lives only in Cuba, and, like so many other species around the world, it is also endangered.

Another very unusual animal from Cuba is the *almiquí.* It has furry feet like a rabbit, the tail of a mouse, and a long snout like an opossum. It's an insect-eating animal about the size of a cat, and one of the few remaining native mammals of Cuba. Catching sight of an *almiquí* is really difficult, because there are so few of them left.

Why are these species disappearing? It's a long process that started with the first human settlements in Cuba about 7,000 years ago.

In recent years, more species have become endangered because of population growth and the redevelopment of the tourist industry, which has again become an important aspect of the Cuban economy.

Learning about these species has been a group effort. A team of Cuban scientists from the Museo Nacional de Historia Natural and U.S. scientists from the American Museum of Natural History in New York, among others, have been researching Cuban animal and plant life. This project is an example of how people around the world are pooling their efforts to study ecology and preserve its biological wonders. The Cuban–U.S. scientific team is also a good example of cooperation between the people of Latin America and the people of the United States.

Este animal, de casi 3 pies de alto, está extinto desde hace más de 7.000 años.

Options

Strategies for Reaching All Students

Spanish-Speaking Students
Ask: *¿Por qué es importante proteger a estos animales? ¿Por qué crees que los científicos del mundo se interesan tanto en estos animales? ¿Qué animales quisieras tú proteger? ¿Por qué?*

 Un paso más Ex. 13-H

Students Needing Extra Help
Ex. 1: Make this an interdisciplinary unit with science. Invite your school's Life Science teacher to speak to the class.
Ex. 2: Students should realize that there is no simple answer to this question. Discuss why solutions for one country might not necessarily work for another.

Enrichment
Have students research one of these environmental problems facing Latin America: 1) Pollution and other environmental problems caused by factories in Mexico. 2) The hunt for sea turtles and their eggs in the Gulf of Mexico and what's being done to curb it. 3) Pollution in Mexico City and how residents and the government are trying to deal with it.

El zunzún, el pájaro más pequeño del mundo

La cultura desde tu perspectiva

1 What endangered species in the United States do you know about? How are the threats facing these animals similar to those facing endangered species in Cuba? How do the threats differ, if they do?

2 How might knowing each other's languages and cultures help experts in Latin America and the United States solve problems more effectively? What problems besides endangered species do you think could be solved by cooperation between the United States and Latin America?

Greta cubana

Perspectiva cultural 431

Cultural Notes ☀

Multiple Intelligences
Intrapersonal/Introspective
See Enrichment.
Naturalist
Have students research environmental issues in their community. Let students as a class decide what they can do to be responsible environmentalists.

(pp. 430–431, photos)
Other endangered animals that are native to Cuba are two mammals: a member of the rodent family, the dwarf hutia (*hutía enana*) and the manatee, or sea cow (*manatí*). The manatee was on the brink of extinction in the mid-1950s. Thanks to a very strict endangered species program, however, it was saved and is now thriving in marshes and on riverbanks.

Preview

Teaching Suggestions
Point out the form *pide* to students. Then ask them what they think happens with a command form of a stem-changing verb. Tell them to notice Luis's last statement. Ask them how they have used *sé* before and what its meaning in Luis's statement might be.

Answers
Answers will vary, but students may mention rules or regulations regarding use of the park.

A Answers will vary.

B *Dice* means "he / she says." The *ellos / ellas* form of *decir* is *dicen*. The *nosotros* form is *decimos*.

C These verb forms resemble the *Ud. / él / ella* form in the present tense. *Pon* differs from the others because it is not like the *Ud. / él / ella* form of *poner*.

Gramática en contexto

You might see a poster like this at the entrance to a national park. What information would you expect to find there?

A Did the poster contain the type of information you expected?

B You have seen the word *dice* many times in this book. What does it mean? The infinitive is *decir.* Like *pedir* and *servir, decir* has an e → i stem change. What would be the *ellos / ellas* form of *decir*? And the *nosotros* form?

C In the poster you can see the following commands: *protege, usa, pide, apaga, lleva, pon.* Do these verb forms look more like present or preterite-tense forms? How does *pon* differ from the others?

432   Capítulo 13

Options

Strategies for Reaching All Students

Students Needing Extra Help
A–C: Elicit from students that this kind of poster often has commands for readers to follow. Give an example.
Have students start to fill in the grammar portion of their Organizers.
El verbo decir: Emphasize that the *yo* form is spelled with a *g: digo.*

Extended Written Practice/Homework
Write four sentences telling what different people you know or people who are in the news say about our environment: *Mis padres dicen que tenemos que apagar las luces en la casa para conservar energía.*

Multiple Intelligences
Bodily/Kinesthetic
Have students practice the present-tense forms of the verb *decir* using the cube made of plastic foam.
Interpersonal/Social and Verbal/Linguistic
See Exs. 1–2.
Visual/Spatial
See Overhead 70, Practice Wkbk. 13-5 and 13-6, and Writing Activity 13-D.

El verbo *decir*

The verb *decir* means "to say" or "to tell." Here are all of its present-tense forms:

(yo)	**digo**	(nosotros) (nosotras)	**decimos**
(tú)	**dices**	(vosotros) (vosotras)	**decís**
Ud. (él) (ella)	**dice**	Uds. (ellos) (ellas)	**dicen**

- Notice the *e* of the stem changes to *i* in all forms except *nosotros* and *vosotros*.

1 Túrnate con un(a) compañero(a) para decir cuál es la opinión de estas personas.

La gente dice que las fábricas deben reducir el aire contaminado.

a. Los médicos
b. Mis amigos(as)
c. Los profesores
d. Nosotros/los estudiantes
e. La gente
f. Muchas personas
g. Nadie

el aire contaminado
los abrigos de piel
el agua pura
las botellas de ___
el mayor peligro
las fábricas
el transporte público

2 Ahora túrnate con un(a) compañero(a) para decir la opinión de estas personas sobre lo que es necesario o importante.

La gente dice que hay que reducir el aire contaminado.

a. El (la) profesor(a) de español
b Mis padres
c. Nosotros/los estudiantes
d. Yo
e. El Presidente de los Estados Unidos
f.

(no) tenemos que
(no) vale la pena
(no) hay que
(no) debemos
(no) necesitamos

Gramática en contexto 433

¡NO OLVIDES!

Remember that we must use *que* after *decir: Dice que..., dicen que...*

Present & Practice

Teaching Suggestions
Ex. 1: Point out that *gente* and *nadie* use the singular verb form.

Answers
1 Statement endings will vary.
a. Los médicos dicen que . . .
b. Mis amigos(as) dicen que . . .
c. Los profesores dicen que . . .
d. Nosotros/los estudiantes decimos/dicen que . . .
e. La gente dice que . . .
f. Muchas personas dicen que . . .
g. Nadie dice que . . .

2 Statement endings will vary.
a. El (La) profesor(a) de español . . .dice que . . .
b. Mis padres dicen que . . .
c. Nosotros/los estudiantes decimos/dicen que . . .
d. Yo digo que . . .
e. El Presidente de los Estados Unidos dice que . . .
f. Statements will vary.

 Practice Wkbk. 13-5, 13-6

 Writing Activity 13-D

¿? **Prueba 13-5**

Answers

3 a, d, e, f, g, i, j, l, m, n, p.

4 Statements will vary, as more than one logical choice exists.
a. Pues, bebe jugo de naranja.
b. . . . descansa.
c. . . . compra unas pastillas.
d. . . . llama a la clínica.
e. . . . haz ejercicio.

El mandato afirmativo (tú)

When you tell someone to do something, you are giving an affirmative command. Here are some affirmative commands you might give to a person you address as *tú*.

> Pablo, **apaga** las luces por favor.
> Linda, **recoge** la basura.
> Cristóbal, **sirve** la cena ahora.

- Notice that command forms are usually the same forms that we use for *él / ella / Ud.* in the present tense.

- Certain verbs, like *poner, hacer,* and *decir,* have irregular command forms.

> Isabel, **pon** los libros en la mesa.
> Miguel, **haz** tu cama.
> Elena, **di** lo que piensas.

- Object pronouns are attached to the end of affirmative commands. When a pronoun is attached to a command that has two or more syllables, an accent mark is added to the stressed vowel.

> —¿Qué debo hacer con las botellas y latas?
> —**Sepáralas,** por favor.

¡NO OLVIDES!

Remember that the *Ud./él/ella* present-tense forms of *decir, hacer,* and *poner* are *dice, hace,* and *pone.*

3 Con un(a) compañero(a), decidan cuáles de estas formas son mandatos afirmativos.

a. sacude	e. vive	i. pide	m. di
b. pruebas	f. juega	j. ayuda	n. recicla
c. dice	g. pon	k. pones	o. quitas
d. haz	h. quedas	l. trabaja	p. trae

4 Tus amigos tienen un problema y te piden un consejo *(advice)*. Contéstales usando el mandato del verbo de la lista.

A — *Tengo mucho sueño.*

B — *Pues, duerme un poco.*

a. Tengo catarro.   Llamar a la clínica
b. Me lastimé la pierna ayer.   Comprar unas pastillas
c. Me duele mucho la garganta. Descansar
d. Tengo gripe y quiero ver al médico. Hacer ejercicio
e. Quiero ser mejor deportista.   Beber jugo de naranja

Options

Strategies for Reaching All Students

Students Needing Extra Help
El mandato afirmativo (tú): Emphasize the irregular forms and have students develop commands using them.
Give more examples of attaching the object pronoun to the command.
Write examples of another *-ar* verb and two for *-er* and *-ir* verbs.

Extended Written Practice/Homework
1. Write a five-sentence list of things that people can do to protect our environment. Use a command in each: *Usa menos agua en el baño.*
2. Write three commands that can help students be more successful at school.
3. Write three commands telling someone what to do at a certain restaurant. Include these verbs in your commands: *comer, pedir, probar.*

Multiple Intelligences
Interpersonal/Social
See Class Starter Review.
Verbal/Linguistic
See Exs. 4 and 6.

5 Copia estos mandatos en una hoja de papel. Después, ponle un pronombre de complemento directo a cada uno de ellos. ¿A cuáles de las formas hay que añadir *(add)* un acento?

a. pide	e. apaga	i. cierra	m. corta
b. compra	f. saca	j. reduce	n. separa
c. bebe	g. pon	k. sirve	o. lee
d. di	h. practica	l. haz	p. cocina

6 Túrnate con un(a) compañero(a) para leer estas ideas sobre el medio ambiente. Uno(a) de Uds. lee, agregando *(adding)* *Dicen que . . . .* El (la) otro(a) responde usando el mandato.

A —*Dicen que debemos sacar la basura.*

B —*Pues, sácala.*

> Debemos sacar la basura

a. Hay que apagar las luces.
b. Debemos conservar energía.
c. Vale la pena proteger el medio ambiente.
d. Tenemos que usar el transporte público.
e. Necesitamos conservar agua.
f. Hay que separar la basura.

La Empresa Municipal de Transportes en Madrid tiene autobuses que no contaminan el aire.

Gramática en contexto **435**

5 Add an accent to a, b, c, e, f, h, i, j, k, m, n, o, p.

6 **ESTUDIANTE A**
a. Dicen que debemos apagar las luces.
b. . . . conservar energía.
c. . . . proteger el medio ambiente.
d. . . . usar el transporte público.
e. . . . conservar agua.
f. . . . separar la basura.

ESTUDIANTE B
a. Pues, apágalas.
b. . . . , consérvala.
c. . . . , protégelo.
d. . . . , úsalo.
e. . . . , consérvala.
f. . . . , sepárala.

Cultural Notes

(p. 434, realia)
Bottled water has recently become popular in the U.S., but has been widely consumed in Spain and Latin America for many years. As the label states, this bottle contains *agua purificada sin gas* (non-carbonated purified water). Carbonated water *(con gas)* is also popular.

(p. 435, photo)
In Western Europe, high gasoline taxes have put private car ownership out of the reach of many people. However, governments have provided extensive support for efficient bus, subway, and light rail systems, making car ownership less necessary. This city bus in Madrid runs on clean-burning natural gas. Ask students: What measures would you recommend to improve the air quality in your area or in the city nearest you?

7 Pregúntale a tu compañero(a) qué puedes hacer tú para proteger el medio ambiente. Él(ella) deberá decirte tres cosas que puedes hacer.

A —*¿Qué debo hacer para proteger el medio ambiente?*

B —*Primero, recicla las botellas y las latas.*
Segundo, conserva agua.
Tercero, apaga las luces si no las necesitas.

El verbo *saber*

We use the verb *saber* ("to know") to talk about knowing facts or information. Here are all of its present-tense forms.

(yo)	**sé**	(nosotros) (nosotras)	**sabemos**
(tú)	**sabes**	(vosotros) (vosotras)	**sabéis**
Ud. (él) (ella)	**sabe**	Uds. (ellos) (ellas)	**saben**

- *Saber* follows the pattern of regular *-er* verbs except for the *yo* form: *sé*.

- When *saber* is immediately followed by the infinitive, it means "to know how to."
  Mis amigos **saben esquiar** muy bien.

8 Pregúntale a un(a) compañero(a) si sabe cómo podemos proteger la Tierra. Pregunta y contesta con elementos de las tres columnas.

A —*¿Sabes cómo podemos reciclar las latas y las botellas?*

B —*Sí, lo sé. Debemos llevarlas a un centro de reciclaje.*

a. reciclar	el aire contaminado	apagar las luces cuando no las usamos
b. conservar	las latas y las botellas	reciclar revistas y periódicos
c. proteger	la basura	usar menos papel
d. reducir	energía	montar en bicicleta o usar transporte
	los árboles de la selva	público
		llevar(las) a un centro de reciclaje

436 Capítulo 13

"Mirar los pájaros es un buen pasatiempo."

En las Islas Galápagos, Ecuador

Options

Strategies for Reaching All Students

Students Needing Extra Help
Ex. 7: Have the whole class brainstorm possibilities, using their Organizers. Then divide the class into groups, assigning two or three verbs to each group.
El verbo saber: Emphasize *sé*. Some students will want to use *sabo*.
Have students develop examples of *saber* + inf. Emphasize that there isn't a direct translation for the "how."

Ex. 8: Match the three columns before conjugating the verbs and making other necessary changes.
Model at least one more example.
Point out that *Sí, lo sé* means "I know (it)" and that *lo* does not refer to cans and bottles.
Remind students that the purpose of the exercise is to practice using *saber*.
Do a model using *proteger*.

Ex. 9: Unlike other activities, students will need to draw upon their own experiences for answers. Have them make up an answer if necessary.
Elicit a *nosotros* answer by asking a student directly if he or she and a friend know how to do something.
Ahora lo sabes: Have students write out this section so they can check off what they have mastered.

9 Pregúntale a tu compañero(a) si él(ella), su familia o sus amigos saben hacer estas cosas.

A —¿Sabes esquiar?

B —Sí, sé esquiar bien. Mi amigo Miguel también sabe.
  o: No, yo no sé esquiar, pero mis hermanas sí saben.

a.

b.

c.

d.

e.

f.

g.

Ahora lo sabes

Can you:

► report what people say or tell?
  —Ellos ____ que debemos separar el vidrio y el aluminio. ¿Qué ____ tú?

► tell a friend, a family member, or a child what to do?
  —¿Debo apagar la luz?
  —Sí. No la necesitas ahora. ¡_____!

► say what people know?
  —Mis padres ____ que es importante reciclar.

Cuzco, Perú

MORE PRACTICE

Más práctica y tarea, pp. 544–545
Practice Workbook 13–5, 13–10

Gramática en contexto   437

---

c. . . . proteger . . .
d. . . . reducir . . .

ESTUDIANTE B
Answers will vary, but should include the correct direct object pronoun attached to the infinitive.

9 ESTUDIANTE A
a. ¿Sabes patinar?
b. ¿Sabes jugar fútbol?
c. ¿Sabes nadar?
d. ¿Sabes jugar tenis?
e. ¿Sabes cocinar?
f. ¿Sabes bucear?
g. Questions will vary.

ESTUDIANTE B
a.–g. Answers will vary, but should include the use of sé + inf. and the correct form of saber.

Answers: Ahora lo sabes
• dicen / dices
• Apágala
• saben

 Practice Wkbk.
13-9, 13-10

 Audio Activities
13.4, 13.5

 Writing Activities
13-F, 13-G

 Prueba 13-7

 Comm. Act. BLM
13-3

 Pasos vivos 1 CD-ROM

Bulletin Board, Slide Presentation Maker, Spindle, Treadmill

Cultural Notes

Extended Written Practice/Homework
Write four sentences saying what people know about dangers in our environment: *Mucha gente sabe que el aire contaminado es muy malo para la salud.*

Multiple Intelligences
Verbal/Linguistic
See Audio Activities 13.4 and 13.5.
Visual/Spatial
See Practice Wkbk. 13-7 through 13-10; Writing Activities 13-E through 13-G; and Comm. Act. BLMs 13-2 and 13-3.

(p. 436, photo)
Las Islas Galápagos are a favorite destination of bird watchers. Rare species include a flightless cormorant and a type of mockingbird that is unknown elsewhere. Even penguins can be found on the shores of these small equatorial islands. Darwin's studies of thirteen different species of Galápagos finches and their adaptations to vastly different environments helped him to form his theory of evolution.

(p. 437, photo)
This small Natural History museum in Cuzco bears the name *Apu Condor. Apu* is the native Quechua term for mountain spirit, and condors are the majestic scavenger birds that live in the high Andes. Condors are revered by Andean peoples for their sheer size and smooth, elegant flight. The Incas and their descendants have a strong relationship with the natural world, and the sight of condors gliding has long provided them with inspiration.

Todo junto

Actividades

En un grupo pequeño, haz un anuncio de radio o de televisión sobre el transporte público de tu comunidad. Estas ideas te pueden ayudar:

La gente que sabe usa el metro.
Dicen los pasajeros: ¡El metro es muy rápido!
¡Qué cómodo es!
Úsalo todos los días.
Es la mejor manera de ir a trabajar y a la escuela.

Presenta tu anuncio al resto de la clase.

Prepara un cartel turístico con fotografías o dibujos de un lugar que te gustaría visitar. Usa mandatos para decirle al turista lo que debe hacer. Puedes incluir esta información:

- qué lugar visitar y cuándo
- cómo llegar
- qué hacer en ese lugar
- qué comprar
- de qué sacar fotos
- qué llevar

Prepara una presentación oral sobre tu cartel para la clase.

Una estación del metro en Buenos Aires

438   Capítulo 13

Options

Strategies for Reaching All Students

Conexiones

Áreas protegidas

Mira el mapa de Costa Rica. Las áreas protegidas (parques nacionales, etc.) están indicadas en verde. **Estima** qué porcentaje del área total del país es el área protegida.

Mira la tabla que compara las áreas protegidas con el área total del país. Con un(a) compañero(a):

- **Calcula** qué porcentaje del área total es el área protegida.
- **Compara** la respuesta con las estimaciones que hicieron tú y tu compañero(a).

País o Estado	Áreas protegidas	Área total
Costa Rica	4.459 millas cuadradas	19.652 millas cuadradas

Copia la tabla y agrega estas cifras del estado de California: áreas protegidas, 3,268 m²; área total, 158,706 m². Con un(a) compañero(a):

- **Calcula** qué porcentaje del área total es el área protegida.
- **Compara** ese porcentaje con el de Costa Rica.
- **Averigua** cuántas millas cuadradas tiene tu estado (o algún estado o país) y cuántas de esas millas están protegidas.
- **Calcula** qué porcentaje del área total del estado o país es el área protegida. Con tu compañero(a), presenta un informe a la clase. Por ejemplo:

> El área total de (nombre del estado / país) es de (número) millas cuadradas.
>
> (Número) millas cuadradas están protegidas.
>
> Las áreas protegidas representan (número) por ciento del estado / país.
>
> Costa Rica protege más / menos de su área total que (nombre del estado / país).

Monte Verde, Costa Rica

Teaching Suggestions

Áreas protegidas, estimation: Draw a rough map of Costa Rica on the board and shade in about 50% of the map. Label the map "50%." Draw the map four more times with 40%, 30%, 20% and 10% shaded, and label each map. Ask students to identify the map on the board whose shaded area best matches the total amount of protected land in the map of Costa Rica on p. 439.

Tell students that in most Spanish-speaking countries, large whole numbers are written with decimal points instead of commas (for example, "4,375" is written "4.375" in Spanish) and fractional numbers are written with commas instead of decimal points ("3.5" is written "3,5" in Spanish).

Answers: Conexiones

Áreas protegidas: Costa Rica: 23 por ciento/California: 2 por ciento/ El porcentaje del área protegida de Costa Rica es casi 12 veces más grande que el porcentaje del área protegida de California./Answers will vary according to state.

 Writing Activity 13-H

 Comm. Act. BLMs 13-4, 13-5

 Pasos vivos 1 CD-ROM

A Jugar, Boom Box, Laboratorio de grabar, Maps, Spindle

Cultural Notes

Multiple Intelligences

Interpersonal/Social
See Cooperative Learning and Exs. 1–2.

Logical/Mathematical
See *Conexiones*.

Verbal/Linguistic
See Pronunciation Tape 13-3.

Visual/Spatial
See Using the Video, Writing Activity 13-H, and Comm. Act. BLMs 13-4 and 13-5.

(p. 438, photo)
The subway system in Buenos Aires has long offered an efficient alternative to commuting along the city's traffic-congested boulevards. It was built by the French in 1913 and is the oldest mass transit system in South America. It consists of five lines identified by the letters A–E. Street entrances to the stations are marked *subte* (for *subterráneo*) and show the letter of the line.

(p. 439, photo)
Costa Rica is home to many environmental projects that attempt to preserve forested land and the abundant animal life living there. Monte Verde is a high altitude cloud forest with around 10,000 acres of protected land. Over 450 species of birds have been observed in the area, including the spectacular *quetzal*.

Apply

Process Reading

For a description of process reading, see p. 48.

Teaching Suggestions

Encourage students to use the reading strategies they have practiced in previous lessons—especially prediction and context clues—to get the meaning of this reading selection. Tell them to rely, too, on their prior knowledge of the subject and on what they have learned in this chapter.

Answers
Antes de leer

Answers will vary.

Mira la lectura

The title of the article is *Cuide el mundo desde casa.* The girl in the picture is prepared to clean up the environment by beginning at home. The purpose of the introductory statement is to let the reader know what the article is about.

¡Vamos a leer!

Muchacha ayudando en su comunidad en Honduras

Antes de leer

STRATEGY ➤ **Using prior knowledge**

How can you help protect the environment? Make a list of five things you can do.

Mira la lectura

STRATEGY ➤ **Using titles and photos to predict**

Look over the reading to get an idea about how it is organized. What is the title? What does the picture tell you? What is the purpose of the introductory statement?

Cuide el mundo desde casa

¡Ud. puede hacer mucho para proteger el mundo!

Unidos podemos mantener el mundo más limpio y mejor. Cada uno de nosotros debe hacer algo diariamente para protegerlo. Con la ayuda de todos, ensuciando menos el planeta y ayudando a purificar el medio ambiente, lograremos crear verdaderamente un mundo mejor para nosotros y para nuestra familia. ¡No olvide que su participación es muy importante!

¿Qué puede hacer desde su propia casa?

- Ahorre energía. No use innecesariamente electricidad ni gasolina.
- No desperdicie agua.
- Compre alimentos o productos envasados en materiales reciclables.
- No use atomizadores, o cualquier otro producto que pueda dañar la capa de ozono.

- Consuma productos naturales que no contengan demasiadas sustancias químicas alterantes.
- Revise la salida de gas de su vehículo periódicamente.
- Conserve limpios los lugares públicos y privados: calles, parques, plazas, playas, etc.
- No tale árboles innecesariamente.
- Infórmese sobre campañas ecológicas en su comunidad.
- Lea artículos o vea programas televisión sobre el medio ambiente.

Como ve, hay muchas cosas que puede hacer para ayudar y cuid el mundo en que vivimos. No se desanime si otras personas no contribuyen. ¡Contribuya Ud. c su ejemplo!

Options

Strategies for Reaching All Students

Students Needing Extra Help
Antes de leer: This may be a challenging reading. Have students first read silently, then you can read aloud while students follow along.
Mira la lectura: If students are having difficulty with the last question, ask them: "What information do you get from the introductory statement?"
Infórmate: Caution students that they are not looking for cognates, but rather for families of related words.

Infórmate

STRATEGY➤ **Recognizing word families**

Word families are groups of related words that are used in different ways as nouns, verbs, adjectives, and so on. Often if you know one word in a family you can figure out the meaning of others. Here are some examples from the article:

el día   diariamente

la verdad   verdaderamente

la ayuda   ayudar   ayudando

1 Now read the article carefully. Were any of the suggestions the same as those on your list? Check off on your list the ones they did mention.

2 Find three or four words whose meaning you can figure out because you know the word family they belong to. For example: *sucio / ensuciando.*

3 Divide the suggestions into two groups: those that you do or could easily do and those that don't apply to you.

Aplicación

Make new words out of the following by adding the ending *–mente.* Then use one of the words in a sentence about how you protect the environment. For example: *Reciclo cartón regularmente.*

frecuente   general   rara   regular

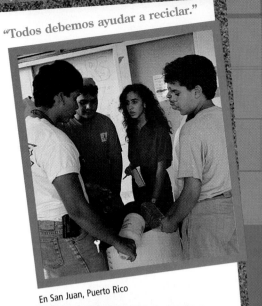

"Todos debemos ayudar a reciclar."

En San Juan, Puerto Rico

Esta niña ayuda a reducir la basura en Buenos Aires, Argentina.

¡Vamos a leer! 441

Infórmate

Answers will vary. For No. 2, students may mention: *ayudando, verdaderamente, innecesariamente, envasados, reciclables.*

Aplicación

Sentences will vary, but should include: *frecuentemente, generalmente, raramente, regularmente.*

www Internet Activities

Cultural Notes ☀

(pp. 440–441, photos)
Environmental awareness has been gaining ground in many Spanish-speaking countries, especially in urban areas where rapid population growth has compounded pollution and overuse of landfills. The teenagers shown here are working on school-sponsored ecology projects. The Argentine girl *(bottom photo, p. 441)* has obviously gotten the message on the garbage can: "put litter in its place."

Apply

Process Writing
For information regarding developing a writing portfolio, see p. 50.

Teaching Suggestions
Point out to students that they can also write free-form or concrete poetry: poetry in the form of the person, animal, or object being described.

 Pasos vivos 1 CD-ROM
Word Processor

¡Vamos a escribir!

How can we express our concern about the environment? One way is through our writing. Write a poem, on your own or in groups, about an animal or a place that you think needs to be protected. Remember, a poem does not need to rhyme. You can follow a pattern of a diamond poem. For example:

1 Think about an animal or a place that needs protecting, and answer the following questions:

- ¿Cómo te sientes cuando piensas en ese animal o ese lugar?
- ¿Qué vocabulario puedes usar en una descripción del animal o del lugar?
- ¿Por qué debemos cuidarlo?
- ¿Cómo podemos protegerlo?

Ballena
grande · buena
bucea · nada · juega
triste · gris
ballena

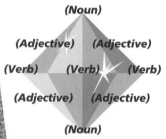

(Noun)
(Adjective) (Adjective)
(Verb) (Verb) (Verb)
(Adjective) (Adjective)
(Noun)

Una ballena gris frente a Baja California, México

2 Use your answers to the questions to write your poem. Organize your ideas in the way you think will be most powerful and effective.

442 Capítulo 13

Options

Strategies for Reaching All Students

Students Needing Extra Help
Step 1: Students may be more successful with something more structured than free verse. Give them a line or two of some poems in English with which they are familiar. Then they can finish them. You might consult with your colleagues in the English department for selections that could be easily translated and / or adapted.
Post pictures of endangered species or natural settings to inspire students.

Step 3: Poetry can be very personal, and students may prefer to work alone. On the other hand, students who are apprehensive about taking ownership of a creative work may be more comfortable working in a group.
Step 4: Have students use their Organizers.

Multiple Intelligences
Intrapersonal/Introspective
See step 1.

442 **Standards** 1.3; 3.1; 4.1

3 Show your poem to a partner. Does your partner understand how you feel about the animal or place? Does he or she think you should change, reorganize, or correct anything? Rewrite your poem.

4 Check for accuracy in spelling and the use of accent marks. Did you use the correct forms of the adjectives and verbs? Did you try to use a varied vocabulary? If necessary, rewrite your poem. You may want to add an illustration to make it more eye-catching.

5 Share your poem by:

- submitting it to the school literary magazine or newspaper
- including it in a collection of class poems called *Vamos a proteger nuestra Tierra*
- posting it on a bulletin board in the school library during Earth Day celebration
- adding it to your writing portfolio

¡Vamos a escribir! 443

CAPÍTULO 13

Repaso ¿Lo sabes bien?

This section will help you organize your studying for the proficiency test, where you will be asked to do similar, though not identical, tasks. There will not be any models on the test.

► Listening
Can you understand when someone talks about the environment? Listen as your teacher reads a sample similar to what you will hear on the test. According to the person making the statement, what is the problem and what are some suggestions for solving it?

► Reading
Can you understand an environmental ad by using word families to guess the meaning of the words you might not know? According to this ad, how can we have a better world?

No corte árboles innecesariamente. No tire papeles en las calles. Recicle. Ayudándonos y trabajando juntos lograremos un mundo mejor.

► Writing
Can you write a letter to a friend in which you describe a place you visited while on vacation and what the people there do to protect the environment? Here is a sample letter:

Querida Luisa,

¡Qué puro está el aire aquí! La gente de esta ciudad sabe que tiene que trabajar mucho para proteger el medio ambiente. Muchas personas montan en bicicleta o usan el transporte público. Por toda la ciudad hay carteles que dicen: Separa la basura, las revistas, las botellas y las latas. La ciudad tiene un parque grande donde hay flores y animales en peligro de extinción.

Tu amiga,
Rebeca

► Speaking
Can you and a partner play the roles of a park ranger and a camper in a national park? Here is a sample dialogue:

A —*¿Qué puedo hacer para proteger el medio ambiente del parque?*

B —*Separa la basura para poder reciclarla después y conserva el agua. También puedes proteger las flores y las plantas del parque.*

A —*¿Y si monto en bicicleta . . . ?*

B —*¡Claro que sí! Necesitamos aire puro. No queremos contaminarlo con los coches.*

► Culture
Can you name two reasons for the gradual disappearance of some species of animals living in the Caribbean region and compare this with other parts of the planet?

www.pasoapaso.com

Estas ranitas doradas de Costa Rica están casi extintas.

444   Capítulo 13

Options

Strategies for Reaching All Students

Students Needing Extra Help
Have students write out this section so they can check off what they have mastered.

Resumen del vocabulario

Use the vocabulary from this chapter to help you:
► describe the natural environment
► list actions to protect the environment
► discuss environmental dangers

to talk about conservation
el centro de reciclaje
la luz, *pl.* las luces
apagar
conservar
proteger
reciclar
recoger
reducir
separar
usar

**to name items that
can be recycled**
el aluminio
la botella
el cartón
la energía
la guía telefónica
la lata
la madera
el periódico
el plástico
la revista
el vidrio

to talk about animals
los animales, *sing.* el animal
la ballena
el caballo

el elefante
el gorila
el jaguar
el lobo
el oso
el pájaro
la serpiente
el tigre
la vaca
la piel

**to talk about nature
and the environment**
el aire
el árbol
la flor
el medio ambiente
el océano
la planta
la Tierra

**to describe
environmental dangers**
la amenaza
contaminado, -a
la fábrica
el mayor peligro
en peligro de extinción
puro, -a

to talk about transportation
la bicicleta: montar en bicicleta
el transporte público

**to talk about
everyday activities**
decir
hacer: (Ud., él, ella) hizo
saber: (yo) sé
         (tú) sabes

to give an opinion
(No) hay que ___.
(No) vale la pena.

**other useful terms
and expressions**
a la vez
formar parte de
la gente
por supuesto

Assessment

 Prueba cumulativa

 Examen de habilidades

 Test Generator

Additional Assessment Options

 Comm. Act. BLMs
Small Group Activities
Situation Cards

 Pasos vivos 1 CD-ROM
Slide Presentation Maker, Video Presentation Maker, Word Processor, Spindle

¿Lo sabes bien? Video Quiz

Internet Activities
Self-Test

Cultural Notes

(p. 444, photo)
Endangered golden frogs in Costa Rica. Although Costa Rica is a relatively small country in area, it is home to an abundance of flora and fauna. Aware of its rich natural life, the government has placed nearly one quarter of its land under protection, giving the country 34 national parks, wildlife refuges, and reserves.

CAPÍTULO 14

THEME: PARTIES AND CELEBRATIONS

SCOPE AND SEQUENCE Pages 446–475

COMMUNICATION

Topics
Parties
Gift-giving
Introductions

Objectives
To discuss teenage parties in Spanish-speaking countries

To talk about parties

To introduce people

To talk about what to wear to a party

To talk about gift-giving

CULTURE
Teenage parties / celebrations

Los quince años

GRAMMAR
Construcciones negativas

El presente progresivo

El verbo dar

Ancillaries available for use with Chapter 14

Multisensory/Technology

Overheads, 71–75

Audio Tapes and CDs

Vocabulary Art Blackline Masters for Hands-On Learning, pp. 73–77/CD-ROM

Classroom Crossword

Video

Pasos vivos 1 CD-ROM

Internet Activities
www.pasoapaso.com

Print

Practice Workbook, pp. 147–156

Writing, Audio & Video Activities, pp. 83–88, 132–134, 178–179

Communicative Activity Blackline Masters
   Pair and Small Group Activities, pp. 99–104
   Situation Cards, p. 105

Un paso más: Actividades para ampliar tu español, pp. 80–85

TPR Storytelling

Assessment

Assessment Program
   Pruebas, pp. 205–214
   Examen de habilidades, pp. 215–218

Test Generator

Video still from Chap. 14

445A

RESOURCE PRO®

Planning Express, Teaching
Resources Library, and Clip Art
Library

¿Lo sabes bien?
Video Quiz

At Home **VIDEO**

Cultural Overview ☼

Fiestas

Celebrations and parties all over the world often include festive decorations. In Mexico, party decorations are usually made by hand. They may consist of long strips of crepe paper folded over each other at right angles and stretched open, or elaborate papier-mâché flowers that are shaped around a wire core.

Piñatas are common at young people's parties. Although *piñatas* are available in stores and markets throughout Mexico and the U.S., they are often constructed by hand of cardboard, papier-mâché, and layers of colored paper. Traditionally, the *piñata* is filled with candy and suspended by a rope. Blindfolded contestants take turns trying to break the *piñata* with a stick to gain access to the contents.

Many celebrations in northern Mexican and Mexican American homes include *mariachis.* These bands usually include eight or nine members who wear outfits derived from the traditional attire of Mexican cowboys, or *charros.* The hat is a large, embroidered *sombrero* made of velvet. The entire *traje de charro* is very expensive.

Mariachis usually consist of two trumpets, four violins, a small guitar called the *vihuela,* and a standard-sized guitar. The *guitarrón,* a large guitar with its back shaped like a bow, provides the bass. *Mariachis* play a traditional form of the *son,* which is native to the state of Jalisco. Most, however, also play other Mexican music, such as *rancheras, boleros, huapangos,* and *corridos,* or ballads. At parties, they may also play dance music *(cumbias, merengues, salsa, tangos,* waltzes, and polkas).

Although formal social affairs include elaborate decorations, formal dress, and live music, social life in Mexico and Mexican American communities in the U.S. mostly revolves around informal gatherings at friends' homes.

Introduce

Re-entry of Concepts

The following list represents words, expressions, and grammar topics re-entered from *El primer paso* to Chap. 13:

El primer paso
Numbers 0–31
Greetings
Calendar expressions

Chapter 1
Adjectives describing personality
Activities
Gustar expressions

Chapter 2
School subjects
School supplies
Time-telling

Chapter 3
Ir a + inf.
Leisure-time activities

Chapter 4
Food

Chapter 5
Family members
Physical characteristics

Chapter 6
Clothing
Colors
Direct object pronouns

Chapter 7
Vacation activities

Chapter 9
Health-related activities

Planning

Cross-Curricular Connections

Math Connection *(pp. 454–455)*
Have pairs of students imagine they are exchange students in Mexico and are planning an end-of-semester party. Have them prepare a list of what they need, along with prices in dollars, and add up the total. Then have each pair figure their totals in *pesos*, using current exchange rates. Rates are available from major banks, newspapers, and on the Internet.

Social Studies Connection *(pp. 460–461)*
Assign pairs of students a Spanish-speaking country. Have them make a chart for a festival or celebration particular to that country. Ask them to present to the class: the time of year it takes place, the cultural / historical significance of the celebration, and any special clothing, food, crafts, games or ceremonies associated with it.

Journalism Connection *(pp. 464–465)*
Have students take turns playing the role of a reporter who arrives at a Hollywood premiere party. The reporter's job is to describe the guests as they get out of their limousines and enter the party. Students can try to guess the names of celebrities as they are described by the reporters. Encourage them to write out their reports the night before their presentations. Tell them that they must use the present progressive and, if possible, negative expressions.

Chapter 11
TV and movies
Indirect object pronouns

Chapter 13
Recycling

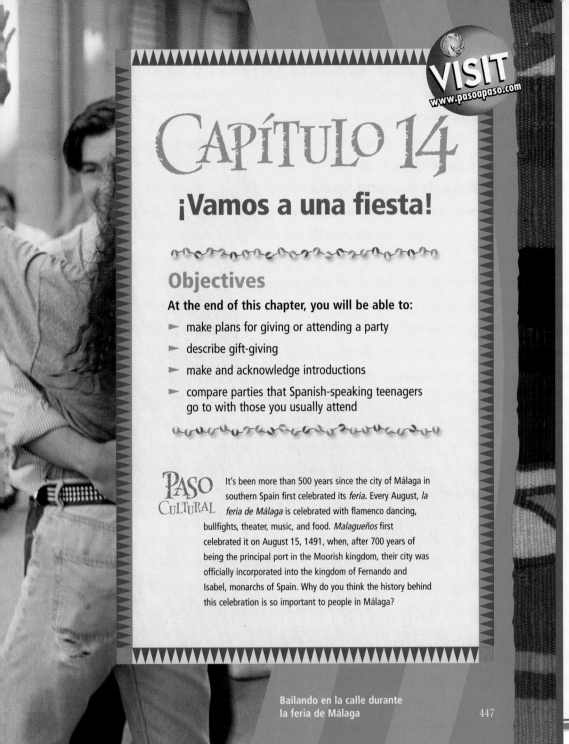

VISIT
www.pasoapaso.com

CAPÍTULO 14

¡Vamos a una fiesta!

Objectives

At the end of this chapter, you will be able to:

► make plans for giving or attending a party

► describe gift-giving

► make and acknowledge introductions

► compare parties that Spanish-speaking teenagers go to with those you usually attend

PASO CULTURAL

It's been more than 500 years since the city of Málaga in southern Spain first celebrated its *feria*. Every August, *la feria de Málaga* is celebrated with flamenco dancing, bullfights, theater, music, and food. *Malagueños* first celebrated it on August 15, 1491, when, after 700 years of being the principal port in the Moorish kingdom, their city was officially incorporated into the kingdom of Fernando and Isabel, monarchs of Spain. Why do you think the history behind this celebration is so important to people in Málaga?

Bailando en la calle durante
la feria de Málaga

447

Cultural Notes ☀

Spanish in Your Community
Obtain (if available) a local Spanish-language newspaper. Ask students to look through it for the announcement of a *quinceañera*. What information is presented in the announcement? How does it compare with the U.S. custom of "Sweet Sixteen"? If there are Mexican restaurants in your area, you might have students interview the manager about *quince años* parties. Look for *quinceañera* cards. If available locally, purchase one and share it with the class.

Paso cultural
Answers will vary. Students may mention that people in Málaga value their traditions and place the city's and country's history and independence in high esteem, just as we do in the U.S. for the Fourth of July.

Preview

Cultural Objective
- To discuss teenage parties in Spanish-speaking countries

¡Piénsalo bien!

Play

Video Activity A

Using the Video
In this chapter's video, host Karina Romera attends a *quince años* party in Guadalajara. After shopping for a gift and choosing her party attire, Karina joins the host family for this special celebration.

To prepare students further for the video, ask them to predict what this chapter's tape will be about. Then have students watch the segment several times. After the first time, you may wish to have them brainstorm possible vocabulary and expressions they will need to talk about what they saw on the video. Ask students to identify: a) activities they saw which reminded them of parties they have attended, and b) activities they saw which are unique to the *quince años* celebration.

Video segment 1: For more teaching suggestions, see the Video Teacher's Guide.

¡Piensa en la CULTURA!

 **At Home** *VIDEO* **Chapter 14** Vocabulary

Parties and *fiestas* in California, Texas, and Spain

Look at the pictures and read the captions.

Teenagers in the Spanish-speaking world usually attend a wide variety of parties, from family occasions like weddings and baptisms to *quince años* celebrations and school dances. What kinds of parties do you usually attend? Are they family occasions, school dances, or get-togethers with friends?

Una madre prepara a su hija para su fiesta de quince años.

"Este collar va muy bien con tu vestido de fiesta."

448   Capítulo 14

"¡Con esta música, todos van a querer bailar!"

What do you suppose *bailar* means? Can you think of an English word that comes from the same root?

Austin, Texas

Escogiendo discos compactos en Austin, Texas

Los Ángeles, California

Options

Strategies for Reaching All Students

Spanish-Speaking Students
Ask: *¿Te gusta recibir regalos? ¿Cuáles prefieres, los prácticos o los personales? ¿Te gustan las fiestas y los bailes? ¿Prefieres fiestas grandes o íntimas (con sólo la familia)? ¿Vas a bailes formales?*

Un paso más Ex. 14-A

Multiple Intelligences
Visual/Spatial
See Using the Video.

"Pasamos toda la noche bailando."

Sevilla, España

¡Piensa en la cultura! 449

Cultural Notes

Present

Chapter Theme
Celebrations: Introductions

Communicative Objectives
- To talk about parties
- To introduce people
- To talk about gift-giving

 Overheads 71–72

 Vocabulary Art BLMs/CD-ROM

 Pronunciation Tape 14-1

 Vocabulario para conversar A

Play

Using the Video
Video segment 2: See the Video Teacher's Guide.

 Video Activity B

Grammar Preview
Dar is presented here lexically. The complete paradigm is on p. 466.

Vocabulario para conversar

¿A quién vas a invitar?

At Home **VIDEO** Chapter 14 Vocabulary

Aquí tienes palabras y expresiones necesarias para hablar sobre las fiestas. Léelas varias veces y practícalas con un(a) compañero(a) en las páginas siguientes.

la fiesta de la escuela

la novia, el novio

bailar

el baile

la fiesta de fin de año

Options

Strategies for Reaching All Students

Students Needing Extra Help
Show how *baile* comes from *bailar*. *También necesitas . . . :* Present the entire *conocer* and *dar* paradigms if necessary. Remind students that they saw some expressions using *dar* in Chap. 11. Give some examples of the use of *soler*. Continue discussion of word families: *regalar* from *regalo* and *encantado* from *encantar*.
Students may think that *parientes* means "parents." Remind them of *los padres*.

Learning Spanish Through Action
STAGING VOCABULARY: *Señalen*
MATERIALS: transparency of the *Vocabulario para conversar*
DIRECTIONS: Direct students to point to the type of party corresponding to the descriptions you give for each (see p. 457, Ex. 15).

Extended Written Practice/Homework
1. Choose five of the events on pp. 450–451 and write a sentence for each telling how much you like/dislike going to them.
2. Write three sentences telling how well you and different members of your family know how to sing and dance.
3. Write three sentences telling how well you know the family and relatives of some of your friends.

la fiesta de cumpleaños

cantar

la fiesta de sorpresa

la fiesta de disfraces

También necesitas...

la reunión	*get-together*
alguien	*someone, somebody*
algunos, algunas	*some*
conocer:	*to know, to be acquainted with:*
(yo) conozco*	*I know*
(tú) conoces	*you know*
Encantado, -a.	*Delighted.*
el pariente, la parienta	*relative*
Te presento a ___.	*I'd like you to meet ___.*
dar: (yo) doy	*to give: I give*
(tú) das	*you give*

recibir	*to receive*
hecho, -a a mano	*handmade*
Depende.	*It depends.*
soler (o → ue) + *inf.*	*to be in the habit of*

¿Y qué quiere decir . . . ?

elegante
¡Feliz cumpleaños!
invitar
personal
práctico, -a
regalar

* *Conocer* is a regular -*er* verb in the present tense except for the *yo* form: *conozco.*

Vocabulario para conversar   451

Practice & Apply

Re-enter / Recycle
Ex. 1: *ir a* + inf. from Chap. 3, family from Chap. 5
Ex. 2: indirect object pronouns from Chap. 11
Exs. 2–3: family from Chap. 5
Ex. 4: family from Chap. 5, direct object pronouns from Chap. 6
Exs. 5–6: *gustar* expressions from Chap. 3
Ex. 7: clothing from Chap. 6
Ex. 8: physical characteristics from Chap. 5

Answers: Empecemos a conversar

1 ESTUDIANTE A
a. ¿A quiénes vas a invitar a tu baile?
b. . . . fiesta de la escuela?
c. . . . fiesta de fin de año?
d. . . . fiesta de sorpresa?
e. . . . fiesta de disfraces?
f. Questions will vary.

ESTUDIANTE B
a.–f. Answers will vary, but look for use of the personal *a*.

2 ESTUDIANTE A
a. ¿Qué sueles regalarle a tu madre para su cumpleaños?
b. . . . hermano(a) . . .
c. . . . primo(a) . . .
d. . . . abuelo(a) . . .
e. . . . amigo(a) . . .
f. . . . novio(a) . . .
g. Questions will vary, but look for the correct use of the personal *a*.

Empecemos a conversar

Túrnate con un(a) compañero(a) para ser *Estudiante A* y *Estudiante B.* Reemplacen las palabras subrayadas con palabras representadas o escritas en los recuadros. 💡 **quiere decir que puedes escoger tu propia respuesta.**

1 A —¿A quiénes vas a invitar a *tu fiesta de cumpleaños*?

B —Voy a invitar a *quince amigos y a algunos parientes*.

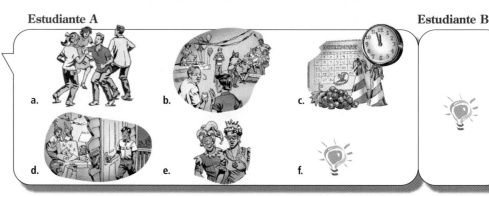

Estudiante A · Estudiante B

a. b. c. d. e. f.

2 A —¿Qué sueles regalarle a tu *padre* para su cumpleaños? padre

B —Depende, pero suelo darle algo *práctico*.
    o: Pues, a veces le doy *sólo una tarjeta de cumpleaños*.

Estudiante A

a. madre
b. hermano(a)
c. primo(a)
d. abuelo(a)
e. amigo(a)
f. novio(a)
g.

Estudiante B

elegante
serio(a) / cómico(a)
romántico(a)
barato(a) / caro(a)
personal
hecho(a) a mano

Options

Strategies for Reaching All Students

Spanish-Speaking Students
Ex. 7: After this exercise, ask: *¿Cuándo fue la última vez que fuiste a un baile? ¿Con quién fuiste? ¿Fue tu familia también? ¿Cómo ibas vestido(a), formal o informalmente? ¿Cómo estuvo la música? ¿Bailaste mucho?*

 Un paso más Ex. 14-B

Students Needing Extra Help
Ex. 1: Remind students of the *a personal.* Insist that students vary answers so that they don't repeat *quince* and *algunos.*
Ex. 4: Review *lo, la.* Give a feminine model.
Ex. 7: Have students use their Organizers from Chap. 6.
Ex. 8: Have students use their Organizers from Chaps. 1 and 5 for descriptive words.

Enrichment
Ex. 1: To extend this exercise, review vocabulary for dates by asking the birthdates of individual students.
Ex. 2: As a homework assignment, have students make a table with three columns headed *Pariente / amigo(a), Personalidad / apariencia,* and *Por eso, suelo regalarle.* In the first column, students should list five family members or friends. In the second, they should describe the personalities and physical characteristics of the people they

3 A —*Te presento a mi amiga Juanita.*   a mi amiga
　　B —*Encantado(a).*

Estudiante A

a. a mi tía, ___

b. a mi madre, ___

c. a mi abuelo, ___

d. a mi profesor, el señor ___

e. a mi profesora,
　la señora (señorita) ___

Estudiante B

Encantado(a).

Mucho gusto.

4 A — *¿Conoces a mi primo Alberto?*   mi primo
　　B — *No, no lo (la) conozco.*
　　　　o: *Sí, lo (la) conozco.*

Estudiante A

Estudiante B

También se dice...

For *regalar*, we can also say *hacer un regalo*.

Empecemos a escribir

Escribe tus respuestas en español.

5 ¿Qué regalos sueles regalar? ¿Qué regalo te gustaría recibir?

6 ¿Te gustaría dar una fiesta grande? ¿A quiénes te gustaría invitar? ¿A toda la familia? ¿A muchos jóvenes? ¿O prefieres las reuniones pequeñas?

7 Cuando vas a un baile, ¿qué ropa sueles llevar?

8 ¿Conoces a alguien famoso? ¿A alguien muy viejo? ¿A alguien fascinante? ¿Quiénes son? ¿Cómo se llaman? ¿Cómo son?

MORE PRACTICE

- Más práctica y tarea, p. 545
- Practice Workbook 14–1, 14–2

Vocabulario para conversar　453

Present

Chapter Theme
Celebrations: Clothes and activities

Communicative Objectives
- To talk about parties
- To talk about what to wear to a party

 Overheads 73–74

 Vocabulary Art BLMs/CD-ROM

 Pronunciation Tape 14-2

 Vocabulario para conversar B

Play

Step

Using the Video
Video segment 2: See the Video Teacher's Guide.

 Video Activity B

 Pasos vivos 1 CD-ROM
Clip Art Album

Vocabulario para conversar

En la fiesta

Aquí tienes el resto del vocabulario necesario para hablar sobre las fiestas y los regalos.

At Home VIDEO Chapter 14 Vocabulary

el traje

el vestido de fiesta

las joyas

los zapatos de tacón alto

la corbata

el collar

el reloj pulsera

los aretes *(m.)*

la pulsera

el lugar: *Virrey Arredondo 255*
la hora: *7:00 de la tarde*
la fecha: *viernes, 2 de julio*

la invitación

454   Capítulo 14

Options

Strategies for Reaching All Students

Spanish-Speaking Students

 Un paso más Ex. 14-C

Students Needing Extra Help
También necesitas . . . : Present the entire *escoger* paradigm if necessary.
Separate *pasarlo bien* from *pasarlo mal.*
Explain the difference between *el ambiente* and *el medio ambiente.*

Learning Spanish Through Action
STAGING VOCABULARY: *Dibujen*
MATERIALS: none
DIRECTIONS: Describe a party from preparation to cleanup. At each stage, direct students to draw the activities on the chalkboard: *Primero hay que escribir las invitaciones, luego hay que preparar la comida, luego hay que decorar,* and so on, up to *¿Quién va a sacar la basura?*

la invitada

el invitado

las decoraciones *(pl.)*

la entrada

decorar

Grammar Preview
Bailando / cantando / comiendo / hablando / viendo are presented here lexically. The explanation of the present progressive is on pp. 464–465.

Teaching Suggestions
Preparing students to speak: Use one or two options from each of the categories of Comprehensible Input, Physical Response, or Limited Verbal Response. For a complete explanation of these categories and some sample activities, see pp. T22–T23.

Class Starter Review
On the day following initial vocabulary presentation, you might begin the class with this activity: Following the example given in this *Vocabulario para conversar,* have students write a very short invitation to their next birthday party, including address, day, date, and time.

www Internet Activities
Juegos

También necesitas...

el ambiente	*atmosphere*	escoger: (yo) escojo*	*to choose: I choose*
bailar: bailando	*dancing*	(tú) escoges	*you choose*
cantar: cantando	*singing*	De ninguna manera.	*Not at all.*
comer: comiendo	*eating*		
hablar: hablando	*talking*	**¿Y qué quiere decir . . . ?**	
pasarlo bien / mal	*to have a good /*	la hora	
	bad time	el lugar	
ver: viendo	*looking*	escribir	
		escuchar (la radio, el disco compacto)	
		preparar	
		tocar música	

* *Escoger* is a regular *-er* verb with a spelling change in the *yo* form of the present tense: *escojo.*

Vocabulario para conversar   455

Practice & Apply

Re-enter / Recycle

Ex. 9: *gustar* expressions from Chap. 1
Ex. 10: clothing from Chap. 6
Ex. 11: calendar expressions from *El primer paso*, time-telling from Chap. 2, *ir a* + inf. from Chap. 3
Ex. 14: *gustar* expressions from Chap. 1

Answers: Empecemos a conversar

9 ESTUDIANTE A
a. ¡Qué fiesta tan aburrida! ¡Nadie está hablando!
b. ...comiendo!
c. ...cantando!
d. ...pasándolo bien!

ESTUDIANTE B
a.–d. Creo que no les gusta(n) ... (*Answers will vary, and should include the correct use of* gustar.)

10 ESTUDIANTE A
a. ¿Necesitas comprar algo para llevar con tu traje?
b. ...tu collar?
c. ...tu vestido?
d. ...tu falda?
e. ...tus pantalones?
f. ...tu chaqueta?

ESTUDIANTE B
a.–f. Answers will vary, but may include: *unos zapatos de tacón alto, una camiseta, una corbata, un reloj pulsera, una blusa, unos aretes.*

Empecemos a conversar

9 A —*¡Qué fiesta tan aburrida! ¡Nadie está* <u>*bailando*</u>!
B —*Creo que no les gusta* <u>*la música*</u>.

bailando

Estudiante A

a. hablando
b. comiendo
c. cantando
d. pasándolo bien

Estudiante B

la comida
la música
el ambiente

10 A —*¿Necesitas comprar algo para llevar con tu* <u>*vestido de fiesta*</u>?
B —*Sí,* <u>*un collar*</u>.

Estudiante A

a.
b.
c.
d.
e.
f.

Estudiante B

Options

Strategies for Reaching All Students

Spanish-Speaking Students
Ex. 15: After this exercise, ask: *Vas a una fiesta de disfraces. ¿Qué disfraz te gustaría llevar? ¿Por qué?*

 Un paso más Ex. 14-D

Students Needing Extra Help
Ex. 9: Discuss word families: *comer, comida.*
Some of these items have only one logical answer; others have a choice.
Exs. 9–10: Remind students that the responses for *Estudiante B* are not in sequential order with the statements or questions for *Estudiante A.*
Ex. 11: Remind students that the word order of dates in Spanish is different from that of English (4 of July as opposed to July 4).

Extended Written Practice/Homework
1. Write three sentences telling how often you wear the clothing and jewelry pictured on p. 454. If you do wear them, indicate when: *Suelo llevar una corbata cuando voy a un lugar elegante.*
2. Write three sentences listing tasks that must be done for a party: *Hay que ...*
3. Write two sentences telling when it is necessary to buy a ticket.

Imagina que vas a dar una fiesta el 2 de junio.

 11 A —¿*Cuándo vas a decorar el lugar para la fiesta?*
B —*El 1° de junio.*

> decorar el lugar

Estudiante A

a. escoger la hora y la fecha

b. escribir las invitaciones

c. escoger la música

d. preparar la comida

e. escoger la ropa que vas a llevar

Estudiante B

Empecemos a escribir y a leer

Escribe tus respuestas en español.

12 ¿Llevas aretes? ¿Y reloj pulsera? ¿Cuándo los llevas?

13 ¿Para qué fiestas necesitas comprar entradas?

14 Para dar una fiesta, ¿qué necesitas hacer? ¿Qué música te gusta tocar?

15 ¿Qué clase de fiesta es? Lee las descripciones y contesta las preguntas.

a. Alejandro le compró un collar a Anita. Llegó a su casa temprano con los otros invitados. Cuando Anita entró en la casa, todos dijeron: "¡Feliz cumpleaños!"

b. María lleva un vestido elegante y zapatos de tacón alto. Su novio, un traje gris con una corbata azul. La música es muy bonita y les gusta mucho la fiesta. Pero a medianoche les duelen mucho los pies.

c. Adela no sabía qué llevar a la fiesta. ¿Jeans, botas y un sombrero vaquero? ¿Un traje de baño, una toalla, anteojos de sol y sandalias? Al final, decidió ir de detective.

¿A qué clase de fiesta fue Alejandro? ¿Y María? ¿Y Adela?

También se dice...

los aros
los pendientes
los zarcillos

el brazalete

el vestido de gala
el vestido de etiqueta

www.pasoapaso.com

MORE PRACTICE

Más práctica y tarea, p. 546
Practice Workbook 14–3, 14–4

Vocabulario para conversar 457

Practice

¡COMUNI

1

Escoge cinco de tus compañeros(as). ¿Qué ropa llevan hoy? Toma notas en español para no olvidarlo. Después, describe a un(a) estudiante. Tu compañero(a) debe adivinar *(guess)* a quién describes.

A —*Lleva aretes azules, un suéter y jeans. ¿Quién es?*

B —*¿Son blancos los jeans?*

A —*Sí.*

B —*Es Sara.*

2

¿Conoce tu compañero(a) a las personas de quienes hablas?

A —*¿Conoces a Mike Smith?*

B —*Sí, lo conozco. Es un estudiante de mi clase de matemáticas. Es muy simpático.*
o:

B —*No, no lo conozco. ¿Quién es?*

A —*Es un estudiante de mi clase de arte.*

B —*¿Cómo es?*

A —*Es alto y rubio.*

458   Capítulo 14

Options

Strategies for Reaching All Students

¡Cuántos regalos! Tu compañero(a) va a comprar regalos para su familia y sus amigos. Ayúdalo(la) a decidir qué comprar.

A —*El cumpleaños de (mi hermano) es (el 10 de junio). ¿Qué le regalo?*

B —*¿Por qué no le compras (un reloj pulsera)?*

¿Qué sabes ahora?

Can you:

► discuss preparations for a party?
—Tengo que preparar ___, escoger ___ y escribir ___.

► tell what kinds of gifts you like to give and receive?
—Me gusta regalar ___. Me gusta recibir regalos ___.

► tell what you wear to a party?
—Cuando voy a una fiesta de cumpleaños, llevo ___ y ___.

► introduce people and acknowledge introductions?
—Te ___ a mi amigo Andrés.
—___.

Vocabulario para conversar 459

Cultural Notes

Cooperative Learning
Assign groups of four students different types of parties or gatherings listed in the first *Vocabulario para conversar*. Then ask each group to list what they would bring to celebrate it. After they have prepared their lists, have one person in each group summarize. As each group reports, have all other students check off the items that also appeared on their lists.

Multiple Intelligences
Interpersonal/Social and Logical/Mathematical
See Cooperative Learning.
Interpersonal/Social and Verbal/Linguistic
See Exs. 1–2.
Verbal/Linguistic
See Audio Activity 14.3.
Verbal/Linguistic and Intrapersonal/Introspective
See *¿Qué sabes ahora?*

(p. 458, realia)
This ad uses the *tuteo* in the repeated phrase *Especialistas en . . .* to suggest a familiarity with the reader's tastes in clothing and, by extension, with the reader as a person. Ask students: Who is this ad's intended audience? How does this ad try to appeal to this audience?

Cultural Objective

• To compare teenage parties in Spanish-speaking countries and the U.S.

Critical Thinking: Identifying Stereotypes

Help students understand that although *quince años* parties are common in many Spanish-speaking countries, the amount of importance given to them varies from country to country. The celebrations themselves also differ greatly, depending upon socioeconomic level and regional or local customs and traditions.

Answers

Answers will vary for inductive questions in Spanish. / Students may mention that the people are celebrating a special occasion. A birthday party or even a wedding might be suggested. / Answers will vary, but may include: The party seems special because of the way the people are dressed.

Perspectiva cultural

Una celebración especial

Dos quinceañeras celebran su día especial en Austin, Texas.

¿Qué fiestas especiales hay en tu familia? ¿Y en tu comunidad?

Based on the photographs, what do you think the people are celebrating? What tells you that this is a very special party?

It's 4 o'clock on a Saturday afternoon in Camuy, a town on the northern coast of Puerto Rico. You can hear the approaching sounds of a ten-car caravan blowing their horns. When the caravan arrives in front of the church,

Una quinceañera con su novio

Tamaris, a young woman in a white dress, steps out of the first car with her mother and father. Inside the church, Tamaris will receive a blessing from the priest while her mother places a crown on her head.

What might look like a wedding party is actually Tamaris's *quince años,* her fifteenth birthday celebration. It marks the girl's entrance into adulthood.

A *quince años* party can be very lavish or very simple. But one thing they all have in common is that family and friends of all ages join together to make it a memorable success. In Tamaris's case, the caravan was driven by her father's closest friends. They all own similar cars and have formed a car club that meets regularly for fun and to serve as escorts for local parties and celebrations, such as a *quince años.*

The white dress Tamaris is wearing was made by her mother, and her grandparents contributed the crown and white high-heeled shoes. Other family members and friends prepared food and refreshments for the party at her home, where a friend from school will act as deejay. Traditionally, the *quinceañera* starts the first dance with her father and then moves on to her escort. Then other couples will join them. The party will continue late into the night.

Options

Strategies for Reaching All Students

Spanish-Speaking Students

Ask: *¿Has participado en un quince años? ¿Has ido a un quince años? ¿Fue muy elegante? ¿Dónde tuvo lugar? ¿Fue mucha gente? ¿Fueron muchos de tus amigos? ¿Te divertiste? ¿Qué piensas de las fiestas de quince años?*

 Un paso más Exs. 14-G, 14-H

Students Needing Extra Help

Talk about the cultural significance of a fifteenth birthday party. Note the difference in the degree of formality and the close relationship with the Church.

Another tradition has the girls at the party
gathering around the cake to pull ribbons
from it. The one who pulls the ribbon with a
ring on it will presumably be the first one to
get married.

However, not all young girls are interested in
having a *quince años* party. Some might ask for
a trip or a special gift instead of a formal party
and a white dress. Tamaris's friend Loida has
asked for a plane ticket so she can spend her
summer vacation with her cousins in New
Jersey and visit New York City. Loida is
looking forward to her first long trip alone.
That will really make her feel like an adult.

www.pasoapaso.com

La cultura desde tu perspectiva

1 Is the party described here
similar to any parties you
have ever attended? How
were they alike or different?

2 What events in the United
States are similar to a
quince años? In what ways
are they similar?

Perspectiva cultural   461

Cultural Notes ☀

(pp. 460–461, photo)
In addition to celebrating the passage of a
girl into adulthood, *quince años* celebrations
are an opportunity for Hispanic Americans
to celebrate their cultural values, chief
among which are *comunidad, tradición,* and
respeto. Ask students: Can you think of any
similar celebrations among other ethnic
groups in the U.S. that affirm both an individual and his or her culture?

Preview

 Overhead 75

Answers

A The ending used on -ar verbs is -ando, and the ending used on -er verbs is -iendo. The meaning of están saliendo is "they are leaving."

B nadie; no, ni . . . ni; nada; and nunca. / No, nunca, and ni . . . ni come before the verb; nadie comes either before or after the verb; nada comes after the verb.

C The sentences in captions 2, 3, and 5 have more than one negative word. When the negative word comes after the verb, the word no is used.

Gramática en contexto

¡La peor fiesta de cumpleaños! ¡Pobre Eugenia!
¡Lo está pasando horrible! ¿Por qué?

Nadie está bailando.

Los invitados no están ni comiendo ni bebiendo.

Mi novio no está hablando con nadie.

Algunos invitados están viendo… ¡la tele!

Muchas personas ya están saliendo, pero nadie me regaló nada.

¡Nunca voy a tener otra fiesta de cumpleaños!

A The verbs in the first four captions are made up of two words. What ending is used on the -ar verbs when they follow estar? And on the -er verbs? What is the meaning of están saliendo in the fifth caption?

B Find all the negative words that Eugenia uses to express her feelings (such as no and nadie). Do these words come before or after the verbs?

C In which sentences do you find more than one negative word? What word is used before the verb in these sentences?

462 Capítulo 14

Options

Strategies for Reaching All Students

Students Needing Extra Help
A: As students identify the tense made up of two verbs, write out the use of estar + a verb form ending in -ando or -iendo to express an action that's happening right now. Ask students from what infinitive pasando comes. Go through each present participle. Then ask for the difference in endings for verbs ending in -ar and those ending in -er or -ir.

B: As students use negative words and note their position, elicit the idea that when the negative word comes before the verb, no is not included. When the negative word comes after the verb, no is included. Students probably won't recognize anything but no as a negative. Point out other negative words: nada, nadie, nunca, etc. Tell them that in English, double negatives are incorrect, but in Spanish they are correct.

Give some examples with and without the no. Remind students of the a personal with nadie. Stress opposites: algo–nada; alguien–nadie; nunca–siempre.

Enrichment
Ex. 1: After students have had the opportunity to answer truthfully about their plans, you may want to ask them to answer every question negatively, pretending they are sick (have them say what's wrong with them) or have other plans.

Construcciones negativas

To make a sentence negative, we put *no* in front of the verb. Some other negative words that you know are: *nada* ("nothing"), *nunca* ("never"), *nadie* ("nobody"), *tampoco* ("neither"), and *ni ... ni* ("neither ... nor"). Recall how we use them:

Nunca saco fotos.
Nadie va a ayudarme con las decoraciones.
No me gusta bailar **tampoco**.
No hay **ni** sandwiches **ni** refrescos.
No quiero comer **nada.**

- Sometimes we can put the negative word before the verb and leave out the *no*. However, if the negative word comes after the verb, we must use *no* or another negative word.

Antonio **nunca** estudia con **nadie**.
No conozco a **nadie** en esta fiesta.

1 Pregúntale a tu compañero(a) qué va a hacer. Usa una palabra *(word)* de cada columna.

A —*¿Vas a leer algo esta tarde?*   **leer**

B —*Sí, voy a leer una revista.*
    o: *No, no voy a leer nada.*

a. comer	hoy
b. jugar	esta tarde
c. ver	esta noche
d. beber	mañana
e. escuchar	este fin de semana
f. hacer	
g. comprar	

Celebrando el Cinco de Mayo en Los Ángeles, California

Gramática en contexto   463

Present & Practice

Class Starter Review
On the day following the presentation of negative constructions, you might begin the class with this activity:
Have students prepare to share a statement about something they never do. Give examples: *Nunca voy a fiestas de sorpresa, Nunca miro programas deportivos*, etc.

Re-enter / Recycle
Ex. 1: *ir a* + inf. from Chap. 3

Answers
1 ESTUDIANTE A
a. ¿Vas a comer algo *(+ choice from right-hand column)*?
b. ...jugar ...
c. ...ver ...
d. ...beber ...
e. ...escuchar ...
f. ...hacer ...
g. ...comprar ...
ESTUDIANTE B
a.–g. Answers will vary.

Extended Written Practice/Homework
1. Imagine that you went to a party but didn't associate with anyone there. Write three sentences about this experience: *No bailé con nadie.*
2. Write four sentences telling about when you went somewhere but didn't do anything: *Fui al restaurante pero no pedí nada.* Use each of these expressions: *ir de compras, ir de vacaciones, ir a la escuela, ir al restaurante.*

Multiple Intelligences
Interpersonal/Social
See Ex. 1.
Visual/Spatial
See Overhead 75.

Cultural Notes ⊛

(p. 463, photo)
Los Angeles was founded by Mexican colonists in 1781 as "El Pueblo de Nuestra Señora la Reina de los Ángeles de Porciúncula." Part of the vast territory that was acquired by the U.S. from Mexico as a result of the Mexican American War of 1846, Los Angeles today has more Mexican Americans than any other city in the U.S. *Fiestas* such as *Cinco de Mayo* are an opportunity for *angelenos* to celebrate the Mexican history of their city.

Standards 1.1; 1.3   **463**

Re-enter / Recycle

Ex. 2: leisure-time activities and *ir a* + inf. from Chap. 3, food from Chap. 4

Ex. 3: direct object pronouns from Chap. 6, TV and movies from Chap. 11, recycling from Chap. 13

Ex. 4: leisure-time activities from Chap. 3, family members from Chap. 5, vacation activities from Chap. 7, health-related activities from Chap. 9

Answers

2 ESTUDIANTE A

a. ¿Alguien va a traer una grabadora?

b. . . . revistas?

c. . . . sandwiches?

d. . . . vasos?

e. . . . videojuegos?

ESTUDIANTE B

a. No, nadie va a traer una grabadora. ¡No vamos a escuchar nada!

b. . . . revistas. . . . leer nada!

c. . . . sandwiches . . . comer nada!

d. . . . vasos. . . . beber nada!

e. . . . videojuegos. . . . jugar nada!

---

2 Quieres hacer una reunión pero nadie quiere llevar nada. Explícale a tu compañero(a) qué problemas van a tener.

A —*¿Alguien va a traer refrescos?*

B —*No, nadie va a traer refrescos. ¡No vamos a beber nada!*

| a. | b. | c. | d. | e. |

3 ¿Cuáles son algunas cosas que no haces nunca? Con un(a) compañero(a), di *(tell)* si siempre, a veces, o nunca haces estas cosas.

A —*Yo nunca llevo aretes. ¿Y tú?*

llevar aretes

B —*Yo tampoco.*
o: *Yo los llevo siempre.*

a. llevar un vestido de fiesta / una corbata
b. escribir cartas / tarjetas postales
c. pasarlo mal en una fiesta
d. regalar algo hecho a mano

e. dar fiestas de sorpresa
f. reciclar botellas de plástico
g. montar en bicicleta
h. ver dibujos animados

El presente progresivo

We use the present tense to talk about an action that always or often takes place or that is happening now.

Ellos **comen** hamburguesas.

They eat hamburgers. (always / usually)
They're eating hamburgers. (now)

We use the present progressive tense when we want to emphasize that something is happening right now.

Ellos **están comiendo** hamburguesas.

They're eating hamburgers. (right now)

Options

Strategies for Reaching All Students

Spanish-Speaking Students
Ex. 3: Have students write out this exercise.
Ex. 4: For Spanish-speaking students, replace Ex. 4 with: *Escribe un párrafo explicando lo que está haciendo cada persona.*

Students Needing Extra Help
Ex. 2: Have students match the artwork with a corresponding verb; for example, sandwiches with *comer,* video games with *jugar.* Stress that *algo* and *nada* are used with things and that *alguien* and *nadie* are used with people.
Brainstorm with students the verb that will be used in the second statement of the *Estudiante B* response.

El presente progresivo: Go through a list of verbs from earlier chapters, changing them to the present participle.
Ex. 4: Have students use their Organizers from Chap. 7. Remind them that the form of *estar* changes with the subject while the participle remains the same.

The present progressive uses a present-tense form of *estar* + the present participle of another verb. To form the present participle, we drop the ending of the infinitive and add *-ando* to the stem of *-ar* verbs and *-iendo* to the stem of *-er* and *-ir* verbs.

(yo)	**estoy**	bail**ando** comi**endo** escrib**iendo**	(nosotros) (nosotras)	**estamos**	bail**ando** comi**endo** escrib**iendo**
(tú)	**estás**	bail**ando** comi**endo** escrib**iendo**	(vosotros) (vosotras)	**estáis**	bail**ando** comi**endo** escrib**iendo**
Ud. (él) (ella)	**está**	bail**ando** comi**endo** escrib**iendo**	Uds. (ellos) (ellas)	**están**	bail**ando** comi**endo** escrib**iendo**

4 Tienes unas fotos de tus vacaciones en Yucatán. Túrnate con un(a) compañero(a) para explicar qué están haciendo las personas en cada foto.

Aquí nosotros estamos explorando la selva.

nosotros

a. mi papá

b. mi hermana

c. mis padres

d. mi familia y yo

e. unos amigos mexicanos

f. yo

Gramática en contexto   465

3 ESTUDIANTE A
a. Yo (siempre / a veces / nunca) llevo un vestido de fiesta / una corbata. ¿Y tú?
b. ...escribo cartas / tarjetas postales. ...
c. ...lo paso mal en una fiesta. ...
d. ...regalo algo (nada) hecho a mano. ...
e. ...doy fiestas de sorpresa. ...
f. ...reciclo botellas de plástico. ...
g. ...monto en bicicleta. ...
h. ...veo dibujos animados. ...
ESTUDIANTE B
a.–h. Answers will vary.

  Practice Wkbk. 14-5

  Writing Activity 14-D

  Prueba 14-5

  Comm. Act. BLM 14-2

4 Answers
a. Aquí mi papá está haciendo ejercicio.
b. ...mi hermana está tomando el sol.
c. ...mis padres están buceando.
d. ...mi familia y yo estamos subiendo una pirámide.
e. ...unos amigos mexicanos están jugando fútbol.
f. ...yo estoy bailando y cantando.

Enrichment
Ex. 4: To extend this exercise, you may want to have students bring their own vacation photos (or those from a magazine for a "pretend" vacation) and take turns presenting one or two of them to the class. Encourage students to be as detailed as possible in their descriptions of the photos, naming people, place, and time (season, month) as well as what's happening.

Extended Written Practice/Homework
1. Find six photos in *Paso a paso* and write sentences telling what is happening:
(p. 441) *Los jóvenes están reciclando botellas de plástico.*
2. Write four sentences telling what you, your friends, and your family members are doing right now.

Multiple Intelligences
Interpersonal/Social
See Ex. 3.
Verbal/Linguistic
See Enrichment and Exs. 2 and 4.
Visual/Spatial
See Practice Wkbk. 14-5, Writing Activity 14-D, and Comm. Act. BLM 14-2.

Re-enter / Recycle
Ex. 5: activities from Chap. 1, leisure-time activities from Chap. 3, vacation activities from Chap. 7
Ex. 6: *gustar* expressions from Chap. 1, school subjects and school supplies from Chap. 2, clothing from Chap. 6
Ex. 7: family members from Chap. 5

Answers

5 ESTUDIANTE A
a. ¿Qué están haciendo Paco y Jorge?
b. ... están haciendo Uds.?
c. ... estás haciendo tú?
d. ... está haciendo Julia?
e. ... está haciendo Carlos?

ESTUDIANTE B
a. Están comiendo tacos.
b. Estamos escuchando música.
c. Estoy hablando por teléfono.
d. Está tocando la guitarra.
e. Está sacando fotos.

 Practice Wkbk.
14-6, 14-7

 Writing Activities
14-E, 14-F

 Prueba 14-6

 Comm. Act. BLM
14-3

---

5 Tu amigo(a) está enfermo(a) y no puede ir a la fiesta de fin de año. Por eso, te llama por teléfono para preguntar qué están haciendo todos los invitados.

A —¿Qué están haciendo Raquel y Fernando?
B —Están bailando.

Raquel y Fernando

| a. Paco y Jorge | b. Uds. | c. tú | d. Julia | e. Carlos |

El verbo *dar*

The verb *dar* means "to give." Here are all of its present-tense forms.

(yo)	**doy**	(nosotros) (nosotras)	**damos**
(tú)	**das**	(vosotros) (vosotras)	**dais**
Ud. (él) (ella)	**da**	Uds. (ellos) (ellas)	**dan**

- Except for the *yo* form, *dar* takes the same present-tense endings as regular *-ar* verbs.

- Because we often say to whom we give something, *dar* is usually used with the indirect object pronouns *me, te, le, nos,* and *les.*

  Nuestro profesor **nos da** mucha tarea.
  Nunca **les doy** nada a mis primos.
  Mis abuelos van a **darme** un libro para mi cumpleaños.

Una muchacha celebra el fin del año escolar en Cuernavaca, México.

466   Capítulo 14

Options

Strategies for Reaching All Students

Students Needing Extra Help
El verbo dar: Do students remember other verbs that have a similar *yo* form? *(soy, voy)*
Have them review their Organizers from Chaps. 9 and 11 for indirect object pronouns.
Point out the position of the pronoun when there are two verbs.
Show that in English we drop the "to" in the statement "to give to someone." ("I gave Mary a gift" as opposed to "I gave to Mary a gift.")

Ex. 6: Because the indirect objects are all singular, you may want to add some plural ones.
Ex. 7: Do the exercise using the first response, then again using the second.
Ahora lo sabes: Have students write out this section so that they can check off what they have mastered.

Enrichment
Ex. 7: As a homework assignment, have students do this exercise with plural names for the people named as "givers." As another assignment, students can list other people (singular and plural) who give them other things.

6 ¿Qué les regalas a las siguientes personas? Trabaja con un(a) compañero(a) para escoger el regalo apropiado.

A —¿Qué le das a un amigo que juega béisbol?

B —Le doy algunas entradas a un partido.

> un amigo que juega béisbol

a. un amigo a quien le gusta dibujar
b. una amiga a quien le gusta esquiar
c. una amiga que estudia álgebra
d. un amigo que escribe mucho
e. una amiga que ve muchas películas
f. un amigo que va a menudo a la playa
g. una amiga a quien le gusta la ropa

7 Dile a tu compañero(a) quién te da estas cosas.

A —¿Quién te da dinero?

B —Mi padre me da dinero.
   o: Nadie me da dinero.

> dinero

a. ropa nueva
b. poca tarea
c. regalos hechos a mano
d. los exámenes más difíciles
e. regalos prácticos
f. tarjetas de cumpleaños

Ahora lo sabes

Can you:

► express a negative statement?
—No tengo hambre. ___ voy a comer ___ ahora.

► tell what is happening right now?
—Marta y Rosa ___ unas enchiladas porque tienen hambre.

► tell what someone gives to someone else?
—Yo siempre les ___ regalos a mis amigos.

¡QUÉ FANTÁSTICA, FANTÁSTICA ESTÁ LA FIESTA!

IDEAS
para su hogar
FIESTAS Y CUMPLEAÑOS, No. 7

MORE PRACTICE

Más práctica y tarea, pp. 546–547
Practice Workbook 14–5, 14–9

Gramática en contexto **467**

Apply

 **Pronunciation Tape
14-3**

 Todo junto A

Play

Todo junto B

Play

Using the Video
Video segment 3: See the Video
Teacher's Guide.

 Video Activity C

 **Pasos vivos 1
CD-ROM**
Video Monitor, Video Presentation
Maker

Answers: Actividades
1 Invitations will vary, but look
for logical responses and a wide
variety of chapter vocabulary.

2 Ads will vary, but should contain a wide variety of vocabulary.

Todo junto

Actividades

1 Quieres dar una fiesta.
Con un(a) compañero(a),
decidan:

- qué clase de fiesta
  va a ser
- cuándo la quieren dar
- dónde
- a quiénes van a invitar
- qué van a servir
- qué ropa llevar
- qué música tocar

Luego escriban una
invitación para la fiesta y
compártanla *(share it)* con los
miembros de la clase.

2 Trabaja con un(a) compañero(a) para crear un anuncio para
un regalo. Si quieren, pueden incluir esta información:

- descripción del regalo
- para qué tipo de persona es
- precio
- por qué es el regalo perfecto
- dónde comprarlo

Luego compartan el anuncio con sus compañeros de clase.

468   Capítulo 14

Options

Strategies for Reaching All Students

Spanish-Speaking Students
Exs. 1–2: Pair bilingual students with non-
bilingual students if possible.

Students Needing Extra Help
Ex. 1: To keep the comments appropriate,
you should decide on the kind of party.
Perhaps you can suggest the anniversary of
grandparents, a party honoring a local
celebrity, etc.
Have students use their Organizers from
Chaps. 4, 6, and 12 (food and clothing).
Brainstorm additional questions.
Ex. 2: If possible, bring in an extra ad aimed
at gift-giving from a Spanish-language
newspaper or magazine to serve as a model.

Conexiones: After students have written as
many combinations as they can, ask them
how many there are (without counting dupli-
cates). Then give students the formula: $N = 2^n$. Tell them to use the number they count-
ed (8) as N and the number 3 for n
(because there are 3 pieces of jewelry). Ask
them if the formula is true for this case.
(Yes, because $8 = 2^3 = 2 \times 2 \times 2$.)

Conexiones

Las matemáticas

¿Qué llevaré?

1 Una mujer tiene una pulsera de oro, un collar de diamantes y aretes de oro y plata. Predice cuántas combinaciones diferentes puede llevar sin repetir *(without repeating)* una combinación.

2 Haz una lista de las combinaciones posibles.

3 Escribe una fórmula para ilustrar esas combinaciones.

4 Prueba la fórmula al añadir *(by adding)* un reloj pulsera.

3 de mayo.
DÍA DE LA MADRE

Un beso y un regalo. Te lo has ganado.

El Corte Inglés

ESPECIALISTAS EN TI.

Todo junto 469

Answers: Conexiones

1. Predictions will vary.

2. Hay 8 combinaciones posibles, y son:

pulsera	collar	aretes
1. sí	sí	sí
2. sí	sí	no
3. sí	no	sí
4. sí	no	no
5. no	sí	sí
6. no	sí	no
7. no	no	sí
8. no	no	no

3. La fórmula para calcular el número N de posibles combinaciones es 2^n, donde n es el número de joyas *(pieces of jewelry)* que se pueden llevar. En este caso, n = 3, y usando la fórmula $N = 2^3 = 2 \times 2 \times 2 = 8$ posibles combinaciones.

4. Si se puede llevar también un reloj pulsera, ya n = 4. Según la fórmula, $N = 2^4 = 2 \times 2 \times 2 \times 2 = 16$. Al escribir la lista de posibles combinaciones como hicimos arriba, se confirma que hay 16.

 Writing Activities 14-H, 14-I

 Comm. Act. BLMs 14-4, 14-5

 Pasos vivos 1 CD-ROM
A Jugar, Boom Box, Laboratorio de grabar, Maps, Spindle

Cooperative Learning
Have each student bring to class a small item that relates to an interest, hobby, personality trait, etc. For example, a tennis ball represents someone good at tennis, sheet music indicates interest in singing or playing an instrument, and so on. The next day, divide the class into groups of three or four. Have students put the items in a bag so that classmates cannot see them. Place all of the items in a larger bag. Now tell students that they will be going shopping for a gift for someone in the class. One by one, have them select an item from the bag. Groups then discuss to whom the item should be given. Set a time limit. After they have chosen the person, a representative gives the item to him or her. As the item is given, the student uses a form of the verb *dar,* an indirect object pronoun, and a reason for giving the object. Afterward, check to see how many objects were "correctly" given as gifts.

Multiple Intelligences
Bodily/Kinesthetic
See Cooperative Learning.
Logical/Mathematical
See *Conexiones.*
Verbal/Linguistic
See Pronunciation Tape 14-3.
Visual/Spatial
See Using the Video, Writing Activities 14-H and 14-I, and Comm. Act. BLMs 14-4 and 14-5.

Apply

Process Reading
For a description of process reading, see p. 48.

Answers
Antes de leer
Students may say that the story is about two boys and a girl, and that the setting might be a dance held somewhere, possibly involving a contest of some kind.

Mira la lectura
Answers will vary.

¡Vamos a leer!

Antes de leer

STRATEGY ➤ **Using titles and pictures to predict**

Look at the title of the story and the pictures to predict who the characters are and what the setting might be.

Mira la lectura

STRATEGY ➤ **Skimming**

Remember that you can get an overview of a story by skimming it. Skim the story now. Were your predictions correct?

Uno, dos, tres, ¡rumba!

Roberto es un muchacho cubano que acaba de llegar a Chicago. No sabe una palabra de inglés. Los primeros meses yo le ayudo con las clases y las tareas. También le ayudo con otras cosas. Cada viernes por la tarde, los muchachos tienen que llevar pantalones negros, camisa blanca y una corbata negra para ir a las clases de baile. Nos reunimos en el gimnasio de la escuela por una hora. El primer viernes, Roberto me dice: "Antonio, ¡no sé bailar! ¿Qué voy a hacer? ¡No voy a entender a la profesora y no puedo hablar con las muchachas!"

Le digo a Roberto que sólo tiene que observar lo que hacen los otros. Y eso es lo que hace. Cuando baila con las muchachas no puede decirles nada. Pero no importa, porque debe pensar en lo que hace.

Un día la profesora anuncia que va a regalar un disco compacto a la mejor pareja de la clase. Entonces una muchacha llamada Susan le dice: *"Come on, Roberto, we have to win!"*

"Pero ¿qué me dice?" me pregunta el pobre Roberto. Cuando le explico que la profesora va a dar

Options

Strategies for Reaching All Students

Students Needing Extra Help
Infórmate: On the chalkboard or overhead, write out the entire sentence that contains the phrase *lo que hacen los otros* (second panel) so that students can understand the context.
Aplicación: If necessary, help students with writing an ending for the story.

Multiple Intelligences
Visual/Spatial
See *¡Vamos a leer!*

Infórmate

STRATEGY> **Using cognates**

Remember that you can use what you know about cognates to figure out the meaning of new words. For example, if you think *observar* means "observe," two facts support that guess. First, if you don't know how to dance, observing

un regalo a los mejores bailarines y que Susan quiere bailar con él, Roberto está un poco nervioso. "No te preocupes," le digo. "Estás bailando muy bien."

La profesora toca una rumba—¡un baile cubano! —y Roberto empieza a bailar bien. Todos lo miran con sorpresa. ¡Roberto y Susan ganan el disco compacto! Después, Susan dice algo y yo interpreto: "Está preguntando si quieres escuchar el disco compacto con ella después de la clase." Y de esta manera Roberto y Susan se hicieron novios. Él aprendió un poco de inglés y ella un poco de español, y los dos aprendieron a bailar.

the other dancers is something you might do. Second, the phrase *lo que hacen los otros* makes sense after the word *observar*. So *observar* probably means "observe."

1 What do you think *interpreto* means? What information helps you figure it out?

2 Which word makes sense in this sentence?

> *Roberto no sabe ___ sus ideas en inglés.*

> a. imitar
> b. expresar
> c. solucionar

3 How did Roberto solve his problem in the dance class?

Aplicación

Write an ending for this story in one or two sentences. Compare your ending with that of a partner.

Infórmate

1 It means "I interpret." First, it is a cognate, and second, we know from the story that Roberto doesn't know English. His friend helps him out when Susan asks if he wants to listen to the CD with her.

2 The word that makes sense is *expresar.*

3 Roberto and Susan became boyfriend and girlfriend. He learned a little English from her and learned to dance.

Aplicación
Story endings will vary.

www **Internet Activities**

Process Writing

For information regarding developing a writing portfolio, see p. 50.

Multicultural Perspectives

People celebrate festivals throughout the Spanish-speaking world. One important festival is *las fallas* in Valencia, Spain. *Las fallas* is a carnival held from March 12–19 that honors the patron saint of the carpenter, San José. In addition to bullfights, processions, and street vendors, there is a contest that consists of each neighborhood teaming up weeks before the start of the festival to build decorative, elaborately made statues of wood, cardboard, and papier-mâché. Each team bases its statue on a different current social or political theme. At the beginning of *las fallas,* each team exhibits its statue. Judges go from neighborhood to neighborhood to evaluate and select the best one. On the last night, *las fallas* culminates in the burning of the statues, all-night dancing, a tremendous fireworks show, and orchestras playing music. Ask students: What are some popular festivals or celebrations held in your community? What kinds of *fiestas* are popular in other cultures?

Pasos vivos 1 CD-ROM
Word Processor

¡Vamos a escribir!

Una celebración en Montevideo, Uruguay ►

You have just been to a party or a prom *(un baile de graduación).* What do you want to remember about it? Write a diary entry about the party. Follow these steps.

1 First, think about the dance and answer these questions.

- ¿A qué hora empezó la fiesta?
  ¿A qué hora terminó?
- ¿Con quién fuiste?
- ¿Qué ropa llevaron?
- ¿Viste a muchos amigos en la fiesta? ¿A quiénes viste?
- ¿Qué comieron?
- ¿Qué tipo de música tocaron? ¿Bailaron?
- ¿Qué te gustó más: la música, la comida, las decoraciones?
- ¿Cómo lo pasaste?

2 Use the answers to these questions to write in your diary. You can start your entry with the words *Querido diario.*

3 Show your entry to a partner. Does he or she think you should add or change anything? Using your partner's recommendations and your own ideas, make the necessary changes and rewrite your entry.

4 Check carefully for accuracy in spelling, the use of written accents, the form and placement of adjectives, and the form of verbs. Rewrite if necessary.

5 Share your entry by

- including it in a collection of writings called *Las fiestas de este año*
- posting it on the bulletin board in your classroom
- adding it to your writing portfolio

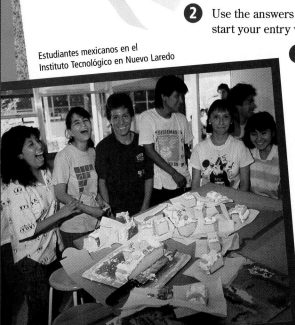

Estudiantes mexicanos en el Instituto Tecnológico en Nuevo Laredo

472   Capítulo 14

Options

Strategies for Reaching All Students

Students Needing Extra Help
Have students use their Organizers to help answer the questions.

Enrichment
Have students write about the same party from two opposite points of view. In each case, they can begin writing by telling who they are and describing their tastes or themselves in a way that would explain their viewpoint. For instance, what would a younger sibling have to say about the party? What would a snobby or envious guest say? What would a true friend say?

¡Vamos a escribir! 473

Answers: ¡Vamos a escribir!
Diary entries will vary. Encourage use of vocabulary from this chapter and previous ones.

Using Photos
(p. 472) Ask: *¿Qué hacen estos estudiantes? ¿Dónde están?*

Cultural Notes ☀

(pp. 472–473, photos)
Gatherings of friends and family members are an important part of life in Spanish-speaking countries. Close relationships provide not only companionship, but often emotional support during difficult times.

Repaso ¿Lo sabes bien?

This section will help you organize your studying for the proficiency test, where you will be asked to do similar, though not identical, tasks. There will not be any models on the test.

► Listening
Can you understand when someone talks about a party he or she is planning to give? Listen as your teacher reads a sample similar to what you will hear on the test. As a guest invited to this party, what two things should you do and why?

► Reading
Can you understand a written description of a party? Here's a written transcription from a radio announcer. What kind of party is described here? Which words or phrases tell you that?

> Todos lo están pasando bien y nadie está aburrido. La actriz Manuela lleva zapatos de tacón alto para su traje de disfraz y Kati Rojas lleva joyas y un vestido de fiesta. Está bailando con Enrique Salas, que nunca lleva corbata ni traje. ¡Me encantan las fiestas de ambiente informal!

► Culture
Can you describe how girls in Spanish-speaking countries celebrate their fifteenth birthday?

► Writing
Can you write a letter describing the arrangements you need to make for a special occasion? Here is a sample letter:

> Querida Susana:
> Me gustaría tener una fiesta para nuestra abuelita, una reunión con toda la familia. No me gusta preparar las fiestas grandes. Nunca lo hago. Pero mi mamá dice que tengo que hacerlo. Mi hermana puede ayudar con las decoraciones. (Ella está decorando su cuarto otra vez, pero suele hacerlo bien.) ¿Qué piensas? ¿Me puedes ayudar?
> Tu prima, Lina

► Speaking
Can you and your partners play the roles of teenagers introducing one another at a party? Here is a sample dialogue:

A —*Laura, ¿conoces al novio de mi hermana?*

B —*No, no lo conozco.*

A —*Pues, Laura, te presento a Jaime Fernández.*

B —*Encantada, Jaime.*

C —*Mucho gusto, Laura.*

MORE PRACTICE

• Más práctica y tarea, pp. 548–551

Una muchacha celebrando sus quince años en Novato, California

474 Capítulo 14

Resumen del vocabulario

Use the vocabulary from this chapter to help you:
- ► make plans for giving or attending a party
- ► describe gift-giving
- ► make and acknowledge introductions

to talk about parties
el ambiente
bailar
el baile
cantar
las decoraciones *(f.pl.)*
decorar
escribir
¡Feliz cumpleaños!
la fiesta
   de cumpleaños
   de disfraces
   de fin de año
   de la escuela
   de sorpresa
la hora
la invitación
el invitado, la invitada
invitar
el lugar
pasarlo bien / mal
preparar
la reunión

to introduce people
alguien
conocer: (yo) conozco
       (tú) conoces
Encantado, -a.
el novio, la novia
el pariente, la parienta
Te presento a ___.

to talk about what to wear to a party
los aretes *(m.pl.)*
el collar
la corbata
las joyas *(f.pl.)*
la pulsera
el reloj pulsera
el traje
el vestido de fiesta
los zapatos de tacón alto

to talk about gift-giving
dar: (yo) doy
    (tú) das
escoger: (yo) escojo
       (tú) escoges
recibir
regalar
el regalo
   elegante
   hecho, -a a mano
   personal
   práctico, -a

other useful terms and expressions
algunos, algunas
De ninguna manera.
Depende.
la entrada
soler (o → ue) + *inf.*

Assessment

 Prueba cumulativa

 Examen de habilidades

 Test Generator

Additional Assessment Options

 Comm. Act. BLMs
Small Group Activities
Situation Cards

 Pasos vivos 1 CD-ROM
Slide Presentation Maker, Video Presentation Maker, Word Processor, Spindle

 ¿Lo sabes bien? Video Quiz

 Internet Activities
Self-Test

Cultural Notes ☀

(p. 474, photo)
Young girl with her parents at her *quince años* celebration, Novato, California. There are many similarities between *quince años* celebrations and weddings. For both events, announcements are usually made in the society pages, formal invitations are sent, a formal dress is required, and a mass is held, followed by a banquet with a fancy cake and a band.

Verbos

INFINITIVE	PRESENT		PRETERITE	

Regular Verbs

estudiar	estudio	estudiamos	estudié	estudiamos
	estudias	estudiáis	estudiaste	estudiasteis
	estudia	estudian	estudió	estudiaron
comer	como	comemos	comí	comimos
	comes	coméis	comiste	comisteis
	come	comen	comió	comieron
vivir	vivo	vivimos	viví	vivimos
	vives	vivís	viviste	vivisteis
	vive	viven	vivió	vivieron

Stem-changing Verbs

(You will learn the verb forms that are in italic type next year.)

cerrar (e → ie)	cierro	cerramos	cerré	cerramos
	cierras	cerráis	cerraste	cerrasteis
	cierra	cierran	cerró	cerraron
costar (o → ue)	cuesta	cuestan	costó	costaron
doler (o → ue)	duele	duelen	dolió	dolieron
dormir (o → ue)	duermo	dormimos	dormí	dormimos
	duermes	dormís	dormiste	dormisteis
	duerme	duermen	*durmió*	*durmieron*
empezar (e → ie)	See *cerrar.*		*empecé*	empezamos
			empezaste	empezasteis
			empezó	empezaron
jugar (u → ue)	juego	jugamos	jugué	jugamos
	juegas	jugáis	jugaste	jugasteis
	juega	juegan	jugó	jugaron
llover (o → ue)	llueve		llovió	
nevar (e → ie)	nieva		nevó	
pedir (e → i)	pido	pedimos	*pedí*	*pedimos*
	pides	pedís	*pediste*	*pedisteis*
	pide	piden	*pidió*	*pidieron*
pensar (e → ie)	See *cerrar.*			

INFINITIVE	PRESENT		PRETERITE	
poder (o → ue)	See *Irregular Verbs.*			
preferir (e → ie)	prefiero	preferimos	*preferí*	*preferimos*
	prefieres	preferís	*preferiste*	*preferisteis*
	prefiere	prefieren	*prefirió*	*prefirieron*
probar (o → ue)	pruebo	probamos	probé	probamos
	pruebas	probáis	probaste	probasteis
	prueba	prueban	probó	probaron
querer (e → ie)	See *Irregular Verbs.*			
servir (e → i)	See *pedir.*			
soler (o → ue)	suelo	solemos		
	sueles	soléis		
	suele	suelen		

Verbs with Spelling Changes

(You will learn the verb forms that are in italic type next year.)

apagar	apago	apagamos	apagué	apagamos
	apagas	apagáis	apagaste	apagasteis
	apaga	apagan	apagó	apagaron
buscar	busco	buscamos	busqué	buscamos
	buscas	buscáis	buscaste	buscasteis
	busca	buscan	buscó	buscaron
conocer	conozco	conocemos	conocí	conocimos
	conoces	conocéis	conociste	conocisteis
	conoce	conocen	conoció	conocieron
creer	creo	creemos	creí	creímos
	crees	creéis	creíste	creísteis
	cree	creen	*creyó*	*creyeron*
empezar	See *Stem-changing Verbs.*			
escoger	escojo	escogemos	escogí	escogimos
	escoges	escogéis	escogiste	escogisteis
	escoge	escogen	escogió	escogieron
jugar	See *Stem-changing Verbs.*			

leer	See *creer.*	
llegar	See *apagar.*	
pagar	See *apagar.*	
practicar	See *buscar.*	
proteger	See *escoger.*	
reducir	See *conocer.*	
sacar	See *buscar.*	
tocar	See *buscar.*	

Irregular Verbs

(You will learn the verb forms that are in italic type next year.)

Infinitive	Present		Preterite	
dar	doy	damos	*di*	*dimos*
	das	dais	*diste*	*disteis*
	da	dan	*dio*	*dieron*
decir	digo	decimos	*dije*	*dijimos*
	dices	decís	*dijiste*	*dijisteis*
	dice	dicen	*dijo*	*dijeron*
estar	estoy	estamos	*estuve*	*estuvimos*
	estás	estáis	*estuviste*	*estuvisteis*
	está	están	*estuvo*	*estuvieron*
hacer	hago	hacemos	hice	*hicimos*
	haces	hacéis	hiciste	*hicisteis*
	hace	hacen	hizo	*hicieron*
ir	voy	vamos	fui	fuimos
	vas	vais	fuiste	fuisteis
	va	van	fue	fueron
poder	puedo	podemos	*pude*	*pudimos*
	puedes	podéis	*pudiste*	*pudisteis*
	puede	pueden	*pudo*	*pudieron*
poner	pongo	ponemos	*puse*	*pusimos*
	pones	ponéis	*pusiste*	*pusisteis*
	pone	ponen	*puso*	*pusieron*

querer	quiero	queremos	*quise*	*quisimos*
	quieres	queréis	*quisiste*	*quisisteis*
	quiere	quieren	*quiso*	*quisieron*
saber	sé	sabemos	*supe*	*supimos*
	sabes	sabéis	*supiste*	*supisteis*
	sabe	saben	*supo*	*supieron*
salir	salgo	salimos	salí	salimos
	sales	salís	saliste	salisteis
	sale	salen	salió	salieron
ser	soy	somos	*fui*	*fuimos*
	eres	sois	*fuiste*	*fuisteis*
	es	son	*fue*	*fueron*
tener	tengo	tenemos	*tuve*	*tuvimos*
	tienes	tenéis	*tuviste*	*tuvisteis*
	tiene	tienen	*tuvo*	*tuvieron*
traer	traigo	traemos	traje	trajimos
	traes	traéis	trajiste	trajisteis
	trae	traen	trajo	trajeron
ver	veo	vemos	vi	vimos
	ves	veis	viste	visteis
	ve	ven	vio	vieron

Verbos   479

VOCABULARIO ESPAÑOL-INGLÉS

The *Vocabulario español-inglés* contains all active vocabulary from the text, including vocabulary presented in the grammar sections.

A dash (—) represents the main entry word. For example, **pasar la —** after **la aspiradora** means **pasar la aspiradora.**

The number following each entry indicates the chapter in which the word or expression is presented. The letter *P* following an entry refers to *El primer paso.*

The following abbreviations are used: *adj.* (adjective), *dir. obj.* (direct object), *f.* (feminine), *fam.* (familiar), *ind. obj.* (indirect object), *inf.* (infinitive), *m.* (masculine), *pl.* (plural), *prep.* (preposition), *pron.* (pronoun), *sing.* (singular).

a at (2); to (3)
  a la, al *(a + el)* to the (3)
el **abrigo** coat (7)
abril April (P)
abrir to open (10)
el **abuelo, la abuela** grandfather, grandmother (5)
los **abuelos** grandparents (5)
aburrido, -a boring (11)
aburrir to bore (11)
el **actor, la actriz** actor, actress (11)
acuerdo: estar de — to agree (8)
adiós good-by (P)
¿adónde? (to) where? (3)
agosto August (P)
el **agua** *f.* water (4)
el **aguacate** avocado (12)
ahora now (9)
el **aire** air (13)
algo something (4)
  — más something else (12)
alguien someone, somebody (14)
alguna vez ever (12)
algunos, -as some (14)
allí there (2)

— está there it is (2)
el **almacén,** *pl.* **los almacenes** department store (6)
el **almuerzo** lunch (2)
  en el — for lunch (4)
alto, -a tall (5)
el **aluminio** aluminum (13)
amable kind, nice (1)
amarillo, -a yellow (6)
el **ambiente** atmosphere (14)
  el medio — environment (13)
la **amenaza** threat (13)
el **amigo, la amiga** friend (3)
anaranjado, -a orange *(color)* (6)
el **animal,** *pl.* **los animales** animal (13)
anoche last night (10)
los **anteojos (de sol)** (sun)glasses (7)
antiguo, -a old, traditional (8)
antipático, -a unfriendly, unpleasant (5)
el **anuncio (de televisión)** ad, commercial (11)
el **año** year (P)
  la fiesta de fin de —

New Year's Eve party (14)
  tener . . . —s to be . . . years old (P, 5)
apagar to turn off (13)
el **apartamento** apartment (8)
aprender to learn (2)
aquí here (2)
  — está here it is (2)
  por — around here (6)
el **árbol** tree (13)
el **arete** earring (14)
arreglar to clean up (8)
el **arroz** rice (4)
el **arte** art (2)
artístico, -a artistic (1)
asco: ¡qué —! yuck! that's disgusting! (4)
así, así so-so, fair (P)
la **aspiradora** vacuum cleaner (8)
  pasar la — to vacuum (8)
atractivo, -a attractive (5)
atrevido, -a bold, daring (1)
el **autobús** *pl.* **los autobuses** bus (10)
  la parada del — bus stop (10)

la **avenida** avenue (10)
**aventura: la película de
—s** adventure film (11)
¡ay! ouch! (9)
ayer yesterday (10)
ayudar to help (1)
el **azúcar** sugar (12)
azul, *pl.* **azules** blue (5, 6)

bailar to dance (14)
el **baile** dance (14)
bajo, -a short *(height)* (5)
la **ballena** whale (13)
el **banco** bank (10)
el **baño** bathroom (8)
el traje de — bathing
suit (7)
barato, -a cheap,
inexpensive (6)
básquetbol: jugar — to
play basketball (3)
bastante rather (8)
la **basura** garbage (8)
beber to drink (4, 12)
la **bebida** beverage (4)
béisbol: jugar — to play
baseball (3)
la **biblioteca** library (10)
la **bicicleta** bicycle (13)
montar en — to ride a
bike (13)
bien well (P)
el **bistec** steak (4)
blanco, -a white (6)
la **blusa** blouse (6)
la **boca** mouth (9)
el **bolígrafo** pen (P)
bonito, -a pretty (5)
la **bota** boot (7)
el **bote** rowboat (7)
pasear en — to row (7)
la **botella** bottle (13)
el **brazo** arm (9)
el **bronceador** suntan lotion (7)
bucear to skin-dive (7)

bueno (buen), -a good (P)
bueno OK, fine, all right
(10)
la **bufanda** winter scarf (7)
el **burrito** burrito (12)
buscar to look for (6)

el **caballo** horse (13)
la **cabeza** head (9)
tener dolor de — to
have a headache (9)
el **café** coffee (4)
el **calcetín,** *pl.* **los calcetines**
sock (6)
la **calculadora** calculator (2)
callado, -a quiet (1)
la **calle** street (10)
calor:
hace — it's hot (out) (7)
tener — to be hot
(person) (9)
la **cama** bed (8)
la **cámara** camera (7)
el **camarero, la camarera**
waiter, waitress (12)
la **camisa** shirt (6)
la **camiseta** T-shirt (6)
el **campo** countryside (3)
el **canal** (TV) channel (11)
canoso: pelo — gray hair
(5)
cansado, -a tired (3)
cantar to sing (14)
cariñoso, -a affectionate,
loving (5)
la **carne (de res)** beef (12)
caro, -a expensive (6)
la **carpeta** pocket folder (2)
la — de argollas three-
ring binder (2)
la **carta** letter (10)
a la — a la carte (12)
el **cartel** poster (8)
el **cartón** cardboard (13)
la **casa** house (8)

el **quehacer (de la —)**
household chore (8)
en — at home (1)
la **especialidad de la —**
house specialty (12)
casi almost (11)
castaño: pelo — brown
(chestnut) hair (5)
las **cataratas** waterfall (7)
la **catedral** cathedral (7)
catorce fourteen (P)
la **cebolla** onion (4)
la **cena** dinner (4)
el **centro** center (13)
el — comercial mall (3)
el — de reciclaje
recycling center (13)
cerca (de) near (8)
el **cereal** cereal (4)
cero zero (P)
cerrar (e → ie) to close
(10)
el **césped** lawn (8)
el **champú** shampoo (10)
la **chaqueta** jacket (6)
el **chile** chili pepper (12)
el — con carne beef
with beans (12)
el — relleno stuffed
pepper (12)
el **chocolate** hot chocolate
(12)
el **churro** churro (12)
cien one hundred (5)
la **ciencia ficción** science
fiction (11)
las **ciencias** science (2)
— de la salud health
(science) (2)
— sociales social studies
(2)
**ciento uno, -a; ciento
dos; etc.** 101, 102, etc.
(6)
cinco five (P)
cincuenta fifty (2)
el **cine** movie theater (1)

ir al — to go to the movies (1)

la **ciudad** city (7)

claro:

¡**— que sí!** of course! (3)

¡**— que no!** of course not! (3)

la **clase (de)** class (2); kind, type (11)

después de las —s after school (3)

la sala de —s classroom (P)

la **clínica** clinic (9)

el **coche** car (8)

la **cocina** kitchen (8)

cocinar to cook (1)

el **collar** necklace (14)

el **color** color (6)

¿**de qué —?** what color? (6)

en —es in color (11)

la **comedia** comedy, sitcom (11)

el **comedor** dining room (8)

comer to eat (4, 12)

los **comestibles** groceries (10)

cómico comical (11)

la **comida** meal (4), food (12)

¿**cómo?** how? (P)

¿**— eres?** what are you like? (1)

¿**— está (usted)?** how are you? *formal* (P)

¿**— estás?** how are you? *fam.* (P)

¡**— no!** certainly! (12)

¿**— se dice . . . ?** how do you say . . . ? (P)

¿**— se llama(n)?** what is his/her/their name? (5)

¿**— te llamas?** what's your name? (P)

la **cómoda** dresser (8)

cómodo, -a comfortable (8)

el **compañero, la compañera**
classmate (P)

comprar to buy (6)

¿**me compras . . . ?** can you buy me . . . ? (10)

compras: ir de — to go shopping (3)

la **comunidad** community (10)

con with (3)

el **concierto** concert (11)

conmigo with me (3)

conocer to know (14)

conservar to conserve, save *(energy)* (13)

contaminado, -a contaminated, polluted (13)

contigo with you (3)

la **corbata** tie (14)

el **correo** post office (10)

cortar to cut, to mow (8)

corto, -a short *(length)* (11)

la **cosa** thing (8)

costar (o → ue) to cost (6)

creer to think, to believe (4, 9)

creo que no I don't think so (4)

creo que sí I think so (4)

el **cuaderno** spiral notebook (2)

la **cuadra** block (10)

cuadrado, -a square (8)

el **cuadro** picture (8)

¿**cuál(es)?** what? which? which one(s)? (11)

¿**cuándo?** when (P)

cuando when (7)

¿**cuánto?** how much? (6)

¿**— (tiempo) hace que . . . ?** how long has it been since . . . ? (9)

¿**cuántos, -as?** how many? (5)

¿**— años tiene . . . ?** how old is . . . ? (5)

¿**— años tienes?** how old are you? (P)

cuarenta forty (2)

cuarto, -a quarter (2); fourth (2, 8)

y — *(time)* quarter after, quarter past (2)

el **cuarto** room (8)

cuatro four (P)

cuatrocientos four hundred (10)

la **cuchara** spoon (12)

el **cuchillo** knife (12)

el **cuello** neck (9)

la **cuenta** bill *(in restaurant)* (12)

el **cuero** leather (8)

de — (made) of leather (8)

el **cuerpo** body (9)

el **cumpleaños** birthday (P)

¡**feliz —!** happy birthday! (14)

la fiesta de — birthday party (14)

la tarjeta de — birthday card (10)

dar to give (14)

— + *movie* or *TV program* to show (11)

— miedo a to scare (11)

de from (P); of — 's, — s' (5)

de la, del *(de + el)* of the, from the (10)

— la mañana / la tarde / la noche in the morning / afternoon / evening (11)

— + *material* made of (8)

— nada you're welcome (3)

— postre for dessert (12)

¿**— veras?** really? (1)

debajo de under(neath) (12)

deber ought to, should (4)

decir to say (13)

  ¿cómo se dice . . . ? how do you say . . . ? (P)

  ¡no me digas! really?, you don't say! (3)

  ¿qué quiere — . . . ? what does . . . mean? (P)

  se dice . . . it is said . . . (P)

la **decoración** *pl.* las **decoraciones** decoration (14)

decorar to decorate (14)

el **dedo** finger (9)

  — del pie toe (9)

delante de in front of (12)

demasiado too (11)

el/la **dentista** dentist (9)

depende it depends (14)

los **deportes** sports (1)

deportista athletic (1)

deportivo: el programa — sports program (11)

depositar to deposit (10)

derecha: a la — (de) to the right (of) (10)

derecho, -a right (9)

el **desayuno** breakfast (4)

descansar to rest (7)

el **descuento: la tienda de —s** discount store (6)

desear: ¿qué desea Ud? may I help you? (6)

desordenado, -a messy (1)

después de after (3)

detective: el programa de —s detective show (11)

detrás (de) behind (10)

devolver (o → ue) to return *(something)* (10)

el **día** day (P)

  buenos —s good morning (P)

el **plato del —** daily special (12)

¿qué — es hoy? what day is it? (P)

todos los —s every day (3)

dibujar to draw (1)

el **dibujo: los —s animados** cartoons (11)

el **diccionario** dictionary (2)

dice: ¿cómo se — . . . ? how do you say . . . ? (P)

diciembre December (P)

diecinueve nineteen (P)

dieciocho eighteen (P)

dieciséis sixteen (P)

diecisiete seventeen (P)

diez ten (P)

difícil difficult, hard (2)

digas: ¡no me —! really?, you don't say! (3)

el **dinero** money (10)

disfraces: la fiesta de — costume party (14)

la **diversión: el parque de diversiones** amusement park (3)

divertido, -a amusing, funny (11)

doce twelve (P)

el **documental** documentary (11)

el **dólar** dollar (6)

doler (o → ue) to hurt, to ache (9)

dolor: tener — de . . . to have a . . . ache (9) *see also* **cabeza, estómago, garganta, muelas, oído**

domingo Sunday (P)

  el — on Sunday (3)

¿dónde? where? (3)

¿de — eres? where are you from? (P)

dormir (o → ue) to sleep (9)

el **dormitorio** bedroom (8)

dos two (P)

doscientos two hundred (10)

durar to last (11)

la **educación física** physical education (2)

educativo: el programa — educational show (11)

ejercicio: hacer — to exercise (9)

el **the** *m. sing.* (P, 2)

él he (2); him *after prep.* (3)

el **elefante** elephant (13)

elegante elegant (14)

ella she (2); her *after prep.* (3)

ellos, ellas they (2); them *after prep.* (3)

emocionante exciting, touching (11)

empezar (e → ie) to begin, to start (2)

en in, at, on (P)

  — + *vehicle* by (10)

encantado, -a delighted (14)

encantar to love (5)

  le encanta(n) he/she loves (5)

  me encanta(n) I love (4)

la **enchilada** enchilada (12)

encima (de) on, on top of (12)

la **energía** energy (13)

enero January (P)

la **enfermería** nurse's office (9)

enfermo, -a ill, sick (3)

enfrente (de) facing, opposite, in front of (10)

la **ensalada** salad (4)

enseñar to teach (2)

la **entrada** ticket (14)

entre between (10)

entrevista: el programa de —s talk show (11)
enviar to send, to mail (10)
el **equipo de sonido** stereo (8)
eres you *fam.* are (1)
es it is (P); he/she is (2)
escoger to choose (14)
escribir to write (14)
¿cómo se escribe . . . ? how do you spell . . . ? (P)
el **escritorio** desk (8)
escuchar to listen to (1)
la **escuela** school (1)
ese, -a; -os, -as that; those (6)
eso: por — that's why, therefore (11)
la **espalda** back (9)
el **español** Spanish *(language)* (2)
la **especialidad de la casa** house specialty (12)
el **espejo** mirror (8)
esquiar to ski (7)
la **esquina** corner (10)
la **estación,** *pl.* **las estaciones** season (3); station (10)
el **estadio** stadium (10)
estar to be (3)
¿cómo estás? how are you? (P)
la sala de — family room (8)
este, -a; -os, -as this; these (6)
el **estómago** stomach (9)
tener dolor de — to have a stomachache (9)
el/la **estudiante** student (P)
estudiar to study (1)
la **estufa** stove (8)
explorar to explore (7)
extinción: en peligro de — endangered (13)

la **fábrica** factory (13)
fácil easy (2)
la **falda** skirt (6)
faltar to be lacking, to be missing (12)
la **familia** family (3)
fantástico, -a fantastic (7)
la **farmacia** drugstore (10)
fascinante fascinating (11)
fascinar to fascinate (11)
favor: por — please (P)
febrero February (P)
la **fecha** date (P)
¡feliz cumpleaños! happy birthday! (14)
feo, -a ugly (5)
la **fiebre** fever (9)
tener — to have a fever (9)
la **fiesta** party (3)
el vestido de — party dress (14)
el **fin:**
el — de semana the weekend (3)
la fiesta de — de año New Year's Eve party (14)
física: la educación — physical education (2)
el **flan** flan (12)
la **flor** flower (13)
formar: — parte de to be a part of (13)
la **foto** photo (7)
sacar —s to take pictures (7)
fresco: hace — it's cool outside (7)
el **frijol** bean (12)
los —es refritos refried beans (12)
frío:
hace — it's cold outside (7)
tener — to be cold *(person)* (9)

la **fruta** fruit (4)
fui, fuiste I went, you went (7)
el **fútbol** soccer (3)
el — americano football (3)

la **ganga** bargain (6)
el **garaje** garage (8)
la **garganta** throat (9)
las pastillas para la — throat lozenges (10)
tener dolor de — to have a sore throat (9)
el **gato** cat (5)
el **gemelo,** la **gemela** twin (5)
generalmente usually, generally (3)
generoso, -a generous (1)
¡genial! great! wonderful! (3)
la **gente** people (13)
el **gimnasio** gymnasium (3)
el **gorila** gorilla (13)
el **gorro** ski cap (7)
la **grabadora** tape recorder (2)
gracias thank you (P)
gracioso, -a funny (1)
grande big (5)
la **gripe** flu (9)
tener — to have the flu (9)
gris *pl.* **grises** gray (5, 6)
el **guacamole** avocado dip (12)
el **guante** glove (7)
guapo, -a handsome, good-looking (5)
el **guardarropa** closet (8)
la **guía telefónica** phone book (13)
el **guisante** pea (4)
la **guitarra** guitar (1)
gustar to like (1)
le gusta(n) he/she

likes (5)

me, te gusta I like, you like (1)

me gusta más I prefer (1)

(A mí) me gustaría I'd like … (3)

¿(A ti) te gustaría? would you like …? (3)

hablar to talk (1)

— **por teléfono** to talk on the phone (1)

hablando talking (14)

hacer to do, to make (8)

hace + *(time)* … ago (6)

hace + *(time)* **+ que** it's been *(time)* since (9)

— **ejercicio** to exercise (9)

se hace(n) con … it's (they're) made with … (12)

hice/hiciste/hizo did/made (10, 13) *see also* **calor, fresco, frío, sol, tiempo, viento**

hambre: tener — to be hungry (4)

la **hamburguesa** hamburger (4)

la **harina** flour (12)

la tortilla de — flour tortilla (12)

hasta until (11)

— **luego** see you later (P)

hay there is, there are (P)

¿cuántos(as) … —? how many … are there? (P)

— **que** it's necessary to (13)

hecho, -a made (14)

— **a mano** handmade (14)

el **hecho** fact (11)

el **helado: el té —** iced tea (4)

el **helado** ice cream (12)

el **hermano, la hermana** brother, sister (5)

los **hermanos** brothers; brother(s) and sister(s) (5)

el **hijo, la hija** son, daughter (5)

los **hijos** sons; sons and daughters (5)

la **hoja de papel** sheet of paper (P)

¡hola! hi!, hello! (P)

el **hombre** man (5)

la **hora** period (2); time (2, 14)

¿a qué —? at what time? (2)

¿qué — es? what time is it? (2)

el **horario** schedule (2)

horrible horrible (4)

el **hospital** hospital (9)

el **hotel** hotel (10)

hoy today (P)

— **no** not today (3)

el **huevo** egg (4)

la **iglesia** church (10)

igualmente likewise (P)

impaciente impatient (1)

el **impermeable** raincoat (7)

incómodo, -a uncomfortable (8)

el **inglés** English *(language)* (2)

el **ingrediente** ingredient (12)

inteligente intelligent (5)

el **interés: el lugar de —** place of interest (7)

interesante interesting (11)

interesar to interest (11)

el **invierno** winter (3)

la **invitación** *pl.* **las**

invitaciones invitation (14)

el **invitado, la invitada** guest (14)

invitar to invite (14)

ir to go (3)

— **a +** *inf.* to be going to + *verb* (3)

— **a la escuela** to go to school (1)

— **a pasear** to take a walk (10)

— **de compras** to go shopping (3)

— **de pesca** to go fishing (3)

izquierda: a la — (de) to the left of (10)

izquierdo, -a left (9)

el **jabón** soap (10)

el **jaguar** jaguar (13)

el **jamón** ham (4)

los **jeans** jeans (6)

joven *adj.* young (5)

el **joven** young man, sir (6)

la **joven** young lady (6)

los **jóvenes** young people (6)

las **joyas** jewelry (14)

las **judías verdes** green beans (4)

jueves Thursday (P)

el — on Thursday (3)

jugar (u → ue) to play (3)

el **jugo** juice (4)

— **de naranja** orange juice (4)

julio July (P)

junio June (P)

la **the** *f. sing.* (P, 2); her, it, you *dir. obj. pron.* (6)

lado: al — de next to,

beside (10)

el lago lake (7)

la lámpara lamp (8)

el lápiz, *pl.* **los lápices** pencil (2)

largo, -a long (11)

las the *f. pl.* (2); them, you *dir. obj. pron.* (6)

lástima: ¡qué —! that's too bad! what a shame! (3)

lastimar to hurt (9)

la lata can (13)

el lavadero laundry room (8)

lavar to wash (8)

le (to) him, her, it, you *ind. obj. pron.* (9)

la leche milk (4)

la lechuga lettuce (4)

leer to read (1)

lejos (de) far (from) (8)

les (to) them *ind. obj.* (11)

la librería bookstore (10)

el libro book (P)

la limonada lemonade (4)

limpiar to clean (8)

limpio, -a clean (8)

llamar to call (9)

¿cómo se llama(n)? what is his /her /their name? (5)

¿cómo te llamas? what's your name? (P)

me llamo my name is (P)

se llama(n) his / her /their name is (5)

llegar to arrive (10)

llevar to wear (6); to take, to carry along (7)

llover: llueve it rains, it's raining (7)

la lluvia rain (7)

lo him, it, you *dir. obj. pron.* (6)

— siento I'm sorry (2)

el lobo wolf (13)

los the *m. pl.* (P, 4); them *dir. obj. pron.* (6)

— + *day of week* on + *day of week* (3)

luego then, afterward, later (10)

el lugar place (14)

— de interés place of interest (7)

lunes Monday (P)

el — on Monday (3)

la luz, *pl.* **las luces** light (13)

la madera wood (13)

de — (made of) wood (8)

la madre mother (5)

el maíz corn (12)

mal:

menos — que . . . it's a good thing that . . . (7)

me siento — I feel ill (9)

la maleta suitcase (7)

malo, -a bad (4)

manera: de ninguna — not at all (14)

la mano *f.* hand (9)

hecho, -a a — handmade (14)

el mantel tablecloth (12)

la mantequilla butter (12)

la manzana apple (4)

mañana tomorrow (P, 3)

la mañana morning (3)

por la — in the morning (3)

el mar sea (7)

el marcador marker (2)

marrón, *pl.* **marrones** brown (5, 6)

martes Tuesday (P)

el — on Tuesday (3)

marzo March (P)

más else (8, 12) more, *adj.* + -er (11)

el / la / los / las — + *adj.* the most + *adj.,* the + *adj.* + -est (11)

— o menos more or less (4)

— tarde later (11)

— temprano earlier (11)

las matemáticas mathematics (2)

mayo May (P)

mayor older (5)

el — peligro greatest danger (13)

me me *obj. pron.* (9)

media:

— hora *f.* half an hour (11)

una hora y — an hour and a half (11)

y — half-past (2)

la medianoche midnight (11)

el médico, la médica doctor (9)

el medio ambiente environment (13)

el mediodía noon (11)

mejor better (9)

el / la (los / las) —(es) the best (11)

menor *pl.,* **menores** younger (5)

menos less (4, 11)

el / la / los / las — + *adj.* the least + *adj.* (11)

más o — more or less (4)

— mal que . . . it's a good thing that . . . (7)

el menú menu (12)

menudo: a — often (12)

la merienda afternoon snack (12)

de — for a snack (12)

el mes month (P)

la mesa table (P)

metal: de — (made of) metal (8)

el metro subway (10)

mi, mis my (3)

mí me *after prep.* (12)

miércoles Wednesday (P)
  el — on Wednesday (3)
mil one thousand (10)
el minuto minute (11)
mismo: lo — the same thing (12)
la mochila backpack (2)
moderno, -a modern (8)
la montaña mountain (7)
montar en bicicleta to ride a bike (13)
el monumento monument (10)
morado, -a purple (6)
el muchacho, la muchacha boy, girl (5)
mucho, -a a lot of, much (2)
  muchas veces many times (12)
  — gusto pleased / nice to meet you (P)
los muebles furniture (8)
las muelas: tener dolor de — to have a toothache (9)
la mujer woman (5)
el museo museum (7)
la música music (2)
musical musical (11)
  el programa — music program (11)
muy very (1)

nada nothing (9)
  de — you're welcome (3)
  no me duele — nothing hurts (9)
  no me gusta — . . . I don't like . . . at all (1)
nadar to swim (1)
nadie nobody (5)
la naranja orange (4)
la nariz nose (9)
necesitar to need (2)

negro, -a black (5, 6)
  en blanco y — in black and white (11)
nevar: nieva it snows, it's snowing (7)
ni . . . ni neither . . . nor, not . . . or (1)
la nieve snow (7)
ninguna parte nowhere, not anywhere (7)
no no, not (P)
  creo que — I don't think so (4)
  ¿no? don't you?, aren't I . . . ? (9)
la noche evening (P)
  buenas — s good evening, good night (P)
  de la — at night (11)
  por la — in the evening (3)
el nombre name (5)
nos us *obj. pron.* (11)
nosotros, -as we (2); us *after prep.* (3)
las noticias news (11)
novecientos nine hundred (10)
noventa ninety (5)
noviembre November (P)
el novio, la novia boyfriend, girlfriend (14)
nuestro, -a our (8)
nueve nine (P)
nuevo, -a new (6)
el número number (P)
nunca never (4)

o or (P)
el océano ocean (13)
ochenta eighty (5)
ocho eight (P)
ochocientos eight hundred (10)

octavo, -a eighth (2)
octubre October (P)
ocupado, -a busy (3)
el oeste: la película del — western (11)
el oído ear (9)
  tener dolor de — to have an earache (9)
el ojo eye (9)
once eleven (P)
ordenado, -a neat, tidy (1)
el oso bear (13)
el otoño fall, autumn (3)
otro, -a another, other (6)

paciente patient *adj.* (1)
el padre father (5)
los padres parents (5)
pagar to pay (6)
el país country (7)
el pájaro bird (13)
el pan bread (4)
  el — tostado toast (4)
los pantalones pants (6)
las pantimedias pantyhose (6)
la papa potato (4)
  la — al horno baked potato (4)
  la — frita French fry (4)
el papel paper (P)
  la hoja de — sheet of paper (P)
para for (2)
  — + *inf.* to, in order to (7)
la parada del autobús bus stop (10)
el paraguas umbrella (7)
el pariente, la parienta relative (14)
el parque park (3)
  el — de diversiones amusement park (3)
el partido game, match (10)
pasado, -a last, past (7)

el **pasaporte** passport (7)
pasar to pass (12)
  — la aspiradora to vacuum (8)
  —lo bien (mal) to have a good (bad) time (14)
  ¿qué pasa? what's the matter? (9)
el **pasatiempo** pastime, hobby (3)
pasear:
  ir a — to take a walk (10)
  — en bote to row (7)
la **pasta dentífrica** toothpaste (10)
el **pastel** cake, pastry (12)
la **pastilla** tablet, lozenge (10)
patinar to skate (1)
pedir (e → i) to order, to ask for (12)
la **película** film, movie (11)
el **peligro** danger (13)
  en — de extinción endangered (13)
pelirrojo, -a red-haired (5)
el **pelo** hair (5)
pensar (e → ie) to think (11)
  — + inf. to plan (7)
peor worse (9)
  el / la (los / las) —(es) the worst (11)
pequeño, -a small, little (5)
perdón excuse me (6)
perezoso, -a lazy (1)
el **periódico** newspaper (13)
pero but (1)
el **perro** dog (5)
la **persona** person (5)
personal personal (14)
pesca: ir de — to go fishing (3)
el **pescado** fish (4)
picante spicy, peppery, hot *(flavor)* (12)
  no — mild *(flavor)* (12)
el **pie** foot (9)

a — walking, on foot (10)
  el dedo del — toe (9)
la **piel** fur (13)
la **pierna** leg (9)
la **pimienta** pepper (12)
la **pirámide** pyramid (7)
la **piscina** pool (3)
el **piso** story, floor (8)
la **pizarra** chalkboard (P)
la **planta** plant (13)
el **plástico** plastic (13)
  de — (made of) plastic (13)
el **plátano** banana (4)
el **platillo** saucer (12)
el **plato** dish, plate (12)
  el — del día daily special (12)
  los —s principales main dishes (12)
la **playa** beach (3)
la **plaza** town square (10)
poco: un — (de) a little (11)
poder (o → ue) can, to be able to (3, 7)
la **policía** police (10)
el **pollo** chicken (4)
poner to put, to place, to set (8)
  — la mesa to set the table (8)
por for (6)
  — aquí around here (6)
  — eso that's why, therefore (11)
  — favor please (P)
  — la mañana / la tarde / la noche in the morning / afternoon / evening (3)
  ¿— qué? why? (4)
  — supuesto of course (13)
porque because (4)
el **postre** dessert (12)
  de — for dessert (12)

practicar to practice (1)
práctico, -a practical (14)
preferir (e → ie) to prefer (4, 8)
preparar to prepare (14)
presentar to introduce (14)
  te presento a . . . I'd like you to meet . . . (14)
la **primavera** spring (3)
primero (primer), -a first (P, 2, 8)
el **primo, la prima** cousin (5)
probar (o → ue) to try, to taste (12)
el **profesor, la profesora** teacher (P)
el **programa** program, show (11)
el **pronóstico del tiempo** weather forecast (11)
proteger to protect (13)
prudente cautious (1)
puedo, puedes *see* **poder**
la **puerta** door (8)
pues well *(to indicate pause)* (1)
la **pulsera** bracelet (14)
  el reloj — wristwatch (14)
punto: en — sharp, on the dot (11)
puntualmente on time (11)
el **pupitre** student desk (P)
puro, -a pure, clean (13)

que that, who (5)
qué what (2)
  ¡— + adj.! how + *adj.!* (6)
  ¿— tal? how's it going? (P)
quedar to fit (6); to be located (10)
  me queda(n) bien it fits (they fit) me well (6)
  —se (en la cama) to stay (in bed) (9)

el **quehacer (de la casa)**
household chore (8)

querer (e → ie) to
want (3, 7)

¿qué quiere decir ...?
what does ... mean? (P)

(yo) quisiera I'd like (7)

la **quesadilla** quesadilla (12)

el **queso** cheese (4)

¿quién(es)? who? whom?
(2, 5)

quince fifteen (P)

quinientos five hundred
(10)

quinto, -a fifth (2)

quisiera see **querer**

quitar la mesa to clear the
table (8)

razón: (no) tener — to be
right (wrong) (8)

real real (11)

realista realistic (11)

recibir to receive (14)

el **reciclaje: el centro de —**
recycling center (13)

reciclar to recycle (13)

recoger to pick up (13)

el **recuerdo** souvenir (7)

redondo, -a round (8)

reducir to reduce (13)

el **refresco** soft drink (4)

el **refrigerador** refrigerator
(8)

regalar to give (a gift) (14)

el **regalo** gift (10)

la tienda de —s gift
shop (10)

la **regla** ruler (2)

regresar to come back, to
return (7)

regular so-so, fair (P)

el **reloj pulsera** wristwatch
(14)

el **resfriado** cold (9)

el **restaurante** restaurant (10)

la **reunión,** *pl.* **las reuniones**
get-together (14)

la **revista** magazine (13)

rojo, -a red (6)

romántico, -a romantic
(11)

la **ropa** clothes (6)

rosado, -a pink (6)

rubio, -a blonde (5)

las **ruinas** ruins (7)

sábado Saturday (P)

el — on Saturday (3)

saber to know (13)

(yo) no lo sabía I didn't
know that (10)

sabroso, -a delicious, tasty
(4)

sacar to take out (8)

— dinero to withdraw
money (10)

— fotos to take pictures
(7)

— un libro to check out
a book (10)

sacudir to dust (8)

la **sal** salt (12)

la **sala** living room (8)

la — de clases
classroom (P)

la — de estar family
room (8)

salir to leave (7)

la **salsa** sauce (12)

la **salud** health (4)

el **sandwich** sandwich (4)

sed: tener — to be thirsty
(4)

seguida: en — right away
(12)

segundo, -a second (2, 8)

seis six (P)

seiscientos six hundred
(10)

el **sello** stamp (10)

la **selva** forest (7)

la — tropical rain
forest (7)

la **semana** week (P)

el fin de — on the
weekend (3)

el **semestre** semester (2)

sentir:

¿cómo te sientes? how
do you feel? (9)

lo siento I'm sorry (2)

me siento bien / mal I
feel well / ill (9)

señor Mr. (P); sir (6)

señora Mrs. (P); ma'am (6)

señorita Miss (P); miss (6)

separar to separate, to sort
(13)

septiembre September (P)

séptimo, -a seventh (2)

ser to be (5)

serio, -a serious (1)

la **serpiente** snake (13)

el **servicio: la estación de
—** gas station (10)

la **servilleta** napkin (12)

servir (e → i) to serve (12)

sesenta sixty (5)

setecientos seven hundred
(10)

setenta seventy (5)

sexto, -a sixth (2)

si if, whether (10)

sí yes (P); do *(emphatic)*
(1)

siempre always (4)

siento, sientes see **sentir**

siete seven (P)

la **silla** chair (8)

el **sillón,** *pl.* **los sillones**
armchair (8)

simpático, -a nice, friendly
(5)

sobre about (11); on (12)

sociable outgoing (1)

el **sofá** *m.* sofa (8)

el **sol** sun (7)
  los **anteojos de —** sunglasses (7)
  hace — it's sunny (7)
  tomar el — to sunbathe (7)
soler (o → ue) + *inf.* to be in the habit of (14)
solo, -a alone (3)
sólo only (5)
son (they) are (4)
  — las it is … *(in telling time)* (2)
sonido: el equipo de — stereo (8)
la **sopa** soup (4)
la **sorpresa: la fiesta de —** surprise party (14)
el **sótano** basement (8)
soy I am (1)
su, sus his, her (5); your *formal,* their (8)
subir to climb (7)
sucio, -a dirty (8)
la **sudadera** sweatshirt (6)
sueño: tener — to be sleepy (9)
el **suéter** sweater (6)
el **supermercado** supermarket (10)
supuesto: por — of course (13)

tacaño, -a stingy (1)
el **taco** taco (12)
tal: ¿qué —? how's it going? (P)
también also, too (1)
  a mí — me too (1)
tampoco either, neither (1)
tarde late (10)
la **tarde** afternoon (P)
  buenas —s good afternoon, good evening (P)

por la — in the afternoon (3)
la **tarea** homework (2)
la **tarjeta** card (10)
  la — postal post card (10)
el **taxi** taxi (10)
la **taza** cup (12)
el **tazón,** *pl.* **los tazones** bowl (12)
te you *fam. obj. pron.* (9)
el **té** tea (4)
  el — helado iced tea (4)
el **teatro** theater (10)
el **teléfono** telephone (1)
  hablar por — to talk on the telephone (1)
  el número de — phone number (P)
la **telenovela** soap opera (11)
la **tele(visión)** television (1)
  ver la — to watch television (1)
el **templo** temple (10)
temprano early (10)
el **tenedor** fork (12)
tener to have (2, 5)
  ¿qué tienes? what's wrong? (9)
  — que + *inf.* to have to (8)
  see also **año, calor, dolor, fiebre, frío, gripe, hambre, razón, sed, sueño**
el **tenis** tennis (3)
los **tenis** sneakers (6)
tercer, tercera third (8)
terminar to end (2)
terrible terrible (9)
terror: la película de — horror film (11)
ti you *fam. after prep.* (12)
el **tiempo** weather (7); time (11)
  hace buen, mal — the weather is nice, bad (7)
  el pronóstico del — weather forecast (11)
  ¿qué — hace? what's the weather like? (7)
la **tienda** store (6)
  la — de ropa clothing store (6)
la **Tierra** Earth (13)
el **tigre** tiger (13)
el **tío, la tía** uncle, aunt (5)
  los tíos uncles; aunts and uncles (5)
típico, -a typical (12)
tocar to play (1)
todavía still (9)
  — no not yet (11)
todos, -as all; everyone (5)
  — los días every day (3)
tomar to take (9)
  — el sol to sunbathe (7)
el **tomate** tomato (4)
tonto, -a silly, dumb (11)
la **tortilla (de harina, de maíz)** (flour, corn) tortilla (12)
tostado: el pan — toast (4)
trabajador, -a hard-working (1)
trabajar to work (10)
traer to bring (12)
el **traje** suit (14)
  el — de baño bathing suit (7)
el **transporte público** public transportation (13)
trece thirteen (P)
treinta thirty (P, 2)
el **tren** train (10)
  la estación del — train station (10)
tres three (P)
trescientos three hundred (10)
triste sad (11)
tu, tus your *fam.* (2, 3)
tú you *fam.* (2)

un, una a, an, one (P, 2)
  es la una it's one o'clock (2)
único, -a only (5)
uno one (P)
unos, -as a few, some (4)
usar to use (13)
usted (Ud.) you *formal sing.* (2)
ustedes (Uds.) you *formal pl.* (2)
la **uva** grape (4)

la **vaca** cow (13)
las **vacaciones** vacation (7)
  ir de — to go on vacation (7)
  valer: (no) vale la pena it's (not) worthwhile (13)
el **vaso** glass (12)
  ¡vaya! my goodness! gee! wow! (7)
veinte twenty (P)
veintiuno (veintiún) twenty-one (P)
vender to sell (12)
la **ventana** window (8)
ver to see, to watch (1)
  a — let's see (2)

el **verano** summer (3)
veras: ¿de — ? really? (1)
¿verdad? isn't that so?, right? (4)
verde green (5, 6)
las **verduras** vegetables (4)
  sopa de — vegetable soup (4)
el **vestido** dress (6)
  el — de fiesta party dress (14)
vez, *pl.* **veces:**
  a la — at the same time (13)
  a veces at times, sometimes (1)
  alguna — ever (12)
  dos veces two times (twice) (12)
  muchas veces many times (12)
  una — one time (once) (12)
vi, viste *see* ver
la **vida** life
  el programa de hechos de la — real fact-based program (11)
la **videocasetera** VCR (8)

el **videojuego** video game (3)
el **vidrio** glass *(material)* (13)
  de — (made of) glass (13)
viejo, -a old (5)
el **viento** wind (7)
  hace — it's windy (7)
viernes Friday (P)
  el — on Friday (3)
visitar to visit (7)
vivir to live (8)
el **vóleibol** volleyball (3)
vosotros, -as you *pl.* (2)

y and (1)
ya already (10)
  — no no longer, not anymore (9)
yo I (2)

la **zanahoria** carrot (4)
la **zapatería** shoe store (6)
el **zapato** shoe (6)
  los —s de tacón alto high-heeled shoes (14)
el **zoológico** zoo (10)

ENGLISH-SPANISH VOCABULARY

The *English-Spanish Vocabulary* contains all active vocabulary from the text, including vocabulary presented in the grammar sections.

A dash (—) represents the main entry word. For example, — **party** following **birthday** means **birthday party.**

The number following each entry indicates the chapter in which the word or expression is presented. The letter *P* following an entry refers to *El primer paso.*

The following abbreviations are used: *adj.* (adjective), *dir. obj.* (direct object), *f.* (feminine), *fam.* (familiar), *ind. obj.* (indirect object), *inf.* (infinitive), *m.* (masculine), *pl.* (plural), *prep.* (preposition), *pron.* (pronoun), *sing.* (singular).

a, an un, una (2)
able: to be — poder (o → ue) (3, 7)
about sobre (11)
ache el dolor (9)
actor, actress el actor, la actriz (11)
ad el anuncio (de televisión) (11)
adventure film la película de aventuras (11)
affectionate cariñoso, -a (5)
after después (de) (3)
  — school después de las clases (3)
afternoon la tarde (P)
  — snack la merienda (12)
  good — buenas tardes (P)
  in the — por la tarde (3)
ago hace + *(time)* ... (6)
to **agree** estar de acuerdo (8)
air el aire (13)
all todo, -a (5)
  — right bueno (10)
almost casi (11)
alone solo, -a (3)
already ya (10)
also también (1)
aluminum el aluminio (13)
always siempre (4)

amusement park el parque de diversiones (3)
amusing divertido, -a (11)
and y (1)
animal el animal, *pl.* los animales (13)
another otro, -a (6)
anywhere: not — ninguna parte (7)
apartment el apartamento (8)
apple la manzana (4)
April abril (P)
arm el brazo (9)
armchair el sillón, *pl.* los sillones (8)
around here por aquí (6)
to **arrive** llegar (10)
art el arte (2)
artistic artístico, -a (1)
to **ask for** pedir (e → i) (12)
at en (P); a (2)
athletic deportista (1)
atmosphere el ambiente (14)
attractive atractivo, -a (5)
August agosto (P)
aunt la tía (5)
  —s and uncles los tíos (5)
autumn el otoño (3)
avenue la avenida (10)

avocado el aguacate (12)
  — dip el guacamole (12)

back la espalda (9)
backpack la mochila (2)
bad malo, -a (4)
  that's too —! ¡Qué lástima! (3)
banana el plátano (4)
bank el banco (10)
bargain la ganga (6)
baseball el béisbol (3)
basement el sótano (8)
basketball el básquetbol (3)
bathing suit el traje de baño (7)
bathroom el baño (8)
to **be** estar (3); ser (5)
  — from ser de (P)
  to — able to poder (o → ue) (7)
beach la playa (3)
beans los frijoles (12)
  green — las judías verdes (4)
  refried — los frijoles refritos (12)
bear el oso (13)
because porque (4)
bed la cama (8)
bedroom el dormitorio (8)

beef la carne (de res) (12)

to **begin** empezar (e → ie) (2)

behind detrás (de) (10)

to **believe** creer (4)

beside al lado (de) (10)

best el / la mejor (11)

better mejor (9)

between entre (10)

beverage la bebida (4)

bicycle la bicicleta (13)

    to ride a — montar en bicicleta (13)

big grande (5)

bill (*in restaurant*) la cuenta (12)

binder (3-ring) la carpeta de argollas (2)

bird el pájaro (13)

birthday el cumpleaños (P)

    — card la tarjeta de cumpleaños (10)

    — party la fiesta de cumpleaños (14)

    happy —! ¡feliz cumpleaños! (14)

black negro, -a (6)

    in — and white en blanco y negro (11)

block la cuadra (10)

    how many —s (from . . .)? ¿a cuántas cuadras (de . . .)? (10)

blond rubio, -a (5)

blouse la blusa (6)

blue azul, *pl.* azules (5, 6)

body el cuerpo (9)

bold atrevido, -a (1)

book el libro (P)

bookstore la librería (10)

boot la bota (7)

to **bore** aburrir (11)

boring aburrido, -a (11)

bottle la botella (13)

bowl el tazón, *pl.* los tazones (12)

boy el muchacho (5)

boyfriend el novio (14)

bracelet la pulsera (14)

bread el pan (4)

breakfast el desayuno (4)

    for — en el desayuno (4)

to **bring** traer (12)

brother el hermano (5)

    —(s) and sister(s) los hermanos (5)

brown marrón, *pl.* marrones (5, 6); *(hair)* castaño (5)

burrito el burrito (12)

bus el autobús, *pl.* los autobuses (10)

    — stop la parada del autobús (10)

busy ocupado, -a (3)

but pero (1)

butter la mantequilla (12)

to **buy** comprar (6)

by por (6)

    — + *vehicle* en + *vehicle* (10)

cake el pastel (12)

calculator la calculadora (2)

to **call** llamar (9)

camera la cámara (7)

can poder (o → ue) (3, 7); la lata (13)

cap el gorro (7)

car el coche (8)

card la tarjeta (10)

cardboard el cartón (13)

carrot la zanahoria (4)

carte: a la — a la carta (12)

cartoons los dibujos animados (11)

cat el gato (5)

cathedral la catedral (7)

cautious prudente (1)

center:

    recycling — el centro de reciclaje (13)

    shopping — el centro comercial (3)

cereal el cereal (4)

chair la silla (8)

chalkboard la pizarra (P)

channel el canal (11)

cheap barato, -a (6)

to **check out a book** sacar un libro (10)

cheese el queso (4)

chestnut(-colored) castaño, -a (5)

chicken el pollo (4)

    — soup la sopa de pollo (4)

chili pepper el chile (12)

chocolate: hot — el chocolate (12)

to **choose** escoger (14)

chore: household — el quehacer (de la casa) (8)

church la iglesia (10)

churro el churro (12)

city la ciudad (7)

class la clase (de) (2, 11)

classmate el compañero, la compañera (P)

classroom la sala de clases (P)

clean limpio, -a (8); puro, -a (13)

to **clean** limpiar (8)

    — up arreglar (8)

to **clear the table** quitar la mesa (8)

to **climb** subir (7)

clinic la clínica (9)

to **close** cerrar (e → ie) (10)

closet el guardarropa (8)

clothes la ropa (6)

coat el abrigo (7)

coffee el café (4)

cold frío, -a (7)

    it's — out hace frío (7)

    to be (very) — tener (mucho) frío (9)

    to have a — tener (un) resfriado (9)

color el color (6)

  in — en colores (11)

  what —? ¿de qué color? (6)

comedy la comedia (11)

comfortable cómodo (8)

comical cómico -a (11)

commercial el anuncio (de televisión) (11)

community la comunidad (10)

concert el concierto (11)

to **conserve** *(energy)* conservar (13)

contaminated contaminado, -a (13)

to **cook** cocinar (1)

cool: it's — out hace fresco (7)

corn el maíz (12)

  — tortilla la tortilla de maíz (12)

corner la esquina (10)

to **cost** costar (o → ue) (6)

costume party la fiesta de disfraces (14)

country el país (7)

countryside el campo (3)

course: of — ¡Claro que sí! (3); por supuesto (13)

  of — not ¡Claro que no!

cousin el primo, la prima (5)

cow la vaca (13)

cup la taza (12)

to **cut** cortar (8)

daily special el plato del día (12)

dance el baile (14)

to **dance** bailar (14)

danger el peligro (13)

daring atrevido, -a (1)

date la fecha (P, 14)

  what's today's —? ¿cuál es la fecha de hoy? (P)

daughter la hija (5)

day el día (P)

  every — todos los días (3)

December diciembre (P)

to **decorate** decorar (14)

decoration la decoración *pl.* las decoraciones (14)

delicious sabroso, -a (4)

delighted encantado, -a (14)

dentist el / la dentista (9)

department store el almacén, *pl.* los almacenes (6)

to **depend** depender (14)

to **deposit** depositar (10)

desk el escritorio (8); el pupitre *(student)* (P)

dessert el postre (12)

  for — de postre (12)

detective show el programa de detectives (11)

dictionary el diccionario (2)

difficult difícil (2)

dining room el comedor (8)

dinner la cena (4)

  for — en la cena (4)

dirty sucio, -a (8)

to **disagree** no estar de acuerdo (8)

disgusting: that's —! ¡qué asco! (4)

dish el plato (12)

  main — el plato principal (12)

to **do** hacer (8)

doctor el médico, la médica (9)

documentary el documental (11)

dog el perro (5)

dollar el dólar (6)

door la puerta (8)

dot: on the — en punto (11)

to **draw** dibujar (1)

dress el vestido (6)

  party — el vestido de fiesta (14)

dresser la cómoda (8)

to **drink** beber (4, 12)

drugstore la farmacia (10)

dumb tonto, -a (11)

to **dust** sacudir (8)

ear el oído (9)

  —ache el dolor de oído (9)

early temprano (10)

earring el arete (14)

Earth la Tierra (13)

easy fácil (2)

to **eat** comer (4, 12)

educational show el programa educativo (11)

egg el huevo (4)

eight ocho (P)

eighteen dieciocho (P)

eight hundred ochocientos (10)

eighth octavo, -a (2, 8)

eighty ochenta (5)

either tampoco (1)

elegant elegante (14)

elephant el elefante (13)

eleven once (P)

else más (8)

  anything — algo más (12)

enchilada la enchilada (12)

to **end** terminar (2)

endangered en peligro de extinción (13)

energy la energía (13)

English *(language)* el inglés (2)

environment el medio ambiente (13)

evening la noche (P)

  good — buenas noches, buenas tardes (P)

  in the — por la noche, por la tarde (3)

ever alguna vez (12)

every day todos los días (3)

everyone todos, -as (5)

exciting emocionante (11)

494   English-Spanish Vocabulary

excuse me perdón (6)

to **exercise** hacer ejercicio (9)

expensive caro, -a (6)

to **explore** explorar (7)

eye el ojo (9)

facing enfrente (de) (10)

fact el hecho (11)

— **-based program** el programa de hechos de la vida real (11)

factory la fábrica (13)

fair regular, así, así (P)

fall el otoño (3)

family la familia (3)

— **room** la sala de estar (8)

fantastic fantástico, -a (7)

far (from) lejos (de) (8)

to **fascinate** fascinar (11)

fascinating fascinante (11)

father el padre (5)

February febrero (P)

to **feel** sentir

how do you —? ¿cómo te sientes? (9)

I — well / ill me siento bien / mal (9)

fever la fiebre (9)

to have a — tener fiebre (9)

few: a — unos, unas (4)

fifteen quince (P)

fifth quinto, -a (2, 8)

fifty cincuenta (2)

film la película (11)

finger el dedo (9)

first primero (primer), -a (P, 2, 8)

fish el pescado (4)

to go —ing ir de pesca (3)

to **fit** quedar (6)

five cinco (P)

five hundred quinientos (10)

flan el flan (12)

floor el piso (8)

flour la harina (12)

— **tortilla** la tortilla de harina (12)

flower la flor (13)

flu la gripe (9)

to have the — tener gripe (9)

folder la carpeta (2)

food comida (12)

foot el pie (9)

on — a pie (10)

football el fútbol americano (3)

for para (2); por (6)

forest la selva (7)

rain — la selva tropical (7)

fork el tenedor (12)

forty cuarenta (2)

four cuatro (P)

four hundred cuatrocientos (10)

fourteen catorce (P)

fourth cuarto, -a (2)

French fries las papas fritas (4)

Friday viernes (P)

on — el viernes (3)

friend el amigo, la amiga (3)

friendly simpático, -a (5)

front: in — of enfrente de (10); delante de (12)

fruit la fruta (4)

funny gracioso, -a (1); divertido, -a (11)

fur la piel (13)

furniture los muebles (8)

game el partido (10)

garage el garaje (8)

garbage la basura (8)

gas station la estación de servicio (10)

gee! ¡vaya! (7)

generally generalmente (3)

generous generoso, -a (1)

get-together la reunión (14)

gift el regalo (10)

— **shop** la tienda de regalos (10)

girl la muchacha (5)

girlfriend la novia (14)

to **give** dar (14)

to — a gift regalar (14)

glass el vaso (12); *(material)* el vidrio (13)

(made of) — de vidrio (13)

glasses los anteojos (7)

glove el guante (7)

to **go** ir (3)

— **on!** ¡vaya! (7)

to be —ing to + *verb* ir a + *inf.* (3)

to — fishing ir de pesca (3)

to — on vacation ir de vacaciones (7)

to — shopping ir de compras (3)

to — to school ir a la escuela (1)

good bueno (buen), -a (P)

— **afternoon** buenas tardes (P)

— **evening** buenas noches (P)

— **morning** buenos días (P)

— **night** buenas noches (P)

it's a — thing that . . . menos mal que . . . (7)

good-by adiós (P)

good-looking guapo, -a (5)

goodness: my —! ¡vaya! (7)

gorilla el gorila (13)

grandfather el abuelo (5)

grandmother la abuela (5)

grandparents los abuelos (5)
grape la uva (4)
gray gris, *pl.* grises (5, 6)
— **hair** pelo canoso (5)
great! ¡genial! (3)
green verde (5, 6)
— **beans** las judías verdes (4)
groceries los comestibles (10)
guest el invitado, la invitada (14)
guitar la guitarra (1)
gymnasium el gimnasio (3)

habit: to be in the — of soler (o → ue) + *inf.* (14)
hair el pelo (5)
half:
— **an hour** media hora (11)
— **-past** y media (2)
ham el jamón (4)
hamburger la hamburguesa (4)
hand la mano (9)
— **made** hecho, -a a mano (14)
handsome guapo, -a (5)
hard difícil (2)
hard-working trabajador, -a (1)
to **have** tener (2, 5)
to — a good (bad) time pasarlo bien (mal) (14)
to — to tener que + *inf.* (8)
he él (2)
head la cabeza (9)
— **ache** dolor de cabeza (9)
health la salud (4); *(class)* las ciencias de la salud (2)
hello! ¡hola! (P)
to **help** ayudar (1)
may I — you? ¿qué desea (Ud.)? (6)

her su, sus (5); *dir. obj. pron.* la (6); *ind. obj. pron.* le (9)
here aquí (2)
around — por aquí (6)
— **it is** aquí está (2)
hi! ¡hola! (P)
high-heeled shoes los zapatos de tacón alto (14)
him *dir. obj. pron.* lo (6); *ind. obj. pron.* le (9)
his su, sus (5)
hobby el pasatiempo (3)
home: at — en casa (1)
homework la tarea (2)
horrible horrible (4)
horror movie la película de terror (11)
horse el caballo (13)
hospital el hospital (9)
hot *(flavor)* picante (12)
it's — out hace calor (7)
to be — *(person)* tener calor (9)
hotel el hotel (10)
house la casa (8)
— **specialty** la especialidad de la casa (12)
household chore el quehacer (de la casa) (8)
¡how! qué + *adj.* (6)
how? ¿cómo? (P)
— **are you?** ¿cómo está (usted)? ¿cómo estás (tú)? (P)
— **long has it been since** . . . ¿cuánto (tiempo) hace que. . . ? (9)
— **many?** ¿cuántos, -as? (5)
— **much?** ¿cuánto? (6)
— **old are you?** ¿cuántos años tienes? (P)
— **old is . . . ?** cuántos años tiene . . . ? (5)
— **'s it going?** ¿qué tal? (P)

hundred cien (5); ciento (6)
hungry: to be — tener hambre (4)
to **hurt** doler (o → ue) (9); lastimarse + *part of body* (9)

I yo (2)
ice cream el helado (12)
iced tea el té helado (4)
if si (10)
ill enfermo, -a (3)
I feel — me siento mal (9)
impatient impaciente (1)
in en (P)
— **order to** para + *inf.* (7)
inexpensive barato, -a (6)
ingredient el ingrediente (12)
intelligent inteligente (5)
interest: place of — el lugar de interés (7)
to **interest** interesar (11)
interesting interesante (11)
to **introduce** presentar (14)
invitation la invitación *pl.* las invitaciones (14)
to **invite** invitar (14)
it *dir. obj.* lo (6)

jacket la chaqueta (6)
jaguar el jaguar (13)
January enero (P)
jeans los jeans (6)
jewelry las joyas (14)
juice el jugo (4)
orange — el jugo de naranja (4)
July julio (P)
June junio (P)

kind amable (1); la clase (11)
kitchen la cocina (8)
knife el cuchillo (12)
to **know** saber (13); conocer (14)

lacking: to be — faltar a (12)
lake el lago (7)
lamp la lámpara (8)
to **last** durar (11)
last pasado, -a (7)
— **night** anoche (10)
late tarde (10)
  see you —r hasta luego (P)
laundry room el lavadero (8)
lawn el césped (8)
  to mow the — cortar el césped (8)
lazy perezoso, -a (1)
to **learn** aprender (2)
least el / la / los / las menos + *adj.* (11)
leather el cuero (8)
  (made of) — de cuero (8)
to **leave** salir (7)
left izquierdo, -a (9)
  to the — (of) a la izquierda (de) (10)
leg la pierna (9)
lemonade la limonada (4)
less menos (4, 11)
  more or — más o menos (4)
letter la carta (10)
lettuce la lechuga (4)
library la biblioteca (10)
life la vida (11)
light la luz, *pl.* las luces (13)
to **like** gustar (5)
  he / she —s le gusta(n) (5)

I / you — (a mí) me / (a ti) te gusta(n) (1)
I'd — quisiera (7)
likewise igualmente (P)
to **listen** escuchar (1)
little pequeño, -a (5)
  a — un poco (de) (11)
to **live** vivir (8)
living room la sala (8)
located: to be — quedar (10)
long largo, -a (11)
to **look for** buscar (6)
lot:
  a — mucho (1)
  a — of mucho, -a (2)
to **love** encantar (5)
  he / she —s le encanta(n) (5)
  I — me encanta(n) (4)
loving cariñoso, -a (5)
lunch el almuerzo (2)
  for — en el almuerzo (4)

ma'am señora (6)
made hecho, -a (14)
  — of de + *material* (8)
magazine la revista (13)
to **mail** enviar (10)
to **make** hacer (8)
mall el centro comercial (3)
man el hombre (5)
March marzo (P)
marker el marcador (2)
match el partido (10)
mathematics las matemáticas (2)
matter: what's the —? ¿qué pasa? (9)
May mayo (P)
me *obj. pron.* me (9); *after prep.* mí (1, 12)
meal la comida (4)
to **meet:**
  I'd like you to — te presento a… (14)

pleased to — you mucho gusto (P); encantado, -a (14)
menu el menú (12)
messy desordenado, -a (1)
metal el metal (8)
  (made of) — de metal (8)
midnight la medianoche (11)
mild *(flavor)* no picante (12)
milk la leche (4)
minute el minuto (11)
mirror el espejo (8)
miss la señorita (P, 6)
miss: to be —ing faltar a (12)
modern moderno, -a (8)
Monday lunes (P)
  on — el lunes (3)
money el dinero (10)
month el mes (P)
monument el monumento (10)
more más (4, 11)
  — or less más o menos (4)
morning la mañana (3)
  good — buenos días (P)
  in the — por la mañana (3)
most: the — el / la / los / las más + *adj.* (11)
mother la madre (5)
mountain la montaña (7)
mouth la boca (9)
movie la película (11)
  — theater el cine (1)
  to go to the —s ir al cine (1)
  to show a — dar una película (11)
to **mow the lawn** cortar el césped (8)
Mr. (el) señor (P)
Mrs. (la) señora (P)
much mucho, -a (2)
  how —? ¿cuánto? (6)

English-Spanish Vocabulary   497

museum el museo (7)
music la música (2)
  — program el programa
    musical (11)
musical film la película
  musical (11)
my mi, mis (3)

name el nombre (5)
  his / her / their — is se
    llama(n) (5)
  my — is me llamo (P)
  what's your —? ¿cómo te
    llamas? (P)
napkin la servilleta (12)
near cerca (de) (8)
neat ordenado, -a (1)
necessary: it's — to hay
  que (13)
neck el cuello (9)
necklace el collar (14)
necktie la corbata (14)
to **need** necesitar (2)
neither tampoco (1)
  — . . . nor ni . . . ni (1)
never nunca (4)
new nuevo, -a (6)
New Year's Eve party la
  fiesta de fin de año (14)
news las noticias (11)
newspaper el periódico (13)
next to al lado (de) (10)
nice amable (1); simpático, -a
  (5)
night noche
  at — de la noche (11)
  good — buenas noches (P)
  last — anoche (10)
nine nueve (P)
nine hundred novecientos
  (10)
nineteen diecinueve (P)
ninety noventa (5)
no no (P)
  — longer ya no (9)

nobody nadie (5)
noon el mediodía (11)
nor: neither . . . — ni . . . ni (1)
nose la nariz (9)
not no (P)
  — anymore ya no (9)
  — at all nada (1); de
    ninguna manera (14)
  — yet todavía no (11)
notebook el cuaderno (2)
nothing nada (9)
November noviembre (P)
now ahora (9)
nowhere ninguna parte (7)
number el número (P)
  phone — el número de
    teléfono (P)
nurse's office la enfermería
  (9)

ocean el océano (13)
October octubre (P)
of de (5)
  — course ¡Claro que sí!
    (3); por supuesto (13)
  — course not ¡Claro que
    no! (3)
often a menudo (12)
ok bueno (10)
old viejo -a (5); antiguo, -a (8)
  how — are you? ¿cuántos
    años tienes? (P)
  how — is . . . ? ¿cuántos
    años tiene . . . ? (5)
older mayor (5)
on en (P); sobre (12)
  — the dot en punto (11)
  — time puntualmente (11)
  — top (of) encima (de)
    (12)
once una vez (12)
one uno (un), -a (P)
  it's — o'clock es la una
    (2)
onion la cebolla (4)

only sólo (5)
  — child el hijo único, la
    hija única (5)
to **open** abrir (10)
opposite enfrente (de) (10)
or o (P)
  not . . . — ni . . . ni (1)
orange *(color)* anaranjado, -a
  (6)
orange la naranja (4)
  — juice el jugo de naranja
    (4)
to **order** pedir (e → i) (12)
other otro, -a (6)
ouch! ¡ay! (9)
ought to deber (4)
our nuestro, -a (8)
outgoing sociable (1)

pants los pantalones (6)
pantyhose las pantimedias (6)
paper el papel (P)
  sheet of — la hoja de
    papel (P)
parents los padres (5)
park el parque (3)
  amusement — el parque
    de diversiones (3)
part: to be a — of formar
  parte de (13)
party la fiesta (14)
to **pass** pasar (12)
passport el pasaporte (7)
past pasado, -a (7)
  half- — y media (2)
  quarter — y cuarto (2)
pastime el pasatiempo (3)
pastry el pastel (12)
patient *adj.* paciente (1)
to **pay** pagar (6)
pea el guisante (4)
pen el bolígrafo (P)
pencil el lápiz, *pl.* los lápices
  (2)
people la gente (13)

pepper la pimienta (12)
   stuffed — el chile relleno (12)
peppery picante (12)
period la hora (2)
person la persona (5)
personal personal (14)
phone el teléfono (1)
   — book la guía telefónica (13)
   — number el número de teléfono (P)
photo la foto (7)
physical education la educación física (2)
physician el médico, la médica (9)
to **pick up** recoger (13)
picture el cuadro (8)
pink rosado, -a (6)
place el lugar (14)
   — of interest el lugar de interés (7)
to **place** poner (8)
to **plan** pensar + *inf.* (7)
plant la planta (13)
plastic el plástico (13)
   (made of) — de plástico (13)
plate el plato (12)
to **play** jugar (u → ue) (3); tocar (1)
please por favor (P)
pleased to meet you mucho gusto (P); encantado, -a (14)
pocket folder la carpeta (2)
police la policía (10)
   — station la estación de policía (10)
polluted contaminado, -a (13)
pool la piscina (3)
post card la tarjeta postal (10)
post office el correo (10)

poster el cartel (8)
potato la papa (4)
   baked — la papa al horno (4)
   French-fried — la papa frita (4)
practical práctico, -a (14)
to **practice** practicar (1)
to **prefer** preferir (e → ie) (4, 8)
   I — me gusta más (1); prefiero (4)
to **prepare** preparar (14)
pretty bonito, -a (5)
program el programa (11)
to **protect** proteger (13)
public transportation el transporte público (13)
pure puro, -a (13)
purple morado, -a (6)
to **put** poner (8)
pyramid la pirámide (7)

quarter cuarto, -a (2)
   — past y cuarto (2)
quesadilla la quesadilla (12)
quiet callado, -a (1)

rain la lluvia (7)
to **rain** llover (o → ue) (7)
   it's —ing llueve (7)
raincoat el impermeable (7)
rain forest la selva tropical (7)
rather bastante (8)
to **read** leer (1)
real real (11)
realistic realista (11)
really? ¿de veras? (1); ¡no me digas! (3)
to **receive** recibir (14)
to **recycle** reciclar (13)
recycling center el centro de reciclaje (13)
red rojo, -a (6)

   — -haired pelirrojo, -a (5)
to **reduce** reducir (13)
refrigerator el refrigerador (8)
relative el pariente, la parienta (14)
to **rest** descansar (7)
restaurant el restaurante (10)
to **return** regresar (7); devolver (o → ue) (10)
rice el arroz (4)
right? ¿verdad? (4)
right derecho, -a (9)
   — away en seguida (12)
   to be — tener razón (8)
   to the — (of) a la derecha (de) (10)
romantic movie la película romántica (11)
room el cuarto (8)
round redondo, -a (8)
to **row** pasear en bote (7)
rowboat el bote (7)
ruins las ruinas (7)
ruler la regla (2)

sad triste (11)
salad la ensalada (4)
salt la sal (12)
same: the — thing lo mismo (12)
sandwich el sandwich (4)
Saturday sábado (P)
   on — el sábado (3)
sauce la salsa (12)
saucer el platillo (12)
to **save** *(energy)* conservar (13)
to **say** decir (13)
   how do you — …? ¿cómo se dice …? (P)
   it is said … se dice … (P)
   you don't — ! ¡no me digas! (3)

to **scare** dar miedo a (11)
scarf: winter — la bufanda (7)
schedule el horario (2)
school la escuela (1)
   after — después de las clases (3)
science las ciencias (2)
science fiction la ciencia ficción (11)
sea el mar (7)
season la estación, *pl.* las estaciones (3)
second segundo, -a (2, 8)
to **see** ver (1)
   let's — a ver (2)
to **sell** vender (12)
semester el semestre (2)
to **send** enviar (10)
to **separate** separar (13)
September septiembre (P)
serious serio, -a (1)
to **serve** servir (e → i) (12)
to **set** poner (8)
   — the table poner la mesa (8)
seven siete (P)
seven hundred setecientos (10)
seventeen diecisiete (P)
seventh séptimo, -a (2)
seventy setenta (5)
shame: That's a —! ¡Qué lástima! (3)
shampoo el champú (10)
sharp en punto (11)
she ella (2)
sheet of paper la hoja de papel (P)
shirt la camisa (6)
   T- — la camiseta (6)
shoe el zapato (6)
   high-heeled —s los zapatos de tacón alto (14)
   — store la zapatería (6)
shopping:
   — center el centro comercial (3)

to **go —** ir de compras (3)
short *(height)* bajo, -a (5)
   — *(length)* corto, -a (11)
shorts los pantalones cortos (6)
should deber + *inf.* (4)
show el programa (11)
to **show** *movie or TV program* dar (11)
sick enfermo, -a (3)
   I feel — me siento mal (9)
silly tonto, -a (11)
since: it's been *(time)* **—** hace + *(time)* + que (9)
to **sing** cantar (14)
sir señor (6)
sister la hermana (5)
sitcom la comedia (11)
six seis (P)
six hundred seiscientos (10)
sixteen dieciséis (P)
sixth sexto, -a (2, 8)
sixty sesenta (5)
to **skate** patinar (1)
to **ski** esquiar (7)
ski cap el gorro (7)
to **skin-dive** bucear (7)
skirt la falda (6)
to **sleep** dormir (o → ue) (9)
sleepy: to be — tener sueño (9)
small pequeño, -a (5)
snack *(afternoon)* la merienda (12)
   for a — de merienda (12)
snake la serpiente (13)
sneakers los tenis (6)
snow la nieve (7)
to **snow** nevar (e → ie) (7)
   it's —ing nieva (7)
soap el jabón (10)
   — opera la telenovela (11)
soccer el fútbol (3)
social studies las ciencias sociales (2)

sock el calcetín, *pl.* los calcetines (6)
sofa el sofá (8)
soft drink el refresco (4)
some unos, unas (4); algunos, -as (14)
someone, somebody alguien (14)
something algo (4)
   — else algo más (12)
sometimes a veces (1)
son el hijo (5)
   —s; —s and daughters los hijos (5)
sorry: I'm — lo siento (2)
to **sort** separar (13)
so-so así, así, regular (P)
soup la sopa (4)
souvenir el recuerdo (7)
Spanish *(language)* el español (2)
special: daily — el plato del día (12)
specialty: house — la especialidad de la casa (12)
spell: how do you — ...? ¿Cómo se escribe ...? (P)
spicy picante (12)
spoon la cuchara (12)
sports los deportes (1)
   — program el programa deportivo (11)
spring la primavera (3)
square cuadrado, -a (8)
stadium el estadio (10)
stamp el sello (10)
to **start** empezar (e → ie) (2)
station la estación, *pl.* las estaciones (10)
to **stay (in bed)** quedarse (en la cama) (9)
steak el bistec (4)
stereo el equipo de sonido (8)
still todavía (9)
stingy tacaño, -a (1)

stomach el estómago (9)
  —ache el dolor de estómago (9)
store la tienda (6)
  clothing — la tienda de ropa (6)
  department — el almacén, *pl.* los almacenes (6)
  discount — la tienda de descuentos (6)
story *(of a building)* el piso (8)
stove la estufa (8)
street la calle (10)
student el / la estudiante (P)
to **study** estudiar (1)
subway el metro (10)
  — station la estación del metro (10)
sugar el azúcar (12)
suit el traje (14)
  bathing — el traje de baño (7)
suitcase la maleta (7)
summer el verano (3)
sun el sol (7)
to **sunbathe** tomar el sol (7)
Sunday domingo (P)
  on — el domingo (3)
sunglasses los anteojos de sol (7)
sunny: it's — hace sol (7)
suntan lotion el bronceador (7)
supermarket el supermercado (10)
surprise party la fiesta de sorpresa (14)
sweater el suéter (6)
sweatshirt la sudadera (6)
to **swim** nadar (1)
swimming pool la piscina (3)

table la mesa (P)
  to clear the — quitar la mesa (8)
  to set the — poner la mesa (8)
tablecloth el mantel (12)
tablet la pastilla (10)
taco el taco (12)
to **take** llevar (7); tomar (9)
  to — out sacar (8)
  to — pictures sacar fotos (7)
  to — a walk ir a pasear (10)
to **talk** hablar (1)
  to — on the phone hablar por teléfono (1)
  — show el programa de entrevistas (11)
tall alto, -a (5)
tape recorder la grabadora (2)
to **taste** probar (o → ue) (12)
tasty sabroso, -a (4)
taxi el taxi (10)
tea el té (4)
  iced — el té helado (4)
to **teach** enseñar (2)
teacher el profesor, la profesora (P)
teeth las muelas (9)
telephone el teléfono (1); *see also* **phone**
television la tele(visión) (1)
  to watch — ver la tele(visión) (1)
temple el templo (10)
ten diez (P)
tennis el tenis (3)
  — shoes los tenis (6)
terrible terrible (9)
thank you gracias (P)
that ese, esa; (6); que (5)
  isn't — so? ¿verdad? (4)
  —'s too bad! ¡qué lástima! (3)
  —'s why por eso (11)

the el, la, los, las (P, 2)
theater *(movie)* el cine (1); el teatro (10)
their su, sus (8)
them *after prep.* ellos, ellas (3); los, las *dir. obj. pron.* (6); les *ind. obj. pron.* (11)
then luego (10)
there allí (2)
  — is / are hay (P)
  — it is allí está (2)
therefore por eso (11)
these estos, estas (6)
they ellos, ellas (2)
thing la cosa (8)
to **think** creer (4); pensar (e → ie) (11)
  I don't — so creo que no (4)
  I — so creo que sí (4)
  to — about pensar en (11)
third tercer, -a (2, 8)
thirsty: to be — tener sed (4)
thirteen trece (P)
thirty treinta (P)
this este, esta (6)
those esos, esas (6)
thousand mil (10)
threat la amenaza (13)
three tres (P)
three hundred trescientos (10)
three-ring binder la carpeta de argollas (2)
throat la garganta (9)
  sore — el dolor de garganta (9)
  — lozenges las pastillas para la garganta (10)
Thursday jueves (P)
  on — el jueves (3)
ticket la entrada (14)
tidy ordenado, -a (1)
tie la corbata (14)
tiger el tigre (13)

time la hora (2, 14); el tiempo (11); la vez (12)

  at the same — a la vez (13)

  at —s a veces (1)

  at what — ¿a qué hora? (2)

  many —s muchas veces (12)

  on — puntualmente (11)

  to have a good (bad) — pasarlo bien (mal) (14)

  what — is it? ¿qué hora es? (2)

tired cansado, -a (3)

to a (3)

  in order — para + *inf.* (7)

toast el pan tostado (4)

today hoy (P)

  not — hoy no (3)

toe el dedo del pie (9)

tomato el tomate (4)

  — soup la sopa de tomate (4)

tomorrow mañana (P, 3)

too también (1); demasiado (11)

  me — a mí también (1)

toothache el dolor de muelas (9)

toothpaste la pasta dentífrica (10)

tortilla la tortilla (12)

touching emocionante (11)

town square la plaza (10)

train el tren (10)

  — station la estación del tren (10)

tree el árbol (13)

to **try** probar (o → ue) (12)

Tuesday martes (P)

  on — el martes (3)

to **turn off** apagar (13)

twelve doce (P)

twenty veinte (P)

twice dos veces (12)

twin el gemelo, la gemela (5)

two dos (P)

two hundred doscientos (10)

type la clase (11)

typical típico, -a (12)

ugly feo, -a (5)

umbrella el paraguas (7)

uncle el tío (5)

uncomfortable incómodo, -a (8)

under(neath) debajo de (12)

unfriendly antipático, -a (5)

unpleasant antipático, -a (5)

until hasta (11)

us *after prep.* nosotros, -as (3); *obj. pron.* nos (11)

to **use** usar (13)

usually generalmente (3)

vacation las vacaciones (7)

  to go on — ir de vacaciones (7)

to **vacuum** pasar la aspiradora (8)

vacuum cleaner la aspiradora (8)

VCR la videocasetera (8)

vegetable la verdura (4)

  — soup la sopa de verduras (4)

very muy (P, 1)

video game el videojuego (3)

to **visit** visitar (7)

volleyball el vóleibol (3)

waiter, waitress el camarero, la camarera (12)

walk: to take a — ir a pasear (10)

walking a pie (10)

to **want** querer (e → ie) (3, 7)

to **wash** lavar (8)

to **watch** ver (1)

water el agua (4)

waterfall las cataratas (7)

we nosotros, -as (2)

to **wear** llevar (6)

weather el tiempo (7)

  the — is nice (bad) hace buen (mal) tiempo (7)

  — forecast el pronóstico del tiempo (11)

  what's the — like? ¿qué tiempo hace? (7)

Wednesday miércoles (P)

  on — el miércoles (3)

week la semana (P)

weekend el fin de semana (3)

welcome: you're — de nada (3)

well bien (P); *(to indicate pause)* pues (1)

went fui, fuiste (7, 10)

western la película del oeste (11)

whale la ballena (13)

what qué (2); cuál(es)? (11)

when ¿cuándo? (P); cuando (7)

where? ¿dónde? (3); donde (7)

  from —? ¿de dónde? (P)

  (to) —? ¿adónde? (3)

whether si (10)

which? ¿cual? (11)

  — ones ¿cuáles? (11)

white blanco, -a (6)

  in black and — en blanco y negro (11)

who que (5)

who? whom? ¿quién(es)? (2, 5)

why ¿por qué? (4)

  that's — por eso (11)

wind el viento (7)

windy: It's —. Hace viento. (7)

window la ventana (8)

winter el invierno (3)

  — scarf la bufanda (7)

with con (3)
  — me conmigo (3)
  — you contigo (3)
to **withdraw** *(money)* sacar (10)
  wolf el lobo (13)
  woman la mujer (5)
  wonderful fantástico (7);
    ¡genial! (3)
  wood la madera (13)
  (made of) — de madera
    (8)
to **work** trabajar (10)
  worse peor (9)
  worst el / la (los / las)
    peor(es) (11)
  worthwhile: it's (not) —
    (no) vale la pena (13)
  wow! ¡vaya! (7)
  wristwatch el reloj pulsera
    (14)

to **write** escribir (14)
  wrong:
    to be — no tener razón (8)
    what's —? ¿qué tienes? (9)

year el año (P)
  New —'s Eve party la
    fiesta de fin de año (14)
  to be . . . —s old tener . . .
    años (P, 5)
yellow amarillo, -a (6)
yes sí (P)
yesterday ayer (10)
yet: not — todavía no (11)
you *fam.* tú ; *formal* usted
    (Ud.), *pl.* ustedes (Uds.)
    (2); lo, la, los, las *dir. obj.*
    pron. (6); te *fam. dir. obj.*

pron. (8); le, les *ind. obj.*
  pron. (9, 11); ti *fam. after*
  prep. (1, 12)
young *adj.* joven (5)
  —er menor *pl.* menores (5)
  — lady la joven (6)
  — man, sir el joven (6)
  — people los jóvenes (6)
your tu (2); tus (3); su, sus
  (8)
yuck! ¡qué asco! (4)

zero cero (P)
zoo el zoológico (10)

ás práctica y tarea
Vocabulario y gramática

Here's an additional opportunity for you to practice new vocabulary and grammar. Write all of your answers on a separate sheet of paper.

El Primer Paso

Sección 1 (páginas 4–6)

1 **Los cognados** Write the cognate for each of the Spanish words.

alfabeto   *alphabet*

1. béisbol
2. clase
3. conversación
4. estudiante
5. laboratorio
6. teléfono
7. tigre
8. vocabulario

Sección 2 (páginas 7–9)

1 **Mucho gusto** Rewrite the following two conversations in Spanish using correct punctuation.

Buenos días   *¡Buenos días!*

A
1. —Hola Cómo estás
2. —Bien gracias Y tú
3. —Así así

B
4. —Cómo te llamas
5. —Me llamo David
6. —Mucho gusto

2 **La conversación** Rewrite the scrambled conversation in the order that makes the most sense. There should be four lines of conversation.

Muy bien, gracias. ¿Y tú?
¡Buenos días! Hola, ¿cómo estás, María?
Así, así.

(Do Practice Workbook P-1.)

Sección 1
Exercise 1
1. baseball
2. class
3. conversation
4. student
5. laboratory
6. telephone
7. tiger
8. vocabulary

Sección 2
Exercise 1
1. ¡Hola! ¿Cómo estás?
2. Bien, gracias. ¿Y tú?
3. Así, así.
4. ¿Cómo te llamas?
5. Me llamo David.
6. Mucho gusto.

Exercise 2
1. ¡Buenos días!
2. Hola, ¿cómo estás, María?
3. Muy bien, gracias. ¿Y tú?
4. Así, así.

Sección 3
Exercise 1
1. c
2. b
3. e
4. f
5. a
6. d

Exercise 2
1. Buenas
2. usted
3. Estoy
4. tú
5. eres
6. de
7. Señora
8. Soy
9. luego

Sección 4
Exercise 1
1. estudiante
2. libro
3. bolígrafo
4. pizarra
5. pupitre
6. hoja de papel

Sección 3 (páginas 10–12)

1 **¿De dónde eres?** Match each question or statement from Column A with the most appropriate response from Column B.

A	B
1. ¿De dónde eres?	**a.** Muy bien, gracias.
2. ¿Cómo te llamas?	**b.** Raúl.
3. ¡Hola!	**c.** Soy de Paraguay.
4. Me llamo Carolina.	**d.** ¡Hasta luego!
5. ¿Cómo está Ud.?	**e.** ¡Buenas tardes!
6. ¡Adiós!	**f.** Mucho gusto.

2 **Profesor y estudiante** Write the word that best completes each line of these dialogues. Use the words in the box.

Buenas	Estoy	Soy
de	luego	tú
eres	Señora	usted

—_1_ tardes, Profesor Santos.
—Hola, señor López, ¿cómo está _2_ ?
—_3_ bien, gracias, ¿y _4_ ?

—Hola, Ricardo. ¿De dónde _5_ tú?
—Soy _6_ Puerto Rico.

—_7_ Aranda, ¿de dónde es usted?
—_8_ de Madrid.
—¡Hasta _9_ !

(Do Practice Workbook P-2.)

Sección 4 (páginas 13–15)

1 **¿Cómo se dice?** Tell how you would say the following words in Spanish.

¿Cómo se dice *"teacher"* en español?   *profesor(a)*

1. ¿Cómo se dice *"student"* en español?
2. ¿Cómo se dice *"book"* en español?
3. ¿Cómo se dice *"pen"* en español?
4. ¿Cómo se dice *"chalkboard"* en español?
5. ¿Cómo se dice *"student desk"* en español?
6. ¿Cómo se dice *"sheet of paper"* en español?

(Do Practice Workbook P-3.)

Sección 5 (páginas 16–19)

❶ Uno, dos, tres Complete each sequence by writing the correct number or month in Spanish.

uno, dos, ___   *tres*
junio, ___, agosto   *julio*

1. dos, tres, ___
2. nueve, diez, ___
3. diecisiete, dieciocho, ___
4. veinticuatro, ___, veintiséis
5. veintinueve, treinta, ___

6. febrero, ___, abril
7. abril, ___, junio
8. septiembre, ___, noviembre
9. junio, julio, ___
10. ___, enero, febrero

❷ ¿Cómo o cuánto? Complete each sentence by writing the correct interrogative: *¿cómo?, ¿cuánto?, ¿cuántos(as)?, ¿cuál?, ¿cuándo?, ¿qué?, ¿de dónde?*

1. ¿___ años tienes?
2. ¿___ es la fecha?
3. ¿___ día es hoy?
4. ¿___ eres?

5. ¿___ está Ud.?
6. ¿___ es tu cumpleaños?
7. ¿___ muchachas hay?
8. ¿___ se escribe "pupitre"?

(Do Practice Workbook P-4, P-5, and P-6.)

Sección 5

Exercise 1
1. cuatro
2. once
3. diecinueve
4. veinticinco
5. treinta y uno
6. marzo
7. mayo
8. octubre
9. agosto
10. diciembre

Exercise 2
1. Cuántos
2. Cuál
3. Qué
4. De dónde
5. Cómo
6. Cuándo
7. Cuántas
8. Cómo

Exercise 1

En casa
ayudar en casa
cocinar
dibujar
escuchar música
estudiar
hablar por teléfono
leer
tocar la guitarra
ver la televisión

Afuera
nadar
patinar
practicar deportes

Exercise 2
1. Me gusta mucho leer.
2. No me gusta nada cocinar.
3. Me gusta mucho estar con amigos.
4. Me gusta mucho practicar deportes.
5. No me gusta nada hablar por teléfono.
6. Me gusta mucho ir al cine.
7. Me gusta mucho ir a la escuela.
8. No me gusta nada ayudar en casa.

Exercise 3
1. gusta
2. me
3. ni
4. ti
5. tampoco
6. mí

CAPÍTULO 1

Vocabulario para conversar (páginas 30–33)

1 **¿Dónde lo practicas?** Organize the activities below by indoor *(En casa)* or outdoor *(Afuera)* activities. Make the lists on a separate sheet of paper.

ayudar en casa	estudiar	patinar
cocinar	hablar por teléfono	practicar deportes
dibujar	leer	tocar la guitarra
escuchar música	nadar	ver la televisión

En casa	Afuera
escuchar música	*nadar*

2 **¿Qué te gusta hacer?** Write whether you like or dislike the following activities.

(Sí)/dibujar   *Me gusta mucho dibujar.*
(No)/estudiar   *No me gusta nada estudiar.*

1. (Sí)/leer
2. (No)/cocinar
3. (Sí)/estar con amigos
4. (Sí)/practicar deportes
5. (No)/hablar por teléfono
6. (Sí)/ir al cine
7. (Sí)/ir a la escuela
8. (No)/ayudar en casa

3 **Los sábados** Adán and Irene are discussing what they like to do on Saturdays. Complete their conversation by choosing from the words in the box.

gusta	mí	tampoco
me	ni	ti

Irene: Adán, en general, ¿qué te __1__ hacer los sábados?
Adán: Los sábados __2__ gusta patinar y estar con mis amigos.
　　　No me gusta estudiar __3__ ver la tele. Y a __4__, ¿qué te gusta hacer?
Irene: No me gusta ver la tele __5__. ¡A __6__ me gusta mucho patinar también!

(Do Practice Workbook 1-1, 1-2, and 1-3.)

Vocabulario para conversar (páginas 34–37)

1 **Los opuestos** Write the opposite of each word. Choose from the antonyms in the box.

sociable   *tímido*

atrevido	paciente	tacaño
ordenado	serio	trabajador

1. desordenado
2. generoso
3. gracioso
4. impaciente
5. perezoso
6. prudente

2 **La conversación** Mateo and Eva are describing themselves. Complete their conversation.

Eva: ¿_1_ tú serio?
Mateo: Sí, y _2_ callado también. ¿Cómo eres _3_?
Eva: _4_ soy deportista. ¡Me _5_ practicar deportes!

Now tell something about yourself: Soy _6_. Me gusta _7_.

3 **¿Sí o no?** Write whether you agree *(Sí)* or disagree *(No)* with the descriptions of these fictional characters.

Charlie Brown es serio.   *Sí*

1. Batman es prudente.
2. El león de *El Mago de Oz* es atrevido.
3. Robin Hood es generoso.
4. Donald Duck es serio.
5. Scrooge es simpático.
6. Arthur es sociable.

4 **Yo soy...** Help Carolina describe herself.

Me gusta dibujar. Soy ___.   *artística*

callada	deportista	perezosa	sociable

1. No me gusta ni ayudar en casa ni cocinar. Soy ___.
2. Me gusta nadar, patinar y jugar béisbol. Soy ___.
3. Me gusta mucho estar con amigos y hablar por teléfono. Soy ___.
4. No me gusta hablar en clase. A veces soy ___.

(Do Practice Workbook 1-4.)

Vocabulario para conversar

Exercise 1
1. ordenado
2. tacaño
3. serio
4. paciente
5. trabajador
6. atrevido

Exercise 2
1. Eres
2. soy
3. tú
4. Yo
5. gusta
6. Answers will vary.
7. Answers will vary.

Exercise 3
1. No
2. No
3. Sí
4. No
5. No
6. Sí

Exercise 4
1. perezosa
2. deportista
3. sociable
4. callada

Gramática en contexto

Exercise 1

1. serio
2. callada
3. trabajadora
4. ordenada
5. gracioso
6. perfecto

Exercise 2

1. No me gusta ni nadar ni patinar.
2. No me gusta ni estudiar ni ir a la escuela.
3. No me gusta ni leer ni dibujar.
4. No me gusta ni escuchar música ni ver la tele.
5. No me gusta ni estar con amigos ni hablar por teléfono.
6. No me gusta ni ayudar en casa ni cocinar.

Exercise 3

1. A mí sí me gusta.
2. A mí no me gusta tampoco.
3. A mí no me gusta tampoco.
4. A mí sí me gusta.

Gramática en contexto (páginas 42–45)

Los adjetivos (página 43)

1 **La clase** Write the correct form of the adjective that describes each person in Jorge's Spanish class.

1. Pablo es ___.	(serio/seria)
2. María es ___.	(callado/callada)
3. Ana es ___.	(trabajador/trabajadora)
4. La profesora Martínez es ___.	(ordenado/ordenada)
5. Pedro García es ___.	(gracioso/graciosa)
6. ¡Jorge es ___!	(perfecto/perfecta)

(Do Practice Workbook 1-5, 1-6, and 1-7.)

Ni...ni (páginas 44–45)

2 **¡No me gusta nada!** Imagine that you don't like to do much of anything.

dibujar/tocar la guitarra *No me gusta ni dibujar ni tocar la guitarra.*

1. nadar/patinar   **4.** escuchar música/ver la tele
2. estudiar/ir a la escuela   **5.** estar con amigos/hablar por teléfono
3. leer/dibujar   **6.** ayudar en casa/cocinar

(Do Practice Workbook 1-8.)

Sí / Tampoco (página 45)

3 **¿Sí o no?** You and Josefina are discussing activities that you like and don't like. Agree or disagree with Josefina, as indicated.

A mí no me gusta ver la tele. ¿Y a ti?/(Sí)
A mí sí me gusta.

A mí no me gusta hablar por teléfono. ¿Y a ti?/(No)
A mí no me gusta tampoco.

1. A mí no me gusta patinar. ¿Y a ti?/(Sí)
2. A mí no me gusta practicar deportes. ¿Y a ti?/(No)
3. A mí no me gusta estudiar. ¿Y a ti?/(No)
4. A mí no me gusta cocinar. ¿Y a ti?/(Sí)

(Do Practice Workbook 1-9.)

CAPÍTULO 2

Vocabulario para conversar (páginas 58–61)

1 **En las clases hay...** Say where you are most likely to find the items mentioned below.

Hay un libro en (la clase de inglés/la clase de educación física).
la clase de inglés

1. Hay un piano en (la clase de arte/la clase de música).
2. Hay un diccionario en (la clase de español/la clase de ciencias de la salud).
3. Hay un mapa en (la clase de ciencias/la clase de ciencias sociales).
4. Hay lápices de muchos colores en (la clase de ciencias/la clase de arte).
5. Hay unas calculadoras en (la clase de matemáticas/la clase de español).
6. Hay una computadora en (la clase de inglés/la clase de educación física).

(Do Practice Workbook 2-1 and 2-2.)

Vocabulario para conversar (páginas 62–65)

1 **¿Qué hora es?** Write what time it is.

3:00   *Son las tres.*

1.	1:00	**4.**	8:15	**7.**	6:20
2.	2:30	**5.**	9:05	**8.**	3:10
3.	12:00	**6.**	5:45	**9.**	4:53

2 **El horario** Tell when each of Catalina's classes begins.

8:00   matemáticas   *La clase de matemáticas empieza a las ocho.*

Catalina García Pasillo	
Hora	**Clase**
8:00	matemáticas
1. 8:50	ciencias
2. 9:45	educación física
3. 11:10	almuerzo
4. 11:40	ciencias sociales
5. 12:30	inglés
6. 1:15	español
7. 2:00	arte

(Do Practice Workbook 2-3 and 2-4.)

Vocabulario para conversar
Exercise 1
1. la clase de música
2. la clase de español
3. la clase de ciencias sociales
4. la clase de arte
5. la clase de matemáticas
6. la clase de inglés

Vocabulario para conversar
Exercise 1
1. Es la una.
2. Son las dos y media/treinta.
3. Son las doce.
4. Son las ocho y cuarto/quince.
5. Son las nueve y cinco.
6. Son las cinco y cuarenta y cinco.
7. Son las seis y veinte.
8. Son las tres y diez.
9. Son las cuatro y cincuenta y tres.

Exercise 2
1. La clase de ciencias empieza a las ocho y cincuenta.
2. La clase de educación física empieza a las nueve y cuarenta y cinco.
3. El almuerzo empieza a las once y diez.
4. La clase de ciencias sociales empieza a las once y cuarenta.
5. La clase de inglés empieza a las doce y treinta/media.
6. La clase de español empieza a la una y quince/cuarto.
7. La clase de arte empieza a las dos.

Gramática en contexto

Exercise 1

1. ellos
2. yo
3. ella
4. nosotros
5. ella
6. él
7. nosotros
8. tú
9. ella
10. ellos

Exercise 2

1. Estudio.
2. Estudia.
3. Estudia.
4. Estudiamos.
5. Estudian.
6. Estudian.

Exercise 3

1. termina
2. cocinas
3. estamos
4. dibujo
5. escuchan
6. hablan
7. nado
8. patina
9. practicamos
10. toca

Gramática en contexto (páginas 71–77)

Los pronombres personales (páginas 71–73)

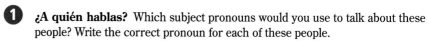 **¿A quién hablas?** Which subject pronouns would you use to talk about these people? Write the correct pronoun for each of these people.

Marta y Cecilia   *Ellas*

1. Clara y David	**6.** Juan
2. you	**7.** Tomás y tú
3. Catalina	**8.** me
4. Miguel y yo	**9.** Isabel
5. la señora Vidal	**10.** el señor Orozco, Carolina y Raúl

(Do Practice Workbook 2-5 and 2-6.)

Verbos que terminan en *-ar* (páginas 73–76)

2 **¿Quién estudia?** Use the correct form of the verb *estudiar* to tell who is studying.

Tú   *Estudias.*

1. yo	**4.** Roberto y yo
2. Sara	**5.** Uds.
3. Alejandro	**6.** Rocío y Patricio

3 **¡El fin de semana!** Write the correct form of the verbs to tell what each person is doing this weekend.

Luz (ayudar) en casa.   *ayuda*

1. José (terminar) la tarea.
2. Tú (cocinar).
3. Nosotros (estar) con amigos.
4. Yo (dibujar).
5. Uds. (escuchar) música.
6. Teresa y Claudia (hablar) por teléfono.
7. Yo (nadar).
8. Ella (patinar).
9. Vicente y yo (practicar) deportes.
10. El profesor Castillo (tocar) la guitarra.

(Do Practice Workbook 2-7 and 2-8.)

Los sustantivos (páginas 76–77)

4 **¿Qué necesitas?** The school principal is preparing a list of suggested school supplies. Help him/her write the list by writing the indefinite articles *un* or *una*.

carpeta   *una carpeta*

1. ___ regla
2. ___ bolígrafo
3. ___ libro
4. ___ cuaderno
5. ___ calculadora

6. ___ marcador
7. ___ diccionario
8. ___ grabadora
9. ___ mochila
10. ___ lápiz

5 **Mi clase de español** Imagine that you're writing a post card about your Spanish class. Complete the post card below by writing the definite articles *el* or *la*.

> ¡Tengo muchas clases! _1_ clase de español es mi clase favorita. _2_ libro es muy interesante. Y _3_ profesor es muy gracioso. Él toca muy bien _4_ guitarra. Hablo bien _5_ español. _6_ tarea no es muy difícil. ¡Hasta luego!

(Do Practice Workbook 2-9.)

Gramática en contexto

Exercise 4
1. una
2. un
3. un
4. un
5. una
6. un
7. un
8. una
9. una
10. un

Exercise 5
1. La
2. El
3. el
4. la
5. el
6. La

Exercise 1

1. Voy al cine los viernes.
2. Voy a la piscina los miércoles.
3. Voy al campo los fines de semana (los sábados y domingos).
4. Voy a la clase de arte los lunes.
5. Voy al gimnasio los lunes, miércoles y viernes.
6. Voy a la clase de música los sábados.
7. Voy al centro comercial los jueves.
8. Voy al parque los martes.

Exercise 2

1. Por la mañana voy a la playa.
2. Por la tarde voy al gimnasio.
3. Por la mañana voy a la clase de música.
4. Por la tarde voy al parque con María.
5. Por la noche voy al centro comercial.
6. Por la noche voy al cine.

Exercise 3

1. de la primavera
2. del verano
3. del otoño
4. del invierno

Capítulo 3

Vocabulario para conversar (páginas 90–93)

1 **¿Cuándo vas?** Imagine that the schedule below belongs to you. Answer Señora Díaz's questions about your schedule.

¿Cuándo vas a la clase de computadoras?   *los lunes*

lunes	martes	miércoles	jueves	viernes	sábado	domingo
clase de computadoras	parque	piscina	centro comercial	cine	clase de música	
gimnasio		gimnasio		gimnasio	campo	campo
clase de arte						

1. ¿Cuándo vas al cine?
2. ¿Cuándo vas a la piscina?
3. ¿Cuándo vas al campo?
4. ¿Cuándo vas a la clase de arte?
5. ¿Cuándo vas al gimnasio?
6. ¿Cuándo vas a la clase de música?
7. ¿Cuándo vas al centro comercial?
8. ¿Cuándo vas al parque?

2 **Mañana, el sábado** Tomorrow's Saturday and you have a very busy schedule. Summarize your schedule using *Por la mañana, Por la tarde,* and *Por la noche.* Write six sentences using the cues.

(2:00 P.M.)/ir al parque de diversiones
Por la tarde voy al parque de diversiones.

1. (8:00 A.M.)/ir a la playa
2. (1:00 P.M.)/ir al gimnasio
3. (10:30 A.M.)/ir a la clase de música
4. (3:15 P.M.)/ir al parque con María
5. (7:00 P.M.)/ir al centro comercial
6. (8:50 P.M.)/ir al cine

3 **Las estaciones** Tell what season the months mentioned in the sentences below belong to.

invierno	otoño	primavera	verano

1. Marzo, abril y mayo son los meses del/de la ___.
2. Junio, julio y agosto son los meses del/de la ___.
3. Septiembre, octubre y noviembre son los meses del/de la ___.
4. Diciembre, enero y febrero son los meses del/de la ___.

(Do Practice Workbook 3-1 and 3-2.)

Vocabulario para conversar (páginas 94–99)

1 **¿Adónde vas?** Tell where you'd most likely go to do the following activities.

Cuando quiero comer... *Voy al restaurante.*

1. Cuando quiero ir de pesca...   voy al campo
2. Cuando quiero nadar...   voy al parque
3. Cuando quiero ir de compras...   voy a casa
4. Cuando quiero jugar básquetbol...   voy a la piscina
5. Cuando quiero jugar fútbol...   voy al gimnasio
6. Cuando quiero jugar videojuegos...   voy al centro comercial

2 **¿Puedes ir conmigo?** Imagine that you're one of Teresa's friends. Tell why you can't accept her invitation to go somewhere.

Graciela/muy cansado, -a   *No puedo. Estoy muy cansada.*

1. Raúl/enfermo, -a   4. Rebeca/enfermo, -a
2. Alicia/no bien   5. Guillermo/no bien
3. Santiago/ocupado, -a   6. Roberto/cansado, -a

3 **¿Quieres ir?** Form questions using the following words.

poder/jugar tenis/a las tres   *¿Puedes jugar tenis a las tres?*

1. poder/ir al cine/conmigo   4. querer/jugar videojuegos/conmigo
2. poder/ir a una fiesta/mañana   5. querer/jugar béisbol/el lunes
3. poder/jugar fútbol/a las cinco   6. querer/ir de pesca/por la mañana

(Do Practice Workbook 3-3 and 3-4.)

Gramática en contexto (páginas 104–109)

El verbo *ir* (página 105)

1 **¡Es sábado!** It's Saturday! Where are all of these people going? Use the correct form of the verb *ir* to complete the sentences.

Carmen y Emilio ___ al campo.   *van*

1. Yo ___ al parque.
2. Benjamín ___ al gimnasio.
3. Uds. ___ a la piscina.
4. La profesora Castro ___ al centro comercial.
5. Tú ___ a la clase de música.
6. Nosotros ___ a la playa.
7. Luis y Sebastián ___ al campo.
8. María Elena y yo ___ a una fiesta.

(Do Practice Workbook 3-5.)

Vocabulario para conversar

Exercise 1
1. Voy al campo.
2. ...a la piscina.
3. ...al centro comercial.
4. ...al gimnasio.
5. ...al parque.
6. ...a casa.

Exercise 2
1. No puedo. Estoy enfermo.
2. No puedo. No estoy bien.
3. No puedo. Estoy ocupado.
4. No puedo. Estoy enferma.
5. No puedo. No estoy bien.
6. No puedo. Estoy cansado.

Exercise 3
1. ¿Puedes ir al cine conmigo?
2. ¿Puedes ir a una fiesta mañana?
3. ¿Puedes jugar fútbol a las cinco?
4. ¿Quieres jugar videojuegos conmigo?
5. ¿Quieres jugar béisbol el lunes?
6. ¿Quieres ir de pesca por la mañana?

Gramática en contexto

Exercise 1
1. voy
2. va
3. van
4. va
5. vas
6. vamos
7. van
8. vamos

Exercise 2

1. regularmente
2. regularmente
3. regularmente
4. mañana
5. mañana
6. mañana
7. mañana
8. regularmente

Exercise 3

1. Esteban va al gimnasio conmigo.
2. Emilia y José Luis patinan con él.
3. Víctor y yo vamos al parque con ellas.
4. Yo quiero jugar tenis contigo.
5. Ana puede ir de compras conmigo.
6. Nosotros(as) podemos nadar con ella.

Exercise 4

1. Estoy enfermo(a).
2. Está enfermo.
3. Estoy enfermo(a).
4. Estamos enfermos(as).
5. Están enfermas.

Ir + a + infinitivo (página 106)

 Las actividades Indicate which of these activities happen regularly (*regularmente*) and which ones are going to happen tomorrow (*mañana*).

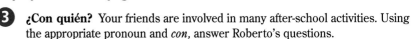

Regularmente	Mañana
Estudian.	*Van a jugar fútbol americano.*

1. Patinan.	**4.** Va a nadar.	**7.** Van a tocar la guitarra.
2. Ayudo en casa.	**5.** Vas a jugar béisbol.	**8.** Escucho música.
3. Hablamos.	**6.** Voy a ver la tele.	

(Do Practice Workbook 3-6.)

La preposición *con* (página 107)

3 **¿Con quién?** Your friends are involved in many after-school activities. Using the appropriate pronoun and *con,* answer Roberto's questions.

¿Quién va al campo contigo? (Carlos y Diana)
Carlos y Diana van al campo conmigo.

1. ¿Quién va al gimnasio contigo? (Esteban)
2. ¿Quién patina con Gerardo? (Emilia y José Luis)
3. ¿Quién va al parque con Yolanda y Luisa? (Víctor y yo)
4. ¿Quién quiere jugar tenis conmigo? (yo)
5. ¿Quién puede ir de compras contigo? (Ana)
6. ¿Quién puede nadar con Isabel? (tú y Dolores)

(Do Practice Workbook 3-7.)

El verbo *estar* (páginas 108–109)

 ¿Cómo estás? Answer each question using the appropriate phrase from the box.

Estoy enfermo, -a.	Estamos enfermos, -as.	Está enfermo, -a.

1. ¿Cómo está Ud.?
2. ¿Cómo está Daniel?
3. ¿Cómo estás?

4. ¿Cómo están Uds.?
5. ¿Cómo están Ana y Laura?

(Do Practice Workbook 3-8 and 3-9.)

CAPÍTULO 4

Vocabulario para conversar (páginas 122–125)

1 **La comida** What do North Americans typically eat? On a separate sheet of paper, list the following foods under the most appropriate headings: *El desayuno, El almuerzo, La cena.*

el arroz	la hamburguesa	las papas	la pizza
el bistec	los huevos	las papas fritas	el pollo
el cereal	el pan tostado	el pescado	el sandwich

El desayuno	El almuerzo	La cena
el cereal	*la pizza*	*el pollo*

2 **¿Qué comes?** Tomás, a four-year-old from Ecuador, asks what North American children typically eat at different meals. Answer his questions with *Sí* or *No*.

En el desayuno, ¿comes huevos? *Sí*
En el almuerzo, ¿comes pan tostado? *No*

1. En el desayuno, ¿comes arroz?
2. En el almuerzo, ¿comes cereal?
3. En la cena, ¿comes bistec?
4. En la cena, ¿comes un sandwich?
5. En el almuerzo, ¿comes papas fritas?
6. En el desayuno, ¿comes sopa de verduras?

(Do Practice Workbook 4-1 and 4-2.)

Vocabulario para conversar (páginas 126–129)

1 **Los ingredientes** Read the list of ingredients and write the name of the foods that are being described.

pan y carne   *la hamburguesa*

1. pan, jamón, queso, lechuga y tomate
2. lechuga, cebollas y tomate
3. plátanos, naranjas, manzanas y uvas
4. pan, pollo, lechuga y tomate
5. cebollas, guisantes y judías verdes

Vocabulario para conversar
Exercise 1

el desayuno
el cereal
los huevos
el pan tostado

el almuerzo
la hamburguesa
las papas fritas
la pizza
el sandwich

la cena
el arroz
el bistec
las papas
el pescado
el pollo

Exercise 2
1. No
2. No
3. Sí
4. No
5. Sí
6. No

Vocabulario para conversar
Exercise 1
1. el sandwich de jamón y queso
2. la ensalada de verduras
3. la ensalada de frutas
4. el sandwich de pollo
5. la sopa de verduras

Exercise 2

1. fruta
2. buena
3. la uva
4. zanahorias
5. comer
6. horribles
7. agua
8. té
9. café
10. hambre

Gramática en contexto

Exercise 1

1. los huevos
2. las naranjas
3. unos guisantes
4. unas zanahorias
5. las frutas
6. unos sándwiches
7. los tomates
8. los plátanos
9. unas cebollas
10. las verduras

Exercise 2

1. graciosos
2. serios
3. ordenadas
4. pacientes
5. trabajadores
6. generosos

---

2 **La comida** Ana María describes what she likes to eat and drink. Help her complete her description.

Me gusta comer (papas/café).   *papas*

Me gusta mucho comer __1__ (fruta/té helado). Es muy __2__ (mala/buena) para la salud. La fruta que más me gusta es __3__ (la uva/la judía verde). A veces como __4__ (refrescos/zanahorias). No me gusta __5__ (beber/comer) cebollas. ¡Son __6__ (horribles/sabrosas)! Cuando tengo sed, prefiero beber __7__ (agua/un plátano). Nunca bebo __8__ (té/pan) ni __9__ (pescado/café). Y a ti, ¿qué te gusta comer cuando tienes __10__ (sed/hambre)?

(Do Practice Workbook 4-3 and 4-4.)

Gramática en contexto (páginas 134–141)

El plural de los sustantivos (páginas 135–137)

1 **En español** Help the grocery store owner with his sign in Spanish. Write the plural form of each food item and beverage.

la papa   *las papas*
un refresco   *unos refrescos*

1. el huevo
2. la naranja
3. un guisante
4. una zanahoria
5. la fruta

6. un sandwich
7. el tomate
8. el plátano
9. una cebolla
10. la verdura

(Do Practice Workbook 4-5.)

El plural de los adjetivos (páginas 137–138)

2 **Las descripciones** Describe the students in Manuel's Spanish class.

Nicolás y Raquel son ___. (desordenado)   *desordenados*

1. Federico y Carlos son ___. (gracioso)
2. Carlota y Samuel son ___. (serio)
3. Julia y Bárbara son ___. (ordenado)
4. Patricio y Elena son ___. (paciente)
5. Lola y Enrique son ___. (trabajador)
6. Manuel y Sara son ___. (generoso)

(Do Practice Workbook 4-6.)

Verbos que terminan en *-er* (páginas 138–139)

3 **¿Hablar o leer?** Write the infinitive of each of these verbs.

debe *deber*

1. lees
2. deben
3. practica
4. estudian
5. bebemos
6. hablas
7. nadamos
8. comes

4 **El desayuno** Read the chart and write what each person has selected for breakfast. Use the verbs *beber* or *comer,* depending on the type of food.

Ceci ___. (beber) *Ceci bebe té.*
Armando ___. (comer) *Armando come cereal.*

	café	té	jugo de naranja	cereal	huevos	pan y mantequilla
Ceci		✓				
Armando				✓		
1. yo		✓				
2. Ángela y yo					✓	
3. tú				✓		✓
4. Uds.			✓			
5. Pepe y Tere	✓					

(Do Practice Workbook 4-7 and 4-8.)

Sujetos compuestos (página 140)

5 **Son las cinco.** It's 5:00 and what is everybody doing? Replace the underlined subjects with pronouns.

Gregorio y Carolina comen papas fritas. *Ellos*

1. Clara y yo escuchamos música.
2. Laura y ella estudian español.
3. Tú y Paco practican deportes.
4. Jesús y él comen fruta.
5. Pedro y Paco beben limonada.
6. Tú y yo vemos la tele.

(Do Practice Workbook 4-9.)

Exercise 3
1. leer
2. deber
3. practicar
4. estudiar
5. beber
6. hablar
7. nadar
8. comer

Exercise 4
1. Yo bebo té.
2. Ángela y yo comemos huevos.
3. Tú comes cereal y pan y mantequilla.
4. Uds. beben jugo de naranja.
5. Pepe y Tere beben café.

Exercise 5
1. Nosotros(as)
2. Ellas
3. Uds.
4. Ellos
5. Ellos
6. Nosotros(as)

Exercise 1

1. Isabel
2. prima/dieciocho
3. Le/nadar/dibujar
4. gusta/estudiar ciencias de la salud
5. abuela
6. hermanos

Exercise 2

1. Mariana tiene quince años.
2. Su hermano tiene diecinueve años.
3. Su madre tiene cuarenta y seis años.
4. Su abuelo tiene ochenta años.
5. Su primo tiene dieciséis años.
6. Su tío tiene cuarenta y ocho años.
7. Su tía tiene cincuenta años.
8. Su prima tiene dieciocho años.

CAPÍTULO 5

Vocabulario para conversar (páginas 154–157)

1 **La familia de José Miguel** Read the items in the chart below and write answers to the questions about José Miguel's family.

¿Cuántos años tiene el padre?
El padre tiene cuarenta y siete años.

La familia de José Miguel		
Nombre	Edad	Le gusta
La madre Isabel	46	leer y jugar tenis
El padre Pablo	47	tocar la guitarra y leer
La abuela Marta	77	cocinar y jugar vóleibol
El tío Beni	45	estar con su familia
La prima Juana	18	tocar el piano
El hermano Luis	14	nadar y dibujar
La hermana Carla	12	hablar y estudiar ciencias de la salud

1. ¿Cómo se llama la madre?
   Se llama ___.
2. ¿Cuántos años tiene la prima?
   La ___ tiene ___ años.
3. ¿Qué le gusta hacer al hermano?
   ___ gusta ___ y ___.
4. ¿Qué le gusta hacer a la hermana?
   Le ___ hablar y ___.
5. ¿Quién tiene setenta y siete años?
   La ___.
6. ¿Es hijo único José Miguel?
   No, tiene dos ___.

2 **¿Cuántos años tienen?** Write sentences telling how old the members of Mariana's family are. Refer to the family tree on page 154.

su hermana   *Su hermana tiene veintitrés años.*

1. Mariana
2. su hermano
3. su madre
4. su abuelo
5. su primo
6. su tío
7. su tía
8. su prima

(Do Practice Workbook 5-1 and 5-2.)

Vocabulario para conversar (páginas 158–161)

1 **Los opuestos** Write the opposite of each word. Choose from the antonyms in the box.

mujer   *hombre*

| antipático | bajo | bonito | grande | menor | viejo |

1. feo
2. alto
3. pequeño
4. joven
5. mayor
6. simpático

2 **¡Hola!** Help Mateo write a letter to his cousin in Bogotá, Colombia. Choose from the words in the box. Each word can be used only once.

| bajo | hermanas | ojos | rubio | tío |
| familia | llama | quince | se llaman | viejo |

¡Hola!

Soy Mateo, hijo de tu 1 José María. Vivo en El Paso, Texas. Tengo 2 años. Tengo el pelo 3 y los 4 verdes. Soy 5 . Aquí hay una foto de mi 6 . Puedes ver que tengo dos 7 menores. Ellas 8 Inés y Laura. También tengo un gato 9 . Se 10 Kiki.

Saludos,
Mateo

(Do Practice Workbook 5-3 and 5-4.)

Gramática en contexto (páginas 166–171)

El verbo *tener* (páginas 167–168)

1 **Mi familia** Help Rocío describe her family. Complete each sentence with the correct form of the verb *tener*.

1. Yo ___ una familia grande.
2. Mis tres hermanos ___ el pelo castaño.
3. Mi hermana menor ___ el pelo negro.
4. Mis hermanas mayores ___ veinte y veintidós años.
5. Lucinda ___ sólo cuatro años.
6. Mi papá y mi mamá ___ cuarenta y ocho años.
7. Cata, Cristóbal y yo ___ los ojos marrones.
8. Mi familia ___ dos gatos.
9. Nosotros también ___ tres perros.
10. ¿___ tú una familia grande?

(Do Practice Workbook 5-5.)

Vocabulario para conversar
Exercise 1
1. bonito
2. bajo
3. grande
4. viejo
5. menor
6. antipático

Exercise 2
1. tío
2. quince
3. rubio
4. ojos
5. bajo
6. familia
7. hermanas
8. se llaman
9. viejo
10. llama

Gramática en contexto
Exercise 1
1. tengo
2. tienen
3. tiene
4. tienen
5. tiene
6. tienen
7. tenemos
8. tiene
9. tenemos
10. tienes

Exercise 2

1. Es sociable.
2. Somos amables.
3. Soy prudente.
4. Eres simpático.
5. Son inteligentes.

Exercise 3

1. son
2. es
3. eres
4. son
5. somos
6. son
7. es
8. soy

Exercise 4

1. su prima
2. su abuelo
3. su hermana
4. su abuela
5. sus padres
6. su tío

Exercise 5

1. c
2. b
3. d
4. a

El verbo *ser* (páginas 169–170)

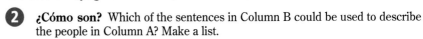

2 **¿Cómo son?** Which of the sentences in Column B could be used to describe the people in Column A? Make a list.

David   *Es paciente.*

A	**B**
1. Samuel	Es sociable.
2. Clara y yo	Eres simpático.
3. yo	Son inteligentes.
4. tú	Soy prudente.
5. David y Clara	Somos amables.

3 **El fin de año** Imagine that it's the end of the school year and time to vote on the personalities of the class. Announce the winners by giving the correct form of the verb *ser.*

Carolina ___ paciente.   *es*

1. Alicia, María y Carlos ___ deportistas.
2. Jaime ___ artístico.
3. Tú ___ inteligente.
4. Rita y Felipe ___ sociables.
5. Gloria y yo ___ graciosos.
6. Juana y Tomi ___ guapos.
7. El profesor Vidal ___ simpático.
8. Yo ___ cariñosa.

(Do Practice Workbook 5-6 and 5-7.)

Los adjetivos posesivos (páginas 170–171)

4 **La familia de Beatriz** Explain the relationship between the members of Beatriz's family by writing down the appropriate response.

El hijo de su tía es ...   *su primo*

1. la hija de su tío es ...	su abuelo
2. el padre de su padre es ...	sus padres
3. la hija de su madre es ...	su prima
4. la madre de su padre es ...	su abuela
5. los hijos de sus abuelos son ...	su tío
6. el hermano de su madre es ...	su hermana

5 **Los amigos** Match each question with the most appropriate response and write it down.

1. ¿Cómo es tu amigo?
2. ¿Cómo es el amigo de Verónica?
3. ¿Cómo son los amigos de Beto?
4. ¿Cómo es mi amigo?

a. Tu amigo es muy inteligente.
b. Su amigo es antipático.
c. Mi amigo es muy simpático.
d. Sus amigos son sociables.

(Do Practice Workbook 5-8, 5-9, and 5-10.)

CAPÍTULO 6

Vocabulario para conversar (páginas 184–189)

1 **¿Qué debo hacer?** Soledad is new to Sara's community. Complete their conversation about clothing customs by writing the appropriate word or expression.

¿Qué ropa prefieres (comprar/costar)?   *comprar*

1. ¿Qué ropa (buscas/llevas) al gimnasio?
2. (Una falda/Unos pantalones cortos) y los tenis.
3. ¿Qué (llevan/llevas) los estudiantes a la escuela?
4. (Los jeans/Las blusas) y las camisetas.
5. En general, ¿cuánto (cuesta/cuestan) una chaqueta?
6. Más o menos (cien/ciento) dólares.

2 **El color de la comida** Write the color of these foods in Spanish. Each color can be used only once.

la manzana   *La manzana es roja.*

amarillo, -a	blanco, -a	morado, -a
anaranjado, -a	marrón	verde

1. el café
2. el guisante
3. la leche
4. la limonada
5. la naranja
6. la uva

(Do Practice Workbook 6-1 and 6-2.)

Vocabulario para conversar (páginas 190–195)

1 **¿Dónde lo compraste?** Tell where you bought the following items by writing the most appropriate answer to each question.

¿Dónde compraste el suéter?   *En la tienda de ropa.*

1. ¿Dónde compraste los zapatos?
2. ¿Dónde compraste esa falda cara?
3. ¿Dónde compraste la camiseta barata?
4. ¿Dónde compraste la mesa?
5. ¿Dónde compraste esa mesa elegante?
6. ¿Dónde compraste los tenis?

Vocabulario para conversar
Exercise 1
1. llevas
2. Unos pantalones cortos
3. llevan
4. Los jeans
5. cuesta
6. cien

Exercise 2
1. El café es marrón.
2. El guisante es verde.
3. La leche es blanca.
4. La limonada es amarilla.
5. La naranja es anaranjada.
6. La uva es morada.

Vocabulario para conversar
Exercise 1
1. En la zapatería.
2. En la tienda de ropa.
3. En la tienda de descuentos.
4. En el almacén.
5. En el almacén.
6. En la zapatería.

Exercise 2
1. b. ¡Qué cara!
2. a. Pagué sólo 15 dólares.
3. c. Es una ganga.
4. b. Hace una semana.
5. a. En el almacén.

Gramática en contexto
Exercise 1
1. Yo prefiero la camiseta roja.
2. Yo prefiero el suéter rosado.
3. Yo prefiero los pantalones cortos grises.
4. Yo prefiero los tenis negros.
5. Yo prefiero la chaqueta cara.

Exercise 2
1. estos
2. esta
3. estas
4. ese
5. esa

---

2 **En el almacén** You overhear different conversations in the department store. Complete each conversation by choosing the most appropriate response.

1. — ¡Esta blusa cuesta cien dólares!
   a. ¡Qué barata!   **b.** ¡Qué cara!   **c.** ¡Qué vieja!

2. — Me encanta tu sudadera.
   a. Pagué sólo 15 dólares.   **b.** Compré unos tenis.   **c.** Perdón.

3. — No pagué mucho por la camiseta.
   a. ¡Qué horrible!   **b.** Es cara.   **c.** Es una ganga.

4. —¿Cuándo compraste los tenis?
   a. Por aquí.   **b.** Hace una semana.   **c.** En la Galería.

5. —¿Dónde compraste esos pantalones?
   a. En el almacén.   **b.** El sábado.   **c.** Sólo veinte dólares.

(Do Practice Workbook 6-3 and 6-4.)

Gramática en contexto (páginas 200–207)
La posición de los adjetivos (páginas 201–202)

1 **Al contrario** You and your friend disagree about clothing. Write your preferences according to the cues.

Me gusta la blusa azul. (anaranjado)
Yo prefiero la blusa anaranjada.

1. Me gusta la camiseta amarilla. (rojo)
2. Me gusta el suéter azul. (rosado)
3. Me gustan los pantalones cortos morados. (gris)
4. Me gustan los tenis blancos. (negro)
5. Me gusta la chaqueta barata. (caro)

(Do Practice Workbook 6-5.)

Los adjetivos demostrativos (páginas 202–204)

2 **¿Qué necesitas?** Help your friend pack for a trip. Choose the correct demonstrative adjective and write it down.

1. ¿Te gustan ___ calcetines? (estos/estas)
2. ¿Te gustaría llevar ___ sudadera? (este/esta)
3. ¿Prefieres ___ blusas? (estos/estas)
4. ¿Necesitas ___ suéter? (ese/esa)
5. ¿Vas a llevar ___ camiseta? (esa/ese)

3 **¿Qué prefieres?** You're helping María Teresa shop. Ask her what she prefers.

camiseta azul/camisa blanca
¿Prefieres esta camiseta azul o esa camisa blanca?

1. chaqueta marrón/suéter verde
2. blusa amarilla/camiseta roja
3. calcetines blancos/calcetines negros
4. falda negra/vestido negro
5. pantalones grises/jeans azules
6. vestido morado/blusa anaranjada

(Do Practice Workbook 6-6.)

El complemento directo: Los pronombres (páginas 204–207)

4 **La ropa** Rephrase the following sentences by replacing the underlined words with a direct object pronoun.

¿Cuándo compraste <u>el vestido</u>?   *¿Cuándo lo compraste?*

1. Compras <u>los pantalones</u>.
2. Quiero comprar <u>este vestido</u>.
3. ¿Cuándo compraste <u>esa falda</u>?
4. ¿Compraste <u>la camisa y los zapatos</u>?
5. ¿Vas a comprar <u>los calcetines</u>?
6. Lola tiene <u>el suéter rosado</u>.
7. Quiero <u>esa chaqueta</u>.
8. Busco <u>las pantimedias</u>.

5 **Todo para la escuela** Read the list of school supplies. According to the chart, write whether or not you've bought each one.

¿Compraste el diccionario?   *Sí, lo compré.*
¿Compraste los bolígrafos?   *No, no los compré.*

Necesito...	Sí	No
3 bolígrafos		✓
1 diccionario	✓	
1 calculadora		✓
5 carpetas	✓	
1 cuaderno		✓
10 lápices	✓	
3 marcadores		✓
1 regla	✓	

1. ¿Compraste las carpetas?
2. ¿Compraste la regla?
3. ¿Compraste los marcadores?
4. ¿Compraste el cuaderno?
5. ¿Compraste los lápices?
6. ¿Compraste la calculadora?

(Do Practice Workbook 6-7 and 6-8.)

Exercise 3
1. ¿Prefieres esta chaqueta marrón o ese suéter verde?
2. ¿Prefieres esta blusa amarilla o esa camiseta roja?
3. ¿Prefieres estos calcetines blancos o esos calcetines negros?
4. ¿Prefieres esta falda negra o ese vestido negro?
5. ¿Prefieres estos pantalones grises o esos jeans azules?
6. ¿Prefieres este vestido morado o esa blusa anaranjada?

Exercise 4
1. Los compras.
2. Lo quiero comprar.
3. ¿Cuándo la compraste?
4. ¿Los compraste?
5. ¿Los vas a comprar?
6. Lola lo tiene.
7. La quiero.
8. Las busco.

Exercise 5
1. Sí, las compré.
2. Sí, la compré.
3. No, no los compré.
4. No, no lo compré.
5. Sí, los compré.
6. No, no la compré.

Vocabulario para conversar

Exercise 1

1. Debe visitar el Museo de las Américas.
2. Deben explorar las selvas de Costa Rica.
3. Debe ir al lago Titicaca.
4. Debe ir a las montañas de Chile.
5. Debe ir a las playas de Costa Brava.

Exercise 2

1. fuiste
2. fui
3. las ruinas
4. quisiera
5. Para
6. museo

CAPÍTULO 7

Vocabulario para conversar (páginas 220–223)

1 **¿Adónde deben ir?** Imagine that you're a travel agent. Based on the interests of your clients, write the best travel suggestions using the words in the box.

A la señora Guzmán le gusta ir de compras.
Debe ir a la ciudad de Guadalajara.

explorar las selvas de Costa Rica	ir al lago Titicaca
ir a las montañas de Chile	ir al mar Caribe
ir a las playas de Costa Brava	visitar el Museo de las Américas

1. A Lupe le gusta el arte.
2. A Santi y a Jesús les gusta ser atrevidos.
3. A la familia Guardo le gusta pasear en bote.
4. Al señor Márquez le gusta esquiar.
5. A Tomás le gusta tomar el sol.

2 **Las vacaciones** Timoteo and Lourdes are discussing winter vacation experiences. Complete their conversation by choosing from the words in the box.

fui	museo	quisiera
fuiste	para	las ruinas

Timoteo: ¿Adónde __1__ tú en las vacaciones?
Lourdes: No __2__ a ninguna parte. ¿Y tú?
Timoteo: Fui con mi familia a __3__ mayas en Guatemala.
Lourdes: ¡Qué interesante! Un día __4__ ir a Madrid.
Timoteo: ¿__5__ ver los lugares de interés?
Lourdes: Sí, especialmente ¡el gran __6__ de arte, El Prado!

(Do Practice Workbook 7-1 and 7-2.)

Vocabulario para conversar (páginas 224–227)

1 **¿Qué tiempo hace?** Weather can vary, so it's a good thing you're always prepared! List the items you have using the cues.

Hace sol. (los anteojos de sol/el paraguas)
Menos mal que tengo los anteojos de sol.

1. Hace calor. (un traje de baño/un abrigo)
2. Hace frío. (un impermeable/una bufanda)
3. Llueve. (una cámara/un paraguas)
4. Nieva. (el bronceador/un gorro)

2 **En los Pirineos** Imagine that you're in the Pyrenees, the mountains that border France and Spain. The weather there is similar to that in the northeastern portion of the U.S. Describe the weather and the clothes you wear during different seasons, using phrases from the two columns below only once.

En el invierno
En el invierno nieva. Llevamos abrigo y botas.

A	B
nieva	pantalones cortos y traje de baño
hace fresco y hace viento	impermeable y botas
hace calor	guantes, gorro y botas
llueve	abrigo o suéter

1. En la primavera...   **3.** En el otoño...
2. En el verano...   **4.** En el invierno...

(Do Practice Workbook 7-3 and 7-4.)

Gramática en contexto (páginas 232–239)

El verbo *poder* (páginas 233–234)

1 **Este sábado** Using the verb *poder,* tell what Irene's friends can and cannot do this Saturday.

1. Marité ___ tomar el sol.
2. Ricardo y Manolo no ___ ir al cine.
3. Julia no ___ salir de casa.
4. Yo ___ bucear en el mar.
5. Mariana y yo ___ regresar a las diez.
6. Y tú, ¿qué ___ hacer?

(Do Practice Workbook 7-5.)

Vocabulario para conversar

Exercise 1
1. Menos mal que tengo un traje de baño.
2. Menos mal que tengo una bufanda.
3. Menos mal que tengo un paraguas.
4. Menos mal que tengo un gorro.

Exercise 2
1. En la primavera llueve. Llevamos impermeable y botas.
2. En el verano hace calor. Llevamos pantalones cortos y traje de baño.
3. En el otoño hace fresco y hace viento. Llevamos abrigo o suéter.
4. En el invierno nieva. Llevamos guantes, gorro y botas.

Gramática en contexto

Exercise 1
1. puede
2. pueden
3. puede
4. puedo
5. podemos
6. puedes

Exercise 2

1. Me gustaría ir a las montañas para esquiar.
2. Quisiera ir al campo para ir de pesca.
3. Rafael piensa ir a la tienda para comprar recuerdos.
4. Elena y Pati prefieren regresar a las cuatro para ver la tele.
5. Quiero comprar una cámara para sacar fotos.
6. Sergio piensa visitar la ciudad para ver los lugares de interés.

Exercise 3

1. quiero
2. quiere
3. quieres
4. queremos
5. quiere
6. quieren

Exercise 4

1. pensamos
2. pienso
3. piensa
4. piensan
5. piensan
6. pensamos
7. pienso
8. piensas

Para + infinitivo (página 235)

2 **¿Para qué?** Tell why these people are going to certain places by forming sentences with *para*.

Debemos ir al restaurante. (comer el almuerzo)
Debemos ir al restaurante para comer el almuerzo.

1. Me gustaría ir a las montañas. (esquiar)
2. Quisiera ir al campo. (ir de pesca)
3. Rafael piensa ir a la tienda. (comprar recuerdos)
4. Elena y Pati prefieren regresar a las cuatro. (ver la tele)
5. Quiero comprar una cámara. (sacar fotos)
6. Sergio piensa visitar la ciudad. (ver los lugares de interés)

(Do Practice Workbook 7-6.)

Los verbos *querer* y *pensar* (páginas 236–237)

3 **¡Fiesta!** The Spanish Club is planning a big party. Tell how everyone wants to help using the correct forms of the verb *querer.*

Alfonso ___ comprar una piñata.   *quiere*

1. Yo ___ tocar la guitarra.
2. La profesora Noguera ___ hacer los tacos.
3. Tú ___ sacar muchas fotos.
4. Juana y yo ___ comprar los refrescos.
5. Anita ___ ayudar con la comida.
6. Ramón y Gabriel ___ escuchar música mexicana.

4 **El sábado y el domingo** Enrique discusses his and his friends' plans for the weekend. Complete his dialogue using the correct forms of the verb *pensar.*

¿Qué _1_ hacer nosotros este fin de semana? Bueno, yo _2_ ir al cine. Mi amiga Teresa _3_ ir al cine también. Si hace sol, Benito y Andrés _4_ ir al parque de diversiones. Si llueve, ellos _5_ ir conmigo al cine. El domingo por la tarde, Gregorio, Reina y yo _6_ jugar béisbol con unos amigos de la escuela. El domingo por la noche (yo) _7_ hacer la tarea con mi hermana Cristina. Y tú, ¿qué _8_ hacer?

(Do Practice Workbook 7-7 and 7-8.)

La *a* personal (páginas 237–239)

5 **¿A quién...?** Tell whom you usually interact with in the following situations. Use *a, al, a la, a los,* or *a las* as you write the answer to each question.

¿A quién ves en la ciudad? (muchas personas)
Veo a muchas personas en la ciudad.

1. ¿A quién escuchas en la sala de clases? (el profesor de español)
2. ¿A quién ayudas en casa? (mi madre)
3. ¿A quién ves en el gimnasio? (la profesora de educación física)
4. ¿A quién ves en tu clase de español? (los estudiantes)

6 **¿Dónde está?** Write sentences telling whom or what señora Reyes is looking for.

sus hijos   *Busca a sus hijos.*
su libro   *Busca su libro.*

1. sus anteojos de sol	3. su perro	5. la cámara
2. su maleta	4. el señor Reyes	6. David

(Do Practice Workbook 7-9 and 7-10.)

CAPÍTULO 8

Vocabulario para conversar (páginas 252–255)

1 **Los quehaceres** Es sábado y la familia Sosa limpia su casa. Escoge el verbo que mejor describa cada quehacer.

Miguel Ángel (limpiar/quitar) el baño.   *limpia*

1. Yo ___ la ropa. (lavar/sacudir)
2. Claudia ___ la basura. (sacar/comer)
3. Los gemelos ___ el coche. (vivir/limpiar)
4. Rafa y Rosa van a ___ los muebles. (sacudir/pasar)
5. Todos nosotros ___ los cuartos. (poner/arreglar)
6. Papá ___ el césped. (quitar/cortar)
7. Mamá ___ los platos. (lavar/hacer)
8. Tú ___ la aspiradora. (lavar/pasar)

2 **¿En qué cuarto?** Escribe los cuartos en que la gente generalmente hace estas actividades. Escoge uno de los cuartos del recuadro *(box)*.

Lavan la ropa en ___.   *el sótano*

la cocina	el dormitorio	la sala
el comedor	el garaje	la sala de estar

1. Los muchachos hacen las camas en ___.
2. La familia come la cena en ___.
3. Los padres hacen la comida en ___.
4. Los muchachos ven la televisión en ___.

Exercise 5
1. Escucho al profesor de español en la sala de clases.
2. Ayudo a mi madre en casa.
3. Veo a la profesora de educación física en el gimnasio.
4. Veo a los estudiantes en mi clase de español.

Exercise 6
1. Busca sus anteojos de sol.
2. Busca su maleta.
3. Busca a su perro.
4. Busca al señor Reyes.
5. Busca la cámara.
6. Busca a David.

Vocabulario para conversar

Exercise 1
1. lavo
2. saca
3. limpian
4. sacudir
5. arreglamos
6. corta
7. lava
8. pasas

Exercise 2
1. el dormitorio
2. el comedor/la cocina
3. la cocina
4. la sala de estar
5. el garaje
6. la sala

529

Exercise 1

La cocina
la estufa
los platos
el refrigerador

El dormitorio
la cama
el cartel
el escritorio
el espejo
el guardarropa
la ropa

La sala de estar
el equipo de sonido
el sillón
el sofá
la videocasetera

Exercise 2
1. cómodo
2. de cuero
3. redondas
4. de metal
5. modernos
6. lámpara
7. cosas
8. Tienes razón.

Gramática en contexto

Exercise 1
1. pone
2. ponen
3. ponen
4. pones
5. pongo
6. ponemos
7. pones
8. ponemos
9. ponen
10. pone

5. Las personas ponen el coche en ___.
6. Los padres hablan con sus amigos en ___.

(Do Practice Workbook 8-1 and 8-2.)

Vocabulario para conversar (páginas 256–261)

1 **¿Dónde deben estar?** Escribe el lugar de la casa donde normalmente están estas cosas. Organiza tus respuestas en tres columnas: *La cocina, El dormitorio, La sala de estar.*

la cama	la estufa	la ropa
el cartel	el guardarropa	el sillón
el equipo de sonido	los platos	el sofá
el escritorio	el refrigerador	la videocasetera
el espejo		

2 **El catálogo de muebles** Carmen y Mario miran un catálogo de muebles. Escoge las palabras que mejor completen su conversación.

Me gustaría tener una videocasetera ___. (nueva/vieja)   *nueva*

Mario: Quisiera comprar un sofá _1_. (cómodo/incómodo)
Carmen: Yo prefiero los muebles _2_. (de basura/de cuero)
Mario: ¿Qué prefieres, las mesas cuadradas o _3_?(de metal/redondas)
Carmen: ¡Mira! Hay muchas sillas _4_. (de metal/cansados)
Mario: Son muy _5_. (cuadro/modernas)
Carmen: Esta _6_ es elegante. (carpeta de argollas/lámpara)
Mario: Hay muchas _7_ bonitas en este catálogo. (cosas/pisos)
Carmen: _8_ (Tienes que ir./Tienes razón.)

(Do Practice Workbook 8-3 and 8-4.)

Gramática en contexto (páginas 266–273)

Los verbos *poner* y *hacer* (páginas 267–268)

1 **¡Vamos a limpiar la casa!** Un grupo de amigos prepara la casa para una fiesta. Escribe cómo cada persona va a ayudar. Usa la forma correcta del verbo *poner.*

Guillermina ___ las mochilas y los libros en el dormitorio.   *pone*

1. Felipe ___ la fruta en la mesa.
2. Roberto y Tomás ___ la basura en el garaje.
3. Susana y Victoria ___ la mesa.
4. Tú ___ los platos en la mesa.
5. Yo ___ los refrescos cerca de los sandwiches.

6. Toño y yo ___ los abrigos en el guardarropa.

7. Tú ___ la limonada en el refrigerador.

8. Nosotros ___ el perro en el sótano.

9. Eduardo y Pepe ___ seis sillas en el comedor.

10. Ud. ___ el paraguas cerca de la puerta.

2 **¿Dónde la hacen?** El profesor de español quiere saber *(to know)* dónde hacen la tarea sus estudiantes. Escribe la forma correcta del verbo *hacer*.

Ana Luisa/la cocina   *Ana Luisa la hace en la cocina.*

1. Pablo/la casa de su amigo

2. Margarita/la cama

3. Armando y yo/la cafetería

4. yo/la sala de estar

5. Antonio y Ramón/su dormitorio

6. tú/la clase de matemáticas

(Do Practice Workbook 8-5.)

Los verbos que terminan en *-ir* (páginas 268–269)

3 **¡Hola!** Becky es una estudiante de intercambio en Ecuador. Completa su descripción para el periódico escolar *(school newspaper)*. Usa las formas correctas del verbo *vivir*.

¡Hola! Me llamo Becky Clayton. _1_ con la familia Gutiérrez. Los Gutiérrez son muy amables. Nosotros _2_ en un apartamento. Mi familia ecuatoriana y yo _3_ muy cerca de la escuela y no muy lejos del centro comercial. En este país, muchas familias _4_ en apartamentos. En mi país, muchas personas _5_ en casas. Don Jorge, el padre del señor Gutiérrez, _6_ en una casa pequeña en el campo. Él me dice, "Mi casa es su casa."

(Do Practice Workbook 8-6.)

El verbo *preferir* (páginas 270–271)

4 **¿Qué prefieren hacer?** Escribe qué actividad del recuadro prefiere hacer cada una de estas personas.

A Papá le encantan los libros.
Prefiere leer.

dibujar	ir a la piscina	ir al almacén	leer
hablar con amigos	ir a la playa	ir al gimnasio	limpiar la casa

Exercise 2

1. Pablo la hace en la casa de su amigo.

2. Margarita la hace en la cama.

3. Armando y yo la hacemos en la cafetería.

4. Yo la hago en la sala de estar.

5. Antonio y Ramón la hacen en su dormitorio.

6. Tú la haces en la clase de matemáticas.

Exercise 3

1. Vivo

2. vivimos

3. vivimos

4. viven

5. viven

6. vive

Exercise 4

1. Prefieres dibujar.

2. Prefiere ir a la piscina.

3. Prefiere ir a la playa.

4. Preferimos ir al gimnasio.

5. Prefieren limpiar la casa.

6. Prefiere ir al almacén.

7. Prefiero leer.

8. Preferimos hablar con amigos.

Más práctica y tarea   531

Exercise 5

1. su gato
2. nuestra casa
3. sus amigos
4. sus hermanas
5. nuestros coches
6. nuestro perro

Vocabulario para conversar

Exercise 1

1. Me duele la espalda.
2. Me duele la nariz.
3. Me duelen las manos.
4. Me duelen las piernas.
5. Me duele la cabeza.
6. Me duelen los dedos.
7. Me duelen los pies.
8. Me duele el cuello.

Exercise 2

1. mal
2. duele
3. duelen
4. izquierdo
5. derecho
6. hace
7. Hace
8. ejercicio
9. gusta
10. Creo que

1. A ti te gusta el arte.
2. A Mamá le gusta nadar.
3. A Papá le gusta el sol.
4. Jaime y yo somos deportistas.
5. Víctor y Elena son muy ordenados.
6. A Susi le gusta comprar cosas.
7. Me encantan las palabras.
8. Mi amiga y yo somos sociables.

(Do Practice Workbook 8-7.)

Los adjetivos posesivos: *Su* y *nuestro* (páginas 271–272)

5 **¿Qué tienen?** Escribe estas frases para indicar de quiénes son estas cosas y cómo están relacionadas estas personas. (Usa *su, sus, nuestro, nuestra, nuestros* o *nuestras.*)

las sillas (nosotros)   *nuestras sillas*

1. el gato (Tina)
2. la casa (nosotros)
3. los amigos de Gerardo (ellos)
4. las hermanas de Ana (ellas)
5. los coches (nosotros)
6. el perro (nosotros)

(Do Practice Workbook 8-8 and 8-9.)

CAPÍTULO 9

Vocabulario para conversar (páginas 286–289)

1 **¡Ay! Me duele...** Escribe las partes del cuerpo que te duelen. Usa *me duele* o *me duelen* en las frases.

el estómago   *Me duele el estómago.*
los brazos   *Me duelen los brazos.*

1. la espalda
2. la nariz
3. las manos
4. las piernas
5. la cabeza
6. los dedos
7. los pies
8. el cuello

2 **Buenos días, Doctora** María José visita a la médica. Completa su conversación con la mejor palabra o expresión.

María José: Buenos días, Doctora. Me siento __1__ . (bien/mal)
La médica: ¿Qué te __2__ , hija? (duele/llama)
María José: Me __3__ los pies. (duele/duelen)
La médica: ¿Te duele el pie __4__ ? (antiguo/izquierdo)
María José: Sí, y el __5__ . (derecho/dolor)
La médica: ¿Cuánto tiempo __6__ que te duelen los pies? (hace/hacen)
María José: __7__ una semana. (Está/Hace)
La médica: Es muy interesante... ¿Haces mucho __8__ ? (ejercicio/sol)

María José: Sí, me _9_ hacer ejercicio por una hora todos los días. (gusta/siento)

La médica: ¡Ah! ¡ _10_ haces demasiado ejercicio! (Tienes que/Creo que)

(Do Practice Workbook 9-1 and 9-2.)

Vocabulario para conversar (páginas 290–293)

① **Es que no puedo porque...** Di *(Tell)* por qué estas personas no pueden hacer estas actividades. Escoge la respuesta que mejor complete cada frase.

1. —¿Quieres jugar tenis conmigo?
—Lo siento. No puedo porque me lastimé (el oído/el brazo).

2. —¿Quieres jugar fútbol con nosotros?
—Lo siento. No puedo porque me lastimé (la mano/el pie).

3. —¿Quieres jugar básquetbol con nosotras?
—Lo siento. No puedo porque me lastimé (la pierna/la nariz).

4. —¿Quieres cantar conmigo?
—Lo siento. No puedo porque me duele (la garganta/el dedo).

② **En la enfermería** Muchas personas están en la enfermería. Escoge la frase que mejor responda a lo que dice cada persona.

1. ¿Qué tienes?
a. Tengo sueño.   **b.** Una muela.   **c.** Me lastimé la pierna.

2. ¿Cómo te sientes?
a. Mejor, gracias.   **b.** En una silla.   **c.** Voy a la enfermería.

3. Tengo dolor de muelas.
a. ¡Qué bueno!   **b.** Debes ir al dentista.   **c.** ¿Vas a hacer ejercicio?

4. ¡Tienes fiebre!
a. Sí, y sueño también.   **b.** Creo que tengo gripe.   **c.** Sí, me gusta el pan.

5. Me duele la cabeza.
a. Ya no tengo calor.   **b.** Me lastimé la mano.   **c.** Debes tomar algo.

(Do Practice Workbook 9-3 and 9-4.)

Gramática en contexto (páginas 298–303)

El verbo *dormir* (página 299)

① **¿Cuántas horas duermes?** El médico quiere saber cuántas horas duermen estas personas cada noche. Usa la forma correcta del verbo *dormir.*

ella/8 *Ella duerme ocho horas.*

Vocabulario para conversar

Exercise 1
1. el brazo
2. el pie
3. la pierna
4. la garganta

Exercise 2
1. c
2. a
3. b
4. b
5. c

Gramática en contexto

Exercise 1
1. Rafael duerme ocho horas.
2. Virginia y Verónica duermen siete horas.
3. Nosotros dormimos nueve horas.
4. Tú duermes cinco horas.
5. Ud. duerme nueve horas.
6. Yo duermo siete horas.
7. El Sr. Rivera duerme seis horas.
8. Elisa y yo dormimos ocho horas.

Exercise 2

1. le
2. le
3. me
4. le
5. te
6. me

Exercise 3

1. Sí, me gusta este suéter.
2. Sí, a Fernando le gustan los tenis marrones.
3. No, a Eva no le encanta este vestido.
4. No, a Ana no le gusta la sudadera rosada.
5. Sí, me gustan los calcetines morados.
6. No, a Mónica no le gustan los jeans blancos.
7. Sí, a Jaime le encanta la camiseta negra.

Exercise 4

1. Hace dos semanas que Nico y Manolo tienen un resfriado.
2. Hace mucho tiempo que Abuelita está en el hospital.
3. Hace seis horas que Paco y yo tenemos fiebre.
4. Hace treinta minutos que estás en la enfermería.
5. Hace cuatro horas que Luz tiene un terrible dolor de cabeza.
6. Hace casi dos días que te duele el estómago.
7. Hace tres semanas que me siento mal.
8. Hace casi una hora que a mi hermanito le duele el oído.

---

1. Rafael/8
2. Virginia y Verónica/7
3. nosotros/9
4. tú/5
5. Ud./9
6. yo/7
7. el Sr. Rivera/6
8. Elisa y yo/8

(Do Practice Workbook 9-5.)

El complemento indirecto: Los pronombres *me, te, le* (páginas 300–301)

2 **Estamos enfermas.** Estas personas están enfermas. Completa las frases con *me, te, o le.*

A mí ___ duele la garganta.   *me*

1. A Francisca ___ duele la cabeza.
2. A Roberto ___ duele el estómago.
3. A mí ___ duelen los ojos.
4. A la Sra. Quino ___ duele la espalda.
5. A ti ___ duelen los oídos.
6. A mí ___ duele la boca.

3 **¿Qué te gusta?** Imagina que estás en un almacén con un amigo. Contesta las preguntas.

¿A Clara le gustan los pantalones cortos?/Sí
Sí, a Clara le gustan los pantalones cortos.

1. ¿Te gusta este suéter?/Sí
2. ¿A Fernando le gustan los tenis marrones?/Sí
3. ¿A Eva le encanta este vestido?/No
4. ¿A Ana le gusta la sudadera rosada?/No
5. ¿Te gustan los calcetines morados?/Sí
6. ¿A Mónica le gustan los jeans blancos?/No
7. ¿A Jaime le encanta la camiseta negra?/Sí

(Do Practice Workbook 9-6 and 9-7.)

La expresión *hace…que* (páginas 301–302)

4 **¿Cuánto tiempo hace que…?** Di *(Tell)* cuánto tiempo hace que estas personas están enfermas.

tres días / Selena / tener gripe
Hace tres días que Selena tiene gripe.

1. dos semanas / Nico y Manolo / tener un resfriado
2. mucho tiempo / Abuelita / estar en el hospital
3. seis horas / Paco y yo / tener fiebre
4. treinta minutos / tú / estar en la enfermería
5. cuatro horas / Luz / tener un terrible dolor de cabeza
6. casi dos días / tú / doler el estómago
7. tres semanas / yo / sentirse mal
8. casi una hora / mi hermanito / doler el oído

(Do Practice Workbook 9-8.)

La sustantivación de adjetivos (página 303)

5 **Las preferencias** A tu amigo le gusta el opuesto *(opposite)* de lo que te gusta a ti. Completa el diálogo con la palabra entre paréntesis.

¿Compras la camisa verde? (rosado)   *No, compro la rosada.*

1. ¿Buscas el tenis rojo? (blanco)
2. ¿Te gustan las chaquetas negras? (marrón)
3. ¿Prefieres los zapatos caros? (barato)
4. ¿Prefieres las uvas verdes? (morado)
5. ¿Comes las manzanas rojas? (amarillo)
6. ¿Compras los bolígrafos negros? (azul)
7. ¿Quieres el coche nuevo? (viejo)
8. ¿Escribes con la mano derecha? (izquierdo)

(Do Practice Workbook 9-9.)

CAPÍTULO 10

Vocabulario para conversar (páginas 316–321)

1 **¿Dónde lo haces?** En general, ¿adónde vas para hacer estas actividades? Escribe el lugar *(place)*.

para comprar pasta dentífrica   *Voy a la farmacia para comprar pasta dentífrica.*

el banco	el correo	la librería	el supermercado
la biblioteca	la farmacia	el parque	la tienda de regalos

1. para comprar comestibles
2. para comprar regalos
3. para sacar un libro
4. para ver un partido de béisbol
5. para enviar una carta
6. para comprar champú
7. para depositar dinero
8. para comprar un libro
9. para ir a pasear
10. para comprar jabón

2 **¿Cuánto te costó?** Imagina que estás en un almacén en España. Escribe, en letras, cuántas pesetas pagaste por estas cosas.

las pantimedias/340 ptas.   *Pagué trescientas cuarenta pesetas.*

1. la tarjeta postal/25 ptas.
2. el sello/35 ptas.
3. el libro/950 ptas.
4. la tarjeta de cumpleaños/220 ptas.
5. el champú/800 ptas.
6. los anteojos de sol/1000 ptas.
7. el jabón/350 ptas.
8. la pasta dentífrica/700 ptas.

(Do Practice Workbook 10-1 and 10-2.)

Exercise 5
1. No, busco el blanco.
2. No, me gustan las marrones.
3. No, prefiero los baratos.
4. No, prefiero las moradas.
5. No, como las amarillas.
6. No, compro los azules.
7. No, quiero el viejo.
8. No, escribo con la izquierda.

Vocabulario para conversar
Exercise 1
1. Voy al supermercado para comprar comestibles.
2. Voy a la tienda de regalos para comprar regalos.
3. Voy a la biblioteca para sacar un libro.
4. Voy al parque para ver un partido de béisbol.
5. Voy al correo para enviar una carta.
6. Voy a la farmacia para comprar champú.
7. Voy al banco para depositar dinero.
8. Voy a la librería para comprar un libro.
9. Voy al parque para ir a pasear.
10. Voy a la farmacia para comprar jabón.

Exercise 2
1. Pagué veinticinco pesetas.
2. . . . treinta y cinco pesetas.
3. . . . novecientas cincuenta pesetas.
4. . . . doscientas veinte pesetas.
5. . . . ochocientas pesetas.
6. . . . mil pesetas.
7. . . . trescientas cincuenta pesetas.
8. . . . setecientas pesetas.

Vocabulario para conversar

Exercise 1

1. El hotel está enfrente de la estación del tren.
2. El correo está al lado del supermercado.
3. El banco está entre el restaurante y la estación de servicio.
4. El zoológico está a la derecha del teatro.
5. La farmacia está detrás del hotel.
6. El estadio está en la avenida de la Reforma.

Exercise 2

1. en autobús
2. en tren
3. en coche
4. a pie
5. en taxi
6. en metro

Gramática en contexto

Exercise 1

1. de la
2. de
3. del
4. de la
5. de la
6. del

Vocabulario para conversar (páginas 322–325)

1 **¿Dónde queda?** Mira el mapa en las páginas 322–323 y escribe dónde quedan estos edificios.

El museo está al lado de(l) ___. (el restaurante/la estación de policía)
El museo está al lado del restaurante.

1. El hotel está enfrente de(l) ___. (la estación del metro/la estación del tren)
2. El correo está al lado de(l) ___. (el supermercado/la iglesia)
3. El banco está entre el restaurante y ___. (la estación del tren/la estación de servicio)
4. El zoológico está a la derecha de(l) ___. (el teatro/el hotel)
5. La farmacia está detrás de(l) ___. (el estadio/el hotel)
6. El estadio está en la ___. (avenida de la Reforma/calle Rivera)

2 **¿Cómo vas?** En general, ¿en qué vehículo vas en estas situaciones? Escribe el vehículo más apropiado.

Cuando quiero ir al campo con mi familia, voy ___. (en taxi/en coche)
en coche

1. Cuando quiero ir a la escuela, que está lejos de mi casa, voy ___. (en autobús/a pie)
2. Cuando quiero ir a otra ciudad, voy ___. (en metro/en tren)
3. Cuando mis padres y yo queremos ir al supermercado, vamos ___. (en coche/en tren)
4. Cuando quiero ir a pasear, voy ___. (en taxi/a pie)
5. Cuando estoy en otra ciudad y no quiero caminar, voy ___. (a pie/en taxi)
6. Cuando quiero ir muy rápido por la ciudad, voy ___. (a pie/en metro)

(Do Practice Workbook 10-3, 10-4, and 10-5.)

Gramática en contexto (páginas 330–337)

La preposición *de* + *el* (páginas 331–332)

1 **¿Dónde queda tu casa?** Eduardo quiere saber dónde vive Federico. Completa su conversación con *de, de la* o *del*.

Eduardo: Federico, ¿dónde queda tu casa? ¿Cerca _1_ tienda María Elena?
Federico: ¡No! Mi casa queda a diez cuadras _2_ esa tienda. Vivo al lado _3_ parque.
Eduardo: ¿El parque que está detrás _4_ iglesia Santa Rita?
Federico: Sí, en la calle Quinta.
Eduardo: ¿Está tu casa a la derecha _5_ plaza?
Federico: Sí, está enfrente _6_ monumento Simón Bolívar; es la casa número ocho.

(Do Practice Workbook 10-6.)

El pretérito de los verbos que terminan en *-ar* (páginas 333–335)

2 **Los quehaceres** El sábado pasado tú y tus amigos hicieron *(did)* muchos quehaceres. Escribe la forma correcta del pretérito de cada verbo que está entre paréntesis.

Josefina (lavar) el coche.   *lavó*

1. Benjamín (comprar) comestibles.
2. Yolanda (enviar) las cartas.
3. Yo (pasar) la aspiradora en la sala.
4. Nosotros (arreglar) nuestro dormitorio.
5. Raquel y Esteban (cocinar).
6. Papá (depositar) dinero en el banco.
7. Mamá y yo (lavar) la ropa.
8. Tú (cortar) el césped.
9. Yo (estudiar) español.
10. Uds. (limpiar) el sótano.

3 **Ayer** Tú y tus amigos hicieron *(did)* diferentes cosas ayer. Escribe la forma correcta del pretérito de cada verbo entre paréntesis.

Yo (tocar) el piano y él (escuchar) el piano.   *toqué/escuchó*

1. Yo (sacar) libros y Marta (comprar) libros.
2. Yo (practicar) el tenis y ella (practicar) el fútbol.
3. Yo (llegar) a las ocho y ellos (llegar) a las diez.
4. Yo (sacar) fotos y tú (comprar) tarjetas postales.
5. Yo (pagar) quince dólares y Ramón e Isabel (pagar) veinte.
6. Yo (mirar) los cuadros en el museo y Ud. (comprar) regalos en la tienda de regalos.
7. Yo (tocar) la guitarra y él (tocar) el violín.
8. Yo (buscar) los zapatos y tú (buscar) los mocasines.

(Do Practice Workbook 10-7 and 10-8.)

El pretérito del verbo *ir* (páginas 336–337)

4 **De vacaciones** Di *(Tell)* adónde fueron estas personas de vacaciones. Escribe los verbos subrayados *(underlined)* en el pretérito.

La familia Soler va al campo.
La familia Soler fue al campo.

1. Emilia va a las ruinas aztecas.
2. Jorge y su hermana van al mar Mediterráneo.
3. Yo voy al parque de diversiones.
4. El profesor Espina va a Perú.
5. Daniel y yo vamos a la selva de Guatemala.
6. Tú vas a Argentina para esquiar.
7. Nicolás y Cristóbal van a la playa.
8. La familia Durán va a la Ciudad de México.

Exercise 2
1. compró
2. envió
3. pasé
4. arreglamos
5. cocinaron
6. depositó
7. lavamos
8. cortaste
9. estudié
10. limpiaron

Exercise 3
1. saqué/compró
2. practiqué/practicó
3. llegué/llegaron
4. saqué/compraste
5. pagué/pagaron
6. miré/compró
7. toqué/tocó
8. busqué/buscaste

Exercise 4
1. fue
2. fueron
3. fui
4. fue
5. fuimos
6. fuiste
7. fueron
8. fue

Exercise 5

1. El doctor Ortiz fue al hospital y ayudó a los pacientes.
2. Felipe fue al correo y envió una tarjeta postal.
3. Yo fui a la farmacia y compré champú.
4. Tú fuiste a la estación de policía y hablaste con ellos.
5. Eva y Ángela fueron al parque y jugaron vóleibol.
6. La Sra. Monterrey y yo fuimos al museo y miramos los cuadros.

Vocabulario para conversar

Exercise 1

1. e
2. c
3. a
4. d
5. b

Exercise 2

1. programas deportivos
2. programas educativos
3. los anuncios
4. los documentales

Exercise 3

1. emocionante
2. aburrir
3. los dibujos animados
4. mejor
5. en blanco y negro

---

5 **En la comunidad** Lee la tabla *(chart)* y escribe adónde fueron tú y otras personas la semana pasada y qué hicieron *(did)* Uds. en su comunidad.

Ella fue a la biblioteca y sacó libros.

Personas	¿Adónde fueron?	¿Qué hicieron?
ella	la biblioteca	sacar libros
1. el doctor Ortiz	el hospital	ayudar a los pacientes
2. Felipe	el correo	enviar una tarjeta postal
3. yo	la farmacia	comprar champú
4. tú	la estación de policía	hablar con ellos
5. Eva y Ángela	el parque	jugar vóleibol
6. la Sra. Monterrey y yo	el museo	mirar los cuadros

(Do Practice Workbook 10-9.)

CAPÍTULO 11

Vocabulario para conversar (páginas 350–353)

1 **Tu programa favorito** Vas a leer una lista de palabras o frases y una lista de definiciones. Empareja *(Match)* cada palabra o frase con su definición.

1. el documental
2. la telenovela
3. las noticias locales
4. el programa musical
5. el pronóstico del tiempo

a. información sobre tu ciudad
b. para saber si va a hacer calor o frío
c. programa romántico
d. concierto
e. programa educativo

2 **La respuesta correcta** Completa estas frases con palabras del vocabulario.

1. Me gustan el básquetbol y el vóleibol. Prefiero ver ___.
2. Quiero ver programas sobre las ciencias. Prefiero ver ___.
3. Veo éstos para saber qué comprar. Prefiero ver ___.
4. Es necesario ver programas de Argentina. Prefiero ver ___.

3 **Antónimos** Escribe las palabras o frases que quieren decir lo contrario *(opposite)* de éstas.

1. aburrido
2. fascinar
3. el programa de hechos de la vida real

4. peor
5. en colores

(Do Practice Workbook 11-1 and 11-2.)

538   Más práctica y tarea

Vocabulario para conversar (páginas 354–357)

1 ¿Quieres ir al cine? Completa el diálogo entre Tina y Alejandro usando palabras o expresiones del recuadro.

corta	larga
dura	más tarde
en punto	

Tina: ¿Quieres ir al cine?
Alejandro: Sí, mi amor. ¿Cuándo? ¿Ahora?
Tina: No, __1__.
Alejandro: ¿A qué hora dan la película?
Tina: La película *El detective y yo* empieza a las 7:00 __2__.
Alejandro: ¿Y por cuántas horas __3__? ¿Es una película __4__?
Tina: No, es una película __5__. ¿Está bien?
Alejandro: Sí. Vamos.

2 Sopa de letras Pon *(Put)* estos grupos de letras en orden para formar palabras del vocabulario.

1. A H T A S
2. D Í D O I M E A
3. E A C I U M S L S
4. T E R U S A V A N

3 La opción correcta Usando las palabras del Ejercicio 2, completa estas frases.

1. Bueno, la película no empieza ___ las 8:00.
2. Vamos a ver los documentales al ___.
3. Hay mucha acción en las películas de ___.
4. Cantan en las películas ___.

(Do Practice Workbook 11-3 and 11-4.)

Gramática en contexto (páginas 362–371)

Los comparativos (páginas 363–365)

1 Comparaciones La gente siempre se está comparando. Usa cada uno de estos grupos de palabras para escribir frases comparativas. No olvides de usar la forma comparativa de los adjetivos. El signo > significa "más que" y el signo < "menos que."

El programa de detectives / > realista / la telenovela.
El programa de detectives es más realista que la telenovela.

Vocabulario para conversar

Exercise 1
1. más tarde
2. en punto
3. dura
4. larga
5. corta

Exercise 2
1. hasta
2. mediodía
3. musicales
4. aventuras

Exercise 3
1. hasta
2. mediodía
3. aventuras
4. musicales

Gramática en contexto

Exercise 1

1. Nosotros somos más prudentes que ellos.
2. Él es peor que ella.
3. El actor es menor que la actriz.
4. Los adultos son mayores que los jóvenes.
5. La película del oeste es menos interesante que la película musical.

Exercise 2

1. Daisy Fuentes es la mejor actriz de la película.
2. Gloria Estefan es la cantante más inteligente.
3. La película de terror es la peor de todas.
4. Las películas de ciencia ficción son las más diferentes de todas.

Exercise 3

1. Las voy a ver / Voy a verlas.
2. Lo quiero ver. / Quiero verlo.
3. Lo necesito ver. / Necesito verlo.
4. ¿Cuándo las vas a ver? / ¿Cuándo vas a verlas?

Exercise 4

1. ¿Por qué viste esa película?
2. ¿Qué películas vieron?
3. Yo vi un documental a las 5:00.
4. ¿Dónde vio Dolores ese programa?

Exercise 5

1. nos
2. les
3. les
4. nos

---

1. nosotros / > prudente / ellos
2. él / < malo / ella
3. el actor / > joven / la actriz
4. los adultos / > viejo / los jóvenes
5. la película del oeste / < interesante / la película musical

(Do Practice Workbook 11-5.)

Los superlativos (página 366)

2 **La mejor, la peor** Usa estos grupos de palabras para escribir frases con el adjetivo en la forma superlativa.

La máscara del Zorro / < mala / película / todas
La máscara del Zorro es la peor película de todas.

1. Daisy Fuentes / > bueno / actriz / la película
2. Gloria Estefan / cantante / > inteligente
3. la película de terror / < mala / todas
4. las películas de ciencia ficción / > diferente / todas

(Do Practice Workbook 11-6.)

El complemento directo: Los pronombres y el infinitivo (páginas 367–368)

3 **¿Qué vas a ver?** Escribe cada una de estas frases usando *lo, la, los,* o *las* en lugar *(place)* del sustantivo *(noun)*.

1. Voy a ver las películas románticas.
2. Quiero ver el anuncio.
3. Necesito ver el programa de hechos de la vida real.
4. ¿Cuándo vas a ver las nuevas películas?

(Do Practice Workbook 11-7.)

El pretérito del verbo *ver* (páginas 368–369)

4 **¿Qué ves ahora?** Cambia los verbos subrayados *(underlined)* al pretérito.

1. ¿Por qué <u>ves</u> esa película?
2. ¿Qué películas <u>ven</u>?
3. Yo <u>veo</u> un documental a las 5:00.
4. ¿Dónde <u>ve</u> Dolores ese programa?

(Do Practice Workbook 11-8.)

El complemento indirecto: Los pronombres *nos* y *les* (página 370)

5 **¡A mí sí me gusta!** Completa estas frases usando *nos* o *les*.

1. A nosotros ___ gustan los programas educativos.
2. A Carlitos y a Donaldo ___ gusta ver programas deportivos.
3. A Patricia y a Ud. ___ fascinan los dibujos animados.
4. A nosotras ___ encantan las películas musicales.

(Do Practice Workbook 11-9.)

CAPÍTULO 12

Vocabulario para conversar (páginas 384–387)

1 **El intruso** Para cada uno de estos grupos de palabras, escoge una palabra que no pertenezca *(belong)* a la misma categoría que las otras.

1. (churros / flan / aguacate)
2. (tacos / enchiladas / chile)
3. (salsa / quesadillas / guacamole)
4. (chile / harina / maíz)
5. (flan / aguacate / guacamole)

2 **La opción correcta** Completa estas frases usando el vocabulario del Ejercicio 1.

1. Un ingrediente principal del guacamole es el ___.
2. De postre quiero un ___.
3. El ___ da un sabor *(taste)* picante.
4. Esta noche quiero comer ___ con carne.

(Do Practice Workbook 12-1 and 12-2.)

Vocabulario para conversar (páginas 388–391)

1 **Definiciones** Decide cuál de las expresiones de la segunda columna define mejor cada una de las palabras de la primera columna. Escribe tus respuestas.

1. el camarero	a. la usas para tu café
2. el menú	b. donde lees tu selección
3. la sal	c. un condimento negro
4. la pimienta	d. la persona que sirve comida en un restaurante
5. la cuchara	e. un condimento blanco

2 **La palabra que falta** Completa cada una de estas frases con la palabra apropiada del vocabulario.

1. El lunes, los tacos, los martes, los tacos, los miércoles, los tacos. Siempre ___.
2. Quiero saber qué pedir. ¿___ el menú?
3. Para pagar, necesito ver ___.
4. Para mi café uso ___.

(Do Practice Workbook 12-3 and 12-4.)

Vocabulario para conversar
Exercise 1
1. aguacate
2. chile
3. quesadillas
4. chile
5. flan

Exercise 2
1. aguacate
2. flan
3. chile
4. chile

Vocabulario para conversar
Exercise 1
1. d
2. b
3. e
4. c
5. a

Exercise 2
1. lo mismo
2. Me trae
3. la cuenta
4. azúcar

Gramática en contexto

Exercise 1

1. pedir
2. servimos
3. pides
4. piden
5. sirve

Exercise 2

1. traigo
2. traen
3. trae
4. traen

Exercise 3

1. me
2. te
3. Les
4. nos
5. le

Gramática en contexto (páginas 396–405)

Verbos con el cambio *e* → *i* (páginas 397–398)

1 **Vamos al restaurante.** Estas personas están en un restaurante. Escribe estas frases con la forma correcta de los verbos entre paréntesis.

1. Voy a (pedir) flan.
2. Nosotros lo (servir) a las 10:00.
3. Tú siempre (pedir) lo mismo.
4. Mis abuelos (pedir) las enchiladas.
5. El camarero (servir) el té.

(Do Practice Workbook 12-5.)

El verbo *traer* (páginas 398–399)

2 **Traer** Completa estas frases con la forma correcta del verbo *traer.*

1. Yo ___ las cucharas.
2. ¿Quiénes ___ los cuchillos?
3. Jaime ___ los tacos y los burritos.
4. Andrea y Patricio ___ muchas cosas diferentes.

(Do Practice Workbook 12-6 and 12-7.)

El complemento indirecto: Los pronombres (páginas 400–403)

3 **Sí, me gusta.** Estas personas están hablando sobre la comida. Completa las frases con el complemento indirecto apropiado.

1. Camarero, ¿___ trae la cuenta?
2. Isabel, ¿___ gusta el helado?
3. ___ compro burritos y quesadillas a mis padres.
4. A Laura y a mí ___ encanta comer en este restaurante.
5. A Juana no ___ gustan los tomates.

(Do Practice Workbook 12-8.)

El pretérito de los verbos que terminan en *-er* e *-ir* (páginas 403–404)

4 **Ayer** Estas personas están hablando sobre las actividades que hicieron *(did)* ayer. Escoge el verbo del recuadro que complete mejor cada frase. Escribe la frase usando el pretérito de ese verbo.

comer	doler	salir	vender

1. Nosotros ___ en ese restaurante ayer.
2. Ellos ___ de la escuela a las cinco de la tarde.
3. Le ___ la cabeza después de comer mucho helado.
4. Él nos ___ cinco tacos magníficos por sólo cincuenta pesos.
5. ¿Tú ___ con don Juan y ___ con él?

(Do Practice Workbook 12-9 and 12-10.)

CAPÍTULO 13

Vocabulario para conversar (páginas 418–421)

1 **Sopa de letras** Pon *(Put)* estos grupos de letras en orden para formar palabras del vocabulario.

1. R E G E T O R P
2. A R A P A G
3. O C E R R E G
4. T E N G E
5. G R N E Í A E

2 **La opción correcta** Usa las palabras del Ejercicio 1 para completar estas frases.

1. Es necesario ___ las luces antes de salir de un cuarto.
2. La ___ tiene que ___ la Tierra.
3. Nosotros tenemos que ___ las latas para la escuela.
4. Las computadoras usan mucha ___.

(Do Practice Workbook 13-1 and 13-2.)

Exercise 4
1. comimos
2. salieron
3. dolió
4. vendió
5. comiste, saliste

Vocabulario para conversar

Exercise 1
1. proteger
2. apagar
3. recoger
4. gente
5. energía

Exercise 2
1. apagar
2. gente, proteger
3. recoger
4. energía

Vocabulario para conversar

Exercise 1
1. El caballo
2. Los árboles
3. Los jaguares
4. La ballena
5. El pájaro

Exercise 2
1. elefantes
2. fábricas
3. Tierra
4. vaca
5. el transporte público

Gramática en contexto

Exercise 1
1. digo
2. dices
3. dicen
4. dicen
5. dice

Exercise 2
1. pon
2. recoge
3. dame
4. apaga
5. recicla

Vocabulario para conversar (páginas 422–427)

1 **La opción correcta** Escoge la palabra que complete mejor cada una de estas frases.

1. (El caballo / El tigre) es un animal domesticado.
2. (Las fábricas / Los árboles) forman parte del medio ambiente.
3. (Las serpientes / Los jaguares) están en peligro de extinción.
4. (El oso / La ballena) vive en el océano.
5. (El pájaro / El elefante) prefiere estar en los árboles.

2 **Nuestro medio ambiente** Completa estas frases con una palabra apropiada del vocabulario.

1. No hay muchos ___ en las Américas porque son de África e India.
2. Las ___ contaminan el aire.
3. Nuestro planeta se llama la ___.
4. La ___ nos da leche y carne.
5. Para conservar energía, todos debemos usar ___.

(Do Practice Workbook 13-3 and 13-4.)

Gramática en contexto (páginas 432–437)

El verbo *decir* (página 433)

1 **¿Qué puede decir?** Completa estas frases con la forma apropiada del presente del verbo *decir*.

1. Yo ___ que debemos proteger los animales.
2. ¿Tú no ___ que es importante reciclar?
3. Mis padres ___ que las flores son muy bonitas.
4. Ellos ___ que el lobo es una amenaza para la vaca.
5. Él ___ que el aire está contaminado.

(Do Practice Workbook 13-5 and 13-6.)

El mandato afirmativo *tú* (páginas 434–436)

2 **Mis padres son mandones *(bossy)*.** A veces los adolescentes piensan que sus padres les dan demasiadas *(too many)* órdenes. Usa los mandatos afirmativos con *tú* para darles órdenes a estas personas.

1. Pablo, ___ (poner) los libros aquí.
2. Mariana, ___ (recoger) las latas y los periódicos.
3. Estefanía, ___ (darme) la madera, por favor.
4. Nico, ___ (apagar) las luces antes de salir.
5. Emilia, ___ (reciclar) el plástico y el aluminio.

(Do Practice Workbook 13-7 and 13-8.)

El verbo *saber* (páginas 436–437)

 El sabelotodo *(The know-it-all)* Completa estas frases con la forma apropiada del verbo *saber.*

1. Miguel, yo ___ que tú ___ reciclar.
2. ¿___ los profesores dónde están las ballenas?
3. Ella ___ recoger las flores.
4. El lobo ___ mucho.

(Do Practice Workbook 13-9 and 13-10.)

CAPÍTULO 14

Vocabulario para conversar (páginas 450–453)

1 La reunión Completa las frases con la palabra más apropiada del recuadro.

conozco	depende	reunión
dar	recibir	

1. Mis padres siempre dicen: "Es mejor ___ que ___."
2. Yo ___ a muchas personas en la fiesta.
3. No sé si voy a la ___.
4. —¿Te gustan las fiestas?
   —Bueno, ___.

2 Definiciones Decide cuál de las definiciones de la segunda columna corresponde a cada una de las palabras o frases de la primera. Escribe tus respuestas.

1. la fiesta de disfraces
2. cantar
3. hecho a mano
4. soler
5. el baile

   a. producir música usando la voz *(voice)*
   b. algo que no se hace *(isn't made)* en una fábrica
   c. reunión o fiesta donde todos bailan
   d. cuando tú llevas ropa diferente de lo normal
   e. tener el hábito de hacer algo

(Do Practice Workbook 14-1 and 14-2.)

Exercise 3
1. sé, sabes
2. Saben
3. sabe
4. sabe

Vocabulario para conversar

Exercise 1
1. dar, recibir
2. conozco
3. reunión
4. depende

Exercise 2
1. d
2. a
3. b
4. e
5. c

Vocabulario para conversar

Exercise 1

1. el collar
2. un reloj pulsera
3. pasarlo bien
4. decoraciones
5. La fecha

Exercise 2

1. los zapatos de tacón alto
2. lugar
3. los invitados
4. corbatas
5. bailando

Gramática en contexto

Exercise 1

1. Nadie baila en la sala.
2. Tú no haces nada.
3. Mis padres no comen tampoco.
4. Ni mis padres ni mis profesores me escuchan.
5. Nunca canto en la fiesta.

Vocabulario para conversar (páginas 454–457)

1 **En la fiesta** Escoge la palabra del recuadro que mejor complete cada una de estas frases, y escribe la frase completa.

el collar	pasarlo bien
decoraciones	un reloj pulsera
la fecha	

1. Mi novia quiere ___ de rubíes y diamantes.
2. Necesito ___ para saber qué hora es.
3. En la fiesta, queremos ___.
4. Si queremos un ambiente menos aburrido, debemos poner más ___.
5. ___ de la fiesta es el 4 de noviembre.

2 **La opción correcta** Escoge la palabra que complete mejor cada una de estas frases, y escribe la frase completa.

1. No le gustan (los zapatos de tacón alto / las decoraciones) con ese vestido.
2. ¿En qué (arete / lugar) vas a dar la fiesta?
3. ¿Quiénes son (los invitados / las entradas)?
4. Los hombres necesitan llevar (relojes / corbatas) para comer en ese restaurante.
5. ¡Qué fiesta tan aburrida! A los invitados no les gusta la música y por eso nadie está (comiendo / bailando).

(Do Practice Workbook 14-3 and 14-4.)

Gramática en contexto (páginas 462–467)

Construcciones negativas (páginas 463–464)

1 **Eres bastante negativo.** Tienes un amigo que siempre dice lo contrario de lo que tú dices. Imagina que tu amigo dijo *(said)* estas frases y cámbialas a la forma negativa.

1. Alguien baila en la sala.
2. Tú haces mucho.
3. Mis padres comen también.
4. Mis padres y mis profesores me escuchan.
5. Siempre canto en la fiesta.

(Do Practice Workbook 14-5.)

El presente progresivo (páginas 464–466)

2 **¿Qué están haciendo?** Cambia las frases afirmativas del Ejercicio 1 al presente progresivo.

3 **El reportero** Imagina que eres el (la) reportero(a) del periódico de tu escuela y tienes que escribir un artículo sobre la fiesta de la escuela. Usa el presente progresivo de los verbos entre paréntesis para describir las fotos que vas a usar en tu artículo.

1. Mi padre (bailar) con mi madre.
2. Mis profesores (conversar) con los estudiantes.
3. Los muchachos (comer) tacos y burritos.
4. Las muchachas (hablar) sobre las decoraciones.
5. Los otros (pasarlo bien).

(Do Practice Workbook 14-6 and 14-7.)

El verbo *dar* (páginas 466–467)

4 **¿Qué le damos en su fiesta de cumpleaños?** Forma frases usando la forma apropiada del verbo *dar.*

Marta / unos aretes / Carmencita
Marta le da unos aretes.

1. (yo) / tarjetas de básquetbol / Antonio
2. mis padres / una pulsera / mi hermana
3. Teresa y yo / entradas para un concierto / nuestros mejores amigos
4. mis abuelos / un reloj pulsera / mí
5. tu novio / un collar de perlas / ti
6. tú / una camiseta rosada / mí

(Do Practice Workbook 14-8 and 14-9.)

Exercise 2
1. Alguien está bailando en la sala.
2. Tú estás haciendo mucho.
3. Mis padres están comiendo también.
4. Mis padres y mis profesores me están escuchando (están escuchándome).
5. Siempre estoy cantando en la fiesta.

Exercise 3
1. Mi padre está bailando con mi madre.
2. Mis profesores están conversando con los estudiantes.
3. Los muchachos están comiendo tacos y burritos.
4. Las muchachas están hablando sobre las decoraciones.
5. Los otros lo están pasando bien (están pasándolo bien).

Exercise 4
1. Le doy tarjetas de básquetbol.
2. Mis padres le dan una pulsera.
3. Teresa y yo les damos entradas para un concierto.
4. Mis abuelos me dan un reloj pulsera.
5. Tu novio te da un collar de perlas.
6. Me das una camiseta rosada.

Examen cumulativo

I.

1. c
2. a
3. b
4. d
5. c
6. b
7. a
8. c
9. b
10. b

Examen cumulativo

Here's an opportunity for you to see how well you have learned the vocabulary and grammar from *PASO A PASO 1*. Write all of your answers on a separate sheet of paper.

I. Write the letter of the response that best completes each statement.

1. Una persona que habla mucho es ___.
   - a. callada
   - b. atrevida
   - c. sociable
   - d. tacaña

2. Para poner mis cosas en orden, necesito una ___.
   - a. mochila
   - b. calculadora
   - c. grabadora
   - d. regla

3. La estación en que no vamos a la escuela es ___.
   - a. la primavera
   - b. el verano
   - c. el otoño
   - d. el invierno

4. Un ingrediente principal en la salsa es ___.
   - a. la cebolla
   - b. la lechuga
   - c. el guisante
   - d. el tomate

5. Los hijos de mis tíos son mis ___.
   - a. gemelos
   - b. hijos
   - c. primos
   - d. hermanos

6. Cuando hace frío llevo ___.
   - a. una camisa
   - b. una sudadera
   - c. un vestido
   - d. zapatos

7. A veces no puedes sacar fotos en ___.
   - a. el museo
   - b. el país
   - c. las montañas
   - d. las pirámides

8. En mi casa tengo que hacer muchos ___.
   - a. sótanos
   - b. lavaderos
   - c. quehaceres
   - d. garajes

9. Celina no puede ir porque tiene ___ de cabeza.
   - a. cuello
   - b. dolor
   - c. nariz
   - d. ojo

10. Para comprar libros necesito ___.
    - a. ir a la biblioteca
    - b. ir a la librería
    - c. comprar sellos
    - d. ir a la iglesia

11. Nunca veo ___ porque me dan miedo.
   a. las comedias
   b. las películas de terror
   c. los dibujos animados
   d. los programas de entrevistas

12. Son las 4:00. ¿Qué vamos a comer para la ___?
   a. merienda
   b. carne
   c. mantequilla
   d. pimienta

13. Vamos a reciclar las botellas de ___.
   a. serpiente
   b. piel
   c. vidrio
   d. madera

14. Necesito comprar un reloj ___.
   a. fiesta
   b. pulsera
   c. fecha
   d. lugar

II. Choose the response that best completes each thought or that best answers each question.

1. Me gusta mucho estar con amigos. Y a ti, Patricio, ¿te gusta estar con amigos?
   a. A mí sí me gusta.
   b. A mí tampoco.
   c. ¿Y a ti?
   d. No me gusta tampoco.

2. ¡Hoy tengo dos clases diferentes de matemáticas en la séptima y la octava hora!
   a. ¿De veras?
   b. ¿A qué hora estudiamos?
   c. ¿Necesitas más tarea?
   d. ¿Qué hora es?

3. ¿Puedes ir al cine conmigo?
   a. ¿Dónde puedes jugar básquetbol?
   b. Lo siento. Estoy ocupado.
   c. ¿A ti te gustaría jugar videojuegos ahora?
   d. No, no voy al parque después de las clases.

4. ¿Qué te gustaría comer para el desayuno?
   a. Un sandwich de jamón y queso.
   b. Cereal y huevos.
   c. Pollo y papas al horno.
   d. Judías verdes y un refresco.

5. José y Julia son gemelos.
   a. ¿Cuántos años tienen?
   b. ¿Julia es hija única?
   c. ¿Cómo se llaman?
   d. ¿Cuántos gemelos hay?

6. ¡Estas camisetas sólo cuestan 10 dólares!
   a. ¡Qué ganga!
   b. ¿Qué desea Ud.?
   c. ¿Dé qué color son?
   d. Me quedan bien, ¿no?

11. b
12. a
13. c
14. b

II.
1. a
2. a
3. b
4. b
5. a
6. a

7. a
8. b
9. b
10. b
11. a
12. c
13. d
14. c

III.
1. b
2. a
3. d
4. d
5. a
6. b
7. b
8. c

---

7. Quisiera pasear en bote.
   a. ¡Fantástico! ¿Cuándo piensas regresar?
   b. ¿Vamos a subir la pirámide?
   c. ¿Vas a las montañas?
   d. ¿No vas a ninguna parte?

8. Tenemos que comprar muebles.
   a. Necesitamos cortar el césped.
   b. Quisiera comprar algo de madera.
   c. ¿Dónde está el guardarropa?
   d. Las ventanas están sucias.

9. Necesito ir a la clínica.
   a. Debo quedarme en la cama.
   b. ¿Qué pasa? ¿Te duele la espalda?
   c. Hace mucho tiempo que no veo al dentista.
   d. No me duele nada.

10. ¿Cuánto cuesta enviar una carta a Uruguay?
    a. Yo devolví la carta ayer.
    b. Quinientos pesos.
    c. ¿Me compras un sello?
    d. Vamos a la tienda de regalos.

11. Es divertido ver la televisión en blanco y negro.
    a. Prefiero los programas en colores.
    b. Las películas románticas no son buenas.
    c. Me da mucho miedo.
    d. ¿Cuándo dan el pronóstico del tiempo?

12. ¿Con qué se hace el flan?
    a. Con aguacates y burritos.
    b. Es la especialidad de la casa.
    c. Con leche, huevos y azúcar.
    d. Muchas veces está picante.

13. Voy a tomar el transporte público.
    a. ¿Vas a apagar las luces?
    b. No vale la pena.
    c. ¿No está en peligro de extinción?
    d. Es bueno conservar energía.

14. Necesito una corbata.
    a. ¡Feliz cumpleaños!
    b. ¿Y también necesitas zapatos de tacón alto?
    c. ¿Vas a una fiesta elegante?
    d. ¿Dónde están tus parientes?

III. Dorotea writes in her diary about her friend Lourdes. Write the letter of the response that best completes each diary entry.

Tengo una amiga muy buena que se llama Lourdes. Ella es muy __1__ . También es muy artística y __2__ gusta mucho dibujar. Tiene una colección de dibujos muy interesante. Lourdes también es mi compañera de clase y __3__ matemáticas en la segunda hora, español en la cuarta hora y arte en la sexta hora. Para Lourdes la clase de arte es muy __4__ porque ya sabe hacer muchas cosas artísticas. A su hermana __5__ también le gusta mucho la clase de arte porque para ella es muy interesante. Pero para __6__ la clase de arte es __7__ . No sé dibujar bien y a mí no me gusta __8__ .

1. a. serio
   b. seria
   c. serios
   d. serias

2. a. le
   b. la
   c. lo
   d. les

3. a. decimos
   b. sabemos
   c. podemos
   d. tenemos

4. a. difícil
   b. ordenada
   c. atrevida
   d. fácil

5. a. mayor
   b. gemelo
   c. canoso
   d. grande

6. a. mi
   b. mí
   c. yo
   d. me

7. a. ganga
   b. aburrida
   c. cara
   d. nueva

8. a. algo
   b. nadie
   c. nada
   d. ninguno

IV.
1. mis
2. Los
3. comemos
4. sirven
5. pido
6. vimos
7. sé
8. gustaría

V.
1. pensé
2. muchas
3. gusta
4. Les
5. escogimos
6. fuimos
7. compró
8. regresamos

IV. Laura writes about what her family and friends like to do on the weekend. Complete the paragraph by using the appropriate form of each word in parentheses.

Mi familia y _1_ (mi) amigos son muy importantes para mí. Nos gusta pasarlo bien. _2_ (el) sábados vamos al Museo de Historia Natural. Luego, _3_ (comer) en un restaurante donde ellos _4_ (servir) helados y frutas de postre. Yo siempre _5_ (pedir) helado de chocolate. El sábado pasado llegamos al museo a las diez de la mañana y _6_ (ver) a muchas personas en la exhibición de animales que están en peligro de extinción. Mañana es domingo y no _7_ (saber) adónde vamos a ir. Es mi cumpleaños y a mí me _8_ (gustar) ir al zoológico para celebrarlo.

V. Claudia writes about her upcoming birthday party and reminisces about last year's party. Complete the paragraph by using the appropriate form of each word in parentheses.

Anoche yo _1_ (pensar) en mi fiesta de cumpleaños. No voy a invitar a _2_ (mucho) personas porque siempre me _3_ (gustar) más celebrar mi día especial con un pequeño grupo de amigos. _4_ (le) voy a decir un poco sobre mi cumpleaños el año pasado. Mi madre y yo _5_ (escoger) las decoraciones para mi fiesta de cumpleaños. Nosotras _6_ (ir) a muchas tiendas. Mi madre me _7_ (comprar) entradas para el concierto de mi grupo favorito *Los perros angélicos*. Después, nosotros _8_ (regresar) a casa y lo pasamos muy bien en la fiesta.

Índice

In almost all cases, structures are first presented in the *Vocabulario para conversar,* where they are practiced lexically in conversational contexts. They are explained later, usually in the *Gramática en contexto* section of that chapter. Light-face numbers refer to pages where structures are initially presented or, after explanation, where student reminders occur. **Bold-face numbers** refer to pages where structures are explained or otherwise highlighted.

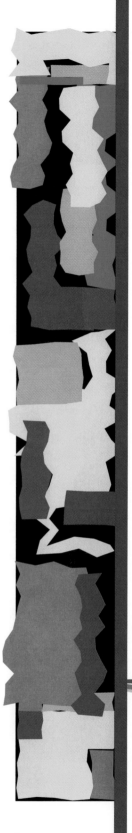

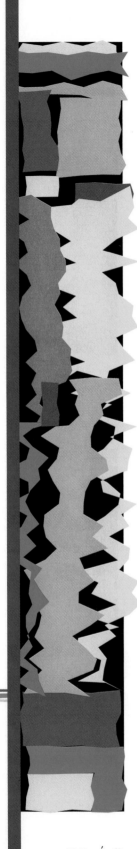

Índice 555

ACKNOWLEDGMENTS

Illustrations Andrea Baruffi: p. 104; Mark Bender: pp. 470-471; Mark Charlier: pp. **XVIII-1, 4, 11;** Rick Clubb: pp. 211, 255, 258-259, 261, 263, 267-277, 281; Lane DuPont: pp. 71, 75, 252-253, 256-259; Tim Foley: pp. 340-341; Joe Fournier: p. 304; Tom Gianni: pp. 30-44, 158-160, 169; Elissé Jo Goldstein: pp. 320, 330-334; David Gothard: pp. 274-275; Seitu Hayden: pp. 7, 10, 13, 15-16, 18, 21-23, 90-91, 94-95, 98, 90-101, 105-108, 209, 234, 266, 318, 324, 326, 335-336, 396; Iskra Lettering Design: Hand lettering on cover and pp. **I-XIII,** 1, 3, 27, 55, 87, 119, 151, 181, 217, 249, 283, 313, 347, 381, 415, 447; Mike Kasun: pp. 376-377; V. Kennedy: pp. 142-144; Hiro Kimura: pp. 350-357, 362, 368; Mapping Specialists Limited: pp. **XIV-XVII;** James Mellett: pp. 58-59, 62, 64, 211, 220-221, 224-228, 234-237; Deborah Melmon: pp. 122-123, 126-130, 136-139, 184-195, 201-206; Susan Melrath: pp. 408-409; Jane Mjolsness: p. 443; Marion Nixon: p. 79; Rob Porazinski: pp. 307-308; Karen Pritchett: pp. 154-155, 162-163, 167; Mike Reed: pp. 418-428, 432, 437; Sandra Shap: pp. 286-295, 299-303 M. Sobey: pp. 384-386, 388-390, 392-393, 399, 401-402; Scott Snow: pp. 450-459, 462-466; Stephen Sweeny: p. 468; Greg Valley: pp. 78, 196, 206-207, 316-318, 322-323; Susan Williams: pp. 174-175

Photographs **Front and back covers, II:** Suzanne L. Murphy/FPG International; **IV:** Otis Imboden © National Geographic Society; **VI:** Peter Menzel; **18:** David Ryan/DDB Stock Photo; **28, 54-55, 63, 71, 219 (t), 250 (b):** Peter Menzel; **57, 89 (b), 297:** Jeff Greenberg/The Image Works; **89 (t):** James Hackett/Leo de Wys; **9, 41, 49 (b), 51, 110 (c, b), 116, 131, 148 (br), 238 (br), 244 (c), 245 (b):** David R. Frazier Photolibrary; **14, 56 (t), 83, 88 (l), 102, 113, 125, 136 (br), 137, 145, 147 (r), 175, 176 (t), 177 (br), 199 (b), 216-217, 231 (tl), 238 (cr), 242 (t), 279, 320, 321 (t), 380-381, 383 (b), 399, 446-447:** Robert Frerck/Odyssey/Chicago; **194, 265, 328-329, 346-347, 382 (c), 397, 406, 416, 438 (l), 441 (t), 473:** Beryl Goldberg; **230-231:** Glenn Randall; **50 (bl), 172 (b), 273 (b), 326:** Owen Franken/Stock Boston; **273 (t):** Gay Bumgarner/Tony Stone Images; **321 (b):** Charles Kennard/Stock Boston; **XVIII (t):** F. Rangel/The Image Works; **XVIII (b), 103 (t):** James P. Rowan; **1 (tl, br), 6 (br), 26-27, 46 (t), 49 (c), 50 (br), 52, 80, 110 (t), 120 (l), 172 (t), 188, 232 (t, b), 238 (t, cl, bl), 240 (b), 309, 333, 395 (b):** Chip & Rosa Maria de la Cueva Peterson; **1 (tr):** Richard Lord; **1 (bl):** Stan Sholik/FPG International; **6 (tl):** Tom McCarthy/PhotoEdit; **6 (tr):** Tony Freeman/PhotoEdit; **6 (bl):** Richard Hutchings/PhotoEdit; **11, 29 (b), 115, 315 (t):** H. Huntly Hersch/DDB Stock Photo; **19:** David Lavender; **24, 29 (tl), 35, 66-67, 69 (t), 70, 73, 74 (t), 74 (b), 77, 88-89, 101, 107, 108, 111 (l), 111 (r), 132 (t), 133 (c), 136 (t), 136 (bl), 162 (l), 162 (r), 164 (b), 165 (tl), 188-189, 189 (r), 195, 197, 200, 212 (b), 231 (tr), 234 (l), 237, 240 (t), 244 (t), 245 (cl), 250 (t), 251 (b), 262, 284-285, 296 (b), 301, 314 (t), 342, 358-359, 365 (b), 370, 374, 398 (b), 402-403, 429 (l, b), 438 (r), 468, 472 (t):** PhotoDisc; **29 (tr), 348 (b):** Owen Franken; **39:** Don Smetzer/Tony Stone Images; **40, 264:** Stuart Cohen/The Image Works; **45, 307:** Bob Daemmrich/Tony Stone Images; **46 (b):** David Young-Wolff/Tony Stone Images; **47 (t):** Private Collection, © Images Modernes, photo: E. Baudoin; **47 (b):** Museo del Prado, Madrid, Spain/Giraudon, Paris/Superstock; **50 (t):** Jack Parsons; **56 (c), 360 (t):** Ulrike Welsch/Stock Boston; **56 (b):** Artville; **60, 448 (r):** Bob Daemmrich/The Image Works; **65:** Karl Weatherly/Tony Stone Images; **68:** Cameramann/The Image Works; **69 (b),120 (r):** Nancy D'Antonio; **74 (c), 103 (b), 133 (b), 152 (t), 165 (tr), 275 (b):** Ulrike Welsch; **83 (inset), 261 (t), 278 (t), 361, 405:** Joe Viesti/Viesti Collection; **86-87:** Oliver Benn/Tony Stone Images; **88 (r):** Diane Joy Schmidt; **102-103, 312-313, 411:** D. Donne Bryant/DDB Stock Photo; **104:** Peter Seaward/Tony Stone Images; **106, 218 (l):** Wolfgang Kaehler; **109, 314 (b):** M. Algaze/The Image Works; **112 (r):** Courtesy Paramount Pictures/United International Pictures, Madrid; **118-119, 278 (b):** Robert Frerck/Tony Stone Images; **121 (b):** Martha Cooper/Viesti Collection; **132 (b):** Steve Vidler/Leo de Wys; **133 (t):** Rob Lewine/The Stock Market; **146 (t), 315 (b), 386, 396 (tl, r, bl), 403, 437, 474:** Robert Fried; **146 (b), 250 (c):** Timothy Ross/The Image Works; **147 (l), 150-151, 156:** Suzanne Murphy-Larronde/DDB Stock Photo; **152 (bl), 176 (br), 274, 284 (b), 343 (inset), 460, 461, 466:** Bob Daemmrich/Stock Boston; **152 (br):** Dale Boyer/Tony Stone Images; **153:** N. Frank/Viesti Collection; **157 (t):** Courtesy Roberto Mamani Mamani; **(b):** John Beatty/Tony Stone Images; **164 (t):** David Baird/Tony Stone Images; **171:** ©Fernando Botero, **On the Park,** 1996, courtesy, Marlborough Gallery, NY; **174 (l):** David Young-Wolff/PhotoEdit; **174 (r):** Mary Kate Denny/PhotoEdit; **176 (bl):** Ilene Perlman/Stock Boston; **177 (t):** R. S. Wagner; **177 (bl):** Spencer Grant/Stock Boston; **180-181:** Barbara Alper/Stock Boston; **182 (t), 296 (t):** Alyx Kellington/DDB Stock Photo; **183 (t), 208 (t), 251 (t), 427, 435, 469:** Stuart Cohen; **183 (b), 260 (b):** David Simson/Stock Boston; **189 (t, b), 395 (inset):** Robert Fried/DDB Stock Photo; **197 (t):** Crandall/The Image Works; **(b):** John V. Cotter/DDB Stock Photo; **198, 236 (b), 240-241:** Macduff Everton/The Image Works; **198-199:** Viesti Collection; **199 (t):** Chad Ehlers/Tony Stone Images; **212 (t):** Tony Arruza; **214:** Peter Menzel/Stock Boston; **218 (r), 305 (t):** Eric Lessing/Art Resource, NY; **219 (b):** Max & Bea Hunn/DDB Stock Photo; **232 (c):** David Wells/The Image Works; **233:** Maria Loxas; **234 (r):** Sonda Dawes/The Image Works; **243 (t):** Corbis-Bettmann; **243 (b):** Randy G. Taylor/Leo de Wys; **244 (b):** Ray Pfortner/Peter Arnold Inc.; **245 (t, cr):** Comstock; **248-249:** Chris R. Sharp/DDB Stock Photo; **261 (b):** Vince DeWitt/DDB Stock Photo; **272:** Robin Smith/Tony Stone Images; **275 (t):** Charles Gupton/Stock Boston; **282-283:** Schalkwijk/Art Resource, NY; **284 (t):** Jeff Greenberg/PhotoEdit; **285:** Victor

Englebert;   **305** (b): Museu Picasso, Barcelona/Index/Bridgeman Art Library, London/Superstock;   **327**: Collection of the Art Museum of the Americas/Organization of American States, Washington DC;   **334** (t): Richard During/Tony Stone Images;   (b): Rob Crandall/Stock Boston;   **338** (t): Ruth Dixon/Stock Boston;   **338** (b): Richard Pasley/Stock Boston;   **343** (inset), **440** (t), **472** (b): Bob Daemmrich Photography;   **344**: K. Preuss/The Image Works;   **348** (t): Courtesy Galavisión;   **349**: Anthony Neste/Gamma Liaison;   **375**: Everett Collection;   **376-377**: Courtesy Coral Pictures Corporation, Miami/Radio Caracas Televisión, Venezuela;   **382** (t): Mark Kelley/Stock Boston;   **383** (inset): Robert Fried/Stock Boston;   **412, 463**: Gary A. Conner/PhotoEdit;   **414-415**: Wayne Lynch/DRK Photo;   **417**: Gerard Lacz/Animals Animals;   **425**: Courtesy Alfredo Arreguín, Collection Dave Anderson;   **430** (t): James A. Hancock/Photo Researchers;   **430** (b): drawing by Eduardo Aparicio/Courtesy American Museum of Natural History;   **431**: Robert A. Tyrrell/Animals Animals;   **431** (inset): Richard La Val/Animals Animals;   **436**: Gerry Ellis/ENP Images;   **439**: Art Wolfe/Tony Stone Images;   **441** (b): Courtesy Waste Management, Inc.;   **442**: Betsy Blass/Photo Researchers;   **444**: Michael Fogden/DRK Photo;   **448** (l): Robert Yager/Tony Stone Images;   **449**: Daniel Aubry/Odyssey/Chicago

Realia **Page 112**: From "Calendario" from EL DIARIO DE JUÁREZ, July 16, 1993, p. 7. Reprinted by permission;   **Page 140**: "Plátano, rico para comer" from MUY INTERESANTE, September 1998, #208, p. 26. Copyright 1998 by G y J España Ediciones S.L.S. en C. Reprinted by permission of G y J España Ediciones S.L.S. en C.;   **Page 223**: "A dónde va la gente con la maleta a cuestas" from MUY INTERESANTE, June 1998, #205, p. 42. Copyright 1998 by G y J España Ediciones, S.L.S. en C. Reprinted by permission of G y J España Ediciones S.L.S. en C.;   **Page 367**: "Héroes de plastilina" from METRÓPOLI, November 1996, #338, p. 120. Reprinted by permission of Metrópoli Unidad Editorial, S.A.;   **Page 372**: "Perdidos en el espacio" by Alma Delia Puga Aguilar from CINEMANÍA, Year 3, #26, November 1998, p. 27. Reprinted by permission of Compañía Editorial Cinemanía, S.A. de C.V.

Acknowledgments 557